Richard F.S. Starr
from a painting by Ruth Starr Rose, ca. 1931

STUDIES ON THE CIVILIZATION AND CULTURE OF NUZI AND THE HURRIANS

Volume 8

Richard F.S. Starr Memorial Volume

Edited by
David I. Owen
and
Gernot Wilhelm

CDL Press
Bethesda, Maryland

Cover Design by Ellen Maidman. Drawing based on a figurine of Ishtar found at Nuzi.

Published by CDL Press, P.O. Box 34454, Bethesda, MD 20827;
E-Mail: cdlpress@erols.com; website: www.cdlpress.com.

ISBN 1-883053-10-2

Library of Congress Cataloging-in-Publication Data:

Richard F.S. Starr memorial volume / edited by David I. Owen and Gernot Wilhelm.
p. cm. — (Studies on the civilization and culture of Nuzi and the Hurrians ; v. 8)
Includes index.
ISBN 1-883053-10-2
1. Nuzi (Extinct city) 2. Hurrians. 3. Starr, Richard F. S. (Richard Francis Strong), 1900-1994 . I. Owen, David I. II. Wilhelm, Gernot . III .Starr, Richard F. S. (Richard Francis Strong), 1900-1994 . IV. Series.
DS70.5.N9R53 1996
935—dc20 96-8532
CIP

Preface

The publication of *SCCNH* 8 in memory of Richard F.S. Starr, 1900–1994, is meant to highlight the enormous contribution he made to the study of the ancient Near East through his masterful and prompt publication of the excavations at Nuzi even though his active, professional involvement in Near Eastern archaeology lasted only for a relatively brief time. Aside from the reminiscences presented or edited by D.I. Owen in the first part of this volume, the articles and notes reflect the remarkably rich and varied research that continues unabated on Nuzi materials — epigraphical as well as archaeological. Nearly sixty years after the final publication of Starr's comprehensive, two volume, excavation report, *Nuzi* I-II (1937–1939), and nearly seventy years since the appearance of the first volume of cuneiform texts (E. Chiera, *Inheritance Texts* [Joint Expedition with the Iraq Museum at Nuzi, I], 1927), we find ourselves still actively engaged in the publication and interpretation of these materials. Volume 8 also contains the first part, texts 1-65, of "Excavations at Nuzi 10" by Jeanette Fincke. EN 10, originally conceived and planned by Owen, contains copies of fragments of Nuzi tablets partially catalogued and transliterated by D.I. Owen, M.A. Morrison, M.P. Maidman and K. Grosz in the Lacheman home during two meetings convened there, subsequently identified by Owen among the papers of the late E.R. Lacheman or identified by Wilhelm and Fincke at the Harvard Semitic Museum.

The dregs of any collection of cuneiform tablets are inevitably the bits and pieces that are usually the last, if ever, of the texts to be studied. Generally a mastery of the corpus must be achieved before smaller fragments can be read, understood, and possibly joined to larger pieces. In the case of the Nuzi tablets, all of the fragments were excavated along with the main tablets. In theory, many should join with one another or with larger fragments published or still in the collections. Indeed, over the years joins have been made internally within the collections and by long distance, between the collections. Now, with virtually all the Nuzi tablets catalogued and mostly read, a major effort is being made to bring all these disparate data together and to maximize the results through careful study and publication.

Studies on the Civilization and Culture of Nuzi and the Hurrians - 8

To this end Wilhelm, Fincke, Owen and Maidman have coordinated their efforts. In this and future volumes, Fincke will provide copies and a catalogue of SMN fragments in the Harvard Semitic Museum. Originally conceived by Owen as a continuation of the EN series, Fincke, under a grant from the DAAD, begins EN 10 with part 1 (hereafter EN 10/1ff.), fragments 1-65. Wilhelm and others continue to contribute "Nuzi Notes" that reflect additions and corrections to SMN texts while adding new data and interpretations to the Hurro-Akkadian from Nuzi. The archaeology of Nuzi continues to be the focus of interest in the contributions of S.J. Andrews and D. Potts. Although the number of scholars currently working on the Nuzi archives remains small, the texts continue to offer unusually rich and fertile ground for important new insights into the language, lexicography and civilization of Mesopotamia in the Middle Assyrian/Babylonian period. The editors hope that the publication of this new data will offer encouragement to others to participate in the elucidation of Nuzi archives and archaeology.

The contents of this volume, dedicated to the memory of Richard F.S. Starr, reflect the broad scope that this series encompasses. Not only are studies on the texts, archaeology and civilization of Nuzi included, but those cultures where the Hurrians played major or minor roles — Urkeš, Kaneš, Hatti, Emar, and Urartu — are also reflected in contributions by Kelly-Buccellati, Hecker, Haas, Wegner, Bassetti, and Donbaz. We encourage all those who are working on these and other relevant sites to consider publishing their results in future volumes in this series.

Support for ongoing research on the Nuzi tablets in the Harvard Semitic Museum by Professor G. Wilhelm and Ms. J. Fincke has come from the Deutscher Akademischer Austauschdienst (DAAD) in the framework of a special program launched together with the American Council of Learned Societies (ACLS). The director of the Harvard Semitic Museum, Professor Lawrence Stager, the Curator of Tablets, Professor Piotr Steinkeller, Dr. Joseph Greene, Assistant Director, and Dr. James Armstrong, Assistant Curator have been most supportive of the study and publication of the Nuzi materials. We are grateful for their support and cordial cooperation.

SCCNH 9 (1997) is now in preparation. The editors will consider articles submitted on historical, philological, geographical, archaeological, religious, and art historical topics relating to Nuzi, Hurrians, Hurrian, Hurro-Akkadian, Hurro-Hittite and Urartian in their widest chronological and geographical contexts. In addition, book-length manuscripts will be considered for publication. Accompanying photos must be printed on gloss paper and clearly labeled. Charts and line drawings should be made so that they can be accommodated in the format size of this volume. Manuscripts from Europe should be sent directly to Professor Gernot Wilhelm, Institut für Orientalische Philologie der Julius-Maximilians-Universität Würzburg, Ludwigstraße 6, D-97070 Würzburg,

Germany. Those from North America and Asia should be sent to Professor David I. Owen, Near Eastern Studies, Rockefeller Hall 360, Cornell University, Ithaca, NY 14853-2502 USA. Inquiries may also be made by electronic mail to DIO1@CORNELL.EDU or by facsimile to (USA) 607-255-1345 or (Germany) 049-931-31-2674. Preferably, manuscripts should be submitted in electronic form (IBM or MAC format) with the name and version of the word processor used accompanied by a printed copy made on a laser or equivalent printer. Closing date for manuscripts for volume 9 will be February 1, 1997. Contributors will be provided with 30 free offprints of their articles. The printing of additional off-prints will not be possible.

Studies on the Civilization and Culture of Nuzi and the Hurrians (*SCCNH*), volumes 1-5 and following, may be obtained directly from Eisenbrauns, POB 275, Winona Lake, IN 46590 USA. Volumes 6 and following also may be obtained directly from the publisher—CDL Press, P.O. Box 34454, Bethesda, MD 20827 USA; E-Mail: cdlpress@erols.com; website: www.cdlpress.com.

David I. Owen &
Gernot Wilhelm
Ithaca and Würzburg
January 1996

TABLE OF CONTENTS

Part I

INTRODUCTION

Richard F.S. Starr, ca. 1953
(1900–1994)

R.F.S. Starr, 1900–1994: An Extraordinary Life*

DAVID I. OWEN

Cornell University

Sixty-five years after he began excavating at Nuzi, Dr. Richard Francis Strong Starr passed away quietly on March 9, 1994 at the age of ninety-four. According to his son Nicholas, he was vigorous and lucid until his death. Starr, was the last of a line of scholars directly associated with the Nuzi excavations. He was best known for his masterful, two volume, Harvard University Press publication of the Nuzi excavations that he directed from 1929–1931 and published in a remarkably short time after their completion. World War II interrupted his relatively brief scholarly career in archaeology to which he never returned. He was a remarkable man whose education, talents and experience were by-products of a special time in our history. Born in Eau Claire, Wisconsin at the turn of this century, he was educated at Cornell University where he graduated in 1924 with a Bachelor of Science degree from the College of Agriculture. Although he majored in agriculture, he took a number of courses in the College of Arts and Sciences.

After graduating, his brother, Nathan, who was an instructor at Harvard, introduced him to Alan Priest, another instructor at Harvard, who had been

* I am most grateful to Nicholas Starr for a copy of Michael Kernan's obituary which formed the basis for the *New York Times* (3/17/94) and other obituaries (*London Times*, 4/1/94) and for his kindness in sharing with me anecdotal and other information about and photos of his father without which this obituary could not have been written. My wife, Susan, and I spent a marvelous afternoon at the Starr home where we were shown numerous mementos of his father as well as taken on a visit to his father's home in Upperville, Virginia, to see his personal collections. A slightly abridged version of this obituary has also appeared in *AfO* 42-43 (1995–1996) 337-39.

Studies on the Civilization and Culture of Nuzi and the Hurrians - 8

invited by Harvard's Professor Langdon Warner to join the Harvard University expedition to the Tun Huang cave temples, an ancient military outpost in western China. When Priest told Starr that the positions of doctor and photographer were not yet filled, Starr volunteered for the photographer slot because, as his son recounts, "he had no idea what he would do for a living, and the adventure of western China was irresistible." En route, he studied Mandarin at the Peking Language School in Peking and fondly recalled ice-skating on the ponds of the old Imperial Palace. He then travelled for nearly four months with the expedition staff by pony and oxcart for 1800 miles along the ancient silk route to Tun Huang. Starr remarked in a letter to his mother that "everything but the barest of necessities had to be carried with us." Because of local hostilities, they were able to spend only three days at the caves where he photographed many of the important, early temple wall paintings. According to his letters, he made those photos with the aid of magnesium flash powder, developed them in a local stream, and printed them by sunlight.

He began his return voyage home from China from Lanchow via a raft buoyed by 120 inflated sheepskins in the ancient Assyrian manner on which he sailed down the Yellow River to Patsebolong from where he returned by train to Peking. His subsequent journey took him to Shanghai and then by boat to Indo-China, Cambodia (Ankor Wat), Malaya, Java (Borobodur), Burma, India, Egypt and Europe. Upon his return to the United States, he worked for a short time as a volunteer at the Cleveland Museum of Art. From Cleveland he moved to Cambridge where he helped to move Harvard's Fogg Art Museum into its new building after which he was hired as its Registrar. In 1927 he joined the first Harvard-Baghdad expedition to Nuzi and participated in the excavations for two seasons (1927–1929) as an assistant to the first two directors, Edward Chiera and Robert Pfeiffer. In 1928, while in Iraq, he became a member of the Harvard Photographic Expedition to Persia as well as an archaeological assistant on the Oriental Institute Reconnaissance Expedition to Khorsabad. He returned to the States in 1929 via India, Malaya, China and Japan. Later that year, he was appointed director for the last two campaigns at Nuzi (1929–1931) during which time he participated also in the survey of the site of Farah for the University of Pennsylvania Museum. Unfortunately, on his return at the end of the expedition, he was asked by an official of the Iraq department of antiquities to deliver a small box to a friend in French controlled Syria. Thinking it to have been a gift, he did not declare it at the customs control. The box was seized by the Syrian border authorities who opened it to find that it contained a number of fine antiquities including cylinder seals. In spite of his disclaimers, Starr was accused of illicit export of antiquities. This created something of a scandal at the time and effectively ended his career as an excavator in Iraq.[1]

---

1 I am grateful to Cyrus H. Gordon for his account of the events.

From 1931–1935, Starr was a Fellow of the Fogg Art Museum for Research in the Near East. During this period he prepared the preliminary manuscript on the Nuzi excavations, repairing and preparing the archaeological objects for study while integrating the objects into the museum's collections. In 1935 he returned to the Near East as field director of the Harvard Expedition to Serabit el-Khadam in Sinai which, according to his memoirs, "included a thorough search of the ancient Egyptian turquoise mines for more examples of the rare Semitic proto-Sinaitic inscriptions." From there he undertook a survey of Van in Turkey. He published the results of the Sinai campaign the following year. From 1935–1941 he completed graduate studies at Princeton University's Institute of Advanced Studies and obtained the M.A. and Ph.D. degrees. His doctoral dissertation was on Indus Valley archaeology. During his stay in Princeton he finished his two-volume, final publication of the Nuzi excavations. In addition, he received a Carnegie Scholarship for independent research in the archaeology of India and a Guggenheim Fellowship for the preparation of a manual on the art of the ancient Near East on which he worked for a number of years but never completed. He was also a visiting lecturer at Princeton University.

In spite of all this extraordinary experience, training and publication, Starr, like so many of his generation, was unable to find a permanent job in academia. As a result, in 1941, he became an examiner for the New Jersey State Civil Service Commission in Trenton (where coincidentally, a number of unemployed Near Eastern archaeologists also found work at local sites). He joined the U.S. Navy Reserve in 1942 as a Lieutenant (J.G.) and returned to Cornell University for a two month, indoctrination course after which he was assigned to Washington, D.C. where he spent the war years.

World War II altered the path of his career dramatically. He served in the Office of Naval Intelligence in Washington, D.C. from 1942–1945. He became the editor and research analyst in charge of publishing, *Foreign Uniforms, Insignia, Comparative Rank* (*J.A.N.* 1), published by the Military Intelligence Service and Office of Naval Intelligence. In addition, he maintained other important positions in the Naval intelligence service until he retired from the Navy Reserve with the rank of Commander in 1945 but remained in the ready reserve eventually retiring with the rank of Captain USNR. From 1945–1948 he remained with Naval intelligence as a civilian administrative officer continuing much of the same intelligence related work he had done in the military. In 1948 he joined the Department of State, remaining there until 1960 as a "Foreign Affairs Specialist, Bureau of Intelligence and Research, Senior Sociologist, Near East Division." He became a research specialist on the Middle East and for the last four years of his career moved to the Central Intelligence Agency where he continued in the same capacity until his retirement in 1965. He had many other interests including Civil War history and collected thousands of early American antique tools. Both he and his wife, Dorothy, were fascinated by Americana and together amassed a virtual museum of antique American handicraft in their Upperville, Virginia home.

According to his son, Nicholas, Starr maintained many friendships with colleagues he met in the Near East, especially those from the Princeton community. Cyrus Gordon, who occasionally visited the Starrs, recounts that he "first heard of Starr when he was working at Beth Zur in Palestine in 1931. Clarence Fisher was visiting the expedition and remarked [to Gordon] that Starr's dig [at Yorgan Tepe] was far and away the scientifically best conducted in all Iraq." In 1989, Carney Gavin, then of the Harvard Semitic Museum, videotaped an interview with Starr in his Upperville home. In it Starr reminisces about China, Nuzi and Sinai among other places. A copy is on deposit at the Harvard Semitic Museum in Cambridge.

Starr was an inveterate correspondent especially with his mother and wife. His many letters were retained by both and in the last few years before his death he typed (and slightly edited) his letters and journals into a manuscript comprising three volumes, each representing the major components of his time abroad — China, Iraq and Sinai. Below, I have edited the sections dealing with Nuzi and Iraq.

Dr. Starr's wife and companion of fifty-two years, Dorothy Clara Simpson Starr, died in 1982. She had been with him during the final season of the Nuzi excavations and had herself written a detailed memoir, *North of Baghdad,* (published below) about her experiences. They are survived by a son, Nicholas, and two grandsons, Richard Kimball and Peter Tristram.

It is fitting that this volume, in a series begun with the *Lacheman Anniversary Volume* (*SCCNH* 1), be dedicated to Starr's memory. Lacheman had written a frequently quoted appendix (on the material culture of Nuzi based on a preliminary survey of the mostly unpublished texts) to Starr's two-volume excavation report. Starr "knew him only as a casual visitor to the Semitic Museum when I was working in the basement. I had my office down there when I was writing the [Nuzi] book." They each represented the pre-World War II generation that contributed so much to the foundations of Near Eastern studies but whose careers, like those of countless others, were unalterably changed by the Great Depression and World War II. We can only be eternally grateful to them for the significant legacy they have bequeathed to us.

Bibliography of Richard F.S. Starr

Books:

Excavations and Protosinaitic Inscriptions at Sarabit El-Khadam (Studies and Documents, No. 6), London: Christophers, 1936 (with R.F. Butin.)

Excavations at Nuzi, I-II (Harvard-Radcliff Fine Arts Series), Cambridge: Harvard University Press, 1937, 1939.

Indus Valley Painted Pottery (Princeton Oriental Series, No. 8), Princeton: Princeton University Press, 1941.

Articles:

"Notes on the Excavations at Nuzi," *Bulletin of the American Schools of Oriental Research* 38, 1930.

"Kirkuk Expedition," *Fogg Art Museum Notes*, 2/1, 1939.

"Excavations in Iraq," *Bulletin of the Fogg Art Museum*, 1/1, 1931.

"Notes on the Tracing of Mud-Brick Walls," *Bulletin of the American Schools of Oriental Research* 58, 1935.

"A Rare Akkadian Head." *Bulletin of the Fogg Art Museum*, 9/1, 1939.

"A Rare Example of Akkadian Sculpture," *American Journal of Archaeology*, 45/1, 1941.

Reviews:

Archaeological Reconnaissance in Northwestern India and Southeastern Iran, by A. Stein, in *American Journal of Archaeology*, 42/2, 1938.

Cylinder Seals, by H. Frankfort, in *Classical Weekly*, 33/10, 1940.

Chanhu-daro, 1935-36, by E.J.H. Mackay, in *American Journal of Archaeology*, 48/2, 1944.

Letters from the Field
1927 – 1930

RICHARD F.S. STARR

Studies on the Civilization and Culture of Nuzi and the Hurrians - 8

The Expedition Staff

From left to right: Mr. Delougaz, Mr. and Mrs. Wilensky, Mr. and Mrs. Pfeiffer, R.FS. Starr

Preface

Richard F.S. Starr was a frequent letter writer. He travelled extensively throughout the world, particularly during his early years, and wrote regularly to his mother, Ida May Hill Starr, and later, also to his future wife, Dorothy. Both his mother and wife retained most of his letters. In the early eighties he edited these handwritten accounts of his experiences and typed them into a manuscript comprising three volumes, each of which is dedicated to the areas of the world where he spent the most time excavating, surveying, or photographing — China, Iraq and Sinai. His son, Nicholas, generously provided a copy of the fascinating, 195 page manuscript of the Iraq years, 1927–1929, for inclusion in his father's memorial volume. The letters reflect the time and places in which Starr worked while at the same moment, provide a sense of the conditions and personalities he encountered during the three campaigns at Yorgan Tepa/Nuzi in which he first participated and later directed. In addition, the letters reflect the intellectual and social attitudes of the time. It was decided to include all the letters since they dispense significant insight into the life of an excavator in those formative years in Near Eastern archaeology and that highlight, in particular, the impressions Starr had of Nuzi, Iraq, its people, and the greater Near East that he visited. No letters from the final season, 1930–1931, were preserved but his wife, Dorothy, who accompanied him in that year, wrote a detailed memoir of those final months in the field entitled, *North of Baghdad*, which is published below. It supplements and brings to a conclusion the remarkable story of the excavations at Nuzi.

Nuzi has recently been described as "... the best available urban site of any size for study anywhere in the ancient Near East."[1] With the publication of Richard Starr's letters and his wife, Dorothy's memoirs, the site assumes an even broader cultural significance. Much has been written of late criticizing the work of the earlier generation of archaeologists without taking into account the difficulties and limitations encountered in those days. The publication of Starr's letters coupled with his wife's memoirs should provide a clearer perspective.[2]

D.I. Owen

---

1 M.P. Maidman, in J.M. Sasson, et al., eds. *Civilizations of the Ancient Near East, II*, p. 931.

2 The letters in the original manuscript have been numbered sequentially 1-78 and placed in square brackets. Titles have been added to most of the letters. Also in square brackets, I have added occasional items for clarification that were not part of the original

manuscript along with footnotes, references, and photos from the Starr family and Lacheman archives. The letters have been left as they were written. Minor editorial corrections have been made where obvious typographical and spelling errors were encountered. One should read, in conjunction with these letters, Starr's introduction to his *Nuzi* I, pp. xxix-xxxviii.

Foreword

A few words of explanation are in order here about the letters that follow. The bulk of them were written to my mother, Ida May Hill Starr ([hereafter] I.M.S.), during the first three seasons, from 1927 into 1930, in which I participated as a member of the Harvard — Baghdad School Expedition excavating ancient Nuzi near Kirkuk, Iraq. For the third season, 1929–1930, I have also added letters to Dorothy ([hereafter] D.C.S.S.)[3] with whom I was later to share my life. There is considerable duplication between the I.M.S. and the D.C.S.S. letters for which I trust I will be forgiven, but each makes its own contribution in its own way. Furthermore, I have taken the liberty of eliminating material of purely personal nature throughout, correcting my eccentric spelling, and straightening out the most obvious of the grammatical tangles.

Unfortunately, at least from my point of view, there were no letters preserved from the 1930–1931 season, the final year of excavation. To fill the gap, I recommend *North of Baghdad*, [my wife] Dorothy's charming but unpublished [see now below] account of that last year when we were together on the dig.

Let me explain how the dig at Nuzi came about and how I happened to be part of it. In 1925, Dr. Edward Chiera, an Assyriologist, was on leave from the University of Pennsylvania and serving as the Annual Professor of the American Schools or Oriental Research in Baghdad. At that time Chiera became curious about certain cuneiform tablets, written in a non-Semitic[4] language, that were turning up in the hands of Baghdadi antiquities dealers. Tracking them to Kirkuk, and more specifically to the village of Tarkhalan some eight or ten miles further west, he actually carried on limited excavations there that year. The results were so promising, and his enthusiasm so infectious, that on returning to America he was able to persuade Harvard to underwrite the expense of a full scale expedition for further exploration. Edward Forbes and Paul Sachs, co-directors of the Fogg Museum of Art and Prof. [David] Lyon, Director of the Semitic Museum, raised the funds for Harvard's participation, and the American Schools of Oriental Research supplied the funds for, and the services of, an Assyriologist in the form of their Annual Professor for Baghdad. Thus the Harvard — Baghdad School Expedition was born. The University Museum (Uni-

3 [According to Nicholas Starr, his mother, Dorothy Clara Simpson Starr, liked to use all four of her initials because her husband also used four.]

4 [What is likely meant here is the Hurrian-influenced Akkadian of Nuzi.]

versity of Pennsylvania) also participated to a certain extent in the latter years of excavations.

Now, how did I come in? After returning from China in 1926 where I had served as photographer and general handyman on the Harvard China expedition, I worked for some months as a volunteer in the maintenance department of the Cleveland Art Museum learning museum management first hand. Then followed a job of transferring the Fogg Museum of Art from its original to its ambitious new building. With that behind me I fell into the job of Registrar at the Fogg. It was just after that that Mr. Forbes and Mr. Sachs realized that they really didn't know anything about this man Chiera who had fast-talked them into committing thousands of dollars and Harvard's prestige to sponsor an expedition into an area and culture that was foreign to any of their previous experience. Someone should be on hand, they thought, to represent Harvard and to keep them appraised of just what would be going on in the field. I was the obvious answer. I was available; I had already weathered the rugged Harvard China Expedition; and I was eager for the adventure.

The expedition headquarters were established in the Turkoman village of Tarkhalan from which we also drew the bulk of our work force. Somewhat less than half of the remainder were Bedouin Arabs from surrounding desert encampments; and a small minority were Kurds from neighboring villages. All were Sunni Muslims. Arabic was our language of communication since it was official for Iraq and since our Turkoman and even our Kurds were more at home in it then we ever were to become. I must say, though, we eventually became quite fluent though spectacularly ungrammatical.

Though we did not know it at first, the cuneiform tablets we unearthed eventually established our site as the city known in antiquity as Nuzi. The people themselves were Hurrians, a race hitherto undiscovered and unknown except for a mention — the Horites — in the Old Testament.

The Director of the Harvard — Baghdad School Expedition for the first season — 1927–1928 — was, of course, Dr. Chiera. For the second season — 1928–1929 — it was Dr. Robert H. Pfeiffer of Harvard and Boston University, who also that year was the Annual Professor of the American Schools of Oriental Research (Baghdad). For the third and fourth seasons — 1929–1931 — the directorship devolved upon me.

These letters reflect, I'm afraid, more the humdrum nature and weariness of work in the field than they do the excitement of discovery. But even some of that may come through if you look hard enough.

R.F.S.S.
Upperville, Virginia, 1982

Letters from Iraq [1–16] to I.M.S.

1927–1928 Season

The Beginning

[1][5]

CAMBRIDGE, MASSACHUSETTS
FRIDAY, SEPTEMBER 1927

My wild telegram has reached you now many hours ago and you know the great news.

You remember that I had held out some hope of going on the Harvard archaeological expedition to Iraq when I was home this summer, but it was a mighty slim hope. When I got back here Mr. Forbes' slow moving machinery got into action again money hunting, but the results were discouraging. Nothing seemed to happen.

Over a week ago, Mr. Forbes said, "Yes, there is a very good chance that you will go; *if* we can raise the money in time. You had better get your passport and steamer reservations so you can hop off on a moments notice." That put me on top of the world.

But somehow that seemed to be the signal for everything to stop dead. Every time Mr. Forbes planned to go out money hunting, some celebrity would turn up and demand attention, or some trivial detail would sidetrack him and tie him to his desk. He did get out a few times, always returning with a long disjointed tale of failure. Here was I all this time a nervous wreck, the sailing time of my boat getting closer and closer, and I getting more and more wrought up. The sudden bang of a door would startle me almost to death, while newspaper accounts of vast fortunes given to establish homes for friendless homing pigeons cause me acute anguish.

Yesterday was particularly discouraging. The fattest and heretofore most susceptible money belt on the whole sucker list refused to disgorge. Oh, it was hard.

Then came the dawn. This morning Mr. Forbes scuttled up to tell me that El Dorado had been found, bound and gagged, and was being delivered to me bag and baggage on this very day. I haven't worked very much today.

My boat, the one I had planned on, sails direct from America to Beirut, Syria, but Mr. Forbes and Mr. Sachs had a better plan. They said, "You are green. You are tackling something about which you know nothing. Wouldn't it, therefore, be the best plan for you to see the great examples of this art which are to be found in Europe? You, as the director and personal representative of the Fogg Museum and thereby of Harvard should, to use the colloquial, know your onion."

---

5 [Often lost in the publication of weighty and serious archaeological tomes are the excitement and frustration associated with projects in the field. Starr's first letter (and others later) captures the feelings many have experienced and serves as an appropriate introduction to his volume of letters.]

So, I sail from New York on October 12th [1927] for England. I spend a few days at the British Museum; then to Paris and the Louvre, and then on to Rome and Naples where I catch my original boat to Beirut. From Beirut to Damascus and from Damascus over the desert to Baghdad. The name of the place where we will be is Kirkuk, a city about 75 or 100 miles north of Baghdad.

I have a mountain of work to do before I leave, both in my job at the Fogg and in outfitting, but I will come home before I leave.

Transatlantic Crossing

[2]

R.M.S. BERENGARIA
12 OCTOBER 1927

I hardly know how to start out on this, my first letter of the great adventure. There is so much to say and I have so little ability to do so. I have a feeling that this trip is going to be a very important event in my life; that it is going to decide whether I continue muddling along in museum work or not. If I do, it should generate for me a much greater interest in my work, a stronger liking for my job, and more of a will to learn. If I don't keep on, heaven only knows what I will do. This trip will not "just perhaps" change things; it has *got* to. We shall see.

Ruth, certainly the best sister a person ever had, and Searls gave me a wonderful sendoff from New York. They were no less impressed with the size and magnificence of this ship than I. Magnificent it certainly is, and the Second Class quarters on the whole are very comfortable although not as good as some of the smaller boats I have been on. However, I have no complaint.

The purser has a huge sheath of letters and telegrams for me when the boat pulled out, and your wonderful wire and others from friends all over. To cap it all, just before the boat sailed, Isobel, my old Peking friend, appeared unexpectedly to bid me God-speed. I never had such a widely spread send off, and it made me almost sorry to be going.

The first couple of days out were quite rough, with relatively few people down for meals, but now the ship has quieted down to a nice, easy, comfortable motion only playfully suggestive of the tricks it could do.

In a few more days we reach England and then off to tour Europe.

The Long Voyage to Yorgan Tepa

[3]

HARVARD — BAGHDAD SCHOOL EXPEDITION
KIRKUK, IRAQ
TARKHALAN VILLAGE
12 NOVEMBER 1927

So long since I have written and so much there is to tell.

The good ship Berengaria brought us safely up the English Channel one fine sunny day preceded, flanked and followed by an escort of thousands of glistening, whirling sea gulls. Glorious birds they are; almost as fine a sight as the orderly, colorful English coastal country on our left.

I spent two days in London, practically all the time at the British Museum although I am ashamed to say that I spent as much time, if not more time, in the oriental department (Far Eastern) than in the Mesopotamian. From there I chased over to "sunny France," that misnamed country. Paris seemed rather dismal this time: a city of manufactured happiness. But my business was at the Louvre, and I learned a lot there; they have some splendid Sumerian things.

After two days of France I left for Italy, a day early to be sure, but the only accommodations that were available. I rode in state on the de luxe Rome express with a compartment all to myself and the most beautiful country. The sun shines there and the people sing. Here, unlike France, when the station porter or news stand keeper charges you a dollar for a ten cent article, he smiles. At least he gives you some return for your money.

From Rome I went straight on to Naples. I would like to have stayed in the Eternal City, but that will have to wait till later. In Naples, however, I had one day to divide between my steamship company and myself, and my half I used to go up Vesuvius. They turned it on when they saw me coming, and it smoked and belched lava in proper style.

The next night on the steamer out of Naples we passed Stromboli, quite active just now; its great flames and showers of red hot lava were quite terrifying. My ship for this leg of the journey was the Patria, loaded to the very scuppers and majestically dirty. Very poor food for a French boat (or for any boat) and as out-of-date as a French bathroom. Jews of all countries returning to Palestine and Egyptians made up most of the passenger list. Some of the Egyptian women were very handsome, and the Jews a very decent lot.

The ship stopped for a short time in Alexandria, and I made the great mistake of going ashore. I should never have done it for it gave a black eye to what I had always believed (and still do) to be a great and wonderful country. The next stop was Jaffa, and profiting by my experience in Egypt, I stayed on the ship. It was too beautiful a sight from the water to have it spoiled by an hour or two among misunderstood people.

Beirut gave me my first real sight of the Near East. There they have trolley cars and taxi cabs, but just ten steps away were the narrow, twisting half-covered, bazaars that I had expected to find. Here Arab, Syrian, Jew and a dozen other races smoke and curse and bargain their wares.

The next day I left on the 500 mile automobile journey to Baghdad. The first stage was Damascus, but since we arrived in the city after dark and left about sunrise, I didn't see much of it. It seemed criminal to race through such a place, but I travel not for pleasure this time. We did see a little of the city that night, though. Mosques with white domes, delicate minarets, and soft colored striped walls. There through that arch you see a black hole that you know to be a street and on the left a blacker spot you know to be a doorway, and you wonder what is behind it. Probably some wretched trinket seller, but again in there might be one of the seven Kalendars of the Arabian Nights.

All the next day we sped across the desert. The most modern American touring car whisked us along at sixty miles an hour over a land more barren and primitive than you can imagine. Hardly a sprig of vegetation to be seen but camel thorn and in places not even that. Sometimes the way would be rough and we would have to stick to the track, but in other places from horizon to horizon in every direction would be hard, flat road. It seemed so incongruous to be on a journey through such country in an automobile. It seemed as though we should be sweating along in the dust of carts as we did in China or swaying slowly along the back of a camel. So it has been done for a thousand years and more; and now we do it in two days. We hurry too much.

Shortly before nightfall, we passed a sign post set up in the desert at a meeting of three tracks. It pointed in three directions and said — Jerusalem, Damascus, and Baghdad! What do those names mean to you? Just think of it.

That night we had a few hours of sleep at a fortified rest house where there was water (Rutba wells); then off again long before daylight. The last hundred miles were about as desolate as anything I have ever seen. Finally we reach a large oasis where there is a health officer who gives you a shot in the arm for cholera, for there is a small epidemic south of Baghdad, then on to a large, muddy river flowing alternatively through flowering and barren country. This the driver tell us is the Euphrates. Over this we go on a pontoon bridge, then on for an hour or more. Finally we sight a host of domes and minarets, cross the noble Tigris on more pontoons, and we are in Baghdad.

The first thing I did on reaching Baghdad was to buy a pair of rubber boots. That describes the conditions pretty well. The fall rains had been heavy there in the last few days, as they had in the last hundred miles or less of the desert (sounds strange, doesn't it?), and the streets, all of which were unpaved, were a sea of mud. My stay in Baghdad was very short, practically all spent in rushing about buying supplies and only a few fascinating hours in the famous bazaars. There one sees the products of the world. There is the peddler who in his dreams is Caliph and behind the shuttered windows on the tortuous, twisting streets whose overhanging houses almost meet overhead, may be a thousand Arabian Nights tales; who knows.

From the long pontoon bridge over the Tigris you see the city again. Houses of all colors with palm trees behind, and in the river those queer, round, oversized baskets covered with bitumen which, from early time, have been typical Tigris boats.

It took almost twenty-four hours by train to get to Kirkuk where the expedition Ford (yes, we have a car), met me and took me out ten miles to our headquarters in the village of Tarkhalan.

I found that Dr. Chiera, the expedition director, had been here some weeks and had fixed for us a most luxurious home. We live in a native house made in the usual style, mud walls and roof, everything of mud, in fact, except for leaky, wooden doors and windows and lime cement floors. The house faces a large compound where we have a garden of sorts, with a smaller one to the left for our donkey and goat, and a huge one further on for our horses and chickens and such when we get them. Inside we have four bedrooms and a large living room, a laboratory, a bathroom with a *real tub*, but no running water of course, kitchen, servants' rooms and a guard room for our three armed sentries who watch at night. On the whole, it is real luxury. Nothing like the China trip. Oh yes, we have a garage.

Our party consists of Dr. Edward Chiera, Assyriologist, on leave from the University of Pennsylvania as Annual Professor of the American Schools of Oriental Research in Baghdad and Director of the Harvard — Baghdad School Expedition; Mrs. Chiera, who is awfully nice and attractive, and their two children, a boy of 12 and a girl of 8; Dr. Ephraim Speiser, Assyriologist, also on leave from the University of Pennsylvania[6]; Emanuel Wilensky, a Russian Jewish architect from Haifa in Palestine to do our plans, etc., and myself.

Mother, it is terribly late. Everyone else has long since been in bed, and we must be up at daylight. I'll tell you about the dig in the next letter.

The Excavations and the Discovery of Armor

[4]

THANKSGIVING DAY, 1927

Yesterday came my first mail from home. The rose petals from [your] garden were almost enough to make me pack up and leave this barren land forever.

Today, being Thanksgiving Day, was unanimously voted a holiday by us all. This day brings back memories of thrilling football games, golden brown turkeys, happy free-for-all rabbit hunts, and the blazing library firs; and around the fire are all those who are dear to me.

---

6 [Curiously, Speiser is hardly mentioned in the subsequent correspondence.]

Mrs. Chiera is doing her best to make this an adequate substitute for the real thing, and great things are going on in the kitchen. Even now I can smell the first whiffs of our Thanksgiving turkey. Also, we are making this an extra special occasion by changing from dirty kakhi breeches and flannel shirts to the black and white of dinner clothes. We're doing all we can to take ourselves away from our surroundings.

I believe my last letter brought you as far as our life on the dig. Our living conditions have certainly been comfortable, and never before have I eaten so much. If I don't put on ten pounds, something certainly must be wrong. My insides are in good shape, and altogether I am feeling very fit.

It is a life that produces an appetite. Not the long, hard marches of China, but from 5:30 in the morning until 9:00 in the evening we are on the go. First of all there is breakfast to put out of the way, then preparations for the day's work to be completed so that we can be in the field and on the job by 7:00. From then until 4:30, except for a half hour lunch period and two fifteen minute rest periods, it is go, go, go; chasing from one hole to another, supervising the excavations, watching over the removal of a cuneiform tablet or an especially nice jar, urging on the workmen, packing objects, piecing together fragments, and a thousand other little jobs. We usually get home at 5:00 with a short wait for cleaning up before dinner. After dinner, with heavy lids, we read or talk for an hour or two and then go to bed. So, you see that our time is very largely spoken for by our jobs; for that reason you must forgive me if my letters are not as frequent as they might be. Friday is our day of rest and mighty welcome it is; that is the Muhammadan Sunday, and since our men are all of that faith, we follow their custom.

The men working on our force are mainly Turkoman and Arabs, and of the two, the Turkoman are the better workers. They are more serious and conscientious in their work, as a rule, and need much less watching. The Arabs, more devil-may-care by nature, are local Bedouin; they are handsome men with their short, black beards and long, braided hair showing underneath flowing head clothes. They wear their rags with a certain air of swagger and grace that is quite appealing. The Turkoman, on the other hand, lack the easy fellowship of the desert people. The Bedouin speak Arabic, of course,; the mother tongue of the Turkoman is Turkish though they are not considered to be Turks in the modern sense but an offshoot from the main Turkic horde of many centuries ago. Intermixed with these two are a sprinkling of Kurds, largely indistinguishable from the Turkoman.

The ancient culture we are investigating is a non-Semitic one dating from around 1500 B.C. The dig itself is centered on two private houses just a short way from a much larger mound, and the yield so far has been rich in things of archaeological interest. Things of artistic value so far have remained hidden from us. That of course is to be expected, for these houses were destroyed by ancient raiders, presumably Assyrians, and it is natural that all things of value would have been carried off. The yield of cuneiform tablets has been good, about ten to fifteen every day; also, a great quantity of pottery and some bronze objects. In the near future we will start exploratory trenches in the big mound in the hope of finding public buildings with their immensely important records or a temple with (from my point of view) their much more important objects of art.[7] If we locate either of these, we are made. A burial ground would be equally rich.

But we need not worry about the success of the expedition, for its name is already on the Golden Book of Memories with a discovery of immense importance, and I had the pleasure of uncovering it. It is a bronze corselet or suit of armor protecting the front of the body from the throat to below the belts and made of two rows of overlapping bronze plates sewn evidently on a fabric or leather jacket. Of course, none of the backing material remains, but the plates were found in their original and proper position so that we know exactly how it looked. Not only has armor never been found before, but our finds prove that all those single objects which were thought to be broad, round ended, knives were, in fact, single armor plates. It was found outside the house, strangely enough, where we were tracing an exterior wall and underneath a huge jar, hidden evidently from the raiding Assyrians. It was exciting.

I find myself still a more or less useless member of the party, but no doubt I do enough to earn my board. I am gradually getting a few words of Arabic, one by one, and I must say it is easier than Chinese.

The weather is getting really cold. We have fires every night, and the early mornings are bitter. The rains have been long due and will keep us, when they come, from the field for many days, but with all the materials we have to process, no one will be idle.

The First Tablet Hoard

[5]

6 DECEMBER 1927

Things go along in our life in about the same way day after day. We have been finding things in pretty good quantities: pottery, scraps of bronze, and scattered tablets, but three days ago we struck a gusher. The big house we have been digging for so long finally yielded up its library, and for three days we have been busy every minute of the day taking care of the cuneiform tablets that came out. In three days (one and a half days working time) we found over 800 complete tablets, not counting the thousands of fragments that will also prove of great value. They are very fragile when they are first taken out of the ground, and it takes great care to make sure they come out complete and not in a thousand fragments. They are made of unbaked clay, and only after we bake

---

7 [One has to remember that Starr was representing Harvard's Fogg Museum of Art and was seeking museum quality objects to bring back to Cambridge for exhibit as the museum's share of the finds. Archaeological research in those times was sponsored by museums with this goal in mind.]

them are they hard enough to handle. In fact, when baked they become brick. We will be setting up our oven soon to put our tablets into durable condition. They are rather dull and uninteresting after the sixth hundredth and your hands and feet are almost frozen. You begin to forget what a treasure you have.

Today the men started on the big mound, and right on the surface were found several tablets which were receipts for temple offerings or taxes. That holds promise that the building may be either a temple or palace. If it is either, we have a very good chance of finding something really good. Up to now the finds have not been exactly art museum material, but there is hope.

The thing of greatest concern to us, outside of the excavations, is the weather, and I must say that it is getting mighty cold. Not cold according to the thermometer, but it seems frigid to those of us who are out in it. The rainy season is long past due, but so far we have had only one good rain. When it rains her it pours, and all work and travel is impossible. However, we can stand some rainy days, for we have a great deal of indoor work to do.

At the moment the great thing in our private lives is the excitement of our latest purchase. Dr. and Mrs. Chiera, Speiser, and myself have just bought personally a horse for each of us, but as yet we have no saddles. We hope to get them from the government post here, but, if that can't be done, I shall buy a native saddle no matter how uncomfortable it may be. Mine is a very handsome, little Arab pony, white, speckled with brown, nine years old, and I am crazy to try him out. The British-controlled troops stationed in Kirkuk are being disbanded and their horses sold. This is one of them, and for that reason they were cheap.

I had wanted a horse so that I could get a change of scenery. Here, in this bleak desert country, everything is alike as far as the eye can see, and one gets fed up with it. Travel to where the prospect might be different is a long walk and a hard one. Iraq is an old and tired country. The weight of its years has taken away its bloom and spirit, and in its old age God seems to have forgotten it....

The Discovery of the Šilwa-Teššup Archives

[6]

21 DECEMBER 1927

A thousand pardons for letting so many days pass without a letter home. When I look back on the days it seems as though I had done nothing at all, but actually our work seldom gives us time for anything else. Since my last letter, the dig has gone along in more or less the same pattern but with a considerable increase in the work force. Now, with our crew expanded to 125 men, it still remains a small group compared to the other excavations in Iraq, but it is enough for us to handle.

I believe I spoke earlier of the armor that we found, so there is no need to speak of that again except say that it still remains our most important single find. Since then we have continued working on the same building and a mighty big establishment it must have been, for though we have been scratching away like badgers for almost two months it still stretches on with no end in sight. Of course the size of the mound that it left tells us the maximum that it can be, but ordinarily a mound of that size should be adequate for several private houses. Eventually, I suppose, we will shift exclusively to the main mound, or city nearby.

Excavation here is particularly difficult in that all of the ancient buildings were built of mud brick, and to be able to detect the stumps of the remaining walls from the dirt surrounding them calls for a pickman of considerable intelligence as well as constant overseeing by ourselves.You see, the soil that had packed down around these remnants of walls is the same composition as the soil from which the mud brick itself was made. You have no idea how easy it is for a pickman to make a mess of things, breaking through walls and creating confusion in our ground plan by following some will-o'-the-wisp that really doesn't exist. However, the correct ground plan is gotten eventually, either from the wall or from the outline of the pack earth floor, and everyone is happy again.

Stone was not used at all here as it was too scarce, but some baked brick was used. Unfortunately it was restricted to occasional floors and foundations so that it is seldom of much use as a guide in tracing our walls. At times, though, it has shown us a doorway or a difference in the shape of a room that we hadn't seen from a higher level.

It is surprising what good condition these bricks are in. Just as good as the day they were made. It sounds almost impossible that here at our living quarters we use bricks that have been waiting for us for 3500 years. Yet it is a fact. We have used them particularly in our walkways and most recently for a very elaborate and big crude oil burning oven in which to bake our tablets. It has just been completed, and the first trial fire is to be today. You see, the tablets, except for official government and temple records (none of which we have yet found), were never baked. They were made of ordinary clay dried in the sun and perfectly capable of standing all the handling that private documents, accounts, and records would get. But when we dig them out of the ground they are damp and extremely fragile; in fact they often come out badly broken, so some means must be found to put them in permanent form. Consequently, we bake them; thus they become small inscribed bricks and almost indestructible.

Getting the tablets out of the ground is always a delicate operation, and it takes a long time to teach these poor dumb people to use sufficient care. The usual procedure in excavating a room is first, if possible, to outline the room from the top. Then the pickmen, the shovelmen, and the dirt haulers work to a foot above the pavement, or a foot above the level of the first objects found. Then three or four picked men are put in with knives to carefully clean down to the pavement. If anything is there they can't miss it. But even these men can do a surprising amount of damage. They dig out a pot and throw away the most necessary fragments, or break a tablet or bronze object through pure carelessness. They have to be watched all the time. Not that they aren't interested in the work; they are very much so and we have a very loyal and honest group of Arabs and Turkoman for our workers, but oh! how dumb they can be.

The kiln where the excavated tablets were baked.

Up until about two weeks ago our yield of tablets had been scattered and slim. The event Dr. Chiera had been hoping for took place: we found the library of the big house we were cleaning. Out of one room there came over 800 tablets almost all in perfect condition: things of great scholarly value. These were lying two and three deep all tangled up on the floor, and the presence of great numbers of bronze nails seemed to indicate that they had been stacked in wooden boxes. Since then our luck has struck again, and several hundred more have been added to our treasure chest.

About two weeks ago we split our force and started excavations on the big mound of Yorgan Tepa. From the size we know that it must have been a city of some importance, but just which one of the many ancient cities spoken of in the tablets of two years ago we do not yet know. However, the tablets from here show this to be the palace or house of the local ruler or governor, so other things of more than usual interest are bound to come along. Already we have found an object of great interest, the best thing artistically so far. It is an incense burner or censor of bronze, about 20 inches in height and in the shape of a truncated cone. The side are pierced with three horizontal rows of triangular holes and on the rim at equidistant points are three lions couchant. It is very heavily encrusted with patina, of course, but when carefully cleaned it should prove to be a piece that any museum would be proud to own. Of course the Iraq Museum has first choice of everything we find, so it may never come to America (the armor certainly never will), but we can always hope. Should we find a temple on this mound (tepa) the chances are good that things of even greater value will be unearthed.

We have been having a few days of much needed rain which gives us a chance to catch up on work at home that has been piling up from the dig. The weather is still mild as a rule, but the heavy Turkoman sheepskin cape I bought in the bazaar at Kirkuk seems mighty welcome.

Never before in my life have I eaten so much. I make a hog of myself at every meal and feel like a starved wolf in between. We live well.

The thought of Christmas makes me feel blue. I see all the glorious gathering at Hope around the blazing fire. All the family, all those I love, together; I don't enjoy the separation. We are doing what we can to brighten things up here, but it will only mean a little bit bigger meal and dinner clothes.

But on Christmas Day I will be at Hope in spirit. Make room for me at the fire for my heart is there.

Christmas in Tarkhalan

[7]

28 DECEMBER 1927

Christmas has come and gone, and a rather dreary day it was. Not that it was actually unpleasant, for we did everything we could to brighten things up, but the thought of our glorious holiday at home kept intruding on our efforts. As I said, we did our best, and it worked out pretty well. We even had two Christmas dinners; the cook being a little hazy as to the real date prepared a great feast for the day before by mistake. However, food is plentiful and our appetites are something to marvel over, so the error was hailed as a blessing rather than otherwise by the cook.

For days before the event Mrs. Chiera and the children had been busy preparing ornaments for the Christmas tree and other little home made surprises. The table fairly bulged with food, and our poor digestive systems were put to no end of overtime work and trouble. Kirkuk gave us a small supply of foreign delicacies, and we put them to mighty good use, too.

We have inaugurated a new style in Christmas trees. The only green we could find was an olive tree, and when the color and glitter of ornaments was added to the soft grey and green of the foliage the effect was quite handsome. Much more appropriate for Christmas, really, than a conifer.

We had dinner about 6:00 (after fasting all day), and afterwards we called in two of our workers to dance for us. All the household staff and all the uninvited, though most welcome, exponents of the dance came along too. It was really one of the most interesting sights I have seen since I have been here. The primitive expressionless face of the man who played monotonously on his little flute; the flashing eyes and glistening teeth of the leader beating his drum (a gasoline can) urging on the rest; then the long row of men stamping in rhythm, their faces expressionless with a far-off, almost hypnotized look, in their eyes. The urge of the dance is a strong one, and once the music started even the kitchen boy could not keep out of it. Unfortunately we did not have enough room for them to really do their group dance, but for solo dancing we discovered right among our guards a man who could make a fortune in New York. Very slow and simple it is, with his long robes swinging, his arms extended with long sleeves almost touching the floor. Very slowly he danced and with a grace that is given to few people. He was splendid.

We had a hard day and I must be off to bed.

Agricultural Finds

[8]

8 JANUARY 1928

There seems to be little to report this week. The dig has been going along steadily yielding the usual amount of pottery and mighty little else though we do have a wealth of interesting architectural features.

No doubt you have heard, or will have by the time this letter reaches you, of Woolley's amazing finds at Ur of the Chaldees. It has all been kept a great secret for some reason. Though we had known for a month or more that things far surpassing his gold objects of last year were coming out, it was not until two days ago that we were let in on it. Certainly he deserves his find for he has had many lean years, years that couldn't show half or on tenth of what we have now, before he struck it rich last year. Should we find a royal burying ground as he has we would startle the world too. We will if we keep at it long enough.

For the last few days we have been going along under reduced force to give our wall tracers a chance to outline enough rooms to keep our rough gang busy. The number of men we have who can do wall tracing is limited. It is slow work, and of course we can't allow the rough gang in to clear a room until all four walls are established. Wall tracing is the most difficult part of this excavation, and it takes a great deal of our time; even the best men must be watched lest they go astray. You wonder how we can be sure of such an unsure thing, and I must admit that it sounds most uncertain, but there is very little chance of going permanently astray. The reason it is so difficult is that the walls must be traced from high up in order to go along fast, and high up they are indistinct and hard to follow. A poor man will have to go way down perhaps to the floor where rain and weather have left them relatively undisturbed. So, when a man gets lost he goes down and there he finds proof for or against; if it shows he is right he picks it up again from the surface. If it is not all right, it means his wall has turned, or he has struck a doorway, or perhaps even that the wall had totally collapsed in antiquity. After a sound wall has been exposed to the air and sun for a few days it is unmistakable as such.

The walls on the big mound, the "*tepa*" or "tell," have been awfully trying because their upper surfaces have been so broken up by relatively recent graves. (Ancient mounds are favorite modern-day burial grounds.) Consequently we must go deep to follow them at all. Generally the depth we must go depend on the weathering that section of the "tell" has been subjected to over the centuries. We have some walls — rooms — ten and fifteen feet deep in the highest part of the mound. From these highest places they get shallower and shallower in the more weathered parts of the mound's surface until they disappear entirely. A room, for instance, that has weathered until the pavement only a foot below the surface is practically undefinable. The walls would be almost impossible to detect, and any objects in such an exposed room would most likely be disintegrated.

We have accumulated quite an interesting agricultural exhibit. We have found great quantities of carbonized wheat, barley, peas, pistachio nuts and date stones; also perfectly preserved loaves or round flat cakes of bread. Imagine, bread 3500 years old! Of course it is carbonized, but everything except the color is as it was the day it was made.

The last two or three days have been quite cold, below freezing in the shade and we feel it considerably.

No work today; the weather is too threatening. However, we got in a lot of work at home, and I had a nice long ride with Mrs. Chiera to whom I am giving riding lessons. Sounds like a joke, and it is. Already she rides as well as I do. Poor Dr. Chiera can't be coaxed near a horse.

The Frescoes

[9]

1 FEBRUARY 1928

The last mail brought your three wonderful letters of Christmas-time. It has been a good many weeks since I had gotten a letter from you at all. The flowers you enclosed were still fragrant, and their faint delicious odor carried me in a second back to Hope and to those I love.

The work is not booming along at the *tepa*. Our workforce has been increased to 170 men, and in spite of the slowness of the task the dirt continues to mount up on the dump higher and higher.

Our prize find since the armor, and of equal value if not greater, have been some large fragments of fresco. They are decorative panels in geometric design with heads (conventionalized) of men and bulls, in fair condition, and the colors fresh and delicate. If they can be preserved they will be of immense importance. They were found in the dirt of a small corridor from which nothing was expected, and had tumbled there with the wall at the time of the destruction. Probably because it was a corridor it had no furniture, etc. to burn in the general destruction, so it was saved. If such an insignificant room yields these things the important rooms must have been even finer. These should please the people at the Fogg.

We found a well the other day, and we are digging it to the bottom. Wells have always been productive for not only have things tumbled down them during their use, but when the destroying Assyrians came down it is not improbably that these people used the wells as hiding places for valuable and sacred objects hoping to fish them out if they themselves survived. Also it is just as likely that the Assyrians used it as a nice place to throw loot that couldn't be carried off. It would be a happy day if we found a couple of statues down there. We are over forty feet down now and should reach the bottom soon. You see, the Assyrians when they destroyed the place for the last time about 1500–1400 B.C. did a thorough job but in doing so they preserved for us many things that otherwise would certainly not have survived. If it had not been for their wholesale destruction we would not have these houses left to us exactly as they were used 3500 years ago. We owe those destroyers quite a bit after all.

About my plans, I don't know much except that I shall probably have to come home, when the season is ended, by the most direct route. It may be necessary in order to make sure of my continuance here next year.

I'm off the dig today with a cold, but all in all I have not been in such good health in years. The amount of food I eat is prodigious.

Visits and Ramadhan

[10]

15 FEBRUARY 1928

One of the American drillers from the Turkish Petroleum Company came over to see the dig the other day, and, as he said, "To get a chance to talk American again," which he did, to my great delight with that soft homely drawl of the Texan. I saw him again in Kirkuk a few days later and he said, "You all don't know how glad I was to see your diggn's out there. It gives me something to write home to my wife about. My wife seems to think that I am going through all kinds of wild adventures and seein' all kind of new sights and I'm runnin' out of material. In fact for the last month or so I've been buying books on Eye-rack (Iraq) and copyin' my letters out of them. That's the stuff she wants."

I feel more or less the same way. Here I am in this far off land of romance and tradition, so called, but with nothing to write about. Unfortunately the only book relating to Eye-rack I have right here is an Arabic grammar, and I'm afraid it wouldn't be very exciting reading. For the last two weeks there has been no digging: the first week because of rains and the second because Dr. and Mrs. Chiera who have gone down to Baghdad for a week and Mr. Wilensky who is off for a week's vacation in the mountains, leaving Speiser, the two children and myself here to work out our own salvation.

It hardly seems possible that our dig is practically over. Just about a week more will finish up our season's work aside from a little exploratory digging in other mounds round about. We had decided long ago to work up until Ramadhan, the Muhammadan holy month which this year begins on February 22, and we just about struck it right for we will have to squeeze pretty hard to make the money last. Very seldom do excavations continue beyond Ramadhan because during that time the men must fast, with no food or water or smoking until after nightfall, which puts them in poor condition and spirit for work. Also, they have certain religious scruples against working at that time. In the south, of course, Ramadhan means also the resumption of summer heat which makes work almost impossible anyway. Here, I am told, the heat is not bad until April. If we had the money and the inclination to work later I don't believe Ramadhan would matter much. Our people are rather broad minded, tolerant Muhammadans whose religious observance would not be so strict as to prevent them from continuing to make a living. They stand in much greater need of money than of salvation.

After the dig closes we will be here until about the end of March finishing up all the inside jobs that have accumulated throughout the year and packing our objects for shipment to America. Packing is going to be a trying job, and I don't look forward to it, particularly when I see our bank balance.

I suppose that I will be coming home right after that, though that depends somewhat on the plans for future excavation. It is also uncertain and trying, for we have as yet no idea whether Harvard is to continue excavations here or not. If they do, I suppose that I will be here again, but if they do not there is no telling what I will be at this time next year. It may be (and most likely) that I will have to come home right away to make sure of my future. There are many things I would like to do before I come home. I would like to see something of the country in which I have been roosting for so long and a little bit of Persia as well. I want to see something of other excavations in the Near East, and some of the Euphrates country. Then, Langdon Warner asked me to join him in Japan (he will have left Cambridge by the time you get this letter), and I would rather do that than anything I know of, but I don't see how that can be managed. However, I hope that I will know about Harvard's plans before I leave here. It would be a great relief to know either one way or the other.

An Invitation

[11]

17 FEBRUARY 1928

Just a note, and such excitement! This afternoon a letter came from a Mr. Edward Austin Waters of Philadelphia, a friend of Langdon Warner's, asking me to travel through Persia with them — Mr. and Mrs. Warner — for three weeks as their guest. They are now in Baghdad and leave for the Persian border tomorrow night. I will come down from the north at the same time and meet them there, for of course I accepted. I never could let such an opportunity go by. From the border we proceed to the capital, Tehran, by airplane, doing in six hours that which before had taken many weeks. Justification for my going is that Fogg Museum asked them to get photographs of the great ruins in Persia at Isfahan, Persepolis, and Pasargadae, and they want me to do the photographic work. Since the season is practically over here I fee free to go.

From Tehran in the north we go south to Isfahan and Lord only knows where else. I know practically nothing about their plans, but I accepted before they had a chance to change their minds. Imagine, a letter coming in casually asking me to meet two perfect strangers at dawn at the eastern railhead for a glorious trip over Persia. Some people are born lucky, and I am the luckiest of all.

Next letter will be from Tehran.

The Persia Excursion

[12]

HOTEL ROYAL
TEHRAN, PERSIA
27 FEBRUARY 1928

If this letter goes out through Russia, as I hope it will, you probably will get it sooner than the wild and hurried note I mailed from Kirkuk about a week ago, so let me explain again how I happened suddenly to be writing from the capital of Persia.

Just about a week ago I was finishing up a long rainy day's work at our peaceful camp-home in Kirkuk when in came a letter from a perfectly strange person, one Edward A. Waters of Philadelphia, a classmate of Roger Warner and a friend of Langdon Warner. The letter went on to say that shortly before leaving America for a trip to Baghdad he had seen Langdon who had implored him to go into Persia for photographs of the great ruins of Persepolis and Isfahan and to see if I could go along to take the photographs, and he proceeded in the letter to ask me to accompany his wife and himself for a three week's trip through Persia entirely at their expense, or rather at the expense of Mrs. Water's mother in Cambridge who is financing their Persia trip for the greater glory and edification of Harvard. That explains my presence here.

Incidentally, they are both delightful people. What is more, they are great boosters of yours. They drove down from Philadelphia to see the gardens of the Eastern Shore last fall just after I left for Iraq, and they haven't stopped talking about you yet.

So much for that.

You can imagine how I snapped up the offer. A chance of a lifetime had been put in my hands.

There is a rail line in Iraq that runs to the Persian frontier at Khanaqin, and the next afternoon saw me aboard the train for the border. About four the next morning I joined the train on which they were coming up from Baghdad, and a few hours later in the cold grey light of dawn we reached Khanaqin. As usual the arrangements they had made with Thomas Cook and Son in Baghdad went wrong, the car that was to take us over the border to Khasr-i-Shirin didn't materialize, but thanks to my few words of Arabic we found a garage and hired a car, a touring car and certainly the oldest Ford in all of Iraq, to take us over. How it ever made it over those roads I don't know, but it got us eventually to the miserable little town of Khasr-i-Shirin, the western end of the airline to Tehran, the capital.

Strangely enough Persia, one of the most primitive countries I know, possessing in all only eight miles of railway, has an excellent air service; not native, of course, but the German Junkers company. We had booked to fly from here to Tehran, but again Cook's plans went wrong and we found it impossible. The war was a great thing for Persia for the English and the Russians had supplied them with excellent roads — at least they were originally — and over these we took a car to Kermanshah, the first big city on our road, some 90 or 100 miles form Khasr-i-Shirin.

The road led us for miles and miles along a broad flat valley with great snow capped mountains on either side which closed in gradually as we sped on east. We knew that we would have to cross the Paitak Pass, and we thought we had reached it a dozen times, but each time our persistent valley, now quite narrow, would wriggle somehow around the seemingly impassable barrier that blocked our way and on we would go for another few miles. But that couldn't last long, and soon we were climbing in earnest, our poor little Ford — yes we were in a Ford again — chattering and roaring over this completely astounding road. Never have I seen such a thing. It was a road that went over a mountain that seemed to deny all passage. At terrific grades it would follow up one side of a little valley to return on the other side where we could see our old road hundreds of feet below us, while at other times it would zigzag back and forth along the face of the mountain like a goat track.

The scenery was splendid, for while the valley had been bare and desolate, the mountain sides, where not sheer rock, had enough vegetation to give a soft green tone to the dull red and brown of the rock. The great vistas down the valleys to the plains and to distant snow covered mountains were breathtaking.

We reached the top of the pass, which is something over 5000 feet, at about snow level, and of course we expected an equally thrilling descent but instead we came out on to what we found out later to be the great Iranian Plateau which covers most of northern Persia. All in all we weren't ungrateful to the plateau for we didn't look forward to going down such grades with that car. Instead we rolled mile after mile over a great bare plain and finally reached Kermanshah long after dark.

Allow me to digress for a minute. I've just read in a book by Sykes on Persia a quotation of Ardeshir, who founded the Sasanian Dynasty in A.D. 226, which struck me as being so remarkable for the time and country and so full of clearly expressed common sense that I thought you would like to hear it. He said: "There can be no power without an army, no army without money, and no money without agriculture, and no agriculture without justice."

Kermanshah was not particularly interesting except for the curious, dark labyrinth of a bazaar where you rubbed shoulders with mobs of strange, picturesque and dirty people. Just at dusk when the little holes in the vaulted roof turn to blackness and the feeble lamps glimmer in the long, winding arcades you might easily imagine yourself a spectator of an Arabian Nights story. As far as things to buy, there seemed to be nothing appealing, though I imagine there is if you know the language and you know the place well enough to dig them out. Like the Baghdad bazaar, it seems to deal largely with things made in Germany and Birmingham.

All in all there seemed mighty little to recommend Kermanshah except the splendid range of snow covered mountains on both sides of the city. Our hotel was pretty bad, particularly the food, but there were no bugs and that was a blessing.

We hired a new car here, a Hudson of fairly recent vintage, with a good looking Arab driver to take us through to Tehran. That man certainly changed my opinion of native drivers, for on those terrible roads he handled his car as beautifully as any driver I have ever been with. He must have been an exception.

We were held up for two days in leaving Kermanshah. The great Asadabad Pass ahead of us was closed by a snowstorm in spite of the 200 shovel men on duty there. But we used our time to good advantage by going out for one day to Takht-i-Bustan, a series of most interesting rock sculptures of the middle and late Sasanian period, and to Behistun to see the rock-cut relief of Darius receiving the homage of captive kings and its world-famous trilingual laudatory inscription.

We got off finally and travelled mile after mile through a broad valley, partially cultivated and bare of trees and grass except where a little mud village huddled at the foot of some towering mountain. Eventually we reached the foot of the pass and started to climb. Here there was nothing of the greenery or life of the Pitak Pass, just bare rock and snow. What we thought had been a bad road on the first pass was like a billiard table as compared to this. For miles we twisted and turned through the snow covered roads up terrible grades with a wall of snow on one side and a drop of too many feet to worry about on the other. It was a thrilling ride. The top is at 10,000 feet, and there was no doubt when we reached it, for here we went through a trench cut through the snow more than twice the height of the car.

The descent was about half that of the ascent, and we were soon rolling along over much of the same flat country as before, reaching Hamadhan after a hard seven hour drive. Everyone had told me that Hamadhan was the garden city of Persia and I agree. It is considerably over 5000 feet in elevation.

Kasvin, the next city on our route, was an uninteresting town except for a glimpse of some nice tiles we could see on two distant mosques. We only stopped there to eat and then off for the long, monotonous drive to Tehran, which we reached some hours after dark.

Tehran is a new city and the capital of Persia. It has funny little horse drawn trolley cars and electric street lights that work now and then. Here again the saving feature is a great mountain range, the highest in Persia, right behind the city, separating the capital from the Caspian Sea.

The most interesting part of the city, I am told, is the bazaar. I haven't been there, however, because it is the center of a bad epidemic of scarlet fever and all foreigners have been warned to stay away. I don't know whether I have had it in my childhood or not, but even if I have and one dose makes you immune I wouldn't like very much to pick up a bug and give it to Mr. or Mrs Waters, who have never had it.

There is nothing here to see and nothing to do but to go to the carpet and antique shops and bargain over things you don't want or can't afford to buy. I haven't gotten much, just a few old textiles and some ancient bronzes and a nice lot of prehistoric pottery, which I though of sufficient importance to buy for Harvard. I have been on the lookout for a pair of beautiful earrings for you, but I have seen nothing so far. In Baghdad they say the only good jewelry is made in Persia, and in Persia you can't find it when you get there.

So far I have not found the Persian people attractive. They seem to have all the bad qualities of the Arab and Turkoman, many times multiplied, and none of the many good qualities. Of course I have no authority on which to express an opinion, but it will be nice to see the handsome face and straight-forward eye of our Kirkuk men again.

We have been out to dinner at the Williamson's, the second secretary of our legation, to dinner with Mr. Phillips, the U.S. Minister, and once for a real meal at the American Mission Hospital. That completes our activities except for a morning I had with Dr. Herzfeld, the great German Near and Middle Eastern scholar. I believe it was the most interesting and exciting morning I have ever spent.

We have been here about five days waiting for good flying weather. We hope to get off tomorrow by plane for Isfahan, Persepolis, Shiraz, Bushire, Mohammera, and thence by train back to Baghdad.

My next letter will probably be from Kirkuk again.

More Impressions of the Persia Expedition

[13]

TARKHALAN VILLAGE
KIRKUK, IRAQ
12 MARCH 1928

Just a note to let you know that I am safely back again at Tarkhalan after my adventurous dash through Persia.

My last letter, from Tehran, you should have received long ago telling of our experience coming into the country and in finally reaching the capital. I'll carry on from there.

The two principal places we wanted to see were Isfahan and Persepolis, the latter just 40 miles north of Shiraz, and there were two ways of doing it, one by car, the other by plane. The motor trip is very long and tiring with very poor stopping places along the way, so we went around to the Junkers Company to see what we could do in the way of a plane. We found, much to our delight, that they had a plane going all the way to Mohamera to bring back radio supplies for the government and that we could go along, stopping a day and a half at Isfahan and the same at Persepolis, then to Bushire, and then to Mohamera. The plane was to go in a few days, but that day never seemed to arrive. Day after day we would pack our bags and pay our bills only to find that the weather reports from Isfahan were bad and we couldn't fly. The only consolation was that we knew they were not taking any chances in sending out passengers over mountains under dangerous conditions.

At last the reports of good weather ahead came in. We rushed down to the field and after the usual red tape over passports and police permits for departure from Tehran we climbed up on our plane, dropped through the manhole at the top of the fuselage into our cramped quarters and before we knew it the lid of our house was clamped down and we were off.

The plane we had was a Junkers all metal monoplane and quite a beautiful thing. I couldn't get over the strangeness of a metal airplane. It seemed so out of keeping with flying. With its corrugated duraluminum sheathing I dubbed it "The Flying Woodshed" and by that name it has been known ever since. As a matter of fact, it was a very famous plane. It had recently, in Germany, set the world's endurance record, beating Chamberlin's record. Now its fuselage, where once I suppose were big gasoline tanks, has been remodeled into space for passengers and their baggage. A hard bench facing forward held two passengers and another facing aft had room for two more.

Our pilot was a splendid one, as we soon found out, and had been on von Richthofen's squadron during the war. His name was Mossbacher and was as nice a chap as I have ever met.

It was very interesting to see the city below us as we left Tehran. Here all in a glance we could see the brilliant tiled domes of the mosques and the gardens and the swarming streets. This was soon out of sight and sooner still we felt the effects of the bad weather that had held us up for so long. Never have I been in anything at sea equal to the roughness of the air that day. Ned Waters, who had been a fighter pilot during the war, said that he had never been in anything equal to it, and we were mighty thankful, all of us, that we had one of von Richthofen's pilots at the controls. Poor Mrs. Waters was miserably sick during the whole trip, and it was only with the greatest effort that I didn't follow suit.

As we left the plain we realized why good weather was needed for flying. We had to climb to 10,000 feet to get over the mountains; I haven't been so cold in all my life. With those great snow-covered crags below us we prayed that our engine would carry on. Fortunately I didn't know enough of the real dangers involved to be scared.

We reached Isfahan in two hours, a hard two day's trip it would have been by car, and we stayed there a day and a half. The town on a whole was not as interesting as I had hoped. The historical monuments, if they may be called such, were not particularly exciting. But we took lots of photographs in case they might be wanted by someone. There was a mighty fine mosque there; at least it should have been for we could only get a glimpse of what the real building was like (we weren't allowed inside), but the huge entranceway and the domes inside were covered with beautiful designs in veri-colored tiles.

The most impressive thing in Isfahan was its immense square. Over a fourth of a mile long and half as wide, it is surrounded by the crumbling blank walls of caravansaries and bazaars; at one end is the great mosque and opposing it the great drum tower, the entrance to the bazaar. On the long side is the imposing High Gate and across from that the beautifully tiled domes of a small mosque.

The great square was very impressive, but the most beautiful was a small mosque elsewhere in the city — the only one we were allowed into. Inside, the courtyard was surrounded by trees and through the center was a long tank in which the ducks played. The surrounding walls were alcoved on three sides and on the fourth was the gate, the dome, and the minarets of the mosque itself, and on all the walls were the soft yellows and blues of the intricately beautiful designs of old ceramic tiles. In that land of dirt and distrust it was a haven of rest I shall never forget.

Isfahan is noted for its silver and gold work and its textiles. The bazaars were particularly interesting, and I had hoped to get some good examples of each, textiles particularly, but these I had no opportunity to see. The silver I thought poor, but I have for you what I believe to be a really beautiful pair of earrings.

The next day to Persepolis was not as mountainous as before and much calmer. It was a bitter disappointment to find that the meadow that served as a landing strip was flooded and we could not come down. We circled several times around the ruins, peering out of the two tiny windows in the cubicle and then went on our way to Bushire over the most glorious tangle of mountains you can imagine. Seven passes we had to cross, as we wormed and threaded our way among the mountains, and then at last after hours of cold and snow and crags came the great drop off the Iranian Plateau to the tropical climate of the coast and Bushire.

That night we spent in a deserted home sleeping on the floor and the pleasantest night of our trip. Everything was quiet except for the rustle of the palms and the soft sound of the surf on the Persian Gulf just beyond our veranda. The full moon shone on the waves and poured over us a feeling of peace and security that we had found no where else in Persia.

The next day we had a very peaceful flight along the coast to the Iraqi border at Mohamera. There we left our pilot and the "Flying Woodshed" for a lowly Ford, and it was with real rejoicing that we crossed back into Iraq.

At Basra we slept in clean beds and renewed our acquaintance with baths, and the next day we boarded the train for Baghdad. The railroad all the way up was heavily patrolled with Britain's Royal Air Force, which is very much on duty here in Iraq. It seems that Ibn Saud, the big man of Arabia, had just declared a Holy War against Iraq, Transjordania, and Palestine, and trouble was expected. We had on our train the chief of the Iraq Police, a particularly objectionable Englishman, and I could not help a sneaking hope that the train would be raided. I would have lost all my stuff, but I would have enjoyed his discomfiture, assuming, of course, that I came out alive myself.

Ned and Peggy Waters came up to Tarkhalan for a couple of days, and they were very interested in our dig. While they were here they got to see an interesting sacrifice of a bull for rain in our village, but I'll tell you of that some other time.

The dig breaks up in two or three weeks. No plans yet.

The End of the 1927–1928 Season

[14]

CARLTON HOTEL
BAGHDAD, IRAQ
6 APRIL 1928
GOOD FRIDAY

Lord only knows when I last wrote you and he being so ashamed of me wouldn't tell. You know as well as I how seldom there is a really good reason for not writing although I kid myself into thinking that I am too busy or too tired or just plain too "ornery."

Almost two weeks ago, a week from Saturday last to be exact, the expedition opened up its bulging suitcases for the last time to put in the last of the post-packing stray socks that are always found under the bed or inside the empty cupboard, and we left our comfortable quarters in Tarkhalan for Kirkuk.

I really had quite a pang leaving the place. We had gotten very much attached to our mud house and particularly to the kindly honest people who had worked there for us. I don't believe that the Occidental in the East is sufficiently willing to forget the accident of race to feel an affection for the native, but we seem to be able somehow to do it. Contrary to most reports we found the Arabs and the Turkoman with whom we worked so closely possessed of a simple honesty and loyalty that draws you to them in friendship in spite of our inherent race prejudices. I feel as though I had some real friends in that miserable little dung heap of a village.

That afternoon and night we spent on the train, and at daylight on Sunday we sighted the domes and minarets of Baghdad including the new Smoking Minaret of the Baghdad light and power plant.

Sunday was a wild day of rushing and cursing, for the whole party was leaving the next day for the desert trip to Damascus, all except me, and there were many things to do. It didn't seem possible that they all could be done, but somehow it was all accomplished, and the next morning I saw them off for the long, hard trip over the desert.

I stayed on to see about getting our stuff sent home, which meant a certain amount of repacking and a great deal of reinforcing our 39 cases of objects, official sealing, permits for export, and many details in anticipation of next year's season, which I ought to do whether I return or not. There was considerable to do, but as you can see by the date on this letter I didn't hurry too much and for my indolence I was richly rewarded.

Dr. Chiera suddenly returned to Baghdad, after having talked in Jerusalem to his new boss from the University of Chicago,[8] to conduct a sort of sounding or exploratory series of excavations up around Mosul and in the Kurdish hills, and he asked me to go along to help him. It will be only a short trip, about two weeks, but it will give me a chance to see new country and to learn about the archaeological value of that region. We leave tonight. Our route takes us through Kirkuk where we pick up equipment, and I honestly look forward to seeing the place again. The route I shall take on my way home I don't know, although I hope I will have enough money to go home by way of Japan. Langdon Warner is living there right now, and it would be a great experience to spend a couple of weeks with him.

So now I say good-bye to the great muddy Tigris and the rustling dusty palms outside my window. No more for a while will I have the intoxicating fragrance of my neighbor's blossoming orange grove; back I go to the hills and the hard invigorating life.

---

8 Dr. Chiera was on leave from the faculty of the University of Pennsylvania, but during our 1927-1928 season he had been offered and had accepted a position as professor of Assyriology at the University of Chicago. R.F.S.S.

Soundings at Khorsabad

[15]

BAGHDAD, IRAQ
24 APRIL 1928

Just a note to let you know that I am back again in Baghdad after a rather trying two weeks or more digging about around Mosul. We found quite a few things of interest (sculptures in low relief mainly) on the mound at Khorsabad, the sight of one of the great palaces of the Assyrian king, Sargon the First. But we couldn't do much except make soundings for prospective future excavations, and this we did in many different places. We didn't live in Mosul, however, but appropriated a room in a mud house in the village of Khorsabad and found it quite comfortable, all together in one room, Dr. Chiera, myself, Bakr, who was our foreman from the dig at Nuzi, our old driver, and our cook. Of course we had with us our faithful army boots and everything necessary for the simple life.

Baghdad is frightfully hot now and considerably ahead of season. This morning at 10 a.m. it was 107 degrees in the shade, and it must be at least 115 now. Think what it must be like in summer.

In about one day more all my work will be finished up here and I will start for home. I go by train to Basra, then a boat from Basra to Bombay, then a train to Ceylon, then a boat to Japan following the usual route. It will be a flying journey, and I don't plan to stop anywhere en route. There I hope to spend a little while with Langdon and leave for home arriving about July 1st. It is rather foolish, and I don't know whether the money will hold out or not, but I am going to try.

I am sick and tired of this country, and the day I leave, headed for home, will be a happy one indeed.

The Voyage Home

[16]

M. S. VIMINALE AT SINGAPORE.
16 MAY 1928

There isn't much to write about except that I am fed up with travelling and bless each day that brings me closer to home.

When I left Baghdad I hadn't much of an idea how I was to get to Japan except, for starters, a British-India Line steamer from Basra to Bombay. I didn't particularly look forward to that awful five day train ride down to Colombo in Ceylon where I knew I could pick up some kind of a boat going further east. But when we came into Karachi, well before getting to Bombay, I found there a ship going direct to Japan, so I hopped ashore, bought a ticket, and had my luggage aboard her before an hour was gone. I am very glad that I did, for it is a very comfortable new ship, though slow, and more reasonable than if I had done the whole journey second class on the route I had first thought to be the only one. Here I travel first class — it is a one class combined passenger and cargo vessel — and as comfortable as one can be on the equator in summer.

This is one of those new Italian motor ships (not a steam ship) with two gigantic oil engines that drive us along. It seems so strange to have a big ship like this chugging along like an oyster boat, and stranger still to see the bob-tailed undressed look that a ship has without a smokestack.

We went straight from Karachi to Ceylon where we had about a half a day to look about on the glorious greenness of Colombo. I didn't see very much because the ship sailed almost a day earlier than we had expected. However, I believe there isn't much of archaeological interest here within easy reach of Colombo. About the only thing you can do beside enjoy the beauty of the tropical vegetation is to wander about the jewel shops and wish you were a millionaire.

Five or six days later we landed in Penang and with a group of more or less congenial people spent the day up on the mountain, the only cool place on the island.

A day and a half more would have had us ashore in Singapore. Instead, we are tied up now at one of the hottest islands yet discovered, taking on fuel oil far out in the Singapore harbor. It is awfully hot here in this part of the world and the sea just about as smooth as you ever could imagine. We often wish for a typhoon or something exciting to come along and cool us off a bit.

There aren't many people on the ship, making it all in all a very pleasant voyage. An interesting crowd they are: an Italian marchioness, Ceylon tea planters, Borneo rubber planters, an Indian Civil Service man, Australian traders, Dutch families for Java, and Italian priests bound for Hankow.

The steward says the passport officer has come aboard so I must be off.

LETTERS FROM IRAQ [17–29] TO I.M.S.

1928–1929 Season

Off Again

[17]

HOTEL WALDORF-ASTORIA
NEW YORK, N.Y.
14 SEPTEMBER 1928

Just a line before I sail away from home.

Ever since leaving Hope, I have been on the rush doing all the things I should have done long ago, or as many as I had time for, and I look forward to the quiet of the steamer.

I sail this time with a very certain feeling of regret. Not that I am not anxious to get back to my work, but it is hard to leave home and you, Mother. You have no idea what you mean to me, and although I may not be a very demonstrative person you know that my love for you is the greatest thing I have. The thought of you is the inspiration for all the worthwhile things I ever hope to do.

Good bye Mother darling. Don't forget that we are to meet next spring in Constantinople.

The Crossing Through the Mediterranean

[18]

BERTOLINI'S PALACE
NAPLES
27 SEPTEMBER 1928

With all those long restless days on shipboard I should have had a letter off to you the first day we reached land, but it seems to be that the only time I can write is when I have a host of other things that must be done at the same time, and shipboard on this last voyage did not seem to be one of those things.

The trans-Atlantic crossing was uneventful and monotonous, and the sea was relatively calm. As far as accommodations were concerned there is nothing that could be asked for aboard the Augustus, even there in second class, except congenial fellow passengers. It being an Italian ship, practically everyone aboard was Italian, and say what you will about international good will and all that, it does not change them or us in the least nor make them any more companionable as shipmates. There were only about half a dozen American-born people in second class, and none of them was particularly exciting either. I saw Alan Priest before sailing, and he gave me a grand send-off. Good cocktails, a good dinner, a good show, and a good friend make up about all that a man can ask for in a fine send-off.

Never have I seen people who can make such a racket at kissing as these Italians. I wandered out on deck just before we sailed to investigate a very strange series of sounds. It seemed as though some one was setting off bunch after bunch of fire crackers down on the dock, but what I found to be was the wet and resounding smacks of countless parting Italians. Everyone was weeping, and all those ladies who could find chairs flopped into them exhausted, partially from the emotional strain and partly from the anticipation of sea sickness to which they became subject even before the ship left the dock.

We passed very close to Gibraltar as we came into the Mediterranean, and although it bore no resemblance at all to my preconceived ideas, showing absolutely no trace of any Prudential Insurance sign, it was nevertheless very impressive.

I had four days to kill in Naples before my next boat sailed which was to take me to Egypt. I had planned to spend two of them in Rome, but when I came to the Bay of Naples and found it even more beautiful than before I put aside the idea. Going to Rome would have meant furious and exhausting sight seeing — seeing a lot and remembering little — and I would rather save Rome until I can spend some time there.

If anywhere on earth there is a Paradise I found it yesterday. I took a little steamer that goes out to the island of Capri, and it is the most lovely place that I have seen west of Angkor. It has been for years the Mecca for artists, and I realize now why. The amazingly beautiful color of the water, its rugged cliffs, the luxuriance of its terraced vineyards, and its picturesque village are lovely beyond compare.

The Blue Grotto at Capri I shall remember as one of the great experiences of all my travels. The steamer stops at the foot of a sheer cliff, and we get into tiny rowboats. We have to lie on the bottom of the boat to get through the opening in the cliff, and when we next look about we find ourselves in another world. The world of matter is gone; that has remained outside. Here is the world of color and the province of azure. It is the color that is around you, in you, and of you. It was like floating on the surface of a sapphire. I can't express how deeply I was moved by it. I remember once when very young you and Dad took me to the Hippodrome in New York where there was a wonderful scene, as I remember it, of an underground fairyland. I will remember that too, as long as I live, for while it was being played I ceased to be one of the audience. I was there and living in that land myself. The Blue Grotto was another such thing. No light entered except that which came up through the water itself. To me everything material ceased to exist. I seemed suspended in a atmosphere of beauty. I was very, very greatly stirred by that experience.

Today I went to Pompeii and had a most interesting though fatiguing day being hauled about by a leather lunged guide. I had always had somewhat of an understanding from the Romans from their history, literature, and art, from things which are available at home, but this showed me an entirely new aspect. There, with practically no stretch of the imagination, we can see them living as they did in the time of Christ. For me it takes them out of the dried apple class and puts them into that of the glorious has-beens. It was a most interesting and valuable experience.

This afternoon I moved from down town to spend my last day here on the hill above the city. This is the most de luxe of all the de luxe hotels in Naples, but it is certainly worth it.

I have just been out on the balcony of my room. Overhead is a brilliant moon just one day from the full; below the lights of the city stretch out on both sides following the line of the bay. To the right are the myriad lights from the villas that cover the hills, and on the left you see across the water a faint glow that you know to be the crater of Vesuvius, boiling in its fury, while all before you is the shimmer of the moon on a silver sea.

I sail tomorrow for Egypt and should reach there before October 1st. From there, after a week looking about, I beat it off to Baghdad hoping on the way to see the ruins of Baalbeck.

My next address will again be: Expedition, Kirkuk, Iraq, Overland Mail (postage 6 cents) or Air Mail (postage 12 cents).

With Reisner at the Pyramids; Jerusalem Impressions

[19]

AMERICAN SCHOOL OF ARCHAEOLOGY
JERUSALEM, PALESTINE
11 OCTOBER 1928

Since my last letter I have done quite a bit of travelling as you can well see, and I shall be a mighty relieved person when I reach my final destination.

By the time I reached Naples, from New York, I was so sick of my Italian fellow passengers that I resolved to travel on to Egypt if it took every cent I had, which it just about did. But it was a foolish extravagance, for on this ship — an Italian vessel again — first class was practically monopolized by wealthy home-coming Egyptians whereas all the interesting English and American passengers seemed to be in second. Never have I seen such luxuriousness on a ship as this Ausonia. Such useless unnecessary luxury.

We reached Alexandria on October 1st, and I took the train straight up to Cairo for a four day stay. I had rather hoped that some of the excavations would be under way so that I could see them in operation, although my better judgement told me that it was too early in the season to expect any such thing. Of course it turned out to be so but I did not go out twice to see Dr. Reisner who was most kind in showing me his plant, methods, and excavations. Reisner, excavating for Harvard and the Boston Museum of Fine Arts, is perhaps the greatest Egyptologist there is now, and it was a great privilege to go around with him. His digs are within fifty yards of the great pyramid of Cheops, and if there is anywhere that an archaeologist might be inspired to great deeds it is in the shadow of that great pile.

After the modest and rather dull nature of our finds at Nuzi Reisner's are truly amazing. He is the one who discovered the tomb of Queen Hetep-Heres, the mother of Cheops, two years ago. He showed me the entrance — a perpendicular shaft — but he couldn't take me down into it. I went into many others, and the beauty of that colored low relief sculpture is astounding. I had never really seen it before, and it made a great impression on me. Beautiful stuff.

He has uncovered also the bases of five or six small ruined pyramids belonging to lesser members of the royal family that were the most interesting; interesting because he was there to tell you how they were made and to whom they belonged. It gave the thing an intimate touch when he would tell you about the family history and inter-relations of all these by-gone royal people. "This," he would say, "is Queen so-and-so whose first husband was the Prime Minister over here (pointing). She afterwards married Prince so-and-so who became King so-and-so; and he is here. This is her cousin so-and-so, that her third child, etc., etc."

Aside from my visit to his expedition house at Giza, I made a special trip just to see the pyramids, and they are without doubt the most amazing monuments to man's vanity, and glory as well, that I have ever seen. Strangely and wonderfully impressive things. I also got out to see the colossal statue of Rameses II, and it was well worth the trouble, as also were the beautiful low relief sculptures on the tomb of King Tai.

In the city itself, aside from the National Museum, I did not see much of great interest except for the Mosque of Sultan Hasan which was really quite fine. Of course I made frequent visits to that treasure house, the National Museum. The things there from the tomb of Tutankhamen are simply beyond description.

From Cairo I went by train directly to Jerusalem, and I recommend to any one who cares to keep his sacred illusions of the Holy City to shun it as if it were the plague. I can see how one with a real knowledge of the Bible and an all-powerful belief in its words would find this a place for reflection, but to one such as myself who would rather know the past through what I can see rather than through imaginative reconstructions I find it most disillusioning. It is a city of strange contradictions. Here the tortuous Oriental bazaar, Muhammadan minarets, and Main Street Methodist church architecture all combine in one mad jumble. The so-called Mosque of Omar, or the Harem esh-Sherif, is the one truly fine thing that I saw in the whole city.

Tomorrow I go to the excavations of the University of Chicago at Megiddo to watch them for about three days, then to the University of Pennsylvania dig at Beisan for two days, then to Damascus to catch the Baghdad desert convoy.

Must pack now.

Reflections on Palestine, Islam and Iraq

[20]

HARVARD-BAGHDAD SCHOOL EXPEDITION
KIRKUK, IRAQ
TARKHALAN VILLAGE
2 NOVEMBER 1928

Since I last wrote many things have happened; nothing of very great import but sufficient to keep me pretty well on the jump.

I believe I have already written my impressions of Jerusalem. Let me say only one thing more and that is of a particularly nice scene that remains in my mind. Right next to the hotel where I spent the first day in Jerusalem was a mosque boasting nothing, on the exterior at least, of any note except quite a fine minaret, originally of Crusader Construction, from which the mullah sang his call to prayer five times a day. This particular man had the finest voice, the softest most melodious tone that I have heard in the East. It was a fine clear night when I heard him give the evening call to prayer, and it was beautiful. Overhead the stars were sparkling and before me the bulk of the tower dimly rose to meet them; at the top the faint outline of the mullah and seeming to pervade everything was the clear querulous call to the Faithful.

It brought to mind something I saw in Mosul last year. I was on the roof overlooking the city — the flat roofs of the native houses are all much used — just before sunset waiting to hear the end-of-day call to prayer. Off to the right was the muddy yellow Tigris in the full strength of spring flood and around below me the roofs of a thousand houses. There must have been fifteen or twenty minarets in sight, and I watched the mullahs as they came out on the balcony of each minaret to await the sunset. I was puzzled as to just how they could all give the call at the right time for their watches, if they had any at all which was most unlikely, could vary from each other an hour or so (such are the watches sold here). Then I saw a great red banner unfurled and waved from the balcony of the most imposing of the minarets, and with that they all began, each with a different tune, each voice different, but from each the same message.

Islam has been subject to the same infiltration of preceding beliefs as Christianity, and we saw an interesting example of it last year in the north of Iraq between Erbil and Mosul. We had stopped to fix a flat tire, and Dr. Chiera and I walked on ahead about half a mile to take a look at a tell. We found it to be an ancient mound as we had suspected, and used now as a modern burial ground as so many of them are. The Muhammadan graves are very plain, for as you know the Koran expressly forbids the setting up or worship of any kind of "graven image." But here we found on one of the graves a complete model of a house with two rooms and a courtyard. In the court were three horses in stalls and on the roof three men seated on chairs with their guns beside them. It was made of clay and modeled with the crudeness that one would expect in such an out-of-the-way spot. No doubt these people, the house, and its belongings were put there for the use of the spirit in the next world just as the Egyptians put models of essential articles and figures in their tombs so that they could accompany them into the hereafter. As you also know much the same thing is practiced in China today. To a strict Muhammadan such a thing would be a great sin, but here on the borderland of wild country previous beliefs and practices persist.

To get back to my travel account: From Jerusalem I went to Haifa, a prosperous town with a beautiful location on the sea, and the place where most, or a great deal, of the Zionist activity has taken place. Then on to Megiddo to visit the University of Chicago's most careful, elaborate, and expensive expedition. They anticipate that it will take about fifteen more years to finish their excavation. After three days there I returned to Haifa and caught the train to Beisan where the University of Pennsylvania is carrying on similar work of equal thoroughness and importance but with a less lavish expenditure of money. There I stayed two days, then on by train to Damascus. It was most interesting to see how others went about the same work that engages me.

As I stand on the *tepa* at Beisan and looked across the valley to the Jordan I wondered what dear black old Aunt Sally would think if she knew where I was. I am quite sure that to her, and to so many others, the Jordan and much of the Holy Land is not of this world but a part of the Heavenly Kingdom to which they hope to go. If I told her that I had crossed the Jordan on a railroad bridge at over 800 feet below sea level and that it was a measly little stream the like of which at home would hardly merit a name I am sure she would merit me a liar.

Just as last year, I reached Damascus in the evening and left early in the morning on the desert convoy for Baghdad, so again I had no chance to see the city.

The trans-desert trip was made, as usual, in large American-made touring cars. It was extremely disagreeable this time with dust enough to last me a lifetime. The side curtains were totally ineffectual in keeping it out and in fact only added to our discomfort. It is a long, hard ride, and after the first time it loses its novelty. During the first half of the trip we went in a convoy escorted by an armored car, so called: in reality just a touring car with the top off and machine guns mounted in the rear. Aside from the moral effect I doubt if it would be of much help, for there is only one for the whole convoy which stretches about thirty miles out along the desert. The only time I ever saw our guardians was when we sped by them as they were wrestling with a flat tire.

I am told on good authority that the danger in the desert arises principally from one man. He works from automobiles, speaks perfect English, French, and of course Arabic, and is extremely courteous to women, never taking their jewelry. He tells his victims that there are only three things he wants: money, petrol, and cars, which he takes whenever he can. My informant unfortunately failed to say whether or not he was handsome.

It seemed good to get back to Baghdad. Here I was joined by Dr. and Mrs. Pfeiffer. He is professor of Semitics at Harvard and will be the Director of the expedition this year. Mr. Wilensky and his new wife and a Mr. Delougaz, our new draughtsman, French educated and, like Wilensky, a Zionist resident of Haifa, have gone on ahead to Kirkuk to get our quarters in shape and to add new rooms to our house. The Pfeiffers and I stayed on in Baghdad four days, then on to Kirkuk. This time it really felt like coming home. All our old workmen were here, and everyone seemed happy to see us. We tried to believe that it was because of ourselves and not just because of the jobs we brought with us.

We started work last Sunday, and today — Friday — is our last day of rest. It is welcome. More later.

P. S. I am enclosing a self explanatory notice. If the people at home knew that I had given a public lecture on this subject they would throw up their hands in horror. But a lecture was demanded and it was the only thing I could speak on. I knew no one here could dispute me.[9]

Mr. Delougaz, Mr. Randolph, R.F.S. Starr, Mr. Wilensky

The Great Flood

[21]

11 NOVEMBER 1928

Yesterday evening I sat down with the full intention of writing a nice long letter, but somehow I just couldn't do it. It had been a hard, tiring day, and everything seeded to go wrong. We had started on what appeared to be promising new ground, but our tracers searched for walls in vain. A few did appear only to fade away to nothing after a few feet. Others appeared at crazy places and did impossible things, strange levels appeared to flourish for a few

9 I have no recollection of what I had the temerity to lecture on or to whom. I console myself in the thought that if it had gone badly, I would still remember it. R.F.S.S., 1981.

feet and then to vanish. Eight scorpions and a giant lizard were about the only finds we had to record at the end of the day. It was most discouraging. When I started to write the only thing that came to me was the distorted vision of a maze of phantom walls.

Today I am just as tired and just as sleepy, but it is the pleasant weariness that comes at the end of a day well spent. Not that we found anything remarkable or particularly valuable but because things are beginning to right themselves. The walls have stopped skittering about and the objects have started in again in their slow steady flow. It doesn't take much to please such simple minded people as ourselves. A few good walls or a cylinder seal fills our hearts with joy, and today we went into raptures over the uncovering of an ancient toilet. Demand what privacy you can in this world for the coming generations of archaeologists will grant you none.

A week ago Thursday the sky began to cloud over and everyone was praying that Allah would grant us a little rain. The countryside was parched, and without rain coming soon the grain sown this fall would have little chance of becoming a harvestable crop in the spring. Even we hoped for it, for we found the powder-dry walls extremely hard to follow, and we also hoped for an early rain to lower the prices of the local food products on which we depend. We were just able to eke out the day's work before the rain came, as nice and gentle a shower as any farmer could hope for. All through the night and most of the next day it continued as a gentle shower, and the country folk saw pleasant dreams of good spring harvests. But there is a limit to the gentleness with all things, and the storm, realizing it, proceeded to show us what real rain could be. All that night it poured in torrents such as I have never seen before. It was like a solid sheet of water coming down. When we woke the next morning everything in the place was flooded. The whole outdoors was flooded. Practically every house in the village was damaged and many washed away completely. The village street was transformed from an arid dung-covered track to a roaring torrent waist deep in places, and most of those houses that had the misfortune of being on the road were nothing now but pitiful heaps of mud. Here where all the construction is of unbaked mudbrick such a downpour causes great havoc. Crops were destroyed, homes washed away, and roads (such as they were) washed out. Destruction was everywhere.

Then as if the storm wanted to show further proof of its virility it started in again and repeated the deluge of the preceding day. Never has there been such a flood here. Even the memories of the imaginative oldest inhabitants could not recall a rainfall equal to it. After seeing this, one can easily imagine how in ancient times another such inundation, with the verbal accretions of many generations of narration, could account in the Biblical account of The Flood.

Even now, more than a week afterwards, our only communication with Kirkuk, eight miles distant, is by donkey; and the railroad has just now succeeded in completing the repairs necessary for the Baghdad-Kirkuk train to run again. Fortunately our house, being sound and on relatively high ground, held up well, and we all weathered the storm safely; but there were few others that did. Sitting here in the evening the sound of the flood rushing down the road by our house to join the larger stream in the village sounded like the surf pounding on the ocean shore.

This storm may not interest those who live in America, but here where rain is not often seen, in this place that we consider more as a desert than anything else, it is a strange experience. Stranger still when you realize that an amount equal to the total yearly average rainfall fell in that one storm.

The people take their catastrophe quite calmly. Their houses are gone, crops are destroyed, but then, it is the will of Allah. Besides, in spite of the present destruction, it still promises well for the spring planting.[10]

Your first letter to Kirkuk came yesterday, and I believe I have reread it ten times. It is wonderful to hear of the stimulating peacefulness of Hope. I heartily approve of your great mural canvases. It's a big idea, and it will take you to do it in a big way. Go to it.

I should say that I did get your flowers sent to the ship at New York, and they were wonderful. I had them on the dining saloon table, and they lasted a week, the envy of this whole ship. Thank you! I feel ashamed for not acknowledging them before this, but when I was in Naples my mind must have been so full of the gloriousness of the present that I allowed the past to go unmentioned. A thousand thanks.

It is ten o'clock and very late for us, so "Good Night."

Boredom Sets In

[22]

21 NOVEMBER 1928

Just a short note to you by this week's mail to let you know that everything is well.

So far as news is concerned there is very little to tell. Things roll along, rather slowly to be sure, but definitely forward. Rain has been rather a nuisance of late holding us up for several days. Today we started off again and went through the most disagreeable day this season. Cold and raw with occasional fits of rain and

---

10 A word is in order here about those soluble houses. Unbaked brick, or mud brick, prevails throughout much of the Near East. In Iraq it is the building medium in all of the rural areas — and much of the urban as well — where stone is not readily at hand, as in the Kurdish mountains. Baked brick was a rarity during the years I was in Iraq because of the scarcity of fuel. The present-day availability of crude oil may now have changed that, I don't know. But during my time there baked brick was available only to the affluent. The few brick kilns that did exist in our area were fired with straw. R.F.S.S. 1983.

a chill in the air that penetrated to the bone. I haven't been able to get over the shivers yet.

The mail goes early in the morning and tonight I don't seem to be able to write. I'm cold, and tired, and cross, and everything seems wrong.

Discouragement

[23]

4 DECEMBER 1928

So long since I have written that I hardly know where to start. Our days go along in so much the same pattern that it doesn't matter much where I begin. This year I have found all my days so completely filled that time has been at a premium. No matter how thoroughly I try to catch up there is always something that should be done in the evening or on Friday. It is getting rather tiresome, after spending so many a hard day on the dig, constantly on the go, to come home dead tired and find each evening I must follow up on some other waiting little job. I have charge of all the money, and that takes time and deserves twice the time that I give it. Then there are the photographs. Besides doing all the field photography, there are plates to develop at night and to load for the following day's need and a seemingly endless number of other things. Just now we are all gathered in our dining-living room recuperating from a rather depressing day. The phonograph is doing its best with the latest dance tunes to clarify the atmosphere.

Things seemed to be ill fated today; my camera tripod broke to start off the bad luck; then Mr. Wilensky found he had an error in his ground plan and would have to do the whole tedious thing over again. Finally, to cap the climax, one of our boys broke a brand new, very expensive surveying instrument which had arrived only two days before from England. True, we have succeeded in fixing it up, but it will never be the same again. There is no reason why it should have been a bad day really; things on the dig went along quite well, a reasonable amount of ordinary objects came out, and the walls went along really quite well. They — the walls — are our great cross. When they fail to materialize there is consternation and havoc, and we have had plenty of both this season.

You see, we are polishing off last year's leftovers, and it isn't much fun. Last year we had so much to choose from that we could pick what went well and just abandon whatever didn't behave, but this year we have really got to finish up all that we possibly can, and it is difficult.

To one who has never done this work or even seen it, it must seem like a lot of foolishness and I am beginning to believe more and more that it is, but we are supposed to be doing serious work in a serious way so we too must be serious.

After all, what is the sense of all this work? We spend years at it and no end of money that could be better used on the poor, and what have we got: a lot of pots that any small town potter could do twice as well and a publication no one will ever read. We say we are working for science, but what good is this kind of science if it doesn't help along the progress of the human race. Science? Bunk! What is all this talk about science and the great benefit? Throughout the whole world there are not more than 300 men who give a hoot for what we are doing here, who even ever heard of this ancient land. Three hundred bespectacled lobsters all clawing and snapping at each other in bitter jealously and in constant controversy over the trivial details. These people constitute science in this field, and they are the ones I had always held in such respect. But now I feel if they represent humanities' great gift to the world — well, how would you feel about it?

Bunk, bunk, bunk; we're all bunk. What earthly good is it to anyone whether King So-and-so rules in one year or another, or for that matter whether he even existed. What is the great gift to mankind in establishing that such-and-such cuneiform character is pronounced ā instead of a. What is the great benefit? What is it all for? God only knows.

In my own case, I know. I have interesting work, good food, a healthy life, and a nice trip, but why anyone should pay me or any of us for it is more than I can see.

I engineered the expedition into buying a phonograph this year, and it is a great comfort. Beside that, I supervised the purchase of the records, and they are good though few. Among them is Dvorak's "New World Symphony" in five double faced records and "*Après midi d'un faune*" and the "*Cathédral engloutie*" by Debussy. Grand.

Lovely weather today, warm and balmy like early autumn, with a clear sky and an uninterrupted horizon. After the almost bitter cold of the last few weeks it is a great relief.

I have so much to do that I am rather praying for a day or two of rain to give me a chance to catch up, but there is none in sight right now.

We are all being vaccinated against smallpox because of an epidemic that is going through the country. Iraq always manages to have some such pleasantry up its sleeve. Either cholera, plague, smallpox, or some other thing. Happy land.

Don't take all this too seriously. Good night.

Christmas, 1928

[24]

26 DECEMBER 1928

Three wonderful letters from you to take away the lonely feeling of our artificially gay Christmas. To hear from you gave me the only real happiness of the Christmas season, because when I am reading your letters I feel that I am really talking with you. Secretly I am glad that your typewriter is out of order (I assume that it is) because it seems a shame that anyone with such an extraordinary and beautiful handwriting should abandon it for a perfectly mechanical and characterless substitute.

You speak so much of the murals, and I am anxious to see them. I have absolutely no doubt as to their worth.

We took a day and a half off for Christmas, and I am rather glad that it is over. It wasn't bad really, we tried our best to be happy and cheerful, but I wished so to be home that I would have given almost anything to have been able suddenly to transfer myself to Hope.

Christmas Eve was about the most dismal I have ever known. That time when everyone is so gay and happy was to us nothing but a shell of merriment that soon wore thin. Poor Mrs. Pfeiffer was passing her first Christmas away from her children and was on the verge of tears the whole evening, and I'm afraid that my spirits were not much higher. But Christmas Day was not as bad. Everyone had prepared most elaborate presents which we distributed to each other during the luxury of a ten o'clock breakfast, and all was very merry. Strangely, the Jews of our party (we are three Christians and three Jews) entered as thoroughly as ourselves, and perhaps more extravagantly, though Christmas is certainly not a holy day to them. Books, carpets, lovely native blankets, Amara silverwork and many other things suddenly appeared and changed hands with the wonderful confusion and exhilaration of Christmas morning.

The rest of the morning was taken up with the Christmas baksheesh to the household and in receiving call from the various important villagers who came to pay their respects and to wish us well on our holiday. Everyone was most kind. Even Ali, the owner of the largest store and general business in Kirkuk, made a special trip out to present us with holiday gifts. That he should have singled us out among all the foreigners even though we are by far not his biggest customers was very gratifying. For a modern Muhammadan businessman he is quite unusual. We asked him whether he furnished the hotel with their supplies, and he replied that the only big demand that they had was for liquor and that he wouldn't sell liquor. When we asked him why, he simply said, "I am a Muhammadan, and I would rather not make money that way." In a European I would think such an attitude that of a prig, but to find a rich man, one of a race whose rich are notedly avaricious, willing to forego a handsome gain for the sake of his faith is truly admirable.

As soon as we could get rid of our callers we all packed into our Ford, and I drove us all out into the desert. It was a grand feeling to be out on that flat plain with every direction a perfect road and the world open to you.

Ours, the most temperamental Ford in Iraq, almost always refuses to go when I am out in it without the driver. Above all things it hates to be cranked, so much so that it just sits back on its hind wheels and refuses to start. The only alternative is for everyone to get out and push it until it gets ready to start. This wasn't so bad for me since I am the one who would sit inside and hold it in gear, and to be at the wheel when and if it started, but after the 10th or 15th time that everyone piled out and put their shoulders to the rear of the car and shoved I noticed that the enthusiasm was beginning to wane a bit. Somehow that joyful anticipation that accompanied each dying spasm of our mechanical donkey gradually faded away, and no one seemed to object when I announced that this time we would push it in the direction of home. We managed to get almost within a mile of home before the car had to be abandoned altogether, but that didn't matter. The walk was a pleasant rest.

The dinner was, if not the best, at least one of the largest with which I have ever mistreated my stomach, and to think that I have been able to eat again today is a marvel to me. After dinner we sat around with dull glazed eyes while the village minstrel, a shepherd, played pleasantly monotonous but never-ending tunes on his pipes while Sulieman, one of our sentries, danced. Even in my stuffed condition I could not but feel the beauty of the superb performance. He is the same one of whom I wrote last year. Such dignity and grace he has. His whole soul is in his motion and rhythm. He might be in trance executing the commands of some higher being but for the occasional flashing of his eyes of a single word to his musician.[11]

Oh well, it was all very merry but it would have been so much nicer at home.

[25]

22 JANUARY 1929

The photographs of your murals arrived yesterday, and I can't tell you what an impression they have made on me. Splendid, splendid things. When I showed these photographs to the other members of our outfit and had their enthusiastic appreciation I felt more proud of you then ever. Carry on, but don't let the glitter of the big city dazzle you.

Nothing very startling has happened here since my last letter. The dig seems to clatter along at about the same pace with very little to distinguish one day from another. The finds have been slim this season when compared with last, which is unfortunate. Not because we are expected to be object hunters (that is the ultimate insult to a conscientious archaeologist), but because those at home who are the ultimate bosses of this work are bound to judge the scientific results of the venture more by the objects sent home than by what we are daily accumulating for publication. Of course you can't blame them for wanting to get something tangible for their money, but they can't expect us to produce where there is nothing to find. The only thing we can do is to carry on and give our best to the work.

Conditions this year have been much more difficult than before. On this particular site the cream was taken last year, as far as easy work is concerned. What is left is in very bad shape and continually presents problems that we never were bothered with last season.

---

11 Quiet, dreamy-eyed Sulieman was a doer, not a talker. He was the one you went to if you have something made to cope with an unexpected need. He also had a reputation as more than usually severe wife beater. R.F.S.S., 1983.

Technically, though, I feel that our work this season is much better than last. However, you have heard all this blowing so many times before that you can probably recite it by heart.

The biggest thing that has happened this week is that I have shaved off my mustache, much to the astonishment of everyone in the community. In fact the sentiment is so strong against my present shorn condition that I have started accumulating a new growth. These people, as a matter of fact all Muhammadans, consider that any one who can produce anything at all is the possessor of a symbol of masculinity of such value that it should be treasured above all other things.

When I tell you that the second thing in importance this week is that I got a haircut at last, you can realize how hard up we are for excitement. Inshallah, I will be able to do better by you next mail day.

Meeting Sir Aurel Stein

[26]

19 FEBRUARY 1929

Shortly after Christmas Dr. and Mrs. Pfeiffer went down to Baghdad for a week, and it left us very shorthanded with no decrease in our over-all work load. Consequently, there was mighty little time that one could call his own. Then no sooner had the Pfeiffers returned that I went off myself on one of the most strenuous and tiring vacations (so called) that I have had in some time from which I have just returned but by no means recovered.

There is the most frightful racket outside my room. Enough to make letter writing almost impossible. The cook and our half-witted house servant are appealing to Dr. Pfeiffer at the top of their voices for justice. One says that the other steals tea, and the other counters with the accusation of attempted murder. We have been entirely too kind with these people. The whole lot ought to be fired. Above all this there is a poor little puppy with a broken paw whose screams rise above those of all the other complainers. It is Bedlam.

We tried our best to bring in the New Year in as congenial and pleasant a way as we could under the circumstances. Our group was rather small, with the Pfeiffers away, but we made up for their absence by eating turkey and Arab bread at our New Year's Eve dinner until we were almost at the bursting point. Everything was merry, the phonograph was kept continually busy grinding out our peppiest records, and a real holiday spirit was in the air, stimulated perhaps a bit by several surreptitious visits to my private liquor closet and to an abundance of Kirkuk red wine. The feeling of righteous pleasure and self satisfaction that fills one when he has dressed for dinner in a camp and feels himself in civilized clothes for the first time in months is a great spur to good spirits.

The greatest obstacle to seeing in the New Year was the turkey. It was too big. At ten o'clock I thought I would never be able to stay awake (we had a hard day on the *tell*, too), but we managed it, and at midnight the pop of the champagne bottle gave the signal to our sentries to startle the sleeping village out of its wits with a great volley at the moon.

The next day, New Year's Day, we took a holiday and clattered over to the oil fields in our antiquated Ford. You probably know that just on the other side of Kirkuk is one of the richest oil fields in the East, a place I had always promised myself to see but where I had never been able to go until now. It was very interesting to see how the thing is done; the chief of the works showed us the whole process of drilling, but he hardly realized that the biggest pleasure he was giving us was the chance of hearing "American" spoken again. All the drilling is being done by Americans; mostly Texans. None of the wells are being worked yet but are being put down as fast as possible then sealed off until they can build a pipeline across the Great Syrian Desert to the coast in Palestine. What vast amounts of money all this represents!

Shortly after this the Pfeiffers returned and brought with them the news of a statue on the market in Baghdad, and since the Fogg Museum is very anxious to get something good, I left the next day for Baghdad to see what it was. Since this would be perhaps the only chance I would have to get away before the end of the season I decided to take off for a week or eight days to visit all the excavations I possible could, and Mr. Wilensky decided to come along with me. To Baghdad from Kirkuk takes from seven in the morning till seven at night on the train, but we didn't mind it. We felt like two school boys off on their vacation.

The next day was destined to be a great one because of one man. We had gone to the Iraq Museum and were talking to the new director, a man I had met curiously enough the year before in the British Museum, when in came a distinguished little grey headed man who, to my utter amazement, turned out to be the great Sir Aurel Stein. This person, who in my China days I had looked upon with the reverence that one pays to a god, suddenly pops up in the moth eaten little museum in Baghdad before my very eyes. Had I been in the center of the Taklamaken Desert, or in Tun Huang, or in the wilds of Afghanistan, I would not have been at all surprised, but this was almost too much to believe. I had carried a letter of introduction to him from Langdon for five years, but I had given up hope of ever having the chance to use it. He is probably the greatest archeological explorer in the world today and one of England's greatest scholars. You probably remember that he was the person who along with Pelliot, brought to the western world the great store of Tun Huang manuscripts. I invited him up to our dig for a day or two, an invitation which he happily accepted.

The next day we had another all day train journey to Ur, the excavations I was most anxious to visit. Of course you have heard of the famous excavations at Ur of the Chaldees, the place where in the last two years they have been finding the those magnificent gold objects from around 3200 B.C. They are the only things that I know of that can compare with the finds of Tutankhamen and Mycenae. They are marvelous.

The general public knows only of these things, but to those who are interested, the private and public buildings at Ur are of as much interest as the rich burials; and it was for these things that I went there. Not just to see the buildings but to see how they were going about the job of excavation. Contrary to most archaeologists, I am a firm believer in seeing other people at work. The way in which others tackle the same difficulties that we have is most instructive, and I believe it would be a very fine thing of everyone, that is every archaeologist, in the country were obligated to visit all the digs that were going on elsewhere in the country.

Ur was a grand place. The ziggurat was a most splendid massive structure, rising up in complicated levels and ramps to the skies. The temple and the private houses were tremendously interesting to us for we had tangled up in more or less the same thing ourselves.

We were received most cordially by Mr. Woolley, and he invited us down into the grave pit to see the work going on. I was very glad of the opportunity for only the select few get in there. He is notoriously close about giving out news of the dig's progress until the end of the season.

We had lunch with them, and afterwards he showed us the finds of the season, the most amazing things I have ever seen. Things of such beauty and workmanship than one wonders where all this progress is that we believe modern man has achieved. Until they are published, at the end of the season, I am not at liberty to describe or enumerate them, but suffice it to say that they are the grandest things I have ever seen from Mesopotamia. He has one storeroom that might almost make you believe yourself in the treasure room of the mythical Caliphs of the Arabian Nights. It is not a small room, it is filled with superb objects, and every object is of gold.

Another long journey brought us back to Baghdad. The train was three hours late because of a head wind! But it was not so slow as to be unable to overtake the four wolves trotting unconcernably along over the desert not more than fifty yards from our puffing locomotive. We spent our last day chasing out to Ctesiphon to see the excavation of the Germans who are working at the great arch on Sasanian stuff, and the Michigan dig where they are getting far beyond their depth in a maze of Greco-Roman levels.

The statue, which was the primary reason for my trip, was a disappointment. Whether it was actually a fake or not I don't know, but it was certainly not right, and I could not recommend it for purchase.

The most valuable result of visiting the other excavations was the encouragement that it gave us in the quality of our own work. Without feeling that I am boasting I can say that I believe that more careful and correct work is being done by us than by any other excavation that I have seen in Iraq. That I believe is due to two things: one, that our problems are so much more difficult (those of actual excavation) than those of any of the other expeditions that the work *must* be done carefully and correctly to get any results. And two, our staff is young and willing to admit that they don't know everything. We are not afraid to say, "I don't know" when we don't, and we are anxious to learn and profit by other people's work in the same line.

We arrived back in Tarkhalan before Sir Aurel Stein left, for he came up a day ahead of us, and I had the great pleasure of spending an evening and morning with him before he rushed on to Mosul.

You have no idea how nice it seemed to be back here. It was like coming home. The dig had carried on and seems in rather a mess, but it will straighten out soon.

In Baghdad I bought a splendid Persian sheepskin coat all embroidered with strange figures on the outside. Something to startle the people with at home, also some Sumerian antiquities. I can't keep money.

A Period of Solitude

[27]

20 February 1929

Today marks the end of almost a week's peace and pleasant solitude, for the rest of our outfit, who had gone off on a bat to Mosul have returned and have taken from me that pleasure and freedom that one can only find alone.

That trip had been planned for a long time, and I felt rather like a quitter not to go along, but I had plenty of reasons. I had been to Mosul and all the places (and more) that they planned to visit over that region at the end of this season, so to hop up there for a couple of days now would be a waste of time. Then, it is a very tiring trip, and somehow the idea of all being uncomfortable together hadn't the appeal to me that it might have had. More important still is that now our time for work is so short I hated to see the dig closed down just for a pleasure trip; and finally I rather looked forward to the opportunity of having a little quiet to myself.

I had a hunch that the car would be crowded, and I was right. The supposed seven passenger car turned out to be only a five seater after all, and with all the baggage aboard and coats and rugs with three people in the front seat and three in the rear there wasn't enough space left for a fly to travel about in comfort. What is more, they tell me that the roads, because of rain, were terrific [sic!]; I already knew from experience that the accommodations in Mosul were bad; and I suspected that the whole outing would become one never-ending dispute. Sour grapes?

Anyhow, it was pleasant here. The dig went along full force in a rather placid fashion with no one to interfere with my pet ideas, and during my hours at home I was the king of the household. I had my meals at the hours *I* wanted them (relatively), and I brought into force all those petty reforms that I had sought before in vain. There was no one to interrupt when I wanted to read, no ladies to be polite to when I felt grouchy, and best of all no one to be grouchy when I was happy. But pleasant though those five days were, they rather scare me, for it (my attitude) seems a sure indication of cranky old bachelorhood.

I said there was no one to interrupt when I wanted to read, but that wasn't quite true. I was right in the middle of a most interesting account of travel in Kurdistan when in walked Jabaar, my shepherd friend, who hearing that I was alone came to visit and to cheer my supposedly lonely soul with music from his pipes. I was annoyed because, as I said, the book was extremely interesting, but Jabaar is one with whom one must be happy. He compels it. Jabaar is not quite right in his head. In fact he is quite definitely off; but he is cracked in the most glorious way that one can imagine, for no matter what happens, be fortune good or bad, he is always happy. Life for him is no grim struggle against poverty and starvation as with most of the people here, it is a glorious gift from Allah of boisterous simple pleasure and happiness. I wish I could be crazy in the same way.

He, as well as the rest of the people, can't imagine why I am not married. It is a source of continual wonder and regret that I persist in this state of singleness. He was so concerned about it, in fact, that although too poor yet to buy a wife of his own, he offered to sell all of his sheep (more dear to him than a thousand lovely wives) and buy me a wife from Tarkhalan if I would bring him a wife from America. Of course she would cost nothing, for everyone knows wives are not bought in America.

He is the chief musician of Tarkhalan, and he ought to be. From sunrise to sunset as he wanders over the desert with his flocks there is hardly a moment that he is not singing or playing his flute or his pipes. I like him.

The work is going along very slowly. This is the month of Ramadhan now during which all the pious fast during the daylight hours, and to expect good work under those circumstances is out of the question. Those who fast, and most of them do, are incapable of good work, and the spirit is contagious to those less pious ones. Neither food nor drink may touch their lips during the daytime of this month. They cannot even smoke. As a result, the night becomes a time for feasting, and endless talking, and they show up the next day bleary eyed, grouchy, and unfit for decent work.

Our work on the dig now is simply that of cleaning up. We close about March 10th. No plans yet for the future.

Frustration and Uncertainty

[28]

26 FEBRUARY 1929

For some reason or other I have been awfully tired for the last two weeks, and tonight I have only one desire and that is to flop into bed. Even dinner fails to appeal when compared with rest. We are getting pretty fed up with things here, and it will be a happy day indeed when we close for the season.

That day is not far off now. Very close, in fact. We close officially on March 3rd, but Wilensky and I will probably carry on for a week or ten days longer to polish off unfinished odds and ends. Dr. and Mrs. Pfeiffer leave on March 5th for Egypt, but there will be so many unfinished and unsolved problems even at that time that the work will have to go on for a while longer.

Whether we continue next year or not we have yet to hear. In fact they (the authorities at Harvard) are driving us almost crazy with their indifference to our work. We try like the devil to do a creditable job, we work ourselves sick over this rotten place, and no one at home seems to give a hoot. We write asking answers to vital questions and receive no reply. We repeat it in a cable and the answer bears no relation to the question. It is damnable. If we do good work no one cares, and if it is poor they would be on us like a bunch of chattering chipmunks.

I will probably come home by the most direct route possible.

The Return Trip Begins

[29]

BEYROUTH, LEBANON
10 APRIL 1929

Tomorrow I sail for home — glory be — but there isn't any great reason for you to get excited yet, for this letter will probably reach you weeks before I arrive. Mine is a very slow boat, and in addition it wanders aimlessly around the map for quite a time before it gets down to the business of heading for America. From here we go down to Haifa and Jaffa in Palestine, then up through the Bosphorus to Constanza in Rumania on the Black Sea, then back to Constantinople, then to Smyrna on the Anatolian coast, then to Piraeus in Greece, then to Sicily, to Algiers, and finally to America. I believe there are a few other places we go to that I have left out. Anyhow, we arrive first in Providence, Rhode Island on the 11th of May, then to New York on the 12th. I will probably get off at Providence and go straight to Cambridge to report to the museum, then on home as fast as I can go. My ship is French, the S.S. Asia of the Fabre Line.[12]

The trip across the desert from Baghdad to Damascus, though not so disagreeably dusty as last fall, was a day longer and very hard. Three days it took this time, and I believe I have never seen anything which looked quite so good to me as the luxuriance of the oasis of Damascus; not only because of the barrenness of the great desert through which we had been travelling but also

12 The Asia was a truly dreadful little boat. Even the food was bad: the ultimate degradation for a French vessel — cockroaches in the stew and the like. She later burned and sank in Jidda harbor with a boatload of pilgrims bound for Mecca. R. F. S. S.

because, except for the dusty gray-green of olive and palm trees, this was the first naturally green spot I had seen since I left home last year.

In order to save money, I came over the desert by a native company carrying pilgrims on their way to Mecca. Two days before I was due to leave I was told that the government had suddenly issued an order that all pilgrim convoys should start a day earlier and take a day longer than the regular cars, and I had to dash around the city in a frenzy of haste in order to get ready. Other than a philanthropic desire on the part of the government to give us pilgrims a day more of torment in the desert than we had paid for, I have not yet been able to fathom their motive.

The four elderly wives and a man servant of a wealthy Baghdadi and myself and the driver completed our cargo. The four poor old ladies had a rather hard time of it, three squatting Arab fashion on the back seat and the other and the servant, disdaining the folding seats, roosting on the floor in the same fashion. The husband rode luxuriously alone in the front seat of another car as I did in this one.

In many places the desert was covered with a sparse green fuzz and dotted with thousands of tiny white and yellow and lavender flowers, the brief result of the winter rain. In a week or two it will be gone and like the greater part of the desert this time will be as barren and arid as a table top. There is something very exhilarating about the vast expanse of this desert, something stirring and fascinating about it that I can't describe.

I had planned to stay several days in Damascus, but after one day I had had enough. It, and all the rest of Syria that I have seen, has become a tourist center, and has given rise to a breed of money grabbing parasites that make travel here very unpleasant. Like Cairo, I didn't see anything much of the city, but I saw enough to know that with all its wealth and size I prefer Baghdad.

The French as colonizers have the ability of imposing their natures, habits, and lives on the people over whom they rule with the result that Syrian cities are simply disgracefully governed, poor imitations of French cities. The English, on the other hand, are quite willing to let a city retain its own character and spirit. The difference probably arises from the fact that the French, who recognize no color or racial line, immediately begin to absorb the population and to make them part of themselves, while the aloof Englishman contents himself purely with trade and government, living his own English life wherever he may be and allowing the natives to live theirs.

From Damascus I went to the great Roman ruins of Baalbek, and it was an inspiring place. It is strange that the most magnificent Roman ruins left in the world today should be in the Near East. The glory of Rome!

The trip over the Lebanon mountains to Beirut, or Beyrouth as the French spell it, is one of the grandest motor rides I have ever taken. I have been over before in bad weather, but it was not until this time that I realized the real splendor of it. As we reached the top and looked over the snowdrifts down and down and down to the sparse vegetation at the tree line, then to the fertile terraced valleys with little red tile roofed houses clinging to the sides of the mountains, and finally to the palm fringed city with the blue Mediterranean beyond that I knew that the Amalfi or any of the other famous drives had found their superior.

Beirut is an uninteresting place. Nothing to do but twiddle my thumbs until steamer time.

Letters to I.M.S. [30–45]

1929–1930 Season

Transatlantic Crossing

[30]

M.S. AUGUSTUS
22 SEPTEMBER 1929

It was really a grand send-off to come aboard the ship and find both a letter and a telegram from you waiting to cheer me on to my renewal of an old adventure. Then yesterday a wireless from you, too. It was wonderful. The best part was the news of great progress toward your usual healthy self. I don't want to hear any more news of ill health.

The last few days in Cambridge were hectic ones, with me trying in a few days to do a great multitude of things. Most of them were done some way or other, and I left Cambridge finally in time to reach New York for a dinner engagement with Horace Jayne with whom I discussed a variety of things pertaining to the expedition. I saw him off on his train to Philadelphia, he having to leave early, dropped in for an hour at a movie and then rode soberly down to the ship about half an hour before sailing time, finding John Earle there to bid me Godspeed.

My ship this time is an imposing new Italian motorship, the M.S. Augustus, recently transferred from the South American trans-Atlantic run. I started out second class as I did last year, but at the end of the first two hours aboard I decided, for the dignity of American scholarship and for my own comfort, to transfer to first class. So, I paid an additional one hundred dollars and left for good the abode of my organ-grinding shipmates. On my salary this is an extravagance, but it is satisfying to be with my own kind for a while — at least before returning to the desert. On English ships one often finds the most interesting and congenial people in second class but not so on any foreign ship that I have travelled on.

We touch at Gibraltar, then on to Naples.

The Egyptian Museum

[31]

S.S. BRASILE AT JAFFA, PALESTINE
FALL OF 1929

How good it seemed to see land again as we came through the Straights of Gibraltar, the smooth gray hills of Europe to the north and the precipitous bluffs of Africa to the south, and then the "Rock" itself towering as if proud of the part it has played in the history of a great empire. Below it the pink and white little city climbed up the steep slope. Scores of little boats clustered around our ship selling five cent baskets of fruit for fifty cents or hydra-like mottled red little octopi to those passengers who might be inquisitively or facetiously minded.

There was great excitement here, for Edda Mossolini, the daughter of "our beloved Duce," came aboard to be our passenger of honor as far as Genoa. The captain, plastered with medals, was at the accommodation ladder to greet her, along with the rest of the officers and row upon row of stewards giving the Fascist salute. The scuffling and scrambling at the rail amongst the passengers in an effort to get a good look would have done credit to a collegiate football team, and the noise of the clicking of cameras (mine among them) was deafening. In spite of all the fuss, she was a rather nice appearing girl, very blonde with a long inquisitive nose and deep set eyes.

Two days more brought us to Naples where I had just enough time to step off one ship and on to another, then back to the Augustus to say good-bye to my shipboard friends and as a lonely figure on a crowded dock to wave the great ship off on its last lap to Genoa. Gone were the great gleaming white boulevards of promenade deck, and gone that pleasant association of shipboard acquaintances. Instead I had a tiny, flea-bitten hulk of a ship that was to carry me on to Beirut, with a broken down French theatrical company on their way to barnstorm Egypt and an odd assortment of Italian, English and Egyptian passengers as companions. Oh yes, an American couple, simple folk from California, he on his second honeymoon, alas; and she on her first, at last. I've seen quite a bit of them (the couple), having more or less taken them under my wing in Egypt out of compassion for their helplessness. In answer to my query of why in going from Egypt to Jerusalem they didn't go by land they answered that the guidebook said that the journey was made by *wagon-lit* and that they didn't want to travel such a distance by wagon.

Our little ship stopped for a day in Catania, Sicily, under the shadow of the every angry Mt. Etna. Along with some other passenger, I took a car and rode over the vine covered hills to the regions destroyed by the eruption of last year. Some thousands of years from now ardent archaeologists will dig these poor little villages out from under the black ragged stream of lava and piece together again a picture of life in 1928. It is too bad that something more representative of our times couldn't be arranged to be put in the way of some convenient volcano.

Catania itself, however, did not intrigue me greatly. The only things that claim any real place in my memory are the picturesquely carved and painted little carts drawn by tiny elaborately caparisoned donkeys.

I hadn't expected to reach Cairo this trip, but when I found that our little boat stopped in Alexandria for three days and one more in Port Said, I packed up and hustled off to the City of the Pharaohs. There were only two places I wanted to go to this time: one was the National Museum and the other was the Pyramids, and I did them both in my own leisurely fashion. The trip to the museum alone repaid me for everything, for in one of the many new cases of material from the tomb of Tutankhamen, which had not been on show before, I found an object the exact duplicate of which we had found in our dig but which we could not explain. It was part of the harness of a chariot and not only tells at last what this thing was, but gives us a most interesting connection with

Egypt. In spite of Dr. Chiera and others, I believe more and more that this was a contact of considerable influence on our people. Those great treasures I could see again and again and neither tire of them or know them well enough.

The next day I went out before lunch to Gizah, at the Mena House Hotel, and sat afterwards until five o'clock on their veranda smoking, thinking, and idling. Before me was a screen of rustling palms trees through which one had vistas of the great bulk of Cheops of few hundred yards away.

Before sunset I took a dragoman, to guard me from petty annoyances, and climbed up to the pyramid terrace, and from high on the western side of Cheops I watched the passing of another desert day. A crescent moon of burnished silver came from behind the pyramidal mass on my left, and a moment later came the stars. With their coming, the twentieth century vanished and though it was not replaced by the twentieth century before Christ, the spirit of that greatness was there as never did I see it before.

The guards soon chased me from my perch, but they couldn't chase from my mind the memory of an enchanted hour. With my silent (by order) dragoman I tramped for an hour through the dark, over stone and through sand, around the site of those ancient monuments. Then back to the dirty city; dirty with trolley cars and *table d'hote* dinners.

The most important part of my trip to Cairo was the purchase of a necklace — yes, it is for you, of course. Why do you ask? Oh well, I bought it because I liked it and now I am scared to death that you won't. Buying jewelry or clothes for others, as you know, is very risky business. It is of silver, dull and mellow with age and dirt with rough hunks of lapis lazuli interspersed; then there is a fascinating dangle of silver and little lapis pebbles. It is crude and barbaric and very handsome. It is from the Sudan.

The ship has just left Jaffa; Haifa this evening; and Beirut tomorrow morning.

Back to Baghdad

[32]

CARLTON HOTEL
BAGHDAD, IRAQ
20 OCTOBER 1929

Just the briefest kind of note to tell you that I am back again in Baghdad and headed soon for Kirkuk.

The journey out was long and on the whole rather pleasant, and now that I am here on the verge of jumping off on my big job I appreciate more than ever before those wonderful days you made possible for me last summer. They seem dream-like now, so long ago and so far away and so completely alien from all that surrounds me now.

I was delayed four days in Beirut on my trip, and it is not a particularly exciting place in which to be stuck. The time for leaving came at last, and I set off by car over the Lebanons to Damascus. That can be one of the loveliest drives I know of, but this time the air was dim with haze. Those wonderful vistas that one usually has, of red-roofed villages padded about with green, were lost in an impenetrable murkiness.

I had only the night in Damascus, unfortunately. I should like to see it sometime outside the tourist season. Being alone and lonely I wandered through the dim deserted streets of the native city to the great mosque and there by the light of the waxing moon made the circuit of its walls. There framed by a ruined Roman colonnade I watched the tall minaret reaching up to the moon and pondered on the limitation of man.

The desert rip was not bad this time except that it took rather long, due to blow outs, losing the track, and getting stuck. Thirty hours steady going with no sleep at the mid-desert station of Rutba Wells, but the desert was not so bad as on previous trips nor was the weather hot.

Here in Baghdad I found everyone most cordial, and it seemed almost like getting home again to reach this filthy, perverse, and lovable city. Dr. Frederick Lutz and his wife are already here. He is this year's Annual Professor (Baghdad) for the American Schools of Oriental Research and will be with us as our epigrapher. This year, as you know, I succeed to the post of Director. Wilensky, on whom I most depend, has been held up by his wife's illness and is not arriving until Thursday. Our anthropologist, Ehrich, should have come in yesterday. God only knows what has happened to him. That leaves only our general handyman, Charles Bache, who is due in about two weeks.

There are a great number of things to be done here, and I find it difficult to get down to them. However, I have gotten started and already purchased a light railway for our dig. The amount of money I will have to spend this year just to get started will cut considerably into our funds. I hope like the very deuce that they send us more. If they don't we are going to be terribly short. I expect to go to Kirkuk on Friday (this being Sunday), driving up in a car which I have yet to find and buy. Sunday doesn't effect business here (unless it is Government, which is controlled by the British who observe their own holidays), and I have a lot to do today and it must be done now.

I am going to be terribly busy this year, but I will write just as often as I can.

Return to Tarkhalan

[33]

HARVARD-BAGHDAD SCHOOL EXPEDITION
KIRKUK, IRAQ
TARKHALAN VILLAGE
1 NOVEMBER 1929

Here at last in my beloved Tarkhalan and on the eve of the new season's work.

Just a week ago this morning I left Baghdad, driving up in the beautiful new Ford that I had bought for the Expedition. It is a sort of station-wagon effect, locally made and, for native manufacture, a fairly good product. It is exactly the thing we have always needed, and I grabbed it up when I saw it. It wasn't even finished when I bought it, but I got it completed, all except the painting which our driver has since done, and done very poorly. Anyway, there is nothing native about the chassis, fortunately.

I had never driven the track from Baghdad to Kirkuk before, having also gone before by the train which goes an night, and I was astounded by the barrenness of the region. For hours on end we travelled over a desert as barren and limitless in appearance as that between Damascus and Baghdad. Only one fertile place, the oasis and town of Deltawah, was in our path between Baghdad and Kirkuk. The car being new I took it very slowly, stopping for the night at the Turkish Petroleum Company's camp at Tuz. The Englishman in charge put me up for the night in an unfinished bungalow, plied me with food and drink, and sent me off on my way early the next morning to Kirkuk.

I only stayed in Kirkuk long enough to do a few errands and then chased out to our village of Tarkhalan eight miles to the west. It seemed just like getting home again. All the way out I would look for, meet, and leave behind old familiar landmarks, maybe a particularly large manure pile, and ancient *tepa*, or a ditch across the road, it didn't matter. They all were pleasant and familiar. Finally I found myself rolling cautiously over the furrowed alleyway that passes for a street in our village, then a little beyond to our house, and around the car as it stopped was a crowd of people in rags and in silk, handsome and ugly, dirty and less dirty, but all bidding me welcome. It made me feel as though I were coming back to another home.

Mr. Wilensky and Ehrich had come up by train the day before and had the house well on the way to being habitable, but there was still a great deal to be done. Alterations had to be made to take care of our increased numbers, roofs had to be remade, and the house generally cleaned and repaired. One of the most important alterations as far as I was concerned was the establishment of suitable quarters for myself, and with that in mind I took over our tiny guest room, cut a door through into the bathroom, moved out the tub and shower to a new place, put in a big window, so now I have sort of a suite of bedroom and study-office. Of course I don't have enough shelves yet and no glass in my window to keep out the dust and rain, but that will come in time.

We started our first day on the dig yesterday with a small crew of 18 men which I expect to increase slowly up to a little over a hundred. This will be a much smaller force than last year but one which I hope will be less liable to error. Nothing particularly interesting came to light, yet it was less discouraging than other first days that I have seen.

Our party is now all assembled except for Charles Bache of Philadelphia; he is due to reach Baghdad tomorrow. We are a rather heterogeneous lot this year being composed of Wilensky, of whom you already know; Dr. Lutz, very German in manner and temperament though he is an American and the champion non-stop talker of the Seven Seas; Mrs. Lutz, a harmless mousy woman who, after fifteen years of competition with her husband, has given up the contest and retired to perpetual silence. The fourth member is Robert Ehrich, a young undergraduate from Harvard, an anthropologist, a Jew, pleasant and oh so young. Bache is still to come, as well as Mrs. Wilensky, who is detained by sickness. Then there is me rounding out our party to seven.

Your wonderful letter was waiting for me when I arrived in Kirkuk, and you have no idea how I lapped it up. You say that I was silent and forbidding this past summer. I know it. I was a beast. I don't know what was wrong with me. There was some indescribable thing that just wouldn't let be happy. If I didn't say "I wish you could be with me in Mesopotamia" it wasn't because I didn't think it. I did many times, but the utter impossibility of it kept me from the subject. I should have said it. I had so many thoughts milling about in my head that would be better said and out of the way. Allah made me so, and I apologize to you for him.[13]

P.S. Letters marked *Overland-Mail* come almost as quickly as those marked *Air mail*, and they take only five cents postage. It's more reliable. I recommend it.

---

13 I realize now, and probably did then, that I was not being entirely candid when I wrote that last paragraph. True, there were lots of tensions in the air. It was evident that Mother would have loved to be invited to be a member of the expedition staff. She viewed my work abroad as a gloriously romantic adventure. I think I could have persuaded the authorities at Harvard to allow it, but her age, her health, her emotional and rather flamboyant character presented, to me, insurmountable obstacles. Then too, her relationship and her commanding presence would inevitably have robbed me of, or diluted, the position of authority I had worked so hard to attain. Yet, I hated so to offend her that I steadily avoided a positive "no" to the idea as I should have.

Perhaps the principal reason for my "silent and forbidding" actions had to do with the change in my personal life. That spring I had met Dorothy; we were much in love and hoped to be married. Mother's ill-concealed opposition to losing her last chick to someone else was a constant source of unspoken tension. Next spring Mother, always the romantic, had met Dorothy and was the first to urge us to elope. R.F.S.S., 1983.

The Work Resumes

[34]

8 November 1929

Bed time already and the end of our day of rest. It doesn't seem possible that this day had gone. I haven't done anything. I haven't even loafed. The only thing that I have done is to take my window off its hinges to fix it, and no power on earth can tell when it will be put back again. One day of rest — what a misnomer. I feel as guilty as a child caught in the jam closet because I haven't been working and, well, I should be. There are a multitude of jobs that cry out to be done: business of the expedition, accounts, notes to write up, journal to complete, and letters to be written to the powers at home.

Our party so far is quite congenial. Bache had arrived and I should have known that I could rely on Horace Jayne's judgment. He is a most likeable fellow, useful and intelligent. Incidentally, his is Horace Jayne's brother-in-law. Ehrich is terribly young for his age and size, somewhat dense and lazy, but he will come around. Dr. Lutz is the champion cross country talker of Iraq; never speaks but what he gives is a lecture; and never lectures but he shouts so as to be heard in the furthermost corner of the largest auditorium. The only consolation is that he really knows a great deal and in that great cataract of sound, a great deal of solid information can be found. He has certain pet theories, of course, and certain far-fetched parallels that are pretty hard to swallow, but happily we are not obliged to accept that which we do not choose to believe.

The work goes on fairly well. Our force of gradually being increased and should reach the 100 mark in about a week. That will be enough for the usual work although more may be needed for occasional jobs. It is our misfortune to be obliged to concentrate this season on the area which we had previously abandoned because of its difficulty. I am extremely anxious to finish up at the top level for the whole *tepa*, and this is the only region left at that level. Whether our earlier trials in this section were haunted with a particular malignant spirit or not, I do not know for we were able to get nothing out of them but an echo of a mad laugh. But this season our work in this section has not been unsatisfactory, and I pray that the ill fortune that haunted us last season has left.

Yesterday was the first day on the dig that bore a resemblance to the good days of the past. Nothing startling; some good pottery of the usual kind and one in fragments of a most unusual type, and good walls. Nothing startling, as I said, but enough happening to keep us going. If the walls come the objects are bound to come too, but with no walls we only have unrelated objects and no material for our architectural plans.

It is long past my bedtime. I rejoice that your last letter shows your health regaining its position of normalcy. Go easy and stay so.

The Well Deposit

[35]

17 NOVEMBER 1929

The dig is going along fairly well now. We started at the concentration points: one on the northwest ridge of the *tepa* and one at the southeastern part of the mound. The first was a region that we had tried and abandoned last season because of its difficulty, but this year it seems to go quite smoothly due probably to more knowledge, more unscientific disregard for the fragmentary upper level, and more luck. All in all it is evolving into a fairly creditable looking excavation. Nothing yet very startling in the way of finds, but that doesn't worry me. What I want are walls. Today has been a good day, and I am feeling cheerful because of this region. Tomorrow evening may see me in the dumps because of a bad one.

The second region started well and interestingly; we struck a massive wall, but it soon developed into such a tangle of seemingly impossible conditions that our wall tracers completely lost their heads. As a result I have abandoned it until such time as I can attack it from a different point. With that in mind I have one of our best men working up hill from this region in the hope that he can establish a base for a fresh attack.

The most hopeful place on the *tepa* right now is a well that we are digging out. Although our worker is only down 69 feet, he seems to have reached a point close to the bottom. Yesterday he went through a heavy layer of tumbled brick, seeming to indicate a catastrophe to the region at the top of the shaft such as the sudden destruction of the building; today a thick deposit of fragments of broken water jars such as one would expect in a well, and slightly below this five jars complete, a jar stand, and a fragment of a very large jar most beautifully decorated. We have this type of painted decoration on very few examples of small cups, but never before has such a vessel as this shown any signs of painted decoration. Of course all of their pottery may have been so decorated, for these people, civilized though they were, had never learned the trick of baking their color. It was merely painted on after the vessel was fired, and only in a very few cases have even the smallest fragments survived. Every sherd that has come up from the well has been saved, and I hope that this piece can be reconstructed completely.

Last week we had the first accident that we have had in three year's work. A wall caved on one of our wall tracers burying him almost completely. We dug him out and rushed him in to the hospital where his is now with a badly injured spine. Poor devil. I hope he isn't injured permanently. Ali Mustafa is his name, and I was fond of him. A good worker, quiet, industrious, careful, and uninspired.[14]

---

14 The British medical officer assigned to Kirkuk maintained a primitive sort of hospital there. It wasn't much, but it was better than nothing. R.F.S.S., 1983.

I like them all here, as you know. Decent self-respecting human people. They think I am a rather hard master, I believe, but I am not really. That is only the outside covering.

Our railway has arrived and carried its first load of dirt yesterday much to the delight of everyone, and later to the dismay of those shovel and basket men whose job it is to fill its insatiable maw. No engine, of course. Just narrow gauge track and dump cars pushed by hand. Great fun.

Forgive me for all this shop talk. I am saturated with it.

[36]

25 NOVEMBER 1929

There is rain in the offing today, within sight often, and for a few hopeful seconds within touch, but never the good steady downpour that we all hope for. That these poor people here need it, you know. Rain is the creator and sustainer of their life. With their few scanty inches of rainfall their miserable crops come to fruition; without it there would be no harvest. We in our work need the rain badly too. The dust on the dig is almost unbearable, our walls are crumbling (I told you of the one that collapsed on one of our tracers), and its very dryness makes the tracing the more difficult.[15]

An abominable day on the *tepa* today. A high south wind springing up about eleven o'clock brought such clouds of dust that work became extremely disagreeable. Every basket dumped and every spade filled seemed to turn immediately into great clouds that got into the eyes, down the back, and into the lungs. Those poor fellows who are in trenches to leeward of a dumping station had afflictions as of Job, and need his patience as well. Good work under such conditions simply can't be done. Yesterday was, if anything, a little bit worse, and the day before it was so bad that I halted the work at the end of half a day.

The day before that was *Juma* (Friday) when I should have written home, but instead I spent it for the first time this year in prefect indolence. The greatest

---

15 Irrigation is available only to the very wealthy who own, or share ownership in, a *shareeez* (Arabic *qanat*). Here's how it works. In the higher ground toward the Kurdish foothills a well is sunk 30 or 40 or more feet until moisture is struck. Then another well is sunk to approximately the same depth 50 yards or so away on the down-grade side (away from the foothills) and the two wells then connected at the bottom by a horizontal tunnel. The same is again repeated over and over again, sometimes for miles. The result, in effect, is a horizontal, level well which eventually, because of the slope of the terrain, emerges at the surface as a flowing stream. Carefully made ones have their tunnel lined with baked brick and last for years though few can afford such luxury. Cut rate unlined ones are correspondingly short lived. Thus only the very wealthy have water for irrigation. The bulk of the people must trust in Allah and the four inches or so of annual rainfall for whatever they grow. R.F.S.S., 1983.

pleasure of *Juma* to my mind is your complete independence for once in the week over the early morning dictatorship of time. I know of no greater pleasure than that of waking up on Friday morning at the usual work-day rising hour, looking at your watch, and settling down in the warmth of the covers for another hour of delicious sleep.

But I have become such a creature of habit that for the life of me I can't sleep more than an hour more in spite of the sleep that I have robbed myself of during the week with the promise of repayment on Friday. These early hours are getting to be a habit which I wish I could retain at home. How different from the days of last summer when to reach the breakfast table by nine o'clock was a struggle. Well, I did get up at last, to linger appreciatively over breakfast, then to my room to clear up the day before's payroll accounts, then out with my little camera to where fate would carry me. I hadn't gone far before I was joined by my "friend," my "servant," my "brother" Jabbar (his devotion is expressed in this way), Jabbar the happy one for whom we have such a liking. Together we head for a Bedouin encampment some miles off.

Along we go, sometimes by fields speckled with the pods of ripe cotton or green with young barley, for we are still in the region of irrigation, or more often as we go farther, over the usual desert ground, barren of everything but camel thorn. Ahead are some twenty black, odd-shaped tents, to the left our scarred *tepa*, and off on the right a herd of camels grazing on the desert thorn.

Jabbar trots beside me, sometimes singing and more often talking about his long desired and soon to be realized marriage, the difficulties he has had arranging matters with the family of the bride, and of the high price asked for wives nowadays.

As usual we are greeted first at the camp by a terrific barking of dogs which was silenced by the judicious and none too gentle use of sticks and stones on the part of the respective owners. Then I see the head man of the camp, the sheikh, advancing to meet us. He is a Sayyid, that is, a descendent of the Prophet, which means little for we have Sayyids carrying baskets on the dig, but he is rich. He has sheep and camels, three wives, and a horse. He is a man of consequence and, moreover, a most genial old soul. He has visited our dig often and for reasons of his own seems to have taken a great liking to me. He receives me with the honeyed and wholesale hospitality that only an Arab of the desert can give. Of course, he means it to a certain extent. It *is* an honor to receive a visit from me,[16] and beside, as I said, he is a genial old fellow. His tent and all his property is not his but mine; the very tent is made as the sweetness of sugar by my coming in, and he is but a miserable beggar who through the honor of my visit has become

---

16 This isn't quite as conceited as it sounds. In their eyes we are fabulously wealthy. As the head of the expedition I am the employer of most of the able bodied men and boys in the poverty stricken area, and I am the final arbiter as to who is employed and who is not. We try to live off the land as much as possible, and the continuous needs of our commissary bring further income to the local households. R.F.S.S., 1983.

great. In that fashion I am greeted, and I am ushered into his tent and given the place of honor on the felts that line both sides of the fire; fresh supplies of dried camel dung are added to the fire, and the ceremonial coffee is started brewing. Several men are already there and more come silently in, murmur the usual greeting and take their places about the fire. The host hustles about preparing unknown things, and blessed continually the day that brought him such honor, while I protest feebly and try my best to carry on even the most faltering conversation. Fortunately, long silences are not considered impolite. Overhead is the black goat-hair tent, shaped like half of a gigantic and distorted football and open along one of its long sides. Inside, in the center, is the fire with its coffee pots, with felts or carpets on either side for the guest to sit upon, and at our end a portion screened off for the women and for cooking.

The coffee is prepared with considerable care, this time being made fresh especially for me, and at last it is ready. My first cup is served with a colossal lump of sugar practically filling the tiny cup, that being his idea of how foreigners take coffee, but the remaining two of the three customary cups I asked to have in Arab fashion — a few drops of black boiling unsweetened brew in the bottom of the cup. This being over I rise to go, but oh no. He will not hear of it. I have three more cups and make a more determined effort with more resistance on his part. I must stay and eat. Food is being prepared. He is humiliated that his sheep are not here so that he could slaughter one and have it prepared in my honor. There is nothing for me to do. Lord only knows what kind of mess will be dished up, but it is about ready for I hear my host discussing with his women in a penetrating stage whisper whether I will eat in Arab fashion or with a spoon.

It is ready at last, and an *aba* is laid on the ground, on this many slabs of round, leathery, pancake-shaped Arab bread and in the center a steaming pewter basin full of dates cooked in that abominable stuff, sheep fat. The spoon is there too, but one look at it decides me to be a thorough-going Arab, and with that determination I tear up the bread into small chunks and scoop up the sweetness and stuff myself. I must say that it was fairly good if you kept on the higher side of the basin where the pools of grease didn't spoil things too much.

I soon had my fill and the basin was passed to the rest of the company who were gathered around it, right knee forward and left hand stuffing themselves to repletion. My host was the last to eat, and I must say that his years have done little to spoil his appetite. He cleaned up the basin to the point where the metal shown or would have had I not made another effort to get home. Great protest, of course, but I succeeded this time in getting away. Even at that I couldn't go as I wished. Nothing would do but that I ride his horse home, and all my protests were in vain. That I would make his saddle as sweet as sugar by riding in it seemed to me to be a bit farfetched, but there seemed nothing to do but to turn his life into one grand confectioner's dream. So I mounted his horse, a dashing flea bitten Arab steed whose fastest gait was a slow walk, with a bridle that was but a halter and a saddle with no stirrups. I reached home half an hour later than I would have had I walked and just in time for dinner.

I thought that eventually I would have to pay for this, and sure enough the next day he came asking for work for one of his men. I was sorry that there was no place. We turn away dozens every day. But I took his man today, so the old sheikh was happy.

The work progresses fairly well. A good number of misses, to be sure, but none impossible of solution.

This long account of a casual outing I hope hasn't bored you. I thought you might like to know what kind of people we have here and how they live. These are nomadic Bedouin and comprise a rather small minority of our work force; the majority — settled Turkoman and Kurdish villagers I think I have already written about in some detail.

Rain: I hear it on the roof. No, it has stopped — only a few drops but it may bring more.

Ten thirty and I should have been in bed half an hour ago to get the eight hours of sleep that I want but seldom get.

Rain, Mud, and Thanksgiving

[37]

3 DECEMBER 1929

For the last five or six days we have been held up by rain. We had been praying for it but we hadn't prayed for quite so much. Two days is the usual time to be held up, but five days no matter how many jobs we may have piled up at home is a bit too much for the nerves. Not that there isn't plenty to do, but somehow rainy days bring with them a feeling of relaxation and self-satisfaction that makes even the most essential jobs seem like unreasonable demands.

Before the rain the work was very disagreeable. The elements took about five days of cloud and wind to produce actual rainfall, and the dust that those winds carried over the work made the days on the *tepa* very trying. Every basketful and shovel-full of dirt seemed to evaporate into dense clouds of penetration discomfort. That is all over now and we, being human in our dissatisfaction with whatever condition exists, complain about the quantity of mud about which such a short time ago was dust.

This country in even the slightest rain becomes a mire of mud, and rubber boots become a necessity. To go outside without them is just about as sensible as going without any shoes at all; less so in fact. Herodotus spoke descriptively when he called Babylonia "the land of mud."

Thanksgiving has come and gone, a holiday which in the past I have always enjoyed so much but which this year seemed to fall flat. The meal, of course, is the big thing on this day but it is a minor factor when compared with the company around it. I had never realized before how much depended on the social ability of the lady of the house until now that I have been confronted by one with none whatsoever. Mrs. Lutz, the wife of our epigraphist, is a pitiful little old woman of thirty-five of hardy, grim, humorless, German-American, Kansas farmer stock, as silent and unresponsive as a potato and utterly lacking in imagination. She doesn't like the bazaar because she can buy so much nicer things in the department stores in California, and she never goes outside of the house because she went out once for a half hour walk and has seen everything there is to see. So you can imagine what a cheery house mistress I have installed here. I feel awfully sorry for her. I don't know what she was like before she was married, but after any woman has been the personal slave and beast of burden to the Herr Doktor for fifteen years I don't wonder that she is as she is.

In my usual thoughtfulness I failed to realize that this letter even at its fastest can hardly reach you before Christmas, but it brings, nevertheless, all the affection and wishes for good cheer that such a short letter can carry. I picture you all at Hope, the open fire and popcorn, the turkey dinner, pancakes and sausage, Pickbourne, duck shooting, and the breathless pleasure of distributing the Christmas morning presents. Even though I am not there I feel it all so distinctly that when the time comes I shall be more with you than in Iraq.

[38]

9 DECEMBER 1929

You up for two flights in an airplane? I simply cannot believe it. What on earth happened that has suddenly given you this urge to outdo the birds? That you ever should have been persuaded to go up leaves me in amazement, yet you have written it and I must believe. Now that the terrible fright of anticipation is over, isn't it a glorious feeling to soar above the walks of man and all his earthly cares? Isn't the Eastern Shore from the air beautiful almost beyond description?

From your letter I should say that you are again back to your wonderful health, and that is the best news I could possibly have. The only trouble is that your good health carries you at such a speed and your momentum is so great that you never can stop on the right side of a danger signal. An elementary rule in driving is to apply the brake before a curve, not after. It is hopeless advice, I know, but I feel better for having given it.

So little has happened here to tell you about that if I say the work continues in between rains I would have told you all there is. No finds and an awful mess of walls that I hope will make sense some day.

You are putting the proper postage on your letters, but the idiot in the Easton post office, because you are not making the letters "Air Mail," is sending them the other way. Your last letter took the almost unbelievable time of six weeks to get here. Use 12 cents postage and write "Air Mail" on the envelope conspicuously, or 6 cents and "Overland Mail."

[39]

21 DECEMBER 1929

Along comes your letter telling of your second airplane flight and in the same mail an account in the *Easton Star Democrat* giving in most glowing terms your sensations and sentiments before and after the great event. Although I don't know enough to have any great fear in going up on flights, I realize just what a great victory over yourself this has been. I marvel. The only trouble is that I am afraid you won't be satisfied now until you have made a parachute jump, and that is one thing I do know enough of to make me good and afraid. Leave that out.

For heavens sake print "Air Mail" on the envelopes of your letters to me. They are taking between five and six weeks to reach me instead of less than twenty days. The postman in Easton evidently thinks that you are overflowing with a great public spiritedness and have assumed that particular type of anonymous philanthropy in order to make the U.S. Postal Service a great self-supporting institution. Why else does he route your letters by sea instead of by air?[17]

We have been digging now for quite some time, but today is the first time I have realized how long it has been. Christmas is the mark that has always been in the far future, and here it is not only four days off. Never has the time passed so rapidly and with so little opportunity for profitable idleness. Of all the worthwhile technical books I brought with me, only three pages of one have been read. It is true that I have read a novel — *All Quiet on the Western Front* — the *Easton Star Democrat*, and the Sunday *New York Times* (all the newspapers are ancient history by the time they get here), but that is little enough recreation. Every evening there is some confounded senseless job that keeps me from devouring by force-feeding those technical books that I should know by heart.

The work booms along; so far we have opened up some 127 rooms and the unexcavated portion of the *tepa* is fast disappearing. If we can complete that this year, along with an extensive series of exploratory trenches in the low mounds surrounding the *tepa*, I shall feel well satisfied. Of course there is a prehistoric *tepa* next to ours on which I hold a permit, and I should like to root around that for a couple of weeks just by way of recreation. I've had that in my head for some time now, and if the money is forthcoming I am going to do it. It would be nice to get a good series of prehistoric material just as a sort of *baksheesh* for all our labor with these liberal-minded Nuzians.

Off the ten miles to Kirkuk tomorrow to do my Christmas shopping again. I've done it once, buying for the different members of our party those things

---

17 There was no trans-Atlantic air mail service at that time. Air mail letters crossed this first hurdle by steamer. At London they connected with the air service to India and proceeded across Europe to Cairo in various hops, then to Beirut (or maybe Damascus or maybe both, I've forgotten), then to Baghdad. From Baghdad the letters continued on to Kirkuk by train. R.F.S.S., 1983.

which I knew they wanted, but they being impatient souls have since provided themselves with the very things that I had bought for them.

Christmas Celebrations and the Bronze Tablet

[40]

Christmas in this out-of-the-way place is at best an inferior substitute for that which we look back on at home. For that very reason we try and make as much of a festive occasion of it as possible, but this year it just didn't go. So much depends on the women of the expedition, and with Mrs. Wilensky in bed with bronchitis and Mrs. Lutz's stolid German apathy to either pleasure or sorrow, it just didn't go off.

We postponed the Christmas Eve celebration until Christmas night in the vain hope that Mrs. Wilensky might be up, but it was to no avail. We did rather enjoy breakfast on Christmas morning when we all gave our laboriously selected presents gathered from the meager market of the Kirkuk bazaar. With so little to draw from it is a wonder that there was no duplication. To one might go a book or a bit of Indian brocade and to another a wicked looking Turkoman dagger. Funny little Mrs. Lutz had bought no presents, being thriftily minded (and why should she if she doesn't care to). Then she came into the room that morning with the astounding statement that since they had bought no presents they would not accept any of ours. That was soon overruled.

After breakfast came a long series of visitors from the village to wish us *Idcum umbarak* on our holiday. They made it most embarrassing since we had to give our household staff their usual Christmas *baksheesh*, and the visitors persisted in staying on and on without the slightest sign of departing. However, Mr. Wilensky had the bright idea of getting them out into the courtyard to see our goat eat cigarettes, and from there is was easy to drift imperceptibly toward the compound doorway until they found themselves already outside and being thanked for their visit.

The goat, by the way, is a beautiful white Angora once brought here by our funny little driver, Muhammad, to whom it belongs, for our amusement. We came out on Christmas morning to find that the servants has so entered in the spirit of the holiday that the goat had been dyed to a nightmare of green, pink, and blue with yellow ears and shiny blue paper pasted over its horns.

Well, we got the household tended to, then all piled into the car (all except Mr. and Mrs. Wilensky) for a spin over the desert. We went *tepa* hunting and come back with great pocketfuls of potsherds and flints from the prehistoric mounds we found.

The dinner that night was not very festive, but there is no law against household alcohol in Iraq so things passed fairly well. I blew the expedition to champagne, and that was a decided help. The only trouble was that I didn't blow hard enough. But Mrs. Lutz did smile before the evening was out so it might almost be called successful.

The next morning at breakfast the amount of water consumed was surprisingly large and the quantity of food the smallest on record. We tottered out to the *tepa* feeling much like boiled owls and entered promptly into the best day we have had this season. The tablets came up so fast that I couldn't take care of them and from all over the dig things of real value: more tablets, figurines, duck weights, cylinder seals, and best of all, a small golden sun disc.

Things break suddenly when they come and without the least warning. We had a slight warning, though, in that the room in which most of the tablets where found had once been very swell. Frescoes had once decorated the walls: large red and grey fields separated by a formal spiral design in red, white, gray, and black. It must have been very handsome. Unfortunately only enough is left to enable us to tell what once was there. A few days ago we found in here what so far is the most valuable find of the season: a bronze tablet. The only inscribed metal object we have found in all the digging. It can only be partially read now, but when it is cleaned it will all come out well. I am tempted to do it here.

I am expecting Dr. Frankfort, the Director of Chicago's dig at Khorsabad near Mosul, today as our guest for a few days. The car goes in for him now, and this letter must go with it.

New Year's Visit of Delougaz and Frankfort

[41]

7 JANUARY 1930

This letter has been on the way, on the very verge of being written, for the last week, but somehow something has always kept it from completion. Once, my pen was lost, twice, it was night work, and three times just plain dog tiredness.

Your latest letter gives just a hint of a visit to your gardener friend in Sing Sing prison and the promise of a fuller account to follow. I am anxious to hear more of it. From the little you said I can see that it must have been a great adventure. I await.

Also, since I last wrote a new year has come into being. What it holds for me I can't say. That is not so much a matter of destiny as it is of personal effort, but I can tell you that whatever I may accomplish that is worthwhile in this new year will be due in no small part to the great example you have set by your own accomplishments and the courage you instill in me in my work. I hope that in this new year we may both reach new heights of achievement.

We had as our New Year's guests Mr. Delougaz, now of the University of Chicago expedition and formerly or draftsman, and Dr. Frankfort, Director of Chicago's combined excavations in Iraq. It was most pleasant to meet again that genial and rotund person Delougaz, and still more pleasant to have made the acquaintance of Frankfort. He is a young man between 35 and 40, a Dutchman speaking English without the slightest accent, and is a widely recognized authority on Near Eastern pottery. Until he was grabbed by the all-powerful Chicago University he had been in charge of the famous Tell el-Amarna excavations in Egypt, and he comes to this country as somewhat of a stranger. He was a most interesting and charming guest, and what endeared him to us more than anything else was his enthusiasm over our dig. He being a big bug in pottery, we hounded him with questions, and it was gratifying rather than disappointing to find that the thing that had balked us were equally balking to him. It made us a little less ashamed of our ignorance.

On New Year's Eve Dr. and Mrs. Lutz and Ehrich went off to spend the evening at one of the neighboring oil camps (Targil), and those of us who were left behind, being freed of certain restraining influences, did the best we could to celebrate the holiday. In the absence of the cautious direction of Mrs. Lutz, we ordered the slaughter of the last remaining turkey (the toughest in Iraq), and all of those liquid refreshments that we could offer were brought into the first line of action.

With this to sustain us it was not long before midnight and, as usual, at the appointed time one of our sentries came in carrying the clock he had been given and asking whether it was time to fire the shot that was supposed to have been a surprise to everyone except him who gave the original order. With a sigh over the futility of precision in the Orient the order was given, the glasses filled, the shot fired, and the New Year was welcomed.

But with guests with us and such a pleasant evening behind us one shot wasn't enough. More were demanded from the sentries, and to add to the racket the shotgun was brought out with a beautiful new full box of shells. Tarkhalan had never heard such a midnight disturbance, and the response was energetic. We were soon answered by shouts from all over the village that before had been so peacefully sleeping, as well as the crack of several answering rifle shots. A minute later a man half dressed and carrying a rifle dashed in from the village, then another, and another, and another. "What was the trouble? Robbers? Raiders?" They were the vanguard, this crowd of men; the whole village was waiting to come to protect us from them. On the whole I believe they were quite disappointed that they didn't have a chance to take part in a good battle, but they took it with good grace and congratulated us heartily though sleepily on the arrival of our holiday.

You have no idea of the feeling it gives one to know that a whole village of the strange and likeable people were up in arms to fight for us at the first hint of disturbance. It shows that the feeling of affection for our people which is so strong in me is, in their own fashion, as strongly returned.

My fountain pen has been acting up in the most outrageous fashion, and I decided that it must be fixed; as with most other things in this country to be done at all you must do it yourself. Well, the result was that I broke the point off of it, and only after great labor with a file and much delicate grinding on the whetstone have I been able to bring it back to this scratchy shadow of its former self. Whether the complaint which I originally set out to cure has been helped or not I don't know yet. Probably not.

Long past my bedtime, and sleep is one thing I must have here.

[42]

25 JANUARY 1930

The reason for my strangely long silence is because of a host of things in such rapid succession, and of such an exciting nature, that letters to anyone were impossible.

First of all, the domestic life has become somewhat disturbed. The situation with Dr. Lutz had become increasingly difficult, and on the 12th the big climax that I had hoped to avoid came about. Dr. Lutz had a big fist fight with Wilensky, considered himself insulted, packed up and left dragging his poor wife along with him. Throughout he acted much like a spoiled child and certainly not the part of a gentleman.

On the same day we found the greatest single thing Nuzi has yet shown us. In the corner of a new room a lion in glazed terra-cotta, 45 centimeters long and showing an artistic feeling and cultivation far exceeding anything I had hoped for. It is absolutely complete and a magnificent thing. It brings to light an entirely new chapter in the area of Mesopotamia, and at last shows us the artistic ability of this un-Babylonian race. It is the best find in Iraq this year.

The next day I had to leave for Baghdad to attend a conference of expedition directors, so I closed the dig and declared a general holiday for that period. You can imagine how I grudged every minute I spent away from that partially cleared room. The conference was a very good thing, and in establishing a basis for willing cooperation between digs; archaeology has been put on a footing not to be found in any other country. Being by far the youngest man there, and in fact the youngest in charge of an important excavation anywhere that I know of, I felt like quite a youngster, and I took every opportunity to pump the other Directors of their knowledge. At the dinner given us by the High Commissioner Sir Francis and Lady Humphreys I cornered Woolley after dinner and kept him going until our hostess literally dragged him away.

This was the first time and certainly the last that I shall ever have an opportunity to refuse an invitation from a king. King Feisal's Master of Ceremonies called up while we were meeting asking that we break up the conference and chase over for an audience, but we simply couldn't do it. It was our last chance to finish up, and the purpose for which the meeting was called had to be achieved.

I could write you volumes about it all, and tell you more that I can't write, but this gives you a picture at least. I stayed with the Advisor to the Minister of Justice, in other words, the Lord Chief Justice, but in spite of their hospitality, I was happy to get back to Tarkalan.

Since then things on the dig have been happening at a fast and furious pace. The room that gave us the lion had yielded a wealth of small objects, tablets and one of the finest ivory figurines I have seen from Mesopotamia. Also a head of a boar in glazed terra-cotta one half life size, the last and completing fragment of which we found today. It shows the same grand development as is seen in the sculpture of the lion.

This is extremely early for glaze, which is important, and throughout it goes more and more to prove the strong connection these people had with the Mediterranean Coast, and their relative freedom from Babylonian tradition.

I have every reason to say that we have at last found the temple for which we have been searching for three years. The design of the room, the wealth of their decoration, the quality of the decoration, the gold found, etc., etc., etc., give us proof even with the few rooms we have uncovered so far. For the last two years we have been looking for excuses to justify our work here. Now none is needed.

Today we commenced on a new room, and it started to give fragile decorative objects in such profusion that I had to take the tracers out of it. They could do too much damage. The whole thing — walls, pavement and all — I'll do with my knife crew. From here this afternoon came lion No. 2, in red painted terra-cotta. He is smaller, slightly, than the other and broken. We have only ¾ of him so far, but the rest — the head and shoulders — will come I am sure. He is different from our first one, more complete in detail and from what I can see now, not quite so fine, but after all a great find.

I could take pages to tell of all the things that have been happening. This description is nothing. I am exhausted and happy. Ten thirty now and I still must write another letter and load a fresh batch of photographic plates. I must close.

More Temple Finds

[43]

1 FEBRUARY 1930

Just the briefest kind of note before I tumble exhausted into bed. Yesterday two grand letters from you telling of all kinds of gay and strange holiday festivities, and of the best news of all, that you are painting and playing the piano. Whenever I hear that I know that things are going well.

We had a guest a short time ago, a young British Royal Air Force officer, who has a taste for good music and he brought his records with him. I wish he had stayed a month instead of three days.

The dig comes on at the same crazy pace, and I am completely fagged out. Things which last month would have sent us shouting for joy we now receive as though they were quite the usual thing. Nothing so grand as our lion has come, but we have fragments of these others which if they could only be completed would be as fine as the first; and all kinds of wonderful little stuff. It is the temple without doubt and found after two and one-half years of searching. Had I not gone against Harvard's wishes and practically disobeyed their orders, I never would have found it. We would be rooting around in the ground somewhere under the palace. Digging holes.

While our temple is giving us nice things, it is not for nothing. The walls are in damnable condition, and tracing them is proving to be the very deuce. I want the objects, but to get the objects without the plan robs an expedition of half its purpose. We are getting down to careful serious work on it now.

[44]

10 FEBRUARY 1930

This has been an abominable day on the dig. A strong cold wind has been buffeting us every minute of the day and bringing with it such clouds of grit and dust that I could wish for nothing but a quiet sunny place ten thousand miles from Iraq. We haven't had such a day since last fall, and I had hoped that we had seen our last but evidently the gods thought that after our pride in our temple we needed humbling.

The finds of the temple region have come to an end, but the architectural plan is not completed yet by any means. Completing that is my goal. If my guess is right it will be immediately abutting the palace, and if this contact can be made we will have completed one of the major tasks that I had set for ourselves this season. In fact we probably have made that contact. It is in one doubtful wall defined today, but we must have more before it is certain. The other remaining task was that of finishing off the remaining upper level of the *tepa*, but I see now that I had set an objective beyond the possibility of attainment. We will be able to come close to it, but it can't be done completely this season. That must be left to work on in the coming years.

A wolf was shot close by the *tepa* today and brought in for us to see. I have never seen such a beast. Simply tremendous. I have seen them here at a distance often but never close up, and I had no idea one could be so large. No wonder the shepherds are so scared of them. I would not like to meet this fellow on a dark night anywhere.

We will stop work here about April 1st, and after that I hope to go off into the mountains of Kurdistan for a week or two. Then for home as fast as I can go.

[45]

23 MARCH 1930

A note at least to let you know that I haven't completely faded out of existence and to tell you how much I appreciate your letters. Two fine ones have come since I last wrote, the last one telling only too briefly of your having seen Mei Lan Fang. I saw him perform once in Peking and I shan't soon forget.

We are closing down the dig, and I feel terribly fagged out. Our division with the government is on the 2nd of April, and by the 15th I should be on my way home. It will be a happy day when I leave here.

I must get to bed and get some kind of night's rest for once.

Letters from Iraq [46-78] to D.C.S.S.

1929–1930 Season

Atlantic Crossing

[46]

M.A. AUGUSTUS
25 SEPTEMBER 1929

Wonderful sight today: our first land. We went between two of the Azores and mighty enticing they were, too. Not that I have a great longing to set foot on solid land just yet, but they were soft and green and made me remember an unforgettable day at Punta del Gada last year. Coming from an arid East where the dusty grey-green of the palm is the only thing to refresh the eye we were ushered suddenly into the paradise of semi-tropical verdure. Such flowers and such enchanting odors, and birds singing with a sweetness and abandon almost unbelievable.

[47]

26 SEPTEMBER 1929

No Azores today, not even a seagull to relieve the monotony of an interminable horizon. A glorious blue sea, though, that we have come into; a blue that shines with warmth reflecting the serenity of the cloudless sky above; a blue with depth and body as has the ocean itself.

Excitement at Gibraltar

[48]

30 SEPTEMBER 1929

Great excitement at Gibraltar the other day. Señorita Edda Mussolini, the daughter of "our beloved Duce," joined our ship on her way home from a visit to Primo de Revera. Tremendous excitement. Passengers fighting for an advantageous place at the rail, cameras clicking (among them mine), the captain and his officers in dress uniform there to greet her, and row upon row of stewards lined up in battle formation all giving them the Fascist salute.

That evening she attended the "gala ball," and so great was the interest of the passengers that I am sure the ship's doctor was called upon afterwards to treat many cases of disjointed necks. She is a rather nice looking girl, in a way; very blonde, long nose, blue eyes, and possessing a sweet and democratic nature, we are told.

It seemed awfully good to see land again, and Gibraltar is a most fitting port of first arrival. All of the military lore and tradition of the place combine with its color and picturesqueness to make it a fascinating port. We couldn't go ashore; we were not there more than an hour, but it was a mightily pleasant one. Scores of little boats surrounded the ship selling five cent baskets of fruit for fifty cents, fishermen offering cuttle fish and other strange sea beasts (of which, oddly enough, they sold quite a few), and the fleet of modern destroyers in the harbor all blended together to make a most interesting water picture. And above all this towered the great rock, grey above and green below with the dusty color of olive trees. We have another celebrity aboard of whom you may have read, The Marquis and Marquise of Something-or-Other. She is the one who was married this summer with a many million dollar dowry, the daughter of Poli, the American theater owner, and the one whose $50,000 engagement ring was confiscated by the customs last spring on her return to America, with great consternation in the newspapers.

We land in Naples tonight, and I will get off this ship and step on another. I don't expect it will be much of a ship. Anyway, it takes a long time getting to my destination, Beirut, ten days, stopping at Alexandria, Port Said, Haifa, and Jaffa, and probably spending a couple of days in each.

Voyage via Egypt

[49]

S.S. Brasile
4 October 1929

Gone is my grand ship Augustus; no more boulevards of gleaming white deck, no longer the pleasant companionship of shipboard acquaintances. All that I have left behind in Naples for this crazy little tub.

We reached Naples about 10 p.m. on the 30th, but most of those disembarking stayed aboard that night, as did I. Up early the next morning to dash up town to get the ticket I had radioed for, then back to the ship to take off my luggage, carry it across the dock to this ship, then back to the Augustus for a final farewell.

This is perhaps the strangest little moth-eaten ship that I have ever contracted to spend ten days upon. I've been on worse, I admit, but they were in the Far East and only for short trips.

A strange group of passengers we have on board: a broken down French theatrical company on its way to play Cairo and Alexandria, and an odd lot of English, Italian, and Egyptian passengers. Oh yes, an American couple from the Augustus whom I never had the chance or desire to speak to while there, but who are now my closest companions. They are honeymooning, he for the second time and she at last for the first. A very plain pair but pleasant in small doses. That makes three at our dining table. The fourth is a stout, pleasant, well educated English Jewess with the most terrifically developed conversational gifts I have ever encountered. It seems particularly surprising in a Briton since I have always considered them as rather sparse and reserved conversationalists. Once this woman starts off you might just as well give in and decide to become an impassive audience for the rest of the meal. It won't do any good to resist.

This letter started off this afternoon in my deck chair, was interrupted by a tour of the engine room, again by tea, and finally by darkness. I am down in my cabin now with a book across my knees carrying on while my cabin mate, whom I have just now seen for the first time, is on the floor wrestling with a very obstinate suitcase. It is the first time during the day that we have been in the cabin awake together, and since he retires later than I and rises earlier he has been until now a complete stranger to me. His only language being French, I am afraid he will remain so.

I had not planned to get off in Egypt, but since I find we stop there three days I suppose I might as well go ashore and run up to Cairo. We land tomorrow in Alexandria, and I can't see three days in part in this flea bitten little boat, especially in Alexandria. Cairo is only three hours off, and I might as well see it again. I'll take another fling at the pyramids and the National Museum, I'll do the bazaar and the antique shops, then join the ship again at Port Said. That will be a lot better than staying on board and feeling sorry for myself. I had hoped that the next time I visited Egypt I would have the time and money to go up the Nile to Upper Egypt, but it isn't possible this time. From Alexandria our boat goes to Port Said, then to Jaffa, then to Haifa, then to Beirut where I disembark to go to Damascus and over the long desert trail to Baghdad.

Whether or not I will have trouble landing tomorrow I don't know for I have no Egyptian visa. I didn't realize when I left New York that we stayed in Egypt so long but rather that it would be just one day in Alexandria which once seen is certainly not worth a ten dollar entry fee. But I'll manage to get one some way, Cairo is worth it many times over.

Outfitting the Dig

[50]

CARLTON HOTEL, BAGHDAD
24 OCTOBER 1929

Confusion all around me, papers strewn over the bed, and bundles stacked in the corners. Yes terrific confusion and of course it means only one thing, packing. Anyway, I have just pushed Wilensky and Ehrich onto the night train to Kirkuk. Dr. and Mrs. Lutz come up in five days, and the Lord only can tell when Bache will show up. The two who went off tonight will have our headquarters establishment somewhat habitable by the time I get there, and the three of us should have things in good running order by the time the Lutz family checks in.

With the car loaded down with stuff of all kinds I push off tomorrow in our brand new automobile. Yes, it is a new one, and a Ford at that, with a beautiful locally made station wagon body. I gave the order only yesterday with the body at that time still uncompleted and with the demand for considerable alteration, and though they promised to have it finished tonight I am astounded to learn that it will be ready for delivery tomorrow. Of course the explanation is that the company is an English one, not native. Unpainted, I am sorry to say, but I couldn't wait for that. We will do that in Tarkhalan in our spare time. Oh, it is beautiful. By the time I get through buying all these expensive necessities there will be no money left for digging, but at least we will ride in style.

Ever since I arrived in Baghdad I have been chasing around in a most hectic fashion seeing to a thousand different foolish things and making purchases that range from pen points to a light railway. Constantly on the go with no apparent diminution in the things to be done. They are over at last; that is, all that I haven't forgotten, and I am off to my real work. Thank God.

Back to Tarkhalan

[51]

KIRKUK, IRAQ
TARKHALAN VILLAGE
28 OCTOBER 1929

Here in Tarkhalan at last and mighty glad to be back in this funny impossibly naive community again. I felt rather as though I were coming home again. All the way out one familiar landmark after another until finally I rolled cautiously over the furrowed alley that passes for a street in our beloved village of Tarkhalan; then a little beyond to our house. The car came to a stop outside the door, and I found myself surrounded by a crowd of swarthy, turbaned, smiling people as happy, apparently, to see me again as anyone could wish. The whole rest of the day a stream of visitors came to bid me welcome. I had become so accustomed to these people that their picturesqueness had ceased to be apparent to me last year, but now that I see them anew and with a fresh mind I am struck by their appearance. Big fellows mostly, with fine aquiline features, big black eyes, and a fearsome countenance belying the good nature that lies beneath. Each has a small rakishly placed turban, a kind of shirt with immensely long sleeves tied together then thrown over their backs, a long robe in tatters reaching to their feet, and a villainous looking curved knife stuck in their sash. From the look of the knife one might imagine that they were skilled in combat, but really they are the most mild and amiable people and I think quite honestly devoted to us. No doubt considerable of their devotion arises from the opportunity we offer of earning quite a decent pay for this country (a rupee a day, 36 cents), but I like to persuade myself that beside the purely financial consideration there is a bond of friendship between us.

They are like children, these people; simple to a degree, patient, industrious, and unbelievably ineffectual. The amount of commotion set up over the simplest task is astounding. That is the east, of course, the indisputable hallmark of the Oriental.[18]

I found Wilensky and Ehrich here a day ahead of me and already well on the way toward making our home habitable. Alterations had to be made to accommodate our larger staff, old roofs had to be remade, the rooms whitewashed, additions put up, and innumerable other jobs. Then, too, all of our stuff had to be hauled out of the storage rooms, cleaned and put in place. We aren't through yet by any means, but we will be soon and then we can think about a little digging.

A Worker's Perspective

[52]

7 NOVEMBER 1929

I am taking the Arab view very strongly this year. They believe that anyone with sufficient money to buy a wife should be married. They are continually puzzled as to why I, rich in their eyes, am not so, and they never cease to urge me toward it. Before this I have laughed away the idea, but this year I haven't the same feeling.

Jasim ibn Muhammad, one of our most trusted workers on the dig, was in my study a short time ago and gently berated me for coming a third time to Tarkhalan without a wife. Jasim, by the way, is a pure Arab type, not Turkoman as most of our people are, and as pathetically almost tragically handsome a man as I have ever seen: jet curly hair and beard, a beak of a nose, hollow cheeks, and big black eyes that hold in them all the silent agony of the desert.

I was about to start writing you when he came in and seeing your photograph on my table immediately asked who it was. Not knowing quite how to put our relationship in Arabic, I told him that you were my wife in spite of just having repudiated the possession of any such thing. That provoked great

---

18 The welcome just described was from the members of our village — Tarkhalan — all of whom were Turkoman. Our Kurdish workers, from the neighboring village of Tabzaowa (phonetic) differed little in dress except for a much larger turban. Their features in general were less sharply defined than those of the Turkoman. Our Arab workers, Bedouin from the near-by desert encampments, eschewed the multi-folded sash, the exaggeratedly long sleeves, and the turban. Theirs was the shirt and baggy trousers, long dark colored cloak or *aba*, and as a headgear the *kafiyah*, or head shawl, held in place by the rope-like *aqal*. Their features tended toward the classic Bedouin hawk-like appearance, with long braids of jet black hair. Incidentally, it was not unusual to see Kurds with blue eyes and relatively fair complexions, unlike the uniformly brunette coloration of the Turkoman and the even darker coloration of the Bedouin. Also, both Kurds and Turkoman often, in fact usually, also wore the Arab *kafiyah*, and wrapped their turbans around it. R.F.S.S., 1983.

rumbling bursts of laughter and a compliment to the readiness of my wit. I didn't press the misrepresentation, and he left with you in his mind as an unsolved mystery.

Today is Friday and being good Muhammadans this is our day of rest too. Usually it is a day to do with as we please, but the first thing I was pleased to do was to write to you and then turn to a day full of paper work. It is not three-thirty and this is still the first on my list. Our guards have orders to let in no one who has not a legitimate purpose, yet they get in by hook or by crook and come to my room and pester me for work. Just plain visitors also get in along with a multitude of other small distracting things.

Yesterday was our first day of work on the dig. We started with a very small crew, 18 men, which I plan to increase slowly to a little over a 100. This will be a much smaller work force than last year and I hope less liable to error. Naturally, all those who were employed before are clamoring to be taken this year at once, and I am bothered almost to death by these people.

Tomorrow mail will come into Baghdad by air and the day after that it should be in Kirkuk. The air mail on the leg from Cairo to Brindisi has just been lost, along with a load of passengers as well. I wonder if one of my letters to you was aboard. Anyway, from now on I send mine *Overland* and not *Air*. It takes a few days longer, but it is safer. It may be held up for a week in the desert because of the winter rains, but it isn't likely to be lost at sea.

[53]

6 NOVEMBER 1929

By the way, the air mail that was lost at sea was that which left Baghdad October 22, but I can't remember for the life of me whether it carried a letter to you or not.

Thirty Sheep for a Wife

[54]

8 NOVEMBER 1929

If I have told you this before stop me. The people here are all very much disturbed over the fact that I am not married. How can it be that I who am wealthy (in their eyes) and who can well afford to buy a wife should remain single? The first year I was here it puzzled them, last year it worried them, and this year they believe something should be done about it. With that in mind my happy friend, that blithe spirit Jabbar came to me the other day and said, "Why, *why* have you no wife? If it can be that you can't afford to buy one I have thirty sheep which I will gladly give you to purchase yourself a wife." The sheep I couldn't accept. I thought they might clutter up your apartment too much. Then, too, prices are very high in America, and I wasn't sure thirty sheep was enough.

Things at the dig are at last beginning to take some kind of shape. Yesterday was the first one which showed signs of being a good day. Nothing outstanding coming up but enough to keep the interest sustained. Some nice pottery of the familiar type, one most unusual one though in fragments, good walls, and the hope for tablets.

Our most principal difficulty is that of good walls. We aren't looking for objects *per se*; we are looking for walls that will establish an accurate ground plan. With the plan fixed, the objects that are there are bound to be found, and within their proper context. We have to concentrate this year on a region which in previous seasons we had abandoned because it was so difficult. We have already started out on it and so far the results have not been bad, but the prospect for the future is not that of a very easy time. A good mudbrick wall, in spite of the fact that the dirt covering it is the same as that of which the brick itself is made, is a fairly easy thing to follow, but one that is poorly made to begin with, that was probably pretty well destroyed before it was covered, and that is tangled up with later superimposed habitations, is the very devil. I can only pray and hope for the best.

Workers' Problems

[55]

UNDATED;
CONTEXT INDICATES ABOUT MID-NOVEMBER 1929

Fate seems to have decided that whenever I start to write you Jasim will appear and squat for interminable hours on my study floor talking and smoking and talking some more. I have told you before about Jasim. I like him and I believe he is honestly devoted to us. He is my brother. A poor, unbelievably poor, desert Arab he, through his intelligence and character, has risen to a position of importance and respect within his community. He is our most trusted knifeman; he gets the colossal salary of 54 cents a day. This year when we heard that he was sick unto death, Mr. Wilensky and I went out to his desert village to help him. We found him with a badly infected boil which he had made no less painful by cauterizing with a red hot iron. I treated it and he got well, and though my treatment was probably not responsible for his recovery, the credit is mine.

Antiquities have been stolen from the dig. In long whispered accounts he tells me about it. He is honest. I believe him. That they have been stolen we know. How and by whom is another question. He is of help there. The offenders are Turkoman. He is an Arab. He has no scruples against telling on them. You could argue that he is shielding his own race, and he probably would have done so no matter how great his attachment to us, but no Arab beside himself has been in a position to take things. Besides, his stories correspond with the fragments that drop from others. A conversation in Arabic is hard enough for me under the best of circumstances, but when it is in whispers it becomes almost beyond my powers.

The dig goes on well in spots. The region of which I was most hopeful is developing into an unintelligible tangle and that region of which I had expected the least is coming out surprisingly well. I have abandoned that first region for the time being. We will have to attack it from a different direction. In the second region we had the first casualty that we have had in three years of digging. A wall collapsed on one of our wall tracers, Ali ibn Mustafa by name. He was dug out and rushed to the Civil Hospital where he is now with a badly injured spine. Poor devil, I hope he isn't maimed for life. I like Ali and I wouldn't want to see him permanently injured. It was hard to see the suffering the poor fellow went through at the time. These people here are a likeable lot, and I don't want to see any of them fall into misfortune. We have had another accident, too; a minor one. One of our men managed, I don't know how, to get his foot under the wheel of one of the big double carts that was delivering our narrow gauge railway with the result that he is in the hospital, too, with a broken foot bone or two. If I had done it I would expect others to feel sorry for me, but somehow I can't work up much feeling for this fellow. Ali is a different case; he took the risk that we must of necessity ask our men to take. The very qualities that make them accept the risk are those qualities that make them admirable. Then, too, it is more our responsibility if he comes to harm.

Night time already. Tea long since past, dinner just over, and as usual for a Friday, I am just starting my grand letter writing session. The question is, why don't I do it on week days? Don't ask me. It just isn't done. On the field at 7 a.m., there until 4:30, then in to clean up and tea at 5:30. Tea means conversation and relaxation, and by the time that it begins to lag, dinner is on the table. An hour afterward, perhaps straightening up the day's notes, half an hour to read before you collapse dead tired into bed. I have with me this year a dozen publications that I should read and want to read. I have only read three pages, and that was last night when I was so sleepy that mighty little of it stayed in my head. It was Dr. Chiera's publication on the Nuzi texts in which he states that which up to now in my innocence I had believed: that our Nuzians were the Hurri. Now, along comes our present epigraphist and says that any child would know that they are not Hurri but Harri! Dr. Chiera and I not being children of course couldn't be expected to know. Considering that Chiera and Lutz (our present man) are deadly enemies, I don't take the controversy too seriously. According to Lutz the Hurri cease to exist after 1800 B.C.

A Bedouin Experience

[56]

23 NOVEMBER 1929

Mail goes off tomorrow and there must be a letter for you aboard that rip snorting, roaring, twenty-mile-an-hour mail train.

A rotten day in the field today: a strong south wind with an unfulfilled threat of rain and dust such as to drive a man crazy. I stopped the work at noon, and I wish I had done it much sooner. Work in that kind of weather doesn't pay. The men can't see properly, and the possibility of the damage they can do is tremendously increased. A man can't trace out even the most obvious wall when his eyes are so full of dust and grit that it is painful to keep them just a little bit open. Even now after half a day's rest mine feel like the proverbial burnt holes in a blanket. Everyone had hoped that this wind would bring the rain that has been threatening for the last week. Rain: the sustainer of life, the creator of life, the origin of life. A few inches of rain, enough to grow their miserable crops or to furnish sparse grazing for their flocks means another year of life, but without it — well, there isn't even miserable life.

The people want rain desperately as always, and even we need it for our work. The ground is so dry that our walls are crumbling to pieces. I told you of the man on whom a wall collapsed. Then, too, a little moisture makes the ground less hard and the cleavage line between dirt and wall a trifle more distinct. Also we count on a certain number of rainy days to allow us to catch up on the work that is piling up ahead of us at home. Another thing not to be forgotten is that a good rain with its promise of a good harvest will bring the local food prices down considerably. We live off the land as much as we can. But I am not worrying; the rain will come and with each little rainfall this whole great alluvial region will turn into a quagmire. Herodotus spoke wisely when he named Babylonia "The Land of Mud."

Yesterday was *Yom al-Juma* (Friday) and, as usual, we good Muhammadans observed this day of rest; I with exercise and stuffing myself to such and extent that I was good for nothing but sleep the rest of the day, and the others with their own chosen pursuits. The greatest pleasure of all on Friday is that of being able to lie in bed in the morning as long as you please. No pleasure here can equal that feeling of luxuriousness which comes when you wake up at the usual time, realize that for today you for once are master over the clock, and roll over for another delicious hour of sleep. But I am so the slave of habit that try as I will to sleep all morning, I cannot continue beyond seven o'clock. That is only an hour more than usual. How different from mornings at home here to get up at nine was a struggle.

I went for a long walk yesterday morning, and before long I found myself joined by my friend Jabbar. We head for a Bedouin encampment some miles off, a group of twenty black tents with a herd of camels grazing on the thorn in the distance. I stride along the path sometimes through barren patches and sometimes by fields of cotton and barley (we are still in the region of irrigation) and Jabbar trots alongside singing and talking at length over the prospects of his coming and long desired marriage, the present high price of wives, and the difficulties he has had in arranging matters with her parents.

At the encampment I am met by the sheikh, a Sayyid — a descendent of the Prophet — and rich. He insists that I come to his tent. His tent and all the property is not his but mine, I am a good man, I am great, his tent is made as sweet as sugar by my coming into it, his was nothing but now his is great because I have so honored him. The place of honor is mine on the felt surrounding the fire; renewed supplies of camel dung are added to the dying flame, and the ceremonial coffee set abrewing. Several guests are already there and more stalk in silently, murmur the usual greeting and squat around the glowing fire. The conversation is carried on principally by my host, an amiable and likable old soul certainly, about the honor he has received today with halting protest from me. We sit on felts and rugs in two rows on either side of the fire with overhead the black woven goat hair in all like half of a distorted football. At one end is a screened off area for the women to which my host retreats frequently to give instructions about the preparation of some special dish.

The coffee is freshly made, and with great care, and I have the ceremonial three cups and rise to go, but the Sayyid's insistence is too strong. I have another three cups and make a more determined effort but with no more results. I must stay and eat. Food is being prepared. Had the sheep not been out in the desert, one would have been slaughtered for a feast in my honor, but that being so he is preparing the best his poor tent can provide. It comes at last after a long discussion in undertone with his wives as to whether I will eat with a spoon or not dates cooked in sheep fat, that abominable stuff. One look at the spoon made me decide to eat Arab fashion which I did with considerable gusto spooning out the sweet greasy stuff with chunks of flat Arab bread. It was really quite good if you kept on the high side of the bowl where the fat was the least. I soon had my fill, then the rest of the company gathered around the big pewter basin, right knee forward and left hand scooping up the food with an energy and satisfaction that I envied.

After that I managed to take my leave but not as I had wanted. Nothing would do but that I ride home on his horse, a dashing arab steed whose fastest gait was a slow walk, on a saddle without stirrups, and a bridle that was but a halter. That I would make his saddle as sweet and sugar by sitting in it seemed to be a bit too much, but there seemed to be nothing to do but turn his whole life into one vast confectioners dream and get out as quickly as possible. I arrived home just in time for lunch, half and hour later than I would have had I walked.

I thought I would have to pay for that hospitality and sure enough, today he arrived at the dig asking for work for two of his men. It was hard, but I had to refuse him. There was no place. We turn away dozens every day.

Thanksgiving Day '29

[57]

23 NOVEMBER 1929

Thanksgiving Day is upon us all of a sudden, appearing unexpectedly out of nowhere to remind me of that which I already know so well. If I remember my history lesson correctly the Puritans instituted this holiday in thanksgiving for a full larder and for another year of life, but to me, one of their descendants, it no longer means that. Life I can't honestly be thankful for because I never asked in the first place to be granted it, and if I hadn't been granted it and didn't exist, there would be no me to regret not existing; and of food, I have come to consider its plentifulness so a matter of course that it has become a matter of acceptance and not of thankfulness.

Our *second* Thanksgiving Day dinner is just over, and I have established myself as a trencherman of unrivaled capacity. You see, we were to have had the principal meal this noon which we did have, but due to mismanagement of some kind on the part of the House Department, there was only twice as much food as one could and should eat. Stuffing to the point of bursting as we all did, I protested the scarcity of food. The house boy, Abdullah, took it to heart and relayed the complaint to the kitchen whereupon the cook proceeded to prepare a dinner of really heroic proportions quite unbeknownst to us all. We complained rather when dinner was announced this evening that we had to eat again, and then came the feast. Well, as I said, I established a reputation at the board which will not soon be forgotten. As a result I envy the python who after a heavy meal curls up for a six week's sleep.

It wasn't a terribly cheerful meal this noon. I am not much at the life-of-the-party business, and even though Bache and Ehrich mixed and contributed a punch of unrequested potency, the meal was rather despondent.

What a difference the right or the wrong lady-of-the-house can make. Last year Mrs. Pfeiffer, young, vivacious, and in many way attractive, could carry off an occasion such as this in grand style, but Mrs. Lutz who through her seniority has fallen heir to the position, just can't and won't do it. She sits a whole mean through without saying a word, rarely smiling, and disappears immediately afterwards to the room and her sewing. Poor little woman. I think she would like to enjoy life, but she can't let herself do it. Her upbringing in a Kansas German-American farming family and fifteen years as the personal slave of her husband has forced her into the belief that her position is with that of the work animals. She is honest, though. She doesn't like the Orient and if asked will tell you so. It is because they don't have department stores here as they do in California.

The dinner this evening, even without the liquid refreshment, was a bit more cheery, and to keep up that spirit I suggested a big game of "I Doubt It," a card game of the kindergarten variety the object of which is to win through rank deception and dishonesty. That went on uproariously for an hour or so and was broken up only when very young Ehrich got huffy because he thought he had been cheated. He had, of course, and I had done it, but his quarrel was with the ladies, and that was not good form.

Rain — that for which the whole country has been praying — is here. Our villagers splash about in the mud and are happy. A few more like this, with a good one in the spring, will mean a good crop year. This last week started badly. Saturday was so dusty that we could work but half a day. Sunday and Monday were as bad, but we carried on for complete full days of grime and grit. Tuesday the rain started, halting the work at noon, and it has carried on since then in driving squalls or in penetrating drizzles with intermission of lowering clearness. A violent ten minute downpour has just stopped. I hope it clears. For our purposes we have had enough, but to those in the village, their mud houses could be washed away (as they were in our cloudburst of last year) and they would be happy and ask for more. Of heat and famine and poverty they have sufficient, but of rain — never.

Vacation Plans in Kurdistan

[58]

6 DECEMBER 1929

You wonder whether your cuneiform professor, Dr. Jacobsen, will be anywhere near us. I should say so! The University of Chicago is digging at Khorsabad, where he will be working, just outside of Mosul which is only 120 miles from our place. I know it well. I was with Dr. Chiera two years ago when he dug there for Chicago. We two put in the first exploratory trenches that convinced Chicago to go into it seriously. It wasn't much of a dig, I must say, two weeks only, but it was enough to show us what was there. You didn't know that I had worked for the University of Chicago, did you?

Whether their group has arrived or not, I don't know. I haven't heard as yet. No, they can't have arrived because I have just loaned them personally 150 rupees to keep their guard alive until they arrive. They left this man there with checks dated ahead for each month, but going only through September, and he has been sent none for the remaining time. He went to the government in Mosul for assistance, and they in turn came to me for information. The result is as you see.

I was quite sure that the temperature was well below zero today, and to verify it I have just looked at the thermometer. Lo, it is only 58 above. It must be wrong; 58 below, yes; but 58 above, never. A cold cloudy day with a threat of rain and me here shivering as though I were suffering from ague.

I have a grand jaunt planned for the future. As long as I have been here I have wanted to go up in the mountain wilderness of Kurdistan. Yesterday Captain Littledale, special police officer for all of this northern country, came out (to see about Chicago's guard) and as we looked at the snow capped peaks on the northern horizon, I casually mentioned my desire to go there. "Fine," he said, "come along with me in the spring when you are through here. We'll go to the end of the motor road and then up through the Rawanduz Pass and around about by pony." Maybe I didn't jump at that! It is sufficiently dangerous country to make permission to travel there by foreigners very difficult to obtain. Even with permission you must take a calvary escort. But he is the man who gives or refuses the requests to travel, and his offer, his knowledge of the country, and his access to all of the difficult places, make it an ideal opportunity. I hope nothing comes to prevent it. It will probably be only for a week or two at the most, but even that will be a great experience. You can't go until spring anyway because of the snows.

Frigid Times

[59]

13 December 1929

Every time I write you I seem to be in a continuing state of the shivers, and this time it became so bad that I have moved outside into the sun. I have a nice new canvas bottomed chair that I ordered from Baghdad. Across the arms I have a small drawing board, and here I sit happy as a clam.

My rooms that were so nice at the beginning of the season have taken on certain definite disadvantages with the coming of cool weather. They face west, north, and east and as a result get on sun at all during the day. It's fine in hot weather, but just now I might as well try and work in a Kelvinator as in my study. One great advantage it still retains is that it does give me a certain amount of privacy. I'll try and show you what our house is like. It is of mud brick, as you know, with mud roof, gypsum floors, and is relatively comfortable. Here it is:

HARVARD–BAGHDAD SCHOOL EXPEDITION
KIRKUK, IRAQ.

CABLE ADDRESS.
EXPEDITION, KIRKUK.

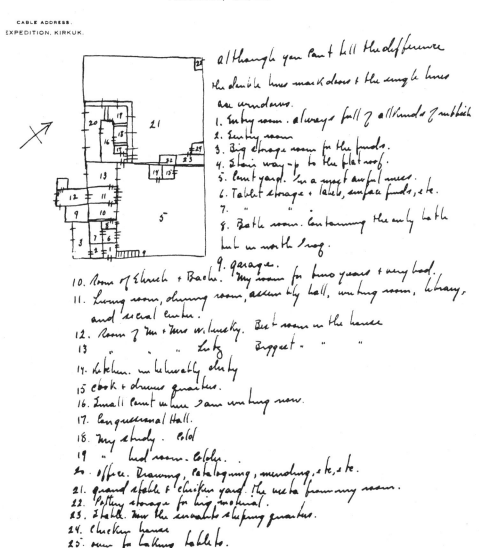

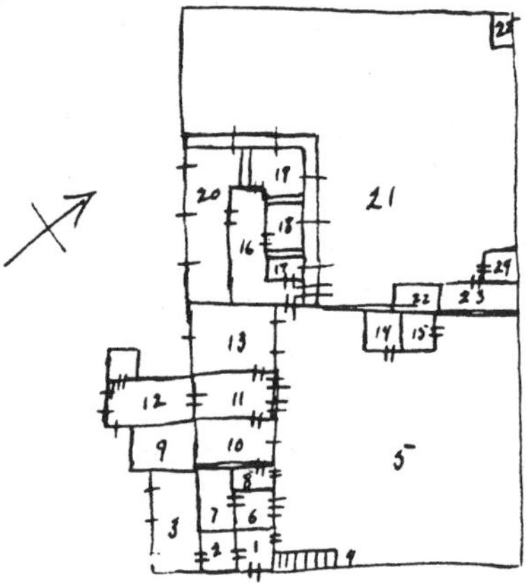

Although you can't tell the difference the double lines mark doors & the single lines are windows.

1. Entry room. always full of all kinds of rubbish
2. Sentry room
3. Big storage room for the finds.
4. Stair way up to the flat roof.
5. Court yard. In a most awful mess.
6. Tablet storage & labels, surface finds, etc.
7. " " .
8. Bath room. Containing the only bath tub in north Iraq.
9. garage.
10. Room of Ehrich & Bache. My room for two years & very bad.
11. Living room, dining room, assembly hall, writing room, library, and social center.
12. Room of Mr & Mrs Wilensky. Best room in the house
13 " " " Lutz Biggest " " "
14. Kitchen. unbelievably dirty
15 Cook & drivers quarters.
16. Small court where I am writing now.
17. Congressional Hall.
18. My study. Cold
19 " bed room. Colder.
20. Office. Drawing, cataloguing, mending, etc, etc.
21. Grand stable & chicken yard. The vista from my room.
22. Pottery storage for big material.
23. Stable. Now the servants sleeping quarters.
24. Chicken house
25. Oven for baking tablets.

There, you have the whole thing before you. Of course it doesn't give much of an idea of what our place looks like. But if you were to come here and if by some chance arrived on a dark night by yourself, with no one at home, and the sentries who are to guard us were all asleep, and the door were unlocked, you would be able to find your way around with the help of this invaluable pocket map.

The number of tablets we have found this year could be counted on the fingers of two hands. This site which usually has been so prolific in this material has proven quite barren this year. Poor Dr. Lutz has become quite despondent and from a continual cross country lecturer has turned into the original wooden Indian. With his wife that makes two who never speak at the table. The feeling between the Lutz's and the Wilensky's is not too good; both are to blame, and that is one of the reasons for his astounding silence.

The good news of more money came in the other day so it looks as though we will be able to put in a full season here, right up to the end of March. Two weeks more for packing and closing the house, and two weeks in Kurdistan, and six weeks of travel brings me home in the middle of June.

Christmas '29 in Tarkhalan

[60]

25 DECEMBER 1929

Christmas is here with us poor sinners in Tarkhalan; Santa Clause has come and gone, and the day is practically over. I wish that it were. It has been a very sad attempt at a holiday. In the first place, so much depends on the women of the party, and with Mrs. Wilensky in bed with bronchitis and with Mrs. Lutz's impenetrable and bovine impassiveness, things have not been too cheery. We postponed the big event (that is, our store-bought tree and the dinner that goes with it) until tonight in the hope that Mrs. Wilensky will be well enough to attend, but she won't. I wish it were all over. I've tried hard to make it go, but I haven't succeeded. We did have fun this morning, though, giving out our various presents laboriously selected from Kirkuk's meager market; to one a bit of Indian brocade, to another a pair of native shoes or a wicked looking Turkoman dagger. Mrs. Lutz being a most economical person, had bought nothing and entered the room with the startling announcement that since they had bought us no presents they could not accept ours. That was soon overruled.

Then came breakfast and a succession of never-departing visitors from the village to wish us *Idcum umbarak* on our holiday. We got rid of them finally, doled out the usual Christmas baksheesh to the household, then piled into the car for a spin over the desert. That was the best part of the day. It is great fun to chase over the desert at top speed with no place to get to and no appointment to keep.

Dinner is due soon, and we are dressing in an attempt to make it a bit more festive. I have champagne for them and, thank God, a bottle of Johnny Walker in my room, but I know it won't help much.

Out of the last six years only once have I spent a Christmas at home, yet the great spirit of this particular day in its connection with those I love seems to have grown stronger rather than diminished. It is a time with us that has always been a time of reunion, accord, and happiness, and particularly within our own intimate group. Here the craving for that which I have foregone is redoubled, and there is no substitute to be found.

The Bronze Tablet and More Frescoes

[61]

27 DECEMBER 1929

Christmas is over, thank the Lord, and yesterday we were on the dig again for the best day we have had this season. I hardly had time to eat yesterday, and this is something that seldom happens to me. First of all, the day started badly. We drifted into breakfast looking in the lamp light of early morning like so many boiled owls. Cheery conversation was not particularly evident and the consumption of water reached a new high level, while the amount of food eaten had never been so low. We staggered out to the field somehow, somewhat revived by the cold morning air, and cursing that on this day we couldn't have had rain and gotten some rest.

The morning was about half over when things began to pop, and they continued so for the rest of the day. Tablets came up faster than I could take care of them, not to mention cylinder seals, animal shaped beads, figurines, duck weights, pottery, and best of all, a little gold sun disc.

Of course on this day we would have a visitor, and we did. A German doctor (naturally) with just enough English to make himself bothersome. I'm afraid he got scant attention from me. Usually we are delighted to have visitors and to see a new face. I detailed Bache to trot him around, but even he had to drop him after five minutes. But we brought him home for tea, and Dr. Lutz was happy to have someone to talk German to.

The room that most of the tablets came from must have been very swell. We had started to clear it before and had found several tablets and perhaps our best find of the year: a bronze tablet. It seems to be in very good shape but unfortunately only a portion of it can be read now. In spots it is badly encrusted with patination and will have to be cleaned carefully before it is all visible. I am much tempted to do it here.

On the walls of this room we found fragments of fresco decoration, broad fields of red and grey separated by vertical strips of red, grey, and black spiral design. Unfortunately, it isn't complete enough to save, but it is sufficiently so to allow a fairly accurate restoration. It is extant only on one wall, the others having been subject to very strong fire, while this was protected by fallen material of mud brick. I think it quite likely that many of the rooms that we find had at one time been so decorated and would be visible to us now had the building been destroyed by any other means other than fire.

I expect the director of Chicago's Khorsabad dig, Dr. Frankfort, and their engineer, Mr. Delougaz who was with us last year, to be our guests for a day or two either today or tomorrow. The reports are that these are the only two members of the expedition who have reached Iraq so far and that others will come along later.

Nuzi Gives Birth

[62]

29 December 1929

Certainly in all the canine world there is no more perverse animal than our dog Nuzi. She drifted in last year, a round wooly ball of a puppy, and with a careless disregard for gender we adopted her. A cuter and more mischievous puppy you couldn't have found in all Iraq. So she was when we took her in, and so she still was when we left last spring.

This fall when we returned Aladj and Goomish were the first to greet us; Aladj big, bushy-tailed, and lazy as ever, and Goomish as sausage-shaped, mongrel, and thoroughly delightful as any dog could be; but no Nuzi. Not a sign of that cute little puppy we had left. In her place was another dog. It simply can't be Nuzi. Our servant swears it is. He should know. His principal job during the summer was to play with the dogs. I don't believe him, but I have outwardly at least to agree with him.

All in all it was a bad trade. We left here a puppy that any one would delight to have, and this cringing yellow bitch is what we find now. Well, there is nothing to do. We accept her but under protest and with the feeling that we have been grievously wronged.

Certainly in all the land you could find no more imbecile a dog. Try to pet her and she rushes away tail between her legs and crying as though you had lashed her with a whip, but if by chance you should dress up on a Friday, she never misses a chance to smear her great muddy paws all over one's only good clothes. Our return to Tarkhalan so upset her mental and moral balance that she is now at this present moment the penitent mother of four puppies. What the final count will be I don't know, but when I last looked the meter showed four.

She, knowing that she is never under any circumstances allowed in the house, set her mind upon it that in my bedroom, nay under my very bed, is the one and only place for the birth of such important new members of our expedition. I have spent half the day hauling her out from under there but nothing would discourage her. Even with my flimsy door bolted, she managed to spring it open at the bottom to squeeze in and dash under the bed.

At great pains I built her a beautiful maternity ward in the courtyard out of petrol tins and matting, but she would have nothing to do with it. Perverse to the end she disregarded it, and finding my room so completely locked, barred, and bolted that access was impossible even to me, she chose the open air of the cabbage patch in which to bring to the light of day her miserable blind little family. Only by my carrying separately and individually each little squealing puppy (at that time only three), could I entice her into her new made-to-order nursery.

Goomish and Aladj remain aloof in masculine indifference, each stoutly denying any connection or even interest in the whole affair, but their attitude isn't convincing. They know more than they care to tell, and personally I suspect Aladj.

Henri Frankfort's Visit

[63]

10 JANUARY 1930

A perfectly villainous day this has been. Friday should be warm and mild and sunshiny instead of like this. The sun had been shining, I grant you that, but as for the rest, no. Cold? I can't begin to tell you how cold it has been today. I haven't even looked at the thermometer because I know from past experience that it will show only fifty or some such foolishness instead of forty below zero. And the wind! It has been blowing a gale all day. So hard that it seems to come right through the flimsy window in front of my writing table as though it were netting and whisk out of the room every particle of warmth that my poor little oil stove can produce. As a result, I gave up all attempts at writing and sat reading such thing as *Liberty* and P.G. Wodehouse until it got colder than I could bear. When that point was reached there was only one thing to do and that was to go outside and warm up.

It is midnight now, and thank God the wind is a bit more reasonable.

One of the hardest things for me to get used to when I came out here was that of going to bed early. Rising early isn't so bad, for any time that I may get up is much too early, but going to bed before midnight and the loss of all those wonderful evening hours is a real privation to me. I am not a night owl. I don't like to stay up until three or four in the morning, but I do like at least a few moments of my own after dinner before tumbling into bed.

Dr. Frankfort, Director of Chicago's two ring circus, along with Delougaz, our former draughtsman and now their general handyman, were our guests here over New year, and I must congratulate Chicago on their new Director; an interesting, intelligent, and scholarly man and a most charming guest. He is a Dutchman, by the way, but by his looks and speech one would call him British at once. He and Delougaz are the only two of the staff here. The rest follow in a month.

Domestic relations at the old homestead are becoming rather strained. We need a vacation from each other. Thank God I go to Baghdad on Monday for five days at the conference of dig directors. Wilensky gets rather tiresome nowadays, and Dr. Lutz has a look as it travels around the table that is more venomous than the bite of a cobra. His vacation comes soon and I expect it will be permanent. The rest of us muddle along as best we can.

My pen has been raising the very devil of late. It got the idea into its head that it should not only be called a pen of the fountain variety but that it should act as a fountain as well. In this country if anything goes wrong there are only two things you can do. One is to throw the offender away and reach into your suitcase for another, and the alternative is to fix it yourself. Naturally I chose the latter. I love to fix things. The result of my operations was that I broke the nib off of the pen, at the same time almost doubling its daily output of ink into the pocket. It was only after the most painstaking and exacting work with file, pincers, and whetstone that it could be brought back to even this scratching shadow of its former self. I wouldn't mind if it scratched consistently, but it has developed a nasty habit of going beautifully for three letters and then letting loose all of a sudden in the most heart and paper rending scratch any pen could devise. I don't like it.

[64]

23 JANUARY 1930

Domestic complications, a conference of Expedition Directors, and finds such as we have never had before have simply swept correspondence out of the realm of possibility. I can't tell you anything about it now. The car has already been waiting too long. This is just sort of a warning to be on the lookout for a more decent letter tomorrow.

While I was at this meeting in Baghdad, I made it an occasion for a general mid-season vacation, and all the members of our party but one came with me to Baghdad to bask in the bright lights of the city. There they met your friend Jacobsen (epigrapher, Oriental Institute, Chicago) and his two associates, and they all agreed that he is about the saddest bird of prey they have ever seen. I haven't met him yet, but he comes here on Sunday (with his two companions) on his way to Khorsabad, so I expect to find out for myself.

The Temple Finds

[65]

25 January 1930

Since the 12th of the month things with me have been going so fast and furious that the opportunity to do those things that I have wanted most to do has been rather slim. First of all, our domestic relations have had somewhat of a jar. The position here with Dr. Lutz for a month past had become more and more difficult, and finally, on the 12th, the climax came which I had so hoped to avoid. He had a big fight with Wilensky, considered himself insulted, packed up, and left, dragging with him his poor, meek little wife. On the whole he behaved most badly. Having behaved in a most insulting manner he finds grounds for finding insult in a retaliation much milder than his own attitude and in all played the part of a rude and spoiled child. I am happy to be rid of him, but it puts me in sort of a hole with those at Harvard.

On the same day we found the finest thing that has ever come from Nuzi: a lion in glazed terra-cotta, 45 centimeters in length and in perfect condition. It shows an artistic feeling that I had never thought possible from this culture. It is a magnificent piece and, judged by those who know it, is the finest thing unearthed in Iraq this year. It is very early for glaze in this country and extremely so for glaze of such fine quality. Of course 1500 B.C. is not so very early for Mesopotamia, but it is early for such intelligent realism. It comes from a time in history when people had evolved from the primitiveness of the early Sumerian tradition but had not yet dropped to the studied conventionalism of the Assyrians. But why speak of these? Our people were neither of these but were Hurrians, under the sovereignty of the King of the Mitanni, and we find here again further proof of the relative freedom from Babylonian tradition in general and of the very strong connection with the Mediterranean cultures.

These and a great wealth of smaller decorative material came from the corner of a small room, and with the rest of the room waiting for me, I had to close the dig and go to Baghdad to attend a conference of expedition Directors. You can imagine how I grudged every minute away for Tarkhalan. Although the conference was only for one day, I had to make five of it, and every minute was filled with the accumulated errand of half a season. Luncheon and dinners were filled with engagements by my over-zealous host and hostess, and the time that I had to myself was nil.

The conference established a basis for willing cooperation between the digs that will put archaeology in the country on a footing such as no other in the East. That alone is a great thing. Of course a multitude of other things were hashed over and decided upon about which I could write pages and a great deal more of which I could tell you but could not write.

Being by far the youngest there, in fact the youngest in charge of any important dig that I know of, I felt very much a youngster. What is more I acknowledged it by pumping the various men of their information at every possible opportunity. At the dinner given us by the High Commissioner, Sir Francis and Lady Humphreys, I was seated between the beautiful Miss Humphreys and Dr. Jordan (in charge of the German dig at Warka), but with Jordan in such a position that I could give my other companion but scant attention. In the same frame of mind I cornered Woolley after dinner and kept him talking until my hostess dragged him from my clutches.

The people with whom I stayed were the Drowers. He is the advisor to the Minister of Justice which makes him to all intents and purposes the Lord Chief Justice of Iraq. She is a most charming author of abominable novels. They were extremely decent, but as I said before I was mighty happy to be back again in Tarkhalan.

While I was away a general holiday was declared, and on my return we started off in great hops for what was ahead of us. The room from which the lion came was re-opened and was practically finished today, several days of rain having come between. All in all it has been the richest room we have ever had. Beside the lion and an important bone goddess figurine it gave us a boar's head in the same green glaze as the lion and showing the same great sculptural sense. Tablets in large quantities also and a wealth of small objects of a decorative nature such as we have never found before.

Today we started into the room adjoining, and such a quantify of fragile decorative beads, plaques, etc. came out that I had to remove the wall tracers altogether. This room I will have to work with my knife crew alone in order to preserve what is there. It will take a little longer, but it will be worth while.

From this room this afternoon came lion no. 2. In painted red clay this time, more elaborate in detail, slightly smaller, and I believe of not quite such fine workmanship. I can't tell yet. He is badly broken, and as yet we have on ⅔ of him, but when the head and shoulders come, as they will, I can tell more.

At last we have our temple. I believe that even with the little we have dug so far there can be no doubt. The thing for which we have been looking for three years has at last come to light. For the last two seasons we have been trying to find a justification for our being here, and now we have it. Had I followed Harvard's advice we would never have found it at all.

The layout of the rooms, the type and wealth of the material, the gold, the profuse decoration, etc., etc., all point to a temple.

It has all been very exciting.

Thorkild Jacobsen's Visit

[66]

31 JANUARY 1930

As to my trip into Kurdistan, I don't know whether it will come about or not. One can never predict the future. Every year I make fantastic plans for journeys to out-of-the-way places on my way home, and usually I am either too anxious to see civilization again or too plain tired to do anything but to catch the next direct steamer to America. I hope I won't have to give up the opportunity, but if I feel as I do now I may. I have never felt so completely exhausted as I have these last two weeks. I've got to turn over a new leaf and lead a more sensible life if the dig will only let me. For the last two months I have averaged six hours of sleep instead of the eight hours I ought to have. I haven't the nerve to weigh myself for fear the scales will tell me the truth. Strangely enough my insides which generally have been more or less of a nuisance to me, have been better this year than ever before. I seem to flourish on mistreatment.

Now about Jacobsen. He and two other members of the Chicago show came last Sunday to stay a day and a night on their way to Khorsabad. Even had I never known Jacobsen before, I think I would have liked him. I liked his manner, and without throwing any bluff he gave the impression of knowing his job. But coming as he did as the one who started you off on cuneiform, of knowing you, and of having been in your vicinity so recently, I looked upon him almost as though he were your personal ambassador. Naturally I asked him about you as soon as I possibly could, and he said so many nice things that he has endeared himself to me for life. He has been unanimously elected a Life Member of the R.F.S.S. Endearment Association, Ltd. First of all he said that he was extremely sorry that he had to give up your class because you were the best pupil he ever had. Naturally. He said, among other things, that you had the best natural aptitude for the language of any beginner he had ever seen. Asking whether you intended to accompany me in future expeditions to Iraq and receiving a positive reply, he said, "I believe that you will have with you a most accomplished Assyriologist." You can imagine the kindly feeling I have toward him. By the way, he is a Dane, not German. I didn't take so kindly to his two companions.

There is a grave threat of rain in the air, and we need it badly to give us an excuse to stay at home and work over the material from the last two weeks. No more lions, that is, no more of the same quality, but better stuff than we have ever had before, this or any other season.

[67]

A perfect avalanche of mail from you has come since I last wrote, and never have I been so lucky. Their dates range all over the calendar, some ante-dating others pre-dating those which came a week earlier. Among them was the one that you wrote on Christmas Eve, another on New Years Day.

Your "A" in Assyrian didn't surprise me in the least. Even if I hadn't seen Jacobsen I would have been sure of such a result. I mustn't act as though it were a great surprise and congratulate you. I knew it would be so.

As to your query of when and what boat I will be coming home on, I cant' tell you a thing. I never know myself until the anchor is up and the boat is under way. The one thing that you can be sure of is that it will be the one which will get me to America in the fastest possible time.

An abominable day on the dig, this. Cold with a high wind that whipped up an almost unbearable dust. We haven't had anything like it since last fall. When I washed up after coming in, the towel brought out from my ears not just dirt like that from the rest of my face but honest-to-God Mesopotamian mud. This, in spite of all you may say, is not the accumulation of a season, but of one day. The only thing that broke the monotonous discomfort of the day was a wolf shot close by and brought for us to see. A huge beast, by far the largest I have ever seen, and with fangs such as would turn the Pepsodent brothers green with envy, so white and large and strong they were. I wouldn't like to meet those in action any time.

Things carry on here in much the same tone as of old. The wonderful finds of our temple have come to an end, and I don't anticipate any more. Its plan is not yet complete, and if we can manage to finish that, it will be a great thing.

Harbingers of Spring

[68]

17 February 1930

Spring is here! The first *hajji laklak* has arrived in the village. He is the stork: *hajji* (pilgrim) because of his predictable migratory return each year and *laklak* for the clacking sound he makes with his bill. I haven't seen him yet, but his arrival has been reported and I heard him this evening clacking his requiem of winter. Soon there will be dozens on their rooftops' nests throughout the village. Winter comes and goes and all the world is changed.

Beads, Beads, Beads

[69]

24 February 1930

Tonight I feel like nothing on earth except the embodiment of a desire to go to bed, put my head under the covers, and forget the cares of the outside world. No great catastrophe has happened, not even an unusually dull day on the dig could bring about this state of mind. Only one thing can do it in this fashion and that is a cold in the head. Spring has come to Tarkhalan, a perfectly innocent and gentle mannered spring to all appearances but harboring under this mask a low and vicious nature. Winter was a clean antagonist. Although it tried all its ways of giving me a cold that it could, it was done in a straightforward masculine fashion, throughout I was able to thwart it fairly successfully. But this low sneaking, double-faced, spring comes along and does me under. I haven't an "ing" in my vocabulary. Thank the Lord you sent me handkerchiefs for Christmas.

For the last ten days we have been held up by rain, and it is a lucky thing that we were. We spent all of that time cleaning beads. Such quantities as came from the temple are almost unbelievable. From one room alone (G 50) there were almost 7000 of the damned things. Considering that only half of those that were once there were in condition to be saved at all you can see what we had. I never want to see another bead as long as I live.

The bad part about the rain was that it held up the Overland Mail, but yesterday it came in with a rush.

Id al-Fitr

[70]

1 March 1930

This has been a funny sort of day. Ordinarily we would be working but being the end of Ramadhan and a great Moslem holiday, we are celebrating by loafing, as is all the rest of the Muhammadan world. Last night a messenger came from Kirkuk saying the new moon had been seen and that the month of fasting was over. With that positive assurance, everyone in the village of Tarkhalan donned his especially prepared holiday clothes and reveled in the luxury of again being able to eat, drink, and smoke during the daylight hours. Little did they know the sin they were committing for about noon another messenger arrived stating that the first one had been misinformed, that the new moon had not been seen, and that *Id al-Fitr* would not be until tomorrow. What a blow that was to all our villagers. They all suddenly became very penitent; gone are the cigarettes they smoked so enthusiastically an hour before and gone is the feeling of holiday spirit that filled the air. I hope that this has not been another false alarm. Anyway, the treat of seeing them in new clothes is a very pleasant one. It is hard often to recognize those who come to the dig in rags and tatters when they blossom forth in such barbaric splendor.

All in all, the local costume is very attractive when well worn, and it is one of the few in which the tall thin man is given an even break. So don't be surprised if I show up in America looking for all the world like a page or two from *The Thousand and One Nights* (expurgated edition).

This moon business is perhaps the most unreliable way of determining the end of a fast that I know of. If the night is cloudy on the expected day and the moon can't be seen, the fast simply isn't over no matter what the calendar may say. Generally, if it is cloudy in one place a telephone or telegraph message from a nearby city will establish it sufficiently well, or maybe a man of not too scrupulous a nature is sent over to the other side of the city in the hope that it isn't raining there and the moon can be seen. He goes out to the prescribed region, picks out the nearest tea house for a game of backgammon, and then rushes back with the news that the moon was clearly visible from where he stood. The side of the city to which he has been sent, on hearing that the other half has seen the moon, presumably from their own quarter, are only too anxious to believe, and since the example is set the fast is ended. They don't question too much. At least this is the way it seems.

But this time there has been some hitch somewhere in the game, and I am anxious to hear just what it is. Of course the Jews are being blamed as having offered the *Khadi* a large sum of money to have the *Id* postponed a day. The *Id* being on Saturday this year when the Jewish shops would have been closed, a colossal amount of business would have been lost to them (I question this).

A Visit by the Nineveh Staff

[71]

3 MARCH 1930

We had the Nineveh dig here last night as our guests: Mr. and Mrs. Campbell-Thompson, Mr. Hutchinson, and a Miss Campbell Shaw. They have just closed down and are on their way to the great outside world. They came bringing bad news: that of their division. They said that the Director of Antiquities had been pretty high handed in taking his share for the government. The division of finds is supposed to be half and half, but the law is so written that the government can take any darned thing it wants, and apparently it did with him. I hope the Director of Antiquities, when he comes here at the end of our season, is in a better mood.

Muhammad brought not only mail yesterday but some delicious looking and nasty tasting cakes from the bazaar. I ate one with the result that I have been in bed all day. Never again. This is the first time I have had any trouble this season, and if I have anything to say about it will be the last.

So you got your Christmas package from Kirkuk! I was hoping that it would be lost. It was such a poor lot. It was all I could find that was truly of the country.

[72]

10 MARCH 1930

It is late and cold and I am dog tired, but a chit at least has to go off to you tonight. When it will be mailed I don't know but written now it will be. It has seemed several eternities since the last grand avalanche of letters from you, and this morning I couldn't stand it any longer. The car wasn't going in, but by a special order a messenger by donkey went and returned bearing for me the *New York Times*, the *Easton Star Democrat*, the *New Yorker*, and that which I sent him for, a letter from you.

Photographic Memories

[73]

12 MARCH 1930

It is late again. I never seem to be able to write to you at a sensible hour in the evening. Going to bed early is a thing that I have long since ceased doing with pleasure. I am enclosing for your personal perusal a photograph of our staff as it is now. Unfortunately I didn't get a photograph of us all before the triumphal departure of the German Legion (Dr. and Mrs. Lutz). Anyway, here is what is left, all lined up for your inspection. Taking them in the usual left-to-right order we have Ehrich, Bache, R.F.S.S., Mrs. Wilensky (bearing not the slightest resemblance to her real appearance), and Wilensky. Perhaps the most important figure in the whole photograph is the modest little creature in the foreground. This, as you should know by now, is Goomish. Beloved Goomish. The favorite of all the expedition pets. He looks very subdued here. Not his usual spritely self at all. In fact, ever since his fight with the *mukhtar's* dog he has been suffering from severe mental depression. I believe his partial defeat in this battle with a dog four times his size has brought to his mind for the first time the distressing realization that youth and life are but transient things.

The big black splotches on my trousers, by the way, are really Goomish's fault. At least, I have to find someone to blame them on. You see, Goomish was being very coy about being photographed, and in my chase around the courtyard after him I encountered difficulties out of all proportion to the size of my objective. These same difficulties manifest themselves as you see.

Also for your delectation is a photograph of our household staff. Again from left to right we have: Muhammad, the shy and ingenious chauffeur, very proud and uncomfortable in a new corduroy suit bought especially for the *Id*; Sulieman, a sentry, silent and a doer of things; Abdullah, the plausible and wily houseboy; Ahmad, the reliable, chief of the sentries; Hidir, the witless likable sentry; Kerim, the industrious kitchen boy; Mustafa, the water boy and even stupider than he looks; and finally, Sammi, the thinnest Indian cook in existence looking in his new suit like a fullback on the Carlisle football team.

Both Sammi and Muhammad took an unfair advantage of the rest. They suspected that a photograph was about to be taken and rushed to their room in a frenzy to make themselves beautiful and quite unrecognizable in their newly bought splendor. Please note the splendid brass watch chain and dangle on the bosom of Abdullah. He, being a devout follower of the Prophet, kept the fast of Ramadhan, as did almost everyone here, and as all the rest, he devoted a good portion of his savings to buying personal adornment to appear in with all the other good Muhammadans to celebrate the end of the fast. The watch chain was an important part of his purchases. In the dangle are two pictures, and I didn't have the heart to tell him what they were. On one side is the Virgin Mary enthroned and on the other is the head of Christ crowned with thorns.

A terrible disappointment today. I came off the field tired and out of sorts. Nothing seemed right any more. Then out of the blue arrived a messenger sent out by our friend, Mullah Ali, bringing mail and, joyous news, a letter seemingly from you. I didn't see that the postmark was Philadelphia, but I tore it open to find to my amazement that it was a wedding invitation of someone you have never seen in your life. After a closer inspection of the envelope, I saw that it wasn't your writing after all but one so much like it that it would fool anyone less of an expert than I. If anyone else plays that trick there is going to be trouble.

It is almost 1 a.m. and I must be up at six.

P.S. *Life* and the *New Yorker* have both arrived. Thanks immensely. The whole expedition, including the goat who prefers *Life*, thanks you.

Winding Down

[74]

16 MARCH 1930

Tonight we pay a call on Hakeem Effendi, the rich man of the village. We have owed him this for five months now and it is time that it be done.

Things are going slowly on the dig nowadays. I have stopped opening up new areas and am spending the all-too-short time left us this season in finishing up that which has been started and is as yet uncompleted. Our railway is being taken up, except which we now need, and is being buried for the summer. Rooms are being cleared, pavements found, followed, and cleaned. Walls that have hitherto failed to materialize are being given one last effort toward solution. The whistle has blown. *Paidost* is over.[19]

Later in the day — the desert blooms. There has been lots of rain this year, and the *chol* or *haweja,* whichever way you want to refer to the desert, is covered with a beautiful but sparse carpet of green. Brave little flowers seek the light of day to bloom for a week before withering.

Closing Down

[75]

21 MARCH 1930

We have all been going rather hard for the last few days in getting things in shape and today in getting Ehrich's things in order for his early departure tomorrow. Being the kind of person he is, his things are in an almost unintelligible mess. It is my fault. I should have checked on his work more closely. He is a nice boy but ineffectual.

As far as I am concerned our dig closed down yesterday on the *tepa,* and tomorrow I start off on the realization of a three years hope, that of prospecting Kudish, a small prehistoric *tepa* near here. I can't do much there, but ten days should give us a fairly good idea of what to expect. The division, when our precious objects are pawed over and snatched from us by the government; then packing, closing the house, and leaving, which way God only knows but certainly for home.

---

19 *Paidost,* a Turkish word I believe, was our 15 minute recess given our men mid morning and mid afternoon. The rest was welcome and it gave the men a chance to perform their required prayers. The devout were not necessarily lazy, but the lazy tended to take so much time off for prayers that eventually they found themselves "no longer needed" on the dig. R.F.S.S., 1983.

My Kurdistan trip is off, at least that part of it which meant the companionship of Captain Littledale, and I doubt very much if I have the energy to do it alone. I want nothing more than to get way from here and sleep. I've been feeling more dead than alive of late, and twelve hours a day in the saddle, fording icy Kurdistan torrents, and floundering through snow drifted passes, doesn't appeal to me as it did earlier in the year.

One-thirty and long past my bed time.

Soundings at Kudish Zagir

[76]

29 MARCH 1930

Ehrich left a week ago, and Mr. and Mrs. Wilensky leave in a few minutes (early). Three more days before our division of spoils with the government, and with only Bache and myself here to defend the expedition from an avaricious Antiquities Department.

The last week I have been running a series of soundings in Kudish Zagir,[20] a prehistoric *tepa* nearby, and the results are very interesting. Nothing spectacular but a very nice series of representative sherds, with a few complete pieces, of painted ware.

I am tired beyond all belief which, coupled with an internal upset, leaves me feeling sorry for myself today. Thank God four days will see us finished, but it staggers me to think that after that will come the packing and shipping of the loot.

Anyway, I should be through here by the 6th (unless I stay on a week in the peace of an empty house to finish off my Kudish material); then to Baghdad for a week; then home. How I will come I never know. I never plan. I never know until I am started, and even then it isn't very certain.

---

20 Kudish the Small. There is also a Kudish the Large in the same general vicinity. R.F.S.S., 1983.

The End of the 1929–1930 Season

[77]

BAGHDAD, IRAQ
18 APRIL 1930

Seventy-seven ages seem to have passed since I have last written. The increasing strain of work culmination in the rush of the division, packing, and all the tens of thousands of trifling jobs connected with closing a dig form a part of my explanation; and the loss of all my writing records (the result of a year's work), the futile attempts to accomplish things quickly in Baghdad, and my natural reaction from the activity of a season to a state bordering on coma constitute the other half of my explanation.

The last two weeks of a dig are always rather trying times, and this season was no exception. Wilensky leaving early made it more difficult in a way, and the arrival of guests from America added two unproductive but pleasant days to our stay in Tarkhalan.

The division of the year's loot was a thing that I had dreaded, but in the end it proceeded most pleasantly and, for Harvard, very successfully. The portion that was allotted to us was much better than I had hoped and certainly should please the people at home. Among the major pieces, we got the lion (hurrah), all of the incomplete animal figurines (except one), the bronze tablet, and the glazed Ishtar. Baghdad took the bone figurine (the most important find of the year to which they are welcome), and the boar's head. In my mind we have much the better half of the collection, and I am extremely pleased.

Packing is one of the least pleasant of all the final chores, and when the 40th and last case was packed, closed, reinforced, and sent off to the station I felt like celebrating. In this country of slipshod habits where anything well done, even down to making the boxes, must be done personally this period is certainly trying.

We had a pleasant distraction in the form of guests. Hoddy Jayne (Horace H.F. Jayne), now Director of the University of Pennsylvania's University Museum, with whom I spent a year on the Harvard China Expedition, and his wife came just after the division along with Freddie Wulsin, also of China days, with a new wife. He is off to take charge of Jayne's new dig at Persepolis. Anyhow it was grand to see them, and we slaughtered the biggest turkey in their honor that had ever been seen in Tarkhalan. Jayne is a peach as is his attractive wife whom I had never met. Freddie Wulsin is in the same category, but I think he didn't do quite so well with his new helping hand. He, by the way, is the man that I almost went to the Belgian Congo with (big game hunting) two years ago.

It is almost too dark to write outdoors. I am sitting on the balcony of my hotel overlooking the Tigris. The lights have just gone on, throwing streaks of gold across the great muddy stream. A dusty grey lizard is frantically using the last minutes of light snatching infinitesimal insects from the wall beside me. The gulls have left the river, and the black erratic flight of bats has taken their place; to the right the whole world passes over the great pontoon bridge and babbles as it goes.

To get back to things: the day finally came when we were ready to leave Tarkhalan. The last box had been sent, the last man paid, the last instruction given to our faithful Fatullah who remains to guard our property and the *tepa* over the summer. The baggage was all in the car, the instruments inside destined for a cool summer in the Consulate storeroom in Baghdad, the lion looking like an accident case in the emergency ward wrapped in hospital absorbent cotton and bandaged from head to tail in surgical gauze nestled in a box of cotton on the rear seat. The crowd of people around the car were those that I had cursed and loved for years now. Each man was a definite personality to me, and each one was sincere in his wishes of Godspeed. It was very pleasant to be leaving, but as the car drew away from this crowd of homely unpretentious people it was even more pleasant to think I would be returning again to them.

Having a more or less decent car I decided to drive down to Baghdad instead of going by train. Bache was along to spell me at the wheel, and small Muhammad was in the back clasping the lion to his bosom. It seems as though we would never get through to Kirkuk. Five last minute errands turned into twenty five, but we did get away finally shortly after ten thirty for the last stage of the journey.

The first third of the 200 miles was over roads unbelievably rough. Roads that had dried and hardened in the fantastic shapes that the traffic of the wet season had put them in. After that, desert — flat, hard, and smooth as a teak deck. Our Ford took wings. Seventy kilometers was the best it would do with its heavy load and a strong wind, but it kept the pace for mile after mile.

We reached Baghdad — why the devil should I bore you with this tedious travelogue? Well, it will be over in a minute. As I started to say, we reached Baghdad that evening, tired, dusty, and thirsty. As we unloaded the car the realization of an almost unbelievable loss struck me. The bag in which I had all of my notes for the year, all of the business records and papers of the season, and *all* of the drawings made during the expedition's *three* years was missing. Lost on the road! It had been tied to the back, and although I had stopped twice to repack, now it was gone. It seemed as though the whole world had dropped from under my feet leaving me dangling helplessly and alone in an eternity that was my loss. The state of depression that it put me in I can never describe.[21]

---

21 The automobile at that time throughout the Near East was beginning to supplant the camel and the donkey as the universal beast of burden. Cars universally were swathed in freight. Cartons, bundles, bags, tins of petrol or water, carpets, and whatever were lashed to the running boards, the back, the top, and even the hood. Ours was such a car. R.F.S.S., 1983.

Of course I notified the police; I saw them all; I waylaid everyone I knew and conscripted their help. I wired to Ali in Kirkuk to scour the country and to get into touch with all drivers. But it was all so hopeless. Two things could have happened. Either it dropped on the road or it was stolen by one of the crowd as we unloaded at the hotel. If it was the first, it might have been picked up on the road by another driver and in that case there was a faint chance that the clothes that I would willingly have sacrificed a hundred times over would be recovered. More likely that it be picked up by wandering Arabs and never seen again. If it was stolen in Baghdad, well the papers were gone. It wasn't a happy culmination of the season.

It was a hopeless task to try and do anything quickly in Baghdad. It just isn't done. But then I haven't been in any great rush because as long as there is any chance of finding my bag I must stay. Business is paralyzed just now. Everything Christian is closed because of Easter; everything Jewish (and Baghdad is about half Jewish, or maybe less) is closed because of Passover. Couple this with a sprinkling of Muhammadan holidays and you can see just what the chances are of doing anything.

It is morning again and the threatening east wind of last night has delivered its inevitable burden. Only the Gobi can rival the sticky copper-colored murkiness of a Baghdad dust storm. It can rival it in intensity but certainly not in frequency. The air is heavy and hot, and I sit in my room by the river clad as only the privacy of my own room would allow. A ragged outline of palm fronds shows the outline of the other side of the river, and the incessant blaring of automobile horns tells me that the outside world is more alive that it appears.

The Jaynes were still in Baghdad when we arrived, and naturally I saw a lot of them. Incidentally, Bache is Jayne's brother-in-law. Jayne's museum is the co-sponsor of the Ur excavation along with the British Museum so he felt he should visit the site even though they had closed it down, but knowing the three day railroad journey there and back he naturally didn't look forward to it. I have done it once, and all the inducements he could offer couldn't persuade me to go along. But Jayne is pretty much awake, and by dint of some pretty clever wire-pulling a special plane was put at his disposal by the Royal Air Force, and by dint of a little subsidiary wire-pulling on my part I joined the party.

We had to make an early start, and by 4 a.m. I was routed out of bed by a remorseless room boy who was quite unconscious of the foul taste of unassimilated Manhattans that bothered me. We were on the field by daylight, signed the necessary papers required of civilians, and climbed into the biggest machine I have ever laid eyes on. It was a carrier. It made the Ford Tri-Motor that you and I took from Boston to New York last year look like a dwarf. The engines roared and we were off.

The party consisted of two pilots, two mechanics, a wireless operator, the famous and jovial Mr. Cooke who engineered the whole thing, Jayne, Bache, and myself. It was a great experience and in truth an archaeological expedition. We covered the 250 miles to Ur by eleven o'clock, spent an hour there, and landed back in Baghdad by three having also hunted out and circled over the mounds and expeditions of Bismya, Kish, Tell Omar, Ctesiphon, Tello, Warka, Nippur, Eridu, Tell el-Obaid, Umma, and chased vainly around over the desert in search of the elusive mound of Farah.

The holy city of Nedjaf that we passed on the long way back was one of the finest sights I have seen in a long time. We were very high because the fanatical Shiah Muslims there feel that their sacred shrine is being violated by infidels and take potshots at planes as they go over. Straight below us was the oval of closely packed houses separated from the waste of desert by a city wall of medieval grandeur, and in the center of the oval was the stately golden dome of the mosque. I shan't soon forget it. Such desolation without and such concentration within and around that great shrine.

I got back to my hotel about four o'clock and found a message that had come in that morning saying to call the police at once. Great God! What could it be? Had they found my bag, or had Muhammad taken out the car and smashed it to bits? I rushed to the phone. "No, Captain Hawthorne has just left. Where are you staying? At the River Front? Well, he will be crossing the Maude Bridge in about five minutes. If you go there you will see him." I did. He came and with him the news that my bag was in his office absolutely intact. A weight such as that of the world left my mind. I wanted to shout the news out to all Iraq. In all the East there couldn't have been a happier person than myself. It had been found on the road outside Baquba and brought into Baghdad by the driver where it was located by the police. Happy day!

It is night again and still my letter is unfinished. I should have known that I couldn't get away from Mr. Cooke's in decent time. I went over to his house for lunch, and by the time we got through looking over his collection of antiquities, it was seven o'clock. After luncheon and tea I couldn't in decency stay for dinner. So I came back to my hotel where I dine with a most amusing Scotsman. He is the most difficult man to understand that ever spoke the English language, not because his accent is Scots, for it isn't, but for a strange habit of speaking with scarcely opening his mouth as though he were afraid of losing a set of oversized false teeth.

My route home has undergone considerable alteration. I had hoped to leave Iraq by an overland route that the Iraq Railway has just initiated: this is, train to Kirkuk, then two days by car via Mosul to the railhead on the Turkish border, then by train to Aleppo, Stamboul, and Europe. But the great difficulty has been that I am determined that the lion and the boar's head (which the Iraq Museum is lending us for repair and exhibition) shall go home with me under my personal supervision and in my own baggage, and the difficulty that I foresaw in taking extremely valuable antiquities into and particularly out of such sticky countries as Turkey and Italy, not to mention the 101 other places en route, made me give it up. By this route Paris is now only seven days away and New York about seven days more.

That being given up, I decided on chasing down to Part Said and catching a Prince Line boat sailing for Boston and New York. That would have been a fine idea if it hadn't been for this perfect pest of holidays that have closed the banks, government offices, and consulates so effectively that I was left only one free day to do three days' arrangements. That I had to give up. The result is that I have wired to that pest hole Beirut for accommodations on a boat sailing for America on the 30th. That will mean about 10 days lost. It would have been much more sensible, probably, to chase off to Part Said and take a chance on picking up a boat there, but it is done now. Only crossing one frontier (into Syria) will make it much easier with this cargo of mine. I've got it boxed up like a set of mummies with big government lead seals all over it and another set to come from the French consulate. It should look pretty formidable by the time it reaches home. All in all it is a darned nuisance and means considerable added expense and delay.

I don't know much about the boat I am taking. It sails on the 30th and goes to some American port, either Boston, Providence, New York, or Kansas City. It's name I don't know, but the line is the Byron Line which means that it is either British or Greek. Since its only scheduled stop is Piraeus, I very much fear that it is Greek. Anyway, if the price charged for passage is any criterion, it should be fairly good (alas that is no criterion at all in these parts), and they say it is fairly fast. I must find out more about it tomorrow.

[78]

S.S. Byron, San Miguel,
Marconi Radio
18 May 1930

Steamer Byron Brooklyn, nineteenth,
love.[22]

Richard F.S. Starr married Dorothy Clara Simpson on his return to the United States in the spring of 1930. In the autumn of that same year she joined him for the last season at Yorgan Tepa. For reasons not stated, none of his letters to his mother were preserved from that final season, but Dorothy later wrote a memoir of those months in the field. She had made some attempt during her lifetime to publish her story, but without success. Immediately below, we have followed with the publication of her charming account that fills in the details of that last season and provides yet another perspective on Tarkhalan, Nuzi, and Iraq of that time.

D.I. Owen

---

22 [The manuscript ends abruptly here.]

North of Baghdad

A Memoir of the Final Season at Nuzi

DOROTHY CLARA SIMPSON STARR

Studies on the Civilization and Culture of Nuzi and the Hurrians - 8

Preface

Dorothy Clara Simpson Starr was born in Chicago in 1906, the fourth child of Dr. Elmer and Clara Simpson. She was raised and educated there and received a bachelors degree in philosophy from the University of Chicago in 1927. In the spring of 1928, she and Richard (Dick) Starr met at a wedding in Chicago and after their relationship became serious, she began the study of Assyriology at the University of Chicago in 1928–29 with Thorkild Jacobsen, who had just arrived from Denmark to work on his Ph.D. Although her Assyriological studies lasted for one year only, she made a very strong impression on Jacobsen who later recalled her excellent language abilities to Starr in Nuzi where the two met the following year.[1] After they were married in the spring of 1930, she joined him for the final season at Yorgan Tepe, the experience which is recalled in her memoir, *North of Baghdad*, printed below. She had tried, without success, to publish this memoir during her lifetime. That it appears here posthumously, together with her husband's letters and in his memorial volume, is of special significance.

Dorothy and Dick Starr had many common interests and their long and happy, fifty-two years of marriage lasted until her death in 1982. He survived her by another dozen years. Her two hundred eleven page manuscript, comprising eighteen chapters, is a fascinating account of life in the village of Tarkhalan, the site of the Expedition compound at Yorgan Tepa, at a time from which there exist few such personal descriptions. She, like her husband, viewed the Near East, its people and customs, from the perspective of her time. Her observations of life on the dig are often more complete and detailed than that of her husband and serve as a valuable supplement to his letters and to our understanding of the dynamics of expedition life in those formative years.

I am indebted to Nicholas Starr for sharing his mother's memoirs with a wider and very receptive audience. I have edited her text very lightly and endeavored to retain the spirit and charm of the original, including some of the idiosyncratic spellings (Muhammed for Muhammad), terminology no longer used (Muhammedan for Moslem), and vocabulary which seems out-of-date today (jollification, etc.). The excavations at Nuzi retain a unique position in Mesopotamian archaeology. Starr's excavation report, the numerous tablet

---

1 See above, "Letters from the Field, 1927-1930," no. 66, 31 January 1930, p. 112.

publications, and now the letters and memoirs of both Starrs, combine to make this site exceptional indeed.[2]

D.I. Owen

2 Bracketed passages and chapter headings have been added to the original manuscript by the editor.

Foreword

Iraq, the country, is no longer unknown to readers of the press and this volume. Even if that modern name does not strike an immediate chord in your memory, it will probably conjure up some vision when you are reminded that Iraq was once Mesopotamia. Lawrence, Yeats-Brown, and others have painted unforgettable pictures of that storm center during the [First World] War. Basrah, Baghdad, and even Kirkuk have taken on the familiar ring of real rather than imaginary cities.

There are two fairly convenient ways of getting to Iraq from the west. The railroad company now offers motor transportation from Nisibin, which is at the end of the railway in Turkey, to Kirkuk, where the metal track begins in this north of Iraq. You may arrange passage from London, Berlin, or from Paris, direct. The other route carries you across the Mediterranean to the seaport of Syria, and thence over the Lebanons by motor car to Damascus. From Damascus another motor car will, in approximately twenty-four hours, take you across the five hundred miles of clay desert to the Tigris and Baghdad.

There are, of course, more daring, more picturesque, more circuitous ways of arriving in Iraq. If you have the money and the nerve, you may reach Baghdad by air, even if you are starting from London. Few have made this passage from England entirely by air. More fly from Cairo. That is easier on the pocketbook. But if you are accustomed to carry more than a toothbrush by the way of luggage, even that is costly; they have a disconcerting habit of weighing the passenger and his baggage together, and the amount of travelling gear allowed to go untaxed depends directly upon the avoirdupois of the traveller. People have been known to diet for months in preparation. What you do when you finally get to Iraq depends largely on why you came.

We were there for a definite purpose: to uncover and investigate thoroughly and scientifically the remains of the buried city of Nuzi (1500 B.C.). Some people, who have no such purpose, avail themselves of the speediest means of getting home again after having inhaled the individual, unmistakable, and inimitable odors of Baghdad. There was a group of tourists who, under the guiding wing of Cook's [Tours] flew from Cairo to Baghdad, spent a few hours in the City of the Caliphs having tea while floating down that stretch of the Tigris between the Maude Bridge and the American Consulate, then flew back to Cairo in the evening. If they are content with so a fleeting a glimpse of the legendary haunts of Harun-al-Rashid, and others, I hope, for their own peace of mind, they indulged in less than three cups of tea. There is a legend which says that he who drinks three times the waters of the Tigris (now filtered, chlorinated, and perfectly safe), must ever return there again. I think there may be some truth in it. Baghdad is still Baghdad, its smells, its filth, its drab aspects notwithstanding. The golden domes of Khadimein retain their brilliance, and the modern city has that fascination which comes from a commingling of the old and the new. Some aspects of the bazaars are as old as the city itself. The conglomerate throng that passes over the great pontoon bridge at night raises its voice in song. Bargeloads of brightly colored pottery float downstream between palm-fringed banks at midday. The most ridiculous-looking little round boats called *gufas* are almost always to be seen, moving leisurely back and forth across the turgid waters. Baghdad has its own special way of charming the eye even while it is offending the nose.

But if your spirit would come close to the soil; if you would stretch your arms skyward and know the whole great expanse of the bowl of heaven; if you would enjoy the desert in its kindlier moods: go north. Take the maddening little train that in twelve hours will accomplish the two hundred miles from Baghdad to Kirkuk. But you must leave even this provincial city behind, and motor over ten brown-rutted miles to Tarkhalan. On the outskirts of this tiny village our Expedition house stands, and it is to this mud mansion I would take you in the following pages. It's only an armchair journey, so it can't be very fatiguing; I have done my best to prevent its being a bore; and if you are in the mood, you may find it pleasant to know "our country" and meet "our people." They are peasants and their raiment ragged, but they are the most likable lot imaginable.

Dorothy C.S. Starr

CHAPTER I

The Road to Tarkhalan

The train puffed its asthmatic way into the station at Kirkuk. It was eight o'clock of an early November evening, and quite dark. Dick opened the door, looking for Muhammed, the Expedition chauffeur. He would surely be there to meet us. I was of no use; I wouldn't know that particular Muhammed from any of the tens of thousands of other Muhammeds in Iraq, since I had never seen him, and at first, all the natives looked very much alike to me. I was the *Sahib*'s new *khatoun* [bride], coming to the field for the first time. Dick had prepared me for the warm reception I was to get from the natives. During the previous three years of excavating for the Harvard-Baghdad School Expedition, the native workmen had all wondered at his wifeless state. How was it, they puzzled, that a man grown to maturity and with surely enough money to buy himself a wife, should remain single? Such a situation was wholly incomprehensible. The year before, one of the older men had approached Dick on the subject. Being told that it was very expensive in America to buy a wife, he had offered his entire fortune of thirty sheep to fill the financial gap.[3] Were they not brothers, he and the *Sahib*? The *Sahib* had to refuse the sheep, writing to me back in America that he was afraid that they might clutter up my father's apartment. But now he had a wife, and she was with him, standing there in the doorway of the compartment, watching the milling crowd of porters and servants on the station platform.

Although this honeymoon introduction to the field — as archaeologists call those distant places where our work takes us in search of greater knowledge about man's remote past — was my first taste of the East, and each of those first impressions stands out in my memory as though carved in relief, I find it difficult to describe the effect of that motley crowd. From the time we had stepped off the ship at Beirut, I had felt like Alice in Wonderland, not quite sure of what I might see next. Syria has a faint European gloss; but this is laid on, and loses itself somewhere in the desert. In Baghdad, notwithstanding its urbanity, and strikingly so here this night in Kirkuk, I felt that I had come to a place where one need not be surprised at anything. Any costume, from rags and tags to velvet gowns, was acceptable, and no detail of dress too incongruous or startling to seem out of place. Certain items like a cheap, very American-looking girl's coat, trimmed with artificial fur and thrown across the shoulders of a burly porter whose Mongol cheekbones and aquiline nose betrayed a mixture of blood, did seem odd. Nevertheless, it wasn't one costume or one face that made so striking a contrast to everything prescribed and typical that I had known in

3 [See above, "Letters from the Field, 1927-1930," no. 27, 20 February, 1929, p. 61.]

American, English or European cities where I had lived until now. It was the mixture, the conglomerate whole. Yet, I know that it was a crowd as would appear quite ordinary to one who had come into many railroad stations "East of the Suez." It seemed to me so when I boarded the train at the end of the season. Not, however, on this night.

Suddenly, a diminutive figure, hardly taller then my own five feet and two inches, popped up out of somewhere; a figure that was dressed in the same kind of khaki drill that Dick wore. A very round, smiling face, surmounted by an unbelievably tall fez, appeared in the doorway of our compartment. It was Muhammed. Greetings were exchanged, hands shaken. It was a gala occasion for us all. Muhammed was so excited and pleased that he could hardly contain himself; Dick knew the exhilaration of returning to this place; while I was experiencing the thrill of a new and strange adventure.

That night Muhammed wasn't just a servant; he was a friend and committee of welcome. Beaming shyly, he produced a somewhat bedraggled bunch of zinnias, and then, to cover his embarrassment, busied himself getting our luggage out. Following him and the luggage, we ploughed through the jostle and noise of the station platform to the waiting Expedition Ford. While Muhammed was piling our duffle into the back, I was able to take in some of the magnificence of this vehicle, with its native-built, station-wagon body.[4] It loomed through the darkness as an ubiquitous reminder of our Western machine age, distinctly out of place in its present setting. Dick elected to drive. We go into the front, Muhammed in back, and soon were off for "home."

The dim lights of the station were soon left behind. Darkness, broken only by the two shafts of our headlights, enveloped us. We bumped our way over an incredibly rough road, over humpy little bridges, through a village where dogs barked harshly but no human resident seemed to attend our passing. There were no lights other than ours. I was aware of the village itself only because there the road narrowed and was hemmed in on either side by vague, low structures silhouetted against a starlit sky. What the buildings were, and how they were constructed, had to be left for daylight to disclose.

After passing the huddle of houses, the road took us again for miles through open places; then through another village with more dogs. We were nearly home, Dick told me excitedly. How odd the word sounded. He explained that the last village was Topazoa, next door to our own Tarkhalan. This explanation was hardly given before we came suddenly upon more walls — the walls of Tarkhalan. There more life was evident. A cluster of children were gathered on a mound — which, I learned afterwards, was the village dung pile. They were clapping their hands and halloing. Evidently they had been expecting us; it was an obvious greeting.

---

4 [See above, "Letters from the Field, 1927-1930," no. 49, 24 October 1929, p. 92.]

A sharp turn to the left, just outside of the village, another sharp turn to the right, and we pulled up at the door. It was a massive wooden door set in a tall mud wall. Inside, a lantern burned dimly. Strange-looking figures hurried to help us out of the car. These were our sentries, I learned. There were *salaams*, and greetings which I could not understand. In the courtyard, the friendly glow of lights from the windows modified the strangeness. Other members of the Expedition, who had arrived before us, poured out the central door. There were the architect, Mr. Wilensky, and his wife, and Charles Bache, who was Dick's assistant. These three had come up from Baghdad a few days before, opened the house, and were on the threshold to welcome us. There were other greetings, too. Dogs, large and small, crowded around us. One little fellow was jumping all over Dick in a laughable mixture of excitement and self-consciousness. It was, it could only be, Goomish, of whom I had heard so much; Goomish, the most intelligent, clever, handsome, superlative of canines. The big, clumsy fellow who bumped and butted his pleasure was Alaj, and the foolish ingratiating one, Nuzi. Nuzi and Alaj had to stay outside, but Goomish, whose manners were above reproach, preceded us into the house, making himself master of ceremonies.

Inside, my first impressions were strong and clear. There was something pleasant about the room we entered. It was the central gathering place, and also the dining room. There was an individuality about it for which its gray cement floor, whitewashed walls, and roughly beamed ceiling could not account. Its charm didn't lie wholly in the fact that it was quaint according to Western standards, nor yet that it was more comfortable than I had allowed myself to hope. Rather it was because here was a room in the heart of a strange land, a room which had been taken over by strangers, had housed and comforted those strangers. It had the aspect of a refuge.

On one wall hung a rough board shelf half full of books, on another was a little box for outgoing mail. There were two kerosene lamps on the long table in the center of the room. I could imagine this room on rainy days in winter when the whole outside world had turned into a sea of mud, and the Expedition had gathered to read, write letters home, or play games. Our discussions, arguments, and laughter of friendly intercourse would take place here; breakfast, luncheon, tea, and dinner would be served here — the table was already set for the evening's meal. Knives, forks, plates, and glasses: implements of living, symbols. It was a room to be lived in, and livable.

Three bedrooms opened off the central dining room: one occupied by the Wilenskys, one reserved for Dr. Meek who had not yet arrived, and the one off to the right that was to be ours. Dick pushed open the rough wooden door, and ushered me in. It was a long, narrow room with whitewashed walls, cement floor, and ceiling of small logs placed side-by-side to hold up the room — a sumptuous chamber in an adobe mansion. A lamp burned on the table, two little cot-beds offered inviting rest after the journey. Dick shouted for Abdulla, and said unintelligible things to him, whereupon pitchers full of hot and cold water were brought. There was a cake of good American soap beside the bowl.

I was glad to see it, because I needed a wash after the train trip. Iraq dust cakes as only clay dust can.

Dinner was a gay affair with chicken. The others, old campaigners all, found amusement in my appreciation of the fowl. They assured me that every meal would be similarly gay. With coffee came the guests, who had been waiting outside in the courtyard. All were men, although the women of the village were probably even more curious to see the new *memsahib*. By that time the people of Tarkhalan were quite familiar with the casual custom we foreigners had of receiving guests, and going calling, in mixed company. But for them to follow suit, for one of their women even to walk in the street beside her husband, would be unthinkable. So these callers were all males, mostly friends and workmen who had known service on the dig in other years. They crowded into the room, their dark faces glowing. Everyone was happy, and there were so many of them. We entertained with coffee and long native cigarettes, and they with strange conversation and appearance.

From a study of proper Arabic, I have since learned that the language they spoke was composed of a slender Arabic core with Kurdish and Turkish words laid lavishly on; but that night it seemed to me that they must be speaking a language as pure as that of the Koran. Mrs. Wilensky translated the gist of the talk for me. This was her third year in the field, and she understood what was being said. First, with true Eastern courtesy, they addressed to Dick and to me extravagant and stereotype compliments of welcome and greeting. The fact that we were both young and robust didn't keep them from inquiring seriously into the state of our health, and giving praise to Allah that it was good. However, after the amenities were satisfied they lost no time in bringing up the subject which most concerned them. When might the work on the dig start? Would there be work for many men this year? And then the most important question of all: will I have my old job again? Dick answered, "Yes, there will be work for many; but *ugga bachir* (day after tomorrow) I want you Aziz, you Jasim, and you, and you to come to the *tepa*."[5] These were the select, experienced men, each of whom had proven his ability in his own specialized task on the complicated business of excavating. Each had a crew of two or three men to assist him; these few, along with their more lowly helpers, would report to the dig on the day after tomorrow, as they had been ordered. Dick's words may not have been couched in very grammatical Arabic, but they brought an eager response from the chosen ones who knew that they had been hired. Their smiles and nods were in such contrast to the blank or even sorrowful expression of the others that Dick was moved to console these disappointed ones by repeating that later there would be work for many. Archaeological excavation must always be tentative and exploratory, and the force must be worked up slowly, new men hired only

5 [The Starrs both use the form *tepa* throughout their manuscripts which I have left as written.]

as they are needed. So the majority, who would eventually have work, must now wrap themselves in a cloak of patience and wait to be called. This having been decided, and a few polite parting generalities having been exchanged, the callers rose, salaamed, and went away.

I remember only two of those first guests distinctly and by name: Aziz and Jasim. The others seemed to form a background for these two. Aziz, a solid villager in the prime of middle life, was somewhat grizzled in appearance, with a kindly face. He wore his head-cloth turban fashion, and his gnarled hands protruded from a coarse brown cloak. On his feet were leather slippers with pointed, turned-up toes, and in his belt was the inevitable *hunjar*, or curved dagger.

Jasim, in contrast, was the picturesque desert Arab. He wore a white robe under a dark cloak. His head-cloth was not wound, but worn shawl-like with a black rope halo keeping it in place, and thin black plaits of hair resting on each shoulder. Jasim was tall, handsome, ascetic, with a lean, Christ-like face, black pointed beard and inscrutable eyes. I couldn't understand his conversation, but his attitude I could. He was deferential but not obsequious. He had a good opinion of himself, but not an exaggerated one.

I suppose that the picture one cherishes as typical of any race or people is never really accurate. Good qualities as well as bad are seldom universal with any clan, and your typical specimen is apt to be that unusual individual in whom most of the likable qualities of his kind are combined: therefore, he is perhaps not truly typical at all. So with Jasim. The memory of his gentle Eastern graciousness, the picture of his splendid noble features, his erect carriage, and the graceful folds of his *aba* flowing from his shoulders will remain for me the epitome of what one likes to think of as typical of the desert Arab. His philosophy, too, I remember as symbolic: born of Eastern thought in which the smallest detail is left to Allah to decide; born of life in the desert, washed by the sun and wind and rain; intelligible if not aggressively intelligent, comforting if not decisive, and very satisfying to the human spirit.

The light of day revealed mysteries made inexplicable by darkness. Our compound, the core of which had originally been a native house, had greatly been added to when it was taken over by the Expedition, until it was now large, comfortable, and adequate according to the standards of life in the field. There were the living rooms, work rooms, courtyards, and high walls. The whole exterior of the structure, innocent of whitewash, remained the dusty, light brown of the earth from which it was built. Within our courtyards, the walls excluded the general landscape, but from the flat roof, accessible by a flight of mud-brick stairs, the whole of our little world was visible: the flat roofs of Tarkhalan near at hand; the walls of Topazoa farther on, and then the undulating brown fields stretching forever away until they faded into the distance and the mountains beyond arrested the eye. Vague, almost indistinguishable shapes, which seemed from the perspective to be nestling at the very foot of the mountains, we knew to be the buildings of Kirkuk, only ten miles away. In the other direction the open desert was broken only by the long, low outline of the mound that marks the sight of ancient Nuzi. Except for the wonderfully blue sky overhead, everything had an opaque, dusty texture like tempera in contrast to the luminous quality of true water color. The overtones and undertones were all brown, the clay earth-brown of Mesopotamia, and our house, like all the village houses, being of the same color and substance, harmonized with and melted into its surroundings.

Time, however, was too precious on that first day to be squandered in contemplation on the roof. I had to meet Sammy the cook, and try to distinguish the other servants as individuals. Sammy was an Indian, black, tiny, shy. He wore European clothes of sorts, and a strip of gunny-sacking wound about his head in lieu of turban or fez. His brand of English was not exactly my own; but that he spoke any at all was very comforting. He greeted me shyly, with downcast eyes, and I felt that he was relieved when I left the kitchen. Kerim, the kitchen helper, was a nice village boy, perhaps eighteen years old. He seemed industrious, quiet — and a trifle cockeyed.

The rather cruelly handsome Abdulla was house-boy. Large brown eyes set not too close to a good straight nose, and fringed with enormously long black lashes, curved lips and smooth bronze skin made him good to look at; but his face was devoid of sympathy. Even his wide, flashing smile lacked warmth. Having been trained to his job from the Expedition's first season, however, he was a perfect servant, as well as being ornamental. He took great pride in his clothes, which were always neat and well cared for. In general cut and character, the garments of all our servants were much the same, being the accepted costume of the villagers in that region. Outside they wear long, coat-like tunics, opening down the front, and having knee-high slits on either side. Around the waist is a wide, intricately wound belt, usually of some printed cotton stuff, which holds the inevitable curved dagger. I once asked Abdulla how he accomplished this complicated and decorative sash arrangement; whereupon he undid his belt and it unwound into at least three or four yards of straight cloth, about half a yard in width. Then he showed me how the trick was turned, by twisting and looping, and passing the long end through the loops; but it took fifteen minutes of careful coaching for me to tie a similar girdle in miniature around a doll I was dressing to send home to one of my nieces.

Beneath the belted tunic, voluminous white cotton pants hang in bulky folds between the legs, but are caught in tightly at the ankles. A white cotton shirt with full sleeves and tight wristbands completes the visible undercostume. Sometimes the shirtsleeves, Turkoman fashion, have pointed elongations which fall to the ground. These inconvenient appendages must originally have been intended to signify a gentleman of leisure; but for practical modern purposes, they are wound about the wrist, forming a rather clumsy cuff. On the head, a square of silk or cotton cloth is rolled turban-fashion, with a second square sometimes worn underneath, hanging shawl-like to the shoulders. If only one cloth is worn, it is wound around a kind of skull-cap. Abdulla's cap was embroidered in black and yellow. His turban of gray and black silk harmonized admirably with his smooth brown complexion.

Muhammed and Sammy were the only exceptions to the general fashion. They wore European clothes, Muhammed affecting a fez as the mark of urbanity.[6]

Ahmet, Sulieman, and Hiddir were the three sentries. They took turns guarding the compound at night. One of the three would always be on duty on the roof, shrouded in a heavy cloak, and proudly armed with a rifle. It mattered little that, as the hour grew late, the man on duty usually slept almost as soundly at his post as the other two in their bunks in the sentry-room by the gate. It was the gesture that counted. In any case, there was no great danger. We felt nothing but friendliness around us; even if our neighbors had not been kindly people, they would have gone a long way to protect and preserve us for we were valuable to them. We meant employment; not just ordinary employment either, but the kind that resulted in tangible silver rupees to an amount undreamed of before we came. Dogs of Infidels that we were, we might have run some risk had we ventured to penetrate into some of the wilder parts of the Near East; but from the friendly, peaceable, agricultural population in that part of Iraq, we were in no danger. It is true that our compound was somewhat isolated, removed as it was some hundred yards from the village, and on the very edge of the desert. But the wolves that run in the desert, and sometimes howled at the moon, would hardly dare to invade a human habitation. Besides, our nine-foot walls were stout and solid. Once or twice during the season wolves did come within shooting distance. On these occasions the luckless creatures made noise enough to waken the sentry, and it was fortunate for them that Ahmet, Suleiman, and Hiddir held no medals for marksmanship.

Ahmet was the aristocrat of all our servants. He came from a very good family, his blind, old octogenarian of a father still being called by the honorary title of Mayor. Besides all this, Ahmet was one of those unusual persons who would have stood out from the crowd in any country. His intelligence and character made his sensitive face rather handsome in spite of its pock marks. He had long, tapering hands and a proud, exaggeratedly erect carriage which was accentuated because he had somehow acquired a frock coat of European cut which he invariably wore over his native costume. His Arabic was much purer than most in that region, and he had the ability to explain things lucidly. If a word gleaned from the vocabulary in the back of my copy of Van Ess' *Spoken Arabic of Mesopotamia* failed to make an impression on any of the other servants, Ahmet would usually recognize it and be able to translate it into the local dialect.

---

6 [For a photograph of the staff, see "Letters from the Field, 1927-1930," no. 73, 12 March 1930, p. 117.]

It was whispered that Sulieman beat his wife more often and more severely than was usual, even in this community where wife-beating was one way for a man to gain prestige. However unfortunate his private life may have been, he was valuable to us. He was clever with tools and carpentry, and if there was any small job of work to be done which required this ability, Sulieman was the man for it. Hiddir, the foolish, was happy and amiable, one of the most likable of the lot. Part of Hiddir's job was to purchase chickens, milk, and eggs for us from nearby villagers. He always seemed to have both hands full of frantic, squawking birds, and at the same time to be trying to retie his turban, which, unlike Abdulla's smart headgear, was forever falling down.

Zen Abdin Mustafa presented a Mongoloid appearance, with long drooping mustaches and high cheek-bones. In black tunic-coat and black turban, it was he who cared for the donkey, and with this good strong beast fetched water from the *cheriz*, a mile distant. He also took the noontime lunches out to the *Sahib*s on the dig, and filled the kerosene lamps for the house. His voice was deep and startling because he seldom used it for more than a monosyllabic yea or nay, or a brief curse at our stout gray donkey's stubbornness. Awad Atiya, a half-wit Arab boy, was also attached to our menage. He worked lazily on the dig all day, but in the evening he tended the privy. The natives called him *Hamfeesh*, which means wild-man-without-much-sense. Indescribably ragged clothes, an open mouth, and a vacant stare did not add to his beauty.

Almost before I had completed my introductory tour of the kitchen, sentry-room, and courtyards, Muhammed had the Expedition Ford chugging at the gate. We were going out to the dig for a picnic lunch and a look around — through Tarkhalan, where children ran after us and shouted and held out their hands for *baksheesh*, where dogs barked us on our way, idle men moved out of the path, and an old blind woman sat in the sunny street close to the wall of a house, clinking wonderingly. We travelled past newly turned fields, over a humpy bridge or two, and through an irrigation ditch where no one had bothered to make a bridge. Automobiles are rare in that part of the world outside of the large cities, and highways unheard of. Our car was the only vehicle of its kind in the vicinity of Tarkhalan, and the roads it travelled were casual, nothing more than donkey trails. After bumping along for several kilometers, we came to the *tepa*, chugged up its steep sides, and jerked to a stop at the very brink of an excavated wall.

The mound was huge and very impressive. The maze of already excavated rooms gave it the appearance of a tremendous honeycomb of mud-brick walls. These ruined walls vary in height with the outline of the *tepa*. One, two, and sometimes as much as five feet of their original structure has remained intact, buried through the centuries in debris of their own making; for it was the upper portion of these same stumps of walls, and the caved-in roofs, that molded the city into a desolate mound at the time of its final destruction. Then nature went on from where Nuzi's human conquerors left off, and the process of disintegration has continued.

As I stood on the *tepa* that afternoon, before the season's work had started and the everyday details of scientific excavation had become of prime importance, my mind was filled with the romance of Archaeology. The work never lost this fascination for me. Later in the year, when material finds were rare, we used to somewhat ruefully console ourselves by saying that, after all, we weren't treasure hunters. It would be ridiculous to minimize the incomparable thrill that comes with finding a beautiful, or important, or even merely intrinsically valuable object; but in the final analysis, it is what we can discover about the *people* of these ancient cities that remains most fascinating and valuable: how they lived, carried on business, and worshipped their gods; what they ate and drank, what they did and said and even what they thought. All this and more is sometimes betrayed in the written records they left behind; in the hasty remains of a meal or the contents of a half-filled granary, in the shape of their pottery, or the incidental arrangement of their rooms. Even when an object of rare beauty is found, its real value lies deeper than the fact that it may be fashioned of gold or silver and encrusted with jewels; for behind all this are the hands that fashioned it, the human progress that developed its technique — and, above all, the human mind. This is what I mean when I say that even the mute, bare walls of an ancient city are intriguing and worthy of adequate description.

Probably everyone who has lived in a modern city has stopped on the street to watch men working on the foundations for a new building; everyone has seen the bleak ruins of similar foundations after the building that had towered over them has been razed. That is what the dig was like, with the brick and mortar of modern construction translated into mud brick, and floors of hard-packed clay.

These ancient walls made a convenient path and if one didn't mind jumping an occasional gap, it was easy to reach any part of the mound. Atop them, I explored a great section of closely huddled rooms that once housed the citizenry of Nuzi. One might think that with the whole plain to build upon, and building material no more costly or rare than the clay of the plain, even the poor could have had spacious quarters. The contrary, however, was true. Even the rich and powerful had to dwell in narrow rooms because of the roofing problem — which in the villages even today had been no more adequately solved than it was four thousand years ago. There was also the problem of protection. The rich and poor of Nuzi were cramped alike within the confines of the great city wall. The need for vigilance was greater in those days than it is now. On first inspection, the most striking differences between the buildings that housed the aristocrats and holy men of Nuzi, and the homes of the masses, lay in the size of the open courtyards, and in the fact that only in important places did baked brick ever supplement the universal sun-dried brick.

The superior quality of this baked brick was surprising. That it was evidence of grandeur is proven by the fact that it was used sparingly, even in important places: in the courtyard of the palace, forming a walk in the temple courtyard, and for the construction of the remarkable Nuzi drainage system.

Some of the wells had baked-brick facings, but the place where it was most extravagantly displayed was in the palace courtyard. This great square court was completely paved in baked brick, and had a low wall facing of the same; but the rest of the construction even here is done in sun-dried brick — the same material used in the native villages today, and of which our Expedition house and compound were built.

In the courtyard of the temple I picked up a tiny carnelian bead, probably washed up by an early rain. It was my first *antiqua*, much to be prized, although by no means rare. The year before they found more than seven thousand beads of different kinds in that courtyard — temple loot.[7]

Later in the day we motored back over the donkey road, over the humpy little bridges, through the village, to the house for *chay*. Tea is the universally gracious ceremony. Sammy had made a fruit cake, and there were sandwiches. It was pleasant to gather around the table, Mr. and Mrs. Wilensky, Charles Bache, and ourselves. The only one missing was the epigraphist, Dr. Meek, who had not yet arrived. He was the Annual Professor loaned to our Expedition by the American Schools of Oriental Research, and is connected with the University of Toronto. He was the cryptic member of our group. None of us had ever seen him, and our curiosity would have to wait. We made all sorts of conjectures about him, and so with laughter, talk, and guesses, we munched Sammy's good sandwiches as though we had not lunched off chicken a few hours earlier.

A walk on the roof as evening fell, and my first day in the field came to an end, brought home to me how free and peaceful this place was to be. The open fields about us and the desert stretching forever away at our backs, the village just at hand and the calm serenity of the mountains in the far distance made us walk close to each other in a mute but profound sense of happiness and well-being. Ahmet joined us presently, speaking shyly at first, and then, as he saw our interest quickened, to tell us such tales as might have formed the basis for an epic of native folklore. I wish that I had then understood Ahmet's words, and taken time to put his stories onto paper; but such formality might have made him self-conscious and spoiled it all. As it was, walking on the roof together in the deepening dusk, even such brief translations as Dick could manage, while Ahmet paused understandingly, were exciting enough. He told of life in the desert in the days his grandfather remembered, and his simple delight at having an appreciative audience might have kept him going for hours if the night had not brought with it a chill that sent us regretfully indoors. We found a fire burning in the little sheet-iron stove in our room, and time for a wash and rest before Abdulla knocked at our door to announce supper. We ate again: chicken.

---

7 [See "Letters from the Field, 1927–1930," no. 69, 24 February 1930, p. 114.]

CHAPTER II

Kirkuk Impressions

Work started on the dig as soon as possible after our arrival. The force had increased in a few days to a hundred and fifteen men, and later even more would be employed. The salaries ranged from one rupee to a rupee and twelve annas for grown men, and from ten to twelve annas for boys. A rupee is worth about thirty-seven cents, and each rupee may be divided into sixteen annas. If I had a mathematical mind I could figure up the amount of the week's payroll in dollars and cents. It was enough so that we did not wish to keep it in the house far in advance. Since we were good Muhammedans, Friday would be our rest day, and Thursday payday. We always had to go to Kirkuk on Wednesday for payroll.

In daylight, the ten miles of donkey road to Kirkuk seemed more natural and even a little less bumpy than it did on the first night on the way from the station. It wound a willful way up and down over every little rise and dip in ten miles, sometimes dropping precipitously into an abandoned irrigation ditch that cut across its path. It skirted bare brown fields and others where the green leaves of cucumber plants were a welcome variation. Living on this plain, one comes quickly to feel that any other than the all-pervading brown tones of the soil is something to be noticed and enjoyed. There are practically no trees. Certainly none standing in the open fields; no hedges, no lawns of grass or flower beds. Even in the few villages along the way, all looking very much like Tarkhalan, scarcely a sprig of green was to be seen: just brown mud walls between which ran the neglected brown dirt street, filled with dirty brown children whose inevitable cry was *baksheesh*! Past the villages, the road emerges to run again for miles through an open country, almost flat except where an artificial mound or two humps itself up from the plain. These long-deserted mounds, whose cryptic slopes embrace the earthly remains of some forgotten people, always set me wondering.

On the outskirts of Kirkuk, a few low, modern structures with corrugated iron roofs mark some of the Iraq Petroleum Company's receiving depots and offices, which reminded us that here, in the immediate neighborhood of Kirkuk, are the richest oil fields in the world. Past these oil buildings we were almost immediately in the streets of the city. Here the houses often rise more than one story from the ground, but they hug each other even more closely than those of the villages. The facades on the street are secretive; these dwellings turn in on themselves jealously. We picked our way with much tooting through a narrow bazaar where open-fronted stalls spilled their stock of foodstuffs and merchandise over the counters and into the street. Haggling, veiled women, intent on driving a bargain, and lounging idle men almost blocked the way.

Unlike their country cousins, these women of the city shroud themselves in black all-enveloping cloaks, worn over the head, drawn close about the face, and falling almost to the ground. They wear nondescript shoes, and black or white cotton stockings that wrinkle over bulbous silver ankle ornaments. It seemed odd to me that these anklets, which were intended for personal adornment, should be worn underneath the stockings. A Western woman, if she would tolerate them at all, would certainly wear them outside; but to the mind of the Oriental female, any such gesture would appear to utterly brazen.

Children played in the streets, and snatched at any chance the dropping of manure, valuable for fuel. Plodding donkeys stepped philosophically to one side, willing to oblige: patient, overworked, abused little toilers. Their lives spent in carrying staggering loads of bricks, or melons, or whatever else chances their owner's way — loads that wear ugly raw places in the flesh under the saddle.

Buggies, drawn by pairs of restless little horses, not so patient as the donkeys, pulled up where the road widened a bit, to let the automobile pass. Then we encountered something that would not wait: a long cavalcade of army wagons, drawn by mule teams, transporting equipment of the Iraqi Army. The uniformed drivers didn't appear to have the large beasts under control. I wondered what was going to happen. The road wasn't wide enough for us both. They kept coming; we hugged the wall as closely as possible, and stopped breathing. The drivers behind were crowding up on those in front. With a crunch and a rip, the first three wagons squeezed past, heedless of our fenders. Muhammed was shouting with all the vehemence his agitated, small frame could muster, the mule drivers swearing. An officer, who was both shouting and swearing, rode up on horseback. He backed the rest of the column up to make way for us, surveyed the damage, and wrote Muhammed's name in a notebook.

Breathing again, we left the suburbs for the city proper. Here we came on a wide thoroughfare in the process of being paved and full of attendant commotion, with swarms of workmen and one small steamroller. On this street fronts the hospital, the Eastern and Ottoman banks, Singer Sewing Machine Company, British Supply store, Ali's and other miscellaneous shops. On a paved cross street are the telegraph and post offices, and the *Serai* where the government offices are located.

The interior of the Eastern Bank, where our money was deposited, with its tellers' cages and benches was very like many a bank in many an American town of three or four thousand inhabitants. What one wouldn't find at home, however, was the walled garden in the back. It wasn't a very immaculately kept garden, but at least it boasted a few trees and bushes, and a romantic well. It is said that a nimble-witted clerk once threw the bank's money bags into this well when he heard that the city was being invaded by a raiding party from the mountains. Of course the brigands never thought to look there for loot, and so an obscure clerk became a hero and a brackish well became romantic.

The Singer Sewing Machine Company has a modern, Western look about it, as has the British Supply Company's store with its tidy rows of tinned goods, wines, liquors, shelves of imported candies and other delicacies. With these establishments one has discovered everything about Kirkuk that is very much like home, although Ali's shop, where we stopped to leave our order, might pass in a pinch for a very disorderly, very small town, very general store. The stock consisted of an assortment of imported canned goods, yard goods, shoes, hardware, and other things all jumbled together. It did have a glass showcase full of toilet articles, and a wooden counter over which goods might be passed. Behind this was a shelf of used books from which one might borrow thrillers by Edgar Wallace, vague, worn-looking novels, whose illustrations proclaimed them to be of another decade, or a copy of "Martin Eden" in Italian.

Much more interesting than his shop was the proprietor, Mullah Ali, a learned and devout gentleman who spoke excellent English. He had submerged himself in the study of his religion and adhered, even more steadfastly than is usual in this devout land, to the tenets of the Muhammedan doctrine. He not only believed, but he lived his faith. Illustrative of the man's high-mindedness is the fact that he had named his adored and only son, A'dl, which means, "the fair and just." Ali was never without his fez, although he had abandoned native costume for European clothes, which seems a pity. There was about him that aura of Eastern mysticism which would have been more effectively framed by native dress. He was such a kindly person, and did so many nice things for us, that we came to regard him as a great friend.

Next door to Ali's was a lovely little Persian rug shop, and then a sprinkling of native *chay-hana*s, or tea houses, that always spill their tables and chairs out into the street, and where a number of men are always lounging over their tea or coffee cups, and water-pipes forever gurgling. Across the street are a few shops of some pretense: tailors, drug stores, and the Iraq Sporting Goods Depot with squash rackets displayed in the window. Beyond these was the Kirkuk Palace Hotel which also belonged to Mullah Ali. Ali was, in fact, a man of considerable property, for he owned not only this hotel and his general store, but a *chay-hana*, an apothecary shop, and an interest in numerous other businesses in the city.

The Kirkuk Palace was the best, most modern, in fact the only possible hostelry in the city. It tried hard to live up to its pretentious name, but remained unlike any hotel I had experienced before. It is remarkable how to the Eastern mind a few unfamiliar details such as electric lights — with exposed wiring — and the letters W.C. painted on a door — comprise the last word in modern convenience. The dining room looked out upon a courtyard where chickens and turkeys foraged half-heartedly and some pretty white ducks swam at intervals in a little stream, only to paddle out upon dry land again, to prune and worry with their feathers for hours. Infinitely more pathetic than the rather forlorn creatures of the courtyard were some of the human inhabitants of the Kirkuk Palace. There was a Russian couple, refugees from revolutionary days, who had sung and danced their way through Persia, and finally somehow arrived in

Kirkuk. Here they would pause for as long as they could attract an audience. When we came in for a sip of tea during the forenoon, they were busy practicing their act in the deserted dining room. Not wishing to disturb them, we sat at a table near the door. They didn't seem to notice us, for they continued, the man at the piano, the woman perfecting the pattern of her dance. The same routine they must have been over countless times before: tum tee tee, one two three, and then one of them would strike a snag. They would stop to squabble loudly in their own language before starting again from the beginning. The man no longer gay and gallant, the woman no longer young and pretty; nevertheless, for them there was no turning back, no time for going home to anticipate. They must always go on, constantly practicing old tunes and steps, forever searching for new ones. What a life, to travel gypsy-like in strange lands, content to make a living without quarreling with the manner of this achievement. Yet they had always ready a proud, if somewhat tawdry, cloak of sophistication to throw over their weariness. As the waiter came to take our order, they noticed us. The tune was finished. The woman sat down upon the raised platform that held the piano, tapped the floor nimbly with her gold kid slippers, and lighted a cigarette with studied nonchalance.

I wanted to visit the main bazaar. To get there it was necessary to cross over the great bridge at the end of the street that was being paved. During the autumn and winter months one may go as dryly over the broad river bed far below, as on the bridge. I was told that during spring floods, the Kirkuk Chi becomes a raging torrent, but now if not completely dry, it was negligible as a river. Heavy motor lorries and trucks were forced to take the lower way at this time in order to save wear on the bridge. A policeman stopped our car, mistaking the station-wagon body for a truck. One glance at the black leather upholstered seats inside, however, was all that was needed to convince him of his error. It was really an honest-to-goodness passenger vehicle, in spite of its eccentric exterior.

Across the bridge was the old part of Kirkuk, the citadel, towers aloft. Over it, and tumbling down its steep slopes, runs a hodge-podge of native dwellings. The consequent debris from such habitations continues, year by year, to add more inches to the citadel, which in reality is another artificial mound, built up by the accumulation from successive hoary civilizations. It is a pity, from the archaeologists' point of view, that it cannot be excavated. Who knows what treasures lie below the modern jumble of living quarters. However, you can't evict the population of half a city, even in the name of science.

Skirting the citadel, we came to a place where we had to abandon the automobile, since the streets within the covered bazaar are strictly pedestrian. Sending Muhammed on his way to do the shopping, we proceeded on ours, prepared to enjoy whatever adventures might lie before us. Through the narrow and interlacing alleys we made slow progress. High above our heads, ancient vaulting spanned the street; in the gloomy half-light, crowds of people swarmed and jostled. Women in black, like flocks of crows, stood about the stalls, gesticulating, arguing, bargaining. They held those enveloping cloaks so close about their faces that only one eye remained visible; this and their shrill, voluble — to me unintelligible — words made them seem more bird-like than human. Men were lounging and gossiping, idly sauntering, or hurriedly elbowing a way through the more sluggish stream of humanity. Flies buzzed restlessly, and dust rose in the shafts of sunlight that fell through the holes in the vaults above. Three or four little boys with baskets popped up beside us, hoping to be engaged to carry bundles; and a big, rugged fellow appeared from somewhere, eagerly volunteering to act as our guide. The others paid no attention to us. Somehow their very indifference made us feel that we belonged, and were at home.

Here was a stall decorated by festoons of brightly colored skull caps, like bells that did not tinkle. We passed through the yard-goods section where merchants ran after us carrying bolts of printed cotton stuff. There were other stalls where the proprietors and their friends sat about drinking coffee, heedless of business. A booth full of honey and dates and assorted sweetmeats had become a haven for a myriad of hungry flies. The trays full of massed stickiness were black with them. Beyond, a maker of clay pipes squatted at his work. At the shoe vender's stall, the tasks of sewing and turning were going on behind a swaying curtain of shoes, strung together end to end. There were red and green and black pointed-toed slippers, and enormous sandals with a special compartment built in to accommodate the big toe. In the same section, saddle makers displayed their tooled, studded wares of great magnificence. Donkey trappings of brightly colored, braided wool and ornamented with tassels and beads swayed in the breeze beside the heavier and more luxurious leather work.

We turned a corner and came to the street of the tailors, and its rows of Singer Sewing Machines making the air whir. Men were clipping bolts of cloth into suit patterns. Just a step farther on was the rug section. We stopped to see what they had to offer, whereupon two salesmen from opposite stalls set upon us, each claiming us for his own. They vied with each other for our attention, spreading rugs in the street for us to see. It did not seem to matter that the passing throng planted their muddy feet upon these rugs, or spat upon them carelessly, or that a herd of sharp-hooved little goats trotted nimbly over them. This didn't surprise us for in Baghdad, where the rug market is more active, we had seen the same thing being done for a purpose. If rugs are left out in the streets of the bazaar, before very long they will become so covered with mud and filth that nothing but their outline is visible. After several months, when they are taken up and washed in the Tigris, they will have acquired a premature appearance of antiquity. Whether these modern forgeries will then be sold as antiques, semi-antiques, or ultra-antiques is left entirely to the discretion of the merchant. In Kirkuk, however, there isn't enough foreign trade to make such a practice profitable. The carelessness we saw here was without design.

A horrible old hag of a beggar came sidling up, clawing at me, whining for *baksheesh*. One of the rug merchants pushed her away with a rough hand and phrase. Gratefully, I explained to him the type of rug I wanted: the long-piled native *Jaf*. These are cheap rugs, made for home use, and not considered fine enough for export. Most of them were too garish for our taste, and none that our merchant-friends spread out were pleasing enough to tempt us to buy. We thanked them and started to walk away. Then these two, who had been rivals, at once became partners in a conspiracy to detain us. While one ran after us and held our attention, the other scurried away to borrow from the stock of a third booth. He had gone to get just what we wanted. We wavered, and went back. One of the borrowed rugs did prove to be livable. In fact, it was quite nice. It was also seventy rupees. We offered forty. The merchants were insulted, but when we started again to leave they held us, arguing its worth until we finally said that we didn't want it anyway and began to walk determinedly away. At this point they gave in. We found that we had bought the rug at our own price, and a small ragged follower carried it away for us. I realized that it would be a mistake to bargain for something one didn't really want, just for the sake of bargaining.

We climbed three steps to leave the bazaar; but before we passed through its old arched gateway and into the open street, we stopped to look at the scene we had just come through. From that perspective it took on unexpected loveliness. The dusky half-light of the narrow street was pierced by oblique shafts of streaming sunlight where dust particles glinted lazily upward, and through these bars of light and shadow the changing throng moved on a background of kaleidoscopic color of great variety.

Passing through the archway, across the street, and down a few steps we came to the second-hand bazaar, so-called because here in shoddy array all manner of goods were set out for sale. But there were also the stalls of one or two metal-workers. We came to a narrow, open-fronted booth where an old man squatted before an anvil, industriously hammering out some golden trinket. A boy apprentice worked the hand bellows, fanning the coals in a charcoal brazier to a glowing heat. When we stopped to watch, the old man paused at his work, fumbled in a box at his side, and drew forth a golden bangle which he presented for our inspection. It was an ornament for the forehead of a male child, and would serve also to keep the baleful glance of the "evil eye" from resting upon the helpless infant. The old man asked if we had a male child; was saddened by a negative answer; but expressed hope for us some day, by the grace of Allah. The trinket was shaped like an inverted crescent, decorated with circles of appliqued gold wire and three small blue stones, which may have been either turquoise or bits of opaque, colored glass. A third point had been added to the center of the concave lower edge, and from this and from each point of the crescent dropped tiny leaf pendants of thinly hammered gold in *repoussé* design. I thought it would make a nice earring. Dick asked the metal worker if he had another like it. The old man looked surprised, but if our faith in Allah was as great as it seemed, he must rise to the occasion; he would make another. It was agreed; we paid a deposit and arranged to call for the finished product the following week.

Dick's watch told us that it was time to go. Muhammed would surely be through with his shopping by now. We trusted him to bargain for fresh foodstuffs for us in the bazaar, since we, being foreigners, could never have traded at the accepted rate of exchange, no matter how long we might haggle. He always took considerable time over his marketing; more, we suspected because he probably also paid a flying visit home to see his wife who lived in Kirkuk, than from any conscientious and long winded attempt to beat some merchant down for a few pennies. Today, however, we had given him ample time for both, so we picked our way back to the appointed meeting place. There was no sign of the little fellow, but we waited, and after a while he arrived in a breathless hurry, with the car full of vegetables, sugar, and other staples. We drove back to the center of town, picked up our order from Ali's, got the precious mail from the post-office, and the full money box from the bank. These things done in a hurry, we were off for home, tired but happy with our excursion into town, and our purchases, and ready for a large and substantial tea when we arrived.

Mrs. Wilensky, who had studied at the Agricultural College in Palestine, and was therefore versed in plant culture, had the large courtyard broken up into plots for flower beds. We had ordered the flowers from Ali, and that night, just as Abdulla was clearing away at the dinner dishes, the truck arrived at our gates. All the lamps were pressed into service to illuminate the planting. Our servants in their flowing garbs and the men from Ali's made a fantastic picture in the moon and lamplight, putting zinnias and marigolds into place. It was as though we had waited until the flowers were asleep so that they might waken in the morning and not know that they had been disturbed. And when we woke it was strange to find our garden grown overnight.

CHAPTER III

The Daily Routine

The quiet routine of the days in our compound was both busy and pleasant. The men usually went off to work in the very early morning, and didn't return until tea time when they would bring back stories of what had happened on the dig, and a box or two of antiques that had come to light in the course of the day's work. The long, rough board shelves in the office were rapidly becoming filled with these objects, every one of which Mrs. Wilensky entered in the catalogue before it was removed to a less temporary resting place in the storeroom. Objects that were either typical or unusual, or for any reason especially interesting were also recorded pictorially by Mr. Wilensky, who made most beautiful and accurate pen drawings.

The majority of the booty was pottery, much of it broken. These pieces had to be mended, whenever the missing sections could be found and mending was possible. I did most of this work, with the help of our versatile chauffeur, Muhammed, who had a certain amount of talent for mending pottery, and infinite patience which is even more essential. We had a special table in the office, and a Primus stove and a double boiler to heat the glue. There were great piles of odd sherds, which would have sent a jigsaw puzzle enthusiast insane with joy. Muhammed scrubbed them clean of the last remnants of the earth in which they had lain for so many centuries, and set them out to dry. Then we would sort them according to color and texture, into little homogenous piles that might eventually be transformed back into pots and jars in their original shapes. The first step was to pick two pieces that would fit together. This might require a lot of patience, but no great skill because the broken edges were extremely irregular, and if the pieces did not fit there was no mistaking it. The real sport began when two more pieces had been glued together. Then their outline made a jagged pattern, the distinctive shape of which, when mentally reversed, would show what to look for in the next piece. It was apt to be exciting work, as well as good fun, because when an object was shattered beyond all recognition and came from the dig in a pile of potsherds, it is fair to say that its real discovery took place on the table beside the glue pot. The possibility that such a discovery might be important, lent a thrill to the sticky job of mending.

Today, however, the latest batch of sherds were drying; we couldn't begin working on them for hours. I had finished settling the week's accounts with Hiddir for the eggs, milk, and chickens he had bought for us from the villagers. Since we consumed from four to six chickens daily, Hiddur was kept busy providing them. But he had been on his job, and there was now a reserve supply of about a hundred scratching contentedly in the service courtyard, oblivious to the certainty that each in his turn would be served up in one of Sammy's numerous dishes. Therefore, with the food supply for the near future assured, and other household duties not very pressing at the moment, I was in the mood for lazy contemplation. It was a perfect autumn afternoon. There was a crisp chill in the wind, but warm penetrating sunshine flooded our world — the kind of sunshine that has a way of seeping into the very bone, making you feel at peace and content.

The roof was the place. Abdulla put up a comfortable canvas chair for me. The dog, Nuzi, followed me up the mud steps, wagging rather stupidly as though she thought I might have something for her to eat. Goomish, who was continuing his morning siesta on the far end of the roof, moved closer. He was somewhat jealous of the other dogs, and rather demanded first attention. Of course, he deserved it. Was he not the most intelligent, handsome, and superlative of canines? To be sure, his chassis was swung rather low, and his wheel-base was somewhat longer than might seem necessary. But then, he was a dog, not a motorcar; and he should be judged for what he was. His beautiful, plumy tail was indeed a true mark of aristocracy.

The dogs settled themselves on the warm sunny roof at my feet, and I let my eye wander over this scene that was mine to observe. It was a splendid vantage point from which to enjoy not only the immediate surroundings, but the distant panorama. The view disclosed our location in what seemed at first glance to be an incredibly flat plain, surrounded, or nearly so, by distant mountains. Some sixty miles away towards Suleimania in Kurdestan, Pit Magudrun reared its great triangular pile. To the north lay the Persian range, more monumental but seemingly less so because of its greater distance. The mist that usually hid these far-away peaks had lifted, and they emerged clear and magnificent — white-mantled outlines cutting sharply into the sky.

During this month of November, and throughout the winter, the fields around our house were bare. The rich browns of the soil mingled with the dusty green of the ever-present camel thorn, and the yellow stubble of last year's crop. Beyond the fields, to the northeast, was Kirkuk; but from our roof it could be only vaguely distinguished, and therefore it did not exist as an immediate detail of our surroundings. Tarkhalan, on the other hand, was very much in evidence. With flat roofs and vertical walls it presented such effects in light and shade as to delight the soul of an artist. A little farther on, the cluster of mud houses that marked the village of Topazoa could be discerned rising like earthly excrescences from the plain.

Beside our gates ran an irrigation ditch, which was fed by the *cheriz*. This ingenious system is the source of the precious water supply for the community. In principle, the *cheriz* is much the same as those shallow wells, used in the arid sections of California. It is a series of wells, extending for a mile of two, sometimes even farther. The individual wells are spaced some thirty yards apart, and are connected by an underground tunnel. Because the land slopes imperceptibly but truly away from the Kurdish mountains, this underground connection comes at length to the surface. Accumulated seepage feeds a running stream of water. From the mouth of the *cheriz* the water is carried in any desired direction by means of an irrigation ditch, or *waddi*. It is over these *waddies* that the humpy little bridges are built along the road. Unfortunately, the construction of a *cheriz* is costly, and only a rich man can build one. The poor must either buy their water, paying for it by dividing their crops, or must hire themselves out to till the lands of the rich. The clay soil of the plain is extremely fertile as far as the water supply reaches. Beyond, all is desert. The excavations at Nuzi have revealed archaeological evidence that our plain was not always so arid; and from the same source we know that in ancient times the region was not, as it is today, so completely denuded of trees. Microscopic examination of the charcoals from our site has shown that oak, poplar, palm, and boxwood existed there in Nuzi times. While numerous causes other than the stripping of trees from the foothills of Kirkuk have probably contributed to this process of dehydration, it must have been a considerable factor.

The natives today do not prize growing trees, and they certainly do not regard the lack of them as a reason for their insufficient water supply. A tree cut down and transformed into lumber for building purposes, or faggots for fuel is of more immediate use than a tree left standing, and they are often desperately in need of wood. The Iraq government, however, is more enlightened. While we were there, a general order was issued requiring a tree or bush to be planted in every courtyard in the village. It is unfortunate that the practical reasons behind this order could not have been brought home to the rural population in some forceful manner. It is one thing to issue a blanket order that trees be planted, but quite another problem to coax the easy-going peasants into caring for them. When I saw the pitiful little dry sticks that were hastily poked into the ground to satisfy this government requirement, I could not feel very sanguine about the outcome of Iraq's reforestation program. Any such project would be bound to meet with the natural inertia of the people, since it is contrary in principle to their inborn philosophy. Their trust in Allah is simple and implicit. He will protect and provide for them; and if He does not, it is His will that they must suffer. Why concern oneself with the future? Particularly a future so remote as to be of possible use only to one's grandchildren?

The water for our house was brought by Zen Abdin Mustafa, with the help of the donkey, in large tins, or *tannica*s, that had once held petrol. (I am sure I don't know how that country got along before the advent of the petrol *tannica*. It is pressed into service for every possible use now-a-days). Although we boiled all of our water before using it, we made sure that it came from the *mouth* of the nearest *cheriz*, about a mile from the house, where it gushed from the ground, clear and cool. From this point the main *waddi* ran past the gates of our compound, and the bridge at the corner of the house was the nearest spot for the women of Tarkhalan to fill their water jars. They were not as particular as we; to them it didn't matter if someone happened to be washing feet or clothing a few yards upstream.

From my vantage point I could see them coming, plodding along the road from the village, with heavy water jars strapped to their backs. Here was a woman who had a donkey to carry the load; she was probably the wife of a rich man. Behind, two little girls came chattering along, apparently oblivious to the weight on their backs. The women tarried at the stream, to gossip, or to pound clean some article of clothing, before they filled their jars, and trudged back to the work of their homes. I couldn't help thinking how pleasant it was to live so close to this scene of activity, particularly when we did so without forfeiting our privacy. In that respect the roof in Iraq surpasses the front porch on Main Street in America.

The native women were shy but friendly. They were unsophisticated enough to appear in public unveiled. Some of the younger ones were strikingly lovely, with dark eyes, and soft brown skin suffused with the pink glow of health. And their clothes were such a welcome contrast to the colorless garb of the city women. The outer garment was colored to suit the fancy of the wearer. Brilliant tones of orange and purple and yellow predominated. It was a simple, untailored cloak, really just a length of woolen cloth the upper corners of which were caught over the left shoulder, while the length of the material fell in graceful, toga-like folds under the right arm. Underneath, a long cotton dress partly covered the baggy pantelettes that were shirred in close at the ankles. Heads were becomingly coifed with black silk or cotton kerchiefs; and sometimes a wealth of thinly hammered gold or silver trinkets betrayed that universal quality of femininity — vanity. A more practical reason for such a display was often that it represented not only the wife's dowry, but also the family savings account. If a man did not wish to be encumbered with livestock, he would invest his weekly pay in jewelry which he could strip from his wife's person at any time, to sell or barter with in the bazaars. Although Kirkuk boasted two banks, these country people did not avail themselves of the convenience of formal banking; they could never bring themselves to trust such flimsy evidence of possession as a slip of paper or a bank book.

So the women came and went all day long, bare brown feet treading firmly on the rough road from the village, heads held high, and bodies straight. Their dress, their carriage, their attitude was one of quiet dignity, yet their days are strenuous with manual labor. They must work hard and tirelessly at many a task for which our Western minds would find a man's strength more suitable. Woman's lot in this country is not an enviable one from our point of view. She must be obedient, thoughtful, and wifely. So far so good, but she has few rights or pleasures to reward her for these virtues. She does not usually choose the man she is to marry. If she finds that she does not like her husband, she may divorce him — if her family is willing to take her back on their hands, and return the goods or money he has paid for her. If not, it is just unfortunate. On the other hand, if she happens to love her husband, there is always the possibility that he may take another wife. What a situation! Small wonder she often becomes a quarrelsome scold — it is her only emotional outlet. This is one reason polygamy is not more prevalent than it is, since to live peaceably with two wives means that a man must be sufficiently wealthy to keep two separate establishments. Unless, as was the case in one menage in our village, both wives so dislike their mutual husband that they are drawn together in a bond of friendship.

Pondering this, one searches for the basic reason why such situations are possible. One is apt to suspect the Muhammedan religion, which is essentially masculine and gives woman only a minor place in the community. This is certainly a contributing factor, but I do not believe that it can be accepted as a complete explanation. Even more fundamental than their religion, is the fact that these people are still essentially primitive. The male with his greater physical strength, symbolizes superiority; and notwithstanding the fact that these village women accomplish, as a matter of daily routine, such tasks as call for more strength than they can spare, brawn is still a man's attribute. Because she is an inferior creature, the female must, paradoxically, do most of the work.

The scene at the *waddi* was not the only interest in this quarter. Just over the bridge some desert Arabs had made their abode in an abandoned mud-brick sheep pen. The overflow was housed in adjacent tents. These were the usual, low-roofed Arab tents of black goat hair, the open sides of which had been banked with brush, indicating that our neighbors intended to stay for the winter. They were probably more than one family, for there was an incredible number of ragged children, as well as a few goats, a donkey, and some dogs. One of the latter was a husky, big fellow who had only three legs. Abdulla said that the missing leg was shot off by a shepherd who had caught the dog killing sheep. I didn't doubt this story, for the animal looked savage enough. His constant companion was a bony white bitch with mean eyes and a litter of fat puppies. These were the camp hangers-on, apparently ignored as untouchables. The only dog the Arabs took any notice of was a poor, half-grown *selugi,* who shivered constantly even though one of the women had made a blanket for him. He was a privileged member of the settlement because he was of a breed highly esteemed as hunters. Like a greyhound in appearance, with low sloping forehead and slender legs, the *selugi* is streamlined and swift; he can outdistance even a deer. By springtime this miserable fellow would have grown enough to be of use in supplying the community larder with game from the desert, and therefore his well-being was a matter of importance.

The picture of these low black tents, the children and the animals, was never complete without the old Arab woman who occupied herself with weaving. She squatted on the ground in front of a primitive loom, throwing the shuttle to and fro, pulling up the wool and batting it down with an antelope horn, to make it firm. She always held the feed-thread between her bare toes. Day by day the strip of heavy white cloth, with its narrow stripe of red at each edge, grew longer under her skillful fingers. It was serviceable stuff, destined to be made into saddle bags that would not wear out for many a year, no matter how full they might be stuffed with grain or vegetables.

While I was watching, the smallest of this woman's ragged children interrupted the weaving to demand his dinner. He must have been well over a year old, for he walked without a trace of hesitation, but he had no intention of being weaned. She nursed him, unembarrassed, and when he had been satisfied, she took up her work again. The older children, still more ragged, played and fought together all around. It was somewhat shocking to notice one little fellow, six or seven years old, puffing happily at the butt of his father's cigarette. The oldest was a girl of nine or ten who, on close observation, would have been quite pretty had it not been for the long enamelled nose-ring dangling down over her mouth. But then, this too was a matter of taste. I had to remind myself that I was just as incomprehensible to this little girl as she was to me. Even my blond hair and blue eyes, and the fact that I wore no nose-ring, must have seemed strange to her. As for the way we carried on — according to quite normal Western etiquette — these people had long since given up trying to understand.

And so the scene intrigued, wherever the eye happened to wander. If one scrutinized some detail closely or gazed into dreamy distance there would be something quaint, bizarre, or colorful or peacefully satisfying to wonder about or enjoy in the always changing panorama of human activity or in the changeless face of nature. In no other place have I felt so strongly the illusion that the whole small world was there within my grasp, apparently visible, comprehensible, circumscribed by the distant mountains. Here it was easy to forget post-Columbus geography, and believe the mountain peaks to be the earth's fringes. It was pleasant, this illusion of completeness; it lent a sense of power to the mind. America, England, and Europe were but vague memories — for the moment they ceased to exist. In the center of this flat and limited world of our own, one felt like opening his arms to the saucer-domed heavens above, believing that here it was possible for the inner spirit to be free, to expand. There were no tall buildings to hem it in, not even trees to obstruct the free passage of the spirit. It was safe and would return home again at evening, because the mountains guarded the horizon.

CHAPTER IV

The Discovery of Nuzi

Mrs. Wilensky and I were going to take Tiffin on the dig. Sammy had been notified in time, and had prepared an ample picnic lunch for us. So we called for Zen Abdin Mustafa and the old donkey to carry the lunch, and one of the sentries to act as bodyguard — which was merely a gesture for no one would have thought of harming us — and started across the bare fields, towards the southwest, where the low outline of the *tepa* was silhouetted against the clear desert sky. As we walked along, we could see, rising here and there, other less pretentious mounds — sites of other ancient cities or towns, as yet unexcavated. What had appeared from the roof of our headquarters as a perfectly flat plain was, in reality, full of dips and rises, and dotted with ancient mounds. These were as alluring as the uncut pages of a book. They gave one the restless desire to know what was written therein, what dim stories of magnificence and decay they might reveal under the scientific spade! One wonders how the willing excavator knows which site to choose among so many. The story of how our dig started shows just how much the element of chance and a villager's tale may have to do with so important an undertaking.

It seems that a few years ago a well was put down on the old citadel in Kirkuk, and clay tablets were thus accidentally unearthed. As often happens with such *antiques*, these tablets found their way to Baghdad; learned men read the writing inscribed upon their surfaces, and were excited. Here were new words, something which would add to the still incomplete knowledge of an ancient written language. Here were the records of a people who must have inhabited the north country many hundreds of years ago, and about whom scholars were ignorant. So it was that in 1924–25, the late, great Dr. Edward Chiera went up to dig the mound of Kirkuk. This, of course, was found to be impossible. It would have been out of the question to buy out the scores of citizens whose homes overrun the site. Therefore, he consulted with Dr. Corner, who was the British Medical Officer for the district, a man with keen interest in things archaeological.

Corner knew a lot about the folklore of the vicinity, he had heard tales of a native named Atiya. Rumor had it that twenty years ago, or more, this man had dug on a mound thereabouts and had unearthed twenty donkey loads of tablets. These he was reported to have carried to Baghdad and sold. Chiera and Corner realized that the truth was being exaggerated, but that Atiya or anyone who had found tablets was of sufficient importance. They set out to run down the source of the story. In the village of Tarkhalan, ten miles southwest of Kirkuk, they found someone who knew about Atiya, and knew in general the location of the mound where he had dug. Further investigation brought them to our *Yorgan Tepa*, and to what seemed to be the marks of Atiya's scratching — not on the big mound itself, but on an adjacent mound of smaller size.

Dr. Chiera established his headquarters in the village of Tarkhalan. He started digging on the small mound, which later came to be known as the T-house, by reason of the subsequent discovery of the ancient owner's name. When this happy discovery took place, they uncovered a great store of tablets pertaining to the goods and house of one Tehiptilla, ancient dignitary, whose family records were there in order for five generations — ample proof that the site was worth more complete investigation. In this way our dig was started. During the first season two small bordering mounds were completely excavated, revealing what seemed to be the villas of rich men who could afford the luxury of country houses outside the city walls, and work was begun on the large mound which turned out to be the city of Nuzi. Now, during this fourth season of digging at Nuzi, I was privileged to be on the spot. Discoveries equally as important as those of other years might be made at any time. That was why the lone, low, irregular silhouette of the mound seemed always to be beckoning, tempting me to walk out there and see what was happening.

When we arrived, Goomish was the first to greet us. He had anticipated lunch time, and didn't believe in being late. He jumped around, wagging, as though to say, "Well, well, so the ladies are joining us today!" Dick and Mr. Wilensky came to take their respective wives in tow, and we waved hello to Charles across a network of ancient mud walls.

The dig was strikingly like an enormous beehive, where somewhat leisurely activity went on with all the effect of hurry and bustle. There were the crews of basket boys, wearing a path from the rooms where excavation was going on to the place where the narrow-gauge railway car waited for a load of dirt. There was a rumble of the full car being trundled over its track to the edge of the *tepa* where it was dumped. There were the shovel men who filled the baskets full of loose earth, and the pick men clearing away fallen debris. It was an endless cycle, where pick men made work for shovel men, who made work for basket men, who made work for the *trambilchis*, who trundled the railroad cars to the edge of the *tepa*.

Then, there were the specialized jobs that went ahead more seriously and with less abandon. Wall-tracers had to be able to recognize the almost infinitesimal differences between the standing remains of mud walls and the fallen debris of the same walls — debris that had filled the rooms of the ancient city, making of its streets, palace, temple, and unintelligible mound. Because there was so little difference between this clay fill and the walls themselves, all had been packed together by the rainfall of thousands of humid winters, wall-tracing at *Yorgan Tepa* was perhaps the most exacting task of all. Also, there was relatively little baked brick or stone to help determine the outline of the separate rooms. It looks so simple when you are introduced to the completely excavated, freestanding ruins, or even when you see fresh walls evolving in rooms adjacent to these that have fully emerged; but it is quite a different matter to start from the beginning.

I saw this happen early in the season when we explored an untouched area over by the edge of the *tepa*. Before setting the men to work, Dick and I walked over the smooth hard surface that was soon to be disturbed in the search for ancient walls. "How in the world," I asked, "do you know where to start?" "Well," he answered candidly, "unless the contour of the ground tells you something, or unless you're blessed with second sight, you might just as well close your eyes, turn around three times, and point. It will be as good a choice as any." That may not sound very scientific, but it is correct; the first thing is to get below the surface — anywhere. Dig a hole and start a trench. Eventually you *must* strike a wall, and when you do, all guesswork stops; follow its surface and it will bring you to a corner. Then you are fairly safe. The right-angle wall will terminate in another corner and so on, until the room has been completely outlined. Then, and not until then, can the rough crew come in to clear the interior. Once the first room in a virgin area is traced, the possibility of speed is quadrupled, for additional tracers can be set to work to find the reverse faces of each of its four walls. The first wall is the most baffling mystery, and when it has been solved, the biggest hurdle has been taken.

Volumes could be written on the science of wall-tracing in mud-brick. It is such exacting work, the kind where error cannot be countenanced, and yet where the possibility of error is omnipresent. The mental equipment to keep a man constantly on the alert was most essential. He had to stay on his toes, or else be demoted. It is not surprising that good wall-tracers were few and far between; yet we always had an eye peeled for wall-tracing potentialities. New tracers were necessary not only to take care of the ever expanding area of activity, but to fill vacancies for even expert workers sometimes lost their flair — either through over-confidence or through the stubbornness born of increasing years. There was no dearth of applicants for a job that carried its prestige home with it at night, and the opinion of a wall-tracer was valued by his fellow villagers. In choosing new recruits for this work, we were fortunate to have in the vicinity of Tarkhalan, many who had previous experience as pick-men in the construction of their horizontal wells. Men who had worked on the *cheriz* at least knew how to handle a pick, and it remained to be seen whether they had any sense for walls.

A healthy inquisitiveness may help to solve difficult problems in tracing, but it is dangerous unless accompanied by intelligence and intuition. There was the amusing if maddening example of Ismail. In following a wall, every seepage crack and joint would hold a possibility of utmost importance to him. So great was the fascination of false clews that, if left unwatched, he would break through a sound wall in their pursuit; he would dig himself into a maze within, and finally emerge on the other side, as satisfied as a worm that has just burrowed through a rotten apple. Ismail was obviously not suited for wall-tracing, yet he had admirable traits of character. Putting these to work in other fields eventually won him a top place among the knife men, specializing in skeletal material.

Being a knife-man also required quick intelligence, equal in its specialized way to that necessary for wall-tracing. It was the knife-men who went into the room after the wall-tracers had discovered its outline and the pick-men had cleared away the general debris inside, and when it was possible that valuable material was just within a knife thrust of the ancient dirt pavement. With infinite care, and skill comparable to surgeons in the operating room, they took from the earth the precious objects that had reposed there for thousands of years.

I made the rounds, and saw some of the puzzles of yesterday made clear. Here a series of walls, yesterday so meaningless, had evolved into a suite of perfectly sensible rooms; the place where the pavement ended unreasonable had become a wall. Little by little, the mysteries were being cleared up, knotty problems solving themselves. Everywhere I went the workmen looked up with a friendly greeting. Jasim, Aziz, Bakir, Ahmet Hama: I had begun to distinguish them by name. Jobar was a foolish shepherd whom the rest of the men called crazy. His job on the dig was to wield a shovel; and when I came by he stopped work, shouted good-day, and made some foolish remark intended to amuse. I think that he was consciously playing a part — trying to appear a little mad before an appreciative audience.

Ahmet Hama (short for Muhammed) was known variously as Ahmet the wolf, because of his prowess as a hunter, or Ahmet the windy, because he liked to talk about it. The latter nickname infuriated him. It was generally used behind his back, because it was also a good pun. *Howa* means wind or windy, and since his real name, Ahmet Hama, is so similar, it was hard to keep my tongue from slipping.

Jasim and Aziz we know of old. Jasim was one of the best knife-men, Aziz a trusted wall-tracer. Bakir was also a wall-tracer, and a sort of foreman. Fortunes of war had made him widely travelled beyond the ordinary man's dreams. He spoke English, picked up in a British prison camp during the war, where he had enjoyed a safe internment and the comparatively pleasant life of an orderly. At the moment, he was consulting a fat, impressive looking watch. The minutes ticked off, it was time for lunch. Bakir blew a shrill blast on his official tin whistle — the signal to stop work. Baskets, picks, shovels were abandoned. Round flaps of unleavened bread appeared, and then disappeared with apparent relish. Dusty brown hands searched in baggy trousers pockets for cigarettes. These long, strong-smelling smokes were lighted by little juice-less flint machines that struck a spark onto the frayed end of a piece of string; and our workmen settled down to rest and gossip. We repaired to our "dining room."

This was a small excavated room in the area of last year's activity, the rather unusually high walls of which gave us privacy for our meal and some protection from the sun. Here ancient baked brick paving blocks from the palace courtyard were piled for chairs, and more for a table, on which Zen Abdin Mustafa had set out the picnic fare. Lunch on the dig varied remarkably little as to menu, and that day's was no exception to the general rule. We had roast chicken, potatoes in gravy, beans, custard pudding and lukewarm coffee, followed by nuts and oranges. If Mrs. Wilensky and I had stayed at home for lunch we would have had roast chicken, potatoes in gravy, beans, custard pudding, and coffee, followed by nuts and oranges. It was much nicer to partake of it out in the open in this three-thousand-year-old dining room in the good company of our husbands and Charles.

The end of the meal was the best. We cracked the nuts on our palace-courtyard-paving-brick dining table, with any small stone that happened to be handy, and threw the orange peelings in a corner we had used on previous picnics as a repository for such clean refuse. In the next room a colony of big black ants had built itself an enormous hill. We dropped bits of walnut meat to the scouts of the ant commissary department, who had come to visit our table. They seemed to prefer walnut meat to any other tidbit. One ambitious fellow tried to haul away a piece three times his size. He wasn't making any headway, but refused to relinquish his find. We took pity on him, stopped him, and cut the piece in two. The ant, mystified, but apparently pleased with the lighter burden, carried it quickly away.

This impromptu class in natural history was interrupted by Bakir's whistle. Lunch period was over. I almost said lunch hour, but that would be incorrect, as the noon *pidost* was limited to half an hour.

After lunch I went to sit in the part of the excavation which we had named "the deep room." Not that its outline marked any actual walls of an ancient room, it was the beginning of an arbitrary shaft which was to be carried down to virgin soil. Although the main purpose of the Expedition was to uncover as completely as possible one simultaneously existing level of the city of Nuzi, we wished to investigate what lay below. It was suggested, from the height to which the mound rose above the surrounding plain, that our Nuzians had not been the only inhabitants of this site. So an exploratory shaft was started through the center of the *tepa* in an effort to discover what lay below the Nuzi strata. The convenient square shape of this shaft made it resemble an excavated room; hence its name.

The scribes of Nuzi who had recorded the legal and personal transactions of their time, in the customary manner on small clay tablets, had been its unwitting historians. These ancient men of learning had no such altruistic purpose in mind when they pressed their reed styluses into the soft clay to make the documents that were to endure for so many centuries. They did it as a business, and for a price; but it resulted in history — the only written history we have of them. As a result, we knew that the years between 1500 and 1400 B.C. saw the zenith of Nuzi prosperity; and we also knew that the city had existed for several hundred years before that time, and was destined to thrive still one or two centuries after. Our work each season brought a clearer understanding. A tremendous amount of data had been collected about the Nuzians, not only from these written records, but from other significant relics as well, especially the pottery.

Consider for a moment how essential a role the container plays in modern life, from the paper sack on the grocer's shelf and the shining aluminum sauce pan in the kitchen to the beautiful service plates and fragile baubles of glass on the dining room table. Translate all and more of these common articles of convenience into pottery, and you will begin to have a picture of home life in antiquity. Nowadays if, when dining out, one were impolite and curious enough to turn one's soup plate upside down to see the maker's mark, it might reveal its origin from any country in the world. Not so in ancient times, when every common article of daily life had to be indigenous. That is why pottery plays such an important part in determining archaeological chronology. The skill with which it was made, the color and texture of the clay, the type of decoration if any was used, the shapes — all these points are eloquent links in the chain of evidence.

We had come to know our Nuzi pottery types well, just as we had become familiar with their language and what to expect from them architecturally. But what lay *below* Nuzi was wrapped in earthy mystery. We were determined to have a look, at least a cross-section of the unknown, in the deep room area. We had not penetrated very far before we came upon evidence of habitation — pottery, made according to Nuzi technique but from what would seem to have been foreign models. These were differences that perhaps would have been striking only to the trained eye — variants in shape, texture, and the like — but they were exciting to us because they pointed to what we had hoped to find: transition. Then gradually all that tied up with Nuzi, even the technique of manufacture, disappeared; the variant characteristics of the transition period had become purified, and resolved finally into something quite foreign to Nuzi. Then came the burials.

I went to the deep room that afternoon because I wanted to watch the knife-men at their delicate task of unearthing these bones. Unearthing is not the proper word, for they were not being taken out. The earth around them was being removed, gently, gently, with knife point and brush, so that the bones and their grave furniture could be photographed *in situ*. Such photographs of any important find were always necessary, but in the case of these crumbling bones they were all we would have for our pains — photographs and field notes. It was a great disappointment to us that the skeletons of these pre-Nuzi people were of so little anthropological use, but it couldn't be helped. The bones were too disintegrated to allow for accurate measurements. We could blame the dampness of the soil for their condition, and a contributing cause was the fact that these skeletons had already been disturbed, centuries ago. As the work progressed we realized that we had stumbled upon a popular burial ground, a place where the bones of one had hardly settled before they were jarred from rest by a new interment.

However badly we may have felt over the loss of anthropological data, we were consoled by the object finds, grave furnishings, mostly of *terra-cotta*. These were simple vessels, undecorated but of beautiful shapes. There were also some metal objects that had to be treated with almost as much delicacy as the bones.

When I walked down the manufactured steps into the deep room, Jasim and Ismail and the other knife-men looked up to smile a welcome. Jasim gave me his usual courteous *"Shloam khe fik?"* Then they all turned quietly again to work, brushing, loosening a few more flakes of earth with a knife-blade, and brushing again. Jasim's long black braids got in his way, and he threw them back with a toss of his head. I had thought that these men might be superstitiously averse to working with grave material, but when I asked Jasim about it he just laughed. He was indifferent to the bones except as fragile material which he could be proud of cleaning with skill in the manner the *Sahib*s wished them to be cleaned. But the objects that lay alongside intrigued his fancy. He pointed out some little shell cosmetic cups that still contained a greenish pigment, and a copper vanity case which he thought must have held *kohl* to beautify the eyes. He was as delighted as a child to be able to identify these things. Ismail, on the other hand, was more stolid. Perhaps he left his imagination back within the walls where he used to love to burrow as an amateur wall-tracer. Here he was working on an intensely interesting burial where a shell cylinder seal, a small, symbolic copper hatchet, and a dagger were all grouped around their unfortunate owner's chest, but the fact didn't seem to excite him. He was cleaning these objects methodically and well, but with no great show of enthusiasm.

Exciting though it was, the finding of objects was not the only thing of importance happening on the dig. I wandered out of the deep room, across the *tepa*, stopping here to see a crumbling fragment of Nuzi wall painting materialize — patches of red, gray, and black plaster that might eventually hook up into a formal design under the hand of a knife-man who was flaking away the last stubborn sheath of fill; there, to watch Aziz conjure an ancient wall out of the earth. Mr. Wilensky was busy with plane table and instruments, recording the magic on paper. The plans of Nuzi will not again be lost with the crumbling of what remains of its walls. For these fragments of the foundations and lower sections of what were once good high walls, will also crumble with time, just as did the upper mud bricks that once made them whole. It would not take many seasons of wind and rain to complete their ruin, when they are excavated and left to the elements.

That day I was not the only spectator watching Aziz at work. Abu Yorgan, the old man who owns the *tepa*, hovered about. He had his monetary compensation, but he was fascinated by the things that were happening in the place where he used to raise grain, oblivious of the city of Nuzi over which he had ploughed, planted, and reaped for so many seasons. The workmen jokingly told him that he now had the largest house in the whole countryside. It was true that on his land hundreds of rooms had been excavated, but poor old Abu Yorgan could hardly avail himself of such grandeur. It would be uncomfortable to live in the unroofed remains of the 3000 year old palace and temple. I could understand that Abu Yorgan was even then looking to the future, to the time when our work there would be completed, and disintegration had gone far enough so that the site would no longer be of value as a "national monument," and when it would again be possible to plough, plant, and reap. When that might be, Allah alone knew. The old man was deeply concerned about it all, for if we insisted in digging such great holes in the ground, how could he in his lifetime, or his sons, or his sons' sons ever carry enough dirt to fill them up? Natural erosion would help, but even so, it would be highly inconvenient to cultivate land too full of sudden dips and rises. As for the deep room — that promised to be a positive menace to the house of Yorgan. The curve of the old fellow's back as he squatted quietly on the wall, his head slightly bent as though by the weight of his thoughts and of the voluminous *khefia* that enveloped it, the loose sleeve of his *aba* lying in pensive folds in his lap, all made him seem more thoughtful than perhaps he was; like Rodin's famous "Thinker" whose attitude is concentrated, but whose primitive physiognomy seems to belie the possibility of such intensive reflection. I was aware of the danger of reading my own thoughts into the minds of these people.

On top of a wall some distance away I could see Dick's spare frame silhouetted beside the camera on its tripod, and the outline of Osman's wiry form in action. Osman was Dick's little shadow, a trim, intelligent lad about fourteen years old, a somewhat exalted member of the force. The way he got his start was rather amusing. Dick needed a shadow, a kind of agile secretary who could follow him about the dig, fetch and carry, and help with routine work such as calling the roll and checking the names of the men as they were paid on Thursday afternoons. It was an important job that would carry with it some responsibility. Bakir recommended small Osman because he was the only young man of the village who could read and write his own language. Obviously, his family were aristocrats in Tarkhalan! At the time, however, Osman was then even younger than when I knew him, and didn't look very prepossessing. There was also the obstacle that he could neither read nor write English. With a field of only one to pick from, the choice did not seem very difficult, but Dick had some misgivings. Then, one day, he came upon the boy trying to learn English by deciphering the labels on old gramophone records in the village teahouse. Anyone with that much ambition deserved his opportunity — and Osman got his. It wasn't long before he made himself a valuable member of the Expedition. His parents were inordinately proud, and they had a right to be.

While I was thinking about all this, Charles rushed past headed their way, apparently with some news. I left Abu Yorgan unceremoniously to his own reflections, and tagged along, scenting excitement. Jasim had found a bronze adze head which still contained a fragment of ancient wood. It was no use! When things on the dig began popping, I couldn't keep up with them. It was like trying to watch all the acts at once in a five ring circus — physically impossible.

But tomorrow would be another day. Bakir's shrill whistle meant four-thirty o'clock, and the end of this day's work. The men made no pretense of staying overtime. With greater activity than they had evinced all day, they flung shovels, picks, baskets over their shoulders and ran, laughing, shouting, down the steep sides of the *tepa*. It was a kind of game, to see who could reach his donkey the first. Half an hour earlier, little brothers and sisters, sons and daughters of the workmen, had brought donkeys out from the village. They were waiting in the adjacent field, and up on the backs of the sturdy little beasts went the grown men, with the little ones clinging on behind. Off they raced in gray cavalcade, each intent on being the first to reach the village.

Of course, every one of the hundred and twenty-five workmen did not own a donkey. A donkey was a luxury, and most of the thirty or forty beasts brought out to the dig every afternoon had been bought by Expedition pay. It had become more or less a matter of prestige, like the ownership of a motor car in America. Those hardy souls who had not succumbed or could not afford to succumb to fashion's dictum, followed after, with easy swinging strides. The days work had not been strenuous enough to tire their toughened muscles. Only Jasim, who lived in the Arab village of Shergat, a couple of miles out in the desert, stopped for a moment to speak to the *Sahib* about some detail of his work. Down along the road which passed the foot of the *tepa* trotted four or five horsemen, riding leisurely home from the desert hunt, their lithe *Selugi* dogs loping easily in front of the horses. They were rich men from Topazoa, returning home after a day's sport in the desert.

Meantime, Dick's little shadow, Osman, piled the day's loot into the waiting Ford. Mr. Wilensky's special helper, Fathulla, packed the precious instruments on the tailboard. This done, we all piled in. The old car groaned, but was game, and with Osman and Fathulla, each perched on a running board, we were off for home and for tea.

CHAPTER V

A Village Wedding

Our sentry, Hiddir, was to be married. For days the villagers had been anticipating the event with a series of celebrations, according to their age-old customs. The *calabala* in Tarkhalan, although quite different from the wedding parties we were accustomed to in America, still fulfills the same social purpose. We had been invited to all of these parties, but politely declined except for this night, immediately preceding the ceremony. After dinner we bundled into warm coats against the evening chill, took walking sticks against the village dogs, and started out on foot.

At the gate of the compound we called for a sentry to accompany us; we were somewhat startled to see that it was Hiddir himself who responded. Why had he not gone to the party long since? Hiddir just grinned and shrugged at our surprise. Nor from his appearance would we have known that he was even remotely connected with the festivities. He wasn't at all dressed up, not even a new *khefia* or girdle to distinguish the occasion; and the only emotion he betrayed was of embarrassment. Muhammed and Abdulla, who were always on hand for something doing, didn't find anything strange in this. I could only conclude that these people were more candid than we: after all, the wedding was only an excuse for jollification, and having furnished the excuse, the bridegroom had no further responsibility. He could have come to the party or not, as he pleased. Imagine the consternation Hiddir's attitude would have caused at home under similar circumstances! I was thinking about that as we trooped to the village — the dogs, Goomish, Alaj, and Nuzi frisking on ahead.

The air was crisp and the moon was full, riding high in the heavens. Our spindling shadows, bobbing on the deserted road, looked like grotesque marionettes. Somehow the night seemed less uneventfully peaceful than usual, either because of the excitement of anticipation in my own mind, or some radio-like emanations from the dark, silent village. Festivity was afoot. Once we reached the village our dogs disappeared, probably to the house of Abas, their real owner, but other fiercer beasts popped out of the dark alleys and doorways, menacing. Charles put about with his walking stick to keep them off, and Muhammed, who had gone bravely ahead, overworked his short legs in fancy dodging. No one seemed to be quite sure just where the *calabala* was being held. The narrow, crooked village streets were dark, except for the eerie light cast by the moon. The high mud walls on either side seemed shrouded in secrecy. Gates were closed — the village had turned its back on us.

Then the noises of merrymaking floated out from somewhere beyond the walls. There was the sharp report of a shot — sure sign of revelry. We tried to follow the sounds, and presently someone came out of a dark doorway and led us through a maze of small courtyards to a large open court where the *calabala* was in full swing. We climbed over a low wall and up some treacherously broken-down stairs to the roof of a house. A blanket was spread for us to sit upon. It gave one a strange feeling of unreality to be sitting in this high place, the freedom of the wintry sky above with its star-gleam uninterrupted, the light of the great round moon cutting deep shadows in the courtyard below. Two or three small gray donkeys, bored with the fuss, had retired to the least congested corner to roll on the ground, or stand in quiet disregard of the human excitement. And the humans were all having a wonderful time. The main attraction was a large circle of young men. In the center of the circle, a giant of particular talent piped on a shepherd's double reed. Around him the company moved, always towards the right and rhythmically up and down to the music, arms twined about waists, knees flexing and unflexing. Now and then they executed a simple dance step in unison. The circle was never broken, even when one dropped out to rest, or another, inspired to greater action, moved into the center beside the piper, to step out in a solo dance.

Now there were two men dancing within the circle, their daggers out and gleaming as the moonlight caught the polished surfaces, a clink of tempered steel as blades were brought together in mid-air; arms and legs moving with smooth, cat-like coordination. Simplicity and muscular grace, this was their dance.

Characteristically enough, the women did not take part, but squatted silently in the shadows, watching. The piper was indefatigable. He had mesmerized the dancers and the audience and himself as well. The attenuated notes that flowed from his shepherd's reed had a fragile quality as though they had congealed for an instant in mid-air, and one might reach out and shatter them with a blow; yet the trick of endless repetition lent persistence to a simple tune until those frozen notes pierced one's very being, to melt and flow again, along a quickened pulse. We found ourselves swaying to the rhythm, fascinated; the key so different that it could not be other than weird to our ears. Everything was weird. As time passed unnoticed this quite ordinary courtyard acquired a mysterious glamour as though the *calabala* were a part of some magnificent primitive drama; and the hard-trodden earth stage and mud walls became mere properties, the cold moonlight a clever illusion. As the dancing circle moved, the figures in the segment of light changed. Individual details were accented, then lost — the contrast of white *aba* against black, the gleam of an eye, the flash of a smile, the glint from a dagger's hilt. Now and again a dark face tilted up, then passed into shadow. They would go on like this hour upon hour.

Then someone fired a shot at the moon — spontaneous emotion loosed. Its sharp dissonance was a relief; the spell was broken. We came to find that while the music and rhythm had taken possession of us, the chill of the night had also crept beneath our heavy coats. We stood up to go. Our hosts protested, and Hiddir insisted that at least we must see his house. Climbing stiffly down from the rooftop, we looked inside at a bare, modest mud room, where huge metal pans were set out to prepare the wedding feast on the morrow.

The crowd pressed about the doorway. They were pleased with themselves and would have us stay; but we found that we had stayed almost too long already. We were satiated with the strangeness of the night and of the *calabala*. As we pushed past the eager, friendly crush out into the open air again, we noticed that the circle in the courtyard had momentarily broken up, and the piper was playing to us. We were sensible of the honor and said so with many protestations. Then threading a careful way again through the uncertain debris of the small dark courtyards, we reached the open street and so walked back in the cold moonlight to home and to bed, with the thin, high rhythm of a shepherd's reed still beating in our ears.

CHAPTER VI

Thanksgiving Plans

Our eyes and ears and emotions had been charmed by a native *calabala*, and now the time had come for us to plan a *calabala* of our own. Thanksgiving was near, and although our preparations seemed to provide solely for gastronomical excitement, we might still call it a *calabala*. From the frequent use of the word by our servants, I take it to mean not only a dance, but a celebration or commotion of any kind in which noise, emotion, or collective human activity predominates — a flexible term.

By this time, with more or less general consent, we had omitted cakes and sandwiches from the everyday tea menu, because too much to eat at five o'clock seemed to dampen our appetites for a seven o'clock dinner. We might have been more fashionable and dined later if the men had not been obliged to get up at the uncivilized hour of six in the morning, in order to spend all of the daylight hours on the dig; and since nine o'clock was our normal bedtime, a later dinner would have been inconvenient. Therefore, it was without fear of any satiated lack of enthusiasm that I took a notebook and pencil after one of our foodless teas, late in November, and called for suggestions about the Thanksgiving menu. Dinner would be the big meal of the day, although breakfast had its points. In any case, we had best start from the beginning. What did we want for Thanksgiving breakfast? Everyone had some special desire. Dick's suggestion was emphatically negative: "no porridge!" I didn't blame him. Sammy's usual morning gruel with its complement of boiled skimmed milk was disheartening enough at any time, and out of the question for Thanksgiving Day morning. The others contributed more positive ideas. I included everything on my list — a regular shotgun dose of a meal.

When no one could think of anything more to add, I went out to see that Sammy had killed the turkey and hung it in a cool place. During the winter months we could let a bird hang for two days without fear of its spoiling. But even in cool weather, the sun shone hot at midday; so we had to hang the fowl inside of the house where the night's chill lingered because of the natural insulation afforded by the thick mud walls. For this purpose we had chosen the bathroom — coldest and least used room in the house. It had an added advantage for our present culinary needs, since the bathtub made an ample drip pan. It would have been shocking to have a lifeless turkey or chicken dripping gore into one's bath water. Don't imagine this ever happened: no one took baths. If this revelation is even more shocking, remember the conditions of life in this place. Water was precious, for it had to be carted from a mile away; and the tiny bathroom was the coldest, dampest, most thoroughly clammy room imaginable in a supposedly hot climate. One might suppose that a small stove, such as we had in every other room, would help. There had been one there once, and some hardy soul had tried to take a bath; but the stove had smoked and the bath-in-a-tub fiend had emerged looking somewhat grimier than before. No one could be expected to try such an experiment again. Finally the stove was taken out — to serve usefully and smokelessly in another part of the house. Undoubtedly that bathroom possessed a jinx. So we made our choice: the vote was overwhelmingly in favor of sponge baths in our own several bedrooms, where fires could be made to blaze in the little sheet iron stoves without smoking us out, and where the water in large white enamelled pitchers was really hot. Our beautiful bathtub, which should have been a pride and joy since it was one of the few extant in the north of Iraq, had degenerated into a drip pan.

It had been hard to overcome Sammy's natural prejudices in the matter of hanging the fowl, even though we had given him so sumptuous a hanging-chamber. The whole principle of hanging meat appalled him. He would never be convinced that fresh meat, cooked hot from the slaughter, was not superior; nor that our method was not dangerous. In summertime it would have been, and I suppose that Sammy's attitude was the result of an inherent fear of meat that was not freshly killed — on the whole, a wise taboo in a refrigeratorless, hot region. This time, however, he had obeyed orders, and the turkey was already hanging over the bathtub. Our holiday preparations were started.

The next day I went to Kirkuk, armed with my notebook and its list of potted, tinned, imported delicacies. The things I couldn't find at Ali's store I got at the British Supply. The order was complete, even down to a can of American coffee, except for just one necessity which I couldn't find anywhere in Kirkuk — cranberry sauce. That was a blow. Would it seem like Thanksgiving without cranberries for the turkey? We would have to substitute currant jelly. That I did find, put up in a tin by a reliable British company.

On the eve of the great day, a very shy Muhammed sidled into the dining room after dinner was over, and finally worked up enough courage to ask if he, Sammy, Abdulla, and Kerim might take the automobile and go to Kirkuk for the night. He said that they wanted to go to the *hamam*, or public bath house, which is only frequented at holiday time, so that the request was also meant to be a complement to our Thanksgiving festival. Needless to add, it was a very good excuse for getting into the city. They promised to be back by eight in the morning, so we gave permission and they went happily on their way.

Thanksgiving morning came cold and rainy. It was still pouring when I woke at seven-thirty, thinking how nice it was to cuddle deeper into the warm blankets and listen to the patter on the roof. I dozed off again, not to wake until it was past nine o'clock, and Hiddir pounding on our door to ask if he should make the breakfast. Somehow, I just couldn't imagine Hiddir making the breakfast. Hadn't Sammy and the rest come yet? He cheerfully said "no." "Well," Hiddir, "thank you but I will make breakfast myself." I got up and started to dress. It looked as if we would have to send out a rescue party for the auto, which I imagined must be stalled in the mud somewhere between Kirkuk and Tarkhalan; but before I finished dressing I heard it coughing and sputtering at the gates. Five minutes later I found Abdulla industriously sweeping the dining room, and Sammy in the kitchen, resplendent in a new fez, deep in the little rites and incantations that meant breakfast. They were all painfully conscious of being late, so I said nothing about it.

Half an hour later, with the expedition gathered expectantly in the dining room, Abdulla had a bright fire in the little "tin" stove, and the table nicely laid with a clean white cloth. We sat down to a royal feast. As an ornamental butler Abdulla was a joy. Even when he was late and flustered, his *khefia* was still beautifully tied, and his whole costume quite meticulous. Although he certainly could not have agreed with our choice of holiday food, nothing pleased him more than to serve an elaborate meal like this. We had orange juice, kippered herring, sausages, bacon, pancakes with honey, toast, American coffee with tinned cream — and *no porridge.*

It was a triumphal meal that lasted until noon. Sammy outdid himself on the pancakes. They looked and tasted more like good American flapjacks than I had dared to expect, although I had given him careful directions for concocting a batter that included both baking soda and sour milk. Sammy's natural inclination about pancakes was quite French. Before this, they had always *looked* like the first cousins to a *crêpe suzette;* but there the resemblance ended. Perhaps it was the contrast that made these raised cakes on Thanksgiving morning seem so superlative. Some of them had achieved an elevation of half an inch and more! We all ate a prodigious number — especially Dick and Charles — and drank plenty of coffee which was more like real coffee than anything we had had since we left home.

It was a good thing that we had planned to forego lunch after such a meal as breakfast. We lounged contentedly around the room which Abdulla had transformed into a living room once more. The late visitors to the *hamam* had brought our mail back with them, and there was a sheaf of the *Baghdad Times,* as well as a new copy of that inimitable newsmagazine, *Time,* which Charles received from home. We were totally incapable of anything approaching activity until mid-afternoon.

Then, the rain having stopped, the valiant Charles suggested a walk. Agreed. We needed exercise to put us in shape for tea-time. We put on coats and high gum boots, for the world was a sea of mud after the rain, and sloshed our way to the village. It's rather fun to walk right through deep puddles, and squash inches deep in mud when one is protected by boots. Ahmet and Abdulla who accompanied us were equipped with no such luxury, but they picked the high spots; and when there were no high spots, they didn't seem to mind getting their feet wet and their *caloshes* muddy. These comfortable slippers, with tops crocheted of heavy wool and sewn onto thick leather soles, would dry out quickly before a fire when they got back to the Expedition house.

Whim took us beyond Tarkhalan, to the nearby village of Topazoa. There was a good deal of rivalry between the two villages. The people of Tarkhalan said contemptuously of those of Topazoa, that they worked, worked, worked all the time so it was no wonder that they were rich. I couldn't see a great difference between being "rich" and "poor," since the people of both villages wore the same kind of ragged clothing, lived in essentially the same kind of comfortless houses, and tilled the soil in the same way — unless one of them happened to be lucky enough to get a job on the dig. Preference with the Expedition was, of course, given to our villagers as far as possible. In fact, the only noticeable difference between the two villages was that here in Topazoa some of the houses had slightly pointed roofs. This was a Kurdish village, which may explain the architectural variation.

Vaguely, our objective had been the garden of Husein Bik, beyond Topazoa. He was a really rich man, even according to our standards. His fortune was in oil lands, which seemed a good reason why his family name should be Naphti. His summer villa was surrounded by a garden where grew the only trees in the countryside — with the exception of one or two scraggly palms to be found in Tarkhalan courtyards. The sight of trees and green foliage was welcome to our eyes, so accustomed to arboreal abundance at home. We liked to walk under the olives and pomegranates, beside a little running stream in Husein Bek's garden. His retainers were courteous, and when the rich man himself was at home he would invite us in for coffee.

But today our footsteps were diverted by a friendly Topazoan who joined our group, and asked us to come to see his brother's sand-grouse trap. We walked with him across the ploughed fields to a flat threshing floor, where no sign of life was apparent; but where, when our guide called out, a smiling turbaned head emerged from a cleverly hidden hole in the ground. There was some conversation in Kurdish between the brothers, and then the one crawled out of his hide-away, dragging behind a gunny-sack full of sand-grouse. This he opened, and presented us with half a dozen of the pretty birds, alive and frightened. Their wings had been twisted together so that they were helpless, though unharmed. They are beautiful creatures, about the size of American quail, their soft feathers a mottled brown except for a band of yellow about the neck. It was a shame to think of eating them. Our impulse was to unwind their wings and free them to the winds and sky again; but we couldn't accept a *baksheesh* like that and throw it away, particularly after all the patient trouble and ingenuity that had gone into their catching. And there were so many of them in this country. The sky was often clouded with great flights of them. Also, they are excellent eating, once you have hardened your heart to the idea. It seemed inevitable, like the will of Allah, that we should have sand-grouse for lunch next day.

We were curious to see how this invisible trap worked. One of our host accommodatingly crawled into the pit, touched an unseen lever of some kind, and released the net. It sprang out of its straw-covered groove on the threshing floor with such force and speed that the eye could not follow. But once sprung, there it was, a rope net about twenty feet long, the free edge lying on the ground more than a meter away from the groove where the other edge was fastened. Any unsuspecting birds, lured to that area by a sprinkling of grain, would be hopelessly caught in its meshes. It was a primitive device, yet quite as efficient as some complicated mechanical snare, and much more thrilling. We remembered that the same thing is pictured identically on Assyrian reliefs dating from the eighth century before Christ; and so we had discovered another link with antiquity. Neither our friends from Topazoa nor our own servants understood that this, like so many other things in their lives, was an inheritance out of the dim past. Time has not for them become the comprehensive thing we try to make it; it remains a true abstraction, something to be considered apart from eternity, yet more concrete than even we know since for practical purposes it is bounded by the lifetime of a father or grandfather.

We noticed that the clouds were swinging low and dark above us. Our respite from ruin was at an end. We headed for home, Hiddir and Ahmet carrying the birds, and our friendly Topazoan following to collect the *annas* we insisted on giving him — either as payment or return *baksheesh*, whichever way you look at it. As we arrived, the rain began. Abdulla had anticipated our coming, and the tea table was ready to yield up fruit cake and sandwiches. From adventuring, we always seemed to return to our dining room as to a hospice where warmth and food were forthcoming.

Tea had just been poured when the sound of a motor car at our gates made us wonder who had been brave enough to venture over impossible roads on a day like this. The American Missionaries, prompted by a desire to spend part of this national holiday of ours with us compatriots? No, it turned out to be a telegram from Dr. Meek, delivered by Ali's kindness. Meek would arrive in the morning. We were sorry that he could not have been there to share Thanksgiving with us. Tomorrow we would probably all be feeling dyspeptic — a discouraging introduction for the new member.

Then the sound of another motor car. Perhaps Dr. Meek was coming today after all. Abdulla appeared hurriedly to announce that guests were at the gates, and Dick went out to welcome them, whoever they might be. When he returned he was accompanied by four of five native gentlemen whose appearance indicated that they were from the city. They were introduced by name, but in the small confusion that accompanies unexpected visitors — finding extra chairs and all that — I, for one, did not catch their titles. I wondered idly just who they might be, and why they had honored us with a call on such a rainy day. No matter, it was always pleasant to have guests, and these were obviously men of culture who spoke excellent English. They explained that they had come to visit the dig, but had found no one there but a sentry who had directed them to our Expedition house. So we told them about the American holiday we were observing, and about its origin in Pilgrim times — although, for that matter, the men would hardly have been working on the dig in such weather anyway. Meantime, the understanding Abdulla had whisked away some of our half-empty tea cups off the table, and now he returned with these, all washed and ready for the guests. They would not take tea, however, saying that they could not stay. We protested, inviting them to remain and partake of the festive turkey; but they refused, and then we learned why. Their wives were waiting for them in a second car, outside in the cold. I was distressed about it, for we did not wish to be even unconsciously inhospitable; but I suppose that the reason they had not told us was because it was obvious that we had no separate receiving room for women. A pity, especially since they were gentlewomen and talking with them might have afforded me some understanding of the feminine mode of life in that class, about which I knew nothing. The women of Tarkhalan were of the peasant order, and I do not imagine that women I had observed driving a sharp bargain in the bazaars of the city belonged to the upper strata of society; in any case these latter were always so closely shrouded that whatever personality they may have had was completely hidden, along with their physical charms. And now the opportunity to see and talk with some native *ladies* was lost, all for the want of an extra room! Well, it couldn't be helped.

After they had gone and our own group was once more alone about the table, I casually said that I wondered just who they were. Dick repeated the names, but these names and titles to unaccustomed foreign ears are not as meaningful as they should be. Finally, however, I was made to understand that the gentleman I had been exchanging polite generalities with was none other than the Prime Minister of Iraq. He and the gentleman in the fez — who turned out to be the Egyptian Consul — were visitors from Baghdad. Their host, who had been the genial-looking one on the other side of the table, was the *Mutasarif*, or governor of the Kirkuk District; and the young boy, his son.

CHAPTER VII

The Discovery of the Old Akkadian Tablets from Gasur

With Dr. Meek in our midst and proving to be a great asset to the general good-fellowship of the group, we felt that the party was complete, and we had really settled down to the season's work; and as fate would have it, he was not to find the Expedition dull. When we had taken the deep room area down about eight meters from the top of the *tepa* — and all the material at this depth was pre-Nuzi — we struck a large cache of early tablets. It was an exciting find, not only because of the unusually large number of tablets, but because, when they were read, we might hope to glean some information about the pre-Nuzi people who inhabited the site upon which Nuzi was later built. So that when Dr. Meek arrived, he found dozens of precious chunks of clay waiting for him on our storeroom shelves, and all of us impatient for his knowledge.

Neither the Nuzians themselves nor these people who lived before them were as careful in baking and turning to brick the letters and records they wrote on soft little pillows of clay as were the people in other regions of Assyria and Babylonia. Just why this is, no one knows. Perhaps they were more careful of the actual property to which their records refer. In the case of the Nuzians, the light-fingered way in which they appropriated other people's property, as the tablets record, would indicate a certain delicate care in the retention of their own perishable goods.

At any rate, when the tablets were uncovered on the dig, they were unbaked and as fragile as the clay debris that surrounded them. It was apparent that great care would have to be taken in removing them from the ground lest they be broken to bits. To prevent such a disaster, a large part of the surrounding dirt was, whenever possible, taken out with them for support; the whole mass was wrapped in absorbent tissue paper and again in heavy paper, labeled and tied with a string.

In this manner they stayed on the storeroom shelves for a month, or until they were thoroughly dry before they were ready for baking. By putting them through this ordeal of fire, we were merely completing the job started and left unfinished by their original manufacturers. Not until they had turned to brick in the oven could they be thoroughly cleaned and examined. They emerged soul-seared, hard-hearted but communicative.

In preparation for the baking they were bedded in sand, wrappings and all, within earthenware jars. In each jar was placed a small potsherd with a Roman numeral scratched on it, so that we might tell, by comparison with our written list — which had been prepared beforehand — what was the original location on the dig. The jars were then stacked in the baking chamber of the oven, the door sealed up with mud-brick and plastic mud, a tiny window of glass set into it, and the fire started.

It is interesting to note that the modern pottery of this region today will not stand up under the intense heat of the baking oven. The only kind that is perfectly satisfactory and emerges as sound as when it was put in is the pottery made at Nuzi a thousand five hundred years before Christ. Perhaps the Nuzians believed, as many peoples have, that the objects of their everyday life would accompany them to the next world. In that case they may have prepared their pottery to resist such temperatures as an unrelenting divine judgement might impose.

Our homemade inferno, which was situated in a far corner of the service courtyard,[8] was a thick-walled structure of baked brick, containing two compartments, one over the other. The lower one was the fire chamber and the upper, the baking chamber. In length and width they were the same — about four by two feet. But in height, the baking chamber was about two feet in comparison to one foot in the fire chamber. This was to allow for stacking the jars full of tablets, one on top of another. A large passage, the width of the chamber at the back, gave access to the flames and heat from the lower to the upper chamber, and at the front end the smokestack poured black, oily soot over our drying laundry.

It is a common belief that oil and water will not mix, but paradoxically enough, we baked our tablets with oil and water just the same. This is how it was done: outside of the oven were two five gallon tins, one containing crude oil, the other water. Each had a spigot which allowed regulated quantities to drip into a funnel and through a pipe leading to the upper part of the fire chamber, where it fell upon a heterogeneous mass of scrap iron. At first pure oil was allowed to drip into the oven and burn. When the scrap iron was thoroughly hot, the water was turned on in smaller quantity than oil. The water mingled with oil, fell onto the red-hot iron, immediately exploded into steam, and in so doing scattered and vaporized the oil throughout the entire chamber, giving instant complete combustion.

As the oven became hotter, the quantity of water could be increased to an amount almost equal to that of oil. This produced the hottest fire of all. In the early days, when the technique of our fiery furnace was being investigated, one batch of tablets had been completely melted, along with the surrounding jars, and fused with the embedding sand. That took considerable heat. But nowadays we knew better, and the fire was carefully regulated and constantly watched by the faithful Fathulla.

---

8 [For a photograph of the kiln, see "Letters from the Field, 1927-1930," no. 6, 21 December 1927, p. 26.]

The fire was started in the morning and kept going for six hours at a low heat to allow the tablets to become completely dry, in case the weeks of standing on the storeroom shelves had not done the job thoroughly. Then came six hours of medium fire just to prepare them for what was to come. Finally hell was let loose, and for six more hours they got all we could give them.

At the end of this time, the oil and water were turned off, and the fire went out. The door of the fire chamber was closed and sealed with plastic mud, and the master of the fiery ceremonies, Fathulla, went home to bed. Twenty-four hours later, the oven might be opened and the tablets removed.

When this batch of deep room tablets had undergone its baptism of fire, cooled and been taken out of the oven, Dr. Meek eagerly started the task of cleaning them. I gave what assistance I could, but the job was made difficult by the fact that these tablets had been so packed together in antiquity that they often had come out of the ground almost clean, and without the protection of any quantity of surrounding clay. To this uninitiated it might seem that it would be easier to scrape off a thin layer of hardened clay than to extract a small tablet from the center of a large chunk [of clay]. Actually, this was far from so, for the surrounding dirt that obscured the writing had also undergone the baking process, and had become as hard as brick. It was far easier to grip on a large mass, and pry it gently loose from the face of the tablet. In many cases when this was possible, the surrounding mass would come away with a little pressure, and leave the face of the tablet beautifully clean. When there was only a thin crust, it had to be cleaned off, painstakingly, flake by flake with the help of a needle set into a wooden handle. We had evolved this excellent and easily made instrument for just such work, and although it was the most satisfactory tool we had, it was not without drawbacks. There was always the hazard of scratching the tablet with the needle. This danger was, of course, minimized by the fact that the tablets were very hard after baking, but they were not absolutely impenetrable; and the ever-present necessity for caution slowed us up.

Another difficulty — also the result of the tablets having come from the ground with no great quantity of surrounding clay — was that many were cracked or had actually come up in fragments. Consequently, there was the heart-breaking task of mending and rescuing tiny flakes which had broken away from the surface. If these were lost, part of the writing would be gone; perhaps only one symbol, or even part of one, but that part might be the key to a whole sentence or even a whole tablet. Moreover, these flakes had to be glued back into place precisely, had to be made to fit absolutely or else they were better lost. It was an unpleasant, sticky job but all in a day's work, for archaeologists and their helpers have of necessity to be Jacks of all trades. That is a misleading description, however, for it implies master at none; and in this work we had to insure worthwhile results by seeing to it that caution and patience were made to compensate for any deficiency in technique. Our success pointed to a certain degree of mastery in the art.

Dr. Meek was, of course, very anxious to start deciphering. This he did as soon as the first tablets had undergone a preliminary cleaning. He finished the work of cleaning as he read, picking off the last clinging remnants of the hardened dirt that obscured the incised characters. It was tedious work, much of which had to be done with the aid of a magnifying glass. However, he was rewarded, for he soon discovered that the type of writing on the deep room tablets was much earlier than, and not at all like, the writing on the so-called "Kirkuk tablets" of the Hurrian people who [later] lived in Nuzi. This in itself was significant, for it told us that the older inhabitants of the *tepa* were not Hurrians. Their language was Akkadian with a mingling of Sumerian words. It was all very surprising because, with one or two isolated exceptions, this was farther north than Sumerian inscriptions of any sort had before been found, and here we had a large number of tablets betraying definite Sumerian influence.

What did it all mean? As far as we could make out, it indicated that here on the site of Yorgan Tepa, there existed in the middle of the third millennium before Christ a people of Akkadian extraction who also knew Sumerian influence. At least, they used both languages in their written documents — a strange, thrilling discovery when you realize that the character of their writing indicates that these people were closely related to the early inhabitants of the ancient city of Ashur.[9] A tentative date of 2500 B.C. has been put on the tablets, which makes them antedate the Nuzi tablets by a thousand years.

In our mind's eye we could picture an Akkadian provincial city, whose name as mentioned on the tablets was Ga-Sur, thriving on our mound only to be superseded by an intrusive Hurrian people who came to build under the supervision of the Mitanni kings — the city we know as Nuzi. It was a ghostly city, this Ga-Sur, which our scientific abracadabra had conjured up for us out of the little wedge-shaped marks on clay tablets; far more ghostly than Nuzi whose veil of mystery had been shredded by investigation. Nor did the magic stop with the mere name of the city and a clue as to the genealogy of its inhabitants; it went on, peopling the place with names. There was the princess Da-da, whose letters to the scribe Ili had fallen into our hands. They were not love letters. One would call them, rather, epistles of advice, for the beautiful Da-da (may we not assume that a princess with such a name was beautiful?) seemed to have had her fingers in more than one pie. Did they love each other, these two? One likes to wonder, even if their strange correspondence contained no impassioned declarations.

As more and more of the tablets were cleaned, other things came to light, until suddenly the most interesting and, in a way, spectacular find emerged from one of those lumps of hard, brown clay. This object was not fashioned of gold, nor encrusted with semi-precious stones; it was just another dull-looking little flat tablet, small in size, measuring three by two and five-eighths inches, not very exciting until on closer inspection of its surface its importance dawned with the force of a small explosion: it was a *map*! It cannot be claimed to be an

---

9 Ashur which lies midway between Mosul and Baghdad on the banks of the Tigris to the southwest of Nuzi, was, in later times, to become the seat of the great Assyrian Empire.

absolutely unique discovery, for one or two other maps have come from different ancient sites; but a quick calculation as to the possible limits of dating Ga-Sur brought home the immensely important fact that we had discovered *the oldest map yet known*. With this revelation came a thrill that is seldom experienced, even in the romantic occupation of archaeology.

As to topography, our map is somewhat baffling. Ranges of mountains on either side are represented in the characteristic Babylonian manner. Between these run two sets of lines, meeting and continuing together. The lines might indicate rivers flowing into a sea represented below — although it has been suggested that they might also be trade routes. In fact, almost any conjecture is possible. Place names in cuneiform, and sometimes enclosed in circles, dot the surface. The difficulty is that we do not know if they are the names of cities, villages, tribes — or what. None is familiar, except one that can be read as Ibla. It is a matter of doubt whether this could mean the fortress of Ibla, whose ancient site is in Syria. Such conjectures and controversies are bound to arise concerning a find like this.

One thing has remained clear throughout: it is a map. The cardinal points of the compass are clearly indicated on its four edges.

Now, after many months of study and after the map has been reproduced and reported with varying degrees of accuracy in innumerable journals throughout the world, scholars are still not in complete accord as to what it represents. Not being a scholar, I used to like to touch the map with the wand of imagining, transform its enigmatic lines and circles into a number of things: sometimes an ancient caravan route, winding its dusty way through a long valley hemmed by rugged mountains; sometimes a forked stream, bearing on its surface all manner of strange craft. And since what I was thinking didn't matter anyway, I have felt free to sit dreamy-eyed and romantic through the most learned discussions. I have heard the weight of evidence that the map really indicates nothing more extensive than the boundaries of a private estate — 365 *gan* of farm land belonging to a man of wealth and power, whose name may be translated variously as Azala or Shat-Azala. So be it, then; daydreams are easily altered and the ghost of Azala becomes even more intriguing than the ghosts of camel trains or ancient river craft. Perhaps some day we may return to this place to explore Ga-Sur as completely and successfully as Nuzi was unearthed. In such an event, it would be no more than reasonable to hope that we might come across more data about so important a personage as Azala whose domain was so extensive and valuable. Thus the past beckons alluringly. Thus by mere chance, from the dim recesses of antiquity, a name emerges; the name of a man whose lands, whose memory, even whose grave has been lost these thousands of years.

CHAPTER VIII

Village Feuds, Superstitions and Customs

At about this time when we were all agog over the discovery of the map, Aziz, the old wall-tracer, began to send us frequent presents of ewe's milk *lebon* — that universal and palatable native dish of clotted milk. He also followed up this attention by paying us frequent visits in the evening, after supper. Poor Aziz, I would hardly have recognized him as the same person who came to visit on that first night so long ago when Dick arrived from Baghdad. He had changed greatly. He was now haggard and worn-looking, and showed his years. The object of both his gifts and his visits was, of course, to enlist our aid in some matter of importance. Bit by bit the story came out.

There had been an altercation among some of the villagers over a matter of stolen sheep. Feeling grew, until it assumed almost the proportions of a feud. Then, one of the "bad men" — those who opposed the family of Aziz — was mysteriously shot in the leg. For this, Aziz's eldest son, who meant more to him than anything in the world, was put into jail.

As Aziz told us all of this, it seemed odd that the question of justice, or even whether the boy had actually done the shooting at all, did not enter into his argument. We suspected, perhaps wrongly, that the son was assuming the blame for the sins of the father. This would at least explain why the old man had been taking the matter so to heart until it had become an obsession that was actually affecting his health. It was pitiful to have him implore us to intercede with the British authorities — a thing we could not possibly do.

All that we could do was to write a letter to the police officer, mentioning the fact that the accused boy had worked for us several seasons and had always been a good and honest servant. It was nothing more than a gesture, but it made old Aziz happy, and we sent him away with the assurance that when his son came out of jail his job at the dig, where he had been a basket boy on his father's clearing crew, would be waiting for him.

When a few weeks had elapsed, the lad's sentence was up. He was on the dig again, working quietly and industriously beside his parent, whose old spirit and happy smile had come back to him, proving that all was once more well with the house of Aziz. If our suspicions were correct, this touching little drama serves to illustrate how deep-rooted and sincere a thing filial loyalty is among these people.

One day — it happened to be a Friday, the Muhammedan rest day when we were all at home doing odd jobs about the office — Abdulla came in and told us that some itinerant entertainers were outside and wanted to put on a show. We went out to find an unpretentious group in the big courtyard, one woman dancer and two male musicians. The men were dressed in the usual native costume of long, ragged tunic and the flowing cloak or *aba* that is so universally worn in this country, and they wore *khefia*s wound about their heads. Under the woman's shabby brown cloak was a black cotton dress, embroidered in white, with a voluminous skirt reaching from a short tight bodice almost down to her ankles — quite reminiscent of a European style several decades past. She wore black cotton stockings and down-at-the-heel European slippers, the straps of which had been cut off. Her head was bound with the usual black silk kerchief, old and ragged in this case, and adorned with silver ornaments at odd angles. Her beads and bracelets were confusing both in variety and number, and she had rings on almost every finger.

Mrs. Wilensky and I were keen to see what kind of a show they could put on; so they were given leave to go ahead. Abdulla brought chairs, and we sat down to wait, while the musicians tuned up and the dancer prepared herself for the performance by shedding her *aba* and shoes, exposing a toe or two coming through the cotton stockings. The musicians squatted on the ground, holding their strange-looking instruments in front of them. One had a sort of elongated drum, covered with hide; the other, a primitive lute with only one string. *Webster* says that the Arabic *al-'ud* (the lute) was originally of wood. This fellow's may have been one of the originals, judging from the sounds that issued from it, and the accompanying rhythm from his companion's drum was almost aboriginal. The woman listened to the music for a while, adjusting her belt and then slowly began the dance, keeping time with a pair of copper castanets. The dance was simple, with rhythmic movements of head, shoulders, hips and arms; but the effect would have been quite nice if she had been graceful, which she was not.

Our sentries and household staff enjoyed the show, too, watching it from where they had congregated in the background, squatting against the wall. Every now and then the dancer stopped and asked for *baksheesh*. We gave her some pieces of silver, hoping that the reward would inspire her to greater activity and variation, but it didn't. After she had collected three rupees, we decided that we had seen all she knew about dancing, and told her to stop. She didn't like this very much, but even she could see that she wasn't exactly what might be called a sensation as far as we were concerned, so she tried something else. She picked up one of her slippers, and in the most pitiful manner showed it to us, asking Mrs. Wilensky and me to give her our shoes. It was very sad, but it didn't work, either. Mrs. Wilensky's Paris brogues, and my Chicago boots were too precious to be parted with; but when we refused, the woman began to claw at our clothing — which is an unpleasant trick beggars in that country seem to have. We didn't like it, and so left her for Abdulla to shoo off, still talking and gesticulating.

It didn't take him long to send them packing, but that wasn't the last we were to hear of our itinerant entertainers. A couple of days later Ahmet told us a tale which reveals the astounding gullibility of our villagers — even of such an intelligent one as Ahmet who should have known better. His father, who was popularly believed to be at least a hundred years old, had been blind for years. It was a pity, considering the patriarch's age and the fact that he still found comparative contentment in a sightless existence, that his family could not be satisfied to leave him alone. However, hope springs eternal and one of the gypsies said that he could make the lame walk and the blind see. Apparently he thought himself versed in the art of medicine as well as music, although as it happened, he knew even less about the former than about the latter, and was a thoroughgoing rascal. For a paltry ten rupees he would cure Ahmet's father of his blindness. Ten rupees in reality was a large sum, it meant a week's wages to Ahmet. But he was a dutiful son, and his family was eager for a miracle, so it was agreed and the hocus pocus began.

First it must be understood — and this the charlatan impressed well — that if instructions were not followed to the letter, he could not be responsible for results. Then he plastered the old man's eyes with some sticky substance made of crushed dates and heaven knows what else. This was all, except that the patient must be put to bed and kept *absolutely still* for three days and nights, after which time he would see again.

They put the old man on his couch, and Ahmet's mother took the precaution of sewing her husband's clothing to the mattress so that he could not move. All this disturbed the father who didn't quite understand what was going on, and wasn't sure that he liked it. But his wife and sons quieted him, and presently he fell asleep.

All went well for a time; then he awoke, tried to move, found that he could not. His mind being cloudy, he imagined evil things. When he called for help those who came only tried to hold him fast to the bed, until absolute terror possessed him, and summoning all of his strength in one great effort, he wrenched himself free, and ran from the house swearing that his ungrateful family was trying to murder him because he was old and infirm. His sons brought him back, comforted him and quieted his fears; but the damage had been done. The spell was broken and they were afraid that their ten rupees had been wasted. After three days and nights had passed, and the dates and bandages had been removed, these qualms became reality. The old man was as blind as before. The musician, however, merely shrugged. If his instructions were not obeyed, he could not be blamed. To which flawless logic there seemed no answer; but Ahmet was very sorry about the whole affair. We were sorry too — that he had not told us before he spent his money.

It was rather a shock that Ahmet in particular, of all our natives, should have been so taken in. Such incidents persuade one of the difficulty in understanding these people. There are many examples to illustrate this gulf which separated us and which could never be completely bridged. I always felt that it was these things that have to do with the processes of the mind that set us apart from our villagers, not their rags and their superficial strangeness — for we must have been just as strange to them.

There was the case of the pregnant girl. To understand, one must realize that although the women of our village wore no veils to hide their features, they were circumspect to the point of negation. But sometimes, it seems, even in a place like this, a girl grows up to discover that conventions are galling to a free spirit. Therefore, unheard of though it was, this girl had been fond of smiling at the men. Again it was Ahmet who told the story — Ahmet who possessed more of the milk of human kindness than most Turkoman, and a greater understanding of our ideas of right and wrong. It was the year before when he had come to the *Sahib* in great agitation to say that there was a girl in the village whose father was going to kill her. Surely there must be some mistake; these villagers are kindly people. But no, Ahmet insisted that there was no mistake and no doubt. The reason being that her stomach was swelling suspiciously, and she was not married. That, of course, would be a problem almost anywhere in the world, and here it seemed to be a matter of life and death.

It was an open secret throughout the village that the author of the trouble was a certain particularly unpleasant young man of a well-to-do family. His position as the son of property made it impossible to bring him to justice. In this country nothing would have been done to him anyway, for the fault was considered to be the girl's, completely and entirely.

We always were loath to meddle in native affairs, but to allow this girl to be murdered without interference would have been going too far. Besides, Ahmet was so positive that they were going to kill the girl, and said so in a dramatic fashion, that he succeeded in getting the whole Expedition worked up over it. Dick sat down and wrote a note to the British Police Officer in Kirkuk, telling him the whole story, saying that the Expedition felt that he should know so that he could take whatever steps he deemed necessary. Shortly afterwards a motor car arrived, bringing two Police Inspectors and a note of thanks from their Captain.

The Inspectors heard the story again and quizzed Ahmet for details. Then they proceeded to the village to talk to the father of the girl. When they left, the father had been persuaded — on threat of dire and instant punishment — to change his mind about killing his daughter.

This was a relief, but the Expedition did not feel so happy about it when they had discussed it with the Police Officer in Kirkuk and heard his comments. He was a man with a rare understanding of the native mind, and although he thanked them again officially for bringing the case to his attention, he said that it was doubtful if much could actually be done for the girl. Murder had been averted, but her life would be made unspeakably miserable, and no amount of interference could stop that. She had brought disgrace upon her family; but what was worse, she had made it impossible for them to find her a husband. No man would pay as much as a single goat for her now, and her father could be counted on to avenge the material loss and assuage his disappointment by treating her cruelly. This would be her situation for as long as she lived, or stayed in the community.

The only possible salvation would be to take her away from her family — but what then? In this country a woman can't go out and earn her own living decently. If she were taken away it would only mean that she would gravitate to some brothel in Kirkuk, Basrah, or Baghdad. Perhaps it would have been better to have allowed her people to fulfill their ancient customs. It is so easy to make matters worse by interfering.

Then this year, when something reminded us of the episode, we enquired of Ahmet about the girl with the large stomach. He remembered her and said quite casually that she was all right now. Of course, we couldn't let it drop there. Curiosity is too impelling. And so the "happy ending" was told — if you can call it that. The girl's stomach had grown larger and larger until springtime had come. Spring with its soft sweetness and its luxuriantly fleeting desert pasturage is always the signal for the villagers to quit the restraint of mud walls, and take themselves and their flocks into the desert for a few brief weeks. They go either in groups or singly, so it was not strange that this girl should accompany her father and his flocks, nor that they should separate themselves from the other villagers and be quite lost to their world for several weeks. At the beginning of summer when they returned to Tarkhalan, the girl's swelling had disappeared. She was quite normal again. But the child? There was no child. Perhaps it had been colic.

Ahmet's manner as he said this was so disarming, so intentionally candid that we thought it best to agree. If it could erase the girl's shame, any fabrication, even one out of the mind of a cruel and greedy father, had a right to go unquestioned. At least, it was probably a more satisfactory conclusion to all concerned than any we might have devised, for now the girl was free to be married, and probably would be some day. So there was nothing to be said. Only we couldn't help wondering what enormities and cruelties were endured in the vast silence of the desert, and stifled by its immensity.

CHAPTER IX

Thank God It's Friday

Activity on the dig reached a mid-season level; but there were occasional moments of excitement, as when a whole group of pig-like, gaping-mouthed, grotesque zoomorphic jars came out of the temple well. Because of their short legs and large heads, someone — I think it was Jasim who had a delightful sense of humor — dubbed them "Goomish jars." The dog, Goomish, couldn't have been very proud of it, but the name soon became a fixed part of the workmen's vocabulary. With these four or five practically complete examples from the well, and innumerable broken fragments of "Goomish jars" which were constantly coming from various other sections of the dig to be gradually pieced together — a toe added here and an ear there — the menagerie on our storeroom shelves was growing.

Besides the ugly "Goomishes," whose fat bellies were nothing more than simple "wheel thrown" pottery jars of the common household type, and whose crude features, legs, and tails had been fashioned by hand and plastered over this homely base, there were the more whimsically humorous figurines. These, too, were crude but they were charming, like children's toys which they may indeed have been — miniature horses, sheep, stags that stood quietly on the shelves and yet always managed to give the impression that they had just stopped prancing and capering when they heard your steps outside the door.

These figurines were delightful, and even the "Goomishes" amusing, but we realized that they could not be called important finds. They had never been fashioned by the sensitive fingers of a true sculptor; and yet we know that Nuzi had had its sculptors, men of real genius. A green glazed lion stands in the Fogg Museum in Cambridge, Massachusetts, a red pottery and yellow glazed lion in the University Museum in Philadelphia, in eloquent if silent testimony of this fact. And then, if the slightest doubt remained, I could, like a small boy who had saved the frosting of the cake until the last, point to the magnificent wall plaque fashioned in the form of a boar's head, which hangs in the National Museum in Baghdad. Its subtlety of line, the power achieved through simplification, and above all the direct and knowing technique of modeling bespeaks skilled hands. There is nothing crude or fumbling about these three beautiful examples of the Nuzi sculptor's art. They had been part of the temple furnishing, overlooked or kicked aside when the Assyrians looted Nuzi. And they all had come to light the year before, after so many centuries of indignity, lying on their sides among the debris of the Temple courtyard, or in fragments down its well, and buried deep within the *tepa* where Abu Yorgan had, in recent times, ploughed and sewn his grain.

So it was that we were always hopeful of similar and even greater finds. If these splendid creatures were mere attributes of Ishtar, what might the statue of the goddess herself be like? Sheathed in finely pounded gold leaf perhaps? Unhappy thought, for then the conquering Assyrians would surely have torn her from her pedestal and carried her away. But we continued to hope.

In the face of such aspirations, the work-a-day level into which our activities settled might seem disappointing. But time, marching on quiet, rapid feet brought a certain comfortable monotony to our lives. For days nothing exceptional would occur. The men would be at work on the dig by seven in the morning and would return at evening with a car full of the usual run of antiques — pottery to be washed and mended, baskets full of sherds, a few spindle whorls and perhaps another "Goomish" jar. The highly important scientific work of wall-tracing and recording the ancient plans went on as a matter of course. Occasionally, however, they would have a story to tell at tea time.

There was one about Jasim, an incident which developed almost into a feud. It seems that Jasim, who had been working on a pavement on the far side of the *tepa*, had gone to the deep room during the morning *pidost* to visit with his friends there, and also to see how their work was progressing. He had a somewhat proprietorial attitude about the deep room, because he had worked there for some time before a particularly delicate task in another section had called him away; and this uncommon concern of his proved to be both fortunate and unfortunate. His sharp eyes saw what the others had missed: a tiny edge of something, barely showing above the surrounding dirt. Curiosity coupled with ego prompted a personal investigation, although he really had no right to trespass on someone else's territory. Had he been strictly ethical about it, he would have called attention to the object, and let it go at that; but he didn't. A few deft knife strokes uncovered the prize, and he held in his hand a strange-looking tablet-like object. Pandemonium ensued, and the *Sahib*s were called to the scene. The object proved to be not a tablet, but a little hard-baked square of fine, light-colored clay, on whose surface tiny animals were incised. A little impromptu cleaning — safe because the clay was hard baked — disclosed the fact that there were small grooves running in from the edge of the block to each figure or group of figures, and at the top of each design a minute half-circle was also incised. Jasim had found one half of a clay mould which must have been used in antiquity to cast miniature metal amulets. Perhaps they weren't really amulets, but merely decorative minutiae which our ancients suspended about their persons on cords, or sewed upon their garments to satisfy the undying human love of adornment. In any case, the minuscule proportions of the intaglios precluded the faintest possibility of our finding any of the finished models, for our climate was not favorable to the preservation of metals. In the case of such delicate figures, even if fragments were found, they would certainly be corroded, patinated beyond recognition. But with the original mould in hand, we had not only the proof that such decorative objects once existed, but also their very shapes.

It was an important find, and that was what made trouble for Jasim. A substantial *baksheesh* was due him for finding the object; but on the other hand, he had no business to have found it. He had cheated Ahmet Hama out of the reward. However, Jasim got the *baksheesh,* and he could fight the matter out according to his own code. The affair didn't add to his popularity among the other workmen, particularly since he was a desert Arab and most of the rest were Turkish or Kurdish villagers.

However, that was Jasim's affair. The mould was the important thing to us as we clustered around the tea table to admire it, and Mr. Wilensky went to get some plasticine clay to make an impression. We were familiar with the superb intaglio technique of the ancients from their cylinder seals, and so the delicate modeling of these tiny animals did not surprise us. And they turned out in brave array to be a delightful little circus indeed: a plasticine bull, lion, gazelle, common house-fly, fishes and bird; but best of all was the horse. The mould had come from a Ga-Sur level, and this was early for the horse.

So our category of animals known to this region in antiquity was enlarged. With the exception of the lion, the animals on the mould, or their descendants, are still fairly common in the vicinity today. However, on our storeroom shelves we had the bones of a Nuzi elephant, and the skull of a pre-Nuzi crocodile. I couldn't help thinking with amusement how, although the sight of either of these two creatures in the flesh would fill our villagers with terror, and startling though the discovery of their remains had been even to us, this tiny horse — common and familiar beast though he was — delighted us far more. All because he came from Ga-Sur, which is early, very early for the horse! Archaeologists are funny that way.

So the days on the dig were not without their high spots, even during periods of comparative lull. Although the cache of tablets from the deep room had apparently been exhausted, and early horses can't be expected to prance from the earth every day, the routine tasks which yielded material of purely scientific interest proceeded. We could not let our insatiable appetite for archaeological thrills blind us to the even more substantial importance of routine work. And we reminded each other again that after all we were not treasure hunters.

Mail day twice a week took on exaggerated importance. We tried to manage to send Muhammed to town for provisions on these days; but if he did not get our *posta,* Mullah Ali would usually be kind and understanding enough to send it out to us in one of his cars. It usually arrived around tea time, and conversation was likely to become desultory while everyone was listening for the sound of a motor at our gates. It was inevitable that this precious loot from the post office should often leave someone disappointed, and there were times when we all went begging for mail. Those days we were likely to break our self-imposed rule of "no sandwiches" for tea, and order Sammy to make up a plateful, thereby finding consolation in simple gastronomical pleasures. Or we would raid the cupboard and put together a snack with soda biscuits and tinned cheese.

After tea and just at sunset, the desire to walk frequently took us out of our compound. At that hour the open world would have found its voice in a subdued concatenation of sounds which came from all directions and grew in volume as it converged towards the village, louder and louder with approaching nearness, until each separate sound emerged and identified itself over and above the incessant barking of the village dogs, the baaing of sheep, the thud of cattle's hoofs on the hard clay roads, the laugh of a shepherd, the call of a bird. This was the time, just at the close of the day when the flocks were being herded in from adjacent fields, that the village woke in a babel of noise and activity. But the mood was past as startling as it had come, and the countryside sank within its mute familiar quietude again, and only the occasional sharp bark of a heedless dog disturbed its reverie. During these evening rambles we usually went over the *waddi* bridge and down the donkey road away from the village. Dick and I enjoyed the peaceful freedom of the plains, whose brown tones took on a deeper warmth with twilight. And along other paths that cut through the fields we would often see the remote figures of our expedition mates, who were also enjoying the intimate solitude of the hour.

Over our heads the saucer-dome of the sky curved gently down to the mountains that hemmed the earth's horizontal reaches. The dark purple peaks that fringed our little world seemed very far away. Behind and above them the soft pastel memories of a sun that had set, faded slowly into gray, while behind us the sky was salmon and flame with afterglow. Then quite abruptly the stars pierced through, and as we turned homeward, a great full moon rose rapidly behind Pir Magudrun to the northeast, silhouetting that rugged peak in dark relief against her own bright face, until at last she leaped free and sailed triumphantly into the open sky. Here, in this land where the people live by the lunar months of the Muhammedan calendar, it was strange how time seemed to be accelerated, and how often the mood surprised us by rising round and full.

After supper had been eaten and the white cloth given way to the gay Indian print which transformed our dining room into a living room, we often got out the ping-pong net or a gaming board which vaguely resembled Parchesi. The table was only wide enough to accommodate half of the ping-pong net, so our style in that game was somewhat cramped; but competition was keen all the same. Then Abdulla would be summoned to retrieve stray balls, and when we really got warmed up anyone who craved peace and quiet had to retire to the sanctity of his own room. Bridge, for some reason, was in small favor; in fact, we were hardly aware of its evolution from Auction to Contract, although we plagued ourselves with every version of solitaire and double solitaire that anyone knew or could invent. With these diversions, and letter writing (quite necessary if we were to expect much in return from the twice-weekly *posta*), or the leisurely perusal of novels from Ali's bookshelf, the short evenings flew and our nine-o'clock bedtime was at hand.

It is easy to understand why we went to bed so early. At six o'clock on fair mornings, Abdulla would come to our room, light the kerosene lamp, and call softly to waken Dick; but not so softly that I didn't hear him, too. His summons was sufficiently sibilant.

"*Sahib, Sahib* Mr. Starr," he would say, hissing the s's, "six o'clock." Dick would mumble some unintelligible, muffled reply, but otherwise seem not to have heard. Then I would open one eye to see whether or not the lamp was smoking, which it always was, and I would have to call Abdulla back to attend to it. "Abdulla!" I would grumble, "*el fernous*!" On this second trip, he would invariably forget to close the door when he went out, and that meant shouting to him again, "Abdulla! *Sitt el bab*!!" By this time Dick would be completely discouraged about that last precious cat-nap he was trying to enjoy, and the bed clothing on his cot would begin to jump agitatedly — a sure sign that he was thinking about getting up. After that I would turn over in my little iron bed, away from the light of the lamp, and resume my slumbers, heedless of the faint clatter of dishes and silverware that came from the direction of the dining room, where Abdulla was setting the breakfast table. Some time later, the little sparrows, who had been the sole occupants of our house during the long summer and couldn't accustom themselves to the idea of being dispossessed, came to sit on the bars outside the open window. With endless cheeping and chatter they dared one another to fly inside, and the noisy whirr of their wings about my ears made further rest impossible. And so my day would commence.

This program varied only on Fridays (our Muhammedan day of rest), and on mornings when a gracious downpour of rain made work on the dig impractical. Then the men could also enjoy a day at home, with the accompanying luxury of a late morning sleep. On Fridays we always took full advantage of the opportunity to be lazy, with breakfast at any hour we cared for it, and then, not much later, a large early-afternoon luncheon. For these occasions, Sammy's specialty of the day was always *pilau*, which is another reason for a week-long anticipation of Friday. *Pilau* is a delectable Persian dish built over a heaping foundation of buttered rice and chicken joints, with a sprinkled garnish of crisply fried onions, raisins, and toasted almonds.

In the afternoon, the village always called us; and we would walk idly in that direction in quest of new adventure. As we proceeded, we always picked up a gallery of loitering natives — mostly old friends from the dig, for this was also their day of rest. Each was our willing guide, each would have welcomed the opportunity to be our host if we would only step into his courtyard, honor his house with our presence. But we were looking for something slightly more exciting than the usual social call, which is apt to be tiresome when one is not fully conversant with the language. Besides, they would have insisted upon bringing out precious little offerings of nuts and cakes, which we would find impossible to refuse and still more impossible to eat — especially after the *pilau*. No, we would not be sidetracked. Instead, we asked to be directed to the house of one Ali ibn Mustafa, where the business of weaving would be going on, despite the holiday.

Ali ibn Mustafa was the brother of our water boy, Zen Abdin. He also used to work for us until he had an unfortunate accident on the dig. A heavy mud wall, weakened by a lower stratum of ancient ash which cut under it, had toppled on his back. He had been rushed to the hospital, where he was treated for several weeks.[10] Of course, the Expedition paid his hospital expenses, and he was also pensioned for the rest of the year on half pay. The poor fellow had expected no such fair treatment, and was so delighted by it that he did not regard the accident as a misfortune. As for the rest of the villagers, no one was sorry for him because his family was quite well off anyway — they owned a lot of sheep. Now he spent his time in the comparatively easy, profitable occupation of weaving bright strips of woolen cloth for blankets. The long narrow room in which he worked contained two looms; one he operated himself, and the other was used by a third brother whose affliction was deafness. The looms were primitive contraptions of wood, set up on the earth floor, with the pedals that controlled the pattern sunk into a pit. The operator sat comfortably on the ground, with his feet in the pit and his arms free to throw the shuttle back and forth. Ali's outfit was at the right in one end of the room, his brother's at the left in the other end; the coarse, woolen threads of the warp were stretched along the floor in gay parallel lines, completely filling what space remained; and great bundles of yarn, in all the colors that may have been in Jacob's coat, cluttered every corner and was stored in neat fat balls in niches within the thick mud walls of the building.

The weavers greeted us warmly, but continued with their work when we asked them to do so. They were eager to explain anything we didn't understand, and didn't seem in the least to mind the intrusion, even when some of the children we had picked up along the way scrambled carelessly over the blanket warp, and the grown-ups crowded into the room until its walls bulged. Even Goomish was not unwelcome because he came with us.

On the way home we stopped in the large bare field at the edge of the village to watch some games of marbles. The game is played here with oversize marbles, and it is not limited to the youngsters, as it is in the West. Quite as often as not, grown men play in keen competition for the bets that have been placed. They are natural gamblers, these natives. The marbles are homemade, by beating soft stones together until they are roughly shaped to size; they are then smoothed, polished, and made perfectly spherical by rolling them around inside of a pottery vessel. Wise older brothers have taught tiny ones that a pretty noise can be made by clinking two stones together; and it is seldom one sees wee children in Tarkhalan without this substitute for a rattle. Consequently, half of the actual work of marble making is accomplished by the youngest generation.

Another common game in Iraq is a kind of dice-throwing. Only here the dice are not the conventional cubes we know — which, by the way, were also used by the ancients, in variety with tiny pyramids and other oddly shaped instruments of chance — but they are sheep's knuckle bones, dry and polished

---

10 [See "Letters from the Field, 1927-1930," no. 35, 17 November 1929, p. 76.]

through long use. These are thrown to the ground, and the point is made or lost by which way they come to rest: on smooth or knobby side. Still another game resembles checkers or chess. The board is marked out on the flat ground in rough squares, and the rival chessmen may be small stones, beans, or nuts, whichever happen to be available. On fair Fridays all of these games would be in progress in the untilled fields at the edge of the village. Sometimes there would be broad-jumping or leaping contests, too, when sheer exuberation of spirit had to be worked off.

Knowing that we were homeward bound, most of the following that had been so faithful during our sally into the village, deserted us in favor of the sports. Only Jobar, the foolish shepherd, stuck. He generally followed us all the way back and into our courtyard, and would come into the house to stay for hours on the slightest, even imagined, encouragement. He was forever offering to me, with a great show of generosity, his goats, his lambs, his dog — any and every tempting *baksheesh* he could think of. None of these things were accepted. It was quite understood that they would not be; but that didn't prevent him from getting to the point at last, and asking for a return *baksheesh*. It might be a pair of socks, a pair of shoes, or a new coat that he wanted. Each time it was something different, but each time it was something.

Home again we left Jobar, more often than not disappointed, standing in the courtyard. He would not come inside unless he was asked, but we had had enough of him for one day. Abdulla brought tea — high tea on Friday, with cake and sandwiches.

Rainy days were somewhat different. Often we couldn't budge outside of the house, even to go to some other part of our compound, without raincoats and gum boots. If the rain stopped, as it often did in the late afternoon, gum boots were still needed. One fortunate thing was that the roof did not leak, as, I was told, it had in other years. During the excessively hot summers the outer clay covering would tend to crack, leaving small fissures for rain to seep through during the wet season. When this happened, they used to send some of the servants topside, to skate on the wet roof, thereby forcing the thick mud down into the cracks, and stopping the deluge within. The boys must have loved that job, for none of the natives seemed in the least to mind the rain. Why should they? The more rain, the better the crops would be in the spring, so they had learned to look upon stormy weather as something to be glad about; even a flood, which sometimes occurred to wipe out half the village, was philosophically received as a blessing from Allah. It was easy enough to build a new mud house, but it was beyond human accomplishment to create abundant precipitation.

Our roof proving water-tight this year, however, we were as dry and cozy as we might wish as long as we stayed indoors. Complete hibernation wasn't convenient; but our compound was compact, and only a quick dash was needed to get from one part to another. Dick spent most of a rainy day in his tiny office, which opened onto the small courtyard, and had windows overlooking the large service court.

On sunny days the donkey would have been out there, ferociously attacking the chickens or turkeys who fled from his charges, and dodged his hoofs. But when it rained he took refuge in the outbuilding where Kerim and Abdulla slept. So that the only forms of life visible would be the turkeys and chickens, huddled in miserable groups, and our three white ducks, who squealed with pleasure and paddled ecstatically in the mud. And Dick sat at his desk behind the windows, too busy doing accounts and other routine jobs to enter into any of their debates as to whether the rain was indeed the blessing or the curse of Allah. Goomish snored contentedly in the corner. He recognized and took advantage of the fact that his superior breeding was his open sesame. The more uncouth Nuzi and Alaj huddled together in the semi-shelter of the arched passage outside.

Charles, made restless by forced inactivity, paced up and down, demanding a job — any job — or else just gave in and went to sleep in his room next door. Mr. Wilensky was always occupied with his instruments and drawing table in the long office at the other side of the small courtyard; and his wife was there too, catching up in the business of cataloguing the objects from the dig; while Muhammed fussed and puttered around the gluepot on the primus stove at the table in the center of the room, mending pottery. It was one of my self-appointed jobs to supervise Muhammed's work; and although I hadn't his patience, and couldn't stick by the potsherds for hours on end as he did, I hovered in and out around the gluepot.

It was here, one very wet afternoon, that I made my major archaeological discovery. I am justly proud of it, for the end result stands in somewhat obscure glory in the Semitic Museum at Harvard University. A batch of incised sherds had come in from the dig, and when they had been washed and dried and were ready for mending, I rescued them from Muhammed's clutches — as I always did the finer pieces. This one proved to be exasperating because the sherds couldn't be sorted according to color. They had been burned by fire in antiquity, *after* the object had been shattered. When the last loose sherd was in place, however, I held in my hand a beautiful example of realistic pottery in the form of a waterfowl. The different kinds of feathering were daintily incised on the different parts of its hollow body, and even its webbed feet were represented, drawn on the bottom of the jar in precisely the manner in which a duck would tuck up his feet when floating on a pond. Although the body was hollow and bore the marks of the potter's wheel inside, the billed head was modeled in the round. Only the tail was missing. I was carrying my prize proudly across the courtyard to show Dick and to lament about the lost tail, when I suddenly remembered something. I changed my course and went instead to the storeroom. What I remembered was that amongst the numerous odd and unfittable "Goomish" fragments one had borne the black stains of ancient burning. I recalled that it had looked just like a crude "Goomish" paw, but — well, maybe it wasn't. And when it turned out indeed to be the missing member of my bird jar, I thought myself pretty smart!

Then Abdulla popped his head into the doorway with the summons to tea. Astute Sammy, realizing that the rain might have dampened our spirits, had provided a cake in spite of the fact that this was not Friday. Tea always revived us all sufficiently to take part in some animated discussion, the subject of which might be anything under the sun, and today it was my bird jar — which I insist upon calling a duck although Dick says it isn't a duck at all.

CHAPTER X

Christmas and New Year's Festivities

The *posta* brought a reminder that Christmas was close upon us. There was a package from provident parents in America, which had made a record trip — probably because it had been mailed in plenty of time, anyway. It was hard not to peep into the alluring packets it contained, all wrapped in red and white tissue paper and tied with tinsel ribbons. So I stowed it quickly away in the farthest corner of our clothes cabinet to get it out of sight and away from temptation.

Its arrival, however, brought the Christmas spirit to our compound. From now on, there were secret conferences, whisperings, and a firm taboo against asking questions or noticing strange behavior. There were also frequent mysterious trips into Kirkuk.

Everyone had agreed that a repetition of the Thanksgiving breakfast would be just the thing for Christmas morning. Consequently, one fine afternoon a week or so before the great day, Dick and I made a special trip into town to duplicate the Thanksgiving order of tinned goods, procure appropriate decorations, and do our private Christmas shopping.

We were disappointed to find that our merchant friend, Mullah Ali, was mistaken about the date of our Christian fiesta; and, thinking that it came in January, had neglected to lay in the appropriate stock. It was too bad not to be able to buy from Ali, but time was too short to wait for him to order our Christmas tree from Baghdad, and we had to go elsewhere. Across the street at the Iraq Sporting Goods Depot, we found a tiny artificial table tree, with silver and gilt ornaments, and a string of tinsel to adorn it and also green and white and red paper streamers to hang around our dining room. Besides these suitable decorations, there was a black and white effigy of Felix the Cat, which would have been more appropriate for Hallowe'en but which we found irresistible. The combined stocks of Ali's store and the British Supply Company yielded up the necessary tins of sausages, kippered herring, and jelly. Cranberries in any form were still unheard of in Kirkuk, but marzipan, of all things, was on prominent display.

For the presents we went first to Kashi's — a branch shop recently opened by a Baghdad merchant. Kashi's shop in Baghdad is a joy, with its varied and fascinating contents. It is also, as far as I know, the only place in that metropolis where the prices are fair and fixed. It may indeed be the only place of its sort in the whole of Iraq. To our unimaginative Western minds this was a great advantage. We were so unused to haggling over prices that we soon tired of it as a sport, and found it only an unpleasant waste of time. Our hopes for finding all of our presents at Kashi's, however, were not fulfilled. We discovered that this Kirkuk branch had a very limited inventory, consisting mostly of rugs. We had decided against giving rugs for two reasons. First, good rugs were expensive, and second, since the Expedition members were necessarily travelling with a limited amount of luggage, we did not wish to be giving white elephants. One of the Kashi brothers, who was in charge at Kirkuk, looked after our needs with deference and patience, bringing out everything for us to see and examine. We made a mental note of three objects that pleased us, but we did not buy until we had seen what we might find in the bazaars and elsewhere.

Across the street, in a tailor's shop, there was a case full of trinkets — a sort of sideline to the tailoring trade. We looked these over carefully, but discovered only one object of unusual interest: a marvelously fashioned brass fish with a flexible body and red glass eyes. This we also left for further consideration and proceeded to the bazaar. Here we found nothing that seemed just right. After an hour or two of tramping and gazing, we returned to Kashi's, footsore and somewhat discouraged. The three objects we had seen there before and liked now became most desirable, and we bought them forthwith. The *paper-mâché,* painted Persian book cover, with its dainty human figures and its delicate design picked out on a gold background, we decided was to be for the Wilenskys; the two heavy, handsome round brass boxes decorated in Damascene workmanship, with silver inlay, had a masculine appeal. It remained only to decide which one should go to Dr. Meek, and which to Charles.

By this time, I had had quite enough shopping for one day, and Dick took me to Ali's hotel, ordered tea for me, and left me to rest and refreshment while he went out again on some mysterious errand. Remembering the taboo of the season, I asked no questions. I was secretly gloating because when we were in Baghdad in the autumn, he had seen a rare old travel book which he admired and longed to own, but felt that it was too much of a luxury to buy for himself. Consequently, a letter to the bookshop had solved my most important Christmas problem.

On the afternoon of the twenty-fourth, Mrs. Wilensky and I, with Abdulla's help, put up the paper streamers and the tree. When we were through, our dining room looked like a kindergarten schoolroom dressed up for the holidays. When the men came in from the dig, they were extravagant in their praise over our efforts. High tea, with fruit cake and sandwiches inaugurated the festivities. We found ourselves like a lot of children, all agog with suppressed excitement. The Wilenskys, for whom the season had none of the background of tradition it had for the rest of us, entered into the spirit of gaiety in sportsmanlike fashion.

In the midst of dinner that night, Mullah Ali arrived with a carload of presents and a perfect arbor of greenery which he had brought for us to decorate with. It was another proof that Christmas could be enjoyed and respected by those of other religions than our own. We urged him to join us in food, but he had already dined. He did accept coffee, however, as a sort of rite due to hospitality. He had brought individual presents for every member, and as we sat and talked, his servant carried in armful after armful of palm fronds, great boughs of lemon trees with the yellow fruit hanging, and laurel branches. It was an extravagant gesture. Ali must have denuded his garden for us. We were touched and grateful, but our continuous expressions of thanks seemed to embarrass the good man. As we finished dinner, and he his third small cup of coffee — the ceremonial number — he left us to dispose of his bounty as we desired. Then, with hammer, nails and string, and Abdulla's ready assistance, we fell to tacking palm fronds and laurel sprays against the whitewashed walls, and tying fruit-laded lemon boughs to the ceiling beams. In half an hour the dining room had been transformed for the second time that day — from a festive-looking schoolroom to an indoor garden. The floriate cheer supplied the finishing touch. In high spirits we played games, sang songs, told stories, while the long evening flew, and it was long past nine o'clock when we hung our Christmas stockings to the wooden bookshelf and went to bed.

On Christmas morning I woke up early enough to go stealthily out and weigh down the stockings with foolishness: tools from the workroom, a package of salt from the kitchen, and lots of tangerines which had been ordered up from Baghdad. From the bulginess I encountered, however, I understood that other jokers had been up betimes; but I refrained from investigating too closely. Hours later, when we had all assembled at approximately the same moment, we found that Abdulla had set the table for breakfast and that it had become mysteriously laden with packages. Most of the presents were wrapped in odd sheets of the *Baghdad Times*, because in whatever other respects the merchants of Kirkuk had been foresighted about this holiday of ours, they had all neglected to provide tissue-paper and red ribbon.

During the first general hubbub of "Good morning" and "Merry Christmas!" the door opened and Jasim came in, carrying a bundle of fox skins. He was on his way to Kirkuk to sell them, as Dick quickly explained before I had had a chance to mistake them for Christmas gifts and thank him for them. He had just dropped in for a courtesy call on his way to town. Muhammed was there too — a diminutive, beaming figure hovering about the doorway in his usual agitated manner. Only today, he was more pleased with himself and more embarrassed than ever. Of all our servants, Muhammed took greatest pleasure in our customs and holidays, particularly when there was giving and receiving of gifts. He was an inveterate gift-giver.

We hesitated, hardly knowing where to begin, but Muhammed took the matter into his own hands by pointing out to each in turn a particular present we must look at first — his gifts. They were embarrassingly grand gifts, too: brilliant red and yellow blankets, an ancient seal, and odd trinkets he had picked up in the bazaars, besides a collection of multi-colored socks of coarse goat's hair which his wife had knitted for us. Muhammed was as delighted about giving these presents as we were to receive them, and he almost burst with pride and joy over our expressions of admiration and thanks. Then, his big moment being over, he retired again to hover in the background and see what the other packages on the table might contain. And such grand things as did come out of them! There were yellow Persian boots with red tops, turned up toes, and tassels; boxes of imported sweetmeats; long-piled saddle-bags in soft colors; a delicately cut ancient cylinder seal; a pair of red wool slippers of local manufacture; enamelled Persian nose rings matched up so that they could be converted to earrings; and the Amara work. Those long-bearded Christian natives from Amara can fashion anything you wish in silver, and decorate it with designs from which they first etch out and then fill with black inlay. The effect is strikingly handsome. Dick received a cigarette case and a match box, both made beautiful and precious to him by designs copied from Nuzi cylinder seals. Inside of the cigarette case, which was from Charles, a dedicatory inscription was engraved. The gift was made all the more wonderful by the fact that the artisan, blindly copying a language he could not understand, had made a mistake in spelling. It read:

R.F.S. STARR
PEERLESS LEADER
EXTRRAORDINAIRE

The marvelous flexible brass fish with red eyes was now mine, along with everything else that I had seen and coveted, or might have coveted had I seen. That, and the fact that Dick was delighted with his book, made the morning perfect. We piled our treasures into convenient chairs, and when the hilarity over the nonsense in the stockings had subsided, we were ready for breakfast.

When Charles pulled out his chair a pitiful "ba-a-a" sounded from underneath the table. He investigated to find a tiny black goat tied by a red ribbon to one of the rungs. It was the most diminutive baby goat imaginable. I think that the Arab name for goat, *dik-dik*, is expressive, and this little *dik-dik* was obviously longing for home and mother. Never mind, after breakfast Charles would send him back — on loan — to his mother who lived with our Arab neighbors by the *waddi* bridge.

The pleasurable delay of opening the presents had given an edge to our appetites, and we were able to put away even more sausages, kippered herring, and pancakes than on Thanksgiving morning. Afterwards, we bundled into heavy jackets and voluminous fur-lined *farowa*s, and set out in the Expedition Ford for the traditional Christmas trip to the desert. We were packed in like sardines, so we decided to leave Muhammed in the village and risk a flat tire. Even a drizzly gray day couldn't dampen our spirits as we chased along the road past the *tepa* where Hurshied, the faithful guard, waved to us as we went by.

On the road beyond we passed an occasional shepherd with his flocks and his dogs. One of these was Abdulla's little brother, and he was accompanied by Abdulla's two huge twin hounds: Oslan [lion] and Kaplan [leopard]. I have never found out just what these names mean, but I take it that they are descriptive of lion-like strength; and the animals, bigger than police dogs but with something like their coloring and features, did not belie their names. They dashed at the car with savage ferocity, barking noisily. We had grown used to such a greeting from the native mongrels, and had ceased to pay much attention to it. But in this case Oslan — or Kaplan, I don't know which — miscalculated the distance relative to his own speed. Before we knew what was happening, there was a sickening thud as the wheels went over something fleshy, and the dog's bark turned to a yelp of pain. With a squeak of brakes we all craned out to see if we had killed the noble fellow; but before we could stop he was on his feet again, limping back towards the shepherd. So we proceeded, with a feeling of relief that no great harm had been done, (and Oslan, or perhaps it was Kaplan, never chased a motorcar again. He had escaped this time, but he had also learned his lesson).

A little farther on, even the donkey road came to an end, and we were in the desert. It gave one a great feeling of freedom and exhilaration to be able to throw off the hampering restrictions of roadway and path. We turned in any direction fancy dictated, making our own highway on the broad, flat plain, only taking care to skirt around the chuck-holes and pits that occur, even in the desert.

Here and there the noise of the motor soared up flocks of great blue heron. In awkward flight they took off the ground almost from a standstill, and great wings beat the air. When they had lifted their heavy bodies five or six feet off the ground, they made no further attempt for altitude, but circled slowly until we were past. Then they came down with delicate ease and grace. Since they are not much shot at, even by native hunters, their fear of human beings isn't very serious.

When we came to a deep *waddi* cut, now dry and deserted, we followed along its banks until we found the least precipitous-looking spot to cross. There we made a half-wide circle, turned at right angles to the ditch, and eased our way to the bottom. Then we groaned up the other side to level land again. We passed the tiny Arab village of Wiron Shahir where children ran and pointed at us, and more dogs barked; and a few kilometers farther, came to a large mound, which the natives call "Abu Kaouba." This had been our vague objective, if we had one at all. We gained speed as we approached the mound, raced up its steep sides triumphantly, and rattled to a breath-taking stop at the summit.

Abu Kaouba is not an artificial mound, created like our Yorgan Tepa by epochs burying each other; but is one of those paradoxical natural elevations that do occur in this desert country. Therefore, although we did scan its top and sides hopefully for interesting potsherds or a possible antique seal that might, in the case of an artificial mound, have been washed up by a recent rain, we found nothing. The modern native name for this place, being besides euphonious, has an amusing connotation. It is an example of the practical humor these people exert in coining titles. From what I could gather from our willing native sources, *kaouba* means an edible wild root that grows in certain spots in the desert in springtime. It must be something like a truffle, and since a great many of these grow on the slopes of this mound, it has been dubbed "the father of truffles." On a fine day it would be an ideal spot from which to enjoy a view of the surrounding desert; but now a persistent drizzle had set in, making even the results of our Christmas pictures uncertain. We decided to turn towards home;

but took a circuitous route back, and arrived thoroughly chilled and ready for a cup of hot tea.

For the auspicious occasion of Christmas dinner everyone dressed. I have never seen a solitary Englishman wearing a dinner coat in the fastness of tropical jungles, but I understand that it has been done. If so, I know why; it does something to one's morale. Anyway, our dining room looked so festive with its greenery, and we in our finery, and the table with its caviar canapes that we called Sammy in from the kitchen to see it all and to give him a vote of thanks for having slaved over our holiday menu. He looked smaller and blacker and even more perspiring than ever as he shyly opened the door. He was terribly pleased by this attention, and also terribly embarrassed. He deserved our compliments, because the dinner, from the canapes to the mince pie, seemed all anyone could wish for.

With Christmas falling on Thursday, and Friday being a natural holiday, the week passed quickly, and New Year was soon upon us. Gastronomically speaking, New Year was a repetition of Christmas. The only change in the menu was from turkey to duck. We had been able that season to procure only three ducks, and those after an extensive search that embraced that whole countryside. Perhaps the shortage was due to a certain mysterious duck malady which had been reported in the *Baghdad Times* as having taken innumerable Iraqi ducks off to a happier, wetter land. In any case, since it seemed unlikely that we would find any more, we had been saving our three for some special dinner. New Year's eve seemed to be the occasion, and on the preceding afternoon two of our ducks were scheduled to disappear from amongst the chickens and turkeys in the service courtyard. I had not been warned as to the exact hour of their demise, but in the middle of the afternoon there was a terrible rumpus outside, and Hiddir rushed in to get me, his turban falling agitatedly over one eye. I wasn't quite sure what was happening, but it seemed serious enough, so I followed where he led — to the service courtyard. There a tragic sight met my eyes. Kerim was standing in awkward silence with a pitiful little dead duck's body at his feet, and a second duck, alive and struggling, in his hands; the third duck was running back and forth at the other side of the courtyard, screaming like a demented thing. Hiddir explained that ducks were particularly sensitive creatures, and if we killed the second, the remaining brother would "weep himself to death." Not having been brought up on a farm, I can't vouch for the truth of this statement; but the spectacle was pitiable enough to move even me, to whom the mention of duck is more likely to conjure visions of Tour d'Argent than of the barnyard. I might have said, "Well, then kill all three," but I didn't have the heart. I said, "Use a chicken instead." And when Kerim freed the bird he had been holding, the sight of grief turned to happiness made the sacrifice worthwhile. We would let them have each other's company for a little while longer, and when they must go, they would go together. After dinner on New Year's eve the hours between nine and twelve were spent playing games. Being used to such early bedtimes, we found it hard to stay awake until the stroke of twelve. But finally our watches told us that the hour was at hand, and we clambered to the roof to fire off the sentry's gun in honor of another year. I knew the story of what had happened the year before when they had fired such a midnight volley into the desert.[11] The people of Tarkhalan live by the Muhammedan calendar, and the first day of January doesn't mean anything special to them. Therefore, when they were awakened to all hours by the noise of shots, the idea of merrymaking never occurred to them — they were sure that something dreadful was happening to the foreigners. As soon as it was humanly possible, they came, *en masse*, attired in all manner of hasty garb and armed with a strange assortment of lethal weapons. This prompt and loyal response to an imagined danger must have been both ludicrous and touching. They had all been invited to come inside, and Sammy had been routed out of bed to make coffee, and the whole affair had turned into a sort of impromptu *calabala* which had lasted for an hour or more. I was secretly hoping that the same thing would take place this year, but it didn't. It seems that one of our sentries had carefully warned the villagers that this was the date that the foreigners chose to make hullabaloo in the middle of the night. So it was with something akin to disappointment that we finally bowed to the inclemency of the midnight wind and went indoors with a simple exchange of "Happy New Year" to all.

---

11 [See "Letters from the Field, 1927-1930," no. 41, 7 January 1930, p. 84.]

CHAPTER XI

Baghdad Excursion

A welcome mid-season break in the routine came after the holidays, when Dick and I went down to Baghdad that he might attend the yearly meeting for Expedition Directors. It was a friendly, get-together sort of meeting, sponsored by the Department of Antiquities of the Iraq government, for the purpose of furthering cooperation between the Expeditions, and for the discussion of helpful ideas. Armed with one of Sammy's put-up suppers of chicken sandwiches, hard boiled eggs and cake, we boarded the train just at dusk. The individual compartments are very comfortable, much like those on European trains, except that the seats run the long way of the car instead of across. There are two such leather upholstered seats, couches really, since one sleeps on them at night, in each compartment. It was well that there was plenty of space, for we couldn't stow all of our luggage underneath these low couches — our hand baggage, two great rolls of bedding rented from the Railway Company, and several coarse native blankets of our own which we had brought in case the night turned out to be particularly cold.

The night run along this road has the advantage of seeming shorter than the day run, but the accompanying darkness makes it less interesting. Even when the train slowed down and jerked to a stop at the little wayside stations, we couldn't see much; but we opened the window to throw the crusts from our supper out to station dogs — scavengers who make a practice of meeting all the trains in the hope of just such a hand-out. And when we came to the Diyala region, where a tiny river runs through great rocky bluffs, we were fast asleep. The rocks thereabout are of some soft formation, for they are so thoroughly honeycombed below and so eroded from above, that, with very little imagination, one can make out of nature's carving great herds of buffalo or elephant, their heads down, flanks close, charging the passing train. But they are beasts of daylight. If they continue to charge menacingly down during the night, we did not know it.

When we woke up very early in the morning and looked out, we saw that we were passing cemeteries full of miniature pointed-roofed houses, just on the outskirts of Baghdad. I don't know what native custom of belief prompts the construction of such tiny chapels over every grave. Perhaps they are to house the souls of the dead; but their only visible occupants are jackals. Beyond these graveyards, the city loomed.

In the station the representatives of different hotels greeted us like long lost friends. We had written to the River Front Hotel to reserve our old room — the establishment boasted eight rooms in all, and this was the only one that contained a bathtub. So we singled out the porter from the River Front, allowed him to claim us and put our bags into his car. We were tooted through the narrow little ways by the station and down the broad thoroughfare of New Street, to the corner by the Maude Bridge where the River Front Hotel now occupies the building that used to house the old Y.M.C.A. Even at that early hour the streets were not deserted, but neither were they crowded as they would be later in the day. It was a blow to discover that our coveted room with bath had been rented by the month to the representative of Dunlop Tyres. We had to be content with a room with a fireplace; but judging from the weather which was bleak and cold, and considering the fact that there was no central heating plant, perhaps we had the best of the bargain after all.

The next day while Dick was attending the meeting, I looked around Kashi's shop on New Street, and found all manner of things to help dissolve a Christmas check from home. There was a lovely old pewter-plated copper tray with etched fish swimming all over its border, a Persian pewter teapot, odd, sharp paper shears, silk *abas* — those voluminous native cloaks — in all the colors of the spectrum, interwoven with gold or silver threads. In the Cashmere Shop down by the American Consulate, were gold and lapis lazuli colored *papier-mâché* rose bowls lined with brass, little finger bowls and trays and boxes of the same material, gold embroidered slippers and beads of turquoise chips set into a black paste. I could see that I was not going to have any trouble spending my money.

Besides, there was Muhammed's request to remember. He wanted us to bring him a new fez as *baksheesh* for the Id-el-Fitr — a Muhammedan holiday which occurs at the end of Ramazan and which he called his "Christmas." This errand would take me to the bazaar, but I waited until Dick was free to go along, for he always enjoyed a visit to the *suq* as much as I did. To get there, we stepped into an *arabana*, which is Baghdad's equivalent to a taxi, and as we jogged comfortably down New Street I remarked again how strange this thoroughfare looks. In some ways it is astonishingly modern; it was widened and paved during the war to facilitate the passage of troops through the city. Wartime disregard of private property is still in evidence. Many of the buildings had been literally cut in two when the street was widened, and the owners have either been too poor or too careless to remodel them. I noticed more than one second story front bedroom which had been sliced in two and left that way, reminding one of an open-fronted doll's house.

Then the carriage turned out of New Street, and we paid the *arabanchi* off at the entrance of the bazaar, to proceed on foot for as many miles as we might please through the crooked, picturesque alleyways, teeming with the activity of barter and exchange. We had entered a different world, a different age. Here, except when one's eye happened to light on some incongruous-looking, foreign-made article proudly displayed for sale, is the Baghdad of which one dreams — filled with all of the glamour and some of the filth of countless ages of urban life, countless generations of merchants: the legendary haunts of that famous man-about-town and adventurer, Harun-al-Rashid.

Comparison made one little bazaar which we knew so well in Kirkuk seem like a country fair. Not only was it insignificant in size when compared to the *suq* of Baghdad, but it also lacked the essential flavor of sophistication. Here every available inch on either side of the passage was cramped and overflowing with merchandise. The majority of the shops were those familiar open-fronted stalls; but there were also occasional indoor establishments of more pretentious nature, where obsequious merchants would first have coffee brought for you, and then would proceed to spread at your feet all of the magic carpets of the East — if you believed what they said, and were willing to spend so much time and let them go to so much trouble. After due ceremony and appropriately impressive secrecy, you might even be shown a cylinder seal or a golden bauble that had been new when Babylon was young. Not wishing to buy rugs, however, we refused to be enticed into these dens of persuasion, preferring to wander in the everlasting twilight of the passages and alleys that make up the bazaar, spanned by ancient vaulting, vaulting that rose more gracefully and to dizzier heights than any we know in Kirkuk.

The things one found to buy here, too, were different. There were blankets animated by tiny men driving tiny camels past miniature mosques; and even those which were decorated merely by the conventional plaids and stripes seemed to be more alluring with more color schemes, more daring. Then aimlessly turning a corner, we came upon the bazaar of the chests. Here, piled three deep, were all sorts of chests; some new, some old, some beautiful, some ugly, some ordinary, some rare. The most attractive were the old Indian Dower chests. They are made of teak, studded with brass nails and plaques of etched brass. They are old, having found their way into the City of the Caliphs a hundred years or more ago, brought by Indian brides who came to live beside the Tigris. Those one finds in the bazaar have all been reconstructed to some degree, but it is intriguing nevertheless to think of the bridal dower they once held — shawls from Cashmere, Damascene silks, jewels, perhaps...

But what is the din we hear in the distance? As we walked along it grew louder and louder until we had to shout to make ourselves heard. It turned out to be the metalworkers' bazaar — a broad street where men squatted beside their anvils hammering copper and brass into all manner of useful vessels of every size and shape. They were swift and clever at their work, and it was so interesting to watch the rough metal taking shape, the processes of polishing and plating the finished products with pewter, that we might have remained for hours if the racket hadn't been so trying.

Wandering through the *suq* this way, we enjoyed ourselves thoroughly, but we had completely lost our sense of direction, and it was quite by accident that we chanced upon one of the outer gates. Quite forgetting about poor Muhammed's fez, we passed through these ancient portals, which are locked at night against thieves and vandals, and stepped into a travelled street once more. My feet were aching and it was well that there was no difficulty in finding a carriage to take us back to the hotel.

After the Dig Director's meetings were over, we decided to spend the rest of our week's holiday with a flying trip to Kermanshah. I wanted a glimpse of Persia; and besides, it had started to rain in Baghdad, and at this season it might keep on raining for a month. Arrangements for airplane tickets were made at Cook's, but we would have to wait for telegraphic confirmation of our reservations to come from Kermanshah. We should have the reply by mid-afternoon. At lunch time, Dick happened to bring with him a copy of the day's *Baghdad Times*. In it, quite by chance, he discovered an insignificant two-inch report of an outbreak of plague in Persia. We telephoned to the American Consul and spent the next half hour in suspense, waiting for him to get exact information as to the state of affairs. When his call came, it wasn't too encouraging. We could go to Kermanshah if we wanted, but the Persian-Russian border had already been quarantined, and the Iraq-Persian border might be at any time. If we had had the "shots" against the plague, it would be all right, but if we had not, we faced the possibility of sitting in a quarantine tent on the border for three weeks, before being allowed back into Iraq. We had not been inoculated, and the time was too short now, even if we felt that three days in Kermanshah warranted the discomfiture. Dick rushed around to Cook's to cancel our reservations.

Our next choice for holiday adventure was a river trip down the Tigris to Basra. When we went to inquire about boats, we found that even that alternative was denied us. There was no boat leaving immediately; to wait for the boat down and then wait in Basra for the first boat back would mean taking more time than we could afford to spare from the dig. Even if we went one way by railroad, we could not make it. *Eh wallah, wallah*, "so be it if it is the Will of Allah," it looked as though we were destined to spend our vacation in Baghdad, and a rainy one at that.

Time, however, did not drag. Between showers we decided to see the city again, so we took a car through devious, narrow streets, swarming with people in all manner of dress. There were Kurds from the mountains, big fellows with tremendous headgear, making them look top-heavy, in spite of their six feet or more of stature; Arabs wearing every degree of ragged or fine headcloth and cloak; city men in European clothes and red fezes, some of which were wound about with green cloth to show that their wearer was a descendant of the Prophet; dirty children, who either stared or smiled and touched their foreheads in greeting as we passed; and always a smattering of shrouded women. Mixed in with the crowding humanity were the inevitable donkeys, plodding along with great pack loads, or carrying a man or a boy on their backs. All this in the streets, not to mention the water buffalo — great black beasts, that look fearsome with their horns lying back along their necks — made motoring slow and difficult, particularly since man and beast alike were extremely casual about the possibility of being run down. But then, we were in no hurry.

Down the center of one street ran amusing little narrow gauge rails for a streetcar. To my amazed ears came a toot which sounded for all the world like a French taxi horn. Dick said it was the street car, and sure enough, presently it emerged from a tunnel. There were a couple of stubby cars behind a steam engine that looked more like a toy than part of a public conveyance. The London-made engines are recent acquisitions, too; street cars in Baghdad used to be drawn by horses, not very long ago.

We passed out of the confusion of the market district to a section with residences fronting directly on the road, heavy wooden gates leading to whatever courtyard or garden they might have. Picturesque, crazy little enclosed balconies hung overhead. In some places, where the road narrowed, these balconies met above and formed a roof. On through the crooked streets to the river again, where there was an ancient bridge. It boasted to great steel pontoons as does the Maude Bridge by our hotel, but was supported by wooden ones in a fine state of disrepair. This was the Khadimein Bridge, so-called because it spans the river towards the Shiite mosque of Khadimein, with its famed golden domes. We paid eight annas toll to cross and toured through the Khadimein district, coming as close to the mosque as the road would permit. Then, leaving the car, we walked into the dim cavern that was the Khadimein bazaar. In comparison to the cramped and busy Baghdad *suq*, business here seemed to be very dull indeed, and there were few people in the broad, clean-swept streets. We sauntered slowly past the iron-chained entrance to the great mosque, trying to make our glances seem as little idly curious as possible. Probably nothing would have happened if we had stood and gaped in what is sometimes thought to be true American fashion, for there is no religious festival in progress at this season. But these fanatical Shiites are cold and impolite, if not actually hostile to foreign infidels, and one hesitates to offend such people. Indeed there are times when it would be unwise and even dangerous to go anywhere near the mosque. And so we hovered unobtrusively beyond the iron chains, to enjoy a brief glimpse of its golden domes glowing in the wintry sun, and its minarets rising in delicate beauty heavenward.

Back in the automobile, we returned to the city, past the tomb of Queen Sitt Subeida of Arabian Nights fame, through the residence district on the Khadimein side of the river, past the grounds of the High Commissioner's residency; and, for another eight annas, we were allowed to cross the Maude Bridge, and our hotel was just on the other side.

From the terrace by the river we watched the glories of the setting sun. At this hour between day and night, which we have become accustomed to associate with peace and quiet, the sharp staccato of wooden chips striking gaming boards in the tea house next door broke discordantly on the evening air. There the idle found pleasure in a game of chance while they drank their tea; and out on the river one of those ridiculous-looking little round boats called *gufas* that fringe the opposite shore were silhouetted more and more darkly against the sunset sky; and the flame and purple afterglow began to fade. The sky above and beyond deepened in vibrant silence for this one last moment of the day, and the first star leaped out. The brief spell was broken. One of the throng that passes across the great pontoon bridge burst into song, and a laugh came clearly across the evening air. A laugh and a babble of voices, and the game in the neighboring *chay-hana* was resumed. The day was done. Baghdad had found its voice and the Tigris flowed smoothly, silently, darkly on.

It rained and rained. Every unpaved inch in Baghdad turned into a slushy, sloppy morass of adhesive brown mud. The accompanying rawness of the air made us grateful for our fireplace. Let those who were perhaps more fanatical devotees than we enjoy their bathtub.

One of the city's well-known licensed dealers in antiquities had called on Dick and told of a large collection of Luristan bronzes which had just come out of Persia. I was keen to see them, and fortunately the rain let up towards four o'clock on the appointed afternoon. Fortified with galoshes and umbrella, we started out. We took the inevitable carriage down New Street to the entrance of the narrow, crooked, unpaved apology for a street down which we had to travel on foot if we were to see the bronzes. It was slippery walking, more hazardous than it seemed, because when you put one foot in front of the other you never knew when you might strike bottom again, if at all. Surface liquidation had levelled the depressions, making holes and ruts a menace. It was giddy going even when apparent solidity was only a few inches down. To make matters worse, the damp cold made it necessary for me to wear my winter coat — a lovely light blue creation topped by squirrel fur — and I could imagine what it would look like if I were to sit down in that mud. However, with Dick leading the way, we managed to cover a mile or more, our eyes glued to the ground, testing every advance. Finally, turning the last of countless corners, we arrived at the dealer's gate without mishap.

A servant admitted us and showed us upstairs to his master's study, a tiny room looking out on an open courtyard. There, over small cups of sweet Turkish coffee, we were shown the bronzes which we had come to see. Each piece had to be laboriously extracted from a chest on the floor and then denuded of its newspaper wrappings. It was a lengthy process, for the collection ran into hundreds of pieces, with numerous examples of pins, bracelets, bits and other horse trappings, knife blades, and some thin cups and pots, besides a great number of animal figurines. Many of the bits, pins, and bracelets were also decorated with animal heads, so typical of the Luristan manner, so reminiscent of the Scythian. It was a splendid collection, worth the effort it took to get there and see it.

But we hadn't counted on the return experience. When we finally succeeded in taking our leave, after having unsuccessfully refused tea, it was quite dark. Winter days, particularly rainy ones, are always unexpectedly short. Our host sent his servant to accompany us with a lantern, for those maze-like burrows of old Baghdad have few street lights. It is only where the veneer of Western civilization has cut through a paved street, or thrown a pontoon bridge across the waters of the Tigris, that illumination or anything approaching adequate lighting is to be expected. In these treacherous back ways, the blackness of the night remained almost undisturbed. It was quite useless to try to pick our way as we had done when we came. The wavering glow from the servant's lantern, as he plodded ahead in flat-footed unconcern, served no other purpose than to lend courage.

The overhanging balconies and austere walls of the houses on either side hugged close, to shut out even the emanating glow of the evening sky. Now and then, as we turned a corner, an unexpected street light did emerge dimly, high up on some wall, only making the scene more unreal, the yawning darkness a few feet beyond more mysterious. The mile stretched out in imagination until, after what seemed hours, we glimpsed the lights of New Street at the end of our rabbit warren, and the noise of wheeled traffic came down to us. Our guide stuck faithfully until he had planted us on the sidewalks of the main thoroughfare. Then, as we stepped into a carriage, he turned back unconcernedly to retrace his steps. To him the little jaunt was the commonest of experiences; but to me it remains in memory like a page from the Arabian Nights, where Ifrits and Jinni and other dark creatures of the imagination are wont to appear and accomplish the fantastic.

We spent another rainy day at the National Museum, where we absorbed as much as we could of the beauty of the wealth of famous antiquities which have come from different sites in this country so rich in ancient remains. It was thrilling to see the originals of objects I had long known from reproduction or photograph — glorious, priceless objects from Ur of the Chaldees, lavish in gold, lapis lazuli, and shell. The beaten gold wig-helmet with its elaborate coiffure picked out in delicate *repoussé*, which once belonged, we are told, to Mes-Kalam-Shar.[12] He must have been a mighty prince, for his personality has not been obliterated by time. It seems to have come wraith-like from the grave along with his trappings, and shows itself in every proud line of these personal belongings. But it was before two other equally famous pieces — an inlaid harp and standard — that I bowed in humble and enthusiastic admiration of the skill and ingenuity which the excavator had exercised in taking these unbelievably delicate objects from the ground, at the same time preserving both the order and beauty of the fragile mosaic art.

Quite naturally, however, my greatest thrill came not from objects of gold or semi-precious stone, but from the cases of less pretentious pottery, stone, and badly patinated bronze finds from our site at Nuzi. Such things, along with the seals, tablets, and the few prime examples of glazed terra-cotta sculpture over which I have already waxed enthusiastic in an earlier chapter — all objects which the Assyrian looters of our provincial Mitanni city apparently considered

12 [Now read, Mes-kalam-dug.]

beneath notice — represent almost everything that these ungracious conquerors of Nuzi left for us to discover. Of gold and gems that once belonged in Nuzi, we have found only insignificant remnants — a bead, a tiny gold sun disc, a single earring. Yet the mud walls, which could not be carried off and which were only occasionally vandalized, are of perhaps greater scientific value than the spectacular objects we might have found.

One of the Museum authorities, who had graciously given up his time during our visit, called our attention to a portrait of Gertrude Bell, the original of which was painted by Sargent. Miss Bell, that remarkable British woman traveller and scholar, needs no introduction to anyone who has journeyed to the Near East — by armchair route or any other. It was through her energy and foresight that the Iraq Museum was first established; she was its first Director of Antiquities, its founder, inspiration, and guiding star. Anyone coming there after her death cannot but wish with profound regret that they might have been privileged to know her. The Museum stands as her monument, her friends are legion.

The thought of this courageous and remarkable woman is always arresting to me. It is strange, but the East seems to have a trick of laying the personalities of foreigners bare; it brings out the best in some, the worst in others, and makes everyone seem slightly picturesque. Great *individuals* like Miss Bell are rare; one often feels that one is meeting *types* out here. But the types fascinate me, too. One encounters them throughout the country, in every penetrable spot.

There is the story-book Police Officer who has been stationed for years in the wildest part of the country where the problem of racial hatreds among the natives themselves is a constant source of trouble. Yet he knows his district in and out, as well as the numerous languages and dialects that are spoken there. He knows when to be harsh and sudden, and when to mollify; and he does his job as perhaps no one else could: he keeps peace — a hard-bitten character, but awfully romantic. Stories about his adventures and tactics make good listening over a cup of tea or a glass of beer at the British Club.

There is the breezy young Air Force officer who is as flippant and gay and unconsciously rude over a cocktail at the River Front Hotel in Baghdad as he might be in Piccadilly. Very young Englishmen often seem to combine a high opinion of American cocktails with a low opinion of all Americans; they are a post-war breed of exasperatingly likable puppies who say what they think and do what they please.

Then comes the most sensitive Britisher who is closer than any other foreigner to that ephemeral yet powerfully motivating philosophy of the East; an intangible thing we all can feel but few can fathom. These do not go native, they go mystic. If they wear native clothing and mingle in places where foreigners seldom penetrate, it is merely a means to an end. They do not belong in the same category with their wilder, perhaps Irish, cousins, who drink too much and really go native now and again. The Irishman is a mystic, too, but with him mysticism is the natural means and not the end. Then he frequents the more lowly quarters of the native city, eats queer foods, visits a native burlesque, or smokes a hubble-bubble in a tumble-down *chay-hana,* he is enjoying himself whether or not he is unconsciously absorbing native folklore.

In sharp contrast to these two is the beefy, insensitive soul so often characterized in *Punch.* This man is apt to be quite unfeeling towards the natives, and is always quite aloof from them. He cannot help despising them, and would be powerless to hide his feelings even if he had any wish to do so. But he is perfectly sincere. He is doing whatever job of work he is out there for, and doing it dam' well. He had forgotten — if he ever knew — that *Sahib* means "friend," not "master." Although he has spent all his life watching the sun set on the British Empire, he knows that the sun never does such a thing; and he is doing his unconscious bit to preserve the distinguished destiny of a cog in the magnificent mechanics of that Empire.

All of these types, of course, belonged to the upper middle class at home; but there was the strange case of the wireless operator who was pure cockney. He wouldn't have "belonged" at home, and therefore he didn't "belong" out here. This man, whose greatest sin was that he dropped an 'h' from one word and added it onto another, was a most intelligent and amusing person. We enjoyed his company, and he was so grateful for ours that is was almost painful. That kind of loneliness, when one is isolated amongst one's own people and nationality, must be a very empty thing.

Quite different were the American rough diamonds who visited us occasionally on the dig. They were the expert oil drillers, who had been imported from the United States to work in the great Mosul oil fields. They were excessively well-paid, clever fellows, hearty and friendly and pretty damn homesick for "God's Country" — but not lonesome. They had quite an international colony at Bab-l Gurgur outside of Kirkuk, where they lived and worked; and an American who stresses the wrong syllable in such words as "hotel" and "cement" is likely to be a good mixer. The Cockney wireless operator was thoughtfully curious about archaeology; but the oil drillers were just curious. One of them got under Charles's skin by asking, "How do you know where to dig? Just scratch around and trust to God 'n Providence?" And then, after Charles had patiently explained about the indications and clues we look for in digging, the fellow said, "Oh, I see, you just scratch around and trust in God 'n Providence."

There was the American woman tourist who was shown the "deep room." After it had been carefully explained that this was not a room at all, but an exploratory and arbitrary shaft, she said, "Remarkable that the stairs should be so perfectly preserved!" I wondered if she expected the workmen to use parachutes. And the men who thought it would be a grand idea for us to excavate hydraulically — when we didn't even have enough water to take tub baths.

On the whole, I think that the Americans and the Beefy Britishers were the only ones who remained impervious to the subtleties of the East. Nothing could move them. On the other hand, we ourselves may have been the queerest of the lot. One never knows about that.

Anyhow, our vacation in Baghdad had to come to an end, and I bid the city a rain-soaked farewell as I waited in a carriage at the entrance of the bazaar, for Dick to rush in and get Muhammed's fez. It would have been a shame to disappoint the little fellow.

CHAPTER XII

Ramazan and the Id-el-Fitr

When we arrived at the Kirkuk station at eight o'clock in the morning after our trip to Baghdad, Muhammed and Hiddir were there to meet us. We had been expecting Muhammed, but it was a surprise to see Hiddir. He explained that he had come to buy chickens for the Expedition. Constant demand and limited supply had depleted the countryside around about Tarkhalan. It is understandable, too, since the buying of chickens was Hiddir's special province, why he would not for the world relinquish it, even to the extent of commissioning Muhammed just once to get chickens in the Kirkuk bazaar. We felt that he might have chosen a more opportune time to do his shopping; but then, the old Ford had been overloaded before this. Our luggage would have to go somewhere, on tailboard or roof.

Because of these household commissions, we did not start at once for Tarkhalan, but went into Kirkuk, where Dick and I had breakfast at Ali's hotel, while Muhammed and Hiddir went along to the bazaar. We cautioned them not to be gone too long, and by the time we had eaten, collected and read the mail, and knocked our heels between Ali's store and the hotel for half an hour, our two bright-faced minions appeared. From the amount of stuff that was piled in the back of the car they must have bought out the market. If these were all necessary purchases, then Sammy's larder must have run desperately low. In happy unconcern, Hiddir sat among a confusion of sacks full of green vegetables, potatoes, flour, and live chickens. How Muhammed, diminutive though he was, expected to squeeze in there was a mystery; but squeeze he had to and did, since our luggage completely filled the lowered tail-board, and we ourselves completely filled the narrow front seat.

Just as we were more or less settled, and about to start, Muhammed calmly announced that we must take the long road home, and stop by at the Iraq Petroleum Company's depot for petrol. This was the last straw. We would have rebelled, but he insisted that we hadn't enough gasoline for another trip into town, and that Sammy had no kerosene for the stove, absolutely *maku*. The only thing we could do was curb Muhammed's passion for buying in job-lots, strictly limiting him to one can of each of the necessary kinds of fuel.

Then, groaning and grunting, the poor old station wagon (which was never meant for such heavy work since it was only a built-over touring car), pointed an agonized nose towards home. We were forced to go in first and second gear, slowly, because at every bump the body of the car came down on the back axle in shivering protest. Even with all our caution, it was a dizzy slither from one side of the road to the other, deep in clay mud. I was thankful that Dick was at the wheel. At least I could find comfort in the knowledge that he was more concerned about the car and its contents than any native chauffeur would have been. The fact was that Dick and I were the only ones were at all anxious about the situation. If Muhammed and Hiddir found anything unusual in that wild ride, it was in the nature of a lark. When the poor frightened chickens began to squawk, Hiddir told them to keep still — we didn't want any *calabala* from them!

For more than an hour we kept our snail's pace. When we reached the outskirts of Topazoa, within sight of Tarkhalan, we began to relax and congratulate ourselves and praise Allah for a safe if hazardous journey. Alas, we were somewhat previous. We had not considered with proper respect the condition of the rain-gutted roads of this village. Just at the narrowest place between Topazoan walls the automobile slid giddily into an invisible and apparently bottomless sink-hole of mud. We pulled on our gum boots, which Muhammed had thoughtfully brought along in case of emergency, and cut out across the fields to the Expedition house on foot, leaving Hiddir and Muhammed to extricate the remains as best they could.

The low brown outline of our mud house, looking for all the world like an old hen squatting forlornly in the mud, delighted our hearts. Never did the whitewashed welcome of our dining room seem more gracious. Once inside, in the warmth, with the rest of the Expedition gathered about to hear, our morning's adventures ceased to be hideous and became humorous. We were all full of talk about our various vacations, and in this pleasant reunion the minor mishaps of a mud-clogged road were soon forgotten. When the bedraggled Muhammed finally brought the car to our gates and Abdulla carried in our luggage, I unpacked my Baghdad treasures and exhibited them on the dining room table. Dr. Meek, Charles, and the Wilenskys had taken a jaunt north to Erbil for their holiday, and they, too, had fascinating bargains from the Erbil bazaars to display. What with their bright array of blankets, jackets, belts and quaint slippers, and my brass, *papier-mâché* work, slippers and beads from Baghdad, we might have started a shop without wishing for more varied or colorful stock.

The next day, the rain having stopped, activity started again on the dig, and we fell quickly into our work-a-day routine once more. During that month the short winter days dragged out chill and sodden with frequent downpours of rain. It was the month of Ramazan when all good Muhammedans fast and pray during the daytime, and only with the setting of the sun allow food, water, cigarette smoke, or indeed anything, but medicine, to pass their lips. Ramazan did not effect us as much, except that the servants in the house and the men on the dig spent a great deal of time praying. As the month wore on, the daytime fasting got on their nerves, making them silent and irritable; but with evening came food, and tobacco, and their habitual good-humor returned to them. The noise of feasting, visiting, and general *calabala* kept up late those nights, both in the village and in the kitchen gathering place on our compound where Kerim read aloud from the Koran. The men were likely to be more slow and sleepy than usual at their work in the morning, because of these unwonted midnight hours.

As the month drew to a close, on the appointed day when a thin new moon was to usher in the *Id-el-fitr* and make an end to religious inhibitions, everyone in our compound gathered on the roof at sunset, hoping to be the first to glimpse the sign. But the sun flamed to earth, the afterglow faded, night fell quickly and no moon appeared. Could it be that there was a mistake? Abdulla was glum as he served our dinner. It was quite natural that when these people had made up their minds that the morrow would bring the *Id*, the prospect of another day of fasting and waiting on a willful moon seemed intolerable. We consulted our almanac and found that this indeed was the correct date for the new moon, but unhappily, the time given for it to rise was along in the afternoon. It must have risen and set unnoticed before anyone had thought to look for it. We tried to explain this complicated bit of astronomy to Abdulla. He was quite willing to be convinced that we knew more about lunar activity than he, but it didn't do any good because he couldn't begin to celebrate before the other villagers. Like Easter Sunday in the Western world it is a signal to dress up. The day dawned bright and sunny, with the first soft promise of spring in the air — a welcome harbinger after the long cold of winter. After a late breakfast we walked into the village to see the finery and to greet our friends with appropriate felicitations on this, their "Christmas Day." When we appeared, a number of our friends immediately detached themselves from the idle, gossiping groups of men in the streets, and walked along with us. They were all togged out in new clothes or gorgeous hue, often with the painful-looking accessory of new shoes which were European in design but local in manufacture — and execution. The fashion note for tunics this year was a bright yellow sateen with narrow blue stripes. Any number of these costumes sparkled magnificently against the dull brown background of mud walls and street. This material was certainly stunning in its fresh splendor, but I couldn't help wondering what it would look like after a few months of constant wear had sullied its sheen. However, it is a pity to be too practical. These people were proud and happy in today; they did not look into a worried future, why should we?

Presently, as we walked along, little Nuri, a basket-boy on the dig, appeared with his small brother. Both were blossoming in yellow and blue coats of identical cut, and they wore light brown leather shoes. Nuri was so insistent that we must call on his mother and father and see his house, that we allowed him to lead us to his courtyard. Bursting with importance, he ushered us in and shouted for his parents. All of the family wealth seemed to have been spent on the boys, for the older people were not dressed up. The mother would not have had new clothes anyway, for this is essentially a man's holiday in a man's country; the woman haven't learned to demand new bonnets for the *Id*. But in this family, the father, too, was wearing old clothes. No matter, their welcome was unembarrassed and sincere as they shooed the animals out of our path in the muddy courtyard. Nuri's house, like most of the others in the village, was a simple, one-story structure, entirely innocent of windows. What light there was came in through the open doorway. His parents spread blankets for us to sit upon, and his mother brought out tiny bowls of cakes and nuts. We nibbled sparingly, while the sons of the house took advantage of our presence to stuff themselves. Fortunately our hosts did most of the talking — about the weather, the dig, and the prospects for crops. I entered into the conversation as much as my limited vocabulary would allow, mostly with monosyllabic expressions of agreement. One has a strange impulse to try to make oneself understood in French, German, Chinese — any language except one's mother tongue — when talking to these people. I suppose that the subconscious logic is that any language foreign to one's own ought to do. And as a matter of fact, perhaps it ought, for Nuri's parents were speaking to us in a fantastic mixture of Kurdish, Turkish and Arabic; wouldn't it be fair, then, for us to answer in Spanish, Italian, and Hindustani — if we could? When the proper length of time for a courtesy call had elapsed, Dick rose, and told abu Nuri that he was well pleased with his son's work on the dig. This made everyone happy, and we took our leave amid elaborate protests of friendship and hospitality.

Nuri and his brother accompanied us, and we picked up the rest of our escort again as we continued on our circuit of the village. When we came to the tea house, the owner, who was also employed on the dig, hailed us in. Smiling, beckoning, and finally coming out and taking Dick by the arm, he made it clear that nothing would do but we must tarry to enjoy all the hospitality his establishment could offer. Almost all of the little tables were full, for, since this was the only *chay-hana* in the village, it was also the chief lounging place — something like a corner drugstore in America or a pub in England. A table was cleared for us in the center of the stage, however, and the men who had given us their seats squatted happily on the mud floor at our feet, and the rest of the company circled up close around us. It was an occasion.

Our host scurried away to make flourish, tea, which he brought with a flourish, and poured into the usual small glasses, over huge lumps of sugar. The more honor bestowed upon a guest, the larger must be the lump of sugar that is broken off the sugar for him. The hot brown liquid quickly melted these mountains in our cups, and the result was a syrupy, very strong drink. I detest sweet tea, almost as much as I do strong tea; but if the refreshment was not to my taste, the frank and childlike delight these friends took in our presence there amongst them was pleasant. Presently the small boy who had been sent post haste to the house of the owner of the *chay-hana* to get some cakes, came running back with a rather grubby bandanna handkerchief full of the hard, dark, pastries so typical of this region. These were deposited on the table for us to eat, while our host cleared away the tea glasses and prepared the coffee. It is quite in order to be honored with both beverages on one occasion. He brought the coffee in a little copper pot with an enormous spout. The cup for this — there was only one cup for everyone — was small and handleless, like a Chinese tea cup. Into the bottom he poured about a teaspoonful of the hottest, strongest liquid imaginable and he handed it to me. When I had blown over it, cooled it enough to drink it off, a similar amount was poured into the same cup for *Sahib* Mr. Starr. After that the host drank, and then as many of the other guests as could before the supply gave out.

Everyone seemed to be shyly aware that we had brought our camera with us. They all aspire to cinematographic fame, although they do not quite know what it is all about. None of them had ever seen a movie. They did know, however, that it was something different, because after spending three years teaching them to stand still when a picture was being taken, the Sahib had suddenly changed his tactics and told them not to stand still in front of the camera any more, to move about. In fact, if they did stand rigidly quiet as they had learned to do for the other mysterious machine, he didn't like it. All of which made the movie camera more alluring. So we lined them up in front of the tea house and took a panorama. For this it wouldn't matter if they moved or stood still; the camera would be moving anyway.

Before we knew it, our watches pointed to two o'clock. Sammy would be wondering if we were never coming home to eat luncheon. I had succeeded in procuring three small spring chickens, and had given him directions for making them into what I hoped would turn out to be *Chicken à la Maryland*. We walked back to our compound, little Nuri still at our heels. One the way, he gave me a marble he had made for me — for *baksheesh*. He was sustained in this act by the pleasure he felt and the conscious pride that it was his best marble; otherwise he would probably have expired from embarrassment. When we reached the Expedition house, we invited Nuri to come in, and sent him home loaded with cakes and oranges from our sideboard — return *baksheesh*.

Ramazan and the *Id* passed, but their effect still lingered. Working on the dig we had a tall gaunt man whose red beard and hair were admirably set off by a green *khefia*. He was privileged to wear this color on his head because he was a *sayyid*, a descendant of the Prophet. His name was Sayyid Ghafil, and he had a temporary abode in the village of Topazoa. He didn't look very robust; the hollowness of his cheeks and the unhealthy pallor of his skin, interesting and ascetic though it made him appear, did not indicate that he was a well man. After a month of strenuous fasting appropriate for a religious man during Ramazan, he had appropriately, if not wisely, gorged himself during the *Id*. Next day he reported for work, a very sick man indeed. As soon as Dick noticed his condition, he sent him home in the car. After Muhammed had deposited Sayyid Ghafil in Topazoa, he reported to the compound to tell Mr. Wilensky — who was working in the drawing room that day — about it; and Mr. Wilensky rushed back to Topazoa with first aid. The poor *sayyid* was in the verge of collapse; but the proper medicines soon brought him around and he rested more easily. He was told to keep quite and not report for work again until he was quite well.

It was a clear case of severe indigestion, but Sayyid Ghafil preferred that it should be otherwise. Consequently, the story that filtered back to us was his explanation of the episode, not ours. It seems that there was another *sayyid* up near Mosul who hated Sayyid Ghafil. The exact reason for this enmity was not made clear, but that it existed there was no doubt. Equally certain was the fact that the Mosul *sayyid* had been dabbling in dark magic. At least, he must have been *wishing* Sayyid Ghafil harm: witness the sudden seizure. But Sayyid Ghafil was too much for him, the more powerful *sayyid* was bound to win: witness the recovery. Ah well, the important thing was that our red-headed basket man did not die.

CHAPTER XIII

A Lecture at the Club in Kirkuk

After that rainy Thanksgiving afternoon when the Mutasarif of Kirkuk brought his distinguished Baghdad guests to call, we heard from him several times. He came on another day for a short visit, bringing a carload of local celebrities. His son, who often hunted in the desert beyond the *tepa*, sent us a gazelle which he had shot; and the owner of the tea house in Topazoa grumblingly moved his establishment out of the road because it seems that the Kirkuk official thought that it was obstructing the path our car had to take on trips to town.

All of these courtesies were quite unexpected. The Mutasarif had apparently taken a genuine interest in our work, and seemed to feel an equally genuine friendship towards the Expedition. Then Dr. Meek received a letter asking him to give a talk in front of the Iraqi club in Kirkuk. The speech had to be written and sent into town beforehand so that it might be translated into Turkish — the common language of Kirkuk. The idea was for Dr. Meek to read the English version, while some member of the club would follow him, sentence by sentence, with the Turkish copy. Charles and I had both brought typewriters to the field, and we volunteered to copy the paper. Since this account sketches the ancient history of the region, and tells something about the contents of the Nuzi tablets and the finds from the dig, I am including it here, with Dr. Meek's kind permission:

The neighborhood of Kirkuk is particularly rich in ancient sites. Kirkuk itself is built on the site of ancient Arrapḫa, a city mentioned in the famous Taylor Prism of Sennacherib, but famed in history many years before that. It is unfortunate that it cannot be excavated, because it would undoubtedly give us much information about a period in early Mesopotamian history which is at present very vague. Quite close to Kirkuk is a mound called Tis'in, where there was a city by that name in ancient times. A few kilometers southwest of Kirkuk is the village of Tarkhalan, still preserving the ancient name of a city in that neighborhood, the city of Tarkulu. Round about Tarkhalan are several mounds, Qutush Kebir and Qutush Seghir, the origins of which go back thousands of years to prehistoric days, when men were just beginning the settlement of Mesopotamia. The particular mound which our Expedition is now excavating, is Yorgan Tepa, situated very close to Tarkhalan, and the site of ancient Nuzi. Just why the city was called Nuzi we do not know, but there is no connection between the name and that of the Arab king Nazo.

Ancient Mesopotamia, like modern Iraq, was not a unit, either geographically, ethnically, or linguistically. In the south were the lowlands, and in the north the highlands. In the former, the population today is predominately Arab; in the latter, it is predominately Kurdish in the villages, Turkoman in the towns, with a sprinkling of Arabs here and there. Similarly, in very ancient times, the Sumerians occupied the south country, while the Proto-Elamites (a Caucasian people from the east), at even earlier date established themselves in the north and even made incur-

sions into the south. Between these two there was long and continual warfare, with the Sumerians gradually gaining the ascendancy. Into the region between the two came presently a great horde of Semites from the west, to contest the domination of the land. Gradually but surely, the Sumerian rule was replaced by that of the Semites, now supplemented by the Amorites, who eventually established the first Babylonian Empire with the capital at Babylon. The greatest king of this dynasty was Hammurabi, who was able to overcome the last vestige of Sumerian opposition in the south, and to overthrow the powerful Elamite state that had established its capital at Larsa. Hammurabi then extended his kingdom into the north and west, until finally his empire reached the shores of the Mediterranean Sea. His successors, however, were unable to maintain the empire; revolts occurred in the south, Hittites invaded the land from the north; and the Kassites from the east took advantage of the chaotic state of affairs to establish their sway over the country, a regime that lasted some six hundred years. In the meantime, the Assyrians (a people of Semitic origin, but fused with other stock) had established themselves in the north, with their capital at Ashur; and they gradually began to encroach on their neighbors to the south. In the end, they completely conquered the south, and once more the land was united under a single rule; but this time the capital was in the north.

The cities of Kirkuk (ancient Arrapḫa) and Nuzi lay between north and south — the middle ground that gave them the opportunity at times for more or less independent rule. One such period was during the decline of the Kassite power and the rise of the Assyrian Empire; and it is from this period that most of the tablets excavated at Kirkuk and Nuzi have come. They show that the population was predominately Hurri, an Elamite stock that early spread over a considerable portion of the Near East and are called Horites in the Hebrew Bible. The tablets so far excavated show that the people minded their own business and had little to do with the political capitals of the time (only once is a king mentioned, and he is a king of the Mittani) and hence they became wealthy citizens of the little state of Arrapḫa. They were content to keep within their own borders, trade among themselves, and carry on their own traditions — although powerfully influenced by the culture of the Assyrians and Babylonians, their neighbors to the north and south. Since they were nominally a part of the Assyrian Empire, Assyrian influence is the stronger of the two.

The tablets are almost altogether business and legal documents, having to do with purchase, sale, barter, loans, adoption, marriage, divorce, lawsuits and the like. Only a few letters have been found among the tables and no religious texts at all, but religious texts are likely to appear now as the temple area at Nuzi is being excavated. In fact, some tablets have just been found, but they have not yet been baked and cannot be read until they are baked. A tablet of peculiar interest is one that records the deportation of the leading citizens of the country by the Assyrians as they extended their sway more definitely over the land. Against this the Nuzians seem to have risen in revolt, for the city was sacked and burned, and henceforth remained little more than a ruin and thus remains to the present day. It is fortunate for the excavator, because there is no obstacle to the excavation of the site.

In our recent operations at Nuzi, a shaft has been sunk to the lower levels in the effort to discover what may lie deep beneath the surface. Here there have recently been found a considerable quantity of tablets, only a part of which have been baked. These are very old temple lists of offerings and the like, and are quite different from the tablets found on the higher levels. They are written in the Old Akkadian language, but with some words in Sumerian. Unfortunately the tablets are not dated, but they can scarcely be later than 2500 B.C., and may be earlier than that.

One tablet is quite large, measuring 16 x 17 centimeters, and contains a long list of offerings. Various gods like Nusku, Girru, and Ishtar are mentioned, but no details regarding their worship are given. One tablet of particular interest contains a word list, including the words for a slave, concubine, priestess, and so forth. It is written altogether in Sumerian and is important because no other tablet like it has ever been found before so far north. When the rest of the tablets have been baked, we will doubtless have material of great importance concerning the early history of Mesopotamia, because they are the oldest inscriptions that have been found so far north.

Altogether some four thousand tablets have been found in the excavations at Nuzi, and others are continually appearing. But the tablets have not been our only finds. I mention only a few of the other items. Quite early in the excavation a suit of bronze armor was found, which is now at the Museum at Baghdad. It is the only one of its kind as yet found in Iraq, and shows that Nuzians of 1500 B.C. wore coats of mail in their warfare. Another early find was a copper brazier in the shape of a truncated cone, some twenty centimeters high. It is pierced with three rows of triangular holes, and on the rim are three crouching lions. Another brazier of importance had a chimney, was made of clay, and beautifully decorated. Among the many cups discovered was one twenty centimeters in height made of diorite. Another was beautifully painted with geometrical designs in white and black and most artistically shaped. A most unexpected find was that of a fresco in brilliantly contrasting colors (white, black, red, and gray), which had fallen from the top of a wall. The design was most artistic, having human faces, heads of bulls, and 'trees of life' in a geometrical setting. Thousands of beads, votive offerings, figurines in glazed terra-cotta, and similar articles have been found strewn in the temple, and temple courtyards, the remains of the loot when the Assyrians sacked the place. Among the bronze objects is a bronze tablet which is a very unusual find; and another unusual tablet (this one made of clay) was made in the shape of an egg, hollow, with an opening of top. It contained forty-nine small pebbles corresponding to forty-nine sheep which the owner had entrusted to the shepherd Zikarri. The latter, being illiterate, kept count of the sheep by means of the pebbles. A duplicate tablet of the ordinary sort was kept by the owner of the sheep, and the oval one containing the pebbles was given to the shepherd. The duplicate tablet was also found.

These, and many other objects that have been excavated, indicate something of the culture by which the ancient Nuzians surrounded themselves, and the high degree of their civilization.

There is no more fertile land in any part of the world than right here in Iraq, and under an enlightened government, irrigation will be extended, the people given advantages of modern education in all its phases, and presently there must blossom on the ashes of the old, another and greater civilization to redeem the many years of sterility in the intervening centuries. Iraq has had a most glorious past, and there is no reason why she should not have an even more glorious future.

When the day came for Dr. Meek to read this paper, we all dressed up in our "city" clothes. It seemed like quite an occasion for me to disregard my breeches and woolen lumber shirt for an afternoon dress, and silk stockings. A pair of rubber shoe-gloves instead of gum boots — for the world was a sea of mud again — and the transformation was complete. Divided between two motor cars that the Mutasarif sent out for us, we bumped and skidded over the familiar ten miles to Kirkuk, leaving Muhammed disconsolate over the fact that he and the old Ford had been jilted for two beautiful touring cars smartly chauffeured by city chaps in tight-fitting clothes and jaunty Iraqi caps.

At the club the friendly Mutasarif met us and escorted us to the lecture room which was filling quickly. He led us to a group of reserved seats in the first row, where the other "Europeans" were already ensconced. They were the newly arrived American Missionary to the district, and his wife. We were all introduced, and, as compatriots on foreign soil will, we fell easily into empty conversation. Presently the Mutasarif returned to introduce the speaker of the day, and Dr. Meek and his native interpreter held forth.

I am sure that Dr. Meek will always remember that as one of the most unusual lectures he ever gave. We have often laughed with him about it, since, for it is quite a feat to be suave and eloquent when a too eager interpreter is stepping on the heels of every sentence. I could never be sure, because I didn't understand the Turkish, but I had the feeling that the English and Turkish variations weren't always in perfect accord. In any case, this was a matter of no importance. In spite of the interpreter's interruptions, the talk went well. In fact, having watched this performance with admiration, I am sure that Dr. Meek would be at home in any rostrum. He even managed to forget that most of his audience couldn't understand a word that he was saying, and interpolated a couple of sentences. This startled the native interpreter; but he rose to the occasion by merely reading ahead in the script. When they finally caught up with each other at the conclusion, our applause was not only in appreciation of the text, with which we were already familiar, but also for the facile way in which so awkward a method of delivery — by echo, so to speak — had been accomplished.

Afterwards, in another of the club rooms, there was an elaborate tea with sandwiches and a gorgeous layer cake so tall and thin that it resembled Pisa's famous tower. The Mutasarif continued to show us every courtesy, introducing the prominent club members, and keeping our tea cups filled; and afterwards he showed us all over the building, with its billiard rooms, squash court and tiny garden courtyard. It had been a pleasant afternoon. These kind people made us feel that they had profited not only by hearing interesting things about the past history of their country, but also that we had helped them to learn a little more English, a difficult tongue they would all like to master. And we felt that we, too, had gained in understanding by this contact with our city neighbors.

CHAPTER XIV

Village Diversions

As winter began to relinquish its frigid grip, we felt more and more the need of outdoor recreation. Of course, there were always our favorite walks to take: to the village, along the donkey road that led over the *waddi* at our gates, along numerous other donkey roads in the vicinity, or just anywhere we pleased, skirting the ploughed fields that were beginning to show green. But Charles' ingenuity supplied a new diversion for us to indulge in on fair Fridays. He gave his personal supervision to the construction of an elaborate and very neat miniature golf course on our flat roof. The hazards were built up of clay and old petrol tins, and the holes were simply cut out of the roof. For balls we used the large-sized native marbles, and for clubs we turned walking sticks around so that the crooked handles served as clubheads. The course started at the top of the stairs, went all the way around the small courtyard, and ended up at the stairs again. It wasn't very easy to make it in par; but its difficulties, hazards both natural and artificial, made it interesting. When a too ambitious player knocked a ball off the roof, there was always a willing and greatly amused Abdulla, Hiddir, or someone else down below to throw it back. This happened so often that we found it necessary to inflict a penalty of one stroke for each offense, thereby creating still another — mental — hazard.

One day we were having a hotly contested game after lunch. It was a sort of championship match, to the accompaniment of music. Hiddir and Abdulla had carried the gramophone up to the roof and stood by to wind the machine and see that the records were changed. The game was just ending in great hilarity — the last long putt across a narrow corner of the roof onto the main fairway was being made by the leading contender, when the tinkling of many bells told us that camels were coming our way.

Caravans did not pass our gates every day, although they were not infrequent along that route. But camels are such ridiculous beasts that we never tired of watching them go by. We had the movie camera out and, the day being bright, it seemed a good time to get a picture. We finished our game hurriedly, and were down by the *waddi* bridge, film set, when the first of a long train of several hundred beasts came by. They were heavily loaded with bags full of dates, slung across high wooden pack saddles. They groaned in passing, perhaps with the monotony of life. They had come two hundred miles from Baghdad and had another hundred miles ahead of them before they would reach Mosul. Dates do not grow that far north, and mostly are brought in by caravan. The huge, ungainly beasts were as fussy about where they put their feet as old women might have been. They made so much ado about crossing the slightly slippery hump of the little bridge, and flatly refused to step into the stream below. Finally, the *caravanchis* filled in a portion of the *waddi* with dirt, and covered the full with straw to give the illusion of dry footing. Only then did the more adventurous camels cross. Most of them had to be beaten and coaxed and heartily cursed before they would even attempt it. Poor things, they aren't very well satisfied about being camels, and one can hardly blame them. They seem to be forever sorry for themselves and to be forever grumbling and spitting. There is a legend which says that when the horse was not pleased with his appearance and complained to Allah, the Creator told him to look at the camel and be content. He did, and was.

When the last of the caravan had passed and its human escort, riding on the little gray donkeys, had melted into the dull background of the road, we turned to the village in search of new subjects worthy of the last few yards of our precious movie film. We found what we wanted, in the form of village women coming out of the fields from the direction of the *tepa*. They were carrying great bundles of cotton on their backs, bundles loosely wrapped in brilliant homespun cloth. It was then that I saw my first evidence of shyness and self-consciousness on the part of our village maidens. When Dick innocently tried to take their picture, they hesitated in groups, didn't seem to know quite what to do, but refused to advance. He was just as much surprised as I was, and quickly handed the camera to me. This gesture satisfied everyone. They really did want their picture taken, for they were just as fascinated as the men by this weird mechanical contrivance of ours. While I held the camera they advanced, smiling, and urged us to come into the village courtyard whither they were bound with their burden of cotton.

In a large courtyard, which was also a kind of municipal gathering place, they put down their bundles. Some of them squatted wearily on their heels, but others come to gather around me with a great display of interest and curiosity. I couldn't understand the attention, the like of which I had not before received from these village women, until I began to realize that here we had stumbled upon a strictly feminine ritual. Their unusual shyness back on the road, and here their unusual curiosity and forward attitude, all spoke loudly that this was their show, and of the importance they felt in it. After I had taken off my hat so that they could examine my blond hair (which I would have thought they had seen often enough during our visits to the village, but apparently wanted to *touch* it, and were also interested in the hairpins) after I had unbuttoned my leather jacket and let them see the cut of my dress; after I had replied negatively to their hopeful inquiries about the possibility of a son being on the way for the Sahib and myself, and received their condolences on that subject; after I had, in other words, put on quite a sideshow of my own, I got a chance to ask them about the cotton. We could not speak a common language with any degree of fluency; but with the help of gestures where my Arabic failed, and more signs when I could not understand theirs, I was finally able to get a glimmer of what it was all about. It seemed that cotton picking was traditionally a woman's prerogative. It was the only one of the countless chores they had to do, for which they were paid, and this money was theirs to keep. It was a custom. That was why they were all so keen for the job. It represented their only means of earning pin money. They would go out to the fields, pick as much cotton as they could carry, and bring it in. Then the owner of the crop would divide with them, either buying their share back, or allowing them to keep it for future sale elsewhere. I wondered what they would spend their little fortunes for — a dangle, a new black silk kerchief, a bag of sweetmeats? I would consider them luxuries dearly bought if for them I had carried a burden several times my size for three kilometers. But these women didn't mind. All during the fall and winter their backs were bent with even larger bundles of twigs and brush, like Malcolm's army bearing Birnam wood to Dunsinane.

Spring had come indeed. The tiny, almost transparent lizards that sometimes during the winter would betray themselves by restless rustling in their place of hibernation in our ceiling, now emerged to decorate our walls. The sparrows became even more numerous. They descended upon us in huge flocks, until every twig on the two small bushes in the courtyard was bowed by their weight. Moreover, nothing but the most succulent food would satisfy their appetites. Every new leaf was stripped from the bushes, and they almost ruined our lettuce patch. They even invaded the house at every opportunity, looking, I suppose, for nesting places.

All of these offenses notwithstanding, I was not pleased when I discovered Abdulla about to feed one of the live little beggars to our dog, Nuzi. His arguments were logical enough. He had caught it in the house, where it had no right to be; and besides, all sparrows were a nuisance — he pointed to our lettuce patch. But I couldn't be that logical. I took the frightened bird away from him, and was rewarded by a vicious peck before I had a chance to set it free.

Great flocks of sheep were now grazing in the fields nearby, and every day new lambs were born. When the first one came, Ahmet the sentry was so delighted that he ran in to tell me about it. I went with him into the neighboring field to see the wee wobbly creature. These newborn lambs are adorable, so small and fragile-looking, and at night the shepherd carries them home in his donkey's saddle-bags. It is amusing to see their woolly heads peeping from the sides of the patient donkeys. When they grow up they are sloppy, ungainly creatures with great hanging fat tails. The adult fat-tailed sheep of the East isn't nearly so nice to look at as our Western variety, but while they are so tiny, they are entrancing. One is moved to feel that it is a pity their youth is so fleeting. And the arrival of each new lamb is hailed with satisfaction because their flocks represent the most easily convertible source of wealth among these people.

As if the lambs and lizards were not enough evidence of spring, the first *hajji-laklaks*[13] had come to take up their abode in the village. The *hajjis* are so-

---

13 [See above R.F.S. Starr, "Letters from the Field, 1928-30," no. 68, 17 February 1930, p. 113.]

called because they, like other pilgrims, return every year at the same time; the *laklak* is merely an onomatopoeic addition. Enormous, stork-like birds, with black and white feathering and brilliant red beaks and legs, they come in pairs to build their large loose nests of sticks and brush on the flat roofs of the village. They had never selected our roof, because we used it too much. We were rather glad of this, for they are carnivores and scavengers and thrive on snakes, frogs, and other reptiles which they carry alive to their nests. But they are stately creatures, beautiful to see soaring aloft, easily on strong wings. In the evening we could count the pairs of them on the village roofs, and watch them from afar while they threw their heads over their backs and made their clattering *laklak* noise. It isn't a call, just a racket made by clapping their long beaks together; a penetrating sound such as some little boy might make playing with two sticks of wood.

Nor were the lambs, lizards, and *hajji-laklak*s the only signs of spring. A perfect epidemic of travelling merchants began to plague us. One of these, with a car full of rugs, came on a Friday and deposited his stock in our courtyard, willy-nilly. We refused to notice him, we walked on his rugs without looking at them, and wouldn't talk to him; but nothing daunted him. There he squatted, from morning until night — at least, until he made a sale. I, of course, had to be the one to give in. I really did like one of the rugs, and so finally I was naive enough to violate the boycott and ask its price. A hundred and fifty rupees; well, keep it. The boycott was on again, but I had given the merchant hope. Every time I put my head out of the door, he would hail me and cozen me to buy, reducing his price by a few rupees.

When the afternoon shadows were lengthening in the courtyard, and the price of the rug had come down to seventy rupees, I looked it over critically again, decided that I did want it, and said, "I'll give you fifty." Sold! There was no argument about it, the fellow had squatted on his heels all day over the deal, and now night was coming on. I gave him the money, and he packed the other rugs back into his rickety automobile and went his way rejoicing, while Abdulla spread my new acquisition on the floor of my room, and complimented me on its beauty. When Dick came in from his office where he had been working, I noticed that his expression was somewhat amused when he saw our new rug. I said, "Don't you like it?" He said, "Yes. How much did you pay for it?" "Fifty rupees." The joke was on me. Dick, too, had thought of buying this rug, and had carried on his own campaign of bargaining all day, whenever he happened to pass the rug merchant who had really stationed himself very strategically in the main courtyard; and Dick had *turned down* the rug at fifty rupees, several hours ago. Oh well, I still think it's a nice rug.

CHAPTER XV

The Temple Cella and Other Discoveries

As February [1931] flew with a rapidity worthy of the shortest month of the year, the madness of the March hare got into everybody and everything. On idle Fridays sheer exuberance made the villagers indulge in jumping contests and impromptu hockey games. It was almost ludicrous to see a respected and sedate wall-tracer, or some other equally dignified figure, suddenly blossom into a star athlete. Hockey is a flexible game as they play it, apparently quite indigenous. Any number of men play on a side; an open field is the arena, the mud walls at either end the goals. Whoever could find a crooked stick was in luck, and any old chunk of wood became the ball. It was always a spirited contest, and they all had a wonderful time.

Activity on the dig had been stepped up to a high pitch, too. The basket boys moved more quickly, *trambilchis* trundled the railroad car to the edge of the *tepa* and dumped its contents with greater alacrity, shovel men attacked the loose earth with renewed energy, even the knife men and wall-tracers pursued their tasks more briskly. It was like a slow motion picture speeded up just a little, but the manipulation of an unseen lever. It had become apparent that it might be possible to finish up the Nuzi levels on the dig that season. With this goal in view, the staff had brought pressure to bear on the workmen. But all of this cheerful hustle and bustle couldn't be due to outside influence. Spring got into their bones, and they were joyous. Every now and then one would burst out singing, so if they felt that they were being driven, they didn't resent it.

The greatest archaeological discovery that had come to light was the cella in the northwestern temple group. It is difficult to compare such discoveries; for although we do not, as in the case of the map, call this cella the *oldest* this or that, it was as important archaeologically as was the map cartographically. This was not our first cella. We had been uncovering them, one below another, all season; but it was our finest cella. It emerged in the late fourth level as a long, narrow sanctuary almost completely bare of the elaborate furnishings that once had glorified it. You entered by a door in the far end of one of the long walls, and when you turned to face the length of the narrow room, its beautiful simple proportions made even the mud walls impressive. A pilaster rose directly in the center of the far wall, with a low dais on either side. Some few feet in front of the pilaster was a low, square, much-burned altar. The proportions of the room were so in keeping with the ancient rites that were performed there that some of their austere essence seemed to have endured, to make one speak unconsciously in subdued tones. It is singular how often the architecture and the soul of a religion seem to be in accord. One can hardly disentangle the

Roman Church from the disciplined dignity of the Renaissance columns, or the lofty Gothic arches from a giddy triumph of the spirit over the heavy restrictions of Romanesque vaulting. To say that our cella was as perfect a mud-brick sanctuary as yet has been found in this country so rich in ancient remains, although a true reportorial comment, does not do it justice; it was one of those impressive ruins that makes one want to stop talking and dream.

The mute but significant archaeological evidence of the ground plans of this holy place, compared with the outlines of the older cella that lay below it, and the successive later buildings that had been on top, gave an inkling of what may have been the ancient drama there enacted. Considering the evidence, and bearing in mind the excess of superstition that pervaded all ancient religions, we are able to reconstruct the fanciful details of what may have been its history. In each case, the builders kept the cella in position, following more or less closely the outline used by the early people who built the *early* fourth stratum sanctuary, which lay directly below the perfect cella I have described. We knew, at that time, only the outline of this oldest holy of holies. We did not wish to demolish — nor could we without permission from the Department of Antiquities — the perfect *late* fourth stratum sanctuary in an effort to find the inner fittings of the temple room below. But the builders of our perfect room had considerably narrowed and shortened its proportions by the simple expedient of thickening its walls; and we could keep the room intact and still determine the outer dimensions of the older building underneath by putting trenches through the outer edges of the tremendously thick walls.

Thus it was proven that the builders of the *late* fourth stratum perfect cella had made a compound building over a simpler tradition, for although they had narrowed and shortened the sanctuary, they had also added a pretentious entry room, where their predecessors had only a portico; and in the *late* fourth stratum the great temple courtyard appears for the first time, and also a companion group to the southeast, similar in plan and size, making a double, compound temple. Was it disaster of pestilence or famine that modified — simplified — the architectural trend of succeeding buildings? It may have been for some such reason that the architects of the third stratum, and later of the second stratum, ignored the pretentious innovations of their fathers and grandfathers. Thinking back, perhaps, to the good old days when their grandfathers and great grandfathers, the builders of the *early* fourth stratum temple were righteous men upon whose efforts the gods smiled, they went back to the original tradition, disregarding the innovations and proportions of the *late* fourth stratum group, which we found so beautiful. In the third stratum they did away with the entry room and returned to the simple portico idea. The courtyard they kept, probably because it had proved convenient; perhaps also because their puristic zeal was concentrated on the sanctuary itself. Its ground plan they changed back until it followed, probably as closely as legend preserved it, that of the original *early* fourth stratum cella. They went even farther to wipe out whatever unpleasant associations were attached to the *late* fourth stratum room. They changed the end pilaster to a free-standing pillar, created a hearth of the usual domestic type of four large bricks sunk flush with the pavement, and added a bowl sunken into the pavement in front of the hearth, perhaps to catch the sacrificial blood. And the cella was kept thus, even when it was rebuilt, down to the final destruction of the city — which proved their gods to be fickle even in the face of all their pains and plans.

Let those who are scholars of such matters be tolerant of this reconstruction of motives. The archaeological evidence is there; I have read into it only what I saw, and perhaps I am not more mistaken than time has often proven more learned persons than myself to be in the matter of reconstruction, which is a dangerous pastime at best.

Other exciting finds, in the shape of objects, came to light during the temple excavations. From the fourth level in another section of the same area, a common-looking pottery jar yielded up a great cache of bronzes. In a way it was fortunate that the jar was of a common type, for its narrow neck and curved shoulders had to be broken away before the precious contents could be taken out. Had the jar itself been unusual or valuable, we would not have wished to destroy it; and we might have tried to remove its contents, leaving the jar intact. That would have proved disastrous. Unlike the ancient bronzes from Egypt, where climate is ideal for their preservation in the ground, the bronzes from Mesopotamia, and particularly from our region, are so badly patinated, devoured by the "bronze disease," that usually very little metal is left in the core. The patina does not always greatly effect the shape of the objects, but the chemical change in the substance of the metal itself will have robbed it of its durability, making it more fragile than glass. Consequently, it was an impatiently long job to take the closely packed individual pieces out of the jar. But we were rewarded with a pair of sun discs decorated in *repoussé*; a pair of similarly decorated moon crescents; seven or eight ceremonial sickle blades, one of which was inscribed; long decorated pins; a saucer-shaped object, the pierced edges of which would indicate that it may have been part of some armor plate to be sewn onto a cloth foundation; and most amusing of all, a little bell in which the free clapper still rattled but could not produce a tinkle. In the surrounding earth, hundreds of minute shell beads were embedded.

Also worthy of mention here, where I am touching on only the most dramatic happenings on the dig, are the developments surrounding the well in the temple courtyard, from which you will remember that earlier in the season the grotesque "Goomish" jars emerged. It was the same well that yielded up parts of the magnificent glazed lions the year before. In fact, it was the "white hope" of our temple area, since the cella itself had been stripped bare by the looting Assyrians — how we could have cursed them for it! Kerim, of elfin appearance, who regarded himself as a master at excavating wells, took this one down to a depth of approximately eleven meters, where the walls that had before been so easy to follow, stopped in an inexplicable jumble of meaningless earth. The *Sahibs* were called to examine the puzzle, and despite my fears that the whole thing might cave in on them, Dick and Charles disappeared into the subterranean depths. They came up with the conclusion that the puzzle might be the result of an ancient cave-in; and ordered an expert knife man to go down and probe around and see if he could pick up the traces of the well sides below. Instead, this man found something which neither he nor anyone else could have expected — a pavement. It was a good, firm, unmistakable mud pavement, upon which rested a quantity of archaic seals of the button type; and below it lay virgin soil. The rounded tops of some of these seals represented seated bulls, and one, a boar's head. The seal designs cut into the flat bottom surfaces were not done in the advanced Nuzi manner, which approaches gem cutting as we know it today, but had the crude, pock-marked appearance so typical of archaic motifs achieved by boring connected holes. These seals were obviously not of Nuzi manufacture, but much earlier. Therefore, the pavement on which they were found, meters below the Nuzi strata, must have been earlier even than Gasur. So, our well turned out to be not a well at all, but a matter of conjecture. The most probable guess was that it formed a shaft down which the Nuzians or their priesthood poured libations to the gods of the underworld.

What with theses unexpected developments, I must confess that we were ripe for the joke that Dick and Charles perpetrated. So ripe that it is possible that no cry of "wolf," even less cleverly executed than this one, would have left us unmoved. When one has seen a well end in a pavement which never could have produced water, and to make it even more fantastic, the shaft happens to lead to the one spot on the *tepa* where a cache of archaic seals lay buried, one is ready to believe anything.

One evening after dinner, the two conspirators started a private discussion about an object that had come "from the deep room" that day. These innocent-sounding allusions fired our interest to a point where we demanded to see the object. It was brought in from the storage room, and proved to be something that looked like a brick, completely covered with mud. On one side some modeling in relief was vaguely distinguishable. This discovery caused tremendous excitement, for Dick and Charles pretended not to have noticed it before. They soon had me cleaning it carefully with a needle; and Dr. Meek, who had been hoping for just such a discovery from the Ga-Sur level, was sure that it was a portrait of a king, and that the name would be given. Sure enough, when I had flaked off enough mud, some extremely archaic-looking writing began to show on the back. Finally our excitement grew to such a pitch that we couldn't wait for the long process of cleaning with a needle. The hard surface of the brick under the coating of mud seemed firm, so we decided to try to wash it. We got a tiny brush and a basin of water, and began, very very cautiously. But lo! The clay melted away in a manner that no dirt of ancient laying has ever been known to melt. As more and more of the surface was exposed, first consternation, and then realization broke upon us. Only then did I recall from my subconscious perception a subtle something in Dick's and Charles' attitude which, had it not been for my excitement, would have warned me from the beginning. They had acted their parts well enough to suppress their mirth, but I should have known that if this object had really come from the deep room they would never have been content to stay in the background and let the rest of us toy with the greatest find of the year. Early in the game, Mrs. Wilensky had caught a fleeting grin on Charles' face, and so she, too, had sat back and let us argue and conjecture over the possibilities of our wonderful brick. How we did bite!

After a hearty laugh, closer examination of the prize showed that it was made of plaster of Paris, soaked in creosote to give it a nice antique color. The strange writing turned out to be an incorrect copy of the Greek alphabet. It came, of course, not from the dig, but from a village over near the Euphrates, whose inhabitants are famous for manufacturing fakes. Fortunately most of these are obvious at a glance — as this one would have been if it had not had a coating of genuine mud. Even those which are cleverly made, betray themselves sooner or later. The modern manufacturers can seldom resist putting a little writing onto their masterpieces, just for good measure; and since they do not understand the language of the ancients, their cuneiform is usually as hopelessly jumbled as was the Greek alphabet on our brick. Even when some careful workman takes the trouble to make an exact copy from a genuine piece, being ignorant of the meaning of the symbols, he will put an ordinary memorandum of the sale of grain onto the statue of a king. Such a text, although genuine in itself, is so utterly out of place at the foot of royalty that it betrays the fraud by its mere existence.

Therefore, it is seldom that anyone with even a meagre knowledge of archaeology is taken in — more to our chagrin. But I must say that our chagrin wasn't very serious. Life in the field would grow dull without its jokes and occasional moments of horseplay. It seems that this particular fake had filtered into the village of Tarkhalan and had been brought out to the dig for the *Sahib*s to see and offered for sale at ten rupees. When Dick and Charles saw it, they of course knew that it was not genuine, but sensed the possibility of some fun with the rest of us. So they borrowed it for a few days, gave it its coating of mud, and brought it home. As a joke it was a huge success. In upholding our outraged innocence and defending our gullibility we protested that all of the obvious qualities about it were covered up with genuine dig mud when we were taken in. And with mock indignation we called it willful deception and a low trick.

Another time when the joke was on us, Dick was on the receiving end along with me. It was a case of mistaken identity this time. It was well into the spring, when the sparse crop of tourists had begun to arrive, and we had received word that an eminent scientist and his wife were in the country visiting the various excavations and on their way to call on us. It was no surprise, therefore, when Abdulla came to rout me out of the office one day, saying that a lady and a gentleman had arrived. I went immediately to give them my most cordial welcome. I was somewhat surprised at their appearance, for they looked extremely Anglo-Saxon; and the people we were expecting, although residents of America, and perhaps even American citizens, had not been born in our country. It was well that I did not find it easy to pronounce their somewhat complicated name, for I would surely have called these guests by it, before they could introduce themselves as Mr. and Mrs. West from Devonshire.

They turned out to be an elderly, obviously well-to-do couple who had travelled from Vladivostok to Timbuctoo and are probably still going. In Iraq they had visited every known archaeological site and although we must have been almost the last on their list, they still possessed the admirable intellectual curiosity to hire a car and brave that appalling road from Kirkuk to visit our dig. Having given them such a glad, glad hand of greeting, I had to sustain the tempo, and I doubt if any other casual guests ever got so much attention from a busy Expedition as these two did. I showed them the compound, the store-room full of antiquities, and then had Muhammed drive us out to the *tepa*. When Dick spotted us, walking atop the mud walls towards the temple area, he came to the same conclusion I had, and rushed over to greet those he supposed to be fellow scientists. I was careful to introduce my new friends by name before he had time to catch his breath. I say friends because by this time I had begun to think these people very nice on their own account. Dick thought so, too, after a little, but just at first he found, like I had, that he had a tempo to sustain. We spent a great deal of time showing them all the high spots; nor was it time wasted for they were students of Bible History and as enthusiastic a pair of amateur antiquarians as one would wish for. In fact, they were unusual guests, and they certainly received an unusual welcome. So unusual indeed from busy archaeologists who are always trying to accomplish more work than is possible in one season, that they were quite startled by it. They spoke again and again about our kindness, and on leaving they did something which I have known Americans of such brief acquaintance to do, but never before a Britisher: they gave us their calling card and urged us to visit them in their home. We did not tell them that we had mistaken them for others. It would have been a pity to burst the bubble.

CHAPTER XVI

Death and Rebirth

The first inkling we had of the tragedy was from a guest who had come out to visit the dig. On the road from Kirkuk he had come across a horse bearing a man, a woman and a baby. They had waved the car down and asked for a lift. The woman's face was streaming with blood where she had scratched herself as these people do when they lament. At first she had refused to get into the automobile because she had never ridden in one before, but finally was persuaded. On the way to Topazoa, where they wanted to go, she had moaned and mumbled incoherent words about a brother who was dead or dying.

The next day, being Friday, we were all at home when a sad-faced delegation of Topazoans came to ask us for our car. It was for the woman's unfortunate brother, who was a Dervish of their village. He had been hunting in the desert with some other men, when they ran across a snake. The Dervish, as we surmised, wanting to show off and prove his prowess, dismounted and picked up the reptile, waving it about in the air. On the way home he had fainted from his horse. His companions were not unduly alarmed, however, because he was *dervish*. Then, when he was dying, they came to ask us for aid. Dick wrote a note to the doctor, and sent Muhammed with the car post haste to take the man to the hospital. It was already too late. The unfortunate Dervish died before they could reach the doctor. When I enquired somewhat indignantly of our sentries why these people had waited so long before they did anything about so serious a thing as a snake bite, they merely shrugged. The man was *dervish*. He should not have died; and the fact that he did only proved that the snake did not know that he was *dervish*.

Soon afterwards, another less spectacular but not less unhappy death occurred in our village. The brother of one of our workmen had been a mounted policeman in Kirkuk. Some months before, he had accidentally fallen from his horse, and been kicked in the chest by the animal. He had developed consumption, a disease he probably already had, at least in an incipient stage, since it is very common in this country. After several months in the hospital he had been released, apparently in better health. But now he was bad again, and his brother came one night to ask us for medicine. Realizing that we could do nothing, but hoping to relieve the patient's mind, we gave a malted milk tablet, to be administered in warm milk. The idea was that it might prove to be a psychological sedative and put him to sleep. Our strong advice was for the family to take him back to the hospital.

After a few days the brother came again, this time asking for an orange, which the patient craved. We gave oranges, but refused another tablet, insisting that they take him to the hospital. We were afraid that if the sick man thought that the malted milk was helping him, he would refuse to go to the *hostahana*; but he refused anyway. He preferred to die at home in his own bed, and soon did. It is understandable why these people fear and dread the hospital. Its routine and the ministrations they receive there are strange to them; and when one is sick, the mind can conjure terror from the unknown so easily. On the other hand, used as I am to the immaculate shininess of American hospitals and familiar as I am with the medical methods — having been brought up in a medical atmosphere — I could not blame ignorance, it can be six of one and half a dozen of the other.

Sad though they were, these tragic events touched us only briefly in the exuberant surge of springtime. The days were mild. With brief showers, rainbows often showed through the sun-pierced clouds. On one afternoon of sun and rain, as I stood on the high elevation of the *tepa*, I could see a man ploughing a field not far away. His proud rags, the flank of the donkey and of the oxen — his plough team — the rough-hewn shape of the ancient wooden plough, the rich warm brown of new-turned earth, all showed through a shimmering mist of green, red, blue, and violet. The far dark mountains beyond reared their sombre peaks less darkly behind the iridescent bar of the rainbow; while the deep gloom of other far-flung peaks on either side of the bow's bright path was heightened by contrast. And up and over the great arc soared, oblivious to the wind-whipped challenge of the clouds, until it reached the place where the face of the heaven was torn between light and darkness. Thence it descended rapidly, truly with infinite grace into the sunlight in front of a billowy white bank hanging low over a distant village; and quickening its pace, fell rapidly into the very midst of the eager cluster of low huts that seemed to close in upon their heaven-sent treasure. My Western mind was thinking that *there* indeed the dreamed-of pot of gold might be revealed to one who cared to seek, so permanently transfixed the village seemed by this spectral shaft. But the brother of the ploughman, Muhammed Ali, was standing by my side, respectful of my mood of adoration in the face of unexpected beauty. Eastern dignity, which forbade him to intrude, struggled with a desire to impart Eastern wisdom, which is older than time itself. Finally, when the evanescent glory was quickly fading, he broke the magic silence. When he spoke it was not of gold or pots of gold. He said, "It is the sword of Allah, the *hunjar* of the heavens."

CHAPTER XVII

Visitors and Diversions

One night a group of wandering Persians set up their abode nearby. Daylight revealed their coarse, black goat's hair tents thrown up in the open field beyond the *waddi* bridge, a little distance from those of our Arab neighbors. The women and older boys kept busy during their brief stay plying one craft, that of fashioning crude colanders out of strips of bark bent round, with bits of green-painted screening tacked to the bottom. These articles the men peddled with indifferent success to our villagers. The people of Tarkhalan were suspicious of these foreigners with their grimy appearance and round hard black felt hats that looked like brimless bowlers. We felt that our sentries only reflected the attitude of the community when they told us that the vagabonds were thieves, and kept exaggerated guard over our gateway, shouldering their rifles even in broad daylight.

The Persian children would stare at us from afar, and their huge, sullen dogs came to the roadway to sniff at us suspiciously. The little daughter of our Arab neighbors did not play with the newcomers. She confided to us that these people were dirty! One of the men approached us, trying to sell us a dog. It was a grand, massive brute; and we might have been tempted to bargain had it not been for the realization that it had doubtless been sold countless times before, only to disappear along with its wandering masters when in the dark of the night they quit the community. And so they did go, silently, we know not where, leaving behind no reminder that they had ever stopped beside our gates.

The fine weather brought other visitors, more familiar and more welcome. As the end of the digging season approached, we enjoyed a more or less constant stream of archaeological guests, either from Pennsylvania's northern dig at Tell Billah, who stopped with us on their way to Baghdad, or from Chicago's dig near Baghdad, coming up to their northern site near Mosul. In either case, Kirkuk was a kind of half-way station. There, the railroad begins or ends, depending on which way you are bound; and the rest of the way from Mosul to Kirkuk must be made by motor car. So our house offered rest from the journey, and these welcome guests brought us not only the pleasure of their company, but also interesting news of what had been happening at other digs.

It was pleasant to have a knowing audience for our more spectacular finds of bronzes, seals, grotesque "Goomish" jars, the elaborate temple offering table in the shape of a decorated pottery house, the fine pottery from the early pit burials below Ga-Sur in the deep room, and the two-hundred Ga-Sur tablets, including the map. These were all objects of interest, and everyone agreed that the map was really *something*. Our *ambar*, or big storage room, its rough wooden shelves groaning with treasures, became the center of interest in the compound, a sort of reception room where excitement ran high when some guest made the discovery that this or that piece was related to something they had found elsewhere, thereby forging another link in the endless chain of cultural evidence. The lengthening of that chain, whether it is accomplished formally through publication or informally through such contacts as these, is one of the major aims of archaeology. From a purely personal point of view, however, our big moment was when we took these fellow archaeologists out to the dig to see our perfect temple cella. That was our prize exhibit, and it never failed to make an impression. Then, over luncheon, tea, or dinner, they would stimulate our imagination with descriptions of the season's discoveries at other places. Archaeology must always be a co-operative science, and this fact makes it more exciting, interesting, and pleasant.

I had been looking forward all season to staging a native style *calabala* in our compound on some spring night when there would be a full moon to light up the big courtyard. Our sentry, Sulieman, was reputed to be one of the most accomplished dancers in the village, so I had hopes for a really good show. On the occasion when we had two guests — the Epigraphist and Director from the Tell Billah dig — the time seemed right. There would be a full moon. We asked Jobar, the foolish shepherd, to come that night with his pipes, and I mentioned the possibility of a *calabala* to Sulieman, expecting that he would have his long-sleeved white shirt washed for the occasion. But a raw wind sprang up in the late afternoon, and after dinner it was apparent that we could not hold the dance outside. We were determined to go ahead anyway, so Abdulla cleared as much floor-space as possible in the dining room. Jobar arrived, tremendously pleased at being able for once to take center stage; but no Sulieman. Finally we sent Abdulla out to fetch him. He had been asleep, and when he did appear it was in his ordinary working clothes, his shirt at grimy-looking as though nothing unusual were about to happen, the lovely long sleeves were still dirty and hopelessly wrinkled from being wound up about his wrists. It was clear that he was not in the mood for our *calabala*, nor willing to exert himself in the dance. We were sorely disappointed.

Jobar, on the other hand, outdid himself, playing so loudly on the larger of his two clay pipes that we couldn't stand it in that little room, and had to insist that he use the other, smaller set. Nothing, however, could make Sulieman warm up. His performance was completely lifeless. Clearly something would have to be done or the whole show would be a flop. So we called the rest of the household servants in to sing. They brought a big metal wash pan which they had placed upside down on the floor, and squatted on their heels around it, supplementing Jobar's music with rhythmic beats as on a tom-tom. This racket put some pep into the performance, but it didn't take it long to become monotonous. One or two songs, charming in themselves, became dull with endless repetition. We were forced to conclude that native entertainment must be spontaneous; it couldn't be made to order. We gave Jobar a chit for his services and let the rest of them go back to bed. Our *calabala* then degenerated into a pale imitation of a Western dance to antiquated tunes from the gramophone.

One fine day about this time, I had gone out to the dig in the early afternoon. When Mrs. Wilensky came later she had a good story to tell about the excitement I had missed. After I had gone, one of the sentries came running to her in a great state of agitation to say that there was a fire in the village. He had seen flames and smoke from our roof. She went immediately to the roof, and sure enough, there were signs of a conflagration of some size. She got Mr. Wilensky from the drawing room. He grabbed the fire extinguisher from the wall, jumped into the Ford, and raced to the village. He came back shortly to report it a false alarm; just a pile of old brush being burned intentionally. The sentries, like the children they really were, although in stature grown men, had hoped for more *calabala* than that, and were all disappointed. Nevertheless, they and all the villagers were pleased with Mr. Wilensky's responses. They said that now we owed them nothing. They had come to protect us when they thought the Expedition was in danger on that New Year's eve the session before, and now we had responded when we thought that they were in trouble. They insisted that Mr. Wilensky had risked his life to save them.

Our chauffeur, Muhammed, was so *baksheesh*-minded that it was sometimes quite appalling. During the entire season he had presented Mrs. Wilensky and me with many gifts which he and his wife had made, and now, when the season was nearly over and we were preparing to leave for home, she sent us each an elaborate Turkoman costume made on her little hand-turned Singer Sewing Machine. These attentions, of course, called for return gifts, but even that was not enough to satisfy Muhammed. He was socially-minded as well, and though it probably didn't prevent him from beating her occasionally, he was very proud of his wife. They had a house in Kirkuk to which we had been invited many times; but we never quite got around to making the effort to go. Our occasional trips to town were always filled with business of one sort or another, and we were too well satisfied with the rural aspect of our lives to squander a precious Friday on the journey just for a call. Although Muhammed usually lived on our compound, Mrs. Muhammed lived at home; but just now he had brought her out for a visit in the village. She was going back to Kirkuk the next day, so we had to call that afternoon or they would both feel hurt. We did so at four-thirty, on the way home from the dig. Dick stopped the car in the village and let Mrs. Wilensky, Muhammed, and me out. Muhammed led the way up a tiny side street, through innumerable courtyards, to the house where his wife was staying. She met us at the door, smiling. We were glad to see her, glad to have arrived, especially because in getting there we had to run a gamut of apparently ferocious village dogs who seemed to wish for nothing more than a juicy bite out of our legs.

Muhammed's wife was quite young. She had a flat face and used too much kohl around her eyes; but she had nice little hands and feet that did not show signs of hard work. Her palms were stained a deep henna, as is the custom. She placed two pillows on the floor for us, and going to a chest in the corner of the small dark room she unlocked it and carefully extracted two cigarettes, which she offered. Then she went to a shelf and produced a bag full of nuts, from which she filled two small dishes. These she placed on the floor beside us, and when these gestures of hospitality were accomplished, she squatted on her heels on the earthen floor in front of us and smiled.

Picture a long, narrow, cell-like room with no windows, lighted only by the open doorway, the floor of hard-pounded clay, the walls of sun-dried brick, and the whole interior as bare of furniture as a barn. Imagine Mrs. Wilensky and me sitting on pillows, and little Mrs. Muhammed on the floor beside us, resplendent in a lavender cotton dress. Being a city woman, she wore what might be called a dress but would be more adequately described as an abbreviated Mother Hubbard. She had no head-cloth over her shiny black locks that were caught into two braids on the sides, with curled bangs in front. About her neck was an elaborate, dangling necklace of gold, wide gold and red glass bracelets on her arms, and golden rings on her fingers, silver anklets under black cotton stockings, and thick-soled wooden sandals on her feet. This is a picture of the adored wife of an unusual man who had saved his money and become *shwaya zengine* — a little rich. By way of background, picture innumerable dirty children, and a sheep with two lambs crowded into the room. Other women of the village had arrived and also squatted on their heels, staring at us, but smiling whenever we looked at them — filling every available inch in the small room, and spilling out the doorway. One of them was nursing a pair of twins.

The main attraction about Mrs. Muhammed that I could gather was that she was a *hajji* — she had been to Mecca. That is, of course, a great thing, especially for a woman. It gained her any amount of respect. She was quite willing to carry the burden of the conversation during our visit, and her main discourse was about what a fine house she had in Kirkuk, and how *muchi*, insignificant, was this house where she was staying. She had no inhibitions as to opinion; and the women of Tarkhalan didn't seem to mind such frankness, for they must have understood what she said, since she did not speak English. The difference between these women was striking. Muhammed's wife was unmistakably urban and sophisticated, while these others were rustic. Perhaps that is why we liked them so well, for with them rustic meant a simplicity and lack of affectation that was in itself charming, as well as an adherence to a traditional costume which was both graceful and appropriate.

Very soon, having exhausted our conversational powers, we terminated the call, refusing the jewelry which Muhammed's wife would strip from her person to give us. But this was not the last we were to hear from Mrs. Muhammed. A few weeks later when Mr. and Mrs. Wilensky were ready to leave the Expedition for their journey back to their home in Haifa, she came again to the village — to bid the architect's *khatoun* farewell. Mrs. Wilensky, who had been ill with bronchitis, was so busy packing that she simply couldn't find time to go herself to make another call, so she told Muhammed to bring his *khatoun* to see her at our house. Muhammed demurred, which was rather aggravating. Was our house not fine enough for his wife to visit? She would be received in Mrs. Wilensky's room, from which even Mr. Wilensky would be temporarily excluded. Muhammed was greatly embarrassed, but finally consented, and brought her for a short call. Later he explained his hesitation, complaining bitterly that by doing this thing he had laid himself open to ridicule from the villagers who asked him who he thought he was, an Englishman, to walk in the street with his wife!

CHAPTER XVIII

A Tearful Departure from Tarhalan

The car, piled high with our luggage, was chugging at the gates; but I tarried for a last, long glance about our compound which, in a few moments, would no longer be ours. Only then did the sadness of this departure, with its touch of finality, strike home. Before, the excitement of getting off and going home had been foremost; but at that moment, all their zest for the journey was gone. Leaving that place, even to be going home, was a bitter-sweet experience. But go, we must. Our sad-faced servants, and friends who had come from the village to see us off, followed us silently to our car. The departure of the Expedition was not this year as it had been in other times when they knew that another autumn would bring with it the return of their American employers. This time, the future was a great question mark. What it might bring of good crops or bad they did not know, but that it would not bring steady wages as they had enjoyed from the Expedition — this they knew for a certainty. They would get along, of course, as they had before we came; but there would be no extra rupees to squander on donkeys and other luxuries. They would have to work harder for smaller gain. Ah well, I told myself that all things are in the hands of Allah. Who knows, perhaps some day we will come again to Tarkhalan, to unfold from the earth the mysterious pages of Ga-sur history. I did not say *adieu* in a tone of finality, but rather, a hopeful *au revoir*.

When Charles met us at the depot, he said that the Expedition house had become a scene of bedlam after we had left, with Ali auctioning off our erstwhile belongings, and the owner of the house trying vainly to take immediate possession. The auction of Ali's was a smart idea. It saved him the trouble and expense of carting the stuff into town, and it also got rid of it for him while there was still a ready market for Expedition relics, and still rupees in the village pockets.

Mohammed was driving the Ford to Baghdad for us, and Hiddir had begged permission to go along. He had never seen Baghdad. So, they were both at the station to see us off before they started their journey by road. When we all met again in the City of the Caliphs, it was amusing to see Hiddir's reactions to the sights and wonders he beheld. He looked like a perfect country bumpkin in his pleasant, loose-flowing garb, and his inevitably untidy *khefia*. Muhammed, who considered himself quite a sophisticate, had blown himself to a gaudy checked suit. They were certainly a funny looking pair. We couldn't resist taking them to the bazaar and buying them black ebony walking sticks. And Charles treated Hiddir to his first and only movie in the ramshackle cinema palace on New Street.

The evening before we were to start on our journey across the Great Syrian Desert to Damascus, the Lebanons, and Beirut, and our ship, Muhammed came up to our hotel room to be paid off. He had a very long face as he presented his final accounts to *Sahib* Mr. Starr, and when Dick began to count out the rupees, the little fellow began to snivel, and then great sobs shook him and he broke down entirely. He couldn't see to count his money, which was a considerable sum. In fact, he seemed helpless, and I was afraid that in such an emotional state he might lose some of the precious *flus*. So, I got an old, clean bandanna out of my suitcase and tied it up in that. Then Dick propelled the little man gently to the door, and when it had closed upon him, I took out my handkerchief and wiped my own eyes. However, the next morning at six o'clock, Muhammed popped up in Nairn's garage, as bright and smiling as ever, to help us into the enormous lorry that was to take us across the desert and to wave frantically as we started on our way. He was our last link with Tarkhalan and all it meant, and I hated to see his funny little form disappear as we turned off New Street to cross the great pontoon bridge and start our six hundred mile journey to the coast.

We could not foresee that the poor benighted villagers we left behind were not the only ones who were going to know times of depression; nor that, because of it, our hope of returning to explore Ga-sur would grow very dim indeed. We could not know that the fond wishes of the Tarkhalan women for Dick and me to have a son would be so beautifully fulfilled in the person of a small, golden-haired Nicholas. And I certainly had no idea that I would ever be pounding out such wistful memoirs on my typewriter.

Part II

General Studies

Duck Tales at Nuzi:
A Note on the Trussed-Duck Weights Excavated at Yorgan Tepa

STEPHEN J. ANDREWS
Southeastern Baptist Theological Seminary
Wake Forest, North Carolina

The seven stone trussed-duck weights excavated at Yorgan Tepa from 1927 to 1931 help provide additional proof that the Nuzian system of mensuration essentially followed the widespread Babylonian model. Since six of the seven weights contained incised marks or notches on the neck and tail, R.F.S. Starr suggested, although tentatively, that the position of the incisions served as guides to the unit value of each weight. A reexamination of the problem proves Starr to have been correct — each notch on the neck of the duck indicated a ten-unit value, and each one on the tail, a one-unit value.

During the course of excavations at Yorgan Tepa from 1927 to 1931, seven stone duck-shaped weights were unearthed.[1] Four were fashioned from marble and three from gray or white limestone. All of the weights came from the Nuzi level of occupation, but apparently the findspots for only the four marble ducks were published.[2] Since such trussed-duck weights typically were found in Mesopotamia,[3] these examples help provide additional proof that the Nuzian

---

1 See R.F.S. Starr, *Nuzi: Report on the Excavations at Yorgan Tepa near Kirkuk, Iraq, Conducted by Harvard University in Conjunction with the American Schools of Oriental Research and the University Museum of Philadelphia 1927-31* (Cambridge, Mass: Harvard University Press, 1937, 1939), I:464-67 and II:33, pl. 122. Starr compared certain features of these weights with another large unpublished trussed-duck weight in the Iraq Museum (I:466). However, he did not state that this weight was found at Nuzi. Powell, on the other hand, did include this as a Nuzi weight suggesting that the total number of duck weights found at Nuzi was eight. See M.A. Powell, "Masse und Gewichte," in *RlA* 7:514.

2 See Starr, II:33. Three of the four marble weights were found in room 33 of the suburban house of Zigi.

3 Zoomorphic weights of stone and metal were very popular in antiquity, and trussed-duck weights dating from 1575-730 B.C.E. have come from Babylon, Erech, Nimrud, Nineveh, and elsewhere. See B. Kish, *Scales and Weights* (New Haven: Yale University Press, 1965), 80, 95, 113-22 and A.E. Berriman, *Historical Metrology* (New York: Dutton, 1953), 8, 62. These so-called "duck" weights may also represent geese or swans.

Studies on the Civilization and Culture of Nuzi and the Hurrians - 8

system of mensuration essentially followed the widespread Babylonian model.[4]

The following tabulation demonstrates that incised marks or notches on the neck or tail were characteristic features of the Nuzi trussed-duck weights:[5]

No.	*Weight*	*Unit*	*Description*
30.	16.36 g.	2 shekels	Marble duck weight (Pl. 122, N [?])[6]
38.	159.50 g.	20 shekels	Marble duck weight, two notches on neck (Pl. 122, O)
39.	480.00 g.	1 mina	Limestone duck weight, one notch on tail
40.	492.50 g.	1 mina	Marble duck weight, one notch on tail (Pl. 122, W [?])[7]
41.	976.00 g.	2 minas	Marble duck weight, two notches on tail (Pl. 122, P)
42.	3,401.97 g.	7 minas	Limestone duck weight, seven notches on tail[8]
43.	10,047.06 g.	20 minas	Limestone duck weight, two notches on neck

R.F.S. Starr recognized the identification value of the markings.[9] Hence, weights 39 and 40, both of which had one notch on the tail, weighed one mina each. Weight 41 had two marks and weighed two minas. Finally, No. 42 which had seven notches on its tail predictively weighed seven minas. Consequently, Starr concluded that the marks incised on or near the tail represented a value of one mina each.[10]

Incisions on the neck presented Starr with a more perplexing problem. Duck weight 43 with two notches on its neck weighed the equivalent of twenty minas. In this case, each mark would stand for one ten-mina unit of weight.

Also, Starr had seen an unpublished duck weight three times the size of No. 43 in the Iraq Museum.[11] Again, Starr reasoned that the six markings on its neck

---

4 See Powell, *RlA* 7:514 and S.J. Andrews, "The *Šupe''ultu* 'Exchange' Transaction at Nuzi" (Ph.D. diss., Hebrew Union College, 1994), II:283-92. The Nuzi duck weights return a mean average for the mina at 488.30 grams with a high and a low range of 502.35 and 478.50 grams, respectively. The median stands at 488 grams.

5 See Starr, I:466.

6 Powell connects figure N on plate 122 with weight 43 (see Powell, *RlA* 7:514). Starr's description, however, notes that 43, a twenty-mina weight was made of limestone and had two marks on the neck. Figure N, on the other hand, appears to represent a marble weight with no marks. Weight 30 fits this description. Regardless of the correct identification, it is obvious that figure N is not drawn to the same scale as O, P, and W.

7 Cf. Powell, *RlA* 7:514.

8 Starr noted that this weight was badly chipped away under the breast of the duck. He felt that it was originally a ten-mina weight "carefully chipped away until the desired value of seven units had been achieved." The seven roughly cut notches would then be a later addition. See Starr, I:467. Unfortunately, Starr does not note if this weight originally contained a notch on the neck.

9 Starr, I:466-67. Trussed-duck weights from elsewhere in Mesopotamia often carry cuneiform inscriptions identifying the weight value. The Nuzi duck weights may be the only examples marked in this manner.

10 Ibid.

11 Ibid., 466. Cf. n. 1 above.

stood for six units of ten minas each and that its weight would be equal to sixty minas or one talent.[12] Together, these two examples suggested to Starr that each incision on the neck represented one ten-mina unit of value.

However, Starr maintained that one of the other duck weights unfortunately disproved this theory. This third example was "a relatively small weight, badly chipped, and originally two minas in value." The two notches on its neck could not stand for twenty minas (two units of ten minas each). Hence, Starr concluded, "The position of the two incisions blasts the hope that this alone would serve as a sure guide to the unit value."[13]

Starr was certainly correct in stating that a mark on the neck does not represent a ten-mina unit. But it might represent another ten-unit value. In fact, another explanation does exist which suggests that position can be taken as a reliable guide to unit value.

Starr did not identify specifically the small weight which disproved the issue of position. The only other duck weight with markings on the neck is No. 38. Two marks on the neck clearly show in the drawing on plate 122, O.

Now this marble duck has a published mass of 159.50 grams. If this was originally a two mina weight, as Starr states, then more than 800 grams or 80% of its mass would have been chipped away to bring it to its current weight.[14] One other duck weight appears to have been remanufactured in such a manner. According to Starr, No. 42 was carefully reduced to seven minas from an original ten-mina weight, and the seven notches were secondarily added to the tail to indicate its new mass.[15] If this was true also for No. 38, then the two notches on the neck were probably added to represent its new weight.

What did the two marks indicate? When divided by two units of ten, No. 38 returns a value of 7.975 grams which is equivalent to the weight of the shekel at Nuzi.[16] Consequently, No. 38 turns out to be a twenty-shekel weight, and the incisions on its neck represent two units of ten shekels each, or twenty shekels.

Duck weight No. 30 confirms that a series of shekel weights were employed at Nuzi along with the mina weights. Hence, although the sample is small, the position of the incisions on the trussed-duck weights at Nuzi did "serve as a sure guide to the unit value." For both the mina and shekel weights, a notch on the neck indicates a ten unit value. On the mina weights, a one-unit value was customarily represented by one mark on the tail.

---

12 Based on the average mean of 488.30 grams per mina for the other Nuzi examples, this hefty duck weight should bend the scales at 29.298 kilograms. The Babylonian talent contained sixty minas and weighed thirty kilograms. See Powell, *RlA* 7:510.

13 Starr, I:467.

14 The final result of such a destructive procedure would probably not look much like a trussed-duck weight, at least, not as recognizable as the one depicted as Plate 122, O.

15 See note 8 above.

16 The Nuzi duck weights return a mean average for the shekel at 8.138 grams with a high and a low range of 8.372 and 7.975 grams, respectively. The median stands at 8.134 grams.

Anat in a Text from Emar

STEFANO BASSETTI

Cotignola – (Ra), Italy

The contract Emar VI/3, no. 26, dated to the second year of MelišiḪU, king of Babylon (1186-1172 B.C.), contains two occurrences of a city read by Arnaud as URU AN-*x*. Quite likely the text should be read URU *An-at*, a well-known city in the country of Sūḫu. Supporting evidence for this reading is the occurrence of Nabunni in this text and in a letter in which he is referred to as *Na-bu-ni ša* KUR *Su-uḫ*.

Emar VI/3, no. 26 (Msk 73.273 [*Emar* VI/1, p. 59]) is a (sale ?) contract concerning the house of Kidin-[Gula][1] son of Sîn-uṣu[r] by Nabun[ni], son of Ulamb[ur]iaš$^{!}$ (^{2}*i-na* É ^{m}*ki-din-*^{d}[*Gu-la*] ^{3}DUMU ^{md}30-UR[Ù] ^{4} ^{m}*Na-bu-u*[*n-ni*] ^{5}DUMU *Ú-lam-*[*bu/bur-r*]*i*$^{!}$ *-iá-áš*$^{!}$).

The text further records that the transaction took place in the city X (lines 7 and 14), thus, according to Arnaud's transliteration: ^{7}*i-na* URU.KI A[N]-*x* ; ^{14} URU AN-*x*.

This document belongs to a small group of tablets unearthed in the "House A V." It is dated to the second year of MelišiḪU, king of Babylon (1186 -1172 B.C.), and, together with the texts *Emar* VI/3 nos. 24, 25, and 27, it is distinguished by the peculiarity of its cuneiform writing which looks quite different from those of the "Syrian" Emar tablets.[2]

As concerns the toponym(s) recorded in lines 7 and 14, Arnaud is inclined to believe that they are one and the same, although he is unable to suggest any identification for it.[3]

To judge from the cuneiform copy,[4] there should be no hesitation in reading *i+na* URU.KI *An-at*$^{!}$ (l. 7) and URU *An-at* (l. 14). Obviously, this is the well-known city of the country of Sūḫu, located on the middle Euphrates.[5]

---

1 For the restoration cf. *Emar* VI/3, no. 25: 6.

2 Cf. Arnaud, *Emar* VI/3, pp. 35 and 37.

3 Cf. *Emar* VI/3, p. 37.

4 Cf. *Emar* VI/1, p. 59.

5 Cf. RGTC 5, p. 31 and M. Liverani, *Studies on the Annals of Aššurnaṣirpal II. 2: Topographical Analysis*, Roma 1992, pp. 67-68.

Studies on the Civilization and Culture of Nuzi and the Hurrians - 8

It is not without interest that another occurrence of Nabu(n)ni — one of the two contracting parties of *Emar* VI/3, no. 26 — is recorded in a still unpublished tablet from Emar (or from its vicinity); a (copy of a ?) letter sent from *Tal-mi-*Lugal-*ma ša* KUR.URU *I-mar* to *Na-bu-ni ša* KUR *Su-uḫ*.

Notwithstanding the anomalous spelling *Su-uḫ*, it seems very likely that the Nabu(n)ni who acts in Anat is the same Nabu(n)ni from the country of Sūḫu. The presence at Emar of people of Sūḫu and the existence of Emar – Sūḫu interrelations are sporadically, yet well attested. See, e.g., *Emar* VI/3, no. 32:25 and no. 263:19, 22; cf.(?) no. 120:18 (PN DUMU *sú-uḫ-ḫi*)

The spelling URU *An-at* does not occur in Middle Assyrian and Babylonian sources (cf. RGTC 5, p. 31). But, on the other hand, it is well attested in Neo-Assyrian sources (cf. *NAT*, p. 19) and in the inscriptions of the rulers of Sūḫu (A. Cavigneaux - B. Kh. Ismail, *BaM* 21 [1990], p. 408).

Nuzi Viewed from Urkesh, Urkesh Viewed from Nuzi

Stock Elements and Framing Devices in Northern Syro-Mesopotamia

MARILYN KELLY-BUCCELLATI

California State University, Los Angeles

Newly excavated inscribed seal impressions have led to the identification of Mozan with the Hurrian city of Urkesh. One of the artistic styles preserved in the non-inscribed seal impressions from the same floor deposit is characterized by the inclusion of stock elements and framing devices. Seal impressions excavated at Brak (probably ancient Nagar) exhibit similar stylistic features. Centered in northern Syro-Mesopotamia in the third millennium, this style is viewed as having an influence in the region still in the Nuzi period, exemplified here by the Nuzi painting.

The recently excavated Akkadian seal impressions from Mozan, located in the Khabur Region of northeastern Syria, have led us to identify the site with the ancient third-millennium Hurrian city of Urkesh (Fig. 1). In the excavations on the western side of the tell just inside the city wall and near a presumed city gate a large building was discovered between 1992 and 1994 (Fig. 2). Over 600 seal impressions were found *in situ* on one floor of a large room in Sector B of this building which we can now identify as a Royal Storehouse (Fig. 3). This identification of Mozan as Urkesh came from our study of both the iconography and seal inscriptions, as over 170 of the rollings were inscribed. In this excavated corpus six seals could be attributed to *Tupkish endan Urkesh*, "Tupkish king of Urkesh." The queen, Uqnitum, had eight seals; on one she is called DAM Tupkish, on the others NIN or simply DAM.[1] While the queen has an Akkadian name, both the king and a member of the queen's household, the nurse Zamena, have Hurrian names. The king's title is *endan*, well known from the inscription on the bronze lions of Tiš-atal. In two instances members of the queen's household have scenes depicted on them which are directly connected with their professions. The nurse has two seals on both of which she is represented holding the hands of a royal child sitting on the lap of the queen. One other seal shows a

1 Buccellati and Kelly-Buccellati 1995 and 1996a; all the Urkesh drawings published here were made in the field by Cecily J. Hilsdale. Lily Tsai produced the line drawings in Figs. 11-14.

Studies on the Civilization and Culture of Nuzi and the Hurrians - 8

kitchen scene with a woman churning and a man about to butcher an animal. This seal belonged to the female cook of the queen; unfortunately her name is not preserved in the very worn inscription box reserved for it.[2]

The scenes on the seals belonging to the king and queen are an embodiment of royal power and dynastic succession, as seen later in Hittite art. In the seals the king, queen and probably four royal children are depicted. The older children (a boy and a girl) are shown touching the lap of either the queen or the king. Two smaller children are sitting on the lap of the queen. The intimate touching gesture of the older children is interpreted as a dynastic act of dependence and continuity.[3]

An even larger number of uninscribed seals could be reconstructed from the seal impressions. The uninscribed sealings are divided into two major categories: those which are closer to southern models and those which are in a style characterized by the inclusion of stock elements, with a special emphasis on the placement of discrete heads of animals, and geometric frames. In this article, I will concentrate on this second style represented in the Urkesh corpus. In fact, I think they are particularly appropriate for a volume dedicated to Richard F.S. Starr since these sealings are part of a northern style found not only at Urkesh but on sealings excavated at Brak by Mallowan and also found in the recent excavations of David and Joan Oates and those of R.J. Matthews. This style was influential as late as the Nuzi period and is most spectacularly seen in the reconstructed portion of the Nuzi painting which emphasizes the positioning of discrete heads within complex geometric frames. Although unsuspected this parallelism can be seen clearly in the iconographic and the formal aspects of the art of both Urkesh (and other northern third-millennium art) and Nuzi. Given the preliminary nature of the research, I will emphasize the presentation of the data from Urkesh, as yet unpublished, and will suggest a line of inquiry in the way of comparative and stylistic analysis, leaving for a later date a fuller study along the same lines.[4]

---

2 See Buccellati and Kelly-Buccellati 1996c.

3 For a fuller discussion of this topic see Buccellati and Kelly-Buccellati 1996b.

4 The evidence for this third-millennium northern art is found for the most part in seal impressions excavated in a stratified context from Urkesh/Mozan and Nagar/Brak. The Mari seal is from a pit while the seal impression from Khafaje is from the surface. Thus the basic evidence comes first of all from the stratigraphic context and subsequently from the style. What we have then is a major corpus of well stratified evidence from modern excavations for this third-millennium art. The Urkesh/Mozan stratigraphic evidence and precise distributional patterns will be published along with all the seal impressions from the Royal Storehouse in the Mozan series. For a recent summary of the status of Nuzi and Hurrian studies, see Owen and Wilhelm 1995.

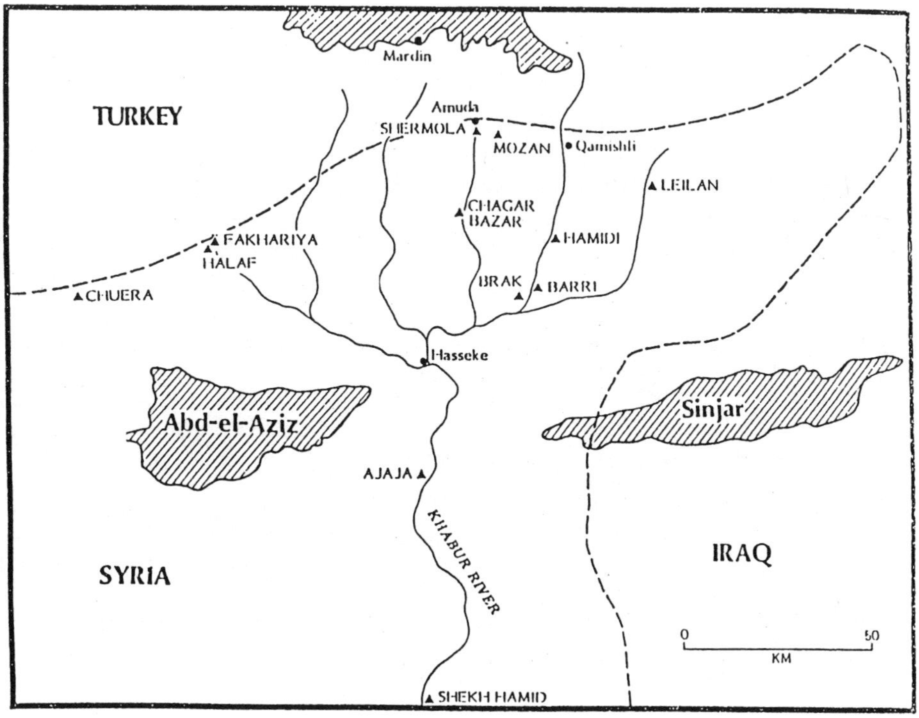

FIGURE 1
Map of the Region of Urkesh/Mozan

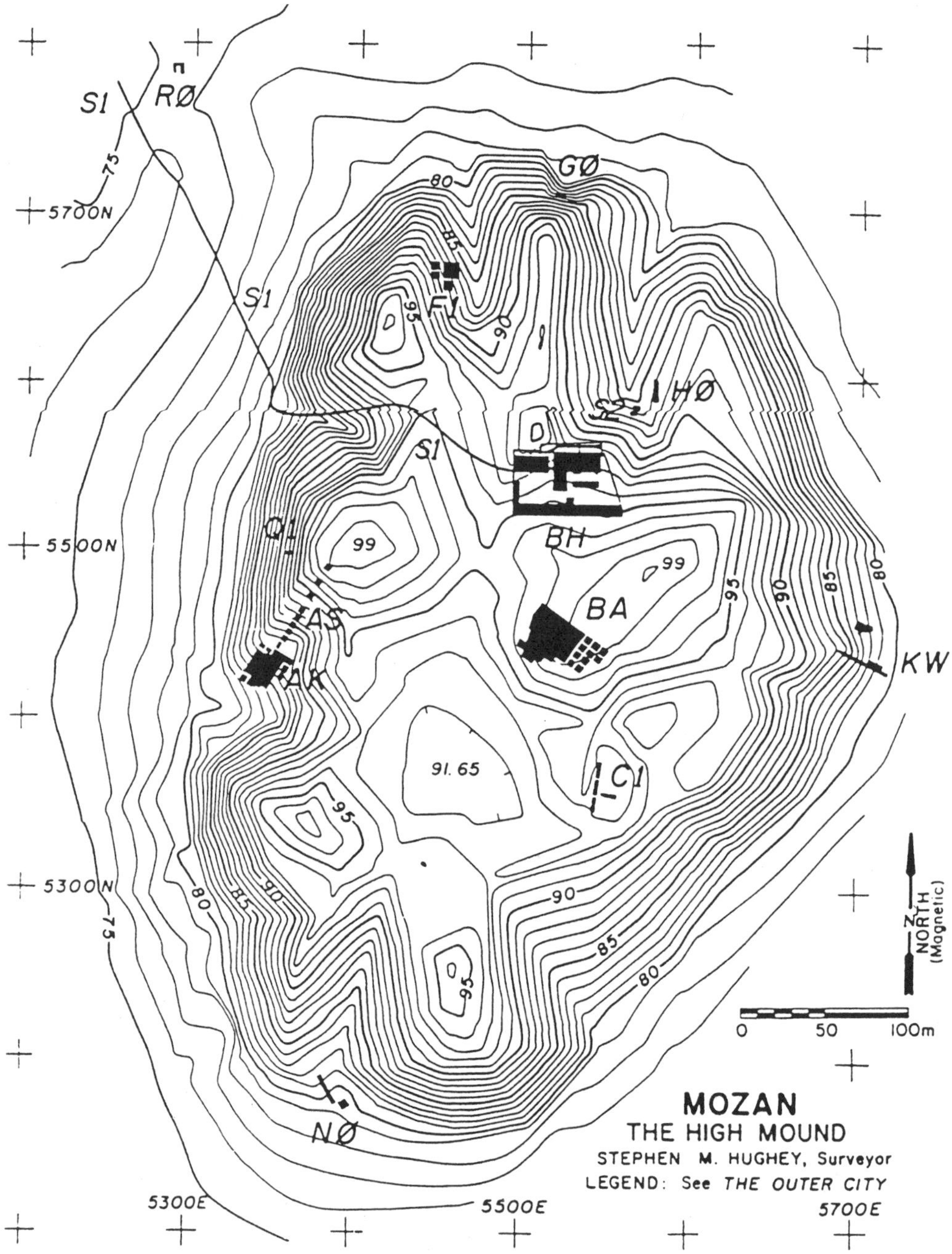

FIGURE 2

Urkesh/Mozan: Topographic Map of the High Mound

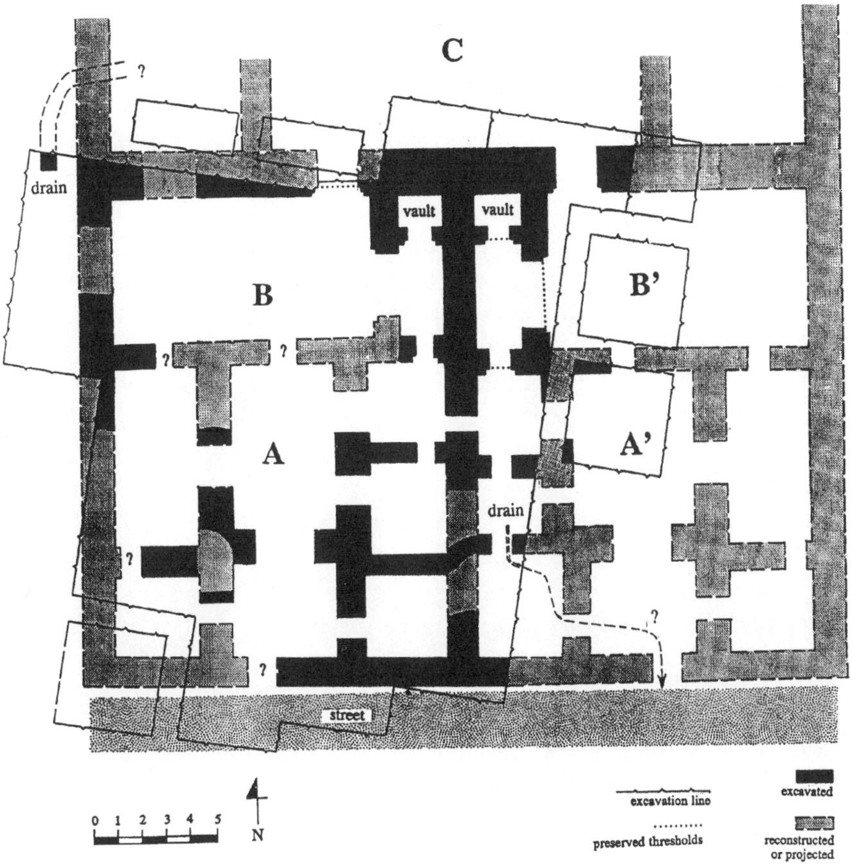

FIGURE 3

Urkesh/Mozan: Plan of the Royal Storehouse (Building AK)

THE URKESH EVIDENCE

The group of stratified seal impressions from the Royal Storehouse under discussion represents a seal style characterized by small seals with a number of figurative elements including humans, animals, trees and other natural elements carved in a simple, somewhat schematic style including short lines and sharp angles. Individual parts of the animal figures can be articulated with long naturalistic lines but other portions of the same animal are shown with geometric-type patterns achieved through the use of short incisions creating segmented forms, as for instance in the faces of most of the animals. In most of the figures large eyes fill the heads. The bodies show little emphasis on details such as hair patterns.The designs include large figures which fill the space but are differentiated in that some of these are interacting with other figures in the composition, while others are more in the nature of static elements placed there for reasons other than the course of the action, somewhat after the fashion of filler motifs. The figures can be arranged in a variety of ways, including the placement of reclining elements below a scene which is otherwise filled with standing figures or figures placed at right angles or even reversed with respect to other elements in the design. Particularly important is the fact that framing devices composed of geometric patterns take on a major compositional function.

Some motifs are in the category of animal combat scenes with human participants. This is the case of A5.180 (Fig. 4) which shows on the far right a human wearing a patterned hat holding a long spear near a lion attacking a bull. On the left there is a seated person wearing a round patterned cap.

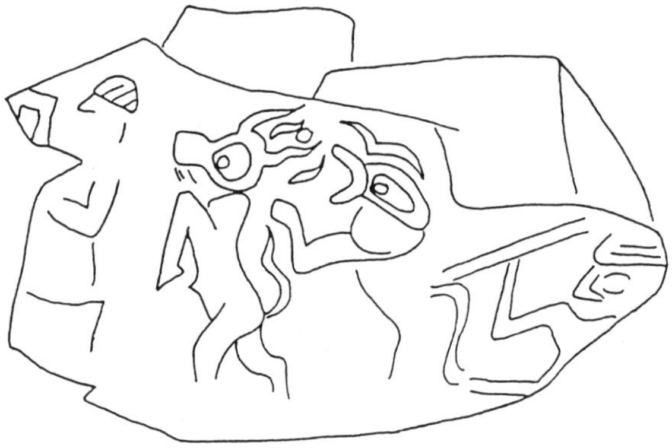

FIGURE 4

Urkesh/Mozan Seal Impression (A5.180). Scale 3:1

In a second scene, A5.178, with two rollings (Fig. 5), two short skirted figures face right toward a horned animal which is clearly depicted on his back. Above this portion of the scene is a geometric design with rectangular panels. Beyond the horns of the bull is an unknown geometric pattern.

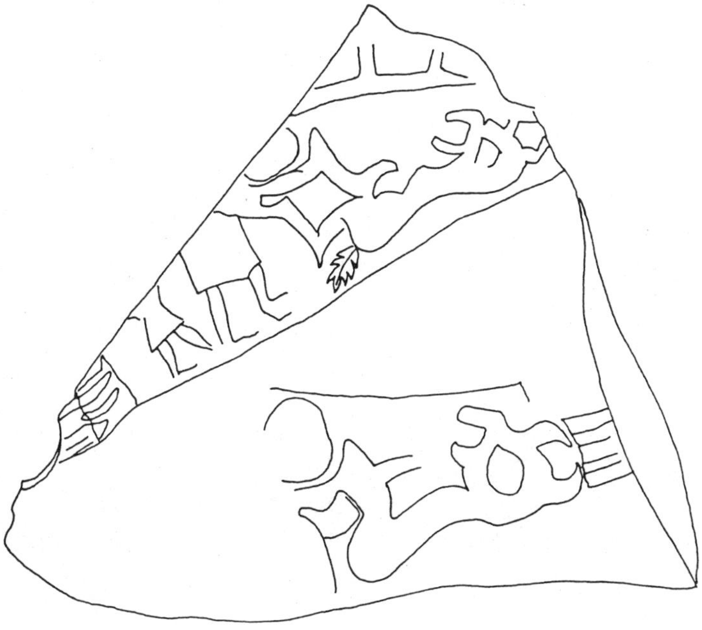

FIGURE 5

Urkesh/Mozan Seal Impression (A5.178). Scale 3:1

A1q1048.9 (Fig. 6) is a small sealing which depicts a short skirted figure with a triangular shaped head behind a standing horned animal.[5] The figure does not appear to be holding a weapon but a large oval object is placed in front of him. Above the animal is a scorpion while a short stylized tree is shown behind the man.

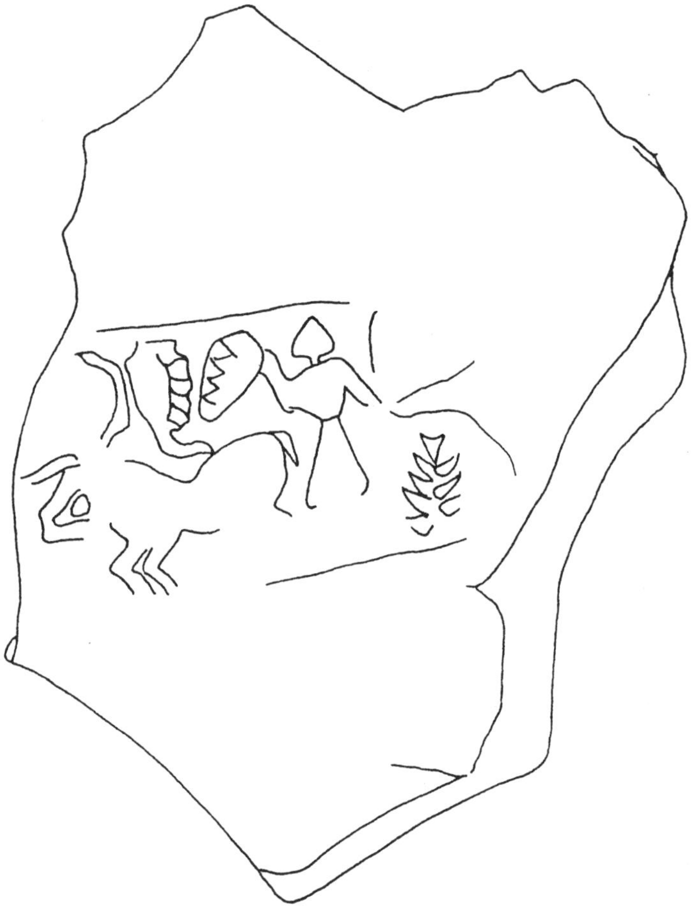

FIGURE 6

Urkesh/Mozan Seal Impression (A1q.1048.9). Scale 2:1

---

5 A thin, elongated figure with a rounded triangular head can be seen as one sealing from Brak, Buchanan 1966: 757, which came from a context dated to the Akkadian period or later by Mallowan; his body is rectangular in form while ours is constructed of two triangles as in Fig. 7.

A human with a triangular shaped head is also represented in Fig. 7 (a composite from 4 rollings: A1.500, A5q923.6, A5q939.9, A1.486). In addition, this figure has a triangular torso with the articulation of his arms and body depicted as attached on the exterior. He holds a long sword; beyond him, may be an animal whose front hoof he grasps. The second figure in the scene is a human carved in a more rounded style with a large eye in the middle of his head which is shown in profile; this style of head is characteristic for some of these seals. He may be nude and has one arm raised.[6]

FIGURE 7

Urkesh/Mozan Seal Impression (A1.500+). Scale 3:1

The next scene, A1. 380 (Fig. 8), is also connected with this group in the way the profile head is shown with a large eye in the center, the large geometric object next to him (possibly the same type of object as in Fig. 5), and the emphasis on the two triangles (flowers?) protruding from a large unknown shape decorated with a geometric pattern.[7]

The two remaining seal impressions from the Royal Storehouse to be discussed here are connected both on stylistic and iconographic evidence to other sites in the area. One impression, A1q704.1 (Fig.9), contains a discrete head and the other (Fig. 10, for which we had three rollings: A5.153, A5.165, A5.115) contains a geometric border separating two seated figures, perhaps part of a banquet scene. In Fig. 9 the scene is generally an animal combat scene

6 The extreme difference in the depiction of the two figures in this scene appears to single out the triangular headed man as a special figure. In one of the Brak impressions (Buchanan 1966: 756, the context of which is dated by Mallowan to the Akkadian period but by Buchanan to ED I) all four figures have a triangular head although the articulation of the arms and bodies is shown differently in the published drawing.

7 The shape is too large to be a basket but the pattern is similar to one.

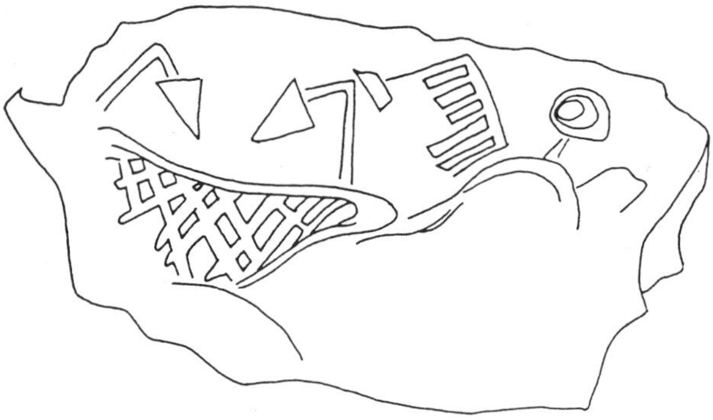

FIGURE 8
Urkesh/Mozan Seal Impression (A1.380). Scale 2:1

representing in the upper rolling a figure, with a head depicted similarly to those in Figs. 7 and 8, standing with an outstretched arm before a horned animal. Isolated in the field is a large bird which by its position does not appear part of the animal combat portion of the design.[8] Below is a second rolling representing another section of the design: a human is placed behind a standing animal with a long tail. Above this animal is the isolated head, neck and a portion of the front leg of a horned animal. This can be compared with a row showing similar parts of a horned animal published by Buchanan[9] and discrete heads and legs in a row dating to the Akkadian period from Brak.[10] Another group in the seal impressions dating to the Akkadian period have discrete heads which occur in connection with geometric borders[11] but also occur

---

8 See the head of a bird in the Mari bone seal with large discrete head (Parrot 1956c: Pl. LXV: 329), discussed below. Detached heads already appear in ED III (see Porada 1948, No. 85, human-headed bull, *ibid.* No. 75 horned animal head in profile; Buchanan 1966, No. 202 horned animal head in profile).

9 1966: 811, from an Ur III context in Brak.

10 Matthews *et al.* 1994: Fig. 13:3, see also no. 11 and Matthews 1991: Fig. 1:1, impressions of a seal with a number of heads of a horned animal perhaps indicates an animal herd: this was used to seal triangular dockets and also dates to the Akkadian period. See Frankfort 1939: Pls. X:h, XI:e.

11 Buchanan 1966:808; Mallowan called the context Akkadian or later. Buchanan published these seal impressions in his chapter on peripheral Early Dynastic styles and dated them on stylistic grounds to ED III. However in some cases Mallowan had dated the archaeological context to the Akkadian period, noted here. The recent finds of excavated seal impressions at Brak dating to the Akkadian period and some of the Urkesh seal impressions from the Royal Storehouse, published here, make it clear that many of these impressions excavated by Mallowan can be attributed to the Akkadian period.

without them.[12] In the last several years, the Brak excavations have found a number of Akkadian seal impressions of this type which can be considered along with Mallowan's excavated corpus. The new impressions have both elements among the motifs represented in the seal impressions: geometric borders,[13] a guilloche,[14] and strikingly arranged discrete heads showing a stylized horned animal, a lion and a human headed bull each repeated a number of times.[15] The human headed bull and lion heads as discrete elements, the

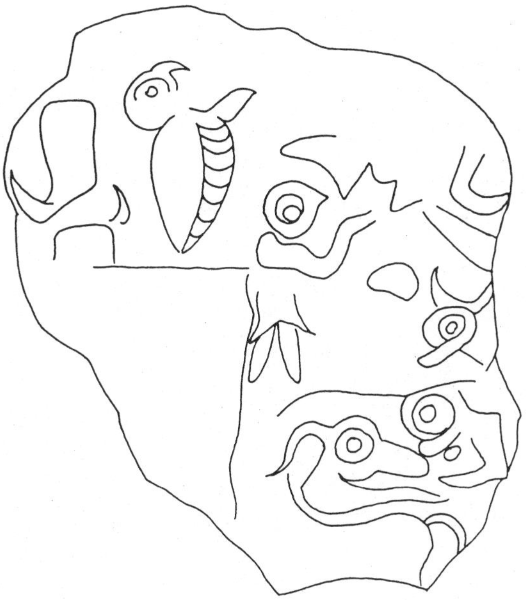

FIGURE 9

Urkesh/Mozan Seal Impression (A5q704.1). Scale 3:1

12 Buchanan 1966:807 where there are 3 lion heads placed sidewise; Mallowan called the findspot an Ur III context; 806 also shows discrete heads of lions and a bearded man, possibly with horns; there is no geometric border in the scene.

13 Matthews 1991: Fig. 1: 7.

14 *Ibid*. Fig.1:4; in this seal impression the guilloche runs through the middle of the design with two rows of discrete heads above and below showing lions and two scorpions.

15 Matthews 1991: Fig. 1: 15 and Matthews *et al*. 1994: Fig. 13: 10, 13. While carved in a different style, the Ebla seal impressions contain geometric borders as well as one seal with the same stock elements of a cat head, human-headed bull, female with long curls, and profile views of horned animal heads. These isolated heads along the upper and lower borders repeat the heads of some figures in the main portion of the design, Matthiae 1977, Fig. 18.

geometric borders, and the guilloche had already been known from the impressions excavated by Mallowan.

FIGURE 10

Urkesh/Mozan Seal Impression (A5.153+). Scale 3:1

From the Temple of Ishtar at Mari, Parrot published a bone cylinder seal, found in a pit in cella 17, with a mask (Fig. 11).[16] The large frontally positioned bearded head, with bull ears and horns, large eyes, long braided hair[17] and what may be a feathered crown is another third-millennium example of the prominent use in a larger composition of a discrete head.[18] The smaller frontal lion head above the "mask" in the Mari seal is also represented on a seal impression found on the surface at Khafaje[19] and in the Brak sealings.[20] In addition the Mari seal has a frieze of animal heads below wearing what appears to be a type of feathered crown consisting in three feathers(?). This is paralleled on lion heads from Brak[21] and appears to be the same crown as shown on some

16 Parrot 1956: pp. 187-88 and Pl. LXV: 329.

17 Braided hair is the usual hair style of the queen of Urkesh, Uqnitum, and her daughter.

18 The ends of the bull's beard are curled; a seal impression from Brak showing a similar head appears from the drawing to also emphasize these curls, Matthews *et al.* 1994: Fig. 13:10.

19 Frankfort 1955:Pl. 35:362; Buchanan 1966: p. 151 says of the Khafaje seal impression "it was probably made by a seal imported from the north."

20 Buchanan 1966: 8067; Matthews 1991: Fig. 1:2,4,5; Matthews *et al.* 1994: Fig 13:13.

21 Buchanan 1966:806; he notes this comparison between the Brak example and Mari. Amiet pointed out that the heads below the mask in the Mari seal can be viewed in reverse as lions' heads, Amiet 1985, pp. 477-78. Reversals are a prominent feature in the Urkesh royal seal impressions. For Chuera the central large head on the Mari seal was cited in connection with the seven-goddess relief, see Moortgat and Moortgat-Correns 1976, p. 53.

examples of the woman's head in the later Nuzi painting.[22] Parrot notes a large discrete head on a seal impression from Nuzi.[23] The inclusion of dots in filling empty spaces also is characteristic of this northern style.[24]

Fig. 10 renders a seated figure on the right with a second figure on the left raising his arm; this second figure is characterized by the typical large dotted eye. Between them is a double v-shaped geometric border which may have originally been inspired by a palm trunk; this border appears to continue into the upper portion of the design. On the left the frame, a horizontal geometric pattern extends above the head of the figure; there may have been a similar horizontal extension of the frame above the figure on the right but this part of the design is not preserved. The function of the frame is fundamental to the overall design of the seal and can be seen as such even if we do not have the whole of the figural motif. The frame in this case serves as a major geometric element in itself and therefore gives a geometric focus to the design; it also serves to encase the figural portion of the design, thereby pointing up the fundamental difference between the figural portion of the design and the geometric one. In addition, given that the figures are shown in such a way that their bodies are indicated by a segmented line (as is the case for many of the human and animal figures in this style), they, too, mirror the geometric pattern in their own way.

In the excavations of Mallowan at Brak, a group of seal impressions were discovered which emphasize a horizontal geometric border placed at the bottom, top or in the middle of a design which is otherwise figurative. In some cases this horizontal frame was purely geometric[25] or represented a guilloche.[26] In the more recent excavation this style of seal impressions continue to be found with examples of both geometric borders[27] and the guilloche.[28] From an Akkadian stratum at Tell Chuera an animal combat scene is framed on three sides with a V-shaped geometric border.[29]

22 Starr 1937 and 1939: Pl. 128.

23 Parrot 1956:185; Starr 1937:p. 444 and Pl. 119:B. Starr notes in his description: "a seal impression from early Nuzi, and appears as an interesting combination of Ga.Sur and Nuzi traditions."

24 Both this Mari seal and the seal which was used to make the Khafaje impression must be from the north as are Frankfort 1939: Pls. X:h, XI:e. An example from Tell Taya shows in two friezes separated by lines a series of dots and isolated animal heads, Reade 1973, Pl. LXXII:a.

25 Buchanan 1966:808 Mallowan described the context as Akkadian or later.

26 Buchanan 1966: 803; Mallowan called the context possibly Akkadian.

27 Matthews 1991: Fig. 1:7,8; Matthews *et al.* 1994:Fig. 13:4,5,10.

28 Matthews 1991:Fig. 1:4; Matthews *et al.* 1994:Fig. 13:6 (similar to a dotted guilloche) and 16.

29 Moorgat 1960, Fig. 14; Amiet 1963, Fig. 32.

URKESH AND NUZI

However, it was the discovery in our corpus from the Royal Storehouse of the two scenes shown in Figs. 9 and 10 which made me think of the Nuzi painting (Fig. 12). Wall paintings at Nuzi were found both in the private houses and in the palace. In the private houses only one wall of what was usually the most important room in the house was painted. The most common type of decoration was a wide panel of solid red color between panels of gray; a vertical guilloche could be used as a divider.[30] While none of the painted designs were found still adhering to the walls, a large painted section with the designs preserved came from the floor of a palace corridor, L15B of Stratum II.[31] From the number and preservation of the fragments, Starr reconstructed the painting as having gone around the whole room above the height of the doors.

FIGURE 11

Drawing of scene from Mari seal rearranged to emphasize the composition

Early Dynastic/Old Akkadian. Scale 1:1.

Cf. Parrot 1956: PL. LXV:329.

The "mask" (with horns above a headdress consisting of a single large tuft in the center, and three small tufts on either side, shown as a band around the forehead) and a cat-like lion head above are interpreted as a vertical element encasing a figurative scene (hero and animal combat). A row of stylized heads can be viewed as reversed lions' heads or as heads with three large tufts in the center, and two or three small tufts on either side, in lieu of the forehead, serves as an horizontal border at the base; scattered dots in the field.

---

30 Starr 1937-39: 57-59; 186-87; 217-18 and Plan 23.

31 Starr 1937-39: 143-44, Pl. 128-29, and Plan 13.

In his description of the Nuzi painting Starr writes: "It is of interest to note the extreme formality and conventionalization of all the designs, and the tendency toward geometrical patterns both in the detail and in the arrangement into vertical and horizontal panels."[32] While elements of the design do occur in the Nuzi seal impressions and to some extent in the painted ceramic designs (he noted the guilloche and the tree), it is the combination of geometric patterns with the discrete heads which is of interest to us here.

Small fragments of geometric design decorated with a number of dots placed in the empty spaces of the design[33] occur in the panels of the stylized tree and discrete heads. These dots appear arbitrarily placed since they are present at times but missing in other panels. Single dots are also seen in the middle of triangles (usually in red on white triangles and in black on the red examples) and in the center of the white rectangles in the alternating black and white borders. The center of the guilloche can also be dotted.[34] Large triangles in a red field are dotted and have a large black dot in the spaces between triangles. They make up a portion of a larger pattern which may be an imitation of a building facade as well as the top of a half oval next to them.[35] These dots then are an

FIGURE 12

Drawing of frieze from Nuzi wall painting

15th century. Scale 1:10

Cf. Starr 1937-39: Pl. 128.

Portions of a frame with geometrical patterns, a guilloche, and rows of stylized bull heads and masks(?) with a crown of three large tufts emerging from an horizontal band around head, bull ears, and long curls. Scattered dots near floral motifs and crossed circles near the bull heads.

---

32 Starr 1939: 492.

33 Starr 1937:Pl. 128:A,E and around the floral motif and bull head in Pl. 129:D.

34 Starr 1937:Pl. 129D; see Matthews *et al.* 1994: Fig. 13:6 for an Akkadian period guilloche with circles in the center.

35 Starr 1937:Pl. 128:H.

integral part of even the smaller patterns in the elaborate geometrical scheme and at times partially fill the field of the discrete heads and floral motifs. In Buchanan's description of the seal impressions from Mallowan's excavations from Brak he notes that one of the iconographic characteristics of what he called the "ED III style distinctive of Brak" is the use of filler motifs composed of dots.[36] A triangular tag from Brak was rolled on both faces with a scene of a row of figures placed above a row of reversed rams' heads; notable about this design is that twelve dots are interspersed between both the figures and the row of discrete rams' heads.[37]

FIGURE 13

Drawing of scene from Nagar/Brak seal

"From pre-Akkadian rubbish." Scale 2:1.

Cf. Buchanan 1966, p. 151

A human-headed bull's head, lion's head with three large tufts above the forehead (placed sideways) and a T-shaped geometrical pattern behind the browsing quadrupeds serve as a vertical frame, encasing a figural scene which is also highly symmetrical.

The Urkesh sealings published here belong to a larger third-millennium style characteristic of the north. In this style the original seals were small and uninscribed; they have prominent geometric aspects, compositions with many figures filling the space, and compositions which are more varied in the arrangement of figures. Iconographically, the choice of the figures and groups come from a limited range of scenes, including some which are well known in the south, such the human and animal combat scenes, and perhaps banquet scenes as well.

---

36 Buchanan 1966: 146, no. 783.

37 Buchanan 1966: 787; dots are also a feature of the design in the Mari seal, see Fig. 11.

But what is most characteristic of this style are two particular features: first, the use of discrete elements which are taken out of a figurative context, and second, a veritable delight for repetition, resulting in sequences which acquire a compositional value of their own. We may briefly address both points in turn. (1) The discrete elements include lion heads, a type of cat head different from the lions (which may represent a lioness), bearded bull heads, the head and foreparts of horned animals, scorpions, dots, various types of the guilloche pattern, and a wide variety of geometric borders. The heads of both humans and animals depicted in profile exhibit a strong outline and a single large dotted eye in the center; those animal heads viewed from the top or shown frontally also place a strong emphasis on the eyes. (2) These stock elements are combined in a somewhat organic manner through repetition by means of linear patterns, as in the case of rows of discrete heads. This fluid arrangement of stock elements is held together additionally by the emphasis on geometric frames which are, in

FIGURE 14

Projected scene from late third-millennium Khabur region

Scene A from Mozan/Urkesh, see above, Fig. 10. It is encased by a geometrical pattern which may be meant to resemble a palm log (column?).
Element B a guilloche (as found in Brak seals and Nuzi painting).
Element C a row of lion heads with tufts as found in Brak seals (sideways). See also Mari seal and Nuzi painting.
Element D a geometrical frieze as found in Brak seals and similar to those in Nuzi painting.
It is proposed that such a composition might have been used for wall paintings in the late third-millennium Khabur region.

this style, raised to the status of major compositional elements. In themselves these borders are extremely varied in their geometric patterns and as frames give a limit to both the space and the number of stock elements included. While the figurative scenes can be more varied compositionally, they can also reflect the geometric emphasis found in the borders and the positioning of discrete heads through the use of symmetry (as shown in Fig. 13).

The basic characteristics of this northern style are still influential as late as the Nuzi period. Compositionally the Nuzi painting is a monumental representation of those formal and compositional characteristics already seen in the third-millennium. The emphasis on the guilloche and geometric patterns serving as frames were multiplied at Nuzi to include a number of nested frames in intricate geometric patterns with complimentary color combinations.[38] The emphasis on discrete heads of figures seen already in the third-millennium is striking. While the long expanse of the Nuzi wall paintings provide the largest compositional evidence for the characteristics of this style, many of these characteristics also occur in the Nuzi seal impressions. Given that we do find this style in both Nuzi painting and seal carving, it seems possible to speculate that there are also third millennium wall paintings in this style.

The presence in the north of this type of seal carving style during the third-millennium did not preclude the coexistence of other carving and painting styles. While this has been clearer in seal carving, (and will be even more so when the inscribed seals from Urkesh are published) it is now beginning to be evident in wall painting. The recently excavated wall paintings from Halawa and Munbāqa emphasize very distinctive large eyed, oval headed figures which either can be placed in a composition as oversized figures in the middle of a group of smaller figures painted in a different style, or can be shown in the composition as smaller figures in the area of this larger figure (Halawa).[39] The Munbāqa figures are placed in a panel having a geometric border[40] but are distinctive in their details from the Urkesh and Brak examples cited and have

38 I have not included here the evidence from the Nuzi seal impressions. Many elements seen in the Nuzi paintings, such as the dotted guilloche, the mask-like heads and the friezes of discrete heads, are also found in the seal impressions. I am also not discussing here the evidence from seals or the Mari painting which would provide connecting elements over this time span, just as I have not discussed southern parallels for single elements or the wider question of the role of the south in the formation of this northern art. When the Akkadian cylinder seals first began to be excavated at Brak, D. Mathews (1991) called this style "provincial." With my current reassessment of the material, including the new evidence from Urkesh/Mozan and Nagar/Brak, it is now clear that this style cannot be considered provincial because it is a dominant northern style in the third-millennium, with its influence lasting into the later periods.

39 Lueth 1989. The stela from Halawa has geometric decoration on a register band, Orthmann 1985.

40 Machule *et al.* 1986.

a different overall effect. In fact these oval headed figures are closer in tone to the later Mari figure of a bearded man with an amorphous body in a single panel surrounded by dots.[41]

In my reconstruction of a hypothetical third-millennium Urkesh painting (which I think is not specific to Urkesh but rather could be found throughout the northern area symbolized by the two poles of Urkesh and Nuzi), I have tried to project back from the Nuzi composition and iconographic motifs onto what is now known from the seal impressions of Akkadian Urkesh/Mozan and Nagar/Brak. (Fig. 14). There are two assumptions behind this suggestion. The first is that wall paintings and seals may share similar stylistic and iconographic features. This is supported by the recurrence of stock elements and of special framing devices in both art forms, and is based, for the wall paintings, only on the later evidence from Nuzi. The second assumption is that seals might occasionally be a representation of scenes which are also shown on wall paintings, and that such might be the case with the seal impression published here as Fig. 10.

In any case, what unites the northern artists over the span of about a thousand years, roughly from the prominence of Urkesh to Nuzi, and singles them out from their southern counterparts, is their innate appreciation for strong geometric designs and the possibility of using disarticulated human and animal heads as part of the overall compositions. Geometric frames and borders are basic to their sense of design just as their arrangement of the frontally positioned discrete heads more often falls into a geometric pattern. Their inclusion of certain types of discrete animal and human combinations more than likely reflects other elements in their culture such as northern mythological figures and events which we have still to recognize.

In pointing out parallel features in the third-millennium art of northern Syro-Mesopotamia and second-millennium Nuzi, I am at this point not addressing, nor attempting to address obliquely, a more fundamental question of who

---

41 Parrot 1958: Pl. XVII. The widespread presence of wall painting in northeastern Syria in the third-millennium is indicated by fragments from Tell Gudeda, level 1 (Fortin 1990: p. 573, Fig. 35) and Tell al Raqa'i, level 4 (Dunham 1993: p. 128, Fig. 1). Painted figures placed in rectangular panels are also seen in the early third-millennium in the Scarlet ware tradition. Scarlet ware was known and probably produced in the north but only with geometric designs on vessel stands. At Urkesh/Mozan we excavated a number in a tomb (Ob1) in the Outer City dating to the ED II period. See the description of the Scarlet ware, late Ninevite V and early Metallic ware from this tomb in Buccellati and Kelly-Buccellati 1991. However the composition of the Scarlet ware designs is very different than the later third-millennium painting now being discovered in Syria. Figures in framed geometric panels existed in the north in the painted Ninevite V tradition (for a collection of these designs, see Numoto 1992). The emphasis on frames is also seen in the Akkadian period "Tigris Group" of cylinder seals published by Boehmer 1965 Nos. 33, 527-28, 664, 665-66 (Wilajeh), 690, 691 (Wilajeh) all Akkadian Ia; Nos. 467 (Susa), 468, 469 (Khafaje), 470-72, 600, 601 (Wilajeh) all Akkadian Ib.

made this art, of whether we can connect the seal impressions at Urkesh/Mozan with an ethnic group, namely the Hurrians. We do know that the king of Urkesh contemporary with the use of the seals discussed here is called Tupkish, a Hurrian name; also we have determined that an important figure in the household of the queen is the nurse Zamena who has a Hurrian name. The royal titulary is also Hurrian. Finally, the two lions of Tiš-atal can now be connected with our site. The queen however has an Akkadian name, Uqnitum, and one of the other important individuals whose goods were kept in the Royal Storehouse is Innin-Šadu, an Akkadian name known from the south.[42]

Attempting to attribute art, or indeed any aspect of material culture, to a specific ethnic group,[43] needs to be approached with a great deal of caution and with theoretical awareness. This question will be taken up later, after we publish our primary data on which it will be based.[44]

---

42 Any attempt to reconstruct the history of northern Syria in the third millennium must take into account the relations between Urkesh and Nagar, which is presumably to be identified with Brak. The seal impressions I have published here are shown to be very similar in style to some early Akkadian sealings from the Brak excavations. However, from the viewpoint of the wider historical situation it should be noted that Nagar plays a role in the Ebla tablets while Urkesh does not. Also Brak is very much connected at a slightly later period in the third millennium with Naram-Sin. Geographically there is no physical obstacle between Urkesh and Brak, but Brak appears to have been throughout its history close to the south. From what we know thus far, Urkesh was not. This may suggest that there was some kind of political boundary between Urkesh and Brak, at least in the Akkadian period. See also Archi, 1996, forthcoming.

43 More than thirty years ago, in a seminal article on Syrian glyptic, Pierre Amiet (1963) gathered the small amount of material then available of this type of Syrian art and reached conclusions which pointed in the same direction I have taken here. More recently, he considered again the possible connection of this material with Hurrian art, specifically thinking in terms of the Nuzi painting (1985).

44 See Mellink 1975, a fundamental early survey of Hurrian art.

ABBREVIATIONS

Amiet, Pierre

1963 "La glyptique Syrienne Archaïque," *Syria* 40, pp. 57-83.

1985 "La glyptique de Mari: Etat de la question," *MARI* 4, pp. 475-85.

Archi, Alfonso

1996 "The Regional State of Nagar According to the Texts of Ebla." *Subartu* 4, (forthcoming).

Boehmer, Rainer Michael

1965 *Die Entwicklung der Glyptik während der Akkad-Zeit*, Berlin.

Buccellati, Giorgio and Marilyn Kelly-Buccellati

1991 "Introduction," in Lucio Milano *et al.*, "The Epigraphic Finds of the Sixth Season," *Syro-Mesopotamian Studies* 5/1, pp. 3-9.

1995 "The Identification of Urkesh with Tell Mozan (Syria)," *Orient Express* 1995/3, 67-70.

1996a "The Royal Storehouse of Urkesh: First Preliminary Report," *AfO* (forthcoming).

1996b "The Seals of the King of Urkesh: Evidence from the Western Wing of the Royal Storehouse AK," *WZKM* (forthcoming).

1996c "The Seals of the Royal Household," *Subartu* 4 (forthcoming).

Buchanan, Briggs

1966 *Catalogue of Ancient Near Eastern Seals in the Ashmolean Museum.* Vol. I *Cylinder Seals.* Oxford: Clarendon Press.

Dunham, Sally

1993 "A Wall Painting from Tell al-Raqa'i, Northeast Syria," *Levant* 25, 127-43.

Fortin, Michel

1990 "Rapport preliminaire sur la 3e campagne de fouilles a Tell 'Atij et la 2e à Gudeda, sur le Khabour (Automne 1988)" *Syria* 67, pp. 535-77.

Frankfort, Henri

1955 *Stratified Cylinder Seals from the Diyala Region.* Chicago: OIP 72.

1939 *Cylinder Seals.* London.

Lueth, F.

1989 "Tell Halawa B," in W. Orthman, ed. *Halawa 1980-1986.* Saarbrücker Beiträge zur Altertumskunde, Band 52. Bonn, pp. 85-100.

Machule, D. *et al.*

1986 "Ausgrabungen in Tall Munbaqa 1984," *MDOG* 188, pp. 67-145.

Matthews, Donald

1991 "Tell Brak 1990: The Glyptic," *Iraq* 53: 147-57.

Matthews, R.J., W. Matthews, and H. McDonald

1994 "Excavations at Tell Brak, 1994," *Iraq* 56: 177-94.

Matthiae, Paolo

1989 *Ebla. Un impero ritrovato. Dai primi scavi alle ultime scoperte.* Torino.

Mellink, Machteld

1975 "Hurriter, Kunst," *Reallexikon der Assyriologie* 4, 514-19.

Moortgat, Anton

1960 *Tell Chuera in Nordost-Syrien. Vorläufiger Bericht über die zweite Grabungskampagne 1959.* "Schriften der Max Freiherr von Oppenheim-Stiftung, Heft 4." Berlin.

Moortgat, Anton and Ursula-Correns

1976 *Tell Chuera in Nordost-Syrien. Vorläufiger Bericht über die siebente Grabungskampagne 1974.* "Schriften der Max Freiherr von Oppenheim-Stiftung, Heft 9." Berlin.

Numoto, Hirotoshi

1992 "Painted Designs of the Ninevite V Pottery — Part 2," *Al-Rafidan* 13, 105-37.

Orthmann, Winfried

1985 "Art of the Akkade Period in Northern Syria and Mari," *MARI* 4, pp. 469-74.

Owen, David I. and Gernot Wilhelm

1995 "Preface," *Studies on the Civilization and Culture of Nuzi and the Hurrians*, Volume 7: *The Edith Porada Memorial Volume*. Bethesda: CDL Press, pp. v-viii.

Parrot, André

1956 *Le Temple d'Ishtar*. Mission Archéologique de Mari, Vol. I. Paris.

1958 *Le Palais: Peintures murale*. Mission Archéologique de Mari, Vol. II. Paris.

Porada, Edith

1948 *The Collection of the Pierpont Morgan Library, Corpus of Ancient Near Eastern Seals in North American Collections*, I, the Bollingen Series XIV, Washington.

Reade, Julian

1973 "Tell Taya (1972–73): Summary Report," *Iraq* 35, 155-87.

Starr, Richard F.S.

1937 *Nuzi*. Vol. II *Plates and Plans*. Cambridge: Harvard University Press.

1939 *Nuzi*. Vol. I *Text*. Cambridge: Harvard University Press.

Eine Stele des urartäischen Königs Minua für die Gottheit Šebitu

VEYSEL DONBAZ and GERNOT WILHELM

Arkeoloji Müzeleri, Istanbul

Julius-Maximilians-Universität, Würzburg

An Urartian inscription on a stele of king Minua, son of Išpuini (ca. 800 B.C.), is published here from a hand-copy by a layman associated with the present owner. The find-spot and present location of the original are unknown. The stele is dedicated to the god Šebitu known from the sacrificial tariff of Meher kapısı dating to the time of Išpuini's and Minua's coregency and from an inscription of Rusa I found at Mahmud Abad in Azerbaijan.

1994 und 1995 wurde den Istanbul Arkeoloji Müzeleri durch laienhafte, aber gut lesbare Kopien sowie durch ein kaum brauchbares, schlecht belichtetes Photo eine urartäische Inschrift bekannt, die von besonderem Interesse ist, weil sie eine Weihung an die Gottheit Šebitu enthält. Die Herkunft und der Verbleib der Inschrift sind leider unbekannt. Der Schriftträger ist eine Stele (Z. 4: *pulusi*); die Breite beträgt ca. 60 cm, die erhaltene Höhe ca. 50 cm und die Dicke ca. 40 cm.

Die hier veröffentlichte Kopie beruht auf den uns vorgelegten Materialien, nicht auf dem Original, so daß der an eine Autographie zu stellenden Forderung nach größtmöglicher Genauigkeit nicht entsprochen werden kann. Zwar scheinen die Zeichen im einzelnen recht sorgfältig abgeschrieben worden zu sein, doch fehlt es der Abschrift offenkundig an Maßhaltigkeit, was die Zeilenlängen betrifft, da alle bekannten Stelen Minuas (und anderer Könige) auf möglichst exakte Rechtsbündigkeit Wert legen. Für das Verständnis des Textes reicht die Materialgrundlage aber aus. An eine Fälschung wird man angesichts des Gottesnamens in der ersten Zeile, der in dieser Inschriftform ein Novum darstellt und sonst schlecht bezeugt ist, nicht denken wollen.[1]

Die neue Inschrift lautet:

1 ^{d}*Še-bi-tú-ú-*⌜*a*⌝$^{sic!}$

2 ^{m}*Mì-i-nu-ú-a*<-*še*>

---

1 Zur Möglichkeit der Fälschung einer urartäischen Inschrift cf. M. Salvini, *SEL* 2 (1985) 143-46.

Studies on the Civilization and Culture of Nuzi and the Hurrians - 8

3 ^{m}*Iš-pu-u-i-né-ḫi-né-še*$^{!}$
4 *i-ni pu-lu-si ku-gu-ni*
5 ^{d}*Ḫal-di-ni-ni al-su-ši-n*[*i*]
6 ^{m}*Mì-i-nu-ú-a-ni*
7 ^{m}*Iš-pu-u-i-né-ḫi*
8 MAN *DAN-NU* MAN *al-su-ni*
9 MAN ^{kur}*Bi-i-a-i-na*<*-ú*>*-e*
10 ⸢*a*⸣*-lu-si* ^{uru}*Ṭu-uš-pa* UR[U]

„Der Gottheit Šebitu hat Minua, der Sohn des Išpuine, diese Stele geweiht. Durch die Größe Ḫaldis ist Minua, der Sohn des Išpuine, mächtiger König, großer König, König der (Leute) des Landes Bia, Herr von Ṭušpa-Stadt".

Die Gottheit Šebitu ist bereits aus dem Opfertarif der Inschrift Išpuinis und Minuas vom Meher kapısı bekannt, wo sie an achter Stelle nach dem Reichsgott Ḫaldi, dem Wettergott Teišeba, dem Sonnengott Šiwini sowie den Gottheiten Ḫuṭuini, Ṭurani, Ua und Nalaini aufgeführt wird:

> ^{d}*Še-bi-tú-ú-e* 2 GUD 4 UDU „zwei Rinder (und) vier Schafe der Gottheit Šebitu (Dativ)" HchI 10 II 6, mit Voranstellung der Opfermaterie auch X 39; cf. UKN 27:6, 39.

Die Gottheit wird außerdem mehrfach in der Inschrift Rusas I., des Sohnes Sardures II., aus Mahmud Abad in Aserbaidschan[2] genannt. Sie besitzt dieser Inschrift zufolge ein Kulttor (Z. 4: *Še-bi-tú-i̯-na-ú-e* KÁ, Genitiv mit Suffixaufnahme Dativ Pl.[3]: *Šebitu=i=na=u̯e*). Ihr Name erscheint teils im Genitiv (^{d}*Še-bi-tú-i* Z. 9), teils im Dativ (^{d}*Še-bi-tú-e* Z. 2, 5, 8), einmal auch mit der Postposition *-kai* „vor" (^{d}*Še-bi-tú-ka-i* Z. 9). Aus dem Fundort der Inschrift hat M. Salvini geschlossen, es handele sich um eine lokale Gottheit von Rezaiyēh.[4]

Da alle bisher bekannten Formen den Namen als *u*-, nicht als *a*-Stamm erweisen, wird man das letzte Zeichen als Fehler des Steinmetzen oder — wahrscheinlicher — des Kopisten für *e* halten, zumal das als *a* wiedergegebene Zeichen teilweise beschädigt ist.

Im Typus schließt sich die Stele an mehrere bis auf die erste Zeile gleichlautende Inschriften Minuas an, die alle aus nur zwei Sätzen bestehen, nämlich (1) einer Weihformel und (2) der Herrscherprädikation. Die Mehrzahl dieser Stelen wurde in Van (HchI 63 = UKN 101, HchI 71 = UKN 108) oder nicht weit östlich davon (Yedikilise: HchI 64 = UKN 109, HchI 65 = UKN 103) und an der Nordostspitze des Van-Sees (Artswapert: HchI 66 = UKN 104, Karahan: HchI 69 = UKN 107, HchI 70 = UKN 120, Karahan 3 Seite a, Karahan 4[5]) gefunden, zwei auch westlich von Patnos (Patnoths) (Kızılkaya: HchI 67 = UKN 105, Methsophay Wank: HchI 68 = UKN 106); sie stammen also alle aus dem zentralen Bereich Urartus. Es darf daher vermutet werden, daß auch die Stele für Šebitu in diesem Raum gefunden wurde.

Meist wird die Weihformel in diesen Stelen mit der Wendung *Ḫaldi=i=ni=ni ušmaši=ni* „durch die Stärke Ḫaldis" eingeleitet, und die Herrscherprädikation beginnt mit der parallelen Wendung *Ḫaldi=i=ni=ni alsu(i)ši=ni* „durch die Größe Ḫaldis". In zwei Fällen (HchI 64, 67) fehlt die Einleitung der Herrscherprädikation, während die hier vorgelegte Inschrift auf den einleitenden Bezug auf die Stärke Ḫaldis verzichtet, der sonst auf den Stelen aus der Alleinregierung Minuas selten fehlt.[6]

---

2 M. Salvini, Eine neue urartäische Inschrift aus Mahmud Abad (West-Azerbaidjan), *AMI* NF 10 (1977) 125-36.

3 Cf. G. Wilhelm, *ZA* 66 (1976) 105-19; in der Analyse der Form von M. Salvini, l.c., p. 133, ist — bei richtiger Übersetzung des Dativs — das letzte Suffix versehentlich als „Gen." bezeichnet.

4 M. Salvini, l.c., p. 133.

5 Die letzteren beiden Inschriften sind veröffentlicht von: A.M. Dinçol / E. Kavaklı, „Van Bölgesinde bulunmuş yeni Urartu yazıtları / Die neuen Urartäischen Inschriften aus der Umgebung von Van" Anadolu Araştırmaları, ek yayın 1 / JKF, Beih. 1, Istanbul: Edebiyat Fakültesi Basımevi, 1978.

6 Die Stelen HchI 13-15, in denen die Einleitung *Ḫaldi=i=ni=ni ušmaši=ni* fehlt, gehören noch in die Zeit der Koregenz, wie das Fehlen der Titulatur und die Nennung des Inušpua zeigen. HchI 65, eine Stele mit Weihung an Teišeba aus der Zeit der Alleinregierung, verzichtet sowohl auf diese Wendung als auch auf die Einleitung der Herrscherprädikation *Ḫaldi=i=ni=ni alsu(i)ši=ni*.

Die Mehrzahl der Stelen, darunter alle aus Karahan[7], sind dem Gotte Ḫaldi geweiht. Daneben gibt es eine für Teišeba (HchI 65), eine für Elip'uri (HchI 66) und eine für eine Gottheit, deren Name abgebrochen ist, die aber nicht Ḫaldi sein kann (HchI 71).

In paläographischer Hinsicht gehört die neue Inschrift wie alle anderen der Gruppe bis auf die beiden Inschriften aus Yedikilise und die Stele Karahan 4 zur „Schule der Schnittvermeidung“[8]. Da sie auf Grund der Herrschertitulatur in die Zeit der Alleinregierung Minuas datiert, bestätigt sie einmal mehr, daß das Prinzip, sich schneidende Keile zu vermeiden, in dieser Zeit sich in Urartu allgemein durchsetzte.

7 M. Salvini, BiOr 46 (1989) 402 identifiziert Karahan mit *Ḫaldi=i* URU unter Hinweis auf seine Ausführungen in *SMEA* 22 (1980) 176, wo allerdings diese Identifikation nicht explizit behauptet und begründet wird.

8 Cf. G. Wilhelm, „Bemerkungen zur urartäischen Paläographie“, *AoF* 21 (1994) 352-58.

Weitere Joins von Nuzi-Texten

JEANETTE FINCKE

Julius-Maximilians-Universität Würzburg

This article concerns three joins among the Nuzi tablets in the Ermitaž of St. Petersburg.

The first one is a long-distance join between a fragment of the Ermitaž and a fragment in the British Museum. Urḫi-teššup, son of Tarmia, adopts the brothers Šēlebu and Niḫria, sons of Abbūt-ṭābi, in exchange for a field.

The second join concerns two Ermitaž fragments. The tablet is a loan-contract between the two brothers Teḫit-teššup and Muš-teššup, sons of [x]pia, and Urḫi-teššup, son of Tarmia. A field in the *ugāru* of the town Tain-šuḫ(we) is given in excange for a blanket which is described very precisely.

The last join — consisting of three fragments of the Ermitaž — is a sistership-contract between Šašk[a...], daughter of Ukkaja, and Zilip-tilla, son of Kelip-šarri.

Im September 1991 hatte ich die Möglichkeit, an den unpublizierten Nuzi-Urkunden des British Museums zu arbeiten.[1] Bei der späteren Durchsicht meiner hierbei angefertigten Transliterationen konnte ich ein Fragment des British Museums mit einem Fragment aus St. Petersburg[2] joinen:

1. BM 102356 + I 83272 (= Jank. 26)

Bei dieser Gelegenheit fand ich auch folgende zwei Joins unter den publizierten Nuzi-Fragmenten aus St. Petersburg:

2. I 15348 + 8371 + 8398 (= Jank. 13 + 13a + 21)
3. I 15389 + 15355 (= Jank. 46 + 89)

Diese drei Joins sollen im folgenden vorgestellt werden:

1 Ich danke den Trustees des Bristish Museum für die Genehmigung zur Einsicht in die unpublizierten Nuzi-Urkunden und für die Genehmigung, BM 86401 hier zu publizieren.

2 Die Nuzi-Urkunden aus Moskau und St. Petersburg sind von N.B. Jankowskaja, "Juridičeskie dokumenty iz Arrapachi v sobranijach SSSR, Peredneaziatskij Sbornik," in: Voprosy Chettologii i Churritologii, Moskva 1961, 424-580, 603-4 (Jank.), publiziert.

Studies on the Civilization and Culture of Nuzi and the Hurrians - 8

1. BM 102356[3] + I 8372 (= Jank. 26); Maße des BM-Fragments: 10,35(frg) x 6,59(frg) x 2,56(frg); Kollation des BM-Fragments am 19.9.1991; join gefunden am 24.12.1991; join nicht vollzogen.

Vs. 1 *ṭup-pí ma-ru-ti š*[*a*]
2 ^{m}*Še-le-bu* DUMU *A-bu-*[*ut-ṭá-bi*]
3 *ù ša* ^{m}*Ni-iḫ-ri-i*[*a* DUMU KI.MIN]
4 2 ŠEŠ.MEŠ *an-nu-ti* ⌜*ù*⌝
5 ^{m}*Ur-ḫi-te-šup* DUMU *Tar-m*[*i-ia*]
6 *a-na ma-ru-ti i-te-*[*ep-šu-uš*]
7 17 ANŠE A.ŠÀ *i+na mi-i*[*n-da-ti* GAL *ša* É.GAL-*l*]*ì*
8 *i+na mi-ṣí-ir-*⌜*šu*⌝ [
9 *i+na su-ta-an* x[
10 *i+na il-ta-an* [
11 ⌜*i+na*⌝ *e-le-en m*[*i-iṣ*$^{?}$*-ri*$^{?}$
12 *i+*⌜*na šu-pa*⌝*-al mi-*[*iṣ*$^{?}$*-ri*$^{?}$
13 ^{m}*Še-le-bu* [*ù* ^{m}*Ni-iḫ-ri-ia a-na*]
14 ^{m}*Ur-ḫi-te-š*[*up ki-ma* ḪA.LA-*šu it-ta-ad-nu*]
15 *ù* ^{m}*Ur-ḫ*[*i-te-šup …*
16 *ki-ma* NÍG.B[A-*šu-nu a-na* ^{m}*Še-le-bu*]
17 *ù a-na* ^{m}[*Ni-iḫ-ri-ia it-ta-din*]
18 ⌜*šum*⌝*-ma* A.Š[À *ša-a-šu bá-qí-ra-na*]
19 [*ir-t*]*a-*[*ši šu-nu-ma ú-za-ak-ku-ma*]
20 [*a-na*] ⌜^{m}⌝*Ur-ḫi-te-*⌜*šup i*⌝+[*na-ad-dì-nu*]
21 [*il-k*]*a*$_{4}$*-šu ša* A.ŠÀ ^{m}*Še-*[*le-bu*]
22 [*ù* ^{m}*Ni*]*-iḫ-ri-ia na-š*[*u-ú*]
23 [*ù*] ^{m}*Ur-ḫi-te-šup l*[*a na-ši*]
u. Rd. 24 [*šum-m*]*a* GAL A.ŠÀ *la i+na-a*[*k-ki-sú*]
25 [*šum-m*]*a* TUR A.ŠÀ *la ú-ra-*[*ad-dá*]
26 [*m*]*a-an-nu-um-me-e i+na* [ŠÀ-*bi*]
Rs. 27 [*ša*] 2 ŠEŠ.MEŠ *aš-bu* [*ù*]
28 ⌜A⌝.[Š]À *ú-za-ak-ka*$_{4}$ *a-na* [^{m}*Ur-ḫi-te-šup* SUM]
29 *m*[*a-an-n*]*u-um-me-e i+na* [*be-ri-šu-nu*]
30 *š*[*a* KI.B]AL-⌜*tu*$_{4}$⌝ 1 MA.N[A KÙ.BABBAR]
31 1 [MA.NA KÙ.S]IG$_{17}$ [SA$_{5}$]
__________[
32 IGI [

---

3 BM 102356 ist bereits publiziert und bearbeitet worden von M.P. Maidman, "Some Late Bronze Age Legal Tablets from the British Museum: Problems of Context and Meaning," in: B. Halpern und D.W. Hobson (ed.), *Law, Politics and Society in the Ancient Mediterranean World*, Sheffield Academic Press, 1993, 71-74. Dieser Artikel wird im folgenden als Maidman abgekürzt.

33 IGI [
34 IGI x[
35 IGI *Ḫ[a-*
36 IGI x[
37 IGI x[
38 ⸢IGI⸣ x[
39 ⸢IGI⸣ [*A-ri-wa-al-ti-ú/e*]
40 [DUMU ^{d}IŠKUR-LUGAL]
41 IG[I
42 IGI [
43 IGI *Ta[r-mi-ia* DUMU
44 IGI *K[a-*
45 IGI *Ni-[iḫ-ri-te-šup* LÚ.*na-gi*$_5$*-rù*
46 IGI *A-ri-[*
47 IGI *Ḫa-ši-ip-[til-la* DUB.SAR
48 *i+na ur-k[i šu-du-ti ša-ṭì-ir]*
o. Rd. 49 NA$_4$ ^{m}*Tar-mi-ia* | ⸢NA$_4$ ^{m}⸣[
50 NA$_4$ ^{m}DUB.SAR | [NA$_4$ ^{m}]*D[u-*

---

51 NA$_4$ ^{m}*Ni-iḫ-ri-ia* | EN [A.ŠÀ]
(Siegelabrollung)
l. Rd. (Siegelabrollung) (Siegelabrollung) (Siegelabrollung)
52 [NA$_4$ ^{m}x-x]x-*a+a* NA$_4$ ^{m}*It-ḫi-til-la* NA$_4$ ^{m}*Ni-iḫ-ri-te-šup* LÚ.*na-gi*$_5$*-rù*
(Siegelabrollung)
NA$_4$ ^{m}*Še-le-bu* EN A.ŠÀ

(1) Adoptionsurkunde des (2) Šēlebu, des Sohnes des Abbūt-[ṭābi], (3) und des Niḫri[a, des Sohnes desselben]. (4) Diese beiden Brüder haben (5) Urḫi-teššup, den Sohn des Tarm[ia], als Sohn ad[optiert]. (7) 17 ANŠE Feld, (gemessen) mit dem [großen] Maß [des Palastes], (8) auf seinem Gebiet [...], (9) südlich .[...], (10) nördlich [...], (11) östlich der Gr[enze$^?$ ...], (12) westlich der Gre[nze$^?$ ...], (13) [haben] Šēlebu [und Niḫria dem] (14) Urḫi-tešš[up als seinen Anteil gegeben]. (15) Und Urḫ[i-teššup hat ...] (16) als [ihr] Geschen[k dem Šēlebu] (17) und dem [Niḫria gegeben]. (18) Wenn das [betreffende] Fel[d einen Vindikanten] (19) [erh]äl[t, werden diese (es) von Ansprüchen freimachen und] (20) [dem] Urḫi-teššup überg[eben]. (21) [Die *ilk*]*u*-Verpflichtung des Feldes trag[en] Šēlebu (22) [und N]iḫria. (23) [Und] Urḫi-teššup [trägt (sie)] ni[cht]. (u.Rd. 24) [Wen]n es groß ist, wird man das Feld nicht beschneid[en]; (25) [wen]n es klein ist, wird er das Feld nicht vergröß[ern]. (26) [W]er auch immer vo[n] (Rs. 27) [den] beiden Brüdern anwesend sein wird, [der] (28) muß das Feld von Ansprüchen befreien (und) dem [Urḫi-teššup geben]. (29) We[r] auch immer un[ter ihnen] (30) [Vertragsbr]uch begeht, muß eine Mine [Silber] (31) (und) eine [Mine Gold bezahlen].

(32-38 zerstört und nicht übersetzt.) (39) Vor [Ariwaltiu/e], (40) [dem Sohn des Adad-šarri]. (41-42 zerstört) (43) Vor Ta[rmia, dem Sohn des ...].

(44) Vor K[a-...]. (45) Vor Ni[ḫri-teššup, dem Herold]. (46) Vor Ari[...]. (47) Vor Ḫašip-[tilla, dem Schreiber. (Diese Tafel)] (48) [ist] nac[h der Proklamation geschrieben]. (o.Rd. 49) Siegel des Niḫria. Siegel des [...]. (50) Siegel des Schreibers. [Siegel] des T[u...]. (51) Siegel des Niḫria, des [Feld]besitzers. (l.Rd. 52) [Siegel des ...]aja. Siegel des Itḫi-tilla. Siegel des Niḫri-teššup, des Herolds. Siegel des Šēlebu, des Feldbesitzers.

Z. 2 Die Ergänzung des Patronyms basiert auf BM 17604:7 (= Maidman Nr. 5), BM 80178:3 (= Maidman Nr. 6) und BM 95353:2 (= Maidman Nr. 8).

Z. 3 Die Ergänzung von DUMU KI.MIN stützt sich auf die nachfolgende Zeile, in der Šēlebu und Niḫria als ŠEŠ.MEŠ, Brüder, bezeichnet werden. M.P. Maidman (S. 74) vermutet die Möglichkeit eines vorübergehend stipulierten Bruderstatus beider in Bezug auf ihren gemeinsamen Rechtstitel an dem Feld gegenüber Urḫi-teššup.

Z. 7-12 Šēlebu tritt in zwei Urkunden als Prozeßgegener des Urḫi-teššup, des Sohn des Tarmia, in Taku(we) auf (BM 17604, 80178). Wahrscheinlich wird das in diesen Zeilen beschriebene Feld ebenfalls in dem Gebiet von Taku(we) liegen.

Z. 35 In BM 26290 (= Maidman Nr. 9), einer Urḫi-teššup betreffenden Urkunde desselben Schreibers, wird ein Ḫanaja, Sohn des Eḫli-teššup, genannt.

Z. 39f. Ariwaltiu/e, der Sohn des Adad-šarri, erscheint in drei Urkunden des Urḫi-teššup als Zeuge. In allen drei Urkunden steht das Patronym in der nachfolgenden Zeile (BM 24137, BM 85280 und BM 102359 = Maidman Nr. 11). Daher ist dieser Name wahrscheinlich auch an dieser Stelle zu ergänzen.

Z. 44 Bei einer Transaktion des Bruders Urḫi-teššups, Akam-mušni, ist ein Kaja, Sohn des Qīšteja, als Zeuge aufgeführt (*Qa-a+a*, [*K*]*a-a+a*, BM 85227). Dieser Kaja ist ferner in JEN 154 und JEN 402 genannt (jeweils *Ka-a+a* geschrieben). Er könnte auch hier gemeint sein.

Z. 46 Im Archiv des Urḫi-teššup sind drei mit *A-ri-* beginnende Namen bezeugt: Ariḫ-ḫamanna, Sohn des [...] (BM 24137), der Richter Arik-kani (BM 80178 = Maidman Nr. 6) und Ariwaltiu/e, Sohn des Adad-šarri (cf. hierzu Kommentar zu Z. 39f.).

Z. 47 Ḫašip-tilla hat zwei weitere Urkunden für Urḫi-teššup, den Sohn des Tarmia, geschrieben (BM 26290 = Maidman Nr. 9 und BM 102369 = K. Grosz, CNI 5, 160, 146[4]). Von einem Schreiber dieses Namens stammen die Urkunden JEN 320, 322, Gadd 17 und Gadd 58. Aus AASOR XVI 64 ist ein Schreiber namens Ḫašip-tilla, Sohn des Enna-pali, bekannt.

4 K. Grosz, CNI 5 = K. Grosz, *The Archive of the Wullu Family* (CNI Publications 5) Copenhagen 1988.

Z. 50 In seinen Prozessen begegnet Urḫi-teššup einem Richter namens Turari (*Du-ra-ri*; TCL IX 15, AASOR XVI 70 und BM 80178 = Maidman Nr. 6). Ein Turari (*Du-ra-ri*), Sohn des Ar-teššup, ist in einem Prozeß als *manzatuḫlu* tätig (BM 17598). Nach einem anderen Fragment bezeugt ein [*Du*]-*ra-ar-te-šup*, Sohn des [...], eine Transaktion des Urḫi-teššup (BM 24137).

Z. 52 Die Schrift auf dem linken Rand ist sehr klein. Demnach fehlen am Anfang der Zeile etwa 3 Zeichen. Als Ergänzung kommen zwei Namen in Frage: Ataja, Sohn des Urumpa, und Ḫanaja, Sohn des Eḫli-teššup. Beide Personen sind als Zeugen auf einer ebenfalls von Ḫašip-tilla geschriebenen Urkunde Urḫi-teššups genannt (BM 26290). Die Zeichenspuren lassen hierfür jedoch keine Entscheidung zu.

Diese Urkunde ist wie die anderen Urkunden des Urḫi-teššup, des Sohnes des Tarmia, etwa in die Zeit der 2.-3. Generation der Schreiberfamilie des Apil-sîn zu datieren.

2. I 15348 + 8371 + 8398; Jank. 13 + 13a + 21; join gefunden am 22.12.91; join nicht vollzogen.

Vs. 1 [*ṭup-pí ti*$_4$*-te-en*]*-nu-ti*
2 [*ša* ^{m}*Te-ḫi-i*]*t-te-šup*
3 [*ù ša* ^{m}]*Mu-uš-te-šup*
4 [DUMU.MEŠ x]-*pí-ia* 1 ANŠE A.ŠÀ *dam*^{am}*-q*[*ú*]
5 ⌜*i+na* A.GÀR⌝ [*š*]*a* URU *Ta-i-in-šu-uḫ-*[*we*]
6 *i+na ú-šal-l*[*i a-n*]*a* ⌜*ti*$_4$⌝*-te-en-nu-ti*
7 ^{m}*Te-ḫi-it-te-*⌜*šup*⌝ [*ù* ^{m}*M*]*u-*⌜*uš*⌝*-te-šup*
8 *a-na* ^{m}*Ur-ḫi-te-*[*šup* DUMU *Tar-mi*]*-ia*
9 *i+na-an-dì-nu* ⌜*ù*⌝ [^{m}*Ur-ḫi-te-šu*]*p*
10 *il-te-nu-tù ḫ*[*u-ul-la-an-nu*]
11 SIG$_5$.GA *za-zu-l*[*u* (...)]
12 *ša ki-na-aḫ-*[*ḫi*
13 2 *am-ma-ti* ⌜*ù*⌝ [...]
14 *ù ru-pu-u*[*s-sú ù*]
15 ⌜3⌝ *am-ma-ti m*[*u-ra-ak-šu ša*]
16 ⌜*ḫu*⌝*-ul-la-a*[*n-ni*]
17 *a-na* ⌜*ti*$_4$⌝*-te-*⌜*en*⌝*-*[*nu-ti*]
18 ⌜*a-na* ^{m}*Te*⌝*-*[*ḫi*]*-it-*⌜*te*⌝*-*[*šup*]
19 [*ù a-na* ^{m}]*Mu-uš-te-š*[*up*]
20 [*i+na*]*-din im-ma-ti-me-*⌜*e*⌝
21 [*ḫu*]*-*⌜*ul*⌝*-la-an-nu ša šu-ul-mu-*
22 ^{m}*Te-ḫi-it-te-šup* : ⌜*us*⌝*-sú*
23 *ù* ^{m}*Mu-uš-te-šup*

u. Rd.24 *a-na* ^{m}*Ur-ḫi-te-šup*

25 *ú-ta-ar-ru*

26 *ù* A.ŠÀ-*šu-*[*nu ša i+n*]*a-an-dì-*[*nu*]

Rs. 27 [*i-le-e*]*q-*<*qú-*>*ú*[5]

28 [*ṭup-pu i+na* EG]IR-*ki*

29 [*šu-du-ti eš-ši i*]*-na* KÁ.GAL

30 [*ša* URU *Ta-ku-we*] *ša-ṭì-i*[*r*]

(Rest der Rs. weggebrochen)

o. Rd. (Siegelabrollung)

31′ [ ]…[

(1) [Darleh]ens[urkunde] (2) [des Teḫi]t-teššup (3) [und des] Muš-teššup, (4) [den Söhnen des ..]pia. Ein gutes ANŠE Feld (5) in der Feldflur der Stadt Tainšuḫ(we), (6) im *ušalli*, haben als Nutzungspfand (7) Teḫit-teššup [und M]uš-teššup (8) dem Urḫi-te[ššup, dem Sohn des Tarm]ia, (9) gegeben. Und [Urḫi-teššu]p hat (10) eine Garnitur *ḫ*[*ullannu*-Decken] (11-12) von guter Qualität, in *zazul*[*u*-Art (?) (…)], mit *kinaḫ*[*ḫu* gefärbt …], — (13) 2 Ellen un[d … (beträgt)] (14) [ihre] Breit[e, und] (15) 3 Ellen (beträgt) die L[änge der] (16) *ḫulla*[*nnu*-Decke — als] (17) Darlehen] dem Te[ḫi]t-te[ššup] (19) [und dem] Muš-te[ššup] [gege]ben. Wann auch immer (21) die [*ḫ*]*ullannu*-Decken, (in) ihrer Vollständigkeit, (22) Teḫit-teššup (23) und Muš-teššup (u.Rd. 24) dem Urḫi-teššup (25) zurückgeben, werden sie ih[r] Feld, [das sie (als Nutzungspfand) ge]ben, (26) [zurücknehm]en. (28) [Die Tafel ist na]ch (29) [der neuen Proklamation i]m Stadttor (30) [von Taku(we)] geschrieb-[en]. (Rest der Rs. weggebrochen).

Z. 10-16 Diese sehr detaillierte Beschreibung einer Garnitur *ḫullannu*-Decken ist in den Nuzi-Texten beispiellos.

Z. 11 *zazulu* ist innerhalb der Nuzi-Texte bereits aus HSS V 95:8 bekannt: 1 TÚG *za-zu-lu* SIG$_5$-*tu*$_4$ „ein gutes *zazulu*-Gewand". Die Wörterbücher interpretieren das Wort als „ein Stoff" (*AHw* 1032b: *sas*(*s*)*ullu*) bzw. „a textile" (*CAD* S 197b: *sasullu*).

Z. 13 Die der Elle nächstkleinere Maßeinheit ist *ubānu* „Finger". Mir ist jedoch nicht bekannt, daß in den Nuzi-Urkunden ein Gewand oder Stoff in dieser Einheit gemessen wird.

Z. 30 Die Ergänzung des Ortsnamens Taku(we) stützt sich darauf, daß zwei weitere Urkunden, die von Grundstücken in oder bei Tain-šuḫ(we) handeln, in dieser Stadt geschrieben wurden (BM 102350, BM 102358) und daß Urḫi-teššup hier ansässig war.

Diese Urkunde gehört wie die vorhergehende in die Zeit der 2.-3. Generation der Schreiberfamilie des Apil-sîn.

---

5 Die Lesung dieser Zeile geht auf einen Vorschlag G. Wilhelms zurück.

3. I 15389 + 15355; Jank. 46 + 89; join gefunden am 13.10.92; join nicht vollzogen.

Vs. 1 [E]ME$^{!}$-*šu š*[*a*] ^{f}*Ša-aš-q*[*a*$^{?}$(-)
2 [DUMU].MUNUS-*sú ša Uk-ka-a*+[*a a-na pa-ni*]
3 [*ši-b*]*u-ti an-nu-ti ki-*[*a-am iq-ta-bi*]
4 [^{m}Z]*i*-⸢*líp-til-la*⸣ DUMU *G*[*e-líp*-LUGAL]
5 [*iš*]-⸢*tu sú-qí*⸣ *l*[*a-lu-ia … ù a-na*]
6 ⸢*a*⸣-*ḫa-tù-ti a-na* ⸢*ia*⸣-*š*[*i i-te-pu-uš*]
7 *ù a-na-ku* 30 MA.NA AN.N[A.MEŠ
8 *a-šar* ^{m}*Zi-líp-til-la e*[*l-te-qè-mi*
9 ⸢*a-na*⸣ *ma-ḫi-iṣ pu-ti-i*[*a*/ ⸢*i*⸣-[
10 [$^{f?}$*N*]*u-uḫ-ḫé* DUM[U.MUNUS$^{?}$
11 [x x (x)] x [
(Rest der Vs. weggebrochen)
u. Rd. (weggebrochen)
Rs. (Anfang der Rs. weggebrochen)
12′ [ ]x-*ti* [
13′ [IGI *T*]*úl-pí-ia* DUMU *Ḫu-zi-r*[*i*
14′ [I]GI *Er-wi*-LUGAL DUMU *Šúk-ri*-⸢*ia*⸣ x[
15′ IGI *Nu-ul-lu* DUMU *Ḫa-na-du* IGI *Ni-i*[*ḫ*-
16′ IGI *Ḫé-er-ši* DUMU *Ša-ši-wa-til*
17′ IGI ^{d}30-KUR-*ni* DUB.SAR DUMU *A-mur*-L[UGAL]

(Siegelabrollung) | (Siegelabrollung)
18′ | NA$_{4}$ ^{m}*Te-ḫ*[*i*-
19′ [NA$_{4}$] ^{m}*Túl-pí-i*[*a*
o. Rd. (Siegelabrollung) [| (Siegelabrollung)]
20′ NA$_{4}$ ^{m}*Ḫé*-⸢*er*⸣-*ši* LÚ.⸢SANGA⸣ [
l. Rd. [(Siegelabrollung) | (Siegelabrollung)]
15′ [NA$_{4}$ ^{m}*Nu-ul*]-*lu* NA$_{4}$ [
16′ [N]A$_{4}$ ⸢DUB⸣.S[AR-*rù* (Z. 16 um 180° gedreht)

(1) Aussage der Šašk[a(-…)], (2) [der Toch]ter des Ukkaj[a. In Anwesenheit] (3) dieser [Zeug]en [hat sie] folgen[dermaßen erklärt]: (4) [Z]ilip-tilla, dem Sohn des K[elip-šarri], (5) [habe *ich* a]uf der Straße [*meinen*] Wu[nsch *erklärt*, und] (6) [er hat] mich als Schwester [adoptiert]. (7) Und ich habe 30 Minen Zin[n] (8) von Zilip-tilla ge[nommen]. (9) Als me[in] Bürge […] (10) [N]uḫḫe, die Toch[ter$^{?}$ …] (Rest der Vs., u. Rd. und Anfang der Rs. weggebrochen.)

(12′) […]x-ti […] (13′) [Vor T]ulpia, dem Sohn des Ḫuzir[i]. (14′) [V]or Erwi-šarri, dem Sohn des Šukria. x[…]. (15′) Vor Nullu, dem Sohn des Ḫanatu. Vor Ni[ḫ…]. (16′) Vor Ḫerši, dem Sohn des Šašiwatil. (17′) Vor Sîn-šadûni, dem Schreiber, dem Sohn des Āmur-ša[rrī]. (18′) Siegel des Teḫ[i…]. (19′) [Siegel des] Tulpi[a …]. (o. Rd. 20′) Siegel des Ḫerši, des Priesters. […]. (l. Rd. 15′) [Siegel des Nul]lu. Siegel des […]. (16′) [Si]egel des Schreibe[rs. (…)].

Z. 4 Zilip-tilla, der Sohn des Kelip-šarri, ist in vier unpublizierten Urkunden des British Museum bezeugt:[6] BM 26259:1,6,11,14,18; 80455:1,5,8,11; 85329:1; 85352:1.

Z. 5 *lalû* „Fülle, Üppigkeit" bezeichnet sowohl die Begierde in sexueller Hinsicht als auch allgemein einen Wunsch oder ein Begehren. In den Nuzi-Urkunden steht *lalû* stets mit *ina/ištu sūqi* „auf der Straße" verbunden für die Initiative der Frau, die sich ohne Unterstützung eines männlichen Verwandten oder Vormundes als Schwester adoptieren läßt.[7]

Die Varianten der Formel sind:[8] HSS V 26:4-5: PN *ina sūqi lalûja attadiššu* „Ich habe meinen Wunsch dem PN auf der Straße gegeben". HSS XIX 70:3-5: PN *ištu sūqi lalû ittalak-ma* „PN ist auf der Straße (mit dem) Wunsch gegangen". Yale 12:3-4: PN *ina sūqi lalûšu attalkaššu* „Ich bin auf der Straße (zu) PN (als) sein Wunsch gekommen". Gadd 31:1′-2′: [...] PN *lalûja illikšu-ma* „PN ging [auf der Straße ?] (auf) meinen Wunsch (zu)". AASOR XVI 54:11-12: PN *aḫātīja ina sūqi iṣṣabat-mi* „PN hat auf der Straße 'meine Schwesternschaft' ergriffen".

Z. 6 Die Adoptionsart *ana aḫātūti* ist z.B. von A. Skaist, *JAOS* 89 (1969) 10-17; D. Freedman, *JANES* 2.2 (1970) 77-85; B.L. Eichler, in: M. de Jong Ellis (Hrsg.), *Essays on the Ancient Near East in Memory of J.J. Finkelstein*, 1977, 45-59; K. Grosz, *SCCNH* 2 (1987) 150-152, untersucht worden.

Z. 9 In den anderen Adoptionsurkunden dieser Art wird nie ein Bürge erwähnt. Demnach muß dieser Adoption eine besondere Voraussetzung zugrundeliegen.

Z. 14′ Erwi-šarri, der Sohn des Ḫuziri, wird in EN 9/1 433:30 ebenfalls als Zeuge aufgeführt.

Z. 17′ Der Schreiber Sîn-šadûni nennt in folgenden Urkunden den Namen seines Vaters Āmur-šarrī: HSS IX 22:39; HSS XIX 30:31; EN 9/1 433:31 und in der unpublizierten Urkunde SMN 3601.

Die einzige datierbare Person dieser Urkunde ist der Schreiber Sîn-šadûni. Anhand der Urkunde HSS IX 22 läßt sich dieser Schreiber der III.-IV. Generation der Schreiberfamilie des Apil-sîn zuweisen, wobei er wohl überwiegend in der IV. Generation tätig war.[9]

---

6 Für eine Übersicht über die unpublizierten Nuzi-Urkunden des British Museums siehe M.P. Maidman, *ZA* 76 (1986) 254-288.

7 Cf. B. Eichler, in: *Gs. Finkelstein*, 1977, 51 Anm. 48.

8 In HSS XIX 67 und 143 finden sich keine mit *lalû* gebildeten Aussagen.

9 Die Personen der in HSS IX 22 beschriebenen Transaktion sind Tupkia, der Sohn des Šurki-tilla, und Pai-teššup, der Sklave des Šilwa-teššup. Šilwa-teššup gehört der III.-IV., und die Söhne des Šurki-tilla der IV. Schreibergeneration an; cf. A. Freedman, *SCCNH* 2 (1987) 109-129; D. Stein, *ZA* 79 (1989) 46, Anm. 31 und *AdŠ* 8, Wiesbaden 1993, 27.

Notes on the Mittani Letter

MitN no. 8-1: Mit. III 57-59.

Im ersten Teil des Paragraphen 24[1] des Mittani-Briefs rühmt sich Tušratta, sowohl die Sendungen seines Großvaters Ardadama wie auch die Sendungen seines Vaters Šuttarna an den Pharao verzehnfacht zu haben (III 50-57).

Der doppelte Vergleich ist in dem folgenden Relativsatz (III 57-59) zusammengefaßt:

57 ... *i-i-al-la-a-ni-i-in*
58 *am-ma-ti-íw-wu-uš at-ta-íw-wu-uš at-ta-i-ip-pa we-e-*WA *ma-ka-a-an-na*
59 *ge-pa-a-nu-lu-u-uš-ta-a-aš-še-na* ...

In analytischer Transkription lautet die Passage:

57 ... *îa=llā=nīn*
58 *ammad(i)=iffu=ž atta(i)=iffu=ž attaī=p=pa fē=va magānn(i)=a*
59 *keb=ān=ol=ōš(=)t=ā=šše=na*[2]

---

1 Der ganze Paragraph wurde von Ch. Girbal, *ZA* 78 (1988) 122-136, bearbeitet.

2 Zur Bedeutung von *keb=ān-* „bringen lassen, schicken" (Kausativ) (=akkad. *šūbulu*) s. G. Müller, *Mesopotamia* 21 (1986) 230ff. Die Morphemanalyse dieser durch das Suffix *-šše* nominalisierten Verbalform bleibt unklar. Ch. Girbal, *ZA* 78 (1988) 129, und ausführlicher *AoF* 16 (1989) 79, sieht in *-oš-* das Tempus der Vergangenheit bei transitiv-ergativen Verben und isoliert davon einen Pluralisator /*t*/, den er mit den pluralischen Elementen in Wunschformen identifizieren möchte, indem er den *i*-Vokal als transitives Element abtrennt (z.B. Jussiv 3. Pers. Pl.: *-i=d=e=n*; Desiderativ: *-i=d=anni*). Zu diesem vermeintlichen Pluralisator auf *-t/d* s. auch V. Haas, *ZA* 79 (1989) 265 (zu CHS I/1 Nr. 6 Rs. III 42: *al+ol=t=a*: sic!). Gegen diese Interpretation spricht aber der Jussiv der intransitiven Formen, z.B. *itt=id=e=n* (Mit. III 23), die bei Abtrennung eines Pluralisators den intransitiven *a*-Vokal zeigen müßten, sowie das auf Grund der Indikativformen auf *-id=o* der hurr.-heth. Bilingue aus Boğazköy etablierte Pluralmorphem *-id-* (s. G. Wilhelm, in: *Fs. Heger*, 666 m. Anm. 7 und *Or*NS 61 (1992) 138). G. Müller, *Mesopotamia* 21 (1986) 232, segmentiert die Form *keb=ān=ol=ošt=a-* ohne weitere Analyse. F. Bush, *GHL* 189-190, vermutet in der Form *keban=ol=ošt=a-* das Suffix -*Všt-*. Obwohl die Handlung eindeutig in die Vergangenheit

Studies on the Civilization and Culture of Nuzi and the Hurrians - 8

Die Form *ma-ka-a-an-na* wurde in den bisherigen Behandlungen des Passus abweichend von unserer im folgenden gebotenen Deutung erklärt. Das hier vorliegende Nomen selbst wird als vedisches oder semitisches Lehnwort betrachtet[3]. Nur Kammenhuber bewertet es als seinem Ursprung nach hurritisch[4].

Die Form *maganna* wurde von Laroche wohl als Absolutiv sg. zu *maganni* mit einem von ihm als *-a* angesetzten Possessivpronomen der 3. Pers. sg. gedeutet, denn er übersetzt: „son présent"[5]. Alle anderen Autoren interpretieren die Form als Absolutiv pl., allerdings mit unterschiedlichem Stammansatz. So geht v. Schuler vom Stamm *maganni* aus und sieht in *maganna* eine unregelmäßige Pluralbildung, die er darauf zurückführt, daß es sich um ein hurritisches Fremdwort handelt[6].

---

verweist, zieht er es vor, das Suffix *-ošt-* nicht als Tempusanzeiger zu sehen, der dann außer bei dem Tempus der Vergangenheit intransitiver Verben auch in ergativer Konstruktion gebraucht werden könnte. In dem Satz *ammad(i)=iffu=ž atta(i)=iffu=ž ... keb=ān=ol=ošt=a-* sieht F. Bush, *GHL* 209, 362 Anm. 85, ein Beispiel von „compound subjects" mit singularischem Verb, wie es auch an anderen Stellen des Mit. bezeugt sei (II 65f., IV 21, 27). E. Laroche, *GLH* 145, betrachtet die Form als „Prét. sg. 3", übersetzt sie aber merkwürdigerweise „(les cadeaux), ceux qui ont été apportés". Bei allen Deutungen bleibt unklar, welche Rolle das Suffix *-ol-* an dieser Stelle spielt.

3 F.W. Bush, *GHL* 189, 342, Anm.137, 353, Anm. 32, und *Fs. Gordon* (= AOAT 22) (1973), 43 mit Anm. 39, vertritt die von H. Kronasser, *Die Sprache* 4 (1958), 127 und *EHS* I, 145, vorgeschlagene Deutung des Substantivs als Entlehnung aus dem vedischen *magha-*, „Gabe, Geschenk", welches durch das Suffix *-nni* hurritisiert sei. E. Laroche, *GLH* 164, stellt es dagegen zur semitischen Wurzel *mgn*. Cf. auch H.-P. Müller, in: L. Cagni (Hrg.), *La lingua di Ebla*, Napoli 1981, 213 Anm. 11, der dazu auch eblait. *ma-ga-na-a-tú* sowie amurr. *ma-ga-nu-um* stellt und fragt: „Ist die Vermutung eines indoiranischen Lehnwortes noch aufrechtzuerhalten?". Das Substantiv ist auch in Alalaḫ und Nuzi belegt; s. besonders A.E. Draffkorn, *Hurrians and Hurrian at Alalaḫ*, 1959 (unveröff. Dissertation, University of Pennsylvania), 181f. (mit zusätzlicher Bibliographie). Dazu s. auch *AHw* I, 574f.; *CAD* M/1, 31f. (mit weiterer Bibliographie).

4 A. Kammenhuber, *Die Arier im Vorderen Orient*, Heidelberg 1968, 228ff., lehnt es ab, *maga-* als das eigentliche Lexem zu isolieren, da sie das bei einer solchen Analyse zu segmentierende *-nni* als hurritischen „Artikel" deuten zu müssen meint, der jedoch nicht vor dem Possessivpronomen stehen könne, während doch die Form *magānniffu-* (s.u.) gerade diese Morphemfolge aufweise. Sie setzt daher als Lexem *magan-* oder *magani-* an und vermutet in dem Nomen einen hurritischen Ursprung. Ihre Argumentation basiert also auf einer Verwechslung des Suffixes *-nni* mit dem sog. Artikel (Relator) *-ne-*.

5 E. Laroche, *GLH* 164; zu dem angeblichen Possessivsuffix *-a* s. G. Wilhelm, *Or*NS 54 (1985) 487.

6 E. v. Schuler, *RHA* 19 fasc. 68 (1961) 19-23. Die gleiche Unregelmäßigkeit vermutet er in dem Wort *mažriyanni*. Der Beleg Mit. II 69 zeigt aber, daß der Absolutiv sg. des Adjektivs *māžriani* lautet und die Verdopplung des Konsonanten /*n*/ auf die Anfügung des Relators sg. oder pl. zurückzuführen ist. Einzig die Textstelle III 117f. (nach Kollation am Photo: ^{KUR}*māžriânni* ^{KUR}*ômīni*^{MEŠ}) scheint die Doppelkonsonanz für den Absolutiv sg. nahezulegen.

Kammenhuber, Farber und Girbal setzen an der hier behandelten Textstelle den Stamm als *magan-* bzw. *magani* an (Abs. pl.: *magan-na*)[7]. Dem widerspricht jedoch die Form, die an zwei anderen Stellen des Mit. belegt ist (II 15: *ma-ka-a-an-ni-íw-wu-*[*ú-un-na*][8] und II 54: *ma-ka-a-an-ni-íw-wu-ú-un-na*) und die darauf hinweist, daß der richtige Stammansatz *magānni* ist[9]. Unter dieser Voraussetzung liegt in *ma-ka-a-an-na* in III 58 nicht der bisher postulierte Absolutiv pl. vor, der **magānni=na* lauten müßte[10], sondern ein Essiv sg., *magānn(i)=a*. Der Kasus hat neben der Funktion als Lokativ die Möglichkeit, einen Zustand oder die Überführung in einen Zustand auszudrücken[11]; hier empfiehlt sich die Übersetzung „als Geschenk".

---

7 A. Kammenhuber, l.c.; W. Farber, *Or*NS 40 (1971) 53, setzt an der hier behandelten Textstelle den Stamm *magani* an; Ch. Girbal, *ZA* 78 (1978) 129f., 132 mit Anm. 24; *AoF* 16 (1989) 79 (*magani*).

8 Ergänzung aufgrund der Übersetzung von G. Wilhelm apud W. L. Moran, *The Amarna Letters*, Baltimore 1992, 65.

9 Mit. II 54 (und II 15) ist demzufolge als *magānn(i)=iffū=nn(i)=a* zu analysieren. (So auch F. Bush, *GHL*, 135, und W. Farber, *Or*NS 40 (1971) 64, der hier inkonsequenterweise vom Stamm *maganni* ausgeht (s.o).) A. Kammenhuber, *Die Arier im Vorderen Orient*, 229, argumentiert, wie oben bereits erwähnt, daß in dieser Form kein hurritischer „Artikel" enthalten sein könne, da dieser „gemäß der streng geregelten Suffixfolge des Hurrischen erst auf die Possessivpronomina folgt". Warum ihr Stammansatz aber als *magan(i)* ohne den doppelten *n*-Konsonanten erfolgt, ist nicht ersichtlich und kann sich nur auf den postulierten Absolutiv pl. der Form *maganna* beziehen. Dagegen analysiert Ch. Girbal, *ZA* 78 (1988) 132, die Form als *magan-n(i)-iffu-nna* und sieht aufgrund seines Stammansatzes mit einfachem /*n*/ in dem abgetrennten *-ni*-Suffix „die gleichzeitige Anwesenheit des 'bestimmten Artikels' *-ni* und des Possessivmorphems". Einen Beleg für den Relator vor einem Possessivpronomen bietet Mit. II 77: ^{DINGIR}*ēn(i)=n(a)=iff=āž=ē=n*, wie schon F.W. Bush, in: *Fs. Gordon* (AOAT 22); Neukirchen 1973, 50, gesehen hat. Die Form soll möglicherweise verdeutlichen, daß es sich um doppelte Pluralisierung handelt, also „unserer Götter", nicht aber „unseres Gottes". Darüberhinaus gibt es nur einen einzigen anderen Beleg im Mit., der im Sinne Relator + Possessivsuffix interpretiert werden kann: $^{\mathrm{[DINGIR.MEŠ]}}$*ēn(i)=ni=p=tan* (IV 116) (contra F. Bush, *GHL* 159f., 341f. Anm. 137, übersetzt G. Wilhelm apud W. L. Moran, *The Amarna Letters*, 1992, 71, „by your god"). Dieser Beleg scheint die Anwesenheit des Relators sg. vor einem Possessivpronomen zu erlauben. Eine andere Erklärung wäre möglich unter Annahme, daß das Zeichen-WA- fehlt: $^{\mathrm{[DINGIR.MEŠ]}}$*e-en-ni-íw-<wu->tan*. In dieser Form wäre dann der Relator pl. enthalten: **ēn(i)=n(a)=iffu=dan*, wobei hier durch den Relator verdeutlicht würde, daß es sich bei dem Nomen um den Plural, bei dem Possessivpronomen aber um 1. Pers. sg. handelt „von meinen Göttern". Schließlich könnte es sich bei Annahme einer größeren Auslassung um einen Genitiv handeln (*$^{\mathrm{[DINGIR.MEŠ]}}$*ēn(i)=ne=v<e=ne>=dan*, der sich auf den Ablativ in Zeile 115 (*še-e-er-re-e-tan*) bezieht.

10 F. Bush, in: *Fs. Gordon* (AOAT 22), 1973, 46. In den Grammatiken von E.A. Speiser, *IH* (1941), und F.W. Bush, *GHL* (1964), findet sich diese Regel noch nicht.

11 Zum hurritischen Essiv s. zuletzt ausführlicher E. Neu, *Hethitica* 9 (1988) 157-170 (mit Bibliographie).

Der Relativsatz Mit. III 57-59 ist demnach folgendermaßen zu übersetzen: „Was (Plural) mein Großvater (und) mein Vater deinem Vater (und) dir als Geschenk geschickt haben, ...". Die nominalisierte Verbalform hat in diesem Fall kein Nomen als Bezugswort — anders als in den vorangehenden Nebensätzen III 53 und 56 (*tivē=na tān=ōž=ā=šše=na*).

M. Giorgieri und I. Röseler

Stern, Tag und Segen(?) im Hurritischen

VOLKERT HAAS and ILSE WEGNER

Freie Universität Berlin

Three Hurrian words from tablets found at Boğazköy are discussed in this article: *ilziri*, which twice appears in the syntagm *ilzir(i)=ra ḫavurun=ne=vi=na* "the *i*.s of heaven," is interpreted as "star"; *šu-u-ú-*WA (*šouve*?) is identified as a word for "day" on the basis of the Hurro-Hittite bilingual from Boğazköy; and *ḫudme* from the Hurro-Hittite ritual of Zelliya is explained as a noun with the suffix *-me* based on the verb *ḫud-* "to bless."

Ilziri: In der ungewöhnlichen und fast ausschließlich in hurritischer Sprache verfassten Opferliste für den Teššup der Stadt Šapinuwa KBo 20.119 (Duplikat KBo 17.86) erscheint das hurritische Nomen *ilziri* zweimal in folgendem Kontext:

KBo 20.119

Vs. I

7 ^{D}*aš-ta-a-wi*$_{i}$ ^{D}*nu-pa-ti-* *ik*
8 ^{D}*ḫé-šu-u-i* ^{D}*ḫa-at-ni* ^{D}*bi-i-ša-i-ša-ap-ḫi*
9 ^{D}*e-še* ^{D}*ḫa-wu*$_{u}$*-ur-* *ni*
10 *il-zi-ir-ra ḫa-wu*$_{u}$*-ru-un-ne-*⌜*wi*$_{i}$⌝*-na*
11 *ta-ga-an tag-mi-ia-šu-* *u*[*n*]
12 *un-du*(-)*mi-ku-un a-ta-at-t*[*e*?*-ru*?*-u*]*n*?

Rs. VI

7′ ^{D}U-*up* *šu-ku-úr-ri-* *wi*$_{i}$
8′ ^{D}U-*up* KARAŠ
9′ ^{D}U-*up* URU-*wi*$_{i}$ ^{URU}*ša-pí-nu-wa-ḫi*
10′ ^{D}*da-aš-mi-iš* ^{D}*A-NI*
11′ ^{D}*kum-mar-bi* ^{D}É.A ^{D}XXX-*uḫ*
12′ ^{D}UTU-*ki* ^{D}*aš-ta-bi* ^{D}*nu-pa-ti-ik*
13′ ^{D}*ḫé-šu-u-i* ^{D}*ḫa-at-ni* ^{D}*bi-ša-i-ša-ap-ḫi*
14′ ^{D}*e-še* ^{D}*ḫa-*[*wu*$_{u}$*-ú*]*r-ni*

15′ *il-zi-ir-ra* [*ḫa-w*]*u*$_{u}$*-ru-un-ne-wi*$_{i}$*-*[*n*]*a*
16′ ^{D}*ta-ga-an* ^{D}*tag-m*[*i*]*-ia-šu-un un-du*(-)[*m*]*i-ku-un*
17′ *ša-at-te-ru- un*

Der Begriff *il-zi-ir-ra ḫa-wu*$_{u}$*-ru-un-ne-wi*$_{i}$*-na* „*ilzirra* des Himmels" folgt nach *e-še ḫa-wu*$_{u}$*-ur-ni* „Erde (und) Himmel". Die Form *il-zi-ir-ra* ist der Plural eines Nomens *ilziri*, das E. Laroche im Hinblick auf den durch die hurritisch-hethitische Bilingue (KBo 32.13 Vs. I 13 *e-še-ni-we*$_{e}$ ^{D}*a-al-la-a-ni* // Vs. II 14 *ták-na-a-aš* ^{D}UTU-*uš*) nunmehr überholten Bedeutungsansatz *eše* „Himmel" und *ḫawurni* „Erde" mit „peut-être les 4 'coins'; akk. *tubuqtu*" wiedergegeben hat[1]. Der hurritisch-hethitischen Bilingue zufolge bedeutet vielmehr *eše* „Erde" und *ḫawurni* „Himmel"[2]. Somit legt der Kontext der Opferliste nahe, in *ilziri* das hurritische Wort für Stern zu sehen[3]; *ilziri* ist mit dem Partizipialsuffix *-iri*[4] von einem Stamm **ilz-* gebildet, der (nicht belegt) vielleicht „leuchten, blinken" o.ä. bedeuten könnte[5].

Möglicherweise liegt in ^{D}*ta-ga-an* (VI 16′) die (einzige) hethitische phonetische Schreibung des Namens des syrischen Getreidegottes *Dagān* vor; ^{D}*tagmiašun* scheint ein Epitheton zu sein. Die Reihenfolge der Opferliste ist dann: „Erde-Himmel, Sterne des Himmels" und „*Dagan-Tagmiašun*". Die Formen nach *un-du* „nun"(?), nämlich (-)*mi-ku-un*[6], *ša-at-te-ru-un*[7] bzw. *a-ta-at-t*[*e-*

---

1 E. Laroche, *GLH* 121.

2 E. Neu, in: *Hurriter und Hurritisch*, hsg. von V. Haas, Xenia 21, 1988, 114 Anm. 12.

3 In meiner *Geschichte der hethitischen Religion*, Leiden 1994, 333 nunmehr nachzutragen. Gegen die Möglichkeit, in *ilziri* das hurritische Wort für „Wolke" zu sehen, spricht die auch im akkadischen belegte Regens-Rectum-Verbindung „Sterne des Himmels" sowie der Befund, daß Wolken nur im Zusammenhang mit dem Wettergott beopfert werden (z.B. KBo 13.245 Rs. 3′-7′; vgl. auch die Nennung der Wolken in Staatsverträgen, wohingegen Opfer an Sterne gelegentlich genannt sind, vgl. V. Haas, *Geschichte der hethitischen Religion*, Leiden 1994, 144 sowie die von M. Krebernik erwähnte Opferliste für die Sterne vom Tall Bi'a (Bi. 29/49:116,1), *MDOG* 126, 1994, 35.

4 Vgl. G. Wilhelm, in: *Hurriter und Hurritisch*, hsg. von V. Haas, Xenia 21, 1988, 52-57.

5 Das Sumerogramm MUL „Stern" erscheint einmal in hurritischem Kontext, wo es mit dem Element *-ḫi* verbunden ist, das entweder zum Stamm des Wortes für Stern gehört, oder als das Morphem der Zugehörigkeit -(*ḫ*)*ḫe* zu bestimmen ist: KBo 24.43(=ChS I/2 Nr. 79) Vs. I 13′ *ka-aš-ša-ap-ti* MUL-*ḫi-ni-e*. Für die erstere Möglichkeit spricht der Eintrag des Vokabulars S^{a} aus Ugarit (bearbeitet von J. Huehnergard, *Ugaritic Vocabulary in Syllabic Transcription*, HSS 32, Atlanta 1987) 35/36.1 [MAL/GÁN (*kakkabu*?)] *zu-zu-ḫé* (vgl. auch J. Huehnergard, l.c., 26); Hinweis G. Wilhelm.

6 Eine Wurzel **mig* liegt vor in dem Opferterminus *mi-ki-*[*ḫi-ia* (KUB 32.50 Vs. 6) und in der wohl als Infinitiv zu betrachtenden Form *mi-e-ku-um-mi* in KUB 47.56 Vs. 13′. Das im CAD M/2, 66, mit zwei Belegen gebuchte Wort *mikuḫḫe* ist allerdings nach einem frdl. Hinweis von J. Fincke hier nicht heranzuziehen, da in beiden Fällen *šimikuḫḫe* zu lesen ist; cf. J. Fincke, RGTC 10, 15.

7 Das Verbum *šatt-* (zu trennen von *šad-* „ersetzen, zurückgeben", vgl. A. Dincol, B.

ru-u]*n*?[8] sind wahrscheinlich als Verben im Imperativ[9] zu bestimmen. Eine andere Möglichkeit wäre, einem Vorschlag von G. Wilhelm folgend, *un-du*(-)[*m*]*i-ku-un* als *und=om=i=kk*(*i*)*=o=n* zu analysieren.

šuwa: Als hurritischen Wörter für „Tag" und „Nacht" wurden von C.-G. von Brandenstein und E. Laroche die Namen der beiden Stiere *Še*(*r*)*ri* und *Ḫurri* in Anspruch genommen, wobei *šer-* „Tag" und *ḫur-* „Nacht" bedeuten sollte[10]; I. M. Diakonoff setzte auf Grund kaukasischer Sprachvergleiche umgekehrt *ḫur-* „Morgen" und *šer-* „Abend" an.[11] Bislang jedoch haben sich diese Bedeutungsansätze nicht bestätigt.[12]

Die hurritisch-hethitische Bilingue KBo 32.19 bietet nun einen Absatz, in dem das hurritische Wort für „Tag" enthalten ist; Vs. I 22-23//Vs. II 22-23 (ergänzt nach Rs. III 47′-48′):

22 *ši-in-ti-šu-ú-wa-at šu-u-ú-wa*
23 *ú-ni-wa*$_a$*-at-ta* … .

Die hethitische Entsprechung lautet:

22 *nu nam-ma* U$_4$ 7.KAM-[(*az*?)] …
23 … *ú-wa-mi*

„Und ferner am siebten Tag … werde ich kommen".

Hethitisch *uwami* „ich komme, ich werde kommen" entspricht hurritisch *uniwatta*, das als *un=eva=tta*, einer Form des konditionellen Optativs, zu analysieren ist „ich könnte/will kommen".

U$_4$ 7.KAM-*az*? „am siebten Tag" entspricht dann der hurritischen Fügung *ši-in-ti-šu-ú-wa-at šu-u-ú-wa*. Eines der beiden Wörter muß somit das Wort für

---

Dinçol, J.D. Hawkins, G. Wilhelm, in: IM 43, 1993 [Fs. Neve], 102, Anm. 78), mit unbekannter Bedeutung ist mehrfach in Mittani und Boğazköy belegt, vgl. dazu die *GLH* 219 sub *šatt-* notierten Belege. Die hier vorliegenden Formen werden von Laroche, ibid., *ša-at-ma-ru-un* und *a-ta-at-m*[*a-r*]*u-un* gelesen.

8 Möglicherweise liegt eine Verschreibung für *šatterun* vor.

9 Nach dem Muster von *kirunna* und *pendun* aus der hurritisch-hethitischen Bilingue KBo 32.15 IV 2 und IV 6, die als *kir=u=nna* „laß ihn heraus" und *pend=u=n*(*na*) „schicke ihn" zu bestimmen sind, könnte in *mikun mig=u=n*(*na*) „x-e es/ihn" und in *šatterun* entsprechend *šatt+er=u=n*(*na*) vorliegen. Es würde sich demnach um Imperative der 2. Pers. Sg. auf *-u* /o/ und der Kurzform des enklitischen Pronomens der 3. Pers. Sg. Absolutiv *-n*(*na*) handeln.

10 C.-G. von Brandenstein, Bildbeschreibungen, *MVAeG* 46/2 (1943) 71 Anm. 1 und E. Laroche, Rech. 49; im *GLH* lässt Laroche die beiden Namen unübersetzt.

11 I.M. Diakonoff *HuU* (1971), 165ff. sowie I.M. Diakonoff und S.A. Starostin, *Hurro-Urartian as an Eastern Caucasian Language*, MSS, Beiheft 12 NF, 1986, 37; vgl. auch V. Haas, *RlA* 4 (1972–1975), 506.

12 Wahrscheinlicher ist es, den Namen *šeri* mit *šerše* „Thron, Thronstadt" zusammenzustellen, wobei sich eine ungefähre Bedeutung, „Thronwächter" o.ä. ergeben würde, vgl. V. Haas, *Geschichte der hethitischen Religion*, Leiden 1994, 319.

„Tag" sein, es sei denn, in *ši-in-ti-šu-ú-wa-at* liegt ein Nominalkompositum, etwa **šindi-šuwa*, vor. Dieser Weg wird hier jedoch nicht verfolgt[13].

Für *ši-in-ti-šu-ú-wa-at* wird folgende Analyse vorgeschlagen: *šindi* Kardinalzahl „sieben" + *š(še)* Ordinalzahlen bildender Formant + *uva* + *t(ta)* Kurzform des enklitischen Pronomens der 1. Pers. Sg. (bezieht sich auf *un=eva=tta*). In der noch unklaren Verbindung *-uwa-* könnte der *a*-Kasus vermutet werden. Die Möglichkeit, in *wa-* den Dativ zu sehen, ist unseres Erachtens weniger wahrscheinlich, da dieser Kasus in der Bilingue, wie überhaupt in dem hurritischen Boğazköy-Schrifttum, fast ausschließlich durch die Zeichen WA_a bzw. PA dargestellt wird. Die Form lautet dann: „am siebten ... ich".

Eine identisch gebildete Ableitung vom Zahlwort *šini* „zwei" bietet der Keššì-Text KUB 47.2 Rs. IV 16 *ši-en-zu-ú-wa-at-ta*, i.e. *šin+š(i)* > *šinzi* + *uva* + *tta* (Langform des enklitischen Pronomens der 1. Pers. Sg.). Auch hier ist das Zeichen WA ohne subskribiertes a wiedergegeben, wie es für das Dativkennzeichen zu erwarten wäre.

Das Wort für „Tag" ist demnach graphisch *šu-u-ú-wa*, für das folgende Analyse vorgeschlagen wird: *šuuw*(V) + a Essiv. Ebenfalls zu diesem Wort möchten wir die beiden Formen *šu-ú-u-wa-ta* aus KBo 32.62 Vs.I 2, 3 stellen. Beide Formen stehen im Direktiv auf *-ta*, der Stamm lautet demnach *šuuwa*. Da der Themavokal *a* im Hurritischen aber nur auf einige wenige Nomina, vor allem Verwandtschaftsbezeichnungen beschränkt ist, könnte der Auslautvokal auch ein *e* oder *ə* sein, das als a realisiert ist. Die Unsicherheit in der Schreibung der interkonsonantischen Vokale *-u- -ú-* bzw. *-ú- -u-* lässt vielleicht auf die Wiedergabe eines ungewöhnlichen Dipthongs schließen, so daß das Wort für Tag /*šouve*/ bzw. /*šuove*/ lautete und sich somit von dem Dativ des selbständigen Pronomens der 1. Pers. Sg. mit der Lautung *šova* unterscheidet[14].

Für den hurritischen Satz bietet sich demnach folgende Analyse und Übersetzung an: *šindi=š(še)=uva=t(ta) šouv(e)=a ... un=eva=tta* „Am siebten Tag ... will ich kommen."

Mit *šuwa* „Tag" liegt nun neben *šawala/šawalli*(<*šawala=ni*) „Jahr" ein weiterer hurritischer Zeitbegriff vor. Falls im Hurritischen bislang allerdings noch nicht erkannte klassifikatorische Wortbildungen existieren sollten, würde ein etymologischer Zusammenhang zwischen diesen beiden Termini bestehen.

Zu der immer noch recht problematischen Frage bezüglich der Verwandtschaft des Hurritischen mit modernen kaukasischen Sprachen[15], sei angemerkt, daß das Wort für Tag im Botlichischen oder im Ghodoberischen als

---

13 Komposita sind für das Hurritische, außer vielleicht in Eigennamen, nicht bezeugt, vgl. dazu I.M. Diakonoff *HuU* (1971), 74 Anm. 74; G. Wilhelm, *SMEA* 29 (1992) 239ff., Anm. 4.

14 Zu der Wortfolge *šindai šova* (KUB 27.23+KBo 27.88=ChS I/1 Nr. 16 Vs. II 9''), in der wohl auch von einem 7. Tag die Rede ist, siehe I. Wegner, *SMEA* 29, 1992, 229f.

15 Vgl. I.M. Diakonoff und S.A. Starostin, *Hurro-Urartian as an Eastern Caucasian Language*, MSS Beiheft 12 NF 1986.

zibu, im Andischen als *zubu*, *zuv* sowie im Karatinisch, Tindisch, Chwarschinischen[16] als *zebu* erscheint[17].

ḫudme: In dem hethitischen Ritual des Zelliya, das der Reinigung eines Menschen, welcher an der Išḫara-Krankheit gestorben ist, dient[18], erscheint der folgende, nur bruchstückhaft erhaltene hurritische Spruch:

KUB 30.26

Rs. IV
x+1′ ⸢*ú*⸣-x[
2′ *a-ru-RI-*[
3′ *ta-a-ar-r*[*i-*
4′ *ḫu-ud-me-na an-ni-*[*il-la*
5′ *u-ru-un-ni-na-*⸢*i*⸣ [

6′ *nu ma-aḫ-ḫa-an ki-i u*[*d-da-a-ar zi-in-na-an-zi*]
7′ *nu* GIDIM *a-ra-aḫ-za pí-*⸢*e*⸣*-*[*ḫu-da-an-zi*
8′ *na-an ar-ḫa wa-ar-nu-m*[*i*

Die Übersetzung des hethitischen Absatzes[19]:

6′ Sobald [man] diese W[orte beendet,]
7′ br[ingt man] den Toten hinaus,
8′ und ich verbrenne ihn. [

In *ta-a-ar-r*[*i-* (Zeile 3′) liegt im Hinblick auf hethitisch *warnumi* „ich verbrenne" sicherlich **tari*(„Feuer")=*ni* mit dem sog. Artikel *-ni* vor.[20]

ḫu-ud-me-na ist der Plural eines Nomens *ḫudme*, das von dem Stamm *ḫud-* „segnen"[21] abgeleitet ist[22]. Zur Nominalbildung *ḫudme* vgl. auch *el*(*a*)*me* „Eid",

---

16 Chwarschinisch gehört der Dido-Untergruppe an, die anderen Sprachen der andischen Untergruppe.

17 Vgl. S.M. Chajdakov, *Sravnitel'no-sopostavitel'nyj slovar' dagestanskich jazykov*, Moskva 1973, 96 (Hinweis Chr. Girbal).

18 KUB 30,26, bearbeitet von H. Otten, *HTR* 100-3.

19 Siehe H. Otten, *Hethitische Totenrituale*, 103.

20 In gleicher Graphie auch in KBo 32.14 Vs. I 6.

21 In der hurr.-heth. Bilingue KBo 32.19 Vs. I 14// II 15 mit heth. *šarliye-/šarlai-*, bezogen auf die Waffen, wiedergegeben. Dem Kontext würde auch hier für *šarliye-/šarlai-* eine Bedeutung „segnen" besser gerecht werden als wie bisher „erhöhen, verherrlichen, rühmen, preisen", vgl. auch das luwische Nomen *šarlaim*(*m*)*i-*, das als Götterepitheton erscheint.

22 M. Salvini, Xenia 21, 1988, 169f.

ḫalme „Gesang", *nulme* „Sklavin", *purame* „Diener", *tašme* „Geschenk" und *ulme* „Waffe"[23]. Auf *ḫudme=na* bezogen ist das Pronomen *anni-*, das im entsprechenden Plural *anni=lla* steht. *u-ru-un-ni-na-*⸢*i*⸣ ist, falls richtig gelesen, der Instrumentalis des Adjektivs *urunni* „letzter, hinterer".

23 I. Wegner, *Or*NS 59, 1990, 303, Anm. 14.

Zur Herkunft der hethitischen Keilschrift

KARL HECKER

Westfälische Wilhelms-Universität Münster

The Kültepe tablet kt k/k 4 is published here in transliteration, translation, copy and photographs. The text is a letter sent by a certain Eḫli-Addu to one Unapše. It deals with the sender's silver in the city of Kaniš. The palaeography is not that of the usual ductus of the Kültepe tablets but displays similarities with Old Babylonian texts from Syria. Both the name of the sender and the addressee are Hurrian and so is the place-name Zipuḫuliwe. These names are discussed in detail in the subsequent article of G. Wilhelm. It seems, then, that kt k/k 4 attests to the participation of Hurro-Syrian merchants in Anatolian trade.

Dem mit der Materie vertrauten Leser ist zweifelsohne klar, daß der Titel dieses Beitrags ein Zitat darstellt[1]. Mir selbst, der ich mich auf dem Gebiete der Hethitologie und der Boğazköy-Forschung allenfalls als einen Dilettanten bezeichnen kann, ging dies jedoch erst auf, als ein erster Rohentwurf bereits in großen Zügen fertig vorlag. Ich kann mir nun aber mein weiteres Vorgehen ganz erheblich vereinfachen, indem ich nämlich, statt die verschiedenen Meinungen und Äußerungen zur Herkunft der Boğazköy-Schrift im Detail vorzuführen, das mit der Überschrift begonnene Zitat fortsetze: „Die hethitische Keilschrift entstammt einer altbabylonischen Kursive, wie sie im nordsyrischen Raum z.B. von frühen Texten aus Alalaḫ ... bekannt ist. Allgemein wird angenommen, daß diese Form der Keilschrift im Zusammenhang mit Kriegszügen des hethitischen Großkönigs Ḫattušili I. nach Nordsyrien (um 1550 v. Chr. gemäß der Kurzchronologie) von dort nach Ḫattuša ... gelangt sei". Zu diesen beiden Sätzen gehört inhaltlich auch noch die Fußnote 2) mit folgendem Wortlaut: „Alternativ wurde erwogen, ob dieser Keilschrifttyp nicht schon von Angehörigen der Kuššara-Dynastie (Pitḫana, Anitta) aus Nordsyrien übernommen sein könnte". Dabei fällt dem Philologen natürlich der unterschied-

1 Es handelt sich um die Überschrift von Absatz A der Einleitung von: Ch. Rüster - E. Neu, *Hethitisches Zeichenlexikon. Inventar und Interpretation der Keilschriftzeichen aus den Boğazköy-Texten* (StBoT, Beiheft 2). Wiesbaden: Harrassowitz, 1989, S. 15. Der hier im weiteren Verlauf des Absatzes zitierte Text schließt an diese Überschrift unmittelbar an.

Studies on the Civilization and Culture of Nuzi and the Hurrians - 8

liche Tempusgebrauch in den beiden Zitaten ins Auge: Das Präsens (im Haupttext) für die derzeit gültige und das Präteritum (in der Fußnote) für die veraltete und heute aufgegebene Auffassung.

Wenn ich hier nun die offenbar ruhende Diskussion um die Herkunft der hethitischen Keilschrift neu zu beleben versuche, dann kann das selbstredend nur auf der Grundlage neuen Materials geschehen. Mein Ziel ist dabei nicht unbedingt, die jetzt gängige Meinung als völlig unhaltbar zu erweisen und die Anfänge der Boğazköy-Schrift ganz neu zu datieren; ich will mich vielmehr darauf beschränken zu zeigen, daß syrische Schreibtraditionen bereits im *kārum*-zeitlichen Kleinasien nicht unbekannt waren. Hierzu möchte ich eine vom Kültepe stammende Keilschrifttafel bekannt machen, die nicht dem bekannten Typ altassyrischer Texte entspricht, sondern auf Grund ihres paläo- und orthographischen Befundes, ihrer Sprache und nicht zuletzt ihres Onomastikons aus Syrien stammen muß.

Die Beziehungen zwischen Anatolien und dem nordsyrischen Raum in der Zeit der aA Handelskolonien haben, wenn ich das richtig sehe, in archäologischen Kreisen bisher einen wesentlich höheren Stellenwert als in philologischen. Für die archäologische Seite mag es hier genügen, auf die Arbeiten von Nimet Özgüç zu den Siegelabrollungen syrischen Stils vom Kültepe[2] und aus den Palästen von Acemhöyük[3] zu verweisen. Außerdem sei noch ein längerer Artikel von Tahsin Özgüç in der *Fs. Mellink* genannt, der zwar die Situation des ausgehenden 3. Jtd., also der der klassischen *kārum*-Zeit vorangehenden Periode, untersucht, sich aber ausführlich mit dem großen Reichtum der aus dem syrischen Raum stammenden Traditionen in Kültepe/Kaniš befaßt[4]. Ganz anders ist das Bild, das uns die Kültepe-Philologen zeichnen. Natürlich ist es lange bekannt, daß die Route von Assur nach Kaniš das nordsyrische Taurus-Vorland durchquerte[5], und man weiß auch, daß in einer Reihe von Orten an dieser Route assyrische *kārum*- und *wabartum*-Niederlassungen existierten[6]. Und schließlich werden in den Texten gelegentlich auch Personen genannt, die aus dem syrischen Raum stammen oder mit Ortschaften aus diesem Gebiet in Verbindung gebracht werden können[7]. Aber alles das ist so tief im altassyrischen Kontext verankert, daß die abweichende Herkunft dieser

---

2 Z.B. in: *Seals and Seal Impressions of Level Ib from Karum Kanish* (TTKY V/25). Ankara: Türk Tarih Kurumu Basımevi, 1968, Kapitel IV. „Old Syrian Cylinder Seals and Impressions", S. 53-57.

3 "Seal Impressions from the Palaces of Acemhöyük" in: E. Porada u.a. (ed.), *Ancient Art in Seals*, Princeton: Princeton University Press, 1980, 80ff.

4 "New Observations on the Relationship of Kültepe with Southeast Anatolia and North Syria during the Third Millennium B.C." in: J.V. Canby u.a. (ed.), *Ancient Anatolia. Essays in Honor of Machteld J. Mellink*, Madison: The University of Wisconsin Press, 1986, S. 31-47.

5 Vgl. K. Hecker, *ZA* 70 (1980), S. 187ff.

6 Vgl. etwa die Tabelle bei L.L. Orlin, *Assyrian Colonies in Cappadocia*, The Hague-Paris: Mouton, 1970, 75f.

Personen und die mit dieser verbundenen Konsequenzen eigentlich kaum ernsthaft zur Kenntnis genommen worden sind. Insbesondere ist, soweit mir bekannt, nie erwogen worden, daß Personen nordsyrischer Herkunft in Kültepe und Kleinasien ein vom Altassyrischen abweichendes Idiom gesprochen haben oder der nordsyrischen Schriftkultur verhaftet gewesen sein könnten. A. Ünal hat die *communis opinio* 1983 dahingehend zusammengefaßt, daß „im Anatolien der Handelskolonienzeit außer dem Altass. keine andere Schriftsprache denkbar" sei[8].

Daß das bisher gültige Bild falsch ist und man auch am Kültepe syrische Keilschrift kannte, das belegt nun die dort bereits im Jahre 1959 gefundene Tafel kt k/k 4 (Mus.-Nr. 162-4-64), die ich im Herbst 1988 im Ankaraner Museum kopieren konnte[9]. Es handelt sich dabei um einen privaten Brief geschäftlichen Inhalts, den ein gewisser Eḫliaddu aus einem nicht genauer zu ermittelnden Ort Nordsyriens an einen in Kaniš ansässigen Unapše schrieb. Leider kann ich keine detaillierten Angaben zum Fundort und zu den Fundumständen der Tafel machen. Es scheint mir jedoch sicher, daß wir es, wie auch bei einer Reihe anderer Texte der Grabungskampagne von 1959, mit einem der jüngeren Phase (Schicht Ib) der *kārum*-Niederlassung zuzuweisenden Text zu tun haben[10]. Ich lege den Text in Photo, Kopie und Umschrift vor und möchte hervorheben, daß Übersetzung und Bearbeitung in Anbetracht fehlenden Vergleichsmaterials nur als vorläufig anzusehen sind.

---

7 Leute aus Ebla z.B. werden ATHE 32, 17 und BIN VI 193, 14 erwähnt, ein Puzur-Ištar aus Tadmur/Palmyra wird EL 303 A, 17. B, 2 als Zeuge genannt. Aus Šimala bzw. Šamᶜal stammen ein Šu-Bēlim (TC III 202, 22), ein Aššur-ṭāb (TTC 9, 15) und ein Šerdu (EL 44, 14) und aus Batna ein Šu-Laban. [Nachtrag: Vgl. inzwischen auch H. Klengel, „Syrischer Handel und die Texte aus Kültepe/Kaniš", in: K. Emre u.a. (ed.), *Anatolia and the Ancient Near East*, 263ff.]

8 *RlA* 6, 330ᵃ s.v. Kuššara.

9 Mein herzlichster Dank gilt Herrn Kollegen Emin Bilgiç, dem Vorsitzenden der Kommission zur Publikation der Ankaraner Kültepe-Texte, für seine Einladung zur Mitarbeit wie auch für seine mannigfaltige Hilfe während meiner Aufenthalte und Arbeit in Ankara.

10 Im Jahre 1959 wurden insgesamt 121 Tafeln bzw. Tafelfragmente gefunden. Davon stammen nach der Aufstellung bei N. Özgüç, *Seals and Seal Impressions of Level Ib from Karum Kanish*, S. 62, 31 aus Schicht Ib, darunter dem Katalog ebd., S. 63ff. zufolge k/k 14-16, 18 und 30 (mit Ausnahme von k/k 30 mit Fundortangabe aa-bb/19-20). k/k 11 ist wegen des Limmus Pilaḫ-Suen *mera* Ikūnim und k/k 19 wegen des Limmus Ilī-ellatī in die Schicht Ib zu datieren. Pilaḫ-Suen ist als Limmu auch in Boğazköy (KBo IX 4, 10 [*ša qāt qātim*] und 5, 28) und Ilī-ellatī in Chagar Bazar und Mari (vgl. die Zusammenstellung bei K.R. Veenhof, *MARI* 4 (1985) 205 Nr. 26) nachgewiesen. [Nachtrag: kt k/k 14 und k/k 1 soeben von V. Donbaz in: Kutlu Emre u.a. (ed.), *Anatolia and the Ancient Near East*, S. 81ff., publiziert.]

kt k/k 4, hellbraune Tafel, 5,7 x 4,7 x 1,5 cm[11]

Vs. *a-na Ú-na-ap-šé qí-bi-*ma*
um-ma ^{m}*Eḫ-li-a-du*
KÙ^{pí} 1 *ma-na* 15 GÍN KÙ
iš-ṭù 25 MU.1.KAM *i-*ṣé-**ri-kà*
i-na a-lim Kà-ni-iš KÙ^{pí}
*la ú-ṣí šu-ma lá ta-ša-*pá-**ar-ma*
ki-ma ša Tù-ni-ip KÙ^{pí}
i-na ma-at Ku-uz-zi ša
i-té-né-pé-šu i-pé-eš$_{15}$
IGI *Šu-šu-ku pá-ar-ku-li*
K. IGI *A-mì-ḫe-pá ša Qá-ta-an*
IGI *Du-ḫu-uš-ma-tí*
Rs. *ša ḫa-ra-ni*
IGI *Ì-lí-a ša Zi-pu-ḫu=li-we*
ší-bu an-nu-tum
ša a-lim Ḫa-aš-ši
*i-na ḫa-ra-ni áš-ta=na-pá-ar-*ma*
KÙ^{pí} *lá tu-ša-ba-al*
šu-ma a-wa-at-kà mì-im-ma
i-ba-ši a-ni-ke-e al-kam-ma
i-na alim ša x x *im*
K. x-KI-*ku-um ú ma-ḫa-ar*
ší-bu-tí
l.S. *al-kam*

[1-2]An Unapše, von Eḫliaddu: [3-4]Mein Silber — 1 Mine 15 Seqel Silber — ist seit 25 Jahren zu deinen Lasten. [5-9]Aus der Stadt Kaniš sollte mein Silber nicht hinausgehen. Wenn du nicht schreibst, so wird, wie Tunip mein Silber im Land Kuzzi zu behandeln pflegt, er(/es$^{?}$) handeln. [10-14]Vor dem Siegelschneider Šušuku, vor Ammiḫepa von Qatan, vor Duḫušmati von *der Karawane*, vor Ilīja von Zipuḫuliwe. [15-18]Diese Zeugen aus der Stadt Ḫaššu schreibe ich immer wieder mit der Karawane, ohne daß du mein Silber schickst. [19-24]Wenn dein Wort etwas wert ist, komm hierher, und in der Stadt … … dir. Und vor die Zeugen komm!

11 In der Umschrift bezeichnet ein Sternchen auf der rechten Tafelkante, zwei Sternchen auf der Rs. stehende Zeichen; auf Gleichheitszeichen (=) Folgendes ist unterhalb der laufenden Zeile eingerückt.

kt k/k 4

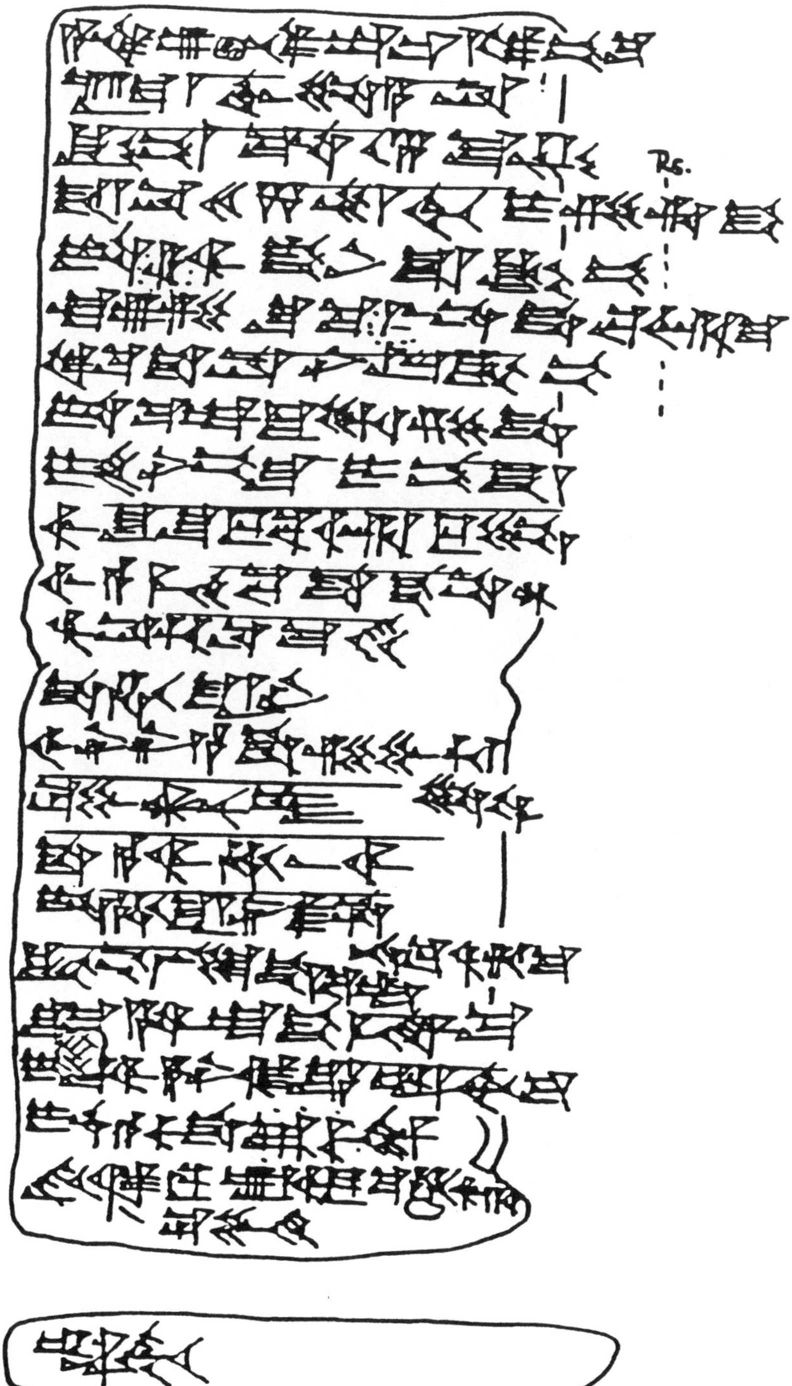

kt k/k 4

Vs.

K.

Rs.

K.

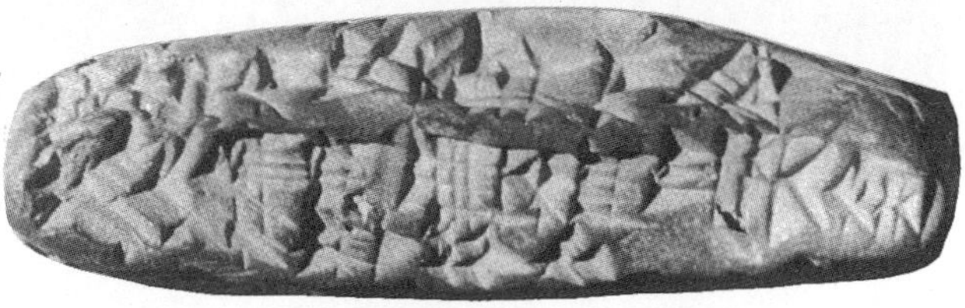

l.S.

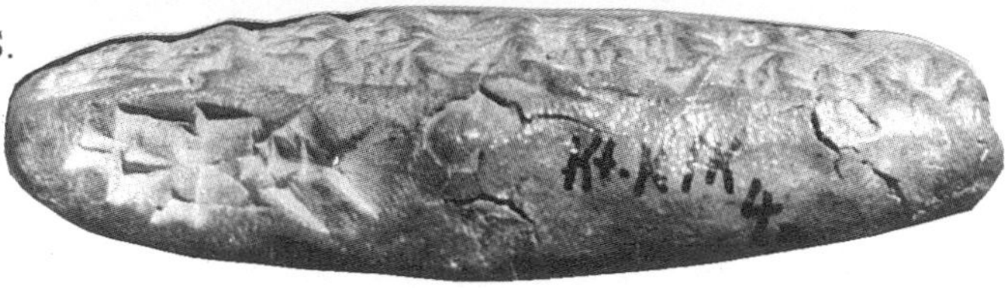

kt k/k 4: Zeichenformen

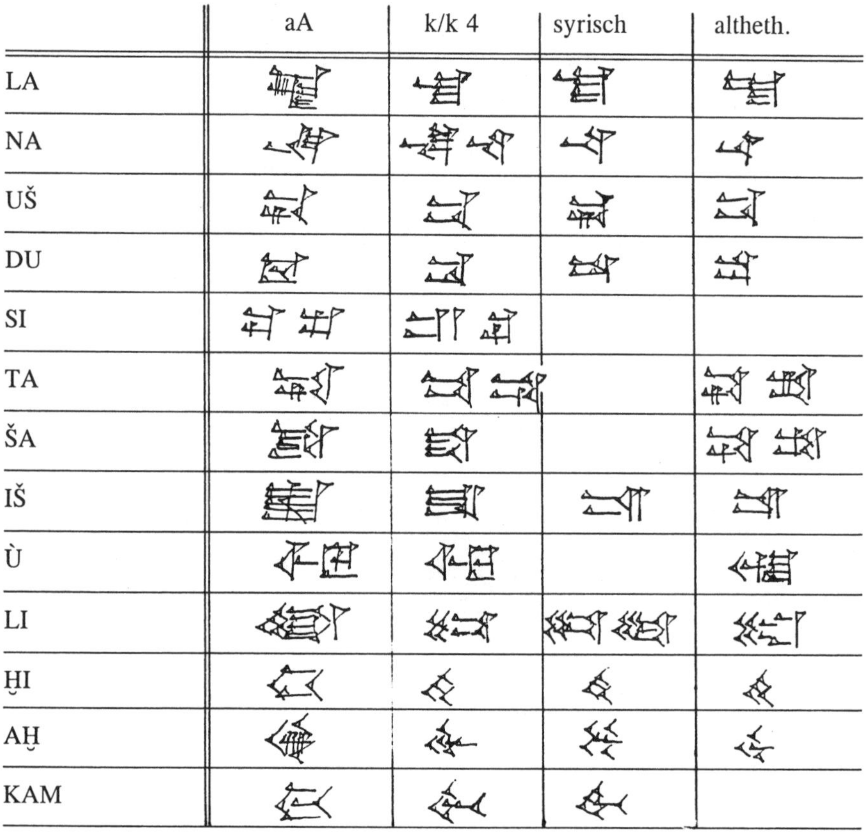

KOMMENTAR:

Daß diese Tafel trotz des Fundortes Kültepe nicht im aA Milieu beheimatet ist, lehrt schon eine äußerliche Betrachtung. Das Format der Tafel mit den leicht zipfelig auslaufenden vier Ecken ist für Kültepe-Tafeln ganz ungewöhnlich. Ferner fehlt der typische, leicht von links nach rechts hängende Duktus der aA Texte. Schließlich fällt auf, daß mehrmals nicht nur auf den rechten Rand, sondern sogar auf die Rückseite hinüber geschrieben ist, ein Phänomen, das auch sonst in älteren Texten aus dem syrischen Raum belegbar ist[12]. Weitere Argumente ergeben sich aus der Paläographie, der Orthographie, aus dem Onomastikon und schließlich auch aus der Sprache des Textes.

a) Zur Paläographie (vgl. auch Tf. 2): Der Schreiber benutzt eine Vielzahl von Zeichenformen, die im „Normal-aA" unüblich sind. Nächste Parallelen finden sich vor allem in altbabylonischen Texten aus Chagar Bazar, Munbāqa und anderen Orten Syriens (außer Mari), aber auch im älteren Hethitischen. Oft aber, und das verdient besonders hervorgehoben zu werden, weichen auch die Zeichenformen der İnandık-Tafel und anderer althethitischer Texte[13] nicht unerheblich von den in k/k 4 benutzten ab. Besonders deutlich fallen die lokalen Unterschiede z.B. bei den Formen von LA, LI, AḪ/IḪ oder IŠ auf. Bei LA steht der komplizierten und keilreichen aA Form eine wesentlich vereinfachte gegenüber, die man fast als AŠ+ŠU beschreiben könnte, während das althethitische Zeichen mit den beiden waagerechten Keilen am Anfang eine eigene Tradition vertritt. Auch bei AḪ/IḪ gehen das „Normal-aA", k/k 4 und das Althethitische jeweils eigene Wege, während etwa bei ḪI alle Gruppen gegenüber dem aA in etwa gleiche Zeichenformen verwenden. Fassen wir den paläographischen Vergleich zusammen, dann muß unserem Text k/k 4 zweifelsohne eine Position zwischen dem „normal-aA" Duktus einerseits und dem altsyrischen und dem althethitischen andererseits zugewiesen werden, wobei wir es einstweilen vielleicht besser offen lassen sollten, ob diese Zwischenstellung historisch oder geographisch zu interpretieren ist[14].

12 Vgl. dazu W. von Soden, „Eine altbabylonische Urkunde (79 MBQ 15) aus Tall Munbāqa", *MDOG* 114 (1982) 71; für eine abweichende Datierung cf. C. Wilcke, *N.A.B.U.* 1990, 28, no. 35.

13 Vgl. die Zeichenliste bei K. Balkan, *Eine Schenkungsurkunde aus der althethitischen Zeit, gefunden in İnandık 1966*, Ankara: Türk Tarih Kurumu Basımevi, 1973, S. 90ff., sowie Ch. Rüster, *Hethitische Keilschriftpaläographie* (StBoT 20), Wiesbaden: Harrassowitz, 1972, passim.

14 Eine detaillierte Untersuchung dieser Problematik dürfte erst nach der Publikation weiterer aB Texte aus Syrien (Tell Leilān, Tell Biᶜa usw.) wie auch aller aA der Schicht Ib sinnvoll werden. Soweit ich das nach Autopsie allerdings nur eines Teils der Kültepe-Ib-Texte in Ankara beurteilen kann, nimmt k/k 4 aber auch unter diesen eine absolute Sonderstellung ein.

b) Auch orthographisch weicht k/k 4 erheblich von dem in aA Texten Üblichen ab. Viermal wird abweichend vom aA Brauch Doppelkonsonanz geschrieben, und zwar in *an-nu-tum* (Z. 15), *mì-im-ma* (Z. 19) und in den ON *Ku-uz-zi* (Z. 8) und *Ḫa-aš-ši* (Z. 16). Zwar verwendet der Schreiber von k/k 4 überwiegend typische aA Zeichen und Lautwerte wie z.B. SI = *ší/é* in *Ú-na-ap-šé* (Z. 1) und *ší-bu* (Z. 15), DU = *tù* in *iš-tù* (Z. 4), *tí* in *Du-ḫu-uš-ma-tí* (Z. 12) und *ší-bu-tí* (Z. 23) oder *lá* in der Negation (Z. 6, ebd. auch *la*), doch kennt er auch im aA seltene oder ganz fehlende: Vor allem *aš* im ON *Ḫa-aš-ši* (Z. 16) und *ši* außer in diesem Namen auch in *i-ba-ši* (Z. 20). Das im aA ganz seltene *tu* liegt in *tu-ša-ba-al*[15] (Z. 18) und *ḫe/i*, falls von mir richtig gelesen, in dem PN *A-mì-ḫe-pá* (Z. 11)[16] vor. Zu den in den „normalen" Kültepe-Texten unbekannten oder zumindest ungewöhnlichen Schreibungen zählen schließlich noch das Ideogramm x MU.1.KAM[17], das Fehlen des Determinativs KI bei *a-lim* (Z. 5, 16, 21) und die Schreibung KÙ^{pí} für *kaspī* (Z. 3, 5, 7, 18)[18].

c) Aus dem Onomastikon des Textes heben sich die Namen des Adressaten *Ú-na-ap-šé* und des Absenders *Eḫ-li-a-du* besonders auffällig ab[19]. Beide PN sind in den Texten aus Alalaḫ gut belegt, der des *Eḫ-li-a-du* sowohl in solchen aus der aB Schicht VII wie aus der jüngeren Schicht IV, *Ú-na-ap-šé* allerdings anscheinend nur in IV[20]. Auch die ON verweisen deutlich auf das nördliche Syrien: Tunip (Z. 7), das wohl im Hinterland der syrischen Mittelmeerküste zu suchen ist[21], *Qá-ta-an* (Z. 11), das ich trotz der Argumente von A. Kammenhuber lieber zu Qatna/Mišrife am Orontes als zu der in der Nachbarschaft von Mari liegenden Ortschaft Qatanum stellen möchte[22], und nicht zuletzt Ḫaššu (Z. 16),

---

15 Zusammen mit *tù* (in *iš-tù* Z. 4) bildet *tu* ein Homophonpaar, wie sie auch in „normal-aA" Texten nicht ganz selten vorkommen (z.B. *ti/tí, la/lá* und *šur/šùr*). In k/k 4 finden sich noch *ši/ší* (*i-ba-ši* Z. 20 : *ší-bu-tí* Z. 23 und *aš/áš* (*Ḫa-aš-ši* Z. 16 : *áš-ta-na-pá-ar-ma* Z. 17).

16 Das von mir *ḫe* gelesene Zeichen (babylonische Zeichenform) entspricht bis auf einen zusätzlichen Winkelhaken weitgehend dem *té/í* in *i-té-né-pé-šu* Z. 9, *Du-ḫu-uš-ma-tí* Z. 12 und *ší-bu-tí* Z. 23. Leider fehlt ein weiterer Beleg für *ḫi* in diesem Text. Den Namen Ammiḫepa kann ich sonst nicht nachweisen, vgl. aber zur Namensform den PNf *Um-mu-ḫe-pa* AT 178, 2 sowie *RlA* 4, S. 328^{b} für weitere mit Ḫepa(t) zusammengesetzte Namen.

17 Im „Normal-aA" wäre MU.x.ŠÈ üblich.

18 Das Determinativ vor maskulinen PN (^{m}*Eḫ-li-a-du* Z. 2), das in den bisher publizierten aA Texten nur recht selten belegbar ist, kann ich in unveröffentlichtem Material ziemlich oft nachweisen.

19 Zu den hurritischen Namen cf. auch den Beitrag von G. Wilhelm in diesem Band, S. 333-345.

20 Den im Index bei D.J. Wiseman, *The Alalakh Tablets*, London: The British Institute of Archaeology at Ankara, 1953 notierten aB Beleg *120, 3 konnte ich dort nicht finden.

21 Vgl. zuletzt M.C. Astour, *Or*NS 46 (1977), 51ff.

22 Vgl. A. Kammenhuber, *Or*NS 46 (1977) 137: Qatanum sei aB in Mari, Alalaḫ VII und Chagar Bazar, Qatna jedoch erst in jüngeren Texten (Alalaḫ IV, Amarna, heth.) belegt. Für mein Empfinden reicht der geographische Rahmen von k/k 4 nicht so weit nach Süden hinunter.

dessen genaue Lokalisierung zwar noch nicht feststeht, das jedenfalls aber südlich des Taurus und in Euphratnähe zu suchen ist[23].

d) Im Bereich von Sprache und Grammatik sind die beiden babylonischen - genauer älter-aB - Formen des Verbums *epēšum* „machen" *i-té-né-pé-šu i-pé-eš*$_{15}$ (Z. 9) von besonderer Auffälligkeit; aA würde man *e-ta-na-pu-šu e-pá-áš* erwarten. Nicht-aA sind ferner *tu-ša-ba-al* (für aA *tù-šé-ba-al*) Z. 18 und die vokalkontrahierten Formen *an-nu-tum* (Z. 15, aA *a-ni-ú-tum*) und *a-ni-ke-e* (Z. 20, aA wäre *annakam* oder von der Bedeutung her auch *annišam* zu erwarten); die Kontraktion von *i+a* zu *ê* gilt zudem als eine typische Erscheinung des Mari-Dialekts. Bemerkenswert ist schließlich noch der Abfall der Mimation z.B. in *pá-ar-ku-li* (Z. 10), *ḫa-ra-ni* (Z. 13, 17) oder *ší-bu-tí* (Z. 23), der in den Mari-Texten erst ganz allmählich einzusetzen beginnt und im aA vorzüglich bei Texten der Schicht Ib auftritt.

EINZELBEMERKUNGEN:

Z. 2) Am Ende der Zeile fehlt *-ma*: Bloßer Schreibfehler oder sprachliche Besonderheit?

Z. 3) Auffällig die Schreibung KÙ für *kaspum* „Silber", die sich aus dem Kontext und der komplementierten Schreibung KÙ^{pí} ergibt. In aA Texten steht KÙ.BI stets am Ende von Abrechnungen und bedeutet dort soviel wie „sein (d.h. der Ware) Wert in Silber".

Z. 5-14) Geht man davon aus, daß bei der Aushändigung des Silbers an Unapše ein Verpflichtungsschein ausgestellt wurde — hierfür könnte vielleicht *i-ṣé-ri-kà* Z. 4 mit dem für solche typischen Terminus *iṣṣēr* sprechen—, dann läßt sich Z. 4-14 am ehesten wohl als Zitat aus diesem verstehen, mit dem U. an die vor 25 Jahren getroffenen Abmachungen erinnert werden soll.

Z. 6) Oder ist *ú-ṣí* Prt. „(das Silber) ist (nicht aus der Stadt Kaniš hinausgegangen" etwa im Sinn von „ist nicht zu mir (dem Besitzer) zurückgekommen"? — Wenn *i-pé-eš*$_{15}$ das Prädikat des Nachsatzes ist, entspricht das *-ma* nach *ta-ša-pá-ar* nicht dem üblichen Sprachgebrauch in *šumma*-Sätzen.— Es ist nicht ausgeschlossen, daß *šapārum* hier nicht „schreiben", sondern „schicken" (Objekt: das Silber) bedeuten soll, doch wird „schicken" Z. 18 durch *šābulum* ausgedrückt.

Z. 8ff.) Wie Tunip als ON Subjekt zu *i-té-né-pé-šu* und $^{(?)}$ *i-pé-eš*$_{15}$ sein kann, ist mir unklar. Handelt das Land durch einen Vertreter? Ein Land Kuzzi ist mir unbekannt.

23 Vgl. *RlA* 6, S. 136f.

Z. 12f.) Da der Ausdruck „PN *ša* ON" in aA Texten und hier Z. 11 wie wohl auch Z. 14 die Herkunft einer Person aus einem Orte angibt, könnte man auch eine Übersetzung „Duḫušmati aus Ḫarran" versuchen. Meine Zurückhaltung dagegen hat die folgenden Gründe: In den aA Texten wird Ḫarran immer *Ḫa-ra-na(-a)* geschrieben (z.B. KTH 14, 18. 24; CCT 29a, 23; KKS 13b, 7), und zudem liegt Ḫarran im Vergleich zu den anderen ON des Textes recht weit im Osten und eigentlich außerhalb seines geographischen Horizonts. Schließlich aber ist, wenn ich Z. 15ff. recht verstehe, die Übergabe des Silbers offenbar in Ḫaššu (erfolgt und) bezeugt worden, Eḫliaddu kommt also häufiger dorthin, wenn er nicht gar dort zuhause ist. Warum sollte er dann dem Unapše die Namen der Zeugen jetzt „immer wieder" aus dem von Kaniš viel weiter entfernten Ḫarran in Erinnerung rufen?

Z. 17) Oder *i-na ḫa-ra-ni* hier eher „von unterwegs"?

Z. 20) Die von mir zunächst erwogene Verbindung *i-ba-ši-a-ni ke-e al-kam* scheitert vor allem daran, daß *kē* vor einem Imperativ wenig Sinn hat. Zudem wäre ein Akkus.-Suf. bei *bašû* nur schwer erklärbar. Ich verstehe *a-ni-ke-e* daher als mimationslose Entsprechung zu dem in Mari häufigen *annikêm* „hier", nach *CAD* auch „hither". Die gleiche Form ist mit leicht abweichender Graphie in einem Vokabular aus Ḫattuša bezeugt, das auch sonst die Kontraktion von *-ki'a* < *-kê* sowie Mimationsverlust aufweist[24].

Z. 21f.) Für das letzte Wort von Z. 21 habe ich ebenso wie für das erste von Z. 22 trotz mehrmaliger Kollation noch keine befriedigende Lösung finden können. In Z. 21 steht nach *ša-* über Rasur anscheinend *-ra-* oder *-lu-* und *-mì-* oder *-ši-*. Nach *a-lim* könnte man wie mehrfach in diesem Text einen ON erwarten, doch ließe sich auch an einen Infinitiv oder ein Verbal-Adjektiv wie *parāsim* oder *parrusim* denken. In Z. 22 würde *-ku-um* zu einem Dativ-Suffix der 2. m. Sg. passen, das sich im brieflichen Kontext am ehesten wohl einem Prädikat in der 1. Person verbinden könnte.

Fassen wir zusammen. Der hier vorgelegte Kültepe-Text stammt gewiß aus der Hand eines nordsyrischen Schreibertraditionen verbundenen Schreibers, ja er dürfte sogar innerhalb Nordsyriens selbst abgefaßt worden sein. Wir werden kaum fehlgehen, wenn wir ihn in die Zeit der Kültepe-Schicht Ib datieren, die auch den Aufstieg der Kuššara-Dynastie erlebte. Damit verliert das aA den Ruhm, die einzige Sprache[25] und Schrift zu sein, die im *kārum*-zeitlichen Anatolien bekannt war; über Nordsyrien vermitteltes Babylonisch tritt nun neu hinzu. Dies bedeutet aber noch nicht, daß schon Pitḫana oder Anitta dem Syrobabylonischen den Weg in die hethitische Schriftkultur gebahnt hätten. Ganz das Gegenteil scheint der Fall zu sein, denn alle bisher bekannten Kültepe-Urkunden, die offiziell im Namen *(iqqāti)* dieser beiden Fürsten ausgestellt sind,

---

24 *an-ni-ke-e* KBo 36,1 Vs. II 3′; cf. G. Wilhelm, *ZA* 79 (1989) 74 und Komm. 76.

25 Abgesehen von den einheimisch-anatolischen natürlich.

stehen ebenso wie alle anderen aA Texte aus dem einheimisch-anatolischen Milieu voll und ganz auf dem Boden der aA Tradition.

NACHTRÄGE:

Da die Erstpublikation dieses Beitrags in den Ulusararası 1. Hititoloji Kongresi Bildirileri (19-21 Temmuz 1990), Çorum o.J. (=1992), S. 53-63, türkische Übersetzung ebd., S. 43-52, nicht allgemein zugänglich sein dürfte, habe ich die Anregung G. Wilhelms auf einen Nachdruck an dieser Stelle dankbar aufgegriffen. Gegenüber dem Erstdruck sind Druckfehler beseitigt und einige kleinere stilistische Korrekturen vorgenommen worden. Der inhaltliche Tenor des Beitrags bleibt aber davon unberührt. Einige Zusatzbemerkungen:

(1) Die Publikation aller 121 Texte der Grabungssaison 1959 (Sigel kt k/-) durch mich, mit einer Darstellung des archäologischen Befundes durch T. Özgüç, ist in Kürze zu erwarten. Aus Schicht Ib stammen die Texte k/k 1-11, 13[26]-25 und 27-30. Unter den nur 27 Texten sind 4 Hüllentafeln, so daß sich vielleicht auf diese Weise die Zahl 31 bei N. Ozgüç (vgl. Anm. 10) ergibt. - kt k/t 115 stammt vom Stadthügel. Zum Schultext kt k/k 23 vgl. inzwischen M.J. Mellink u.a. (ed.), *Aspects of Art and Iconography: Anatolia and its Neighbors. Studies in Honor of Nimet Özgüç*, Ankara: Türk Tarih Kurumu Basımevi, 1993, 285f. [1.5.1995].

(2) Weitere „aA Syrien-Texte" vom Kültepe sind im Ankaraner Museum inzwischen von C. Michel entdeckt worden und werden von dieser zur Publikation vorbereitet. Ich hatte übrigens schon in den siebziger Jahren bei einem meiner Besuche am Kültepe T. Özgüç gegenüber die Erwartung geäußert, daß er eines Tages Häuser oder gar den Kārum der „vielen Eblaiter" (vgl. dazu ATHE 32, 17-18) finden werde. [1.5.1995].

(3) Inzwischen hat mir S. Çeçen eine Anzahl von unpublizierten Texten aus dem Ankaraner Museum zur Lektüre zur Verfügung gestellt. Darunter befindet sich auch der Text kt n/k 1952. Es handelt sich dabei um das Protokoll einer Gerichtsverhandlung zwischen zwei Assyrern, das große Teile von k/k 4 wörtlich zitiert. Eine Publikation des Textes n/k 1952 wird von S. Çeçen vorbereitet. [22.5.96].

ADDENDUM:

In a letter of 15 August 1995, Prof. Klaas R. Veenhof informs the editors that he has identified another letter addressed to Unapše during his work in the Ankara Museum in June 1995. The letter mentions a "scribe who understands and reads Hurrian." Prof. Veenhof hopes to publish an edition of this text in *SCCNH* 9.

---

[26] k/k 12 fehlt im Inventarbuch des Ankaraner Museums: k/k 11 trägt die Inv.-Nr. 162-11-64, k/k 13 folgt unmittelbar mit 162-12-64. Eine Erklärung war nicht zu erhalten.

Eine „Memorandum"-Tafel (*ṭuppi taḫsilti*)

MANFRED KREBERNIK

Ludwigs-Maximilians-Universität München

This previously unpublished "memorandum"-tablet (*ṭuppi taḫsilti*), from Nuzi or its environs, is unusual in that it contains neither the sealings nor the witnesses normally found in such a document. The tablet concerns barley and/or emmer received by various individuals.

Die hier zu veröffentlichende[1] Tafel[2] konnte ich 1989 bei einem Münchner Kunsthändler kopieren. Sie stammt nach Schrift und Inhalt aus Nuzi oder dessen Umgebung — etwa aus Kurruḫanni, wo sowohl ein Na-uṣur (vgl. Z. 2 unseres Textes) als auch ein Tae, Sohn des Ḫanaya, belegt sind (vgl. Z. 10 unseres Textes). Laut Unterschrift handelt es sich um eine „Memorandum"-Tafel (*ṭuppi taḫsilti*), die vielleicht in einem Rechtsstreit Verwendung fand[3]. Siegelabrollungen bzw. eine Liste der siegelnden Personen, womit solche „Memoranden" gewöhnlich versehen sind, fehlen in unserem Falle. Der Text notiert 18 Getreideposten (ŠE „Gerste" und ZÍZ.AN.NA „Emmer", gemessen in ANŠE [= 10 BÁN] und BÁN), die verschiedene Personen erhalten haben (*ilqe* „hat erhalten" ist in Z. 1 syllabisch geschrieben, in der Folge logographisch TI). Zu den einzelnen Personennamen tritt meist Filiation, Herkunfts- (Z. 4) oder Berufsangabe (Z. 13; 22). Fast alle Namen sind bereits in Nuzi-Texten bezeugt. Drei Trennlinien (nach Z. 7, 12 und 21) gliedern den Text in Gruppen von 5, 3, 7 und 3 Einträgen.

---

1 Für die Publikationsmöglichkeit und für bibliographische Hinweise danke ich G. Wilhelm sehr herzlich.

2 Die Tafel ist 7 cm hoch und 8 cm breit.; die größte Dicke beträgt 2, 7 cm.

3 Zur Gattung vgl. M.P. Maidman, *SEANFA* 134. Folgende Texte dieser Art sind bisher bekannt: HSS V 44, 46, 51; HSS IX 71, 94; HSS XIII 404; HSS XIV 644; JEN 138, 191, 195, 198, 388, 390; *RA* 23, S. 133 + 158, Nr. 61; *RATK* 11; SMN 1666; TCL IX, 33.

Studies on the Civilization and Culture of Nuzi and the Hurrians - 8

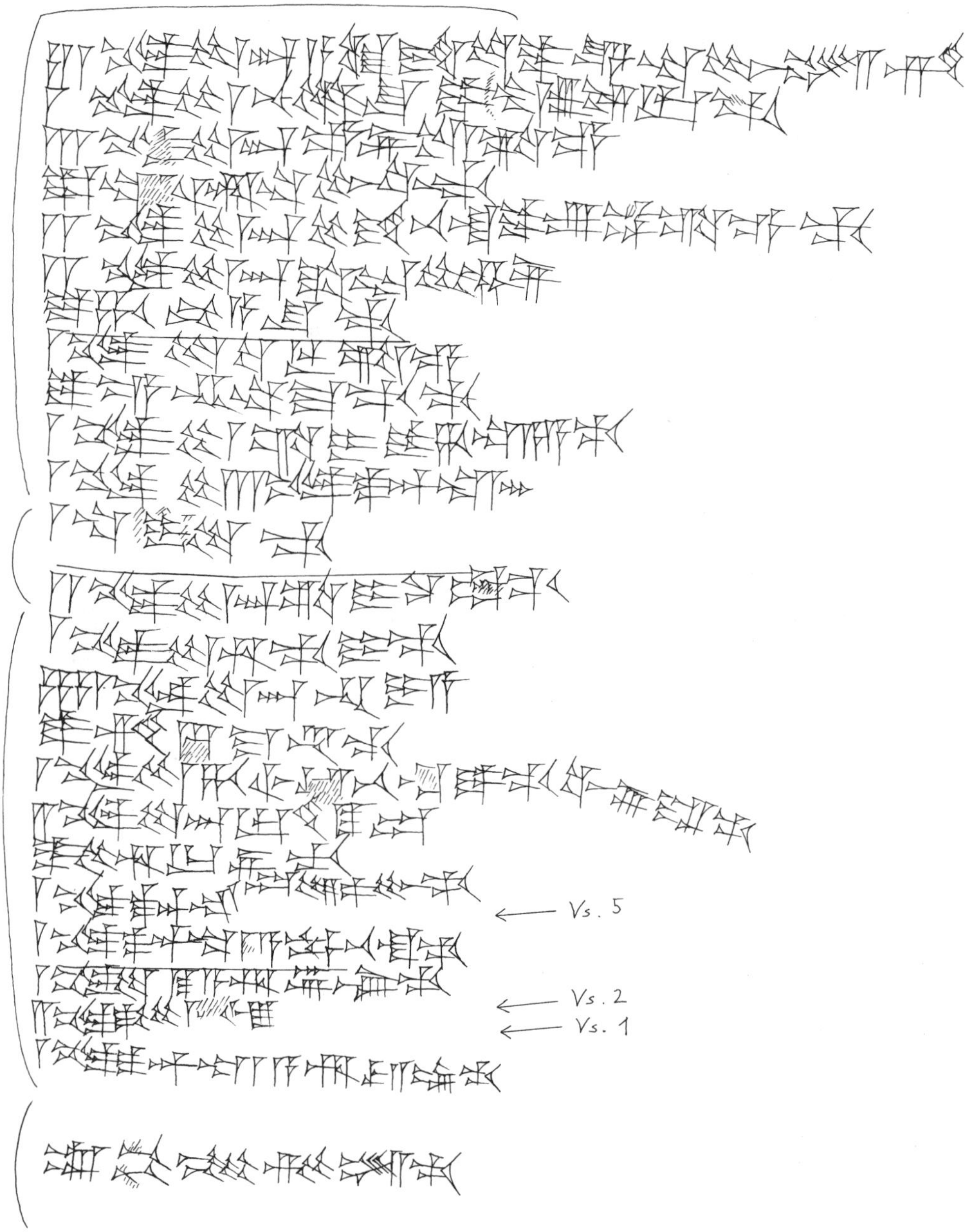
Vs. 5
Vs. 2
Vs. 1

Vs. 1 4 ANŠE ŠE^{MEŠ} ^{I}*A-ki-it-te* DUMU *Pur-na-pu il-qé*
2 1 ANŠE ŠE ^{I}*Be-li-šu* DUMU *Na-ú-ṣú-ur* TI
3 3 AN[Š]E ŠE^{MEŠ} ^{I}*E-ni-iš-ta-e*
4 *ša* UR[U] *Ar-na-bu-we* TI
5 2 ANŠE ŠE^{MEŠ} ^{I}*Še-qar-til-la* DUMU *Ú-nap-ta-e* TI
6 2 ANŠE ŠE^{MEŠ} ^{I}*Ša-du-še-en-ni*
7 DUMU *Ḫa-bi-a-šu* TI

---

8 1 ANŠE ŠE ^{I}*Ut-ḫáp-ta-e*
9 DUMU *E-en-na-ma-ti* TI
10 1 ANŠE ŠE ^{I}*Ta-i* DUMU *Ḫa-na-a-a* TI
11 1 ANŠE ŠE 3 ANŠE ZÍZ.AN.NA^{MEŠ}
Rd. 12 ^{I}*Na-i-te* TI

---

13 2 ANŠE ŠE^{MEŠ} ^{I}*Ta-i-qa* SIMUG TI
Rs. 14 1 ANŠE ŠE ^{I}*Ḫu-ti-i* TI
15 7 ANŠE ŠE^{MEŠ} ^{I}EN-*ia*
16 DUMU *Ge-˹lu˺-ma-tal* TI
17 1 ANŠE ŠE ^{I}*Ḫa-ši-˹ip˺-til-˹la˺* DUMU *Ti-wi-ir-ra* TI
18 2 ANŠE ŠE^{MEŠ} ^{I}*Ur-ḫi-ku-du*
19 DUMU *Še-ḫu-ur-ni* TI
20 1 ANŠE ZÍZ.AN.NA ^{I}*Du-li-pa-pu* TI
21 1 ANŠE ZÍZ.AN.NA ^{I}*A-ki-ip-til-la* TI

---

22 1 ANŠE ŠE ^{I}*Ku-a-ri* ^{LÚ}ZADIM TI
23 2 ANŠE 5 (BÁN) ŠE^{MEŠ} *ù*
24 1 ANŠE ZÍZ.AN.NA ^{I}*A-ri-ip*-LUGAL TI
Rd. 25 *ṭup-pí taḫ-sí-il-ti*

Vs. 1 4 ANŠE Gerste hat Akitte, der Sohn des Purn-apu, erhalten.
2 1 ANŠE Gerste hat Bēlišu, der Sohn des Na-uṣur, erhalten.
3f. 3 ANŠE Gerste hat Eniš-tae aus Arnabu erhalten.
5 2 ANŠE Gerste hat Šekar-tilla, der Sohn des Unap-tae, erhalten.
6f. 2 ANŠE Gerste hat Šatu-šenni, der Sohn des Ḫabi-ašu, erhalten.

8f. 1 ANŠE Gerste hat Utap-tae, der Sohn des Enna-mati, erhalten.
10 1 ANŠE Gerste hat Tai, der Sohn des Ḫanaja, erhalten.
11 1 ANŠE Gerste (und) 3 ANŠE Emmer hat Nai-te erhalten.

---

13 2 ANŠE Gerste hat Taika, der Schmied, erhalten.
Rs. 14 1 ANŠE Gerste hat Ḫuti erhalten.
15f. 7 ANŠE Gerste hat Bēlija, der Sohn des Kelum-atal, erhalten.

17 1 ANŠE Gerste hat Ḫašip-tilla, der Sohn des Tiwirra, erhalten.
18 2 ANŠE Gerste hat Urḫi-kutu, der Sohn des Šeḫurni, erhalten.
20 1 ANŠE Emmer hat Tulip-apu erhalten.
21 1 ANŠE Emmer hat Akip-tilla erhalten.

---

22 1 ANŠE Gerste hat Kuari, der Bogenmacher, erhalten.
23f. 2 ANŠE 5 (BÁN) Gerste und 1 ANŠE Emmer hat Arip-šarri erhalten.
Rd. 25 „Memorandum"-Tafel.

KOMMENTAR

Z. 1. Akitta/e, Akitti: *NPN* 17. Purn-apu: *NPN* 119. *A-ki-it-te* DUMU *Pur-na-pu* ist auch in JEN 365: 20 belegt.

Z. 2. Cf. Bêlšu: *NPN* 113. Na-uṣur: HSS 19, 76: 23; 118:32. Ein *Na-ú-ṣú-ur* kommt auch in einem Text aus Kurruḫanni vor: IM 70764: 15 (Fadhil, *SCCNH* 1, 364f.).

Z. 3. Eniš-tae: *NPN* 46f. URU *Ar-na-bu*: MAH 15867: 2 (E.R. Lacheman, *Genava* NS 15 [1967] Nr. 6).

Z. 5. Šekar-tilla: *NPN* 128. Unap-tae: *NPN* 164f.

Z. 6f. Šatu-šenni: *NPN* 127. Ḫabi-ašu: *NPN* 55.

Z. 8f. Utḫap-tae: *NPN* 168f. *Ut-ḫap-ta-e* DUMU *En-na-ma-ti* ist auch in JEN 636: 28, 38 belegt.

Z. 10. Tae: *NPN* 141; Tai: *NPN* 142. Ḫanaja: *NPN* 52f. *Ta-e* DUMU *Ḫa-na-a-a* ist auch in Kurruḫanni belegt: IM 70878: 42 (Fadhil, *RATK* Nr. 8).

Z. 11f. Cf. Nai-teja: *NPN* 102.

Z. 13. Taika: *NPN* 144.

Z. 14. Ḫute, Ḫuti: *NPN* 64.

Z. 15f. Bēlija: *NPN* 113. Kelum-atal: *NPN* 83.

Z. 17f. Ḫašip-tilla: *NPN* 58f. Tiwirra: *NPN* 156.

Z. 18f. Urḫi-kutu ist sonst, soweit ich sehe, nicht belegt. Šeḫurni: *NPN* 128.

Z. 20. Tulip-apu: *NPN* 157.

Z. 21. Akip-tilla: *NPN* 16.

Z. 22. Kuari: *NPN* 89.

Z. 23f. Arip-šarri: *NPN* 29.

Bemerkungen zu Nuzi-Texten aus dem P.A. Hearst Museum/Berkeley

GERFRID G.W. MÜLLER

Westfälische Wilhelms-Universität Münster

The group of eight Nuzi tablets from Berkeley recently published and discussed by J.W. Carnahan, K.G. Hillard, and A.D. Kilmer (*JCS* 46 [1994] 105-122) contains a number of readings which are reinterpreted here. Collations by the author from the published photos and of the tablets by Prof. Anne D. Kilmer and Mr. J.W. Carnahan provide additional suggestions for improvement. Appended are revised transliterations which incorporate the new readings.

Im Jahre 1987 identifizierte E. Leichty im P.A. Hearst Museum of Anthropology an der Universität von Kalifornien zu Berkeley sieben Nuzi-Tafeln, die kürzlich von J.W. Carnahan, K.G. Hillard und A.D. Kilmer bearbeitet und veröffentlicht wurden[1]. Neben Autographie, Umschrift und Übersetzung wurden ein knapper Kommentar sowie Photos der Siegelabrollungen auf den Tafeln vorgelegt.

Darüberhinaus präsentierten die Autoren eine neue Bearbeitung eines weiteren Textes aus diesem Museum, der bereits mehrfach behandelt wurde[2]. Auch mit dieser Neubearbeitung ist noch nicht das letzte Wort darüber gesprochen. Für das Patronym des Nimki-tilla (Z. 1) wird die Lesung *Šup-*⸢*ri*⸣-*ia* geboten. Das IA ist sicher, das RI beruht auf Kollation der Neubearbeiter und das RU wurde bereits von Lutz vorgeschlagen (als *Ru-* gelesen). Hurritische Namen, die auf /r/ anlauten, gibt es nicht, die Lesung *šup* für RU ist im Anlaut bisher auch nicht belegt und damit unwahrscheinlich[3]. Mit Sicherheit handelt es sich nach dem Photo bei Lutz um ein am Tafelrand etwas mißglücktes *Šúk-*, wobei der erste waagerechte Keil etwas zu schräg geraten ist und der obere schräge durch die später gesetzten drei senkrechten zerdrückt wurde. Der

---

1 *JCS* 46 (1994) 105-122. I wish to thank Prof. Kilmer and Mr. J.W. Carnahan for undertaking the collations and Prof. Owen for facilitating the contacts with Prof. Kilmer.

2 H.W.F. Lutz, "A Legal Document from Nuzi", in: UCP 9/11 (1931) 405-417, sowie E. Chiera, "A Legal Document from Nuzi", in: *AJSL* 47 (1931) 281-286. Ferner P. Koschaker, *OLZ* 35, 405.

3 M.W. ist sie im Onomastikon auf *Te-šup* beschränkt.

Studies on the Civilization and Culture of Nuzi and the Hurrians - 8

Name des Vaters ist also *Šúk-ri-ia.* In Z. 10 steht nach demselben Photo nicht 1 BÁN, sondern lediglich DIŠ. Die Richter sind mit Ausnahme von Šennatil S. Ḫuja sonst nur als Zeugen belegt. Šennatil sitzt jeweils in einem anderen Richterkollegium[4]. Das Siegel, von dem nur ein kleiner Ausschnitt abgerollt wurde, ist identisch mit dem in JEN 370 gebrauchten[5]. Tarmi-tilla S. *Tu-ra-sa-ri-ia*[6] erscheint auch in HSS 15,78:5 als *Du-ra-sa-ri-ia*[7].

In der Bearbeitung des Textes UCLMA 9-3032[8] stößt man auf den ungewöhnlichen Personennamen *Teššа-ḫašuar. Dieser soll laut Bearbeitung ein Sohn des Šimika-aRI gewesen sein (Z.1-2) und einen Esel besessen haben, der laut Kommentar zum Preis einer Kuh verkauft wurde, wobei sich — interessanterweise — die Pönalklausel auf die Kuh, und nicht auf das angeblich gekaufte Objekt, den Esel bezieht.

Laut Kommentar zu Z. 1 ist der Name *Tešša-ḫašuar weder in *NPN* noch in *AAN* zu finden. In Zeile 6 des Textes wird ein Ḫašuar als Empfänger der Kuh genannt. Da sowohl *NPN* als auch *AAN* einen Ḫašuar, Sohn d. Šimika-atal aufführen, schließen die Bearbeiter, daß Ḫašuar die Kurzform für *Tešša-ḫašuar sei. Ein Beispiel für den Ausfall des ersten Namenselementes ist mir nicht erinnerlich, der Abfall bzw. die Verkürzung des zweiten Namenselementes ist dagegen im arrapäischen Onomastikon sehr häufig[9]. Ḫašuar, Sohn d. Šimika-atal ist etwa zwei Dutzend male schlicht als Ḫašuar belegt, der Name Ḫašuar erscheint insgesamt an die hundert male. Dabei ist dieser Name nie mit einem anderen Element verbunden, wie schon *NPN* zeigt[10], und wurde bereits von I.J. Gelb[11] und Oppenheim[12] mit dem kassitischen *ḫašmar* in Verbindung gebracht, das mit akk. *kassūsu*, „Falke", geglichen ist[13]. Daß nun ausgerechnet an dieser Stelle eine Langform des Namens vorliegen soll, ist auszuschließen. Die erste Zeile ist vielmehr 1 ANŠE.ŠE.MEŠ *ša Ḫa-šu-ar* zu lesen.

Das Archiv des Ḫašuar S. Šimika-atal, das von A. Fadhil[14] ausführlich behandelt wurde, lagerte in Nuzi in Raum A 14, worin in der Hauptsache Urkunden des Prinzen Šilwa-teššup gefunden wurden. Es enthält überwiegend

---

4 JEN 370, 663, EN 9/1 397, 423.

5 Porada Nr. 999.

6 In *NPN* 149 u. 159 zu korrigieren.

7 Eindeutig kopiert; gegen *AAN* 152 Du-ra-ar(?)-ri-ia (s.v. Turarija).

8 S. 108ff.

9 Gelegentlich auch bei ein und derselben Person, z.B. Kirzam-pula (mit dem Hypochoristikon Kirzija), Punni-ḫarpa (Punnija) u.a.

10 Siehe das Verzeichnis der nicht-akkadischen Namenselemente in *NPN*, S. 198ff., insbesondere S. 215.

11 Inscriptions from Alishar and vicinity. OIP 27, 1935, S.20.

12 *WZKM* 44 (1937) 184.

13 Vgl. K. Balkan, *Kassitenstudien*. 1. Die Sprache der Kassiten (AOS 37, 1954), S. 4 u.151.

14 *Studien zur Topographie und Prosopographie der Provinzstädte des Königreichs Arrapḫe* (BaF 6, 1983), S. 113-21.

Urkunden über Darlehensgeschäfte. In diesen finden wir auch die beiden Verkäufer der Kuh wieder: In EN 9/1 367 (SMN 1166) leihen *Zi-iq-qa-mi* S. Ḫutija und *Ku-uš-ši-ta-e* S. Enna-pali von Ḫašuar S. Šimika-atal 13 ANŠE Gerste, zurückzuzahlen zur Erntezeit in der *dimtu* Arik-kani. Beide Schuldner siegeln auch (Z.16/17), und an beiden Stellen kann kein Zweifel an der Lesung *-ta-e* anstelle des von den Bearbeitern vorgeschlagenen, bisher in dieser Position im Namen auch nicht belegten *-ta-mar* bestehen. Ob Zikkami in beiden Urkunden dasselbe Siegel verwendet[15], läßt sich auf dem Photo des neuen Textes nicht mit Sicherheit ausmachen.

Auffällig ist auch, daß laut Bearbeitung in UCLMA 9-3023 die Schuldner überhaupt nicht siegeln, hingegen ein Zeuge mit dem Namen *Zi-qa-mi* DUMU *Šar/Tu-ri-ši-te-e* (Z. 13a-b). Der Name Zikkami ist bisher nur aus den genannten zwei Urkunden bekannt, das seltsame Patronym überhaupt nicht. Das Photo auf S. 119 zeigt statt des DUMU ein klares NA4. Das abgebildete, leider sehr schwach abgerollte Siegel ist demnach das des Zikkami S. Ḫutija. Da die Zeugen in den folgenden Zeilen — im Gegensatz zu dem Schuldner Zikkami — alle mit Patronym genannt sind, kann in Z. 13b der Name des zweiten Schuldners Kušši-tae erwartet werden, ebenfalls ohne Patronym, dessen Siegelabrollung, die offenbar noch schlechter auf der Tafel zu erkennen war, nicht abgebildet ist. Das letzte auf dem Photo erkennbare Zeichen nach NA4 ist KU. Dem UŠ fehlt in der Kopie ein waagerechter Keil oben, das ŠI ist klar kopiert und das TA auf der Tafelkante wohl schon im Original so deformiert, daß es nicht mehr gelesen, sondern nur rekonstruiert werden kann. Das E am Ende ist hier im Gegensatz zu Z. 4 und 9 völlig korrekt kopiert.

Als Zeugen erscheinen in EN 9/1 367 u.a. auch die Gebrüder Zilik-kuja und Ḫašija, Söhne des *Ḫa-ri-*⌜*x*⌝-[*x*]. Das Patronym läßt sich nun durch UCLMA 9-3023:15-16 zu *Ḫa-ri-a-ši* ergänzen. Dieser Name ist bisher nicht belegt.

Der Schreibers Teḫija schrieb beide Texte. Das von ihm hier (Photo S. 119 oben links) verwendete Siegel ist nicht identisch mit Stein, *AdŠ* 9, Nr. 764. Ein Schreiber dieses Namens begegnet ansonsten nur in Kurruḫanni[16].

Nach EN 9/1 367:12 läßt sich auch der letzte Zeuge zu [*Ḫa-iš*]*-te* DUMU *Tar-mi-til-la* ergänzen.

Die Urkunde berichtet nicht vom Verkauf eines Esels zum Preis einer Kuh, sondern vom Empfang eines ANŠE Gerste als Kaufpreis für eine Kuh, die dem Ḫašuar zu übergeben ist. Der Kaufpreis erscheint außerordentlich gering. Zu erwarten wäre nach den Berechnungen von Cross[17] etwa das Sechsfache, oder das vierfache wie im Falle eines vierjährigen Rindes (HSS 16,433).

---

15 S. D. Stein, *The Seal impressions* (Das Archiv des Šilwa-teššup 9 [=*AdŠ* 9]), Siegel Nr. 765 auf Text *AdŠ* Nr. 707 (EN 9/1 367).

16 Vgl. G.G.W. Müller, *Studien zur Siedlungsgeographie und Bevölkerung des mittleren Osttigrisgebietes* (HSAO 7, 1994), S. 65, 67f.

17 *Movable Property in the Nuzi Documents* (AOS 10, 1937). Danach ist ein ANŠE Gerste mit 1,6 Schekel Silber, ein Rind etwa mit 10 Schekel zu bewerten.

UCLMA 9-3028 (S. 113f.) gehört zum Archiv des Šilwa-teššup, wie ein Vergleich der Abfolge in der Auflistung von Männern Z. 13-17 (Teḫija, Ḫutip-tilla, Zilip-šenni, *At-ti-lim-mu* [sic!], Namḫi-tilla) mit *AdŠ* 26 (HSS 13,390) Z. 10-13 (Teḫija, Ḫutip-tilla, Zilip-šenni, Namḫi-tilla) und Z. 47 (ebenfalls in der seltenen Schreibung *At-ti-lim-mu*) zeigt. Auch Zilip-erwe erscheint in beiden Texten. In Anbetracht der beträchtlichen Menge von 10 ANŠE Gerste dürfte demnach in Z. 1 ^{f}*Šu-wa-a*[*r-ḫé-bat/ba*] zu ergänzen sein, die Schwester des Šilwa-teššup. Wegen Urḫa-tarmi dürfte UCLMA 9-3024 (S. 110f.) zu demselben Archivkontext gehören, obwohl das hier von ihm gebrauchte Siegel nicht mit Stein, *AdŠ* 9, Nr. 450 identisch ist[18].

UCLMA 9-3027 (S. 111f.) stammt aus dem Palastarchiv, denn Šumpirinni, einer der beiden, die in diesem Text für den Transport von Hausgerätschaften aus Purulliwe verantwortlich sind, erhält in HSS 13,174 von Erwi-šarri, dem *šakin bīti* des Palastes in Nuzi, zusammen mit anderen ähnliche Utensilien aus Purulliwe, die sich in Nuzi befinden. Aus demselben Kontext kommt wohl auch UCLMA 9-3029. Für Utḫaja S. Eḫli-teššup[19] sei noch auf WHM 152.335[20] hingewiesen.

Supplementum:

Auf Wunsch der Herausgeber werden im folgenden revidierte Umschriften aller Nuzi-Texte aus Berkeley gegeben. Frau Prof. A. Kilmer sei für ihre Bereitschaft, die Texte zu kollationieren, herzlich gedankt.

UCLMA 9-2870

Vs. 1 ^{m}*Ni-im-ki-til-la* DUMU *Šúk*$^{!}$-[*ri*]-*ia*
it-ti ^{m}*Zi-li-ḫa-ma-an-na*
DUMU *Pa-ik-ku i-na di-ni*
a-na pa-ni DI.KU$_5$.MEŠ *i-te-lu-ma*
um-ma ^{m}*Ni-im-ki-til-la-ma*
LÚ *ša-nu-ma a-ḫa-ti-ia a-na aš-šu-ti*
il-te-qè ù ^{m}*Zi-li-ḫa-ma-an-na*
a-na ma-ḫi-iṣ pu-ti a-na KÙ.BABBAR-*šu*
ša ⸢*a*⸣-*ḫa-ti-ia it-ta-zi-iz-ma*
⸢2 ANŠE⸣ <<1>> ŠE.MEŠ *ki-ma* ⸢KÙ.BABBAR-*šu*⸣
^{m}*Zi-*⸢*li*⸣-*ḫa-ma-an-na a-na*
na-dá-ni iq-ta-bi
ṭup-pa i[*t-t*]*i-ia il-ta-ṭar*

18 Vgl. Stein, a.a.O. S. 383f.

19 HSS 13,4, HSS 16,433, 435.

20 *SCCNH* 1 (1981), S. 440f.

ù ^{m}*Pa-i[k]-ku a-bi-šu ša*
^{m}*Zi-li-ḫ[a]-ma-an-na*
a-na ši-bu-ti i-na ṭup-pí
ša-ṭì-ir ^{m}*Zi-li-ḫa-ma-an-na*
it-ta-al-kam-ma a-na ia-ši
iq-ta-bi bi-la-am-ma-mi
ANŠE-*ka*$_4$ *ù* ŠE.MEŠ-*ka*$_4$
lu-ú ba-bi-il-mi
ù lu-ú ad-dì-in-mi
1 ANŠE.EME$_5$-*ia* ^{m}*Zi-*⸢*li*⸣*-ḫa-ma-an-na*$^{!}$
u.Rd. *il-te-qè* 1 ANŠE ŠE.[MEŠ]
^{m}*Zi-li-ḫa-ma-an-na*
id-dì-na 1 ANŠE ŠE.⸢MEŠ⸣
Rs. *ù* ANŠE-*ia ik-ta-la*
DI.KU$_5$.MEŠ ^{m}*Zi-li-ḫa-ma-an*$^{!}$*<-na>*
iš-ta-lu-uš
um-ma ^{m}*Zi-li-ḫa-ma-an-na-ma*
a-an-ni-mi it-ti ^{m}*Ni-im-ki-til-la*
ad-bu-bu-mi ANŠE-*šu el-te-qè*
i-na KUR *Nu-ul-lu-ma-a-a-i*
ú-bi-il iš-tu KUR *Nu-ul-lu-ma-i*
iš-tu ŠU-*ia iṣ-ṣa-ab-tu*
DI.KU$_5$.MEŠ *a-na* ^{m}*Ni-im-ki-til-la*
⸢*iq*⸣*-ta-bu-ú*(Rasur)[1] ANŠE-*ka*$_4$
i-na KUR *Nu-ul-lu-ma-a-a-i*
a-na a-bá-li ta-aq-bu-ú-mi
um-ma ^{m}*Ni-im-ki-til-la-ma*
ANŠE *i-na* KUR *Nu-ul-lu-ma-a-a-i*
a-na a-bá-li la aq-bi-šu$^{!}$*-ma* ANŠE-*šu*
ša ^{m}*Zi-li-ḫa-ma-an-na*
it-ta-ra-du$_4^{!}$(AZ)[2] *ina di-ni*
^{m}*Ni-im-ki-til-la*
il-te-⸢*e*⸣*-ma* DI.KU$_5$.MEŠ
a-na 1 ANŠE ŠE
a-na 1 ANŠE *ki-ma* ⸢ANŠE⸣-*šu*
ma-aš-lu ^{m}*Zi-li-ḫa-ma-an<-na>*[3]
a-na ^{m}*Ni-im-ki-til-la*
it-ta-dú-uš um-ma
^{m}*Ni-im-ki-til-la-ma*
ú-ri-ḫul šá a-na 1 ANŠE
la ú-bá-a-mi

o.Rd. NA$_4$ ^{m}*Te-ḫi-ia* NA$_4$ ^{m}*Še-ka$_4$-*[*rù*]
DUMU *Te-eš-šu-ia* DUMU *Eḫ-li-*[*ia*]
l.Rd. NA$_4$ ^{m}*Tar-mi-til-la* NA$_4$ ^{m}*Še-en-na-til*[4]
ŠU ^{md}*Iškur-an-til*
DUMU *Tu-ra-sa-ri-ia* DUMU *Ḫu-ia*

Notae:

(1) Was auf dem Photo aussieht wie ein zu kurzes MA, ist nach Kollation eine Rasur.

(2) „Es (war) sein Esel, mit dem PN normalerweise (ins Lullubärland) hinabging". Auf dem Photo sieht das Zeichen wie ein Zwitter aus AS und TUM aus. Lutz, der zugegebenermaßen nicht sehr verläßlich ist, hat die beiden kleinen Senkrechten unten als Kratzer interpretiert und TUM kopiert. Da hier doch wohl ein Relativsatz mit Ziliḫ-ḫamanna als Subjekt und keine Auflösung der status-constructus-Annexion (vgl. Wilhelm, AOAT 9, 29f.) vorliegt, ist diese Deutung vorzuziehen.

(3) Das Fehlen des *-na* wurde durch Kollation bestätigt.

(4) S.u. Nuzi Notes 35.

UCLMA 9-3020

Vs. 12 *ḫa-ar-*<*wa*>*-ra-*⸢*ḫu*$^{!}$ IN⸣[1].NU.MEŠ
a-na ^{m}*Ta-ak-ku*

---

5 KIMIN-*ma* IN.NU.MEŠ
a-na ^{m}*Ku-uz-za-ri-ia*

---

1 KIMIN-*ma* IN.NU.[ME]Š
a-na ^{m}*Ḫa-i-iš-te-*⸢*ia*⸣
5 KIMIN-*ma* IN.NU
[*a-na* ^{m}*E*]*n-na-ma-*[*t*]*i*
Rs. IN.NU.MEŠ
pu-ḫu-ga$_5$-ru
ina URU *Nu-zi*
(Siegelabrollung)
NA$_4$ ^{m}*Pu-ur-na-pu*[2]

Notae:

(1) Das Zeichen IN ist auf dem Photo S. 117 entgegen der Kopie klar zu erkennen.

(2) Kollationiert (nach Vorschlag D. Stein).

UCLMA 9-3022

Vs. 1 TÚG *lu-bu-uš-tu*$_4$ *ša ši-la-an-ni*
1 TÚG DÁRA.MEŠ (= *nībittu/nēbettu*[1]) *lu-bu-uš-tu*$_4$ *ša a-aš-ši-a-an-ni*
1 TÚG.MEŠ *nu-uḫ-pu-ru ša su-un* ⸢ŠÌK⸣.ZA.GÌN.NA
1 TÚG *ša* MUNUS.MEŠ *ša a-aš-ši-a-an-ni*
2 GÚ.È *tu-ut-tu-bu-ú*
14 TÚG.MEŠ *ši-na-ḫi-lu-ú*
[6!+]1 GÚ.È.MEŠ 2-*ḫi-lu*

⸢6⸣ ^{ha}*ḫar*!*-we*[2] *ša* ⸢3? *x x* (*x*)-*ia*.MEŠ
3 *šu-šu-up-pu-*⸢*ú*!⸣
ŠU.NÌGIN 19 TÚG 2-[*ḫi-lu*]
u.Rd. 9 GÚ.È.MEŠ[3]
Rs. *iš-ka-ru ša* URU! *Kum-ri*![4]
(2 Siegelabrollungen)

Notae:

(1) H. Schneider-Ludorff machte mich darauf aufmerksam, daß DÁRA in Nuzi sonst nicht belegt ist. Daher ist nach der Parallele HSS 14,6:2 vielleicht besser SIG!.MEŠ zu lesen.

(2) Vgl. den Paralleltext HSS 14, 6 z. 7 (*ḫa-ar-we*) und 8 (*šu-šu-up-pu-ú*).

(3) Dahinter folgt nichts mehr (vgl. HSS 14,6:11). Bei *ḫarwe* handelt es sich ebenso wie bei *šušuppu* „(Lenden) tuch" nicht um ein Gewand, da beide sowohl hier als auch in HSS 14,6 nicht in der Summierung enthalten sind, sondern eher um ein Accessoir.

(4) Parallel in HSS 14,6:12: *iš-kà-ru ša* URU *A-šu-ḫi-iš*. Vgl. hierzu noch HSS 14,7, worin die *iškaru*-Abgaben verschiedener Orte an Textilien, die nach Nuzi gebracht wurden, aufgelistet und summiert werden. Diese Tafel trägt das Siegel des Königs Itḫija S. Kibi-teššup.

UCLMA 9-3023

Vs. 1 ANŠE ŠE.MEŠ *ša Ḫa-šu-ar*
DUMU *Ši-mi*!*-ka*$_4$*-tal a-na ši-mi*
a-na 1 GU$_4$.ÁB ^{m}*Zi-ka*$_4$*-mi* DUMU [*Ḫu-ti*]-*ia*
ù Ku-uš-ši-ta-e

DUMU *En-na-pa-li i[l]-qú-ú*
1 GU$_4$.ÁB *a-na [Ḫa]-šu-ar*
SUM-*din-nu [šum]-ma* GU$_4$
pí-ir-qa ir-ta-ši
^{m}*Zi-ka*$_4$*-mi ù* ^{m}*Ku-uš-ši-ta-e*
u.Rd. *ú-za-ak-ku-ma ù*
⌜*i*⌝*-na-an-din ma-an-nu* KI.BAL-*kat*
[1+]1 GU$_4$.MEŠ *na-ás-qú* DIRI-*la*
Rs. NA$_4$ ^{m}*Zi-ka*$_4$*-mi*
NA$_4$ ^{m}*Ku-uš-ši-ta*$^{!}$*-e*
NA$_4$ ^{m}*Ša-ar-te-ia* DUMU *Ši-mi-ka*$_4$*-tal*
[N]A$_4$ ^{m}*Zi-li-ku-ia* DUMU *Ḫa-ri-a-ši*
NA$_4$ ^{m}*Ḫa-ši-ia* DUMU *Ḫa-ri-a-ši*
NA$_4$ ^{m}*Te-ḫi-ia* DUB.SAR
[NA$_4$] ⌜^{m}*Ḫa-iš*⌝*-te*$^{!}$ [DU]MU *Tar-mi-til-la*

Nota:

K. Deller hat sich mittlerweile in *NABU* 1995/76 zu UCLMA 9-3023 geäußert und die meisten Fehllesungen korrigiert.

UCLMA 9-3024

Vs. 2 *li-im*
GI.KAK.SI.SI.MEŠ[1]
a-šar ^{m}*Ti-ša-am-mu-uš-ni*
il-te-qè
a-na URU *Til-pá-aš-te*
Rs. ⌜*uš*⌝*-te-ri-bu*
(Siegelabrollung)
NA$_4$ *Ur-ḫa-tar-mi*

Nota:

(1) Wohl für KAK.SI.SÁ = *šukūdu/šiltaḫḫu*, da sich in Boğhazköy die Form *ka*$_4$*-ak-sí-sí* für *šukūdu*, „Sirius", findet (*AHw* 1265b s.v. *šukūdu* 2b).

UCLMA 9-3027

Vs. 1 *du-ú-dì ša* URUDU
5 *ta-ku-la-at-ḫu ša* ZABAR
2 *sà-aḫ-ḫa-ru ša* ZABAR *ša* ŠU.MEŠ
2 *ka-ap-pá-ar-nu ša* A.MEŠ
ša ZABAR
6 *ḫa-ar-gal-lu ša* GIŠ.IG *ša* ZABAR

5 *sí-ik-ka*$_4$*-tù ša* GIŠ.IG.MEŠ
1 *nam-za-qí ša* ZABAR
1 MUŠEN *ša* ZABAR
u.Rd. 1 *šu-ku-e ša* URUDU
ša GIŠ.IG.MEŠ
Rs. ⸢2⸣ KUŠ.MEŠ *ša* GÌR.MEŠ
an-nu-tu$_4$ *ú-nu-tù*
ša URU *Pu-ru-ul-li-we*
^{m}*Šu-um-pí-ri-in-ni*
ù ^{m}*A-ri-iḫ-ḫa-ma-an-na*
ša URU *Nu-zi*
ú-bi-la
(Siegelabrollung)
NA$_4$ ^{m}*A-ri-iḫ-ḫa-ma-an-na*
l.Rd. (Siegelabrollung)
NA$_4$ ^{m}*Šu-um-pí-ri-in-ni*

UCLMA 9-3028

Vs. 10 ANŠE ŠE.MEŠ *š*[*u-ku-na-a*][1]
a-na ^{f}*Šu-wa-a*[*r-ḫé-pa-a*][1]
na-din

---

1 ANŠE 3 BÁN 6 SÌLA *a-*⸢*na*⸣ 37 ⸢x⸣[2]
a-na ANŠE.KUR.RA *pa-ri-it-ta-*⸢*ni*⸣[3]
^{m}*Zi-li-pè-er-we il-qè*

---

1 ⸢ANŠE 2 BÁN⸣ ŠE *a-na* ANŠE.KUR.RA.MEŠ
a-na ^{m}*Tù-ra-ri-ia* ⸢*na-din*⸣
⸢3 BÁN⸣ ŠE.MEŠ *a-na*$^{!?}$(LA)(-) *am-ba-ra*.MEŠ[4]
a-na ITU-*ḫi Ar-*⸢*ka*$_4$⸣*-bi-in-ni*
a-na ŠU ^{m}*Ba-a-*ḪUŠ-⸢*šu*$^{?}$⸣*-un*[5]
u.Rd. *na-din*

Rs. ^{m}*Te-ḫi-ia*
^{m}*Ḫu-ti-ip-til-la*
^{m}*Zi-li-ip-še-ni*
^{m}*At-ti-lim-mu*
^{m}*Nam-ḫi-til-la-a*
3 BÁN ŠE <*a-na*> ^{m}*Na-ḫi-iš-šal-mu*
2 BÁN ŠE *a-na* ⸢*Túl*⸣-[
u.Rd. 3 BÁN ŠE *a-na* ^{m}⸢*Ḫu*⸣-[

Notae:

(1) Ergänzung nach *AdŠ* 141 (HSS 13,301): 20-21.

(2) Die auf der Kopie wiedergegebenen Zeichenspuren sehen wie KUR aus. Da sie sich auf dem Rand der Tafel befinden, darf man sie aber wohl großzügig interpretieren. Man könnte an ⸢U$_4$.MEŠ⸣ denken, was aber der gängigen Praxis, monatsweise abzurechnen widerspräche. Sollte hier die Zahl der Tiere gemeint sein, hat sich der Schreiber vertan und das ⸢x⸣ am Ende der Zeile wäre nur als Kratzer anzusehen. Alternativ könnte man „37 ⸢x⸣" auch als ŠAḪ$^{!}$.⸢MEŠ$^{!}$⸣ interpretieren; allerdings ist mir kein anderer Beleg dafür in Erinnerung, daß Futterrationen für verschiedene Tiere als ein Posten verbucht werden. Am ehesten wäre an dieser Stelle eigentlich ein Monatsname zu erwarten.

(3) Vgl. *AHw* 107a s.v. *barittannu* etwa „altersgrau". Nach dem dort auch zitierten Text HSS 15,101 bedeutet das Wort, das nach Mayrhofer von sskr. *palitá-* abzuleiten ist, doch eher lediglich die Farbe Grau (Z. 5), da davor in Z. 4 Pferde genannt sind, die mit der Bezeichnung *ṣalmu*, „schwarz", spezifiziert werden. Im übrigen ist mir für das von Kilmer et al. an dieser Stelle herangezogene Wort *parû*, „Maultier", kein Beleg aus Nuzi bekannt.

(4) Unklar.

(5) Das Zeichen ḪUŠ ist in Nuzi ungewöhnlich und daher eher als ḪAR aufzufassen. Dennoch bleibt die Lesung des PN völlig unklar.

UCLMA 9-3029

Vs. 2 *ma-at* SIG$_4^{!}$.MEŠ[21]
ša É.GAL-*lì la-bi-ru*
^{m}*Ut-ḫa-a-a* DUMU *E-ḫé-el-te-šup*
a-na UR$_5$.RA *il-qè*
ina EGIR *e-bur$_{14}$-ri*
2 *ma-at* SIG$_4$.MEŠ
ú-ta-ar
Rs. NA$_4$ ^{m}*Ut-ḫa-a-a*
(Siegelabrollung)

---

21 Kollationiert. [For the reading SIG$_4$ for ANŠE, and additional comments on this text, see now B. Lion, *NABU* 1995/104. EDS.]

A Re-Examination of the Late Period Graves at Yorgan Tepe (Nuzi)

D.T. POTTS

University of Sydney

In light of the considerable amount of work done over the past few decades on the archaeology of Mesopotamia during the Parthian and Sasanian periods, it is now possible to put the discoveries made at Nuzi in the so-called 'Late Period' graves into a new context. Some of the more significant finds are re-examined, and the historical geography of the Nuzi region in the late pre-Islamic era is discussed.

Introduction

R.F.S. Starr's 1939 volume on Nuzi contains a short chapter by him on what he called the "meager" remnants of Late Period occupation at the site, by which he meant "Parthian, Sassanian, and Colonial Roman" (Starr 1939:495), as well as an Appendix by Robert W. Ehrich in which the finds from a post-Hurrian cemetery at Yorgan Tepe and from various soundings in the vicinity of the site were published (Ehrich 1939:545-69). The conclusion to Ehrich's chapter, completed in 1932, commences with the query: "Who were these later people who lived at the base of Yorgan Tepa?" (Ehrich 1939:566). When the Nuzi graves were discovered, little comparable material existed which could aid in their dating and interpretation. During the past few decades, however, considerable advances have been made in the archaeology of the later pre-Islamic periods in Mesopotamia (Map). With the comparable material at our disposal it is now possible to refine the dating, classification, and interpretation of the Nuzi graves. In the pages that follow I would like to return to that question, offering a few observations on the late graves at Nuzi as a modest tribute to the memory of R.F.S. Starr.

The Late Period Graves

With the exception of the large, schematic plan showing the locations of the late period graves at Nuzi (Starr 1939: Plan 39), the only detailed grave plans given in the original excavation report were of tombs located off the mound. For practical reasons, however, a discussion of these graves is beyond the scope of

Studies on the Civilization and Culture of Nuzi and the Hurrians - 8

the present paper. We have, however, descriptions of four grave types encountered at Nuzi itself. These included simple interments, sacrificial infant burials, baked-brick graves with a pitched or saddle-back roof, and vaulted mud-brick graves.

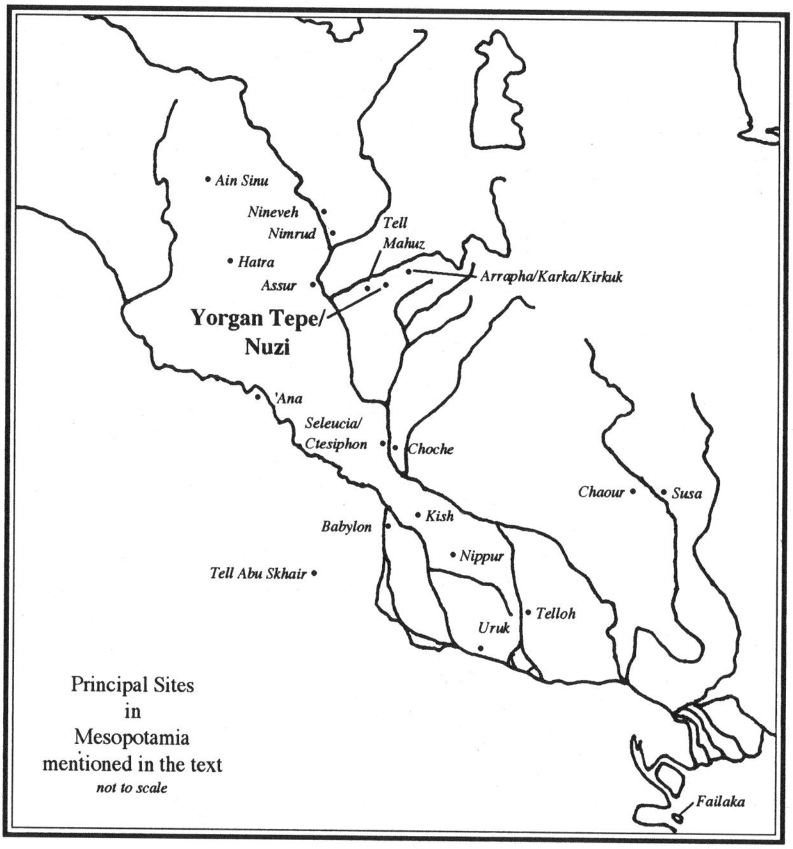

Principal Sites
in
Mesopotamia
mentioned in the text
not to scale

The first type requires no comment, for it involved nothing more than a simple pit dug into the ground. The second type was represented by jar burials in which an infant was laid to rest in a ceramic vessel which was then interred beneath the floor of the house in which, presumably, the child's family lived. As Ehrich noted, this practice was one of great antiquity at Nuzi (Ehrich 1939:549). Starr described one grave of this type, F16, as follows: "In F16, of the Partho-Sassanid period, was a pot (Pl. 138, F), buried upright below the pavement, containing the skeleton of a single newborn babe. The base of the jar was unpierced, and the mouth was carefully covered with a fragment of brick" (Starr 1939:357). Jar burials, or 'Topfgräber', were widespread in both space and time throughout large portions of the Near East (Strommenger 1957–1971:582-84).

The baked-brick grave with pitched roof at Nuzi is virtually identical to the so-called 'Ziegelgräber' of Parthian Assur, the only difference being that at the latter site, the pitched bricks forming either side of the roof of the grave did not touch but were separated by a line of flat-lying bricks (Andrae and Lenzen 1933:96-97 and Taf. 47.k-m). This, however, was undoubtedly a regional distinction of no great significance for at Babylon, where pitched-roof graves identical to those of Nuzi were found (Reuther 1926:Taf. 91.231), various roofing techniques were employed side by side. Similar, pitched-roof graves have also been found by the Italian expedition at Seleucia-on-the-Tigris (e.g., Invernizzi 1967:Fig. 9; Negro Ponzi 1970–1971:Fig. 36). E. Strommenger, who noted the existence of this type of grave at Nippur, Der, Nimrud, and Billa, in addition to Babylon and Nuzi, suggests that a prototype of this form may be found in Achaemenid Nippur (Strommenger 1957–1971:588). Whatever its origin may have been, examples of the pitched-roof or saddle-back grave at Choche/Ctesiphon (Cavallero 1966:Fig. 21;1967:Fig. 34) demonstrate conclusively that this grave type continued in use into the Sasanian period.

Finally, the vaulted mud-brick graves of Nuzi are a somewhat less grandiose version of the 'Grüfte' found at Parthian Assur (Andrae and Lenzen 1933:97-98, Taf. 48, 50), Ctesiphon (Hauser 1993:Abb. 3 and Taf. 125), and Seleucia-on-the-Tigris (Yeivin 1933:Figs. 8-11; Graziosi 1968–1969:Figs. 49-51; Negro Ponzi 1972a:Fig. 9; Invernizzi 19731974:Fig. 4). It is also interesting to note that a related expression of the same type of grave architecture is found at ed-Dur in the United Arab Emirates during the first century A.D., a period approximating the Middle Parthian era (Boucharlat *et al.* 1989:Figs. C, P; cf. Potts 1990:283). That this type of grave had a long heritage in Mesopotamia is proven by the existence of similar graves as early as the third millennium (Strommenger 1957–1971:588). Perhaps the most impressive monuments of this kind were those of Middle Assyrian date excavated at Assur (Haller 1954:100ff.). We turn now to the contents of some of the individual graves at Nuzi.

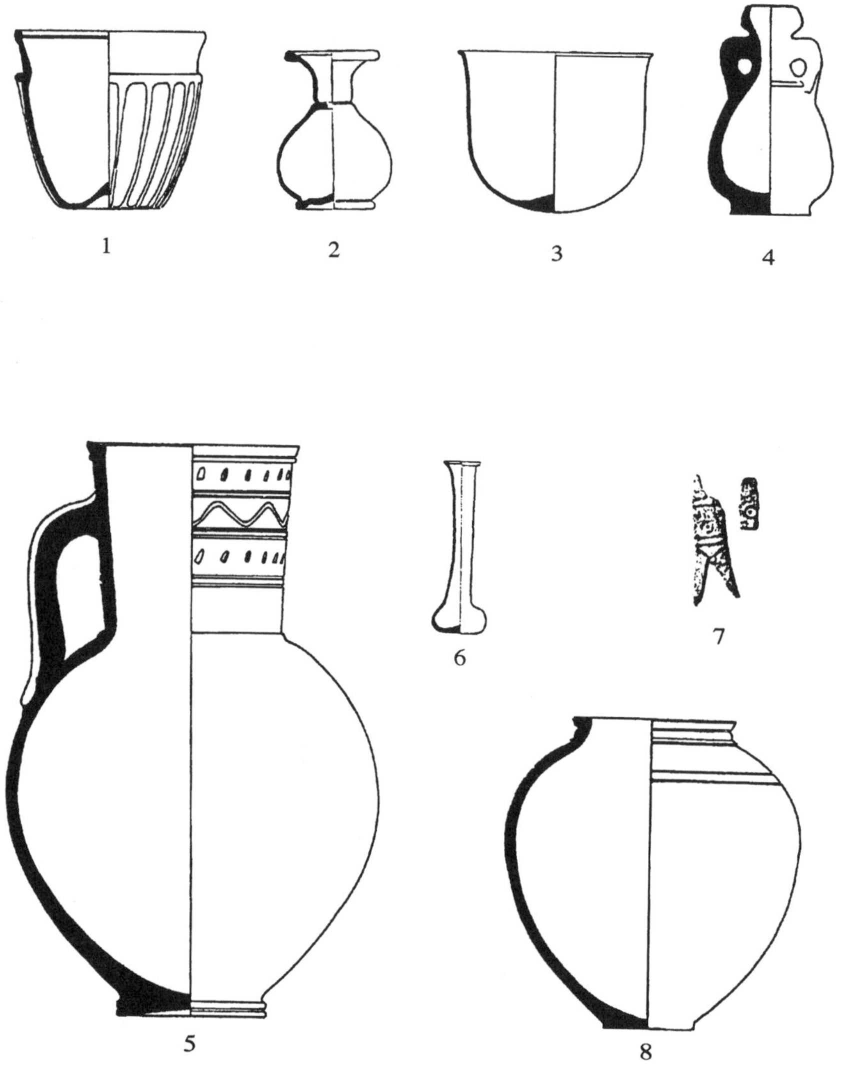

Figs. 1-8. Objects from Yorgan Tepe discussed in the text.

GRAVE 5

Grave 5 was classified as a variant of the vaulted mud-brick grave type. Two pieces of glass found here are important indicators of chronology and cultural affinity. The fluted glass bowl (Fig. 1 = Ehrich 1939:Pl. 140O) with a kick base is an example of the commonest sort of hemispherical glass bowl found in the proto- and middle-Sasanian levels at Choche. Their numbers make it likely that they were being produced in central Mesopotamia during the Sasanian period (Negro Ponzi 1984:34 and Fig. 2.8). On the other hand, the prominence of this type only 50 kms. west of Nuzi at Tell Mahuz on the Lower Zab (Negro Ponzi 1968–1969:Fig. 157.70) suggests the existence of a production center in northern Mesopotamia as well. The Tell Mahuz finds are also extremely important for they are dated by associated coins to between 250 and 400 A.D. (Negro Ponzi 1984:34).

A small bottle (Fig. 2 = Ehrich 1939:Fig. 140M) can be compared generally with late Parthian examples of glass from Tell Abu Skhair (e.g., Negro Ponzi 1972b:Figs. 20.21, 24; 21.25-26) in both body and rim form, although the latter examples have a kick base rather than the pseudo-ring base of the Nuzi exemplar. The fact that these comparisons are by no means exact is no doubt due to a real chronological difference between the two sites, the Nuzi graves being demonstrably later by at least one-and-a-half to two centuries. A close comparison for the neck and rim shape can be found in a fragment from the Sasanian settlement at Kish (Harden 1934:Fig. 5.19). Very similar examples are also known from Tell Mahuz (Negro Ponzi 1968–1969:Fig. 154.32-33), and Negro Ponzi has also identified examples of the same general type at Nineveh, Uruk, Babylon, and Karanis in Egypt (Negro Ponzi 1972b:227, with refs.). The Nuzi vessel is considered an East Roman product, probably of Syrian origin, by Negro Ponzi (Negro Ponzi 1968–1969:337). However, she has stressed the unity of the Nuzi and Tell Mahuz glass *corpora* which differ demonstrably from those of Nineveh, Hatra, and Dura Europos, suggesting that the character of the glass at Nuzi and Tell Mahuz reflects the historic entity Beṯ Garmaï (see below) with its strong ties to the early Sasanian kings (Negro Ponzi 1968–1969:382-83).

GRAVE 8

This vaulted mud-brick grave contained a silver coin of Shapur I (240-70), unfortunately unillustrated (no weight or denomination given). A glass bowl (Fig. 3 = Ehrich 1939:Pl. 140N) found in it is very similar in form to a bowl considered Roman from a grave on Bahrain (During Caspers 1972–1974:Fig. 5c), and finds, furthermore, an exact parallel at Telloh in southern Mesopotamia (Ghirshman 1936:Pl. 133.3).

GRAVE 13

Here we have another example of a vaulted mud-brick grave. A glazed *amphoriskos* (Fig. 4 = Ehrich 1939:Pl. 135C) found in Grave 13 belongs to a category well-known in the Hellenistic-Parthian ceramic repertoire which seems to have developed locally in Hellenistic Babylonia (Hannestad 1990:183). Examples of this form are known, *inter alios*, at Susa in Apadana level 5c (c. 100 B.C.–100 A.D.) (Boucharlat 1987:Fig. 65.5) and in Ville Royale II level 3C (c. 100–150 A.D.) (Miroschedji 1987:Fig. 33.8); on Failaka, where there tends to be slightly more room between the handles and the neck (e.g., Hannestad 1983:Pl. 29.302 or Bernard *et al.* 1990:Fig. 5.131, with a less complex rim); and on Bahrain, where the body may be significantly squatter (e.g., Salles 1990:Fig. 9b). Although no precise comparanda can be found in the corpus of Seleucid and Parthian glazed pottery from Uruk (Finkbeiner 1991), E. Strommenger has pointed to the occurrence of this type at Uruk during the Parthian period, and referred to numerous comparanda from Telloh, Nippur, Seleucia-on-the-Tigris, Dura Europos, and Nimrud (Strommenger 1967:26 with refs. and Taf. 27.7-9). E. Haerinck, who has studied this form exhaustively citing occurrences throughout Mesopotamia and southwestern Iran, has noted that the smaller vessels of this type occur in what he has called Middle (c. 150–1 B.C.) and Late Parthian (c. 1–225 A.D.) times, although the form definitely continued in use into the early Sasanian period (Haerinck 1983:34; Valtz 1984:43). It is, for instance, attested in level 2 at Chaour near Susa (Labrousse and Boucharlat 1972:Fig. 37.5; Boucharlat and Labrousse 1979:Figs. 28.9, 35.2), as well as at Tell Mahuz (Venco Ricciardi 1970–1971:Figs. 87.54, 92.54-57) and Choche (Venco Ricciardi 1967: Figs. 135, 156-60). L. Hannestad has specifically compared the example from Nuzi Grave 13 with a vessel from Choche (Hannestad 1983:39), noting that it "must also be very late Parthian or Sassanian." The Choche and Tell Mahuz comparisons are striking and should, in my opinion, be taken to date the Nuzi exemplar to sometime within the first half of the Sasanian period.

GRAVE 15

Grave 15 was a baked-brick grave with a pitched roof. A large, single-handled amphora with incised decoration found here (Fig. 5 = Ehrich 1939:Pl. 136F) belongs to a category of Sasanian pottery which was widespread throughout the Near East. Commenting on a fragment from Failaka with comb-incised decoration, L. Hannestad drew attention to the Nuzi vessel, while noting other parallels at Nimrud, Ain Sinu, Dura Europos, Tell Mahuz, Assur, and Tell Billa in contexts datable to the 3rd century A.D. and later (Hannestad 1983:61). D. Oates drew a parallel between the amphora from Grave 15 and a large class of incised, two-handled amphorae from Ain Sinu (Oates 1968:148), although in this writer's opinion the absence of a second handle on the Nuzi vessel is a clear indication of a later date than that assigned to the Ain Sinu material, which Oates placed in the first third of the third century A.D. R. Venco Ricciardi has suggested that this type of decoration was commonest in northern Mesopotamia, but examples which are very similar to the Nuzi vessel are known from the Eastern Province of Saudi Arabia (Potts 1989:Fig. 123); the coast of Ras al-Khaimah in the United Arab Emirates (e.g., Kennet 1994:Fig. 11.18); the northern tip of Oman (de Cardi 1972:Fig. 2.29, 34); and Fars province in Iran (e.g., Whitcomb 1984:Figs. 2-3). A two-handled amphora with very similar decoration is known from Choche (Venco Ricciardi 1967:Fig. 141), but perhaps the closest similarities are to be found in a whole group of single-handled vessels from nearby Tell Mahuz (Venco Ricciardi 1970–1971:436 and Fig. 88.7-10).

GRAVE 30

This simple pit interment contained a bronze spatula (Ehrich 1939:Pl. 141N) which is paralleled exactly by an iron one from level 1 at Chaour near Susa (Labrousse and Boucharlat 1972:Fig. 28.3).

GRAVE 32

This 'unclassified' grave showed no signs of either a pit or brick construction. A tall glass vial or *unguentarium* (Fig. 6 = Ehrich 1939:PI. 140K) found here belongs to a category well-attested at Tell Mahuz (Negro Ponzi 1968–1969:Fig. 153.12-15) and Choche (cf. Negro Ponzi 1966:Fig. 34;1984:Fig. 1.9). E. Strommenger has grouped the Nuzi vial together with similar finds from Telloh, Nippur, Babylon, Ctesiphon (for which see Hauser 1993:361-62, no. 42 and Taf. 136c), Uruk, and Assur (Strommenger 1967:34 with refs. and Taf. 47.1). An example with a kick base is attested as far south as ed-Dur in the United Arab Emirates (Boucharlat *et al.* 1989:Fig. 32, center) where it was found in a grave excavated in Area F which dated to the first quarter of the fourth century A.D.

GRAVE 105

This baked-brick grave with pitched roof contained an interesting bone object (Fig. 7 = Ehrich 1939:Pl. 141K). A very similar piece, also made of bone, was found by W.K. Loftus at Uruk in 1854 and is illustrated on a composite watercolor sketch entitled 'ornaments from Coffins', where it appears alongside several examples of Roman glass (Barag 1985 Pl. D, lower right). A similarly shaped bone object from an unstratified context was found in the British excavations at 'Ana on the Middle Euphrates (Bamber 1988:Fig. 57.2), and recently more objects of this type from Uruk and Susa have been published (Boucharlat and Haerinck 1994:188).

Starr believed that the Nuzi object was an arrow nock, the attachment inserted into the butt-end of a hollow arrow into which the bowstring fits. He commented on the functional suitability of bone as follows: "Bone is unexcelled for this purpose, and it is of interest that they should have used at this early date that material so prized for the same purpose by archers of today. The size of the nock presupposes an arrow of extraordinary thickness and weight, and would have demanded a bow of exceptional weight and cast to handle it" (Starr 1939:503). While it is certainly true that hollow arrows (Akk. *qanû*) were used in ancient Mesopotamia, the distal-end diameter of the better preserved examples from Uruk suggests that they cannot have been arrow nocks. While modern arrow shafts are generally less than 1 cm. in diameter, the Uruk bone objects appear, from the illustrations, to be no less than c. 3 cm. in diameter (Potts 1993/

94:137), hence Starr's own astonishment at the 'extraordinary thickness and weight' of any arrow onto which such a nock would necessarily fit.

GRAVE F16

This was one of the sacrificial infant burials found dug into the Nuzi period levels on the site. The type of jar used to house the burial (Fig. 8 = Ehrich 1939:Pl. 138F) is very reminiscent of a somewhat squatter type used throughout the Sasanian period at Choche (Venco Ricciardi 1984:Fig. 4.5).

The sum total of these observations leaves little doubt that the late period graves at Nuzi date to the Sasanian, and not to the Parthian period. The numerous parallels to be found in the material from Choche and Tell Mahuz are, in my opinion, definitive, and in view of the fact that the finds from the latter site have been dated numismatically to between 250 and 400 A.D. (Negro Ponzi 1984:34), I would be inclined to date the Nuzi graves specifically to the first half of the Sasanian period. This would also find confirmation in the presence of a coin of Shapur I in Grave 8. This being the case, we turn now to a more general consideration of Nuzi and the area of Nuzi during the Sasanian period.

Perspectives on the Historical Geography and Anthropology of Nuzi in the Sasanian Period

That Nuzi was relatively unimportant in the late periods is demonstrated by the apparent lack of a substantial settlement on the site. Indeed, by the Sasanian period the site seems to have been used principally as a cemetery. It is hardly surprising, therefore, that no epigraphic finds turned up during the original excavations which reveal the name of the site in the late periods. We can, however, gain some insight into the population inhabiting the region by examining the relevant written sources.

Yorgan Tepe's written history goes back to the Old Akkadian period when the site was known as Gasur (Edzard, Farber and Sollberger 1977:54; Wilhelm 1989:7; Fincke 1993:35-38). Thereafter, of course, it became known by the non-Semitic (Hurrian?) name Nuzi/Nuzu (Fisher 1959:123-26; Fincke 1993:194-209). Nuzi, which flourished in the period between c. 1450/1400 and 1250/1200 B.C., was a town within the kingdom of Arrapḫa [*māt Arrapḫe*] (Fisher 1959:90; Zaccagnini 1979; Fadhlil 1983:1-2). The kingdom took its name from that of the capital city [Arrapḫe^{ki} or ^{URU}Arrapḫe] located beneath the modern town of Kirkuk. The name Arrapḫa can be traced back to the Ur III period where we find *Ar-ra-ap-ḫu-um*^{ki}/*A-ra-ap-ḫu-um*^{ki} (Edzard and Farber 1974:16; Fadhlil 1983:2; Astour 1987:39-40). As F. Delitzsch recognized (Delitzsch 1881:125; cf. Herzfeld 1907:222; Forrer 1921:4) we find a survival of this name much later in Cl. Ptolemy's list of Assyrian toponyms, for he calls the region Arrhapachitis/Αρραπαχιτισ (Forbiger 1844:609) and indeed the name survives to this day in the Arabic toponym *'Arafa*, the name of a suburb of Kirkuk (Fiey 1964:192, n. 7).

There are, however, other important names associated with the region of Yorgan Tepe. During the reign of Tiglathpileser III (744–727 B.C.) an Aramaean tribe known as the Gurumu are attested in the region of the Lower Zab (Brinkman 1968:276; cf. Dietrich 1971:705). Much later Cl. Ptolemy also knew of a tribe in this region called the Garamaei/Γαραμαιοι (Fiey 1968:14; Forbiger 1844:609), a name which survived in Beṯ Garmaï, the name given in Nestorian sources to the area, the capital city of which was Karka of Beṯ Sloḫ (i.e., the 'city of the house of Seleucus'), modern Kirkuk (Fiey 1968:14ff). Long ago F. Delitzsch suggested that the names Garamaei and Beṯ Garmaï perpetuated that of the Gurumu (Delitzsch 1881:240; cf. Herzfeld 1907:222).

Arrapḫa/Karka of Beṯ Sloḫ was thus always the main metropolitan center of which Gasur/Nuzi/Yorgan Tepe was a subsidiary settlement. We are fortunate in having an extant Syriac text entitled *The History of Karka of Beṯ Sloḫ* (Fiey 1964:194; cf. the earlier but still important discussion in Hoffmann 1880:267-70). The very epithet of Karka, 'city of the house of Seleucus', confirms that the ancient city of Arrapḫa was *re-founded* by one of the Seleucids (Tscherikower 1927:97; cf. Dillemann 1962:100; for the Talmudic sources, see Obermeyer 1929:141). During the Parthian period, Karka and its hinterland fell administratively within the compass of the area called *Nwt-hštrkn*/Nodh-Ardashirakan in Middle Persian (Maricq 1958:304, n. 4). We have no extant sources which name the exact date of the evangelization of the region, but the *History of Karka* tells us that as early as the time of the Roman emperor Hadrian (117–138) a persecution of Christians in the West led the bishop Tuqrayté/Theocritus to seek refuge at Karka, where he found an already existing Christian community (Fiey 1964:199, 1970:56). Moreover, it records that "From the time of the king Balash [Vologases IV] to the twentieth year of Shapur, son of Ardashir [Shapur I], which is ninety years, Karka was a blessed field and no weeds grew therein" (Sachau 1919:55; Fiey 1964:196). The implication of this statement is that from a date ninety years before Shapur's twentieth year on the throne (261), i.e., from the year 171 onward for the space of almost a century, Karka was a blessed, Christian city (cf. Fiey 1970:49). We are thus certain that Christianity was well established in the region during the Parthian period, at least by the third quarter of the 2nd century. That there was a large Christian population in the region during the early Sasanian period is a well-established fact. During the reign of Shapur II (309–379) Karka was the scene of notorious persecutions and martyrdoms, as related in the acts of the martyrs of Karka of Beṯ Sloḫ (Labourt 1904:73-74; Fiey 1964:203ff.). By the middle of the fifth century, the region of Karka was referred to administratively as Garmekan (cf. Beṯ Garmaï) when it seems to have formed part of a single unit together with the kingdom of Adiabene (Morony 1982:10; cf. Rahimi-Laridjani 1988:34). The Armenian geography of Ps. Moses Xorenaci, a source composed around 700 and generally taken to describe conditions in the late Sasanian period, distinguished Nodh-Ardashirakan/Norshirakan, the name by which the region had been known in Parthian times, from Garmekan (Marquart 1901:21).

As Herzfeld showed in his discussion of 'Sasanidische Ansiedlungen' in Garmekan, several Arabic sources, as well as the testimony of numerous toponyms ending in *-abadh* (e.g., Kardaliabadh, Balabadh, Khurustabadh [= Khorsabad], Perozabadh), attest to considerable new settlement in the region during the Sasanian period (Herzfeld 1907:116-17), and it is certainly to this phenomenon that the late period graves at Nuzi and the various other nearby settlements sounded by Starr and Ehrich bear witness. We will, undoubtedly, never uncover the name of Yorgan Tepe in this period, for despite the fact that there are many as yet unlocated toponyms in Garmekan/Bet̠ Garmaï which must belong to towns located near Karka (extensively discussed by Hoffmann 1881:267-77, "Städte in Bet^{h} Garmai"; and Sachau 1919:55-57, "Kirchenprovinz Bêth-Garmai, Garamaea"), Yorgan Tepe was essentially a cemetery with, perhaps, a nearby village of no great importance. But of the importance of the province of Bet̠ Garmaï and its capital Karka within the context of the history of Nestorian Christianity under the Sasanians, there can be no doubt, and it is thanks to the hard work of R.F.S. Starr and R.W. Ehrich in excavating and publishing the graves discussed here that we have been afforded an important archaeological perspective on the past of a region for which we have precious few literary sources.

Abbreviations

AnOr	Analecta Orientalia
AOMIM	R. Boucharlat and J.-F. Salles, eds. *Arabie orientale, Mésopotamie et Iran méridional de l'âge du fer au début de la période islamique.* Paris: Editions Recherche sur les Civilisations Mémoire 37,1984.
BaM	*Baghdader Mitteilungen*
BAH	Bibliothèque Archéologique et Historique de l'Institut Français d'Archéologie de Beyrouth
CNIP	Carsten Niebuhr Institute Publications
CSCO	Corpus Scriptorum Christianorum Orientalium
DAFI	Délégation Archéologique Française en Iran
FFF 1986–1988	Y. Calvet and J. Gachet, eds. *Failaka, Fouilles Françaises 1986-1988.* Lyons: Travaux de la Maison de l'Orient 18, 1990.
JASP	Jutland Archaeological Society Publications
RGTC	Répertoire Géographique des Textes Cunéiformes
RlA	*Reallexikon der Assyriologie*
TAVO	Tübinger Atlas des Vorderen Orients
WVDOG	Wissenschaftliche Veröffentlichungen der Deutschen Orient-Gesellschaft

References

Andrae, W. and Lenzen, H.

1933 *Die Partherstadt Assur.* Leipzig: WVDOG 57.

Astour, M.C.

1987 "Semites and Hurrians in Northern Transtigris," in Owen, D.I. and Morrison, M.A., eds. *Studies on the Civilization and Culture of Nuzi and the Hurrians, vol.* 2. Winona Lake: Eisenbrauns, pp. 3-68.

Bamber, A.

1988 "Small Finds," in Northedge, A., Bamber, A., and Roaf, M. *Excavations at 'Ana: Qal'a Island.* Warminster: Aris & Phillips, pp. 126-34.

Barag, D.

1985 *Catalogue of Western Asiatic Glass in the British Museum, vol. 1.* London: British Museum Publications and Jerusalem: Magnes Press.

Bernard, V., Gachet, J. and Salles, J.-F.

1990 "Apostilles en marge de la ceramique des etats IV et V," *FFF 1986–1988:* 241-84.

Boucharlat, R.

1987 "Les niveaux post-achéménides à Suse, secteur nord. Fouilles de l'Apadana-Est et de la Ville Royale-Ouest (1973–1978)," *Cahiers de la DAFI* 15:145-311.

Boucharlat, R., and Haerinck, E.

1994 "Des ewig-weibliche figurines en os d'époque parthe de Suse," *Iranica Antiqua* 29:185-99.

Boucharlat, R., Haerinck, E., Lecomte, O., Potts, D.T., and Stevens, K.G.

1989 "The European Archaeological Expedition to ed-Dur, Umm al-Qaiwayn (U.A.E.): An Interim Report on the 1987 and 1988 Seasons," *Mesopotamia* 24: 5-72.

Boucharlat, R. and Labrousse, A.

1979 "Le palais d'Artaxerxes II sur la rive droite du Chaour à Suse," *Cahiers de la DAFI* 10:19-136.

Brinkman, J.A.

1968 *A Political History of Post-Kassite Babylonia, 1158-722 B.C.* Rome: AnOr 43.

Cardi, B. de

1972 "A Sasanian Outpost in northern Oman," *Antiquity* 46: 305-10.

Cavallero, M.C.

1966 "The Excavations at Choche (presumed Ctesiphon) Area 2," *Mesopotamia 1:* 63-81.

1967 "The Excavations at Choche - Area 2," *Mesopotamia* 2: 48-56.

Delitzsch, F.

1881 *Wo lag das Paradies?* Leipzig: Hinrichs.

Dietrich, M.

1971 "Gurumu," *RlA* 3: 705.

Dillemann, L.

1962 *Haute Mésopotamie orientale et pays adjacents.* Paris: BAH 72.

During Caspers, E.C.L.

1972–1974 "The Bahrain Tumuli," *Persica* 6:131-56.

Edzard, D.O. and Farber, G.

1974 *Die Orts- und Gewässernamen der Zeit der 3. Dynastie von Ur.* RGTC 2, Wiesbaden: Dr. Ludwig Reichert.

Edzard, D.O., Farber, G. and Sollberger, E.

1977 *Die Orts- und Gewässernamen der präsargonischen und sargonischen Zeit.* RGTC 1, Wiesbaden: Dr. Ludwig Reichert.

Ehrich, R.W.

1939 "Appendix E. The Later Cultures at Yorgan Tepa," in Starr 1939: 545-69.

Fadhil, A.

1983 *Studien zur Topographie und Prosopographie der Provinzstädte des Königreichs Arrapḫe.* Mainz: Baghdader Forschungen 6.

Fiey, J.M.

1964 "Vers la rehabilitation de *l''Histoire de Karka d'Beṯ Sloḥ,*" *Analecta Bollandiana* 82: 189-222.

1968 *Assyrie chrétienne, 111. Bét̲ Garmaï, Bét̲ Aramayé et Maišan nestoriens.* Beirut: Dar el-Machreq.

1970 *Jalons pour une histoire de l'église en Iraq.* Louvain: CSCO 310, Subsidia 36.

Fincke, J.

1993 *Die Orts- und Gewässernamen der Nuzi-Texte.* RGTC 10, Wiesbaden: Dr. Ludwig Reichert.

Finkbeiner, U.

1991 "Keramik der seleukidischen und parthischen Zeit aus den Grabungen in Uruk-Warka," *BaM* 22:537-637.

Fisher, L.R.

1959 *Nuzu Geographical Names.* unpublished PhD. dissertation, Brandeis University.

Forbiger, A.

1844 *Handbuch der alten Geographie aus den Quellen bearbeitet.* Leipzig: Mayer & Wigand.

Forrer, E.

1921 *Die Provinzeinteilung des assyrischen Reiches.* Leipzig: Hinrichs.

Ghirshman, R.

1936 "Appendice sur les Fouilles de Medain," in: de Genouillac, H. *Fouilles de Telloh.* Paris: Geuthner, pp. 139-50.

Graziosi, G.

1968–1969 "Excavations in Squares CLXXI, 54/55/56/64/65/66 (Porticoed Street)," *Mesopotamia* 3-4: 43-52.

Haerinck, E.

1983 *La céramique en Iran pendant la période parthe (ca. 250 av. J.C. à 225 apres J.C.): typologie, chronologie et distribution.* Gent: Peeters.

Haller, A.

1954 *Die Gräber und Grüfte von Assur.* Berlin: WVDOG 65.

Hannestad, L.

1983 *The Hellenistic Pottery, vols.* 1-2. Aarhus: JASP 16:1-2

1990 "Change and Conservatism. Hellenistic Pottery in Mesopotamia and Iran," in: *Akten des XIll. Internationalen Kongresses für Klassische Archäologie, Berlin 1988.* Mainz: Von Zabern, pp. 179-86.

Harden, D.B.

1934 "Excavations at Kish and Barghuthiat 1933 II. Pottery," *Iraq* 1:124-36.

Hauser, S.R.

1993 "Eine arsakidenzeitliche Nekropole in Ktesiphon," *BaM* 24:325-420.

Herzfeld, E.

1907 "Untersuchungen über die historische Topographie der Landschaft am Tigris, kleinen Zâb und Ğebel Hamrin," *Memnon* 1:89-143, 217-38.

Hoffmann, G.

1880 *Auszüge aus syrischen Akten persischer Märtyrer.* Leipzig: Abhandlungen für die Kunde des Morgenlandes 7/3.

Invernizzi, A.

1967 "The Excavation of Tell 'Umar," *Mesopotamia* 2:9-32.

1973–1974 "The Excavations at the Archives Building," *Mesopotamia* 8-9:9-14.

Kennet, D.

1994 "Jazirat al-Hulayla - early Julfar," *JRAS*[3] 4/2:163-212.

Labourt, J.

1904 *Le Christianisme dans l'empire perse sous la dynastie Sassanide, 224-632.* Paris: Lecoffre.

Labrousse, A. and Boucharlat, R.

1974 "La fouille du palais du Chaour à Suse en 1970 et 1971," *Cahiers de la DAFI* 2: 61-167.

Maricq, A.

1958 "Classica et Orientalia 5. Res Gestae Divi Saporis," *Syria* 35: 295-360.

Marquart, J.

1901 *Eranšahr nach der Geographie des Ps. Moses Xorenac'i.* Berlin: Abhandlungen der königl. Gesellschaft der Wissenschaften zu Göttingen, phil.-hist. Kl. NF 3/2.

Miroschedji, P. de.

1987 "Fouilles du chantier Ville Royale II à Suse (19751977) II. Niveaux d'époques achéménide, séleucide, parthe et islamique," *Cahiers de la DAFI* 15:11-143.

Morony, M.

1982 "Continuity and Change in the Administrative Geography of Late Sasanian and Early Islamic al-lraq," *Iran* 20:149.

Negro Ponzi, M.M.

1966 "The Excavations at Choche (presumed Ctesiphon) - Area 1," *Mesopotamia 1:* 81-88.

1968–1969 "Sasanian Glassware from Tell Mahuz (North Mesopotamia)," *Mesopotamia* 3-4: 293-384.

1972a "Excavations in the Agora (S.C. Porticoed Street)," *Mesopotamia* 7: 17-25.

1972b "Glassware from Abu Skhair (Central Iraq)," *Mesopotamia* 7:215-37.

1970–1971 "Excavations in Squares *CLXXI*, 54/55/63/64/74 (Porticoed Street)," *Mesopotamia* 5-6:31-39.

1984 "Glassware from Choche," *AOMIM:* 33-40.

Oates, D.

1968 *Studies in the Ancient History of Northern Iraq*. London: British Academy.

Obermeyer, J.

1929 *Die Landschaft Babylonien im Zeitalter des Talmuds und des Gaonats.* Frankfurt: Schriften der Gesellschaft zur Förderung der Wissenschaft des Judentums.

Potts, D.T.

1989 *Miscellanea Hasaitica.* Copenhagen: CNIP 7.

1990 *The Arabian Gulf in Antiquity, ii.* Oxford: Clarendon Press.

1993/94 review of van Ess and Pedde 1992. *AfO* 40/41:136-38.

Rahimi-Laridjani, F.

1988 *Die Entwicklung der Bewässerungslandwirtschaft im Iran bis in sasanidisch-frühislamische Zeit.* Wiesbaden: Beiträge zur Iranistik 13.

Reuther, 0.

1926 *Die Innenstadt von Babylon (Merkes).* Leipzig: WVDOG 47.

Sachau, E.

1919 "Zur Ausbreitung des Christentums in Asien," Berlin: Abhandlungen der Preussischen Akad. d. Wiss., phil.-hist. Kl. 1.

Salles, J.-F.

1990 "Questioning the BI-Ware," *FFF 1986–1988:* 303-34

Starr, R.F.S.

1939 *Nuzi*, vol. I. Cambridge: Harvard University Press

Strommenger, E.

1967 *Gefässe aus Uruk von der neubabylonischen Zeit bis zu den Sasaniden.* Berlin: Ausgrabungen der Deutschen Forschungsgemeinschaft in Uruk-Warka 7.

Tscherikower, V.

1927 *Die hellenistischen Städtegründungen von Alexander dem Grossen bis auf die Römerzeit.* Leipzig: Philologus Supplementband 19/1.

Valtz, E.

1984 "Pottery from Seleucia on the Tigris," *AOMIM:* 41-48.

van Ess, M. and Pedde, F.

1992 *Uruk. Kleinfunde II* [= Ausgrabungen in Uruk-Warka Endberichte 7]. Mainz: von Zabern.

Venco Ricciardi, R.

1967 "Pottery from Choche," *Mesopotamia* 2: 93-104.

1970–1971 "Sasanian Pottery from Tell Mahuz (North Mesopotamia)," *Mesopotamia* 5-6: 427-82.

1984 "Sasanian Pottery from Choche," *AOMIM:* 49-57.

Whitcomb, D.

1984 "Qasr-i Abu Nasr and the Gulf," *AOMIM:* 331-37.

Wilhelm, G.

1989 *The Hurrians.* Warminster: Aris & Phillips.

Yeivin, S.

1933 "The Tombs found at Seleucia (Seasons 1929-30 and 1931-32)," in: Waterman, L. *Second Preliminary Report upon the Excavations at Tel Umar, Iraq.* Ann Arbor: University of Michigan Press, pp. 33-64.

Zaccagnini, C.

1979 *The Rural Landscape of the Land of Arrapḫe.* Rome: Quaderni di Geografia Storica 1.

Zu den hurritischen Namen der Kültepe-Tafel kt k/k 4

GERNOT WILHELM
Julius-Maximilians-Universität Würzburg

The tablet kt k/k 4/4 from Kārum Kaniš Level Ib published in this volume by K. Hecker contains several Hurrian names, including a place-name based on a Hurrian term of profession of the Alalaḫ type. The names are discussed here in detail with ample reference to the verbal and theophoric elements of Hurrian sentence names. For the term *eḫelli* („eḫele") in the census lists from Alalaḫ, a new linguistic analysis is suggested.

Die in diesem Band von Karl Hecker edierte Kültepe-Tafel kt k/k 4, für die er eine Herkunft aus Nordsyrien nachgewiesen hat, enthält einige unzweifelhaft hurritische Namen und stellt damit ein in Hinsicht auf ihre frühe Zeitstellung (wohl Kültepe Schicht Ib) besonders wertvolles Dokument für die Verbreitung des Hurritischen westlich des Euphrats dar. In Ergänzung der Ausführungen Heckers seien diese Namen im folgenden eingehender kommentiert.

1. Der Name **Unapše** ist ein Satzname mit der Verbalform *un=a=b* (3. Ps. sg./pl. intransitiv) „er kam" und einem Element *še*, das als Abkürzung von *šenni* „Bruder" gedeutet werden kann. Wie in hurritischen Satznamen[1] üblich, steht das Verb in Anfangsposition, während die zweite Position von dem Subjekt eingenommen wird, bei dem es sich in aller Regel um ein theophores Element handelt.

Als theophore Elemente[2] treten vor allem auf:

1 Zur Bestimmung des Suffixes *-b* als Personenzeichen der 3. Ps. und zur Erklärung der mit Formen auf *-b* gebildeten Personennamen als Satznamen cf. I.M. Diakonoff, *Hurrisch und Urartäisch* (MSS Beih. 6 N.F.), München: Kitzinger, 1971, 123 Anm. 141; cf. auch M.L. Khačikyan, *SCCNH* 2 (1984) 153-55; G. Wilhelm, „Zum hurritischen Verbalsystem", in: S.R. Anschütz (ed.), *Texte, Sätze, Wörter und Moneme. Festschrift für Klaus Heger zum 65. Geburtstag*, Heidelberg: Heidelberger Orientverlag, 1992, 659-671.

2 Die Beispiele beschränken sich auf Namen aus dem umfangreichsten lokalen Corpus hurritischer Namen, dem von Nuzi. Für Belege vergleiche man die Liste der Elemente nicht-akkadischer und nicht-sumerischer Namen in *NPN*, 183-279.

Studies on the Civilization and Culture of Nuzi and the Hurrians - 8

(a) *enni* „Gottheit" (zu *eni* „Gott"), *šarri* „(Götter-)König", *adal* „der Starke" (wohl als Epitheton eines [bestimmten?] Gottes), *erve* „Herr", *allai* „Herrin, Königin";

(b) Namen von Gottheiten wie Bēl(e)t-ekalli, Bēl(-Ul)amme[3], Kužuġ (Mondgott), Šavuška (Ištar), Šeri(ž), Šimige (Sonnengott), Teššob (Wettergott), Tilla[4], Tirve, Ugur, Umella (= Ištar ḫumella[5]), Sarva (Zarwa), etc.;

(c) Naturnumina wie *pabni* „Berg" (zu *p/faba* „Berg"), Abiġe (= Ebiḫ?[6]), Araššiġ (Tigris);

(d) Stadtnumina wie Arrapḫe, Lumdi/Lupti, Navar (Nawar), Nuzu, Tarbašḫe, Dūr-ubla, etc.[7];

(e) architektonische Elemente der Stadt wie *abulli* „Stadttor", *kerġe* (*kerḫu*) „Oberstadt", evtl. *dūru* „Stadtmauer";

(f) Monatsnamen wie *Šeġala* (*Šeḫala*) und *Šeġli* (*Šeḫli*).

In derselben Position und bei häufig identischen verbalen Vordergliedern begegnen sehr häufig Verwandtschaftsbezeichnungen, die in Nuzi immer, sonst meist das Suffix *-ni* tragen, das nach dem Muster *evri* „Herr" : *everni* „König" als „individualisierendes Suffix" bezeichnet worden ist:[8]

el=li/e (zu *ela* „Schwester"), *men=ni* (zu *mena* [wohl weibliche Verwandtschaftsbezeichnung[9]]), *šal=li* (zu *šāla* „Tochter"), *šen=ni* (zu *šēna* „Bruder").

---

3 Cf. K. Deller, *Or*NS 45 (1976) 44f.; A. Fadhil, *Studien zur Topographie und Prosopographie der Provinzstädte des Königreichs Arrapḫe* (BaghF 6), Mainz: Verlag Philipp von Zabern, 1983, 276.

4 Cf. V. Haas, „Betrachtungen zum Gotte Tilla", in: *SCCNH* 1 (1981) 183-88; idem, *Geschichte der hethitischen Religion* (HdO I 15), Leiden/New York/Köln: E.J. Brill, 1994, 929 s.v.; K. Deller, *Or*NS 45 (1976) 44.

5 Zu dieser Gottheit cf. K. Deller, *Or*NS 45 (1976) 40, 44; A. Fadhil, *Studien zur Topographie und Prosopographie der Provinzstädte des Königreichs Arrapḫe*, 23, 68.

6 Cf. *NPN* 202.

7 Dabei begegnen die Namen jener Städte, in deren Kult eine Göttin an der Spitze steht, in manchen Fällen ausschließlich in weiblichen Personennamen, woraus geschlossen werden darf, daß hier der Ortsname für die Hauptgottheit steht. So sind Namen mit dem Element *-Ninu* (Ninua, mit der Stadtgöttin Ištar/Šavuška von Ninive) in Nuzi stets Frauennamen (*NPN* 239, außerdem [f]Zilim-ninu *AAN* 173); dasselbe gilt für *-Nuzu* (Nuzi/a/u, mit der Stadtgöttin Ištar *nuzoḫḫe*). Andererseits werden Personennamen mit dem theophoren Element *-Arrapḫe* (Arrapḫa/e, alter Kultort eines Wettergottes) nur von Männern getragen (*NPN* 205). Da der ON Navar (Nawar) nur in Männernamen begegnet, möchte man auf eine männliche Hauptgottheit schließen. Allerdings verweist mich M. Guichard auf den Namen Ummī-Nawar „Meine Mutter ist Nawar", ARM 16, p. 209. Die ON Lumdi (Lubdi, Kultort der Ištar *luptoḫḫe*) und Sissa (Zizza) finden sich dagegen sowohl in Frauen- als auch in Männernamen.

8 G. Wilhelm, *ZA* 73 (1983) 100 mit Anm. 12.

9 Ch. Girbal, *SMEA* 29 (1992) 162f. schlägt als Bedeutung „Zwilling" („Zwillingsschwester") vor.

Dabei begegnen die weiblichen Verwandtschaftsbezeichnungen nur in Frauennamen, die männlichen nur in Männernamen.

Bei Namen wie *Un=a=b - el=li* „Die Schwester kam" oder *Un=a=p - šen=ni* „Der Bruder kam" ist man zunächst geneigt, diese Namen auf die Situation der Geburt in dem Sinne zu beziehen, daß das zweite Namenselement sich auf das Neugeborene bezieht, ähnlich wie dies bei akkadischen profanen Begrüßungsnamen wie Aḫu-illika „Ein Bruder ist gekommen!" oder Aḫu-ittabši „Ein Bruder ist da!"[10] der Fall ist. Allerdings müßte man dann für den ganz gleich gebildeten Namen *Un=a=p - Teššob* (*NPN* 165a, *AAN* 157bf.) „Teššob kam" einen gänzlich anderen Sinn suchen, und zwar doch wohl dergestalt, daß hier die Geburt des Kindes mit der hilfreichen Gegenwart des Gottes verknüpft wird. Auch sonst ist nicht selten der Wechsel von Verwandtschaftsbezeichnungen und Götternamen in im übrigen identischen Namen zu finden: *Ag=i=p - šen=ni* „Der Bruder nahm auf" : *Ag=i=p - šarri, -Teššob, -Tilla, -Tirve*; *Ar - šen=ni* „Der Bruder gab ihn" : *Ar - Šavuška, -Teššob, -Tilla*. In diesen und in einer Reihe anderer Fälle scheint die Verwandtschaftsbezeichnung weder auf das Neugeborene, noch auf sein (lebendes) Geschwister bezogen zu sein, sondern eher eine Art Verwandtschaftsnumen zu bezeichnen. Weitere (und systematischere) Untersuchungen zu dieser auch religionsgeschichtlich interessanten Problematik wären wünschenswert.

Die Formen *šenni* und *šena* sind bereits in altakkadischer Zeit bezeugt, und zwar in Tell Mozan *Ú-[n]a-ap-šè-ni*[11] und in einer altakkadischen Personennamenliste *Ú-na-ap-šè-na*[12]. In der älteren Zeit ist jedoch eine Form *šen* häufiger; sie findet sich im Namen des in die Gutäer- oder die frühe Ur III-Zeit zu datierenden Königs Atal-šen von Urkeš und Nawar und in dem des Meisters, der Atal-šens Bronzetafel herstellte.[13] Zu den wohl ältesten Belegen für die Verkürzung von *šenni* zu *še* gehört der Name *Túl-bi-ip-še* (IM 85455:1) in einem altakkadischen Brief aus Tall as-Sulaima im Ḥamrīn-Gebiet.[14] In der Ur III-Zeit

---

10 Cf. J.J. Stamm, *Die akkadische Namengebung* (MVAeG 44), Leipzig: J.C. Hinrichs, 1939, 130.

11 L. Milano, *Mozan 2, The Epigraphic Finds of the Sixth Season* (*SMS* 5/1), Malibu: Undena Publications, 1991, 18; 32, M2, 1 obv.? I 4′.

12 A. Westenholz, *Old Sumerian and Old Akkadian Texts in Philadelphia* (BiMes 1), Malibu: Undena Publications, 1975, Nr. 47 V 4; cf. R. Zadok, „Hurrians as well as Individuals Bearing Hurrian and Strange Names in Sumerian Sources", in: A. Rainey (ed.), *kinattūtu ša dārâti. Raphael Kutscher Memorial Volume* (Tel Aviv, Occasional Publications 1), Tel Aviv: Institute of Archaeology, 1993, 227.

13 *A-dal-se-en, Sa-um-se-en* Samarra-Tafel 4; 21; cf. F. Thureau-Dangin, *RA* 9 (1912) 1-3, Tafel; G. Wilhelm, in: V. Haas (ed.), *Hurriter und Hurritisch* (Xenia 21), Konstanz: Universitätsverlag Konstanz, 1988, 47f.

14 Cf. F.N.H. Al-Rawi, „Two Old Akkadian Letters Concerning the Offices of kala'um and nārum", *ZA* 82 (1992) 180-85 (zur Analyse des Namens G. Wilhelm, S. 181, Anm. 13).

sind Namen mit der Kurzform *šen* öfter bezeugt[15]. Der Name des in der Zeit Šulgis tätigen Schreibers *Ú-na-ap-še-en/in*[16] zeigt mitunter auch die Verkürzung von *šen* zu *še*: *Ú-na-ap-šè*[17]. Die verkürzte Form *Ú-na-ap-še* ist während der altbabylonischen Zeit mehrfach in Mari[18] und je einmal in Chagar Bazar[19] und in Tall ar-Rimaḫ[20] bezeugt. In derselben Form und Schreibung begegnet der Name im 15./14. Jh. auch in Nuzi[21] und in Alalaḫ.[22] In Nuzi, wo das Element *šenni* in zahlreichen verschiedenen Namen erscheint, begegnet die Verkürzung *-še* nur bei einigen wenigen Namen, die aber häufig belegt sind (Akap-še, Unap-

---

15 Cf. I.J. Gelb, *Hurrians and Subarians* (SAOC 22), Chicago: The University of Chicago Press, 1944, 109-115.

16 Cf. u.a. E. Keiser, BIN III 591; M. Çığ / H. Kızılyay / A. Salonen, *Die Puzriš-Dagan-Texte der Istanbuler Archäologischen Museen, Teil I: Nrr. 1-725* (AASF B 92), Helsinki 1954, 34, Nr. 94, Siegel; 74, Nr. 235, Siegel; 95, Nr. 312, Siegel; 224, Nr. 597, Siegel; F. Yıldız / T. Gomi, *Die Puzriš-Dagan-Texte der Istanbuler Archäologischen Museen, Teil II: Nr. 726-1379* (FAOS 16), Wiesbaden-Stuttgart: Franz Steiner Verlag, 1988, 181, Nr. 1267, Siegel; T. Gomi, *Orient* 16 (1980) 53, Nr. 46, Siegel; M. Sigrist, *Textes économiques néo-sumériens de l'Université de Syracuse* (Mémoire n° 29), Paris: Éditions Recherche sur les Civilisations, 1983, Nr. 202, Siegel; 204, Siegel. - Cf. auch R. Zadok, l.c., 228ff.

17 Cf. D.I. Owen, *Mesopotamia* 8-9 (1973/74) 147f., Text Nr. 3 obv. 3 und Siegel; G. Frame / D.R. Frayne / G. McEwan, „Cuneiform Texts in the Collections of McGill University, Montreal", *ARRIM* 7 (1989) 9 Nr. 6:4 und Siegel.

Daß *še* tatsächlich eine Verkürzung von *šenni* ist, geht auch aus dem Wechsel mit der logographischen Schreibung ŠEŠ im Vertrag Šuppiluliumas I. mit Šattiwaza hervor, wo das von einem hethitischen Schreiber geschriebene Exemplar KBo I 1 Vs. 38 und 39 ᵐ*Šar-ru-up-ši* bietet, während das Exemplar KBo I 2, das eine mittanische Handschrift zeigt, in Vs. 21' ᵐ*Šar-ru-up*-ŠEŠ, in Vs. 20' ᵐ*Šar-ru-up-še* schreibt. Der volle Name liegt vor in *Šar-ru-up-še-en-ni* Al.T. *64:12, *-še-ni* 189:49 (= SSAU IV Nr. 8), 194:28 (= SSAU IV Nr. 1) (die Kurzform ist aber ebenfalls in Alalaḫ bezeugt, und zwar vereinzelt schon in Schicht VII: Al.T. 148:56 [= SSAU II Nr. 9], 149:35 [= SSAU II Nr. 31], 214+217:36 [= SSAU V Nr. 25], *376:9); vgl. auch die Formen mit hethitischen Endungen *Šarrup-šenn-a-š/n* (Nom., Akk.); cf. E. Laroche, *Les noms des Hittites*, Paris: Librairie C. Klincksieck, 1966, 160, Nr. 1131.

[Zitate von Texten aus Alalaḫ (Al.T.) erfolgen nach D.J. Wiseman, *The Alalakh Tablets*, London: The British Institute of Archaeology at Ankara, 1953; soweit dort keine Kopie geboten wird, außerdem nach D.J. Wiseman, *JCS* 8 [1954] 1ff. und nach M. Dietrich / O. Loretz, „Die soziale Struktur von Alalaḫ und Ugarit" (= SSAU) (II) *WO* 5 (1969) 57-93, (IV) *ZA* 60 (1970) 88-123, (V) *UF* 1 (1969) 37-64.]

18 Cf. M. Birot, *RA* 47 (1953) 129; J.M. Sasson, *UF* 6 (1974) 371 s.v.

19 C.J. Gadd, *Iraq* 7 (1940) 42a.

20 S. Dalley / C.B.F. Walker / J.D. Hawkins, *The Old Babylonian Tablets from Tell al Rimah* (= OBTR), [London]: British School of Archaeology in Iraq, 1976, Nr. 317:1.

21 *NPN* 164 (JENu 285 = JEN 702:28); *AAN* 157; außerdem EN 9/1, 37:15.

22 Al.T. 180:13 (= *JCS* 8, 11); 197:7; cf. auch das Hypokoristikon *Ú-na-ap-še-ia* Al.T. 214+217:42 (= SSAU V Nr. 25). In Alalaḫ ist außerdem die Schreibung *Ú-nam-še* bezeugt: Al.T. 133:24, 144:2, 148:6 (= SSAU II Nr. 16, 2, 9).

še, Utḫap-še, Wantiš-še); dies spricht dafür, daß die Verkürzung zu dieser Zeit nicht mehr produktiv war.[23]

2. **Eḫli-Ad(d)u** (Eġli-Addu): Das PN-Element *eḫl-* (*eġl-*) ist seit der altbabylonischen Zeit bezeugt[24]. Die Wurzel ist durch logographische Schreibungen mit KAR „retten"[25], durch die Entsprechung von hurr. *eġelli* (*e-ḫe-el-e*)[26] und akk. *šūzubu* in der Bezeichnung einer Sozialklasse in Alalaḫ[27], durch die lexikalische Gleichung KA[R = …] = *eḫ-lu-um-me* = *ḫu*-PI-*ú*[28] sowie durch die Wiedergabe mit heth. *ḫuišnu-* „am Leben erhalten, retten" in der hurr.-heth. Bilingue aus Boğazköy[29] als „verlassen lassen[30]; retten" bestimmt. Neben dem Namenstyp

---

23 Die von *NPN* 253a fragend angeführten Fälle von Wechsel zwischen verkürzten und unverkürzten Namen bei Personenidentität bleiben zweifelhaft.

24 Mari: u.a. *Eḫ-li-ia* ARM XIII 139:18, *Eḫ-li-ip-a-dal* M. 10539:7, cf. M. Bonechi, in: J.-M. Durand (ed.), *Florilegium marianum, Fs. M. Fleury* (Mém. de N.A.B.U. 1), Paris 1992, 14; ARM VII 113:11; cf. D. Charpin / J.M. Durand, *M.A.R.I.* 2 (1983) 79; *Eḫ-li-ip-šar-ri*, cf. J.M. Sasson, *UF* 6 (1974) 359; Ebla: *Eḫ-li-ia* TM.76.G.412:16, cf. J.-R. Kupper, *SEb* II/4-5 (1980) 50 und Fig. 13f.; Tall ar-Rimāḥ: *Eḫ-li-ia* OBTR 229:10; Alalaḫ VII: s.u.

25 In Alalaḫ z.B. KAR-^{d}*Iš-ḫa-ra* // *Eḫ-li-Iš-ḫa-ra*, cf. B. Landsberger, *JCS* 8 (1954) 57 Anm. 111; A.E. Draffkorn(-Kilmer), *Hurrians and Hurrian at Alalaḫ: An Ethno-Linguistic Analysis*, Philadelphia: Dissertation, University of Pennsylvania, 1959, 28f.; in Ugarit: ^{f}KAR-^{d}*Ni-ik-ka-lu* // ^{f}*Eḫ-li-*^{d}*Ni-ik-ka-lu*, cf. E. Laroche, *Les noms des Hittites*, 52; F. Gröndahl, *Die Personennamen der Texte aus Ugarit* (StPohl 1), Roma: Pontificium Institutum Biblicum, 1967, 214, 324.

26 *eġelli* erscheint im Sg. mit akkadischer Deklinationsendung als ^{lú}*e-ḫe-el-lu* Al.T. 211:47 (= SSAU V, Nr. 7; cf. auch *e-ḫe-el-li* ibid. Z. 61) oder mit der gebrochenen Schreibung *-el-e*, die anscheinend ebenfalls Doppelkonsonanz anzeigt: 1-*en e-ḫé-el-e* Al.T. 133:37 (= SSAU II, Nr. 16). Dieselbe Schreibung weisen fast alle Pluralformen auf: *e-ḫé-el-e-na* Al.T. 129:44, 131:45, 132:22, 31, 133:34, 136:40, 54, 143:26, 144:18, 148:52, 62, A 59:21 (alle SSAU II) sowie Al.T. 189:20 (= SSAU IV, Nr. 8). Die Doppelkonsonanz und der anaptyktische Vokal *e* machen deutlich, daß hier noch ein bisher übersehenes Suffix vorliegt, und zwar wahrscheinlich das Berufsbezeichnungen bildende Suffix *-li*, das direkt an die Wurzel treten kann (cf. dazu G. Wilhelm, *SMEA* 29 [1992] 242f.): **eġl=li* > *eġel=li*. Im Absolutiv Sg. würde man statt des tatsächlich einmal bezeugten *e-ḫé-el-e* eine auf *i* auslautende Form erwarten; möglicherweise ist hier die Auslautschreibung von der viel häufigeren Pluralform beeinflußt, die die reguläre Öffnung und Dehnung unter Akzent (R=*i* : R=*ḗ=na*) zeigt. Der Ansatz einer Singularform **eġele* (so M. Dietrich / O. Loretz, *WO* 5 [1969] 92 und passim), die sich morphologisch aus der Wurzel *eġl-* oder der Nominalbildung *eġli* nicht ableiten ließe, ist demnach aufzugeben.

27 Cf. B. Landsberger, *JCS* 8 (1954) 57 Anm. 111; M. Dietrich / O. Loretz, *WO* 5 (1969) 92.

28 E. Laroche, *Ugaritica* 5 (1968) 456; J. Huehnergard, *Ugaritic Vocabulary in Syllabic Transcription* (HSS 32), Atlanta: Scholars Press, 1987, 81f.

29 *e-ḫe-el*$_{5}$*-le-wa*⸢$_{a}$⸣*-aš-ša* (< **eġl=i=l=eva=ž=nna* „wir wollen ihn retten") // *na-an-kán ḫu-*⸢*iš*⸣*-nu-mi-ni* KBo 32,15 Vs. I/II 18′; cf. E. Neu, *Or*NS 59 (1990) 225; G. Wilhelm, *Or*NS 61 (1992) 139.

30 Zu dieser Bedeutung ist sicherlich der Infinitiv *e-*⸢*eḫ*⸣?*-lu-um-ma* DÙ.MEŠ IM 70740, zitiert von K. Deller, *WO* 9 (1978) 300, zu stellen, der die Entlassung aus einem *tidennūtu*-Verhältnis bezeichnet.

Eġl=i-GN ist in Nuzi auch der Typ *Eġl=i=b/p*-GN bezeugt (z.T. mit Metathese *elġ-*). In *Eġli*-GN ist nicht etwa *-b/p-* assimiliert, denn dieser Typ ist wie im hier zu besprechenden *Eġli-Ad(d)u* auch bei vokalisch anlautenden theophoren Elementen bezeugt, und außerdem ist bei solchen GN, die mit *t*, *k* oder *n* anlauten, in keinem Falle eine graphische Verdopplung zur Darstellung der Assimilation anzutreffen (stets *Eḫ-li-te-šup*, nie **Eḫ-li-it-te-šup* wie z.B. bei *A-ki-it-te-šup* neben *A-kip-te-šup* und *A-ki-te-šup*; cf. *NPN* 198b). Auch die Formen mit Synkope und Anaptyxe *E-ḫe-el*-GN (cf. *NPN* 209a) sprechen dafür, daß diese Namen nicht mit der *b*-Form gebildet sind. Da die Formen ohne *-b/p-* bereits altbabylonisch bezeugt sind, können sie nicht als jüngere Entwicklung (Verlust von *-b/p* wie häufig in Namen des 14. und 13. Jhds. v.Chr.[31]) verstanden werden. E. Laroche erklärte den Typ *Eġli*-GN als Nominalsatz unter Heranziehung des Nomens *eġli*[32], das in hurritischen Texten aus Ḫattuša gut bezeugt ist.[33] Seine Deutung von *eġli* als „salut", „Heil"[34] ist allerdings unbegründet, seine Interpretation der *b*-Formen[35] im Lichte unserer heutigen Kenntnis der Struktur hurritischer Satznamen obsolet. Das Substantiv *eġli* zeigt dieselbe Struktur wie *ḫan=i* „Kind" von *ḫan-* „gebären", *ḫalv=i* „Umfriedung" von *ḫalv-* „umfrieden", *ḫezm=i* „Gürtel" von *ḫezm-* „sich gürten" etc. Seine Bedeutung ist wegen der genitivischen Verknüpfung mit Wörtern wie *en(i)=na* „Götter", *šarri* „(Götter-)König" und dem Gottesnamen „Teššob" gewiß „Rettung", nicht „Retter"[36]. Ein Name mit der Bedeutung *"GN ist die Rettung" wäre vielleicht denkbar; wahrscheinlicher ist jedoch eine bisher nicht erwogene Deutung, die *eġl=i* als Imperativ „rette!" auffaßt (wie *ar=i* „gib", *pal=i* „wisse") und damit einen Namenstyp ansetzt, der im Akkadischen Parallelen in Šūzib-GN und Eṭir-GN[37] „Rette, GN!" hat. Schließlich sind die verhältnismäßig wenigen Namen mit der transitiv-ergativischen Form *eġl=o=m* „er rettete ihn" zu nennen: *Eḫ-lum*-AN Al.T. 148:18, *Eḫ-lu-me-ni* (*eġl=o=m - en=ni*) Al.T. 150:13, 17; *Eḫ-lu-up*-LUGAL[38] Al.T. 132:23.

---

31 Cf. G. Wilhelm, „Zum hurritischen Verbalsystem", 669.

32 E. Laroche, in: *Ugaritica* 5 (1968) 456.

33 Cf. z.B. ᵈU-*up eḫ-li-bi* „Teššob der Rettung" ChS I/1 Nr. 3 Vs. 47; *šarri=ne=da eġli=bi=ne=da* „dem (Götter-)König der Rettung" ChS I/1 Nr. 2 Rs. 23′; für weitere Belege cf. E. Laroche, *GLH* 76 und V. Haas, ChS I/1, 347.

34 E. Laroche *apud* J. Friedrich, *HethWb*, 3. Erg., 1966, 48; idem, *Les noms des Hittites*, 351; idem, in: *Ugaritica* 5 (1968) 456; idem, *GLH* 75; M. Dietrich / O. Loretz, *OLZ* 52 (1967) 546 („Heil"); N. Oettinger, *Glotta* 59 (1981) 7 (übersetzt Eġli-Teššob als „(Gott) Tešub (ist) Gruß"), H. Freydank / M. Salvini, *SMEA* 24 (1984) 38 („Heil") u.a.m.

35 E. Laroche, *Ugaritica* 5 (1968) 456 (*b* als Possessivsuffix der 1. Ps. Sg.).

36 E. Laroche, ibid., nennt als mögliche Bedeutung „*sauveur*".

37 Cf. Stamm, *Die akkadische Namengebung*, 170.

38 Zu der Lautentwicklung *m* > *p* vor *š* cf. G. Wilhelm, „Zum hurritischen Verbalsystem", 668.

Der Typ *Eǧli*-GN ist im ganzen hurritischen Sprachraum bezeugt[39], doch scheint er vor allem im Westen stark verbreitet gewesen zu sein, und zwar besonders in Alalaḫ. Als theophore Elemente erscheinen hier die Götter Addu[40], Ammu[41], An[42], Appu[43], Aštabi[44], Išḫara[45], Kūbī[46], Kuža(ġ)[47], Šarruma[48], Teššob (oder ebenfalls Addu)[49]. In Ugarit begegnen Namen dieses Typs u.a. mit den Gottheiten Kužuġ und Nikkal[50], in Emar mit dem Mondgott in seiner für

39 Für Nuzi cf. *NPN* 209a; mA sind noch einige wenige zugehörige Namen belegt, darunter ein *Eḫ-li-Ḫa-bur*; cf. H. Freydank / C. Saporetti, *Nuove attestazioni dell'onomastica medio-assira*, Roma: Edizioni dell'Ateneo & Bizzarri, 1979, 49; H. Freydank / M. Salvini, *SMEA* 24 (1984) 38.

40 *Eḫ-li-a-du* Al.T. *20:14 (= *JCS* 8, 5, und F. Zeeb, *UF* 24 [1992] 478), *36:4, *60:rev.12, *63:17 (*-ú*), *205:27,28 (= *JCS* 8, 14), *238:38, *249:2,12 (= *JCS* 8, 17), *-lì-* *265:6 (= *JCS* 8, 21), *268:21 (= *JCS* 8, 21), *270:5 (= *JCS* 8, 21), *-lì-* *274:16 (= *JCS* 8, 22), *384:2,4. – *Eḫ-li-ia-du* Al.T. 192:29 (= SSAU IV, Nr. 9).

41 *Eḫ-lam-mu* Al.T. 148:25 (= SSAU II, Nr. 9), 214+217:6 (= SSAU V, Nr. 25), A 81/9:22 (= SSAU V, Nr. 17), *-un* Al.T. 144:8 (= SSAU II, Nr. 2).

42 *Eḫ-li-ia-an* Al.T. 197:18 (= SSAU IV, Nr. 17).

43 *Eḫ-la-ap-pu* Al.T. 130:8 (= SSAU II, Nr. 6), 143:2 (= SSAU II, Nr. 14).

44 *Eḫ-li-aš/eš-ta-bi*, cf. Draffkorn, *Hurrians and Hurrian at Alalaḫ*, 27, sowie Al.T. 137:17 (= SSAU II, Nr. 17), 200:6 (= SSAU IV, Nr. 14).

45 *Eḫ-li-*[(d)]*Iš-ḫa-ra*, *Eḫ-li-IŠTAR(-ra)*, KAR-[d]*Iš-ḫa-ra*, cf. Draffkorn, *Hurrians and Hurrian at Alalaḫ*, 28, sowie Al.T. 129:13, 21 (= SSAU II, Nr. 18), 131:30 (= SSAU II, Nr. 1), 191:7 (= SSAU IV, Nr. 2), 195:24 (= SSAU IV, Nr. 6), 197:16 (= SSAU IV, Nr. 17).

46 *Eḫ-li-*[d]*Ku-bi*, KAR-[d]*Ku-bi*, cf. Draffkorn, *Hurrians and Hurrian at Alalaḫ*, 28, sowie Al.T. 129:15 (= SSAU II, Nr. 18), 131:37 (= SSAU II, Nr. 1), A 75:4 (= SSAU II, Nr. 24).

47 KAR-[d]30, KAR-[d]*Ku-š[a]*, *Eḫ-lik-ku-ša*, cf. Draffkorn, *Hurrians and Hurrian at Alalaḫ*, 28, sowie Al.T. 137:4 (= SSAU II, Nr. 17), 138:11 (= SSAU II, Nr. 5), 139:23 (= SSAU II, Nr. 11), 143:5, 32 (= SSAU II, Nr. 14), 144:11 (= SSAU II, Nr. 2), 146:2 (= SSAU IV, Nr. 3), 149:41 (= SSAU II, Nr. 31), 198:28 (= SSAU IV, Nr. 13), 214+217:48 (= SSAU V, Nr. 25), A 30+47:16 (= SSAU IV, Nr. 11).

48 KAR-*šar-ru-ma* Al.T. 197:14 (= SSAU IV, Nr. 17); denselben Namen in der Schreibung *Eḫ-li-*LUGAL-*ma* trägt auch ein König von Išuwa; cf. Laroche, *Les noms des Hittites*, 52, Nr. 229.

49 *Eḫ-li-*[d]IŠKUR, KAR-[d]IŠKUR, cf. Draffkorn, *Hurrians and Hurrian at Alalaḫ*, 28f., sowie Al.T. 131:43 (= SSAU II, Nr. 1), 137:6 (= SSAU II, Nr. 17), 138:38 (= SSAU II, Nr. 5), 143:27 (= SSAU II, Nr. 14), 189:26 (= SSAU IV, Nr. 8), A 30+47:12 (= SSAU IV, Nr. 11), A 80/23:12 (= SSAU IV, Nr. 28).

50 KAR-[d]30 RS 16.276:5, 13, 17, 23, cf. PRU III, S. 69f.; [f]*Eḫ-li-*[(d)]*Ni-ik-ka-lu* RS 17.226:3, 6, cf. PRU IV S. 208, [f]KAR-[(d)]*Ni-ik-ka-lu* RS 17.355:2, 13, 15, 19, cf. PRU IV, S. 209, cf. Gröndahl, *Die Personennamen der Texte aus Ugarit*, 324.

Alalaḫ typischen Form Kuža(ġ)[51] und in Ḫattuša gleichfalls mit dem Mondgott[52] sowie mit Šarruma[53] und Teššob[54].

Der Name Eġli-Addu ist anscheinend nur in Alalaḫ, hier aber — vor allem in Schicht VII — sehr häufig belegt, und zwar oft in derselben Schreibung wie in kt k/k 4. Damit ist, wie schon K. Hecker in seinem vorstehenden Aufsatz gesehen hat, ein wichtiges Argument für die Herkunft der Tafel aus einem nordsyrischen Milieu gegeben.

3. Der Name **Duḫušmati**, bei dem der erste Bestandteil *d/t/ṭuḫ(ḫ)uš* keine Bestimmung als akkadischer *mātum*-Name[55] zuläßt, könnte von seiner Struktur her gut hurritisch sein: Das Vorderglied könnte eine Form auf *-o/už* sein wie in Aluš-tae und Tambuš-kiba (für beide cf. *NPN* s.v.), eine Wurzel *tuḫ-* ist zwar selten, aber immerhin bezeugt.[56] Das Hinterglied könnte das wohlbekannte Namenselement *madi*[57] sein. Da aber weder der Name als ganzer noch das Vorderglied anderweitig bezeugt zu sein scheinen, wird man angesichts kültepezeitlich-anatolischer Namen wie *Du-ḫu-ší-li/lì* und *Du-ḫu-ší-ip-ḫa*[58] auch anatolische Herkunft in Betracht ziehen müssen.

4. Der Ortsname **Zipuḫuliwe** (*Sib=o=ġ(e)=o/u=li=ve*) gehört zu den verbreiteten hurritischen Ortsnamen, die aus einem Personennamen oder — selten — einer Berufsbezeichnung im Genitiv bestehen[59]. Im vorliegenden Fall

---

51 *Eḫ-li-Ku-ša* Msk. 731005:3, Msk. 731016:47 = D. Arnaud, *Textes sumériens et accadiens* (Recherches au pays d'Aštata. *Emar* VI.1), Paris: Éditions Recherche sur les Civilisations, 1985, S. 74, S. 87 = *Emar* VI.3, 1986, Nr. 144; 137.

Eḫ-li-Ku-ša: D. Arnaud, *Textes Syriens de l'âge du Bronze récent* (AuOr Suppl. 1), Sabadell-Barcelona: Editorial Ausa, 1991, 16:45 und sonst.

*Eḫ-li-*ᵈ30 ibid. Nr. 37:7.

52 *Eḫ-li-*ᵈ30*(-aš)*: Cf. Laroche, *Les noms des Hittites*, 52 (583/d+ = KBo 18,153 Rs. 14); cf. ᵈ*Eḫ-li-*[...] KUB 56,1 Rs. IV 1′.

53 *Eḫ-li-*LUGAL*-ma*: Laroche, *Les noms des Hittites*, 52.

54 *E-ḫal-*ᵈU*-up* (aus Ḫalab), *E-ḫal-Te-eš*: Laroche, *Les noms des Hittites*, 52.

55 Zu diesen Namen cf. Stamm, *Die akkadische Namengebung*, 79f.

56 *tu-u-ḫu-u-ši* ChS I/1 Nr. 41 Vs. II 45 (= KBo 15,73 Vs. II 33′).

57 Cf. *NPN* 233f.; Der dort zitierte Bedeutungsansatz von C.-G. von Brandenstein („Verstand, Sinn“) kann jetzt auf Grund der hurr.-heth. Bilingue aus Boğazköy, die *madi* mit heth. *ḫattatar* wiedergibt, präzisiert werden; cf. E. Neu, *Das Hurritische: Eine altorientalische Sprache in neuem Licht*, Mainz/Stuttgart: Steiner-Verlag, 1988, 19 mit Anm. 52.

58 Cf. Laroche, *Les noms des Hittites*, 187f.

59 Cf. J. Fincke, *Die Orts- und Gewässernamen der Nuzi-Texte* (RGTC 10), Wiesbaden: Dr. Ludwig Reichert, 1993, XVIIIf. Für Berufsbezeichnungen als Basis von ONn cf. URU *Paḫḫar(i)=r(a)=aš=fe* „Stadt der Töpfer“ cf. J. Fincke, l.c. 211f., URU *Tupšarri=(ne=)ve* „Stadt des Schreibers“ ibid. 302f.

ist der Suffixkomplex der Berufsbezeichnungen auf *-uḫ(u)li* (*-o=ġ(e)=(o/u=)li*)[60] leicht erkennbar. Solche Berufsbezeichnungen werden in Alalaḫ und sonst vereinzelt auch als Personennamen verwendet[61]. Da der Suffixkomplex mit dem Adjektivsuffix *-ġe* nach Derivativvokal einsetzt, kann er nur an Nomina antreten.[62] Als Ausgangswort darf daher ein *sibV* angesetzt werden. Ein solches Wort ist tatsächlich vereinzelt — auch in Ableitungen — bezeugt[63], doch ist seine Bedeutung aus dem Kontext nicht zu ermitteln. Ob in Zipuḫuliwe die normale Form ohne den Derivativvokal vor *-li* oder die in Alalaḫ charakteristische Form auf *-uḫuli* = *-o=ġ(e)=o/u=li* vorliegt, ist nicht zu entscheiden, da im Genitiv der Relator *-ne-* erscheinen kann und in diesem Falle das regelhafte Ergebnis von Synkope, Anaptyxe und Assimilation (-V_1C*li*+*ne*- > -V_1CV_1*l*+*le*-) formal mit der Alalaḫ-Form übereinstimmen würde. Ein Beispiel hierfür ist der in Boğazköy bezeugte Genitiv der Berufsbezeichnung *taloġli* (*taluḫli*): *t*]*a*-⌜*al*⌝-*lu*-*ḫu-ul-le-wi$_i$* ChS I/5 Nr. 2 Vs. 22′ = KBo 23, 23 Vs. 4′ (*tal(l)=o=ġ=o=l(i)=l(<n)e =vi*)[64].

Ein — auch in der Wurzel — ganz ähnlicher Ortsname ist in Alalaḫ IV bezeugt: [uru]*Za-pu-ḫu-li-e* Al.T. 187:18; [...-*p*]*u-ḫu-li-e* A 78/2:10. Es ist nicht auszuschließen, daß dieser Name auf den mindestens 300 Jahre früher bezeugten Namen Zipuḫuliwe zurückgeht. Wie dem auch sei, deutet jedenfalls auch der Ortsname wiederum auf eine Nähe der Tafel kt k/k 4/4 zu Alalaḫ. Darüberhinaus zeigt er, daß die hurritische Sprache in der Kültepe-Ib-Zeit in Nordsyrien bereits die Toponomastik beeinflussen konnte.

---

60 Zur Analyse dieser Suffixkomplexe cf. G. Wilhelm, „Hurritische Berufsbezeichnungen auf *-li*", *SMEA* 29 (1992) 239-44.

61 m*Ta-ku-ḫu-li/u* Al.T. 131:25 (= SSAU II, Nr. 1), 197:10 (= SSAU IV, Nr. 17), 195:28 (= SSAU IV, Nr. 6) und sonst; m*Ta-ku-uḫ-li-* (mittanischer General) KBo 5,6 Vs. II 17; cf. Laroche, *Les noms des Hittites*, 170f., Nr. 1215; m*Ta-ku-uḫ-li* HSS 15,32:2, 12.

62 Cf. G. Wilhelm, l.c., 243.

63 *sib=i: zi-bi* (Absolutiv) ChS I/1 Nr. 2 Vs. 22′; vielleicht auch ChS I/5 Nr. 2 Vs. 33′ (oder verbunden mit folgendem *zu-ḫu-úw-wu$_ú$*); *si-pa* (Essiv) ChS I/1 Nr. 43 Rs. III 27′;
sib=ar=i: zi-pa-ri-pa (mit iterativer Wurzelerweiterung, Dat.) ChS I/1 Nr. 5 Vs. II 32;
sib=ir(i)=ni: zi-bi-ir-ni (agensorientiertes Partizip mit Suffix *-ni*(?); cf. *tabirni* „Schmied") ChS I/1 Nr. 50 Vs.? 16′, 17′.

64 Cf. V. Haas, in: V. Haas (ed.), *Hurriter und Hurritisch* (Xenia 21), Konstanz: Universitätsverlag Konstanz, 1988, 122f. Cf. auch die dort zitierten Pluralformen aus Nuzi: *taloġolla* (< **taloġli=na*): *ta-lu-ḫul-la(-a)* AdŠ 17:50, 106:19, 109:47, 115:10, 116:31, 119:27, *-ḫu-ul-* 118:8 (jeweils nach akk. *ana*) im Kontrast zu dem Singular *a-na* PN *ta-lu-uḫ$_5$-li* AdŠ 24:39 und dem akk. Plural *a-na* 8 LÚ.MEŠ *ta-lu-uḫ-*⌜*le*⌝*-e* AdŠ 120:21.

Part III

Nuzi Notes, 18-35

Nuzi Notes

18. A new word in *-arbu*: *kirarbu*

It is well known that Hurrian has special numbers for the age of animals formed by a suffix *-arbu* (presumably with the Akkadian nominative ending *-u*). Until now, they have shown up only in the Nuzi tablets where the following forms are attested: *šinarbu* "2-years-old," *kigarbu* "3-years-old," *tumnarbu* "4-years-old," *nariyarbu* "5-years-old,"[1] and *šindarbu* "7-years-old." On the basis of the known cardinal numbers, we might reconstruct **šukk/garbu* "1-year-old,"[2] **šežarbu* "6-years-old,"[3] **tamrarbu* "9-years-old,"[4] and **emanarbu* "10-years-old." The word for "8" has not yet been detected.

The Nuzi fragment SMN 1409 = EN 10/1, 13 contains another form ending with *-arbu*. The first three lines of the poorly preserved tablet read:

Vs. 1 1 ANŠE.KUR.RA MUNUS *ki-ra-ar-pu*()
2 *mi-ša-ma-at-tu*$_4$
3 ⸢*ù*⸣ x[x x (x)]x-*šu ia-nu*

The first preserved line of the reverse ends with another number in *-arbu*, which unfortunately is not fully preserved ( *-ar-pu*). The word *mišamattu* appears here for the first time.

The only number between 1 and 10 still unknown is "8." A meaning "eight-year-old" would be acceptable considering the age of a horse. Another expla-

---

1 Cf. G. Wilhelm, *SMEA* 24 (1984) 223-24.

2 For *šukki* "once" cf. E. Neu, *Hethitica* 9 (1988) 163; idem, *Das Hurritische: Eine altorientalische Sprache in neuem Licht*, Mainz/Stuttgart 1989, 298; cf. also Ch. Girbal, *ZA* 78 (1988) 124 for *šukkanni* "a single," and G. Wilhelm, *ZA* 77 (1987) 235 n. 21 for *šug/kkamġa* (*šug/kk=am=ġ(e)=a*: R=factitive=adjective=essive) as a number adverb (now to be translated as "single").

3 For *šeže* "6" cf. E. Neu, "Neue Wege im Hurritischen," in: E. von Schuler (ed.) *XXIII. Deutscher Orientalistentag* (*ZDMG* Suppl. VII), Stuttgart: Steiner 1989, 298.

4 For *tamri* "9" cf. E. Neu, l.c.

Studies on the Civilization and Culture of Nuzi and the Hurrians - 8

nation would start from the frequently attested word *ke/irV* with its derivatives *ke/irae* (adverb) and *keraššе* "long" (in time), "lasting."[5] The meaning "aged" for animals, however, is represented by the word *sillonni* (*zi-il-lu-un-ni*).[6] [In an article to appear in *SCCNH* 9, M. Giorgieri and I. Röseler will argue for a number *kir-* attested in *kirmana* and *kirmanzeni* KBo 32, 20 Vs. I 5′, 11′.]

G. Wilhelm

19. Hurrian **ašar* "gate"

J. Puhvel explains the Hittite word ^{GIŠ}*araša-, araši-*, for which he adopts the meaning "door," as a loanword from an alleged Hurrian *ašar* "gate, door."[7] Since this etymology seems to find some credit,[8] it is not superfluous to point out that it is based on a misunderstanding of a passage in a Nuzi text. Puhvel does not quote the source for the alleged Hurrian word, but it is evidently J. Friedrich, *HethWb* 320, who refers to E.R. Lacheman's contribution to the Nuzi excavation report.[9] Unfortunately, Lacheman in his essay often does not quote the texts he used. In the case of the passage quoted here, he used SMN 3091 which in 1962 (after the publication of Friedrich's *HethWb*) he published as HSS 19, 96. The relevant passage is the *šaṭir*-clause:

17 *ṭup-pu i-na* <EGIR-*ki*> *šu-du-ti i+na*
18 *pa-ni* KÁ.GAL *a*$^{!}$*-šar du-ri-we*
19 *ina* URU *Nu-zi ša*$_{10}$*-ṭì-ir*

---

5 Cf. E. Laroche, *GLH* 143 sub *keri*.

6 Cf. W. von Soden, *WO* 6 (1971) 255f. (For another attestation [Jank. 59:1] cf. V. Haas / G. Wilhelm, *Or*NS 41 (1972) 7f.; the interpretation of *s*. given there can no longer stand.) v. Soden's emendation of HSS 16 453:1 = AASOR 16 86:1 (=*AdŠ* 443 forthcoming) requires modification, since there is a trace visible () before the break which does not fit *u*[*n*, but is perhaps best read as *n*[*a*.

7 J. Puhvel, *Hittite Etymological Dictionary*, vol. 1 and 2, Berlin: Mouton de Gruyter, 1984, 128.

8 Cf. H.C. Melchert, *Anatolian Historical Phonology*, Amsterdam: Editions Rodopi, 1994, 170 sub (3).

9 E.R. Lacheman, "Epigraphic Evidence of the Material Culture of the Nuzians," in: R.F.S. Starr, *Nuzi*, vol. I, Cambridge: Harvard University Press, 1939, 528-44; p. 530: "There was also a "southern gate" (*abullu šupālu*, and its Hurrian equivalent *ašar du-ri-we*) ...."

"The tablet has been written <after> the proclamation in front of the western gate in the city of Nuzi."

ašar is the Akkadian preposition, which in this context is unusual.[10] The normal construction is found in the Akkadian equivalent of the same location mentioned in HSS 19,46:

55 *ṭup-pí i+na* EGIR-*ki šu-du-ti i+na*!(text: *ša*) KÁ KÁ.GAL
56 *ša šu-pa-li i+na* URU *Nu-zi ša*$_{10}$*-ṭi*$_{4}$*-ir*

"The tablet has been written after the proclamation at the entrance of the western gate in the city of Nuzi."

The meaning of Hurrian *turi* "low" has been established by F. Thureau-Dangin, *Syria* 12 (1931) 248.[11] The meaning "west" is the equivalent of Akkadian *šupālu* "low," which in Nuzi is used as a point of the compass (Hurr. *turišḫe*[12]), as opposed to *elēnu* "east" (Hurr. *pabaḫḫe* "mountainous") . Both meanings are evidently derived from the geographical situation of the areas east of the Tigris.

G. Wilhelm

20. HSS 14, 60 incorrectly joined

The copy of HSS 14, 60 clearly shows that the text has been reconstructed from two fragments which do not fit together very well. The catalogue on p. xi of the same volume, however, attributes only one museum number to both fragments (SMN 3392), which suggests that the fragments have been brought together rather early, maybe already during the excavations. A study of the content of both fragments and an autopsy of the original in the Harvard Semitic Museum leads to the result that the fragments do not belong together.

Both fragments, which we suggest to label "SMN 3392a" and "SMN 3392b," belong to the lists of grain rations for the royal court. Like SMN 3392b, these texts usually commence with the rations for the horses of the GÌR.MEŠ LUGAL; cf. e.g.:

---

10 For a parallel cf. EN 9/1, 381:18-20: *ṭup-pu ina b*[*á-ab*] KÁ.GAL U[RU] *Nu-zi a-ša*[*r šu-p*]*a-li* [*ša*$_{(10)}$-*ṭ*]*ì-i*[*r*].

11 Cf. also E. Laroche, in: K. Bittel e.a. (ed.), *Anatolian Studies Presented to Hans Gustav Güterbock on the Occasion of his 65th Birthday* (Uitgaven 35), İstanbul: Nederlands Historisch-Archaeologisch Instituut in het Nabije Oosten, 1974, 180-183; idem, *GLH* 273; for *du-ú-ri-a* / / heth. *kat-ta-an-ta* "down to" KBo 32, 14 Rs. 35 / / 41 cf. E. Neu, in: *Festschrift für Sedat Alp*, 396; idem, *IstMitt* 43 [*Fs. Neve*] (1993) 60; V. Haas / I. Wegner, *IstMitt* 43 [*Fs. Neve*] (1993) 54; for *du-ú-ri* / / heth. *kat-ta-an-ta* KBo 32, 13 Vs. I/II 10 cf. E. Neu, in: *Festschrift für Sedat Alp*, 393f.

12 Cf. F.R. Steele, *JAOS* 61 (1941) 286-87.

HSS 14, 46: 1 [2]$^{?}$ ANŠE 1 (PI) 1 BÁN ŠE.MEŠ *a-*˹*na*˺ ANŠE.KUR.RA.MEŠ

2 [*š*]*a* GÌR.MEŠ LUGAL *a-na* 2 UD-*mi*

HSS 14, 48: 1 7 ANŠE 2 BÁN ŠE.MEŠ *a-na* 6 UD-*mi*

2 *a-*˹*na*˺ ANŠE.KUR.RA.MEŠ *ša* GÌR.MEŠ LUGAL

HSS 14, 49: 1 6 ANŠE 5$^{?}$ B[ÁN ŠE.MEŠ *a-na* 5$^{?}$ UD-*mi*]

2 ˹*a-na*˺ ˹ANŠE.KUR˺.RA.M[EŠ *ša* GÌR.MEŠ LUGAL]

SMN 3392a (measurements: 49 x 44 x 23 mm):

Obv. 1 [4$^{?}$+]˹4˺ ANŠE 4 BÁN ŠE.MEŠ

2 [*a-n*]*a* ANŠE.KUR.[R]A.MEŠ

3 [*a-n*]*a* 6 UD-*mi*.MEŠ

4 [x+]2 ANŠE ŠE.MEŠ

5 [*a-na* Z]ÍD.DA.MEŠ

6 [*a-na* ^{m}*Ut-ḫ*]*áp-ta-e*

7 [x x x Š]E *a-na* NUMUN

(rest of obverse destroyed)

Rev. (beginning of reverse destroyed)

8 [x ANŠE 2 BÁ]N ŠE

9 [*ša na-a*]*d*$^{?}$*-nu*

---

10 [x BÁN] ŠE *a-na* MUNUS.LUGAL

11 ˹*i+na*˺ ITI-*ḫi Mi-*˹*ti*˺*-ru-un-ni*

Concerning the fragment SMN 3392b (measurements: 49 x 66 x 27 mm), which appears as the lower part of HSS 14, obverse and reverse have to be changed; the text now reads:

Obv. 1 [6+]3 ANŠE ŠE *a-na* ANŠE.KUR.RA<MEŠ>

2 *ša* GÌR.MEŠ LUGAL *a-na* 8 UD-*mi*

3 10 ANŠE 1 (PI) 2 BÁN ŠE *a-na*

4 *ba-la-li ù a-na* x x[

5 *a-na* MUNUS.MEŠ *ša* ˹URU˺ Z[*i-iz-za*]

6 1 ANŠE 2 BÁN Š[E

7 x x[

(rest of obv. destroyed)

Rev. (beginning of rev. destroyed)

8 1 A[NŠE

9 *a-na i-*x[

10 1 ANŠE ŠE *a-na* [

11 *a-na* MUNUS.LUGA[L(-*ti*)]

12 2 BÁN 2 SÌLA ˹ŠE˺ ˹*a-na*˺ [

13 ˹2 BÁN 2˺ [SÌLA ŠE (x)] x x

14 [2 BÁN] ˹2˺ SÌLA ŠE ^{m}*Ú-*˹*i*˺*-ra-at-ti*

U. e. 15 ⸢3 BÁN⸣ ŠE *a-na* LÚ.SUKKAL
16 ⸢3 BÁN⸣ ŠE *a-na ú-bá-ri*
17 *ša* KUR *Ḫa-ni-gal-bat*
Le. e. 18]x-*an-nu*
19] ŠE.MEŠ *i+na* ITI *ḫi-a-r*[*i*]

Michael Klein

21. A missing line in HSS 14, 10

The copy of HSS 14, 10 (SMN 3396), a fragmentary royal edict from the palace archives (D 6), is not complete. On the lower part of reverse there are parts of a seal impression still visible, to which a subscript on the upper edge is nearly completely preserved:

U.e. 1′ NA$_4$.⸢KIŠIB⸣ ^{m}AM-^{d}30

Within the palace archives, a Rīm-Sîn receives rations of barley in the lists HSS 14, 47:16; 49:18; 52:30; 55:19; 135:14; 15, 239:13. The scribe Rīm-Sîn has written the *ṭuppi mārūti* HSS 19, 22 + SMN 1687 (cf. *SCCNH* 7 [1995], 144ff.), his son Tarmi-teššup the declaration HSS 15, 293 (l. 10). Other persons with the same name are mentioned in HSS 19, 2:69 (witness, son of Šumu-libši), JEN 845:27 (father of the witness Sîn-nāṣir), and HSS 16, 339:7.

Michael Klein

22. SMN 1621 joined to HSS 13, 218

SMN 1621 fills the large lacuna in the obverse of HSS 13, 218 (= SMN 218). The tablet is complete now. The register of HSS 13, p. xi, attributes SMN 218 to room A 23 in the house of Šilwa-teššup; a paper slip attached to the fragment SMN 1621 gives the following locus and date: "C 61, Jan 27, 1928." The latter information is wrong, presumably because the paper slip was misplaced. As it becomes clear from various comparisons, the tablet belongs to the so-called *rākib narkabti* lists found in room A 34 of the so-called "House of Zige," next to the tablet rooms A 26 and A 23 in the house of Šilwa-teššup.

The text has been mentioned by G. Dosch, *Zur Struktur der Gesellschaft des Königreichs Arrapḫe* (HSAO 5), Heidelberg: Heidelberger Orientverlag, 1993, p. 8, where the restoration of l. 6 of our text should be corrected now.

Obv. 1 ^{m}*Qa-na-a+*⸢*a*⸣(over erasure) DUMU ⸢*Ku-uš*⸣*-ši-ia*
2 ^{m}*Na-i-*[*t*]*e* DUMU *Ši-i*[*l-*w]a*-te-šup*
3 ^{m}*A-ki-*[*i*]*a* DUMU ÌR-DINGIR-⸢*šu*⸣
4 ^{m}[*Ṣi-i*]*l-la-bu* ⸢DUMU *It-ḫi*⸣*-p*[*u-g*]*ur*

5 ^{m}*E[l]-ḫi-ip-til-la* DUMU *Ar-ru-um-pa*
6 ^{m}⸢*Ša*⸣*-aḫ-lu-*⸢*ia* DUMU⸣ *A-ri-i[a]*
7 ^{m}*Še-eḫ-li-*⸢*ia*⸣ DUMU *A-kap-dug-ge*
8 ^{m}*Šúk-*⸢*ri-te*⸣*-šup* [DU]MU ⸢*Šu*⸣*-b/ma-a+a*
9 ^{m}*T[a]r-mi-ia* [D]UMU *A-zi-ia*
10 ^{m}*Al-pu-ia* [DU]MU ⸢*A*⸣*-ri-ia*
11 ^{m}*I-ri-*⸢*ri*⸣*-ti[l-la* DUM]U *Ma-ša-ar-ta-nu*
12 ^{m}*Še-el-we-e* [DUM]U *E-ni-ia*
13 ^{m}*Wi-ir-ra* D[U]MU *Ḫa-ši-ib-ba-*⸢*ra*⸣*-al-la*
14 ^{m}*En-na-ma-ti* DUMU *Na-aš-we*
15 ^{m}*Ta-i-til-la* DUMU *Lu-mu-ut-ra* (erasure)
16 ^{m}*Pu-i-ta-e* DUMU *Ka*$_4$*-lu-li*
17 ^{m}*Ḫu-ti-ip-*LUGAL DUMU *A-kap-ta-e*
18 ^{m}*Túl-bi-še-en-ni* DUMU *El-ḫi-ip-*LUGAL
19 ^{m}*A-ri-ḫa-ma-an-na* DUMU *A-li-ib-<bi>-ia*
20 ^{m}*Ki-iz-za-ge* DUMU *Ša-aš-ta-e*
21 ^{m}*Eḫ-li-te-šup* DUMU *Ḫu-i-ba-a-pu*
22 ^{m}*A-ki-ip-til-la*[13] DUMU *Na-ni-ip-*LUGAL
L.e. 23 ^{m}*Ki-in-tar* DUMU *Šúk-ri-ia*
24 ^{m}*Šar-ri-ia* DUMU *Ḫu-ta-ar-ra-áp-ḫé*
25 ^{m}*Ge-el-te-e-a* DUMU *Ar-zi-iz-za*
Rev. 26 ^{m}*[K]u-ut-ti* DUMU *Ú-ta-a+a*
27 ^{m}*Ge-el-te-e-a* DUMU *Ú-ta-a+a*
28 ^{m}*A-ki-ip-til-la* DUMU *Ta-a+a*
29 ^{m}*Zi-ge* DUMU *Te-ḫi-ip-til-la*
30 ^{m}*Tub-bi-iz-zi* DUMU *Ge-li-ia*
31 ^{m}*Ḫu-i-til-la* DUMU *Ta-a+a*
32 ^{m}*Šu-ur-te-šup* DUMU *Ar-te-eš-šup*
33 ^{m}*Šúk-ri-te-šup* DUMU *Ar-ru-um-ti*
34 ^{m}*Šúk-ri-ia* DUMU *Zi-il-li-ia*

G. Wilhelm

23. Problematische SMN-Nummern der Texte EN 9/1-3[14]

Nach der Publikation von EN 9/1 in *SCCNH* 2 (1987) und EN 9/2 in *SCCNH* 4 (1993) ist nun mit EN 9/3 in *SCCNH* 5 (1995) die Veröffentlichung der nachgelassenen Kopien von Nuzi-Texten aus der Hand E. R. Lachemans zum

13 ^{m}*A-ki-ip-til-la*, not *-kip-* as in HSS 13, 218:22.

14 [See also Nuzi Note 33 below.]

Abschluß gekommen. Dem Herausgeber D.I. Owen ist insbesondere auch dafür zu danken, daß er den Autographien einen „cumulative catalogue" aller EN 9-Texte vorangestellt hat, dem neben der Textnummer die Museumsnummer (SMN), die Raumnummer und eine kurze Inhaltsangabe der Urkunde zu entnehmen ist. Da ein offizieller SMN-Katalog des Harvard Semitic Museums anscheinend nicht existiert, waren die Angaben zu SMN-Nummern vor allem aus den Unterlagen Lachemans selbst zu gewinnen, wobei in vielen Fällen Widersprüche sowie fehlende oder ungenaue Angaben zu Tage traten. Im Folgenden seien einige Korrekturen und Ergänzungen zu diesem „cumulative catalogue" nachgetragen:

Der Katalog zu den EN 9/2-Texten (*SCCNH* 4, 136) gibt für EN 9/2 83 die Museumsnummer SMN 2010. Diese SMN-Nummer ist laut „cumulative catalogue" jetzt EN 9/3 72 zugewiesen, während die SMN-Nummer für EN 9/2 83 in SMN 2126 verbessert wird. Dieselbe SMN-Nr. ist aber bereits für einen anderen Text, nämlich HSS XIX 145, vergeben.

Die Frage nach der richtigen Museumsnummer für EN 9/3 104 = SMN 363(2?)1 läßt sich dahingehend entscheiden, daß es sich bei SMN 3621 um die Tafel HSS XIX 100 handelt und demnach EN 9/3 104 die Museumsnummer SMN 3631 haben muß.

Das Fragezeichen in der Angabe EN 9/1 127 = SMN 2088+? muß durch SMN 2682 (zuvor als AASOR XVI 45 in Transliteration publiziert) ersetzt werden, wie es so bereits in dem Katalog zu den EN 9/1-Texten (*SCCNH* 2, 363) gesagt wurde.

EN 9/1 131 = SMN 2264 (so auch *SCCNH* 2, 363) ist nicht identisch mit HSS XV 47 = SMN 2264.

EN 9/1 138 = SMN 1154 (so auch *SCCNH* 2, 363) ist nicht identisch mit HSS XVI 357 = SMN 1154.

Die Angabe bei EN 9/3 288 mit SMN 2051 steht im Widerspruch zur Angabe im Register der Tafeln von HSS XV, 1955, S. XV „SMN 2051 has been added to SMN 2229" (= HSS XV 16).

Im Katalog zu den EN 9/1-Texten (*SCCNH* 2, 371) steht bei EN 9/1 368 die wohl richtige Angabe SMN 973. Diese ist im „cumulative catalogue" mit Verweis auf die frühere Angabe in SMN 793 verbessert worden. SMN 793 ist jedoch ein anderer Text, der als HSS XIV 226 publiziert worden ist.

Die Identität von EN 9/3 385 (= SMN 3056) mit HSS XVI 452 ist vermerkt worden, jedoch liegt bei der Raumangabe ein Fehler vor: Es muß C 19 heißen.

Die wohl richtige Angabe im Katalog zu den EN 9/1-Texten (*SCCNH* 2, 372) für EN 9/1 390 mit SMN 2619 ist im „cumulative catalogue" stillschweigend in SMN 2618 verändert worden. Der Text ist jedoch nicht identisch mit HSS XIX 118 = SMN 2618.

EN 9/1 418 = SMN 3152 (so auch *SCCNH* 2, 374) ist nicht identisch mit HSS XIV 11 = SMN 3152.

Der „cumulative catalogue" nennt sowohl für EN 9/1 438 als auch für EN 9/3 446 die Museumsnummer SMN 3764. Die richtige Zuordnung ist nur dem

„cumulative SMN-index" (S. 141/2) zu entnehmen: EN 9/1 438 = SMN 3164 und EN 9/446 = SMN 3764.

Bei EN 9/3 471 (= SMN 1048), das bereits als AASOR XVI 14 in Transliteration publiziert wurde, fehlt die Angabe der Raumnummer: L 2 oder M 2 (frühere Bezeichnung: C 2, cf. E.R. Lacheman, HSS XVI, S. vii).

EN 9/3 476 (= SMN 941) ist bereits unter der Nummer HSS IX 60 (Autographie) bekannt (cf. demnächst auch AdŠ 285).

Laut dem „cumulative catalogue" sei die Museumsnummer SMN 997, die auf den Text EN 9/3 482 bezogen wird, zuvor für den bereits publizierten Text EN 5 (= HSS XIV) 38 vergeben worden. HSS XIV 38 trägt jedoch dem Index zu HSS XIV zufolge die Nummer SMN 3128. [E.R. Lacheman verbucht in seinem unveröffentlichten Manuskript *Personal Names from the Kingdom of Arrapḫa* unter Urḫitilla einen EN 9-Text mit der Museumsnummer SMN 1706, der aufgrund der 9 angeführten Belege für den PN Urḫi-tilla mit EN 9/3, 482 identisch sein muß. - G.W.]

Bei EN 9/3 504 (= SMN 3535) und EN 9/3 519 (= SMN 3541) handelt es sich um dieselbe Tafel.

Für EN 9/3 518 ist die Museumsnummer SMN 2356 angegeben worden. SMN 2356 ist laut G. Wilhelm, *SCCNH* 7 (1995) 152, jedoch ein anderer Text und mit ERL 29 identisch.

J. Fincke

24. Syllabische Schreibungen des Namens Nergal in Nuzi und in Tell Leilān

K. Deller hat 1976 auf eine seit 1926 publizierte, aber anfangs mißverstandene[15], dann falsch gelesene[16] und weithin unbeachtet gebliebene[17] syllabische Schreibung des Gottesnamens Nergal hingewiesen[18], die auf eine Lautung Nerigla führt, wie sie von einigen späteren außerkeilschriftlichen Wiedergaben von mit Nergal gebildeten Personennamen, insbesondere den verschiedenen Formen des Namens Neriglissar, nahegelegt wird. Die entsprechende Stelle, JEN 29:25f., lautet: *a-na pa-ni* ²⁶*ša* ᵈ*Né/Ni-ri-ig-la*. Die—bis auf die altassyrisch übliche Wiedergabe der letzten Silbe mit *lá*—gleiche Schreibung findet sich nun

15 P. Koschaker, *Neue keilschriftliche Rechtsurkunden aus der El-Amarna-Zeit*, Leipzig 1928, 78, footnote 1 from p. 76, 6b.

16 E. Cassin, *L'adoption à Nuzi*, Paris 1938, 220f.

17 Cf. E. von Weiher, *Der babylonische Gott Nergal* (AOAT 11), Kevelaer / Neukirchen-Vluyn 1971, 19.

18 K. Deller, *Or*NS 45 (1976) 43; cf. auch G. Wilhelm, Das Archiv des *Šilwa-teššup*, Heft 3, Wiesbaden: Harrassowitz 1985, 48.

in dem altassyrischen Vertrag aus Tell Leilān[19]: [dN]*i-ri-ig-lá* LUGAL [(*ša*) *Ḫ*]*u-ub-ší-il*$_5$ L 87-442+ Kol. I 9f. (l.c. S. 194f.). Damit wird deutlich, daß die Form in Nuzi in einer Aussprachetradition des Gottesnamens steht und nicht als Nuzi-typische lokale Sonderentwicklung aufgefaßt werden darf.

G. Wilhelm

25. *sabli* „(Metall-)Schale, Schüssel" auch in Nuzi

Das Akkadische kennt seit seiner mittleren Sprachstufe eine Gefäßbezeichnung *saplu*, die nach W. von Soden, *AHw* 1027a, ins Hebräische, Aramäische und Arabische entlehnt wurde. Die ältesten Belege sind ins 15. und 14. Jahrhundert zu datieren und stammen von der Peripherie der Keilschriftkultur, nämlich aus Alalaḫ, Ugarit und Amarna (für Belege cf. *AHw* und *CAD* S s.v.). Das Material, soweit angegeben, ist Metall, und zwar Bronze (Amarna) oder Kupfer (Ugarit), in neuassyrischer Zeit auch Gold. Die für Alalaḫ bezeugte Gewichtsangabe in Höhe von 5600g deutet auf die Dimensionen eines Kessels, doch kann *sablu* auch ein wesentlich kleineres Gefäß bezeichnen, wie die in Ugarit belegte Gewichtsangabe von 1600g zeigt (cf. *AHw* s.v.).

Die in Alalaḫ bezeugte hurritische Pluralform 3 *sà-ba-al-la* Al.T. 435:4 (<**sabli=na*) deutet daraufhin, daß das Wort auch ins hurritische Wörterbuch gehört. Dies wird auch durch einen bisher übersehenen Beleg aus Nuzi gestützt: 3 *kap-tùk-ku sà-pa-al-la ša* GUD.MEŠ (HSS 9, 23: 11f.).

CAD K 191 bucht die Stelle unter *kaptukkû* „jar of two seahs" und liest ohne Übersetzung „4 *pa-al-la*". *AHw* 445a nennt den Beleg unter demselben Stichwort, läßt aber das fragliche Wort aus. Eine Gegenstandsbezeichnung, die, folgt man *CAD*, auf Grund der Pluralform auf -**na* als hurro-akkad. **palu* (hurr. **palV*) angesetzt werden müßte, ist m.W. nicht bezeugt. Die Übereinstimmung mit der in Alalaḫ bezeugten hurritischen Pluralform von **sabli* und der Zusammenhang mit der Gefäßbezeichnung *kaptukkû* dürfen daher als ausreichendes Argument für die oben gegebene Lesung der Nuzi-Stelle gelten. Da *sà-pa-al-la* offenkundig das zuvor genannte Maßgefäß *kaptukkû* qualifiziert, dürfte es sich — auch in Hinsicht auf die höchst unterschiedlichen Dimensionen eines *sablu*-Gefäßes — um einen bestimmten Formtyp handeln.

Obwohl Ort und Zeit der frühesten Belege für eine Ableitung aus dem Hurritischen sprechen, liefert das hurritische Wörterbuch bisher keine plau-

---

19 Cf. J. Eidem, "An Old Assyrian Treaty from Tell Leilan," in: D. Charpin / F. Joannès (ed.), *Marchands, diplomates et empereurs. Etudes sur la civilisation mésopotamienne offertes à Paul Garelli*, Paris: Éditions Recherche sur les Civilisations, 1991, 185-207.

20 Cf. Laroche, *GLH*, 302: *za-ap-la-aš-ši* [KBo 21, 43 = ChS I/1 Nr.7 Vs. I 8′; cf. noch ChS I/1 20 Rs. III 10′, 24 Vs. II 2′(?); alle Stellen ohne semantisch ergiebigen Kontext.

21 Cf. Laroche, *GLH* 300.

sible Anschlußmöglichkeit. Eine Wurzel *sabl-* ist nur schlecht bezeugt[20] und könnte derzeit nur aus dem Wort *sa/ubalgi* „Sünde; Verlust"[21] abgeleitet werden, eine semantische Verbindung wäre aber auch dann nicht erkennbar. Dasselbe gilt für die Wurzel *sab-*, zu der *sabli* eine Ableitung auf *-li* sein könnte; die in Nuzi bezeugten Stellen mit dem Infinitiv *sabumma epēšu*[22] sind am ehesten mit dem Bedeutungsansatz „abschlagen" zu verstehen.

Es erscheint naheliegend, einen Zusammenhang mit der neuassyrisch bezeugten Gefäßbezeichnung *sab/pulḫu*[23] anzunehmen, allerdings würde man auf Grund der bekannten Regeln bei Derivation auf *-ġ/ḫḫe* eine Form mit *a* statt *u* erwarten (**sabalġe*).

G. Wilhelm

26. *ḫušuḫḫe* „(Zier-)Gürtel"

HSS XIII 225 = E.R. Lacheman, *RA* 36 (1977) 202 (= Nuziana II), eine Liste über verschiedene Gewänder und Accessoires, beginnt mit folgenden Angaben:

1 1 TÚG *ši-la-an-nu ša a-aš-ši-a-an-*[*ni* 1 TÚG *aš*]-⸢*du*⸣-*us-sú*
2 1 TÚG *ba-aš-lu ša ta-bar-ri-a-an-*[*ni*]
3 (Rasur) 1 *ka-sú š*[*a*] KÙ.BABBAR.MEŠ *ša* 20 GÍN [1 *ka-s*]*ú ša* KÙ.BABBAR *ša* 2[0 G]ÍN
4 *ù* 1 *ḫu-šu-uḫ-ḫu ba-aš-lu*
5 *an-nu-tu*$_4$ *a-na* MUNUS-*ti*

„Ein *šilanni*-Gewand, *aššian*[*ni*,[24] ein *aš*]*tussu*-Frauengewand,[25] (2) ein mit *tabarri*-Farbstoff (rötlich) gefärbtes (lit.: gekochtes) Gewand, (3) ein Becher aus Silber von 20 Sekeln (Gewicht),[26] [ein Be]cher aus Silber von 2[0 Se]keln

---

22 Cf. *CAD* S sub *sabumma*, *AHw* sub *zapumma*.

23 Cf. *AHw* 1027b ("churr. Fw.?"); *CAD* S 168 (lies: *RA* 69 182!:29).

24 Für *aššianni* „wohl ein Kleiderstoff" cf. *AHw* 84a und „a decoration sewn on garments" cf. *CAD* A II 465b. Für einen weiteren Beleg cf. J.W. Carnahan, K.G. Hillard, A.D. Kilmer, *JCS* 46 (1994) 106f.: TÚG ... *a-aš-ši-a-an-ni* (UCLMA 9-3022:2,4) und nochmals G.G.W. Müller, oben p. 316.

25 *ašt=u=ssi* „einer Frau geziemend (angemessen)" von *ašti* „Frau"; cf. E.A. Speiser, IH (= AASOR XX [1941]) 116, §160; für weitere Bildungen dieser Art cf. G. Wilhelm, *SMEA* 29 (1992) 241 Anm. 6.

26 In einer Tributliste aus Ugarit ist ebenfalls ein Becher aus Silber zwischen Gewändern genannt (17.382+380:46: *1-en ka-sú* KÙ.BABBAR.MEŠ; cf. J. Nougayrol, PRU IV, Paris 1956, 82) (freundlicher Hinweis von A. Hagenbuchner).

Das Gewicht des „Bechers" ist mit 20 Sekeln Silber (= 166⅔ g) sehr gering. Es ist daher anzunehmen, daß es sich bei dem *ka-sú* eher um ein Accessoire handelt.

(Gewicht) (4) und ein gefärbtes (lit.: gekochtes) *ḫušuḫḫu*. (5) Diese (sind) für Frauen (lit.: Singular)".

Die Liste wird folgendermaßen zusammengefaßt:

45 ŠU.NÍGIN 32 TÚG.MEŠ 5 *ta-pa-*⸢*lu*⸣ [*ḫu-ul-la-an-nu*]
46 8 *ta-pa-lu na-*⸢*aḫ*⸣*-la-a*[*p*]*-*⸢tu_4⸣ [1 *a*]*l-lu-rù*
47 <n> *zi-a-na-*tu_4 ⸢*ù*⸣ 1 *ḫu-šu-ḫu*

„Insgesamt: 32 Gewänder, 5 Paar [Decken], (46) 8 Paar Obergewänder (?), [ein *a*]*lluru*-Prachtgewand, (47) <n> *ziānatu*-Decken und ein *ḫušuḫḫu*".

ḫušuḫḫe[27] läßt sich als Zugehörigkeitsadjektiv auf *-ḫḫe* mit dem Derivationsvokal *-o/u-* von einem Nomen **ḫuži*[28] ableiten, dem die hurritische Verbalwurzel *ḫuž-* „binden"[29] (*ḫuž=o=ḫḫe*) zugrundeliegt. *ḫuž=o=ḫḫe* bedeutet demnach „Gürtel". Das Adjektiv *bašlu* (Z. 4) „gefärbt" weist darauf hin, daß der Gürtel aus Stoff hergestellt ist. Der Unterschied zu dem anderen ebenfalls in den Nuzi-Urkunden bezeugten hurritischen Wort für „Gürtel", *ḫezmi*,[30] liegt wahrscheinlich darin, daß der *ḫušuḫḫe* in erster Linie als Ziergürtel verwendet wurde.

J. Fincke

27. *pizipsumma epēšu*

Das Prozeßprotokoll EN 9/1 434 enthält einen bisher unbekannten hurritischen Infinitiv, zu dessen semantischer Eingrenzung die Urkunde insgesamt einer Bearbeitung bedarf.

EN 9/1 434; SMN 3102; keine Maße; C 28.

Vs. 1 ^{m}*Ša-*⸢*ar*⸣*-te-šup* DUMU *Ut-ḫáp-ta-*⸢*e*⸣
2 *it-t*[*i* ^{m}*A-ri-i*]*p*-LUGAL DUMU ⸢*Ku*⸣*-un-*x[
3 *i+na di-n*[*i a-na pa-ni*] DI.KUD.ME[Š] *š*[*a* U]RU *Nu-*[*zi*]
4 *i-te-lu-m*[*a u*]*m-ma* ^{m}⸢*Ša-ar*⸣*-te-šup-*⸢*ma*⸣
5 5 ⸢ANŠE ZÍZ.AN.NA⸣.MEŠ ⸢*ša*⸣ ^{m}[*U*]*t-ḫáp-ta-e a-bi-ia*
6 *i+na* É*-ti qa-ri-ti* ⸢*ša*⸣ ^{m}*A-ri-ip-*⸢LUGAL⸣
7 *at-ta-bá-ak-mi* ⸢*ù*⸣ *a-na* ŠU*-ti* [*ša*]

---

27 Cf. *AHw* 362a „ein Kleid" und *CAD* Ḫ 263 „a garment".

28 Eine direkte Ableitung von der Wurzel *ḫuž-* verbietet sich wegen des Derivationsvokals; cf. G. Wilhelm, *SMEA* 29 (1992) 240 Anm. 4.

29 Cf. G. Wilhelm, *ZA* 73 (1983) 101.

30 HSS XIV 620:1: 3 TÚG.MEŠ *ši-la-an-ni-e* (2) *it-ti ḫe-ez-mi-šu-nu* „Drei *šilanni*-Gewänder mit ihren Gürteln" und (13) 1 TÚG *ši-la-an-nu i*[*t-ti*] (14) *ḫi-iš-mi-šu* „ein *šilanni*-Gewand m[it] seinem Gürtel".
Für *ḫezm=i* „Gürtel" von *ḫezm-* „sich gürten" siehe G. Wilhelm, in: *Fs. Heger*, 1992, 663.

8 ^{m}*A-ri-ip*-LUGAL *at-ta-din*
9 *ù i+na* ŠÀ-*bi ša* 5 ANŠE ZÍZ.AN.N[A.MEŠ]
10 2 ANŠE.ZÍZ.⸢AN.NA⸣.MEŠ *a-šar* ^{m}*A-r*[*i-i*]*p*-LUGAL
11 *el-te-q*[*è-mi*] ⸢*ù*⸣ 3$^{!}$ (Text: 5) ANŠE ZÍZ.A[N.NA].MEŠ *er-te-eḫ*
12 *ù i+na-an-*[*na iš-t*]*u* 3 MU.MEŠ
13 3 ANŠE [ZÍZ.AN.NA.MEŠ] *ša i-ri-ḫ*[*u*]
14 *a-*⸢*šar*⸣ ^{m}⸢*A*⸣-[*ri-ip*-LUGAL] ⸢*e*⸣*-te-r*[*i-i*]*š-ma*
15 [*la i+na-an-din-mi*] ⸢*ù*⸣ DI.KUD.M[EŠ]
16 [^{m}*A-ri-ip*-LUGAL *i*]*š-*⸢*ta*⸣*-lu-*⸢*uš*⸣
17 [*um-ma* ^{m}*A-ri-ip*-LU]GAL-[*m*]*a a-*⸢*an-ni*⸣*-mi*
18 [5 ANŠ]E ZÍZ.A[N.NA.MEŠ *ša* ^{m}*Š*]*a-ar-te-šup*
19 [*i+na*] ⸢É⸣-*ti qa-r*[*i-ti-ia*] *it-*⸢*ta*⸣*-bá-ak-ma*
20 [*ù a-n*]*a* ⸢ŠU⸣-*ti-ia* [*i*]*t-*[*t*]*a-din*
21 [*i+na* ŠÀ]-*bi ša* 5 ⸢ANŠE⸣ [Z]ÍZ.AN.NA.⸢MEŠ⸣
22 [2 AN]ŠE ZÍZ.AN.NA.MEŠ ^{m}*Ša-ar-te-*⸢*šup*⸣ *il-qè*
23 [*ù* 3] ANŠE ZÍZ.AN.NA.MEŠ *iš-tu* ⸢3⸣ MU.MEŠ *i+na* UGU-*ḫi-ia aš-bu*
24 [*ù* ^{m}*Ut*]-⸢*ḫáp*⸣*-ta-e a-bi-šu ša* [^{m}*Š*]*a-ar-te-šup*
25 [^{m}*Ta-ḫi*]-⸢*ri*⸣ DUMU *Un*$^{!}$*-te-šup* ⸢*a*⸣*-na ia-*[*š*]*i*
26 [*a-na le-q*]*è-e a-*⸢*na*⸣ *ku-ni-ši iš-ta-pár*^{ar}
27 [*ù* 3 ANŠE] ⸢ZÍZ⸣.A[N.N]A *a-na* ^{m}*Ta-ḫi-ri a-na-an-din-mi*
28 [*ù* ^{m}*T*]*a-ḫi-r*[*i ku-n*]*i-šu* ⸢*ša*⸣*-a-šu a-*<*na*> *le-qè-e*
29 [*la im-gu*$_{5}$*-ur-mi*[31] *ù*] *a-*[*n*]*a ia-ši iq-ta-*[*b*]*i*
30 [*ku-ni-š*]*u* [*ša-a-šu*] *bi-zi-ip-z*[*u-u*]*m-ma* DÙ-*šu*
u. Rd. 31 [x x x x] x[x x x x x]-*lu*/ ⸢*ù*⸣
32 [ ]x ⸢x x⸣ [*i*]*a* [(x) *ù*] DI.KUD.MEŠ
33 [^{m}*T*]*a-ḫi-ri iš-t*[*a-lu-u*]*š um-ma* ^{m}*Ta-ḫi-ri-m*[*a*]
Rs. 34 *i+na ša-lu-u*[*l-ti*] *ša-at-ti*
35 *a-na-ku* ^{m}*Ut-ḫáp-ta-e a-na le-qè-e*
36 ⸢*a*⸣*-na ku-ni-šu a-na* ^{m}*A-ri-ip*-LUGAL
37 *iš-tap-ra-an-ni-mi ù*
38 ^{m}⸢*A*⸣*-ri-ip*-LUGAL 1 ANŠE ZÍZ.AN.[N]A.MEŠ
39 *a-*⸢*na*⸣ [*p*]*a-ni-ia ul-te-ṣí-šu-ma*
40 *ù ku-ni-šu ša-a-šu*
41 *bi-zi-*⸢*ip*⸣*-zu-um-ma* DÙ-*šu*
42 *ù a-na-*[*ku*] *la el-te-qè-mi*
43 *ù* DI.KU[D.MEŠ] *a-na* ^{m}⸢*A*⸣*-ri-ip*-LUGAL
44 ⸢*iq*⸣*-ta-b*[*u-ú*] *a-li*[*k-m*]*a* LÚ.MEŠ *ši-bu-ti-ka*$_{4}$

---

31 Ergänzung G. Wilhelm, nach Z. 46.

32 Lesung G. Wilhelm.

45 *bi-la-am-m[i ki]-⸢i⸣-m[e]-e ku-ni-šu*
46 ^{m}*Ta-ḫi-r[i a-na l]e-⸢qè⸣-e la [im-g]u*$_5$*-[r]u*$^{!}$[32]
47 *ù* ^{m}*A-r[i-i]p*-LUGAL LÚ.M[EŠ *š]i-bu-[ti-š]u*
48 *a-na pa-n[i* DI.K]UD.MEŠ *uš-t[e-l]i* ⸢*ù*⸣ *im-*⸢*ta*⸣*-nu*
49 ⸢*ù*⸣ *a-w[a-ti-š]u-nu ša* L[Ú.MEŠ *ši]-bu-ti*
50 ⸢*a*⸣*-[n]a pa-ni* D[I.KU]D.MEŠ *ši*$^{!}$*-na-[ap-šum-m]a* DÙ-⸢*šu*⸣
51 ⸢*ki*⸣*-i-me-e* ⸢*a*⸣*-wa-ti-šu-n[u ša* L]Ú.MEŠ *ši-bu-ti*
52 ⸢*ši*⸣*-na-ap-šum-ma* DÙ-*šu* ⸢*ù*⸣ [ZÍZ.AN.NA.M]EŠ LÚ.MEŠ *ši-b[u]-*⸢*ti*⸣
53 *š[a]* ^{m}*A-ri-ip*-LUGAL *a-na [le-qè]-*⸢*e*⸣ *it-tab-lu-u[š]*
54 *ù* EME-*šu ša* ^{m}*A-ri-ip*-[LUGAL *a-na p]a-ni* DI.KUD.MEŠ
55 *iq-ta-bi a-an-ni-mi* 3 AN[ŠE ZÍ]Z.AN.NA.MEŠ
56 *iš-tu* 3 MU.MEŠ-*ti* ⸢*i*⸣*-[na* UGU-*ḫi-i]a*
57 *a-ši-ib ù la ad-*⸢*din-mi*⸣ [^{m}*Š]a-ar-te-šup*
58 *i+na di-ni il-te-e-ma* ⸢*ù*⸣ [DI.KUD].MEŠ
59 ^{m}*A-ri-ip*-LUGAL *ki-i* EME-*š[u]*
60 *a-na iš-pí-ki a-na* 30 ⸢ANŠE.ZÍZ⸣.AN.NA.[MEŠ]
61 *a-na* 30 *ša-ḫi-ir-ri* I[N].MEŠ.NU(sic!)
62 *a-na* ^{m}*Ša-ar-te-šup it-[t]a-*⸢*du*⸣*-u[š]*
(Siegelabrollung) | (Siegelabrollung)
63 NA$_4$ ^{m}*Eḫ-li-pa-pu* NA$_4$ ^{m}*Ur-ḫi-ia* DUMU *Zi-g[e]*
64 NA$_4$ ^{m}*A-kap*$^{!}$*-dug-ge* [0]
o. Rd. (Siegelabrollung) | (Siegelabrollung)
65 NA$_4$ ^{<m>}*Nu-pa-na-ni* DUMU *Qa-ak-ki*
l. Rd. 66 (Siegelabrollung) ŠU ^{m}*Tu-[*
67 DUMU *Z[i-/G[e-*
68 NA$_4$ ^{m}*A-ta-a+a* DUMU *A-ri-ia*

(Vs. 1-4) Šar-teššup, der Sohn des Utḫap-tae, ist mit [Ar]ip-šarri, dem Sohn des Kun-x[ ], bei Gericht [vor] den Richtern der Stadt Nu[zi] erschienen.

(4) Folgendermaßen Šar-teššup: (5-8) „5 ANŠE Emmer meines Vaters [U]tḫap-tae hatte ich im Speicher des Arip-šarri deponiert (lit.: hingeschüttet) und der Verantwortung [des] Arip-šarri übergeben. (9-11) Und von diesen 5 ANŠE Emmer hatte ich (dann) 2 ANŠE Emmer von Ar[i]p-šarri (zurück)genommen und 3 (Text: 5) ANŠE Emmer übriggelassen. (12-14) Und jetz[t] habe ich [nac]h drei Jahren die 3 ANŠE [Emmer], die übriggeblieben sind, von A[rip-šarri] gefordert, aber (15) [er hat (sie) nicht gegeben]".

(15-16) Und die Richter befragten [Arip-šarri].

(17) [Folgendermaßen Arip-ša]rri: (17-19) „Ja, [5 ANŠ]E Emm[er des Š]ar-teššup hatte er [in meinem] Speic[her] deponiert (lit.: hingeschüttet) und (20) [i]n meine Verantwortung [übe]r[ge]ben. (21-22) [Vo]n diesen 5 ANŠE Emmer hatte Šar-teššup [2 AN]ŠE Emmer (zurück)genommen, (23) [und] ich schulde seit drei Jahren [3] ANŠE Emmer. (24-26) [Dann] hat [Ut]ḫap-tae, der Vater des [Š]ar-teššup, [Taḫi]ri, den Sohn des Un-teššup,

zu mir geschickt, [um] den Emmer [entgegenzune]hmen. (27) [Und] [3 ANŠE] Emmer wollte ich dem Taḫiri geben, (28-29) [T]aḫir[i jedoch] hat [sich geweigert], den betreffenden [Em]mer z<u> nehmen, [und] (folgendes) zu mir gesagt: (30) '[Der betreffende Emme]r ist *pizipsumma*'. (u. Rd. 31-32) [...].. [...]".

(32-33) [Und] die Richter befr[agte]n [T]aḫiri.

(33) Folgendermaßen Taḫiri: (Rs. 34-37) „Im dritt[en] Jahr hat Utḫaptae mich(sic!) zu Arip-šarri geschickt, um den Emmer entgegenzunehmen. (38-39) Arip-šarri hat mir (nur) ein ANŠE Emmer herausbringen lassen; (40-41) aber der betreffende Emmer war *pizipsumma*, (42) und ich habe ihn (darum) nicht genommen".

(43-44) Und die Richt[er] sagt[en] zu Arip-šarri: (44-46) „Ge[h u]nd bringe deine Zeugen herbei (, die bestätigen können), daß Taḫiri den Emmer nicht entgegenn]ehmen [wo]ll[te]".

(47-48) Und Ar[i]p-šarri brachte [se]ine Zeugen vor die [Richt]er[33]. (49-50) Und die Aussagen der [Ze]ugen vor den Ri[cht]ern wide[rspra]chen sich[34].

(51-52) Weil sich die Aussagen der Zeugen widersprochen haben (52-53) und die Ze[u]gen des Arip-šarri den [Emmer zum Entgegenneh]men gebracht haben, (54-55) und wegen der Erklärung des Arip-[šarri—v]or den Richtern hat er gesagt: (55-57) „Ja, ich schulde seit drei Jahren 3 AN[ŠE E]mmer, (57) und ich habe sie nicht (in derselben Menge und Qualität entsprechend dem deponierten Emmer) (zurück)gegeben",—(57-58) hat [Š]ar-teššup den Prozeß gewonnen.

(58-62) Und die [Richt]er verurteilten Arip-šarri wegen sei[ner] Aussage zu einem Feldertrag, (nämlich) zu 30 ANŠE Emmer (und) zu 30 Bündeln Stroh, zugunsten von Šar-teššup.

(63) Siegel des Eḫlip-apu. Siegel des Urḫia, des Sohnes des Zik[e]. (64) Siegel des Akap-tukke. (o.Rd. 65) Siegel des Nupanani, des Sohnes des Kakki. (l. Rd. 66-67) Hand des Tu-[...], des Sohnes des Z[i-/G[e-...]. (68) Siegel des Ataja, des Sohnes des Aria.

pizipsumma epēšu (Z. 30, 41)[35] bezieht sich auf den Emmer, und zwar entweder auf seine Qualität oder seine Quantität. Die Aussagen des Arip-šarri und des Taḫiri widersprechen sich in bezug auf die Quantität des strittigen Emmers: Nach Arip-šarri hat er die noch ausstehende Menge Emmer in voller Höhe zur Verfügung gestellt (Z. 27), nach Aussage des Taḫiri hat ihm Arip-šarri jedoch

33 Cf. *CAD* M/1 224a (4b, SMN 3102:47).

34 *šinapšumma epēšu* „sich widersprechen, widersprüchliche Aussagen machen". Cf. hierzu R.E. Hayden, *Court Procedure at Nuzu*. Ph.D. Dissertation, Brandeis University, 1962, 108f., 138. Für andere Bedeutungsvorschläge cf. C.H. Gordon, *BASOR* 64 (1936) 27 Nr. 102; ders. *Or*NS 5 (1936) 322f.; ders. *Or*NS 7 (1938) 53 Nr. 31; K. Grosz, *The Archive of the Wullu Family* (CNI Publications 5), Copenhagen 1988, 145; P. Negri-Scafa, *SMEA* 29 (1992) 189-202. Siehe auch demnächst J. Fincke.

35 Die Auffassung der Verbalform als Stativ folgt einem Vorschlag von G. Wilhelm .

nur ⅓ der Menge bereitgestellt (Z. 38-39). Weil in der Urteilsbegründung eine zweite Aussage Arip-šarris zitiert wird, derzufolge er den Emmer nicht zurückgegeben hat (Z. 57), darf man davon ausgehen, daß die Aussage des Taḫiri über die falsche Quantität des Emmers der Wahrheit entspricht. Demnach wird sich *pizipsumma epēšu* wohl nicht ebenfalls auf die Quantität, sondern eher auf die Qualität des Emmers beziehen. Der Emmer könnte entweder minderer Qualität, für die vorgesehene weitere Verarbeitung unbrauchbar oder sogar völlig verdorben gewesen sein — sei er nun feucht geworden, bereits gekeimt, mit Schädlingen behaftet oder verfault.

pizipsumma ist einer der in den Nuzi-Texten zahlreichen hurritischen Infinitiv auf *-umma*. Bei *pizips-* könnte es sich um eine reduplizierte Wurzel[36] mit Metathese (**pis=pis-* bzw. **pes=pes-* > *piz=ips-* bzw. *pez=eps-*) oder um einen Stamm *pi/es-* mit einer noch unbekannten Wurzelerweiterung *-i/eps-* oder -V*ps-* handeln. Jedoch ist diese Wurzel in hurritischem Kontext bisher noch nicht bezeugt[37].

J. Fincke

28. *aladumma epēšu* „begleichen; kaufen"

EN 9/2, 292 (SMN 2365), eine Tafel aus dem Archiv der Söhne des Pulaḫali (Raum S 132), enthält den hier erstmals bezeugten hurritischen Infinitiv *aladumma*. Der Text lautet:

Vs. 1 *um-ma* ᵐ*Zu-un-na*
2 DUMU *Ur-ḫi-ia*
3 1 ANŠE *ša* ᵐ*Pa-aš-ši-til-la*
4 DUMU *Pu-la-ḫa-*⌜*li*⌝

36 Für reduplizierte Wurzeln vgl. *fir=vir=išt-* „lösen" (Boğazköy; cf. E. Laroche, *GLH* [Teil 2 = *RHA* 35] (1977) 297; V. Haas / H.J. Thiel, AOAT 31 [1987] 245; G. Wilhelm, *ZA* 77 [1987] 237 Anm. 29) und *kel=i=gel=ešt-* „erhöhen; hochlegen" (Boğazköy-Bilingue: KBo XXXII 13 I 6; cf. E. Neu, *Das Hurritische. Eine altorientalische Sprache in neuem Licht*, Akademie der Wissenschaften und der Literatur, Abhandlungen der Geistes- und Sozialwissenschaftlichen Klasse, Jahrgang 1988 Nr. 3, 7 Anm. 13; G. Wilhelm, *Or*NS 61 [1992] 131; V. Haas, *AoF* 20 [1993] 264).

37 Die reduplizierte Wurzel erinnert an das nA bezeugte *pispisu*, dem offenbar ein schlechter Geruch anhaftet: *kī ša pi-is-pi-su bi-'i-šú-u-ni … ni-piš-ku-nu li-ib-ši* „Wie das *pispisu* stinkt bzw. schlecht ist, so soll … euer Atem sein"; cf. D.J. Wiseman, „The Vassal-treaties of Esarhaddon", *Iraq* 20 (1958) 75 VIII 603. Die Deutung des Wortes von Wiseman, „urine", ist in *CAD* B 4b sub *ba'āšu* A eingegangen, wohingegen *AHw* 867b und R. Borger, *TUAT* I, Gütersloh 1982, 175, es aus gutem Grund ungedeutet belassen. K. Watanabe, *BaM* Beiheft 3, Berlin 1987, 173, 204, schließt sich der Interpretation von E. Reiner in: J.B. Pritchard (Hrsg.), *ANET*³, Princeton 1969, 540 („bedbug"), an und übersetzt *pispisu* als „Wanze".

5 *ša*$^{!}$ *i+na* 30 MA.NA *a-na-ku*.MEŠ
6 *a-la-du-um-ma e-pu-uš*
7 *a-na* KASKAL.MEŠ *ša e-kál-lì*
8 *šu-pu-ur ù*
9 ^{m}⸢*Zu*⸣*-un-na* 30 MA.NA [*a-na-ku*.MEŠ]
10 ⸢*i*⸣*+na* ITI ⸢*Ar*⸣*-qa-b*[*i*]*-i*[*n-ni* x] x *ša* UD/GIŠ.TUR
(Rest der Vs. zerstört)
Rs. (Anfang zerstört)
11 ⸢*ú*$^{?}$*-ma-al*$^{?}$*-l*[*a*$^{?}$]
12 [IG]I *Ta-e* DUMU *El-ḫi-i*[*p-til*]*-la*
13 IGI *A-ni-na-bi* DUMU *Šúk-r*[*i-ia*]
14 IGI *Ḫa-ši-ip-til-la*
15 DUMU *Šá-ar-te-e-a*
16 IGI *Ar-te-šup* DUMU *Šum-mu-ku*
17 ŠU ^{m}*Ḫu-ut-te-šup* DUB.SAR
18 *ṭup-pí i+na* URU *Ú-lam-me*
19 *ša*$_{10}$*-ṭì-ir*
o. Rd. (Siegelabrollung) (Siegelabrollung)
20 ⸢NA$_4$⸣ ^{m}*Ta-e* NA$_4$ ^{m}*Ḫa-ši-ip-til-la*
(Siegelabrollung) (Siegelabrollung)
21 NA$_4$ ^{m}*A-ni-na-bi* NA$_4$ DUB.SAR
NA$_4$ ^{m}*Zu-un-na*
(Siegelabrollung) (Siegelabrollung)
22 [NA$_4$ ^{m}*Ar*]*-te-šup*

Folgendermaßen Zunna, der Sohn des Urḫia: „Einen Esel des Pašši-tilla, des Sohnes des Pulaḫali, welchen ich mit 30 Minen Zinn ...., schicke auf eine Handelsreise des Palastes!“[38] Und Zunna [...] die 30 Minen [Zinn] im Monat Arkapinni (=August/September) ...[...] zahlt(?)[39] [...] (Zeugen, Schreiber) Die Tafel ist in der Stadt Ulamme geschrieben. (Siegelabrollungen und -beischriften).

Zunnu, der die Tafel siegelt und also mit dieser Urkunde gegenüber ihrem Besitzer — nach dem Auffindungsort ein Mitglied der Familie des bekannten Kaufmanns (LÚ.DAM.GÀR) Pulaḫali — eine Verpflichtung eingeht, wird mit der Anweisung zitiert, einen Esel, den er von Pašši-tilla, einem der Söhne des Pulaḫali, mit 30 Minen Zinn *aladumma* gemacht habe, auf eine Handelsreise des

---

38 Die Übersetzung von M.A. Morrison, *SCCNH* 4 (1993) 100 gibt den Imperativ *šupur* fälschlich als „it was sent“ wieder.

39 Wenn Z. 11 richtig gelesen, liegt hier die Klausel mit der Konventionalstrafe bei Vertragsbruch vor.

Palastes zu schicken. Anscheinend sind die 30 Minen nicht bereits gezahlt worden, denn sie erscheinen in der folgenden, teilweise zerstörten Klausel im Zusammenhang mit dem Namen Zunna und einer Monatsangabe wieder; offenkundig handelt es sich hier um eine Zahlungsverpflichtung. Es liegt demnach anscheinend ein Kreditkauf vor. Der Esel ist für eine Handelsreise des Palastes bestimmt. Wahrscheinlich beabsichtigt Zunna, sich mit einem Kommissionsgeschäft an einer Karawane des Palastes zu beteiligen, wie dies auch sonst gut bezeugt ist.[40] Wer die Karawane führt, ist nicht gesagt; da jedoch der Vater des Verkäufers des Esels als *tamkāru* bezeugt ist, wird man nicht fehlgehen zu schließen, daß der Sohn das Geschäft des Vaters fortführte.[41] Der Text würde dann wieder die von C. Zaccagnini betonte enge Bindung des *tamkāru* an den Palast[42] bestätigen. Ist dies richtig, so stellt hier der *tamkāru* dem (sonst nicht bezeugten) Zunna durch einen Verkauf auf Kredit einen Esel zur Verfügung, um es ihm zu ermöglichen, sich an einer von ihm, dem *tamkāru*, selbst im Auftrage des Palastes organisierten Handelsreise zu beteiligen. Aus dem erwarteten Gewinn, so dürfen wir vermuten, sollte nach Abschluß der Reise der Kaufpreis entrichtet werden.

M.A. Morrison kommentiert den Infinitiv *aladumma*: „Here, it seems to refer to a kind of financial arrangement"[43]. Mit einer Gleichung des sumerisch-hurritischen ḪAR-ra=*ḫubullu*-Vorläufers aus Ugarit läßt sich indes die Bedeutung der Wurzel *alad-* genauer fassen; S.-H. Vok.[44] II 14 lautet: [ì-dub x x x g]i-gi = min (= *ka-ru*-WA[45]) *a-la-da-mi-né-we*. In der kanonischen Fassung Ḫḫ II[46] 126 entspricht dem: [ì-dub (x x)] íb-gi$_4$-gi$_4$ = *min* (= *iš-pi-ki*) *i-ta-na-pal*, nach der Übersetzung Landsbergers: „he will regularly pay back to the storehouse (the barley due)".

Die hurritische Fassung bietet indes keine finite Verbalform, die der sumerischen und der akkadischen Form (*ītanappal*) entsprechen würde, sondern wie in den vorausgehenden Zeilen (*kade=ne=ve* „der Gerste", *šum(m)ižum(m)i=ne=ve* „des Sesams/Leinsamens", *silumba=ne=ve* „der Dattel", *immur(i)=r(<n)e=ve* „der Wolle") einen Genitiv, so daß hier also ein (Verbal-) Nomen vorliegen muß. Angesichts des auch sonst aberranten Vokalismus des Textes[47] wird man daher nicht, wie es naheläge, **alad=am-* segmentieren und damit ein Faktitiv zu

40 Cf. C. Zaccagnini, „The Merchant at Nuzi", *Iraq* 39 (1977) 171-89, hier: 180.

41 Cf. ähnlich, jedoch ohne Heranziehung dieser Stelle, M.A. Morrison, *SCCNH* 4 (1993) 106f.

42 Cf. C. Zaccagnini, l.c.

43 M.A. Morrison, *SCCNH* 4 (1993) 100 Anm. 29.

44 F. Thureau-Dangin, *Syria* 12 (1931) 225-266, N° 8, Pl. L-LII.

45 Bei E. Laroche, *GLH* 137 sub „*karubi*", sind irrtümlich beide Belege aus dem S.-H. Vok. mit *-bi* statt WA transkribiert.

46 B. Landsberger, MSL V, Roma 1957, 45-80.

47 Cf. M.L. Khačikyan, *VDI* 1975/3, 21-38.

alad- ansetzen, sondern *alad=am(m)i* als aberrante Form des üblichen Infinitivs auf *-umme* ansehen. Die Wurzel *alad-* entspricht jedenfalls nach dieser Stelle sumerisch gi$_4$-gi$_4$ und nach der akkadischen Fassung *atappulu* „i.w. begleichen, bezahlen".

Im Kontext von EN 9/2 292:6 hat das Verb, wie wir gesehen haben, nicht exakt dieselbe Bedeutung im Sinne einer Entrichtung des Kaufpreises, vielmehr müssen wir hier eher „kaufen" (unter Implikation der Möglichkeit einer späteren Entrichtung des Kaufpreises) übersetzen.

G. Wilhelm

29. SMN 708 Vs. 8′: *kalmarḫ[e]*

CAD G p. 20 bucht unter Hinweis auf E.R. Lacheman *apud* Starr, Nuzi I, 535, das Fragment SMN 708 als Beleg für einen Baumnamen *galmar*. Derselbe Beleg wird *CAD* K 86a in Korrektur dieses Eintrags *sub kalmarḫu* mit der Bemerkung wiederholt: „... is probably to be read *gal-ma-ar-<ḫu>*". Eine 1995 vorgenommene Kollation des Fragments ergab, daß unmittelbar hinter *-ar* noch ein zur Hälfte erhaltenes Zeichen deutlich sichtbar ist, nämlich: .

Die Zeile Vs. 8′ ist daher zu lesen: 8 GIŠ *gal-ma-ar-ḫ[é*.

G. Wilhelm

30. SMN 1669 joined to HSS 13, 100

s. 1 2 *nu-bi* GI [*šu-ú*]-*le*$^!$-*e*$^!$(Text: *-e-le*)
2 *a-na šu-ku-du* ⌈*e*⌉-[*pè-š*]*i ša* URU *Nu-zi*
3 **i+na* ŠU *a-na**(über Rasur) ^{m}*Ú-na-a*[*p-te*]-*šup*
4 DUMU *A-ri-iq-qa-a+*[*a*]
5 *ù i+na* ŠU *a-n*[*a*]
6 ^{m}*Ḫé-ri-qa* DUMU ^{f}[(x-)]*na-wa-a+a*
7 *na-ad-nu*
Rs. 8 NA$_4$ ^{m}*Ú-na-ap-te-šup*
(Siegelabrollung)
(Siegelabrollung)
9 NA$_4$ ^{m}*Ḫe-ri-qa*

HSS 13, 100+ stammt aus dem Raum M 79 des Palastes, in dem mehrere weitere Quittungen über die Entgegennahme von Materialien zur Pfeilher-

48 Cf. W. Mayer, AOAT 205/1, 32-38.

stellung gefunden wurden.[48] Das Anschlußstück zeigt, daß Z. 6 und danach auch HSS 13, 99:8 in der Editio princeps falsch ergänzt wurden; diese falschen Ergänzungen haben auch in *AAN* 57a (*sub* Ḫerrikaia) und 128a (*sub* Šilwaia) sowie in W. Mayers Katalog der Tafeln des Palastes Eingang gefunden und sind nun zu korrigieren. Das Original bietet folgenden Befund: . Es ist bemerkenswert, daß Ḫerikka durch den Namen seiner Mutter identifiziert wird. Deren Name ist trotz des Abstandes zu dem vorausgehenden Determinativ wohl Nawaja, ein Frauenname, der auch sonst gut bezeugt ist. Der Abstand würde allerdings für ein weiteres Zeichen ausreichen, wobei man, ausgehend von ^{f}*Na-na-wa* HSS 13, 26:4, an [*Na*]$^{??}$-*na-wa-a+a* denken könnte.

G. Wilhelm

31. SMN 2799 and one unnumbered fragment joined to EN 9/2 455

Obv. 1 [x+]1 ANŠE ŠE.MEŠ *ša* ^{m}[*Pu-ḫi-še-en-ni*]
2 [DU]MU *Mu-ša-pu a+n*[*a ši-mi*]
3 ⸢*a*⸣-*na* 1 GUD ^{m}*Ḫa-š*[*i-in-na*]
4 [D]UMU *A-ki-pa-p*[*u*
5 ⸢1⸣ GUD SIG$_5$ ⸢*lu-ú* ÁB *lu*⸣-*ú* ⸢NITA⸣[
6 [*lu*]-⸢*ú* NITA *ù*⸣ *lu-ú* 40 [
7 [*i+n*]*a* ITI-[*ḫi Š*]*e-ḫa-li ša* ^{d}IŠK[UR
8 ⸢^{m}⸣*Ḫa-ši-in-na a-na*
9 ^{m}*Pu-ḫi-še-en-ni i+na-an-din*
10 *šum-ma ina qa-bu* UD-*mi*
11 GUD ^{m}*Ḫa-ši-in-na*
12 *a+na* ^{m}*Pu-ḫi-še-en-ni*
13 *la i+na-an-din* 1 BÁN ŠE
14 *ú-ri-ḫul-ši*
l.e. 15 *ina* UD-*mi ù ina* UD-*mi*
16 ^{m}*Ḫa-ši*-⸢*in*⸣-*na*
Rev. 17 *a+na* ^{m}*P*[*u-ḫi-še-en-ni*] SA$_5$-*la*
18 IGI *Na*-[ ]
19 IGI *Ḫa*-[-*t*]*a*$^{?}$-*ia*
20 IGI *Q*[*a*-]
21 IGI [ ] 
22 IGI [ ]  (Rasur)
23 I[GI

The fragment SMN 2371 belongs to a similar topic:

Obv. 1 ^{m}*Pu-*[*ḫi-še-en-ni* DUMU *Mu-ša-p*]*u*
2 [-*ti*]*l-la*

3 [-]*še*$^{?}$
Rev. 2′ *ši-mu ša* ⸢GUD⸣ *a-šar Ḫa-ši-in-na*[
3′ *i-leq-qè*
u.e. 4′ NA$_4$ ^{m}*Ge-li-ip*-LUGAL
(Seal impression)

J. Fincke

32. HSS 15, 317

The three fragments HSS 15, 317 F, G and L belong to the same tablet and join directly:

Obv. 1 [2$^{?}$ TÚG.M]EŠ *tu-ut-tu-pu š*[*a aššijanni*]
2 [1 T]ÚG SIG *ša* KI.MIN
3 [1 G]Ú.È SIG *ša* KI.MIN

---

4 [1 TÚ]G SIG *ša* MUNUS *ša sú-u*[*n uq-na-ti*]

---

5 [x] TÚG.MEŠ *ši-na-ḫi-lu*
6 ⸢16⸣ GÚ.È *ši-na-ḫi-lu*

---

7 1 *ḫa-*⸢*ar*-WA⸣
8 2 TÚG *k*[*ab-r*]*u-*⸢*tu*$_4$⸣ *ša ḫa*[*r-ku-na-aš*]
9 3 *šu-šu-up-pu*

---

10 ŠU N≤GIN 36 TÚG.MEŠ *ši-na-*[*ḫi-lu*]
11 16 GÚ.È.MEŠ
12 [*iš-kà-r*]*u ša* URU [*A-šu-ḫi-iš*]
l.e. (destroyed)
Rev. (destroyed)
u.e. (seal impression)

[The join of HSS 15, 317F+G+L was detected by M. Klein in 1985. It shows the text to be a virtual duplicate of HSS 14, 6. The restorations have been adopted from the latter tablet. It can safely be excluded that the tablets are identical, because according to Lacheman's copies the distribution of signs is not exactly the same. Furthermore, though in content the text on both tablets refers to the same administrative procedure and even the division lines are identical, there are some minor differences in ll. 1, 2, 3, 9, 10 and 11. Apart from that, the tablet HSS 14, 6 is registered in the HSM shipment list as having been returned to Iraq in 1982, whereas the fragments HSS 15, 317F, G, L are still (1995) in the HSM. — G. Wilhelm]

The two fragments joined in the copy of HSS 15 317 K do not belong together.

M. Klein

33. Notes to "Cumulative Catalogue," *SCCNH* 5 (1995) 89-135[49]

With the publication of EN 9/3 (*SCCNH* 5 [1955] 85-357), the largest uncompleted project of E.R. Lacheman has been finished and published — in magnificent fashion. Only those immersed in the study of these texts can begin to appreciate the enormous and succesful effort behind this accomplishment. David I. Owen deserves our gratitude and admiration for this painstaking effort.

Now that all of EN 9 is available for study, some few items from the publication — very few given the amount of material published — may now be clarified or corrected. The following represent such comments.

I. Notes to "Cumulative Catalogue," *SCCNH* 5 (1995) 89-135.

p. 94, EN 9/3 51

For adopted Katiri, read: adopted by Katiri.

p. 95, EN 9/3 61

For sons of Tulpiya are adopted by Itti-šarri, read: sons of Tulpiya adopt Itti-šarri For Great Gate, read: gate.
For Tešup-a[tal], read: Tešup-e[rwi].

p. 96, EN 9/3 64

For Ṭab-šar-beli, read: Ṭab-IM beli

p. 96, EN 9/3 65

For concerning land, read: concerning land in Nu[zi].

p. 96, EN 9/3 68

For Great Gate, read: gate.

p. 102, EN 9/1 131

The second line of this entry should start, [*Ṭuppi mā*]*rūti*.

p. 106, EN 9/3 180

In an unpublished manuscript, this text was assigned the publication number 190.

---

49 [See also Nuzi Note 23 above.]

p. 106, EN 9/3 182

In an unpublished manuscript, this text was assigned the publication number 218.

p. 107, EN 9/3 190

In an unpublished manuscript, this text was assigned the publication number 359B.

p. 109, EN 9/3 210

In an unpublished manuscript, this text was assigned the publication number 453.

p. 110, EN 9/3 218

In an unpublished manuscript, this text was assigned the publication number 318B.

p. 111, EN 9/3 228

In an unpublished manuscript, this text was assigned the publication number 156.

p. 112, EN 9/3 235

In an unpublished manuscript, this text was assigned the publication number 224.

p. 112, EN 9/3 237 and 238 have been inadvertantly omitted from the catalogue.

Insert the following entries:

EN 9/3 237 SMN 2847 No room number

Receipt of items received by Eḫli-Tešup in return for(?) buildings ceded to(?) Puḫ-šenni. Context somewhat unclear.

EN 9/3 238 SMN 3705 No room number (but see below) = EN 7 432 (as noted on p. 142, n. 14; the findspot of EN 7 432 is given as Room I 26 [EN 7, p. xii])

Inventory of and receipt for hides. (Line 3 and EN 7 432:3 are not in agreement)

p. 121, EN 9/2 353

Published in transliteration as AASOR 16 22.

p. 123, EN 9/2 371

SMN 2358A appears as SMN 2358X in SMN index, p. 139.

EN 9/2 371 = EN 9/3 514.

p. 123, EN 9/3 228

In an unpublished manuscript, this text was assigned the publication number 480.

p. 128, EN 9/1 438

For SMN 3764, read: SMN 3164 and see page 141, n. 13 and below, note to p. 141, n. 13.

p. 130, EN 9/3 454

In an unpublished manuscript, this text was assigned the publication number 454.

p. 130, EN 9/3 456

In an unpublished manuscript, this text was assigned the publication number 520.

p. 130, EN 9/1 466

The SMN number of this text is not 3468; rather, it is unknown. See D.I. Owen, "Nuzi Afterthoughts,"(*SCCNH* 9 [1997]) for SMN 3468.

p. 131, EN 9/3 476

See p. 137, note 3. The text was previously published as EN 2 60. The publications differ somewhat.

p. 135, EN 9/3 526

In an unpublished manuscript, this text was assigned the publication number 125A.

p. 135, EN 9/3 527

In an unpublished manuscript, this text was assigned the publication number 125B.

p. 135, EN 9/3 528

In an unpublished manuscript, this text was assigned the publication number 311A.

p. 135, EN 9/3 528

In an unpublished manuscript, this text was assigned the publication number 311b.

II. Additions and Corrections to "Cumulative SMN Index," *SCCNH* 5 (1995) 137-42.

SMN 1101 = EN 9/3 131 according to p. 137b with n. 6, based on a manuscript of Lacheman. However, the same text is assigned two other SMN numbers. The first, SMN 2713, originates in a *Randgloss* also by Lacheman (see *SCCNH* 5, p. 140b where SMN 2713 is identified with EN 9/1 45B, which is an error, actually representing EN 9/1 131 (as noted above, an unpublished manuscript assigns to this tablet the number 45B). The second, SMN 2264X, appears in *SCCNH* 5, pp. 102 and 139a. It appears to be an ad hoc correction of *SCCNH* 2, p. 363, which assigns to this text the incorrect number, SMN 2264. SMN 2264 = EN 6 47 (so EN 6, p. viii; *Nuzi-Bibliographie*, p. 225; and *SCCNH* 5, p. 102, n. 6; 137, n. 6; and 139, n. 9).

SMN 1168 = EN 9/1 11, not EN 9/1 8.

SMN 2015 = EN 9/1 8, not EN 9/1 9.

Insert SMN 2088 = EN 9/1 127.

SMN 2150 = EN 9/1 388, not EN 9/1 389. Note that *Nuzi Bibliographie*, p. 228 indicates that 2150 joins 2583 = EN 9/1 389. This is incorrect.

SMN 2264X. See above note to SMN 1101.

SMN 2319+2321. Note that 2009 + 2319 + 2321 = HSS 19 111 which, however, is not the same text.

SMN 2356. This number was assigned to ERL 29 by G. Wilhelm in *SCCNH* 5, p. 152. But these are not the same texts.

SMN 2358X. Or, SMN 2358A. See note to p. 123, EN 9/2 371.

Sub SMN 2583. Note that *Nuzi Bibliographie*, p. 228 indicates that SMN 2583 joins SMN 2150 = EN 9/1 389 (388 is what appears here). This is incorrect.

SMN 2630 = EN 9/1 7 not EN 9/1 8.

SMN 2713. See above, note to 1101.

SMN 2778 = EN 9/1 150, not EN 9/3 150.

SMN 2993. Delete entry.

Insert SMN 3375$^{?}$ = EN 9/1 132 (also p. 162; *SCCNH* 2, p. 363, has 3375 without question mark.

SMN 3468. Delete this entry. See above note to p. 130, EN 9/1 466.

Insert SMN 3489 = EN 9/1 120.

Page 141, note 13 change EN 9/1 418 to EN 9/1 438.

III. Note to "Cumulative List of Scribes to Excavations at Nuzi 9," *SCCNH* 5 (1995) 149-53.

Sub Taya son of Apil-Sîn, delete EN 9/1 147.

IV. Notes to "Plates"

EN 9/3 52; add legend, Fragment A, to first and last pieces on plate.

EN 9/3 72 = EN 9/2 83; slightly different copies of the same text with somewhat different descriptions.

EN 9/3 72 = EN 9/2 83; Almost identical copies of the same text with somewhat different descriptions.

EN 9/2 83 = EN 9/3 72; Almost identical copies of the same text with somewhat different descriptions.

EN 9/2 158. At bottom of reverse, part of a seal impression is preserved. On the left edge parts of two otherseal impressions are preserved.

EN 9/2 177 rev. On the left edge, below the text, two seal impressions are preserved.

EN 9/2 234 obv. At end of line 4, add sign "a" (accidently omitted by haplography?).

EN 9/2 371 = EN 9/3 514. Almost identical copies of the same text with somewhat different descriptions.

EN 9/1 406 obv. For add to L. read: add to L. 1.

EN 9/3 514 = EN 9/2 371. Almost identical copies of the same text with somewhat different descriptions.

EN 9/1 427 rev. After line 46, both seal impressions are on the upper edge.

EN 9/1 432 obv. The number 432 is missing at heading at the top of this plate.

EN 9/3 451 is mislabled 302 (same as page number).

EN 9/3 479. This text is reproduced twice (pp. 319-20).

M.P. Maidman

34. A comment on G. Wilhelm's "*Bīt papāḫi* in Nuzi"

In "*Bīt papāḫi* in Nuzi" (*SCCNH* 7 [1995] 121-28), G. Wilhelm publishes and edits ERL 82 + SMN 2963. Commenting on the term *takurazu* (cf. l. 15), he notes (p. 127) that Lacheman's copy of JEN 709:21 has DUMU *ku-ra-zu*, where one would prefer to have *ta-ku-ra-zu*. Against interpreting the signs as a patronymic, he notes that *Kurazu would be a unique personal name in the Nuzi corpus and that Lacheman himself elsewhere interpreted the sequence as *ta-ku-ra-zu*.

A third reason may be adduced to cast doubt on the accuracy of the copy. Collation of the tablet reveals that DUMU is not there at all, at least not as of the 1980s. Rather, the traces appear as: . The traces could represent many things including TA.

Maynard P. Maidman

35. Zur Lesung des Personennamens *Šenna*BE = *Šennatil*

Aus den Nuzitexten sind mehr als ein Dutzend Träger des Namens *Šenna*BE mit verschiedenen Patronymen bekannt. Dazu kommen etwa zehn Personen, deren Vater diesen Namen trug, sowie eine nicht feststellbare Anzahl von Personen, deren Patronym nicht angegeben ist und die daher nur teilweise identifiziert werden können. Von den an die einhundert Belegen weisen fast alle die Schreibung *Še-en-na*-BE auf.

Die in *NPN* 131 aufgeführte Variante (3) *Še-na-be* (nur SMN 214) wird zwar in *AAN* wiederholt, der Beleg aber bereits richtig der Normalschreibung *Še-en-na-be* zugeordnet, die auch in der editio princeps (HSS 13, 214) angegeben ist. Sie ist also zu streichen, da bisher nicht belegt, wie auch die Neuedition (*AdŠ* 24) zeigt.

Die Variante (4) *Še-en-na-a-be* soll in SMN 352 = HSS 13, 352:10 und UCP IX pl. 12:57 vorliegen. In HSS 13, 352 steht nach der Transliteration von Pfeiffer und Lacheman *Še-en-na-a-*[*be*], was besser zu *Še-en-na-a-*[*a*] ergänzt werden sollte.

---

50 [For a revised transliteration of this text, see above p. 314.]

51 Leider ist der Name auf den beigegebenen Photos der Ränder, die bei Lutz' Erstedition fehlten, wieder nicht abgebildet.

Nach der kürzlich erschienenen Neubearbeitung von UCP IX pl. 12 (Nr. 11; Museumsnr. UCLMA 9-2870[50]) in *JCS* 46 (1994) 115f. steht auch hier einfach die Normalform *Še-en-na*-BE[51]. Damit ist auch diese Variante zu streichen.

In *AAN* 125 wird eine 5. Variante *Ši-*[*en-*]*na-be* aufgeführt, für die aber kein Beleg angegeben wird. Wahrscheinlich handelt es sich um das Relikt einer später wieder aufgegebenen Lesung. So verbleibt nur noch die interessanteste Variante (2), die *NPN* dazu bewog, den PN als ŠENNAPE anzusetzen: In JEN 58 tritt ein Zeuge namens ŠennaBE S. Ḫairalla, dessen Name in Z. 28 in üblicher Weise, in Z. 38 in der Siegelbeischrift aber angeblich *Še-en-na-bi* geschrieben sein soll. Bereits *NPN* bemerkte dazu „fragment with spelling *Še-en-na-bi* now broken away from tablet; impossible to collate". Da auf den Namen direkt die Erläuterung „*ši-bi* aus Ulamme" folgt, ist es wahrscheinlich, daß hier ein Versehen des Kopisten vorliegt.

Die Variante *Še-en-na-bi* wird aber scheinbar in *AAN* bestätigt, das sie für HSS 16, 330:17 bucht. Schaut man dort in Lachemans Transliteration, so findet man [*Š*]*e-en-na-pí* entgegen der sonst in diesem Band anzutreffenden Transliteration *Še-en-na-pè.* Diese Stelle wäre zu kollationieren.

In dem von F. Ar-Rawi in seiner Dissertation vorgelegten Text IM 73.215 (TF_1 442)[52] begegnet in Z. 35 ein Zeuge *Dub-bi-ia* DUMU *Še-en-na-ti-x*[ ], wobei das zerstörte Zeichen mit zwei waagerechten Keilen beginnt. Derselbe Zeuge begegnet noch einmal in IM 70.887 (TF_1 263) und *RATK* 4:12f., wobei das Patronym in beiden Fällen *Še-en-na*-BE geschrieben ist. Über die Identität des Zeugen besteht kein Zweifel, daher darf geschlossen werden, daß der Name *Še-en-na-til* zu lesen ist[53].

Die Verwendung von BE für *til* im Auslaut bereitet keine Schwierigkeiten, wie ebenfalls häufig belegte Namen wie Akawatil und Tampuštil zeigen, wobei allerdings eingeräumt werden muß, daß alternative Schreibungen *-ti-il* o.ä. bei diesen Namen ungleich häufiger auftreten. Wie stark Konventionen wirken können, zeigen andererseits die Namen mit dem Theonym Tilla, das fast immer *Til-la* geschrieben wird. Lediglich für den mehrere hundert Male belegten PN *Teḫip-tilla* erscheint selten die Variante *Ti-la*.

G.G.W. Müller

---

52 Ar-Rawi, "Studies in the Commercial Life of an Administrative Area of Eastern Assyria in the Fifteenth Century B.C.", Ph.D. Diss. University of Wales, 1977, S. 465.

53 So etwa Wilhelm in *AdŠ* (1980ff.) sowie bereits der Index zu *SCCNH* 1 (1981), während in der Textbearbeitung daselbst und auch z.B. in *SCCNH* 6 (1994) die traditionelle Namensform benutzt wird. Etymologie: *Šen=na* („Brüder") + *til* (Kurzform des enklit. Pers.pron. 1. Pers. Pl.).

Part IV

Excavations at Nuzi 10, Editors' Introduction

The Nuzi tablets of the Harvard Semitic Museum for many years were published in a sub-series of the Harvard Semitic Series called Excavations at Nuzi (EN 1-8 = HSS 5, 9, 10, 13, 14, 15, 16, 19). The more than 500 copies of Nuzi tablets left by the late Professor E.R. Lacheman after his death in 1982 subsequently were published by D.I. Owen and M.A. Morrison, as EN 9 in three parts within the series *SCCNH* (EN 9/1 = *SCCNH* 2, 355-702; EN 9/2 = *SCCNH* 4, 131-398; EN 9/3 = *SCCNH* 5, 85-357).

Despite Lacheman's life-long efforts that resulted in the publication of about 2000 tablets from the Nuzi collections of the Harvard Semitic Museum, thousands of fragments and a considerable number of more or less complete tablets still remain unpublished. Many of these fragments carry a SMN-number (Semitic Museum Nuzi). Sometimes a group of fragments has been collected under one SMN-number only, but in many cases such groupings of fragments had no number at all when Professor Lacheman returned them to the museum in the early seventies. The museum staff assigned new numbers to these fragment groupings using the siglum, NTF (Nuzi tablet fragments).[1] According

[1] The system of NTF numbers is not quite clear. It uses the letters M, N, MM, Q and P and numbers the boxes by a non-continuous sequence of figures which sometimes are further subdivided by letters and in some cases even further by index numbers. Some of the NTF fragment collections carry a SMN-number. To give an example of the fragments collections with the siglum "M":

M 1: 10 larger and some tiny inscribed fragments.

M 1A: 6 small fragments, one sealed, most of them without script.

M 1A1: numerous fragments; as far as they contain script, torn surface; one label from room A 23 excavated on Dec. 5 [1927].

M 3A: 10 fragments of a will (Šukria s. of Wa-...), rejoined by G. Wilhelm in 1978.

M 5B: 4 inscribed fragments.

M 5C: 12 inscribed fragments = SMN 2465.

M 6A: 29 inscribed fragments from room C 2 (= L 2 or M 2).

M 7A: 7 inscribed fragments, among which one large sealed fragment with a list of witnesses.

M 7B: 8 inscribed fragments, one fragment of an envelope from room A 14, excavated on Dec. 14 [1927]. ...

Studies on the Civilization and Culture of Nuzi and the Hurrians - 8

to a rough calculation, the NTF collection contains about 3000 fragments, many of which, however, display very few cuneiform signs or none at all. The main value of this collection is in its potential use for joins.[2]

"Excavations at Nuzi 10" was conceived initially by D.I. Owen after hundreds of additional Nuzi fragments had been returned by him to the Harvard Semitic Museum from the Lacheman home where Lacheman had, for many years, been preparing to copy each and every one of them. The majority was not in any order and many of the SMN-numbers had been lost or never assigned. Furthermore, many fragments resulted from breaks that occurred in storage and not in the field. Because time was limited, Owen, together with M.A. Morrison, M.P. Maidman and K. Grosz, began a rough catalogue of these fragments. Those without SMN-numbers were assigned the siglum, ERL. Prior to their return to the HSM, Owen prepared a computer file of transliterations of hundreds of these fragments based on the rapid readings of these texts by himself, Morrison, Maidman and Grosz. In addition, he culled transliterations from Lacheman's unpublished Harvard University dissertation as well as other notes in Lacheman's papers and added them to this file. Copies were then shared with Maidman, Wilhelm, Fincke and others. These data helped greatly with the cataloguing of important new texts, with joins to previously published tablets and with identifications of missing or otherwise confused sources. It was Owen's intention to prepare a volume of transliterations of all fragments as "Excavations at Nuzi 10," thereby continuing and completing the series. Furthermore, Owen made available copies of Lacheman's unfinished personal name collection, *Personal Names from the Kingdom of Arrapḫa* (hereafter *PNKA*), to those working on the Nuzi archives, thereby making it possible to facilitate further identifications. Later on, after discussions with G. Wilhelm, it was decided instead to prepare copies of all these fragments. This plan became a reality because of the enthusiastic and positive response of Jeanette Fincke to our suggestion to take over the charge to copy the fragments. Her intimate familiarity with the Nuzi corpus and her interest in undertaking this demanding project, made her the ideal candidate for such an effort. During her stay in the Harvard Semitic Museum in the autumn of 1995, Ms. Fincke copied the 65 fragments published in this volume as EN 10/1, 1-65. Her work is expected to be continued in fall of 1996 and the results will appear in future volumes.

We decided not to attempt to publish the fragments according to text types or archives because this would have delayed the publication for many years. The sequence of publication basically follows the order of SMN-numbers. The task of reconstructing all the Nuzi archives making full use of all the unpublished materials can only be a prospect for future generations of Nuzi scholars.

---

2 Cf. G. Wilhelm, *Das Archiv des Šilwa-teššup*, Heft 2-4, for which the NTF collection was surveyed. The individual fragments within the NTF fragment collections are unnumbered. In the edition of the Šilwa-teššup archive, a single NTF fragment is referred to as "one fragment from NTF ..." or "NTF ... (1)."

The project enjoyed the full support of the director and staff of the Harvard Semitic Museum; we express our sincerest thanks to the director and curator of the museum, Professor Lawrence E. Stager, to Professor Piotr Steinkeller, curator of the cuneiform collections, to Dr. Joseph Greene, assistant director, and Dr. James Armstrong, assistant curator.

The stays of G. Wilhelm (Sept. 12-23, 1995) and J. Fincke (Sept. 17 - Oct. 28, 1995) at the Harvard Semitic Museum were made possible by a generous grant of Deutscher Akademischer Austauschdienst (DAAD) in the framework of a special program launched together with the American Council of Learned Societies (ACLS).[3]

We are confident that this project will stimulate the study of Nuzi tablets which provide a unique insight into various aspects of the social, economic and legal organization of an ancient Near Eastern society.

David I. Owen
and
Gernot Wilhelm

---

3 Project-based exchange of scholars in the humanities and in social studies (Projektbezogene Förderung des Wissenschaftler-Austauschs in den Geistes- und Sozialwissenschaften).

Excavations at Nuzi 10/1, 1-65

JEANETTE FINCKE

Julius-Maximilians-Universität Würzburg

INTRODUCTION

Some of the previous editions of Nuzi texts from the collections of the Harvard Semitic Museum did not attempt to group the texts according to find spots or text genres but simply followed the sequence of the SMN (Semitic Museum Nuzi) numbers. This is the case in HSS 13, which contains the tablets with SMN numbers between 1 and 500 (as far as they had not been published before) and HSS 14, pp. 1-49, which continued with SMN numbers between 502 to 654. To a certain extent, but not systematically, the same procedure has been applied in the volume HSS 16.

In our edition of unpublished fragments of Nuzi tablets from the collections of the Harvard Semitic Museum, we basically follow this procedure though we are aware of the disadvantages for the user. We felt, however, entitled to do so because it would have taken many years of work to check all the possibilities to assign fragments to specific archives and, in many cases, this would not have been possible at all. The findspots of these fragments are recorded only in rare cases. Also, the SMN numbers do not help much in establishing the archival links of fragments, though in principle they follow the course of the excavations.[1] In addition to that there is considerable confusion of SMN numbers; in many cases different SMN-numbers refer to one and the same fragment or SMN-numbers of unpublished fragments have already been assigned to published tablets.[2]

In some cases SMN numbers could be attributed to unnumbered fragments[3] with the help of the late Professor Lacheman's transliterations and of his unpub-

1 Most of the texts from the archive of Šilwa-teššup, excavated in 1927/28, have SMN numbers between 1 and 1500; but since during the same season, the excavation of the palace was started, tablets from the palace also may have low SMN numbers.

2 Compare also D.I. Owen and M.A. Morrison, *SCCNH* 2 (1987) 341ff.

3 There are three collections in the HSM which contain tablets and fragments without a

Studies on the Civilization and Culture of Nuzi and the Hurrians - 8

lished and unfinished manuscript on Nuzi personal names, both kindly made available to me by Professor David I. Owen.

Whenever a tablet is recorded under two different SMN numbers, and one of these numbers has already been assigned to a tablet in previous editions, the earlier number has been accepted as the correct one. Sometimes, however, a fragment may be registered under one SMN-number which, however, has been assigned already to a published tablet. In these cases the SMN number is marked by an asterisk followed by the former publication number (marked by ≠ "not identical with").

Measurements are given in mm in the sequence, width x height x thickness. In all cases, the maximum dimension is given.

All the copies have been drawn at a scale of 3:1 and reduced in print to a scale of 3:2 (except for EN 10/1, 9). Whenever the surface is abraded, it is marked by dots; when it is completely broken away, it is marked with hatching. A thick line represents the edge of a tablet; a thin line indicates the edge is not preserved.

My research only became possible through the support of several persons and institutions. I am indebted to Professors David I. Owen and Gernot Wilhelm, who initiated this project and helped me in various ways. Professor Owen generously made the manuscript of a remarkable collection of Nuzi personal names (*PNKA*) available to me, that had been prepared by the late Professor E.R. Lacheman during the last decades of his life, as well as transliterations of many unpublished Nuzi tablets and fragments. My teacher, Professor Wilhelm, kindly arranged for my stay at the Harvard Semitic Museum, read the manuscript and made various comments. I also owe sincere thanks to the director and staff of the Harvard Semitic Museum for their support and encouragement: Professor Lawrence Stager, Director and Curator of the museum, Professor Piotr Steinkeller, Curator of the cuneiform collection, Dr. Joseph Greene, Assistant Director, and Dr. James Armstrong, Assistant Curator, who helped me especially with all practical problems during my stay in the museum.

SMN-number: The largest one is the collection of the "Nuzi Tablet Fragments" (NTF), followed by a collection of tablets which has been provisionally labelled "ERL." Some tablet fragments without a SMN number could also be detected within the collection of the Nuzi clay-bullae.

Bibliographical Abbreviations

AASOR 16	R.H. Pfeiffer / E.A. Speiser, "One Hundred New Selected Nuzi Texts" (AASOR 16), New Haven 1936 [quoted according to texts numbers].
AdŠ	G. Wilhelm, *Das Archiv des Šilwa-teššup*, Heft 2, Wiesbaden 1980; Heft 3, Wiesbaden 1985; Heft 4, Wiesbaden 1992 [quoted according to texts numbers].
HSS	Harvard Semitic Series, Cambridge MA.
Lacheman, *PNKA*	E.R. Lacheman, *Personal Names from the Kingdom of Arrapḫa* [unpublished manuscript].
Lacheman, *JAOS* 55	E.R. Lacheman, "New Nuzi Texts and a New Method of Copying Cuneiform Tablets," *JAOS* 55 (1935) 429-31, Plates I-VI.
Müller, HSAO 7	G.G.W. Müller, *Studien zur Siedlungsgeographie und Bevölkerung des mittleren Osttigrislandes* (Heidelberger Studien zum Alten Orient 7), Heidelberg 1994.
RGTC 10	J. Fincke, *Die Orts- und Gewässernamen der Nuzi-Texte* (Répertoire Géographique des Textes Cunéiformes 10 = Beihefte zum Tübinger Atlas des Vorderen Orients, Reihe B Nr. 7/10) Wiesbaden 1993.
Starr, Nuzi I	R.F.S. Starr, *Nuzi*, Vol. I: Text, Cambridge, MA, 1939.

CATALOGUE

No.	*SMN*	*Room*	*Measurements (in mm); Description; Notes*
1	119* ≠ HSS 13, 119		53 (frg.) x 14 (frg.) x 20 (frg.) Fragment of the upper part of a tablet. Seals of Muš-teš[šup] (rev.) and Šilwa[ya/teššup] (u. edge). Possibly belonging to the archive of Teḫip-tilla. For the names compare JENu 1023 = Lacheman, *JAOS* 55 (1935) Nr. 1, or JEN 354.
2	708 + 1744 + 1264 (= ERL 22)	A 23 (referring to SMN 1744)	68 x 86 x 30 (join: Sept. 28, '95) List of different kinds of trees/wood qualified by Hurrian terms. Most of them are classified as *pa-ḫa-ar-ḫu-ul-li-na*.MEŠ (overlaps on reverse); for this term compare HSS 15, 141. Some of the trees mentioned on the fragment SMN 708 (lo. left edge fragment with wormhole) are already quoted by E.R. Lacheman apud Starr, *Nuzi* I, 1939, 535 and *CAD* G 20a, K 86a and *AHw* 426b.
3	770		15 (frg.) 42 (frg.) x 14 (frg.) Fragmentary declaration (upper edge and beginning of obverse). [*lišānšu*] by Aššur-bēlī, the LÚ.[...], concerning [^{f}Aḫaj$^{?}$a]mši, wife of [...]. Seal of Akip-tilla.
4	894		55.8 (frg.) 24.6 (frg.) x 22.5 (frg.) (Identification through Lacheman, *PNKA*). Fragmentary legal text (lower part of the tablet). ^{f}Ummī-nuzu receives houses in the center of the city Nuzi, *ša tikki* PÚ.MEŠ, as her share from Ar-x[...] and Ḫainni, sons of [...].
5	961		49 x 49 x 8 (frg.) Reverse of a tablet (the fragment is black from burning). Seals of Manni, the scribe, of Taena and of Si[l?]-tilla.
6	1026 (= ERL 97)		67.5 (frg.) x 55 (frg.) x 24.5 Fragmentary list of men who had been at the disposal of [...], Urḫi-tilla and Tupki-tilla (*ša* ŠU PN) and now are released to their own houses (*ša ana* É-*šunu muššurū*). Seal of Teḫip-šarri.
7	1103 (= AdŠ 279)		44.5 (frg.) x 44 (frg.) x 22 (frg.) Fragmentary list of personal names (the remaining part of reverse is rubbed off completely).
8	1120* ≠ HSS 14, 102		58 x 82 x 33.5 Memorandum (?) of different amounts of tin, barley, [...] and wheat. Reverse not inscribed.

No.	*SMN*	*Room*	*Measurements (in mm); Description; Notes*
9	1132		73.4 x 98 (frg.) x 28 (frg.) Fragmentary [*ṭuppi mā*]*rūti*. Ezira is [adopted] by Tur-marti and Šukria.
10	1173 (= ERL 2) + 348 (= AASOR 16, 3)	C 2 (=L/M 2) (referring to SMN 348)	1173: 82 (frg.) x 61 (frg.) x 16 (frg.) (join: Oct. 25, '95) Identification of the ERL-fragment by G. Wilhelm (cf. *SCCNH* 7, 152). This fragment joines lines 45-55 (Rev.) of AASOR 16, 3 (declarations of different persons concerning K/Ḫušši-ḫarpe).
11	1272		41 (frg.) x 53.5 (frg.) x 12 (frg.) At the upper break of the fragment are traces of adhesive paste, but the joining fragment could not be found in 1995. A transliteration made by G. Wilhelm in 1987 shows that six lines with personal names are lost.
12	1292		58 (frg.) x 50 (frg.) x 9 (frg.) Fragment of reverse. Statement (*umma*) concerning a field. Preserved are the vindication clause and the renunciation of action. This fragment belongs to the Teḫip-tilla archive (assigned by M.P. Maidman).
13	1409		72.8 (frg.) x 52.6 (frg.) x 24.7 Fragmentary description of horses given to [...], son of Zilia, and *Am?-ḫa-x-x-pu*, son of Teḫit-teššup, by (?) Tupki-tilla, the *aduḫlu*. For l. 1 see G. Wilhelm, Nuzi Notes 18 in this volume.
14	1464		72.9 (frg.) x 64 (frg.) x 15.5 (frg.) (Identification through Lacheman, *PNKA*). Fragment of the right part of a list of women identified by patronyms. The lines are separated by dividing lines.
15	1525		42 (frg.) x 30 (frg.) x 17.8 Work contract; Ḫašip-apu gives materials to Ni[r-...] *ana šipra epēši*.
16	1527 + 2860 (= AdŠ 580)		Main frg.: 68 (frg.) x 46 (frg.) x 5.5 (frg.), Frg. of obv.: 32.5 (frg.) x 30.5 (frg.) x 5 (frg.), Frg. of rev.: 28.5 (frg.) 37.5 (frg.) x x 8.5 (frg.) The box with the number SMN 1527 in 1995 contained five fragments which could not be identified with other SMN numbers. Three of these fragments belong to the same tablet and one of them joins SMN 2860 (join G. Wilhem 1987). (For the other two fragments see below 10/1, 17 and 10/1, 18.) Fragmentary record of a court case concerning a field. Wirreštanni looses the case because of a contradictory declaration ([*awātīšu*] *šinapšumma ītepuš*).

No.	*SMN*	*Room*	*Measurements (in mm); Description; Notes*
17	1527*		41 (frg.) x 36 (frg.) 10.5 (frg.) For the SMN number see above sub 10/1, 16. The palace and a Šelluni are mentioned.
18	1527*		34.5 x 36 x 9 (frg.) For the SMN number see above sub 10/1, 16. Reverse of a record of the delivery of arrows (probably by the palace).
19	1529		66.8 x 70 (frg.) x 23.3 (frg.) Fragmentary list of different goods (6 donkeys, 3 *ṣimitt[u...]*, [*ša* GIŠ *š*]*a-ak-ku-u*[*l-li*], wheels).
20	1530		66 x 25.5 (frg.) x 19.5 Lacheman, *PNKA*, quotes this fragment as SMN 1539; there is no other tablet or fragment known under SMN 1539. Fragmentary statement. If Zili-ḫa!manna does not give ⌜2?⌝ [*x* (*x*)] ⌜*x-ra*⌝*-pu* (l. 3′) he has to pay 5 ANŠE of barley to Ninki-tilla after the harvest.
21	1531 + 2775 (= EN 9/3, 52A)		56 (frg.) x 53.9 (frg.) x 11.5 (frg.) (join: Oct. 23, '95) Fragmentary [*ṭuppi mārū*]*ti*. fTarmennaja, the MUNUS.LUGAL, is adopted by Eḫlip-apu, [son of Šan]ḫari, and receives 7 GIŠ.APIN ⌜A⌝.[Š]À *šīqū* in the *ugāru* of Atakkal. The upper edge shows traces of a seal impression.
22	1537		53 (frg.) x 52 (frg.) x 8 (frg.) "Sammelurkunde" (frg. of the lower part) belonging to the archive of Zike: Delivery of tin to different persons as interest-bearing loans to be repaid aft[er the harvest] (l. 6′).
23	1540		52 x 42 (frg.) x 19 (frg.) Fragmentary (frg. of the upper part; black burned clay) loan contract concerning 10 talents of copper. The *tamkāru* Šummalli (mistake for Šumma-ilī?) is mentioned. He also sealed the document.
24	1561		36.5 (frg.) x 23.5 (frg.) x 19 (frg.) Fragmentary (lower part; deeply black burned clay) statement made by two or more persons concerning the receipt of barley given in favor of five daughters [of the king] by *Er*!-WA-LU[GAL]. Sealed by fKalimt[u]. Compare HSS 13, 77.
25	1584 + JENu 401 (= JEN 13)		SMN 1584: 30.5 (frg.) x 62 (frg.) x 27 (frg.) (long distance join: M.P. Maidman) Black burned clay. *ṭuppi mārūti* of Teḫip-tilla, son of Puḫi-šenni. Transliterated by M.P. Maidman, *SCCNH* 2 (1987) 345ff.

No.	SMN	Room	Measurements (in mm); Description; Notes
26	1585 (= ERL 85)		53.5 (frg.) x 32 (frg.) x 24 (frg.) Fragmentary (lower part) statement made by two or more persons concerning an adoption (?). Pai-teššup receives a field and pays, among other goods, GÚ.È.MEŠ (obv. l. 4′).
27	1586 + 1044 (= HSS 9, 22) (= AdŠ 610)	A 11 (referring to SMN 1044)	1586: 37.5 (frg.) x 59 (frg.) x 10 (frg.) (long distance join: G. Wilhelm, 1987) The tablet HSS 9, 22 is housed in the Iraq Museum, Baghdad, (IM 50834) and could not be used for copying the joining signs. *ṭuppi mārūti* of Tupkia, son of Šurki-tilla, who adopts Pai-teššup, servant of Šilwa-teššup.
28	1588		56 (frg.) x 63.5 (frg.) x 27 (frg.) Fragmentary list of 28 women from Nuzi (u. edge 26′f.); 11 women are MUNUS.MEŠ *esrētu*.M[EŠ] *nuārāti*.MEŠ *ša* U[RU] *Ta-še-ni-we* (rev. l. 23′f.) and four are DUMU.MUNUS LUGAL (l. l. edge 26′).
29	1588* (= ERL 54) + 1635 (= EN 9/1, 148) (= AdŠ 614)		66.4 x 107.3 x 33.5 (join: Sept. 19. ′95) (Identification through Lacheman, *PNKA*. This fragment has the same SMN number as EN 10/1, 28). Fragmentary declaration before witnesses made by Šanḫarua, son of [...]inni; he gives a field in Šelwuḫu to Pai-teššup, son of Ḫanaja, in exchange for barley, wheat and other goods. The field is situated north of the road to Abenaš (l. 10) and cut by the canal of Šilwa-teššup (l. 13f.). The tablet was written *ina* EGIR-*ki šūdûtu ša* É.GAL (l. 26f.) by the scribe Eni[a?], son of Uta-[andul?].
30	1590		63.5 (frg.) x 31.5 (frg.) x 15 (frg.) Fragment (upper part of obverse) of a *ṭuppi mārūti*. Ḫerrea, son of [Teḫip-apu], adopts Muš-apu, son of [Purna-zini]. For the archive of Muš-apu see M.A. Morrison, *SCCNH* 4 (1993) 69ff., and EN 10/1, 56.
31	1593* ≠ EN 9/1, 141		49 (frg.) x 40.5 (frg.) x 12 (frg.) Fragmentary deed mentioning [...], son of Tulpia (l. 1′), and Šilwaja (l. 6′) concerning a donkey. Note l. 5′: *ši-bi-ir-ti*.
32	1594		64 (frg.) x 33 (frg.) x 27 (frg.) Fragmentary *ṭuppi titennūti* (top of the tablet). Tae, son of Ḫuziri, gives a field in the *ugāru* of Nuzi to [...]. For transliteration see D.I. Owen, *SCCNH* 2 (1987) 350.
33	1595		58 (frg.) x 24.5 (frg.) x 20 (frg.) Fragmentary *ṭuppi titennūti* (top of the tablet) of *Ta-*⸢*x x x*⸣ [...]. The tablet is sealed by Wantišše and the scribe.

No.	SMN	Room	Measurements (in mm); Description; Notes
34	1599		76 (frg.) x 21.5 (frg.) x 15 (frg.) Fragmentary (top of the tablet) *ṭuppi tamgurti* between Alkija, son of Tarmi-teššup, and Ilānu, son of [Tajj]uki. Sealed by Kuššia, Taena and Taika.
35	1605	"A 23"	58.4 x 52.8 x 15 (frg.) Obverse and lower edge; dark grey burned clay. According to a slip of paper the fragment was found in room A 23 on Dec. 5 [, 1927]. The tablet, however, belongs to the group of *rākib narkabti*-lists, possibly from A 34.
36	1606		39 x 23 (frg.) x 19. Fragment of the upper part of a tablet: Urḫi-teššup, Utap-tae and Puḫi-šenni, 3 LÚ.ME *pa-aḫ-ḫa-ru* (l. 4). Sealed by Akip-šenni.
37	1607		66 (frg.) x 14 (frg.) x 18.5 (frg.) Fragment of the first three lines of obverse with two Kassite personal names. For transliteration see Müller, HSAO 7, 1994, 74.
38	1608 (= AdŠ 527)		37.5 (frg.) x 48.8 (frg.) x 11 (frg.) Fragment of reverse with personal names.
39	1609		57.5 (frg.) x 46 (frg.) x 11 (frg.) Fragment of reverse; grey burned clay. List with personal names. Only some professions are preserved, e.g. [... *ra-ki*]*b* GIŠ.GIGIR (l. 1′) and [...-*š*]*a-tal* SIPA *ša* É.GAL (l. 2′).
40	1610		52 (frg.) x 21.5 (frg.) x 18.5 (frg.) Fragment of the lower part of a tablet with personal names.
41	1613 (= ERL 77)	C 81 (= R 81)	53.5 x 50 x 22 (Identification through an unpublished transliteration of E.R. Lacheman). List with names of women. Reverse uninscribed.
42	1614		41 (frg.) x 44 (frg.) x 9 (frg.) Fragment of reverse; part of a list of 11 *ṣuḫarātu* handed over to Ammi-x[...], son of Šatum-na[ya].
43	1615		42 (frg.) x 37 (frg.) x 9.4 (frg.) Fragment of obverse with names of women. No join with SMN 1614 despite the similarity of script and content.
44	1616 (= ERL 75)		54.5 x 51.5 x 21.3 (Identification through an unpublished transliteration of E.R. Lacheman).

No.	SMN	Room	Measurements (in mm); Description; Notes
			List of women of various professions; l. 1′: [...]x *birmi*, l. 5′: 3 [MUNUS.MEŠ *š*]*inaḫiluḫlu* (from *šinaḫilu* "of second position / quality"), l. 7′: MU[NUS x]-*annuḫlu*, l. 9′: *sirāšû* (brewer), l. 10′: *ša* GIŠ.GAD, l. 12′: *uzzulikaru*[!].
45	1620		56.8 (frg.) x 52.4 (frg.) x 11 (frg.) Fragment of reverse with list of witnesses and two seal impressions. Iškur-mansum is the scribe.
46	1622		53 (frg.) x 63 (frg.) x 18 (frg.) The upper edge is close to the breach. Fragment of reverse with two seal impressions, one of Iriri-til[la].
47	1623		51 (frg.) x 46 (frg.) x 15.2 (frg) Fragment of the upper part of a tablet. List of objects, only the numbers are preserved. Sealed by Tupkia.
48	1624 + 1567 (= HSS 16, 425) (= AdŠ 448)	A 23	45 x 16.5 (frg.) x 19.5 (frg.) (long distance join: G. Wilhelm 1986) The tablet HSS 16, 425 has been returned to the Iraq Museum, Baghdad, in 1983 and could not be used for copying the joining signs.
49	1625* ≠ HSS 19, 33		41 (frg.) x 41 (frg.) x 7.5 (frg.) Fragmentary list of men with filiation (witnesses ?).
50	1626 + 307 (= HSS 9, 11) (= AdŠ 578)	A 23 (referring to SMN 307)	84 (frg.) 15 (frg.) x x 25 (frg.) (long distance join: G. Wilhelm, 1987) The tablet HSS 9, 11 is housed in the Iraq Museum, Baghdad, (IM 50782) and could not be used for copying the joining signs.
51	1627		63.5 (frg.) x 21.5 (frg.) x 12.5 (frg.) Fragment of reverse and upper edge. Seal impression of Kuššia.
52	1628	C 76 (= R 76)	44.5 x 43 x 22.5 On reverse the names of two seal owners ([f]Unu[š-kiaše] and [f]Tiš-nu[ri]) are preserved.
53	1632		39 (frg.) x 53.3 x 9 (frg.) Fragmentary (right part of obverse and lower edge) statement of Ipša-ḫalu concerning 200 bricks (l. 4′: 2 *li-mi* SIG_4.M[EŠ).
54	1634 (= ERL 99)		68.5 (frg.) x 40 (frg.) x 25 (frg.) (Identification by G. Wilhelm, 1986/7). Fragmentary (upper part of tablet) declaration (*lišān-šu*) of Tultukka and Attija, sons of Innikaja. The tablet was written *ina* EGIR [*š*]*ūdût*[*i*] (l. 5) in Nuzi.

No.	*SMN*	*Room*	*Measurements (in mm); Description; Notes*
55	1637		62.8 x 29 (frg.) x 19.5 Fragmentary (upper part of tablet) declaration (*lišān*[!]*-šu*) of x[...], son of Ḫuti[...]. On reverse the seal impressions of [Tamp]uštil, son of Šeḫal-teššup, and of Turar-[teššup?], son of Z[i-/G[e-...], are preserved.
56	1638 (= ERL 105) + 1 Frg. from NTF P 63		65.7 x 77 (frg.) x 31 (frg.) (join: Sept. 28, '95) For identification of the ERL tablet cf. G. Wilhelm, *SCCNH* 7 (1995) 154ff. Fragmentary [*ṭuppi mārūti*]. Muš-apu (written: *Nu-ša-a-pu*)(, son of Purnazini,) is [adopted] by Ḫerrea (, son of Teḫip-apu,) and receives a field "as his share". The tablet is written by *A-*⌜*ú*?⌝[...]. For the archive of Muš-apu see M.A. Morrison, *SCCNH* 4 (1993) 69ff., and EN 10/1, 30.
57	1639 + ERL 79		64 x 93 (frg.) x 27 (rejoined Sept. 19, '95) Lawsuit between Ezira and Tarmi-teššup concerning a field. An oath by the king is mentioned (*nīš* LUGAL; compare also EN 9/1, 148). Ezira wins the case. Ila-nīšu the scribe.
58	1640		58 (frg.) x 79 (frg.) x 15 (frg.) Traces of a seal impression on the remains of left edge. Protocol of charges against the mayor K/Ḫuššiḫarbe (*Ku-uš-ši-ḫar-pa* l. 4', 13') mentioning 30 GIŠ *ku-pa-nu* (l. 5). For a similar declaration of Zilip-tilla concerning ᶠBizatu (l. 9'), ᶠḪumer-elli (l. 10'), Šimi-tilla (l. 11', 15') and K/Ḫuššiḫarbe cf. AASOR 16, 4 l. 1ff.
59	1641		61 (frg.) x 87 (frg.) x 20 (frg.) Protocol of charges against the mayor K/Ḫuššiḫarbe (*Ḫu-uš-ši-ḫar-be* l. 10) referring to a textile (*pa-am-pa-la* l. 7), the palace (l. 8) and the *ilku*-duty (l. 9') of property given (?) to K/Ḫuššiḫarbe (l. 9'-11'); cf. AASOR 16, 13.
60	1642		36 (frg.) x 58 (frg.) x 27 (frg.) Protocol of charges against the mayor K/Ḫuššiḫarbe (*Ḫu-uš-ši-ḫar-be* l. 6, 8) mentioning a house of Akapu (l. 4') and another (?) house in Atakkal (l. 12') [on the road to] Anzukalli (l. 13').
61	1643 A		42 (frg.) x 52 (frg.) x 7 (frg.) Protocol of charges against the mayor K/Ḫuššiḫarbe (*Ku-uš-ši-ḫar-pa* l. 6') mentionig parts of wagons ( ]x.MEŠ *ša* GIŠ.MAR.GÍ[D.DA.MEŠ]) and 10 sheep (l. 8').

No.	*SMN*	*Room*	*Measurements (in mm); Description; Notes*
62	1643 B		26 (frg.) x 41 (frg.) x 8 (frg.) Fragment (reverse with the beginning of the right edge of the tablet) of a lawsuit concerning theft (rev. 2′: *i-na mu-ši* "in the night"; rev 4′: *nu-uš-te-ri-i*[*q*] "we have stolen"; rev. 5′f.: [... *i*]*š-tu*$_4$ *ma-ag-ra-*[...] / [... (*ni-*)*il*(*-te*)]*-qè*, "from the threshing floor we have taken ...").
63	1644 + 1646		61 (frg.) x 90 (frg.) x 31.5 (frg.?) (join: Oct. 25, '95) Protocol of charges against the mayor K/Ḫuššiḫarbe ([*-u*]*š-ši-ḫar-be* l. 6, 9, 15′, 16′) referring to oil (l. 2). The storehouse ( ]x *ka-ri-*⸢*we*⸣ l. 20′) is mentioned.
64	1645		55 (frg.) x 45.5 (frg.) x 17.5 (frg.) Fragmentary (top of the tablet) statement (*umma*) made by Ḫeru(y[a]).
65	2909 + 4 unnumb. fragments		67.2 (frg.) 100 (frg.) x x 20 (frg.) (join: Oct. 11, '95) Fragmentary [*ṭuppi a*]*ḫḫūti* of Taja who establishes an *aḫḫūtu*-relationship with Ezira concerning 10 ANŠE field in the *dimtu* Šel[wuḫu(we)] (l. 4) and a house (É *ba-i-ḫu*!, l. 5) in the *ṣerītu* of Nuzi.

INDEX OF SMN NUMBERS

Index of ERL Numbers

ERL	SMN	EN 10/1	ERL	SMN	EN 10/1
2	1173+	10	79	1639 (+)	57
22+	1264+	2	85	1585	26
54+	1588*+	29	97	1026	6
75	1616	44	99	1634	54
77	1613	41	105	1638+	56

Index of Previous Publications

Publication	*Museum No.*	EN 10/1
AASOR 16, 3+	SMN 348	10
EN 9/3, 52A+	SMN 2775	21
EN 9/1, 148+	SMN 1635	29
HSS 9, 11+	SMN 307	50
HSS 9, 22+	SMN 1044	27
HSS 16, 425+	SMN 1567	48
JEN 13+	JENu 401	25
M.P. Maidman, *SCCNH* 2 (1987) 345ff.	SMN 1584+JEN 13	25
G. Müller, HSAO 7, 1994, 74	SMN 1607	37
D.I. Owen, *SCCNH* 2 (1987) 350	SMN 1594	32

Index of Scribes

A-⸢*ú*⸣-[...]	EN 10/1 56
Eni[a?], son of Uta-[andul?]	EN 10/1 29
Ila-nīšu	EN 10/1 59
Iškur-mansum	EN 10/1 45
Manni	EN 10/1 5

Index of Room Numbers

Room No.	EN 10/1	SMN	*Room No.*	EN 10/1	SMN
none	1	119*		40	1610
	3	770		42	1614
	4	894		43	1615
	5	961		44	1616
	6	1026		45	1620
	7	1103		46	1622
	8	1120*		47	1623
	9	1132		49	1625*
	11	1272		51	1627
	12	1292		53	1632
	13	1409		54	1634
	14	1464		55	1637
	15	1525		56	1638+ 1 frg. NTF P 63
	16	1527+2860		57	1639 + ERL 79
	17	1527*		58	1640
	18	1527*		59	1641
	19	1529		60	1642
	20	1530		61	1643 A
	21	1531+2775		62	1643 B
	22	1537		63	1644+1646
	23	1540		64	1645
	24	1561		65	2909+ 4 unnumb. frgs
	25	1584+JEN 13	A 11	27	1586+1044
	26	1585	A 23	2	708+1744+1264
	28	1588		48	1624+1567
	29	1588*+1635		50	1626+307
	30	1590	"A 23"	35	1605
	31	1593*	(= A 34?)		
	32	1594	C 2	10	348+1173
	33	1595	(= L/M 2)		
	34	1599	C 76	52	1628
	36	1606	(= R 76)		
	37	1607	C 81	41	1613
	38	1608	(=R 81)		
	39	1609			

1

OBVERSE

1

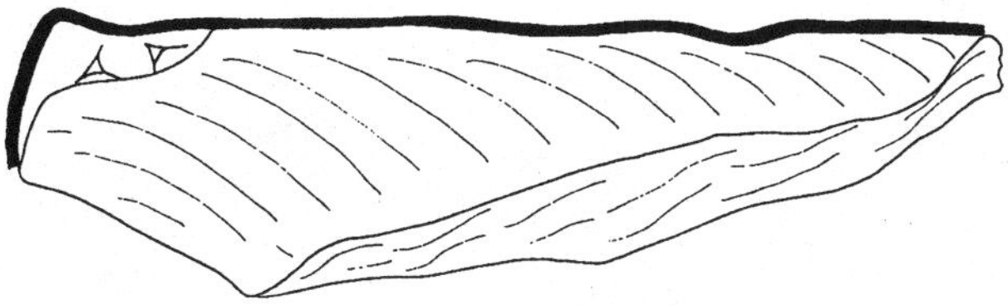

END OF OBVERSE DESTROYED

REVERSE

BEGINNING OF REVERSE DESTROYED

2’

UPPER EDGE

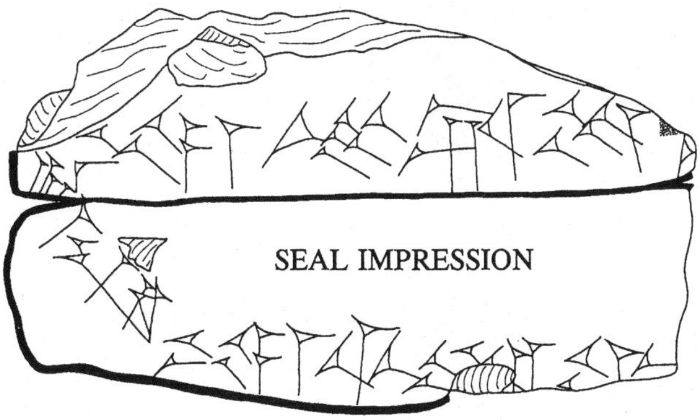

4’

2

OBVERSE

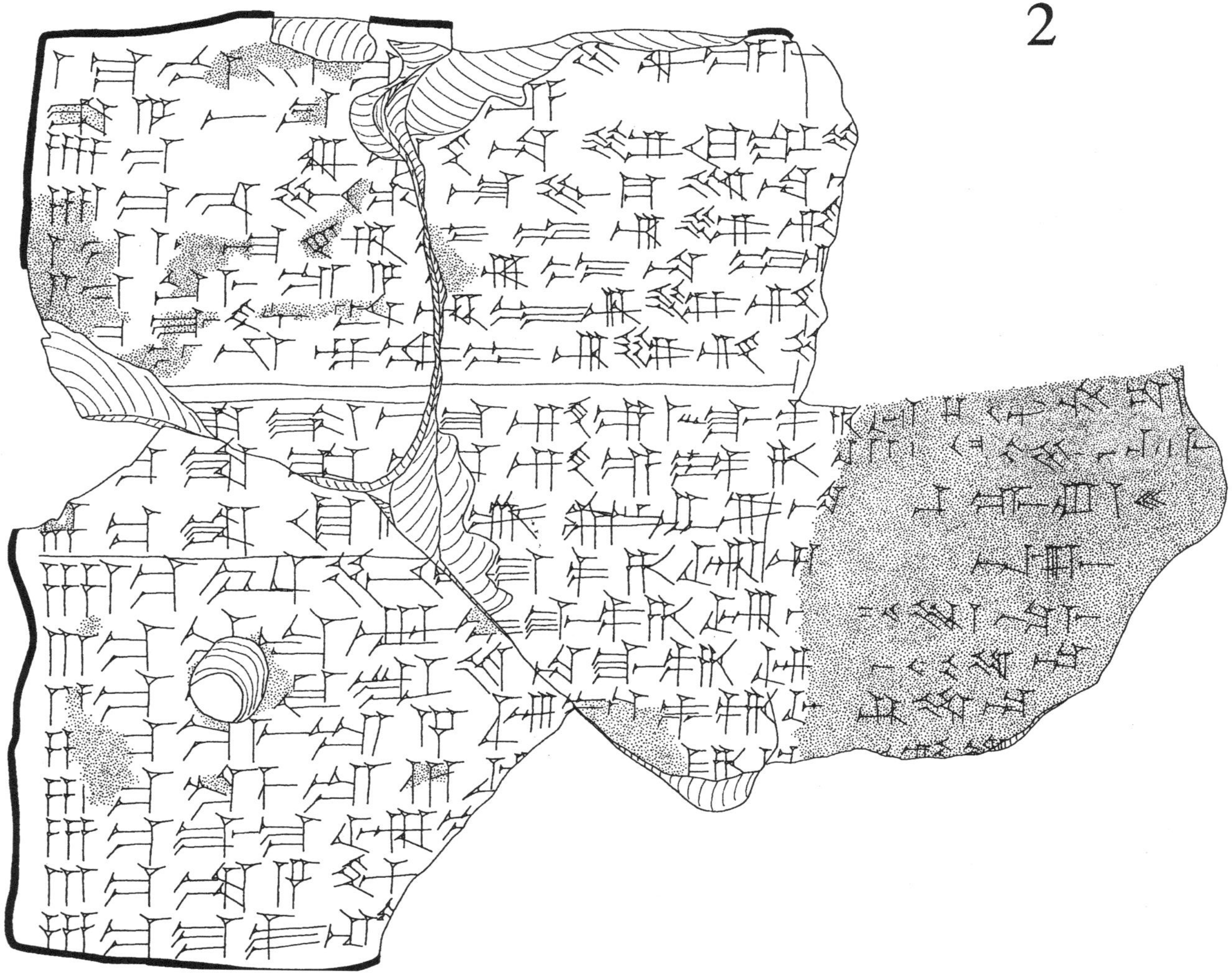

2

LOWER EDGE

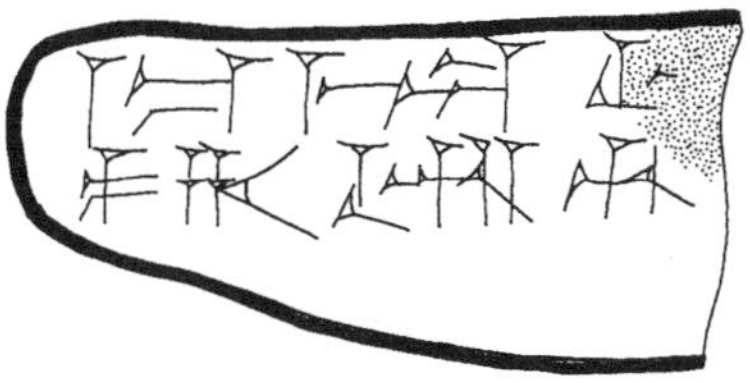

REVERSE

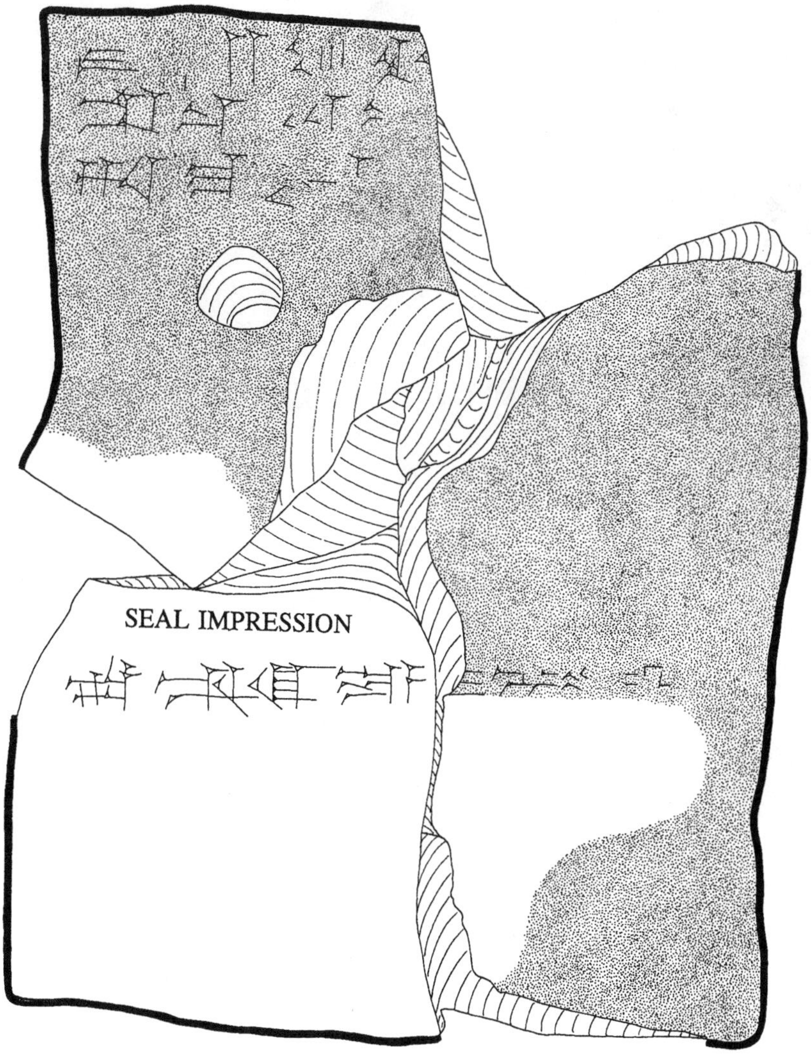

3

OBVERSE

2

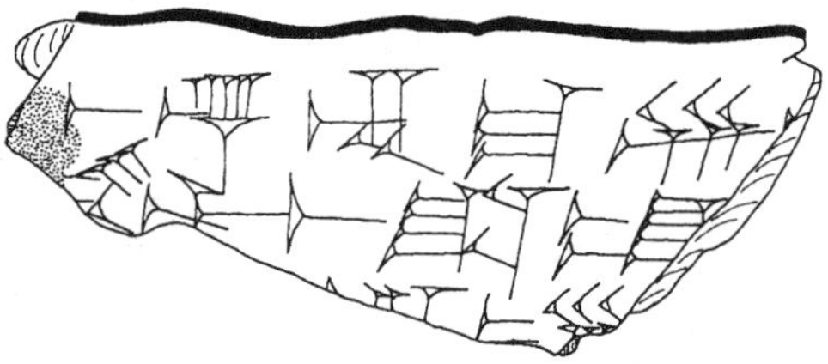

END OF OBVERSE DESTROYED

UPPER EDGE

4'

4

OBVERSE

BEGINNING OF OBVERSE DESTROYED

2'

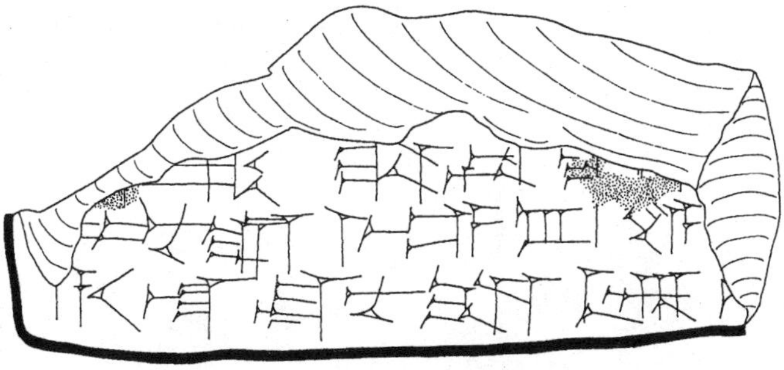

LOWER EDGE

5'

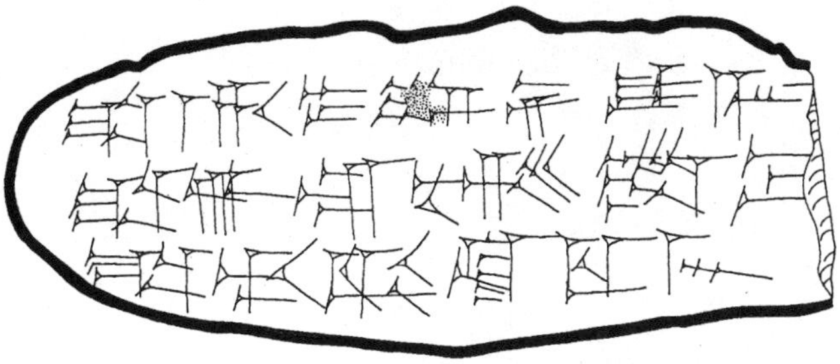

REVERSE

10'

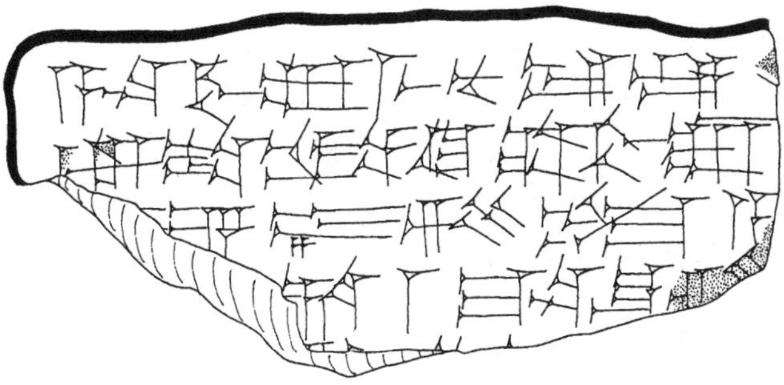

END OF REVERSE DESTROYED

5

REVERSE

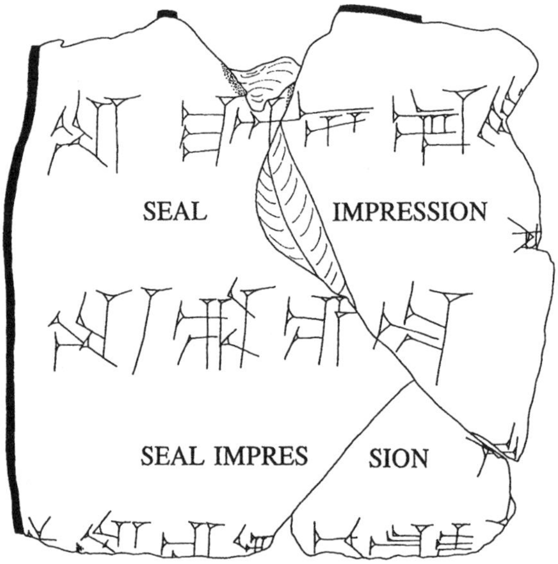

5'

3'
2'
1'

6

OBVERSE

BEGINNING OF OBVERSE DESTROYED

5'

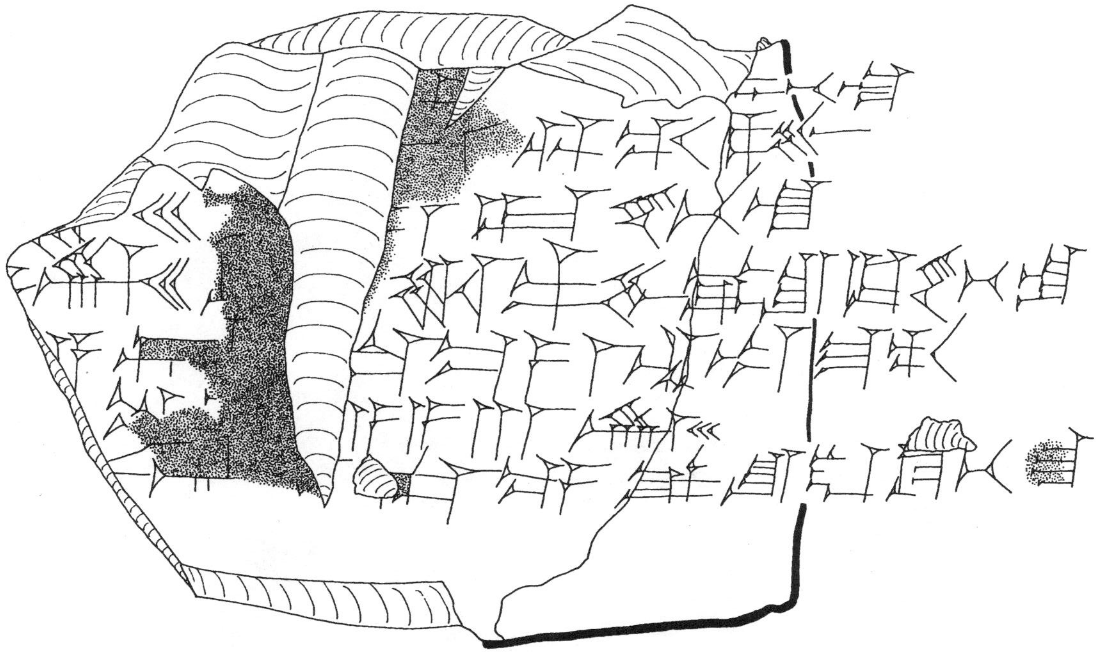

6

REVERSE

8'

9'

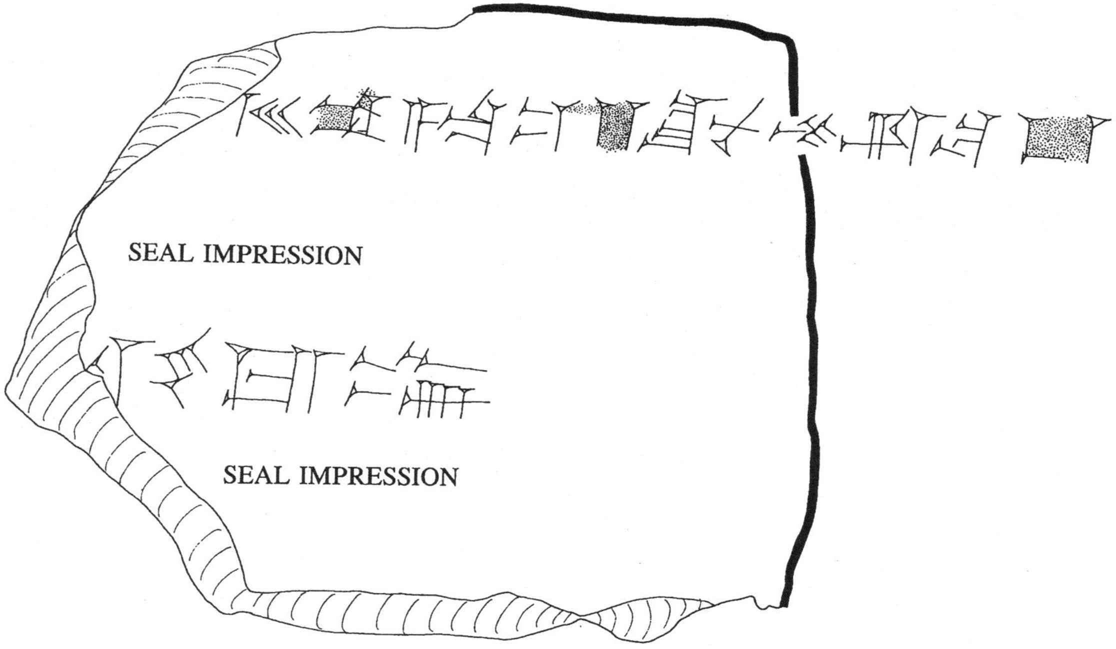

END OF REVERSE DESTROYED

7

OBVERSE

RIGHT EDGE

5'

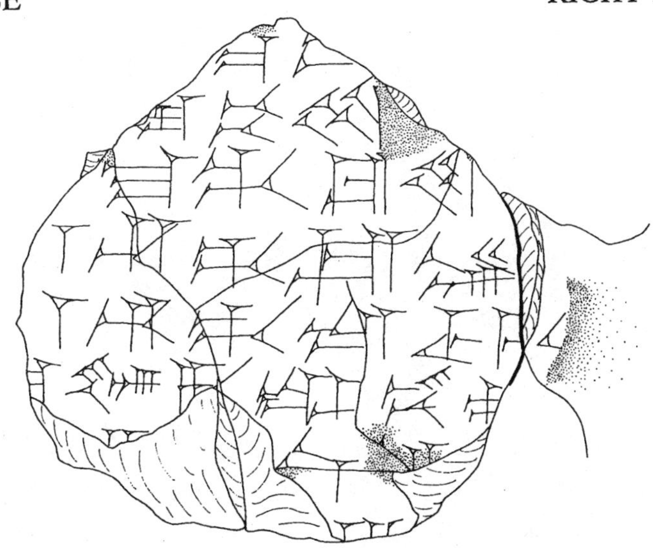

8

OBVERSE

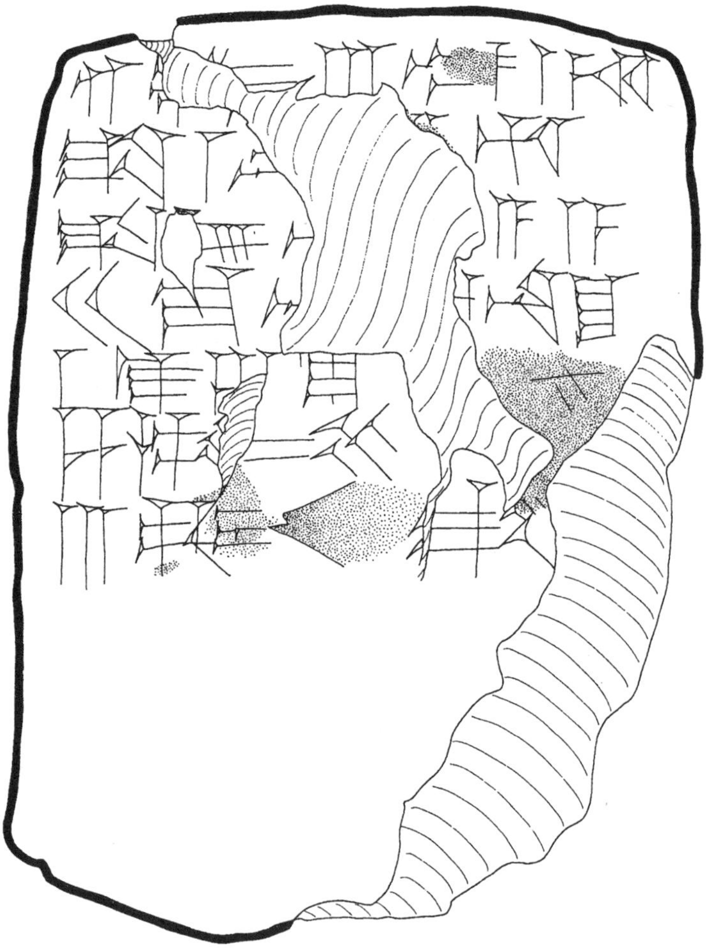

REVERSE UNINSCRIBED

9

OBVERSE

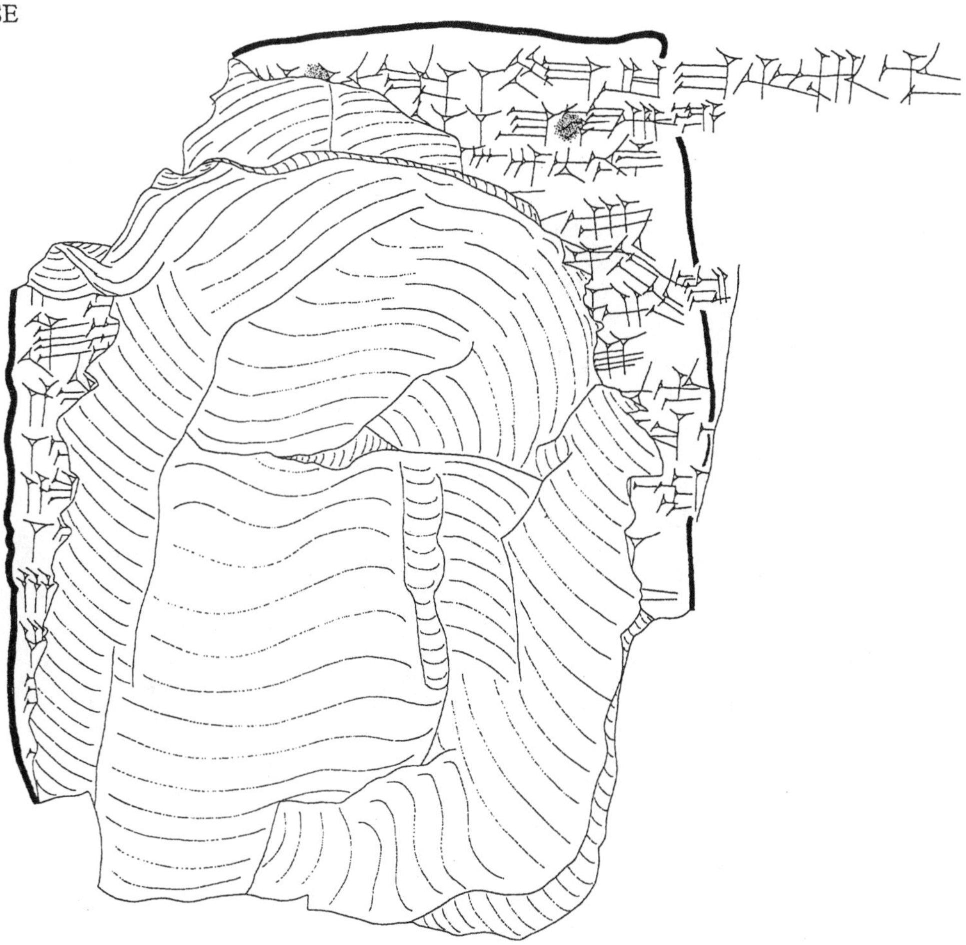

END OF OBVERSE DESTROYED

9

REVERSE

BEGINNING OF REVERSE DESTROYED

16'

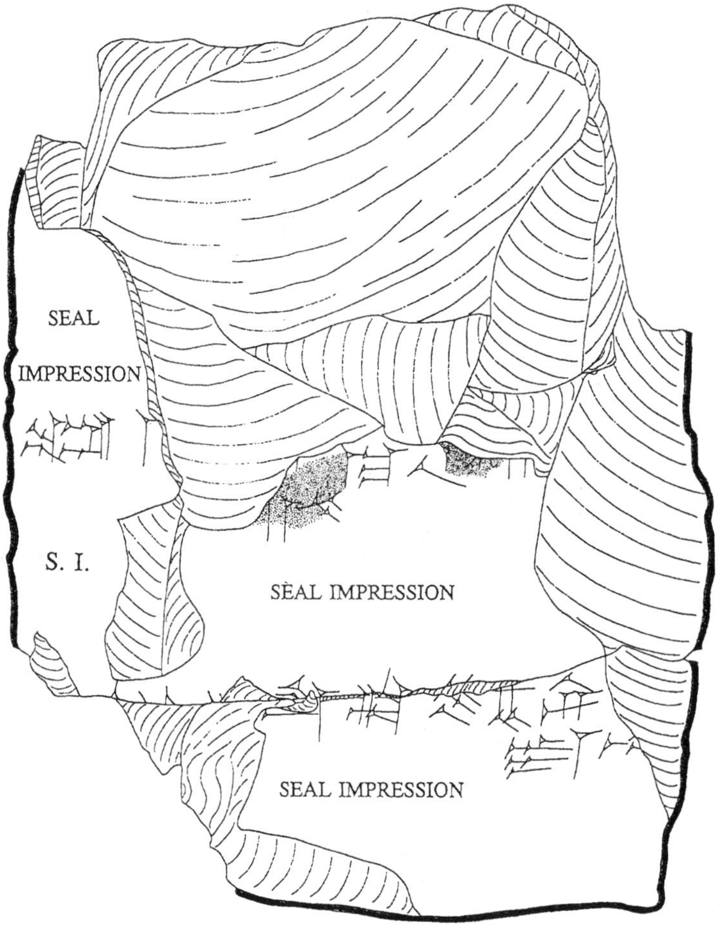

UPPER EDGE

20'

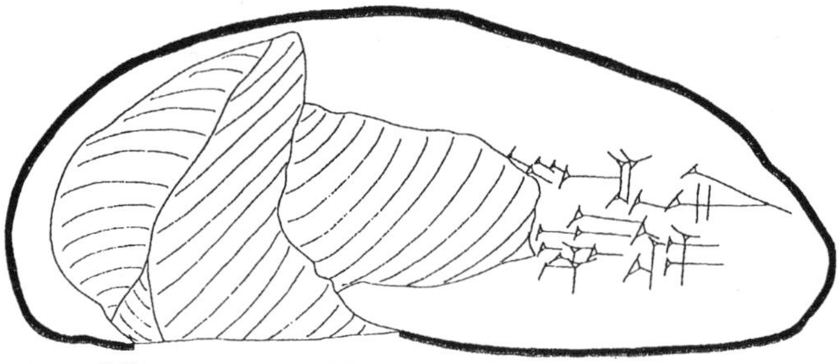

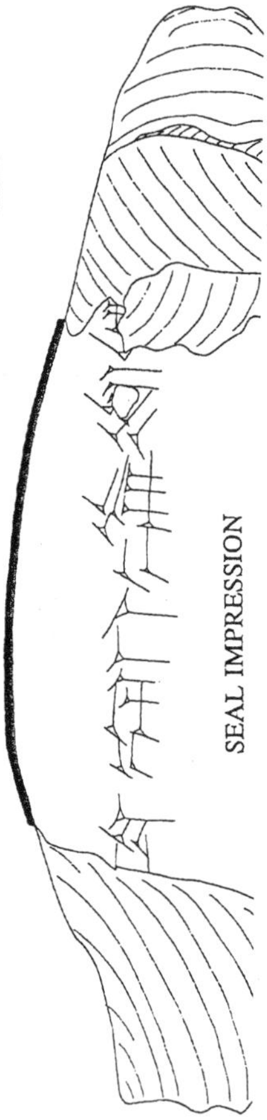

LEFT EDGE

10

REVERSE

FOR OBVERSE AND BEGINNING OF REVERSE
SEE AASOR 16, 3

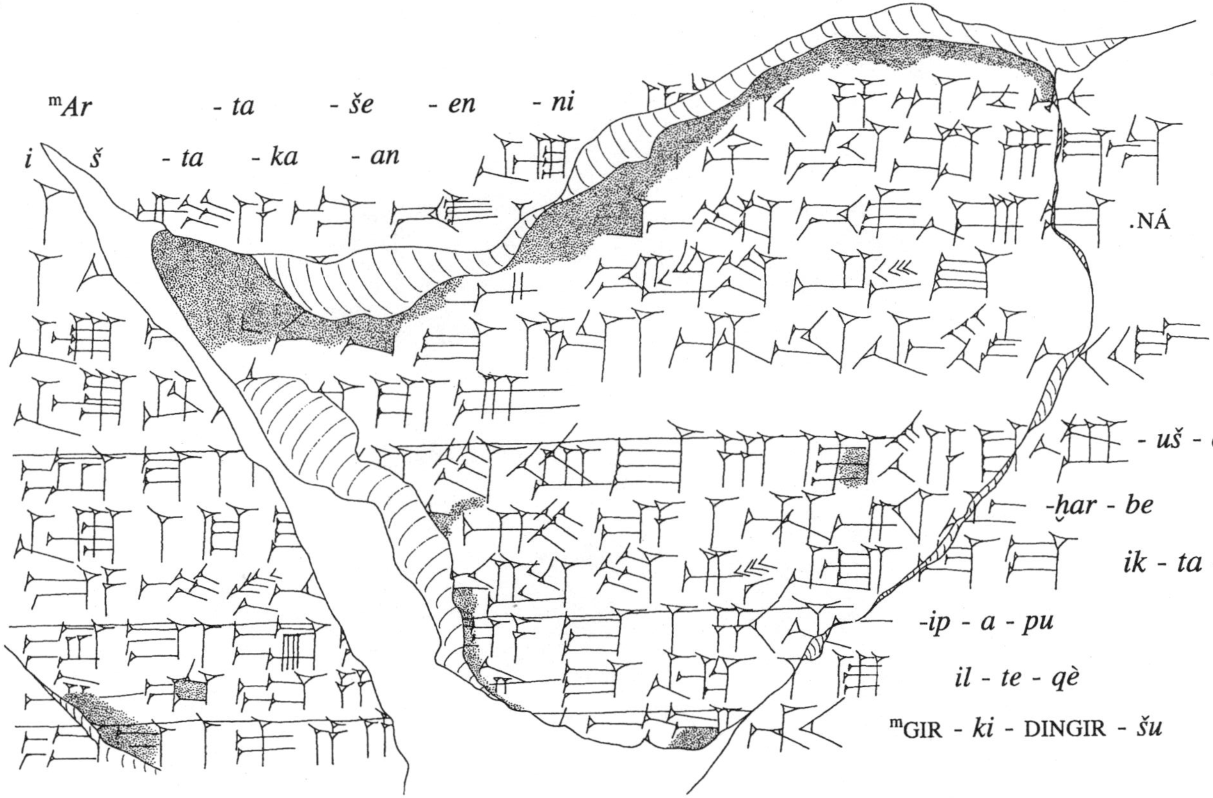

FOR THE END OF REVERSE SEE AASOR 16, 3

11

OBVERSE

BEGINNING OF OBVERSE DESTROYED

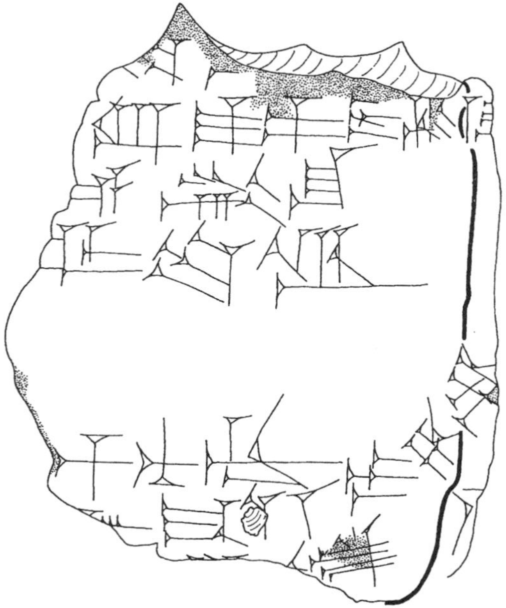

12

REVERSE

BEGINNING OF REVERSE DESTROYED

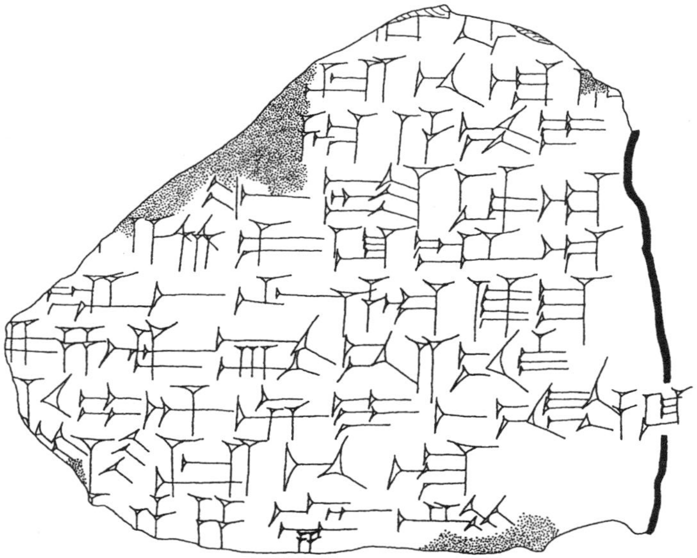

13

OBVERSE

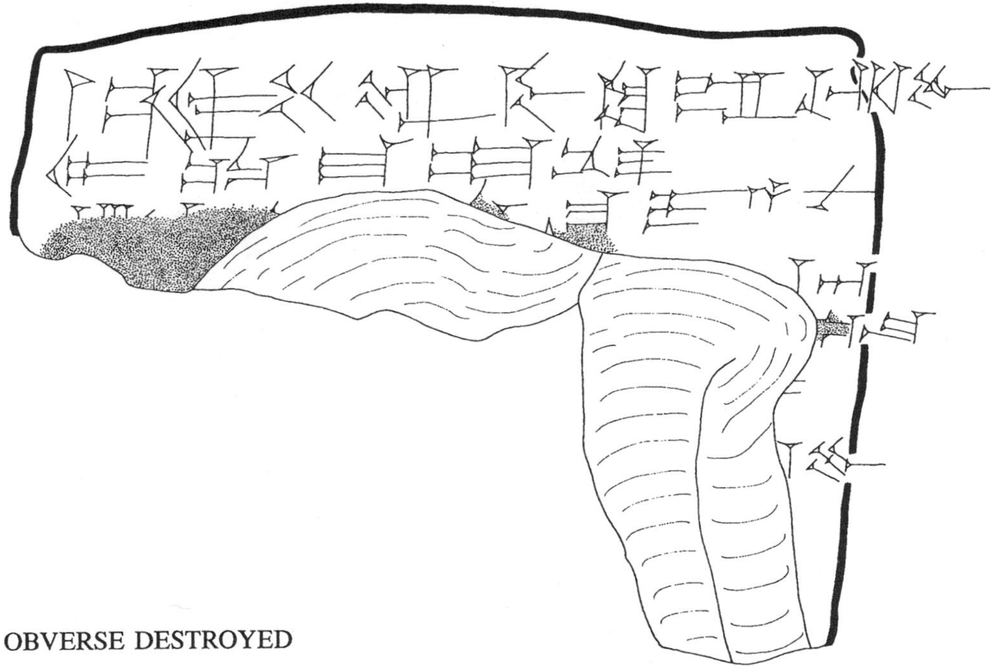

5

END OF OBVERSE DESTROYED

13

REVERSE

BEGINNING OF REVERSE DESTROYED

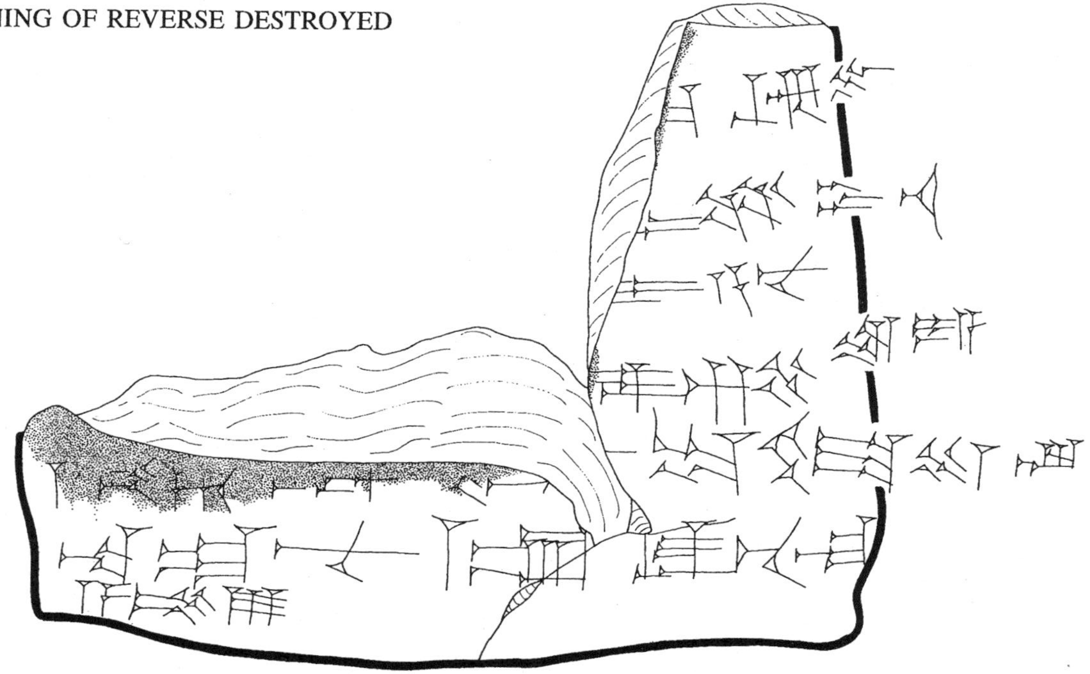

14

OBVERSE

BEGINNING OF OBVERSE DESTROYED

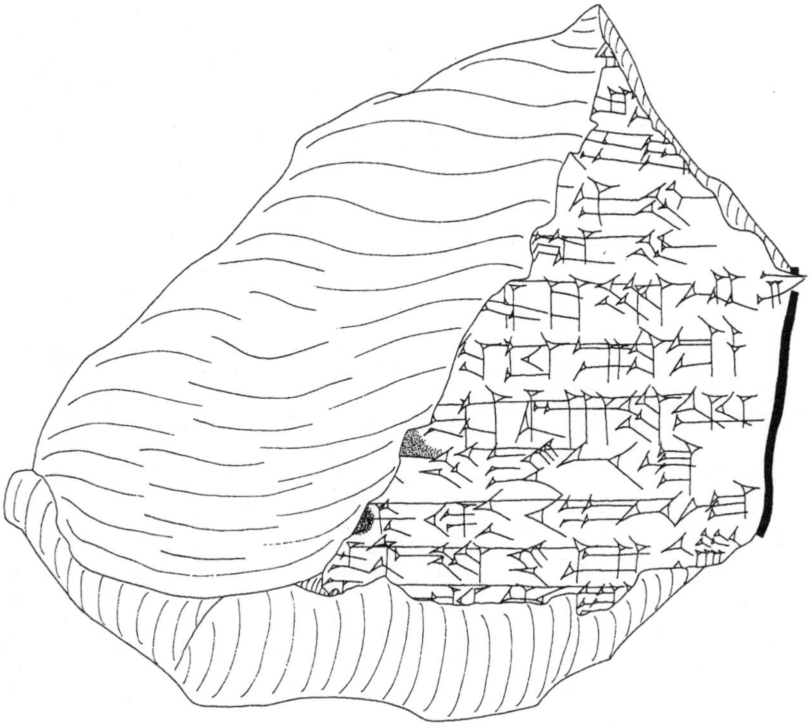

END OF OBVERSE DESTROYED

15

OBVERSE

BEGINNING OF OBVERSE DESTROYED

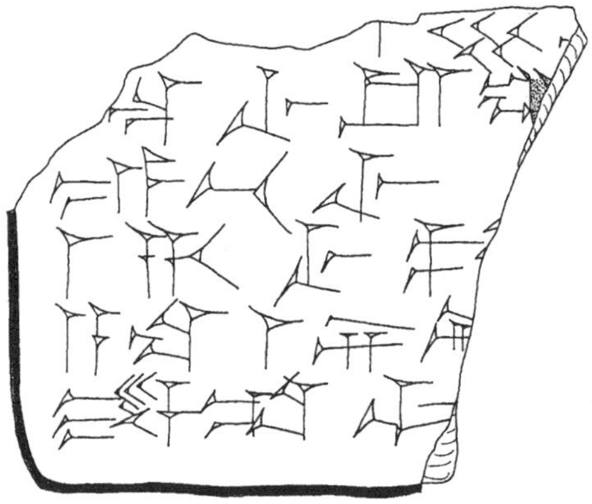

LOWER EDGE

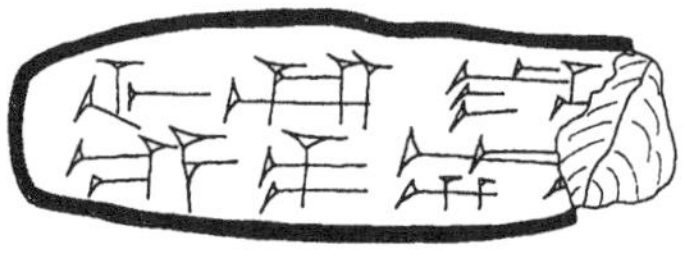

REVERSE

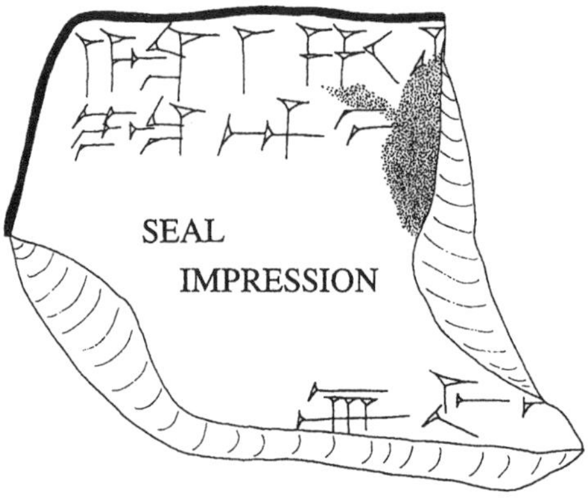

END OF REVERSE DESTROYED

16

OBVERSE

5’

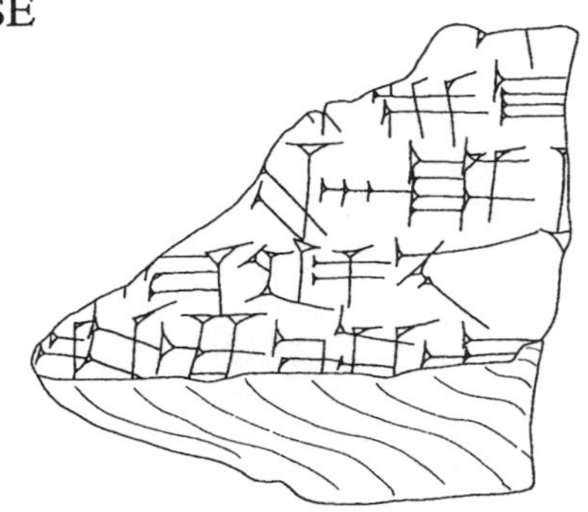

OBVERSE

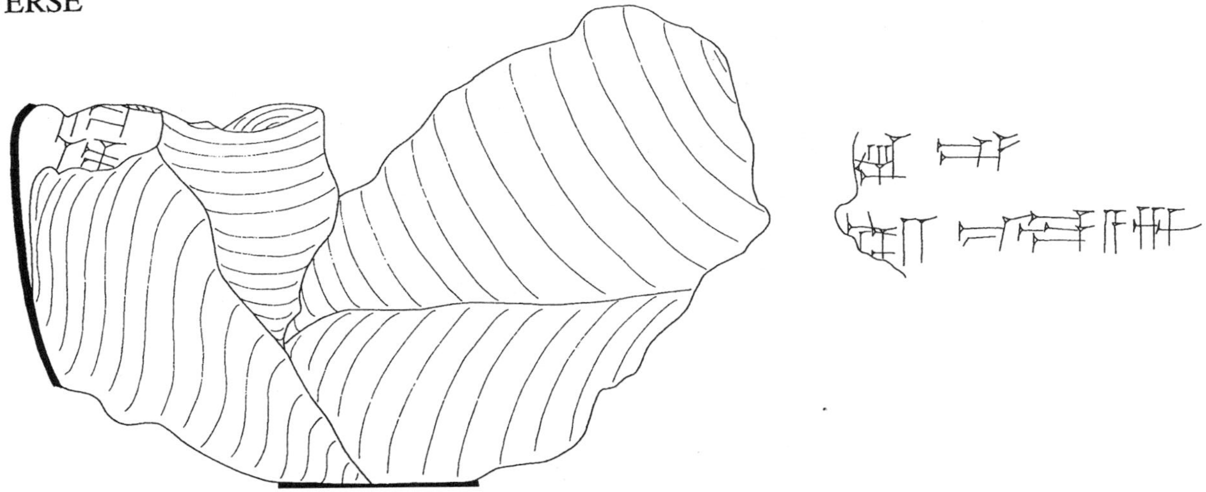

16

LOWER EDGE

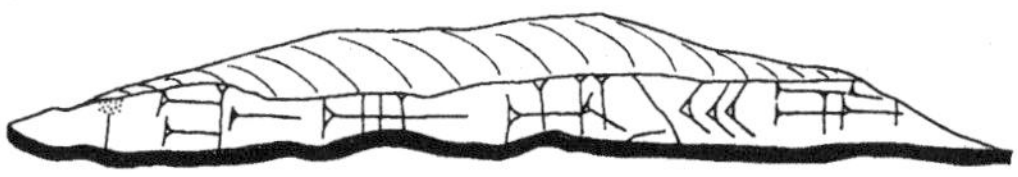

REVERSE

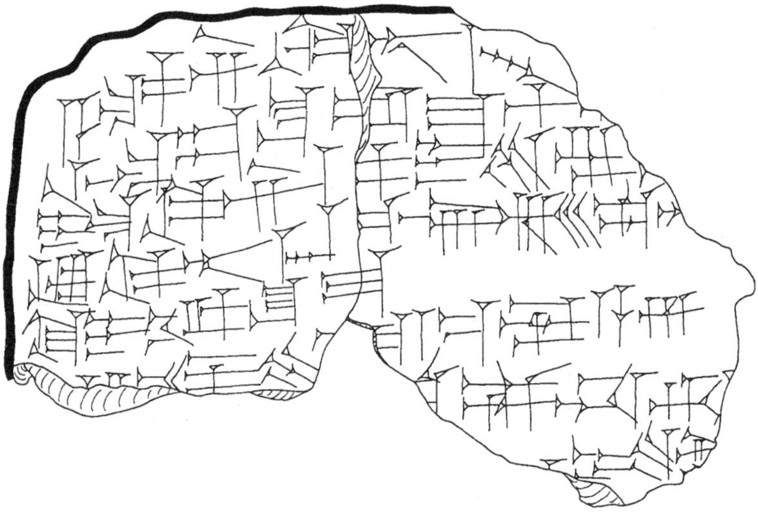

REVERSE

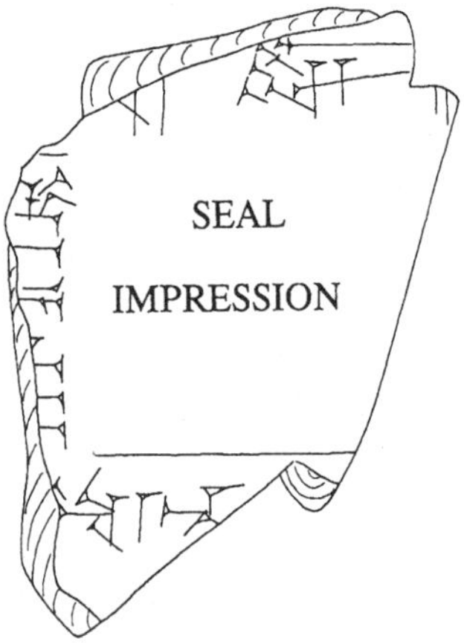

17

OBVERSE

BEGINNING OF OBVERSE DESTROYED

5’

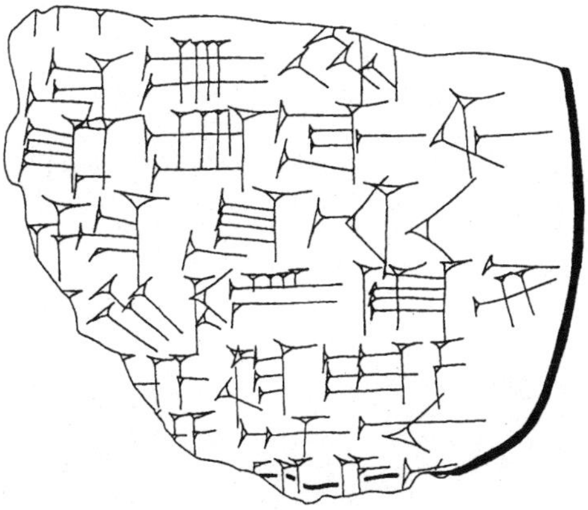

LOWER EDGE

18

REVERSE

OVERLAPS FROM OBVERSE

1

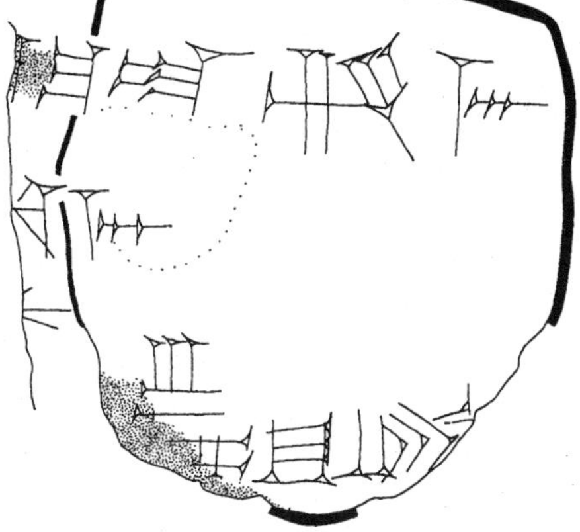

5’

19

OBVERSE

BEGINNING OF OBVERSE DESTROYED

1’

5’

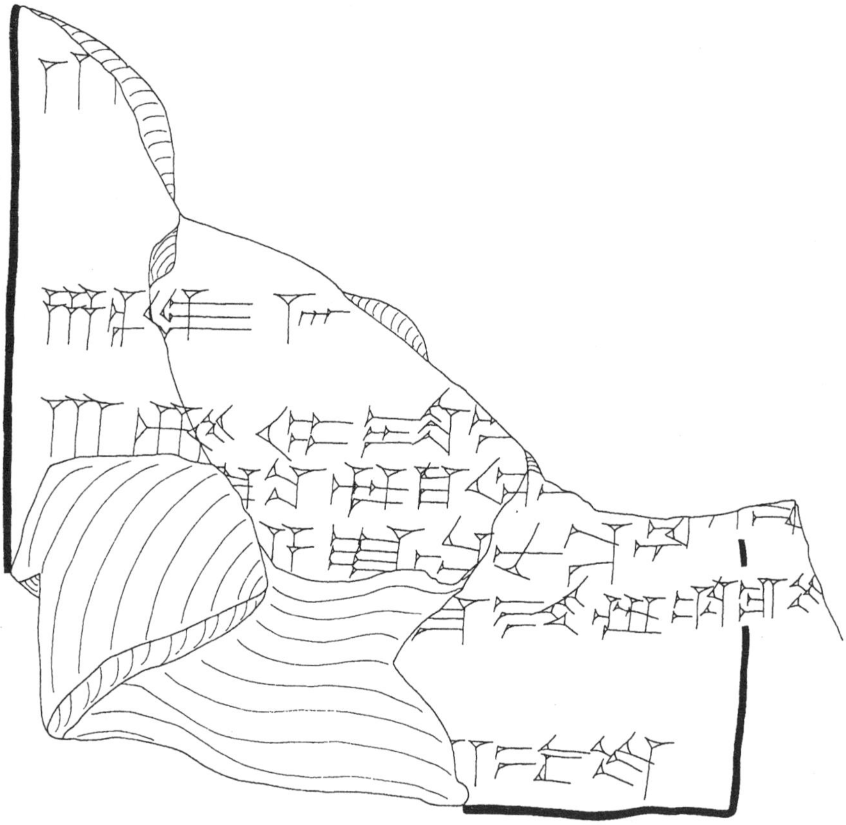

19

REVERSE

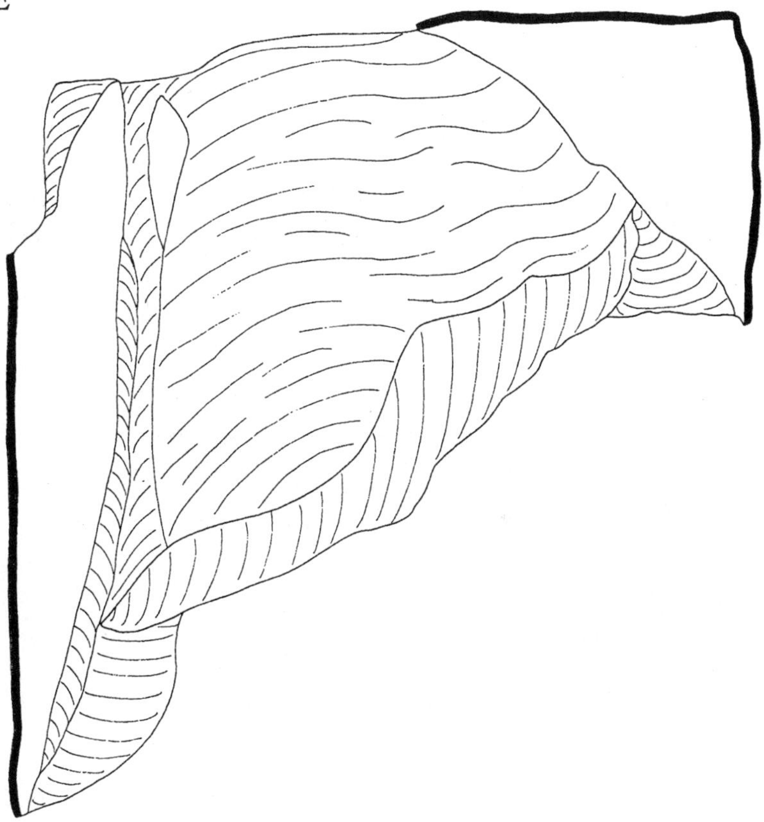

END OF REVERSE DESTROYED

20

OBVERSE

BEGINNING OF OBVERSE DESTROYED

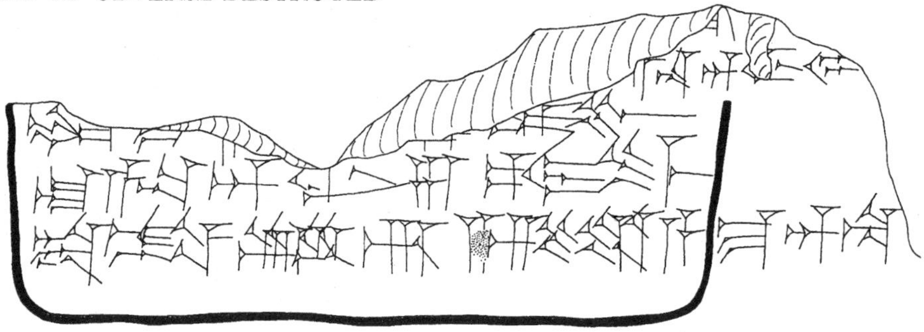

5'

LOWER EDGE

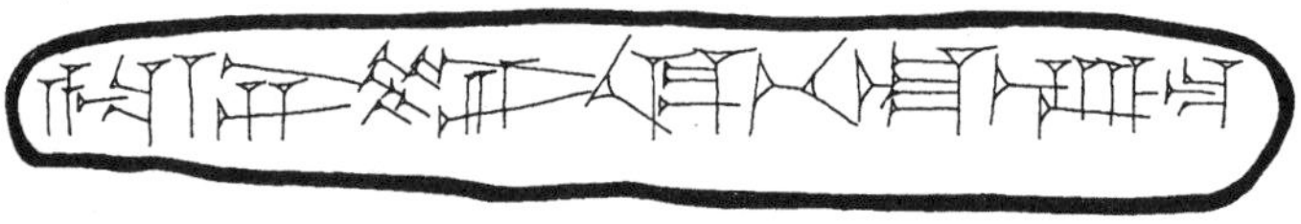

REVERSE

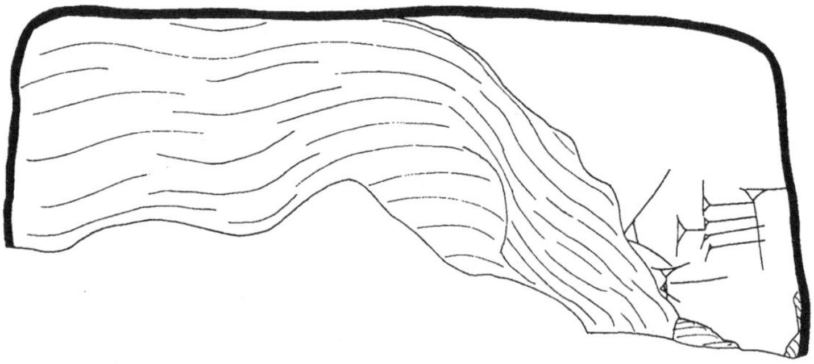

7'

END OF REVERSE DESTROYED

21

UPPER EDGE

OBVERSE

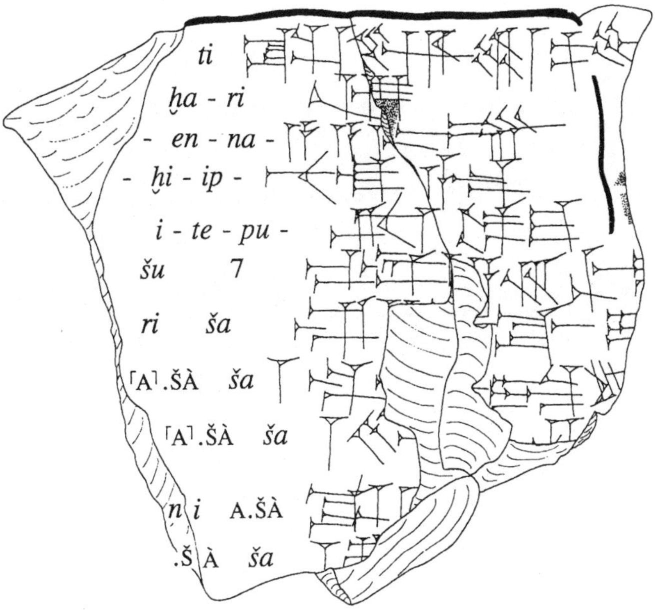

END OF OBVERSE DESTROYED

22

OBVERSE

BEGINNING OF OBVERSE DESTROYED

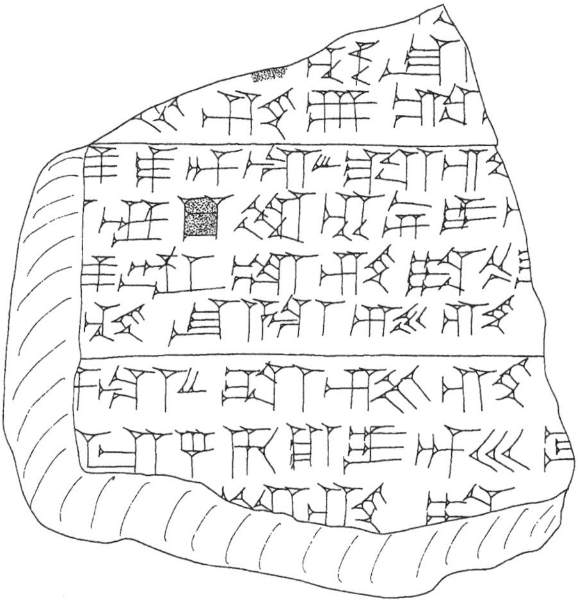

END OF OBVERSE DESTROYED

23

OBVERSE

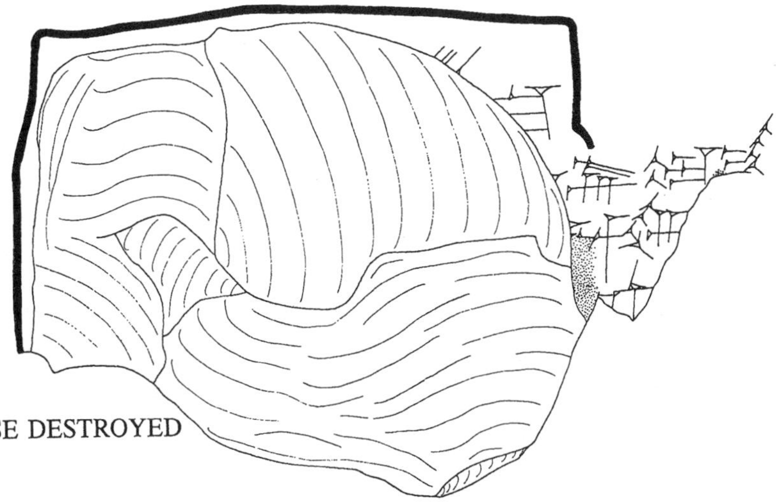

5

END OF OBVERSE DESTROYED

REVERSE

BEGINNING OF REVERSE DESTROYED

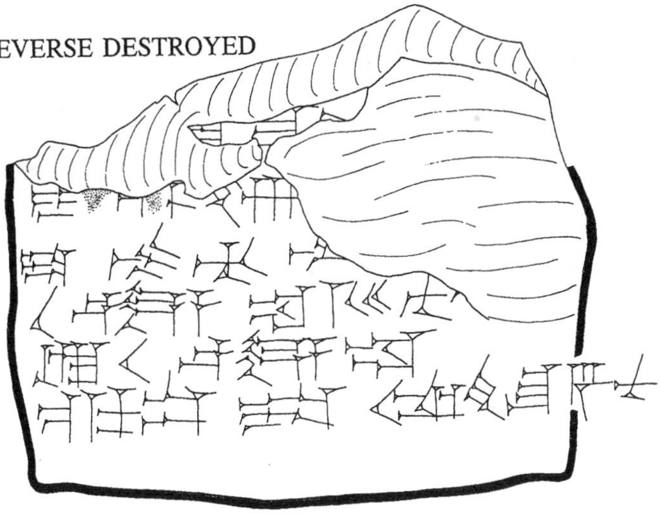

10'

UPPER EDGE

13'

24

OBVERSE

BEGINNING OF OBVERSE DESTROYED

1'

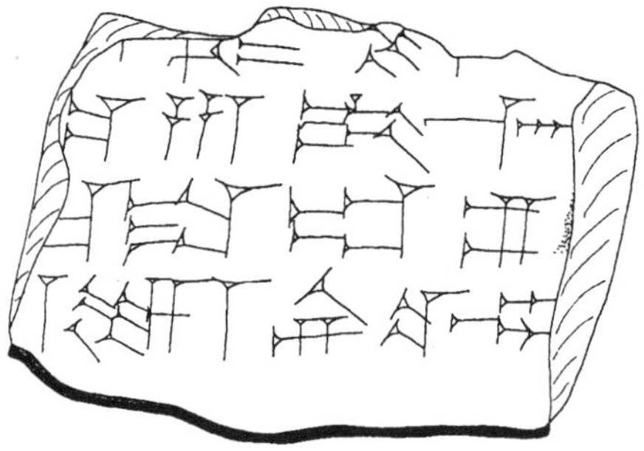

LOWER EDGE

5'

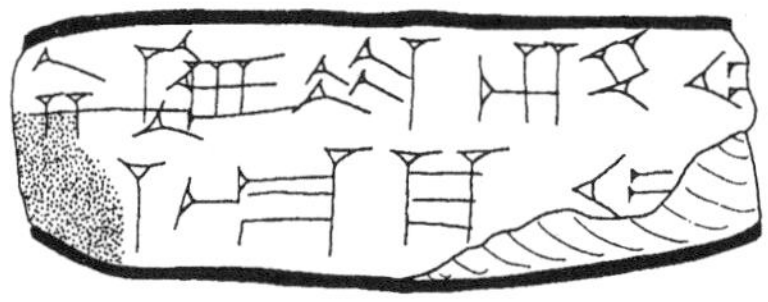

REVERSE

7'

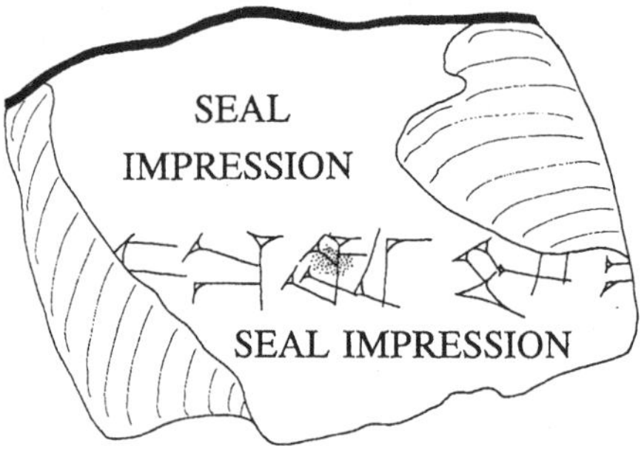

END OF REVERSE DESTROYED

25

OBVERSE

5

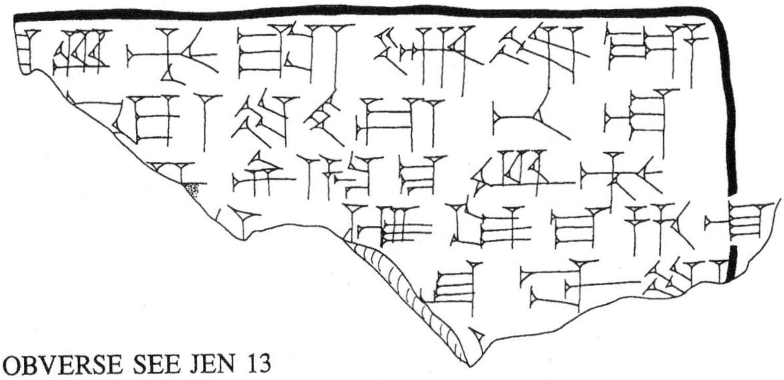

FOR END OF OBVERSE SEE JEN 13

REVERSE

FOR BEGINNING OF REVERSE SEE JEN 13

48

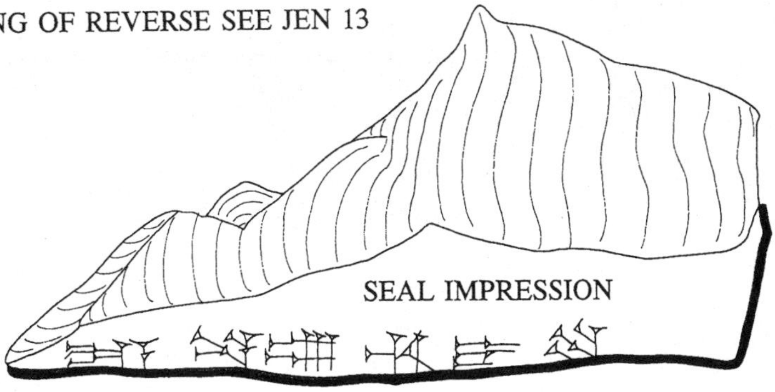

UPPER EDGE

49

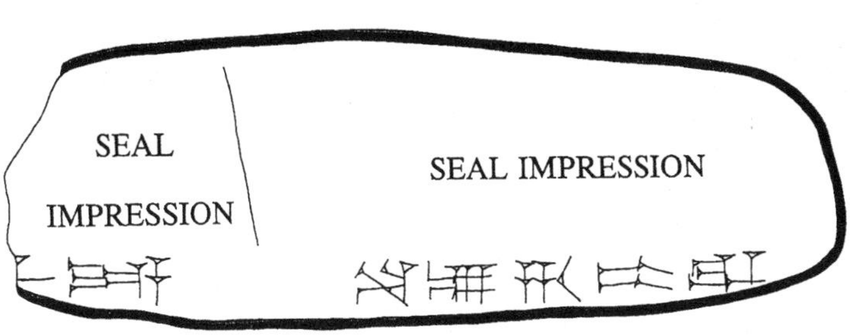

26

OBVERSE

BEGINNING OF OBVERSE DESTROYED

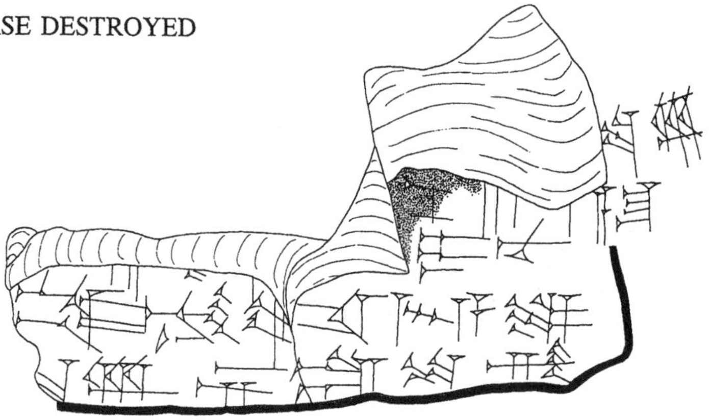

LOWER EDGE

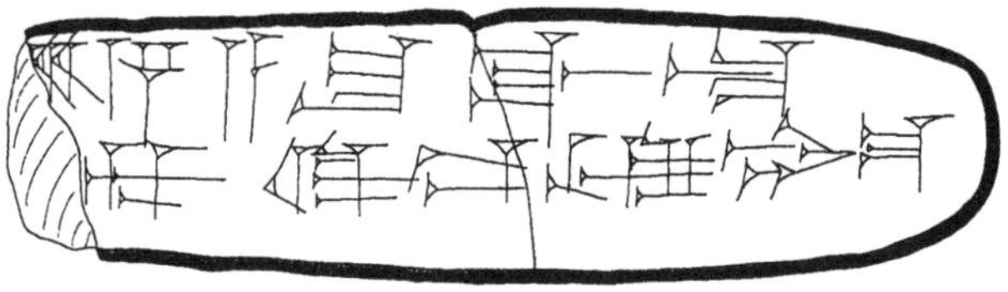

REVERSE

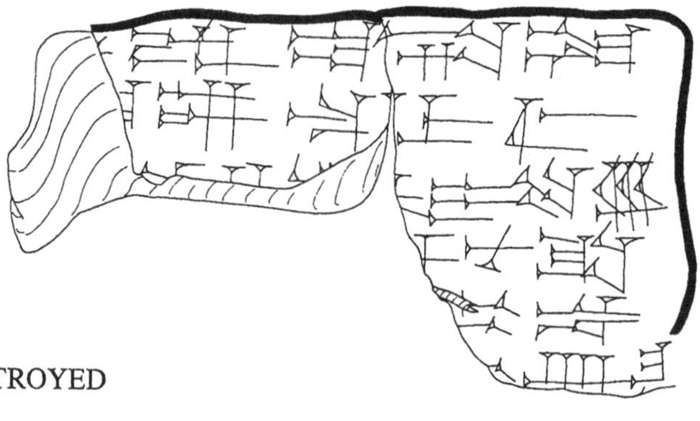

END OF REVERSE DESTROYED

27

OBVERSE

RIGHT EDGE

FOR LEFT PART OF OBVERSE SEE HSS 9, 22

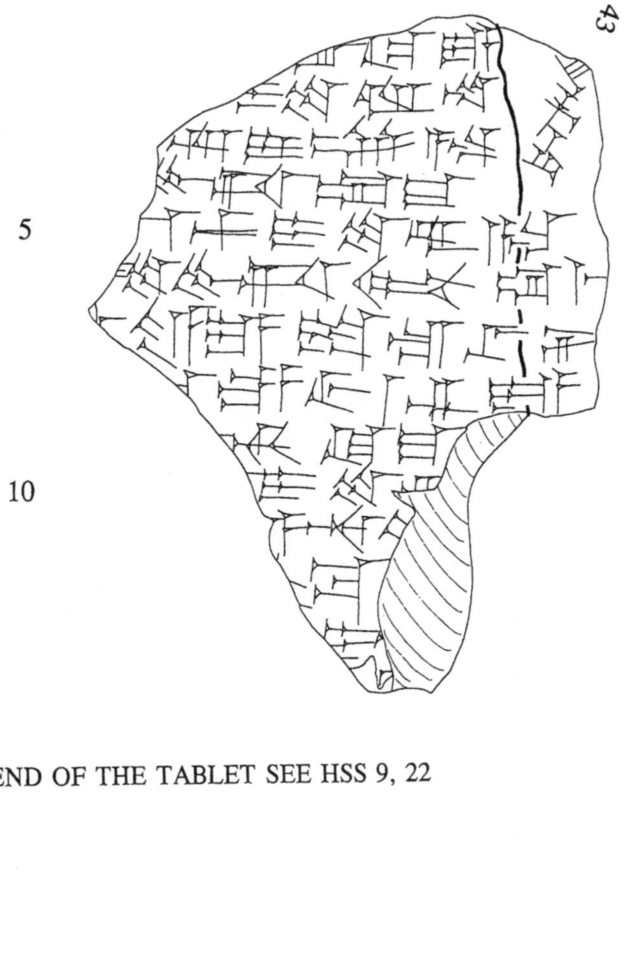

FOR END OF THE TABLET SEE HSS 9, 22

28

OBVERSE

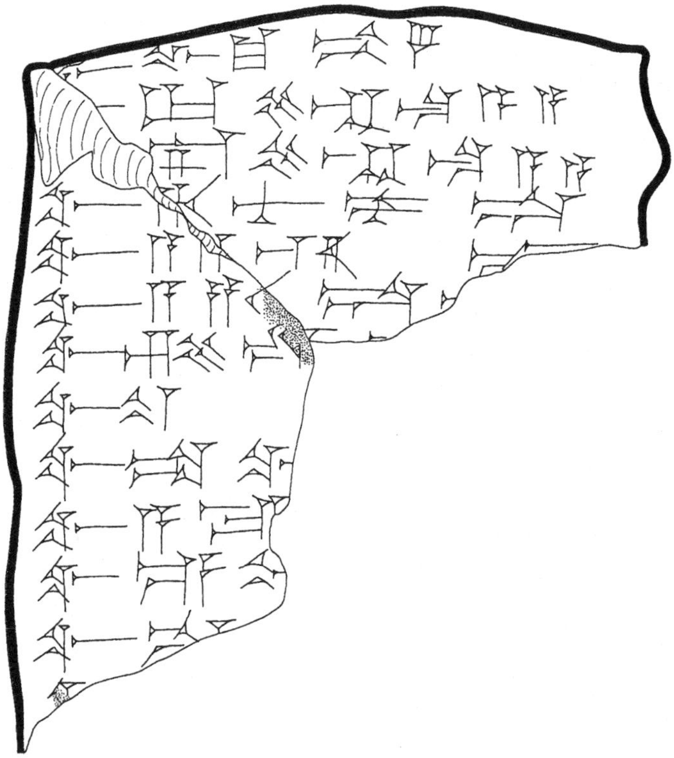

END OF OBVERSE DESTROYED

28

REVERSE

BEGINNING OF REVERSE DESTROYED

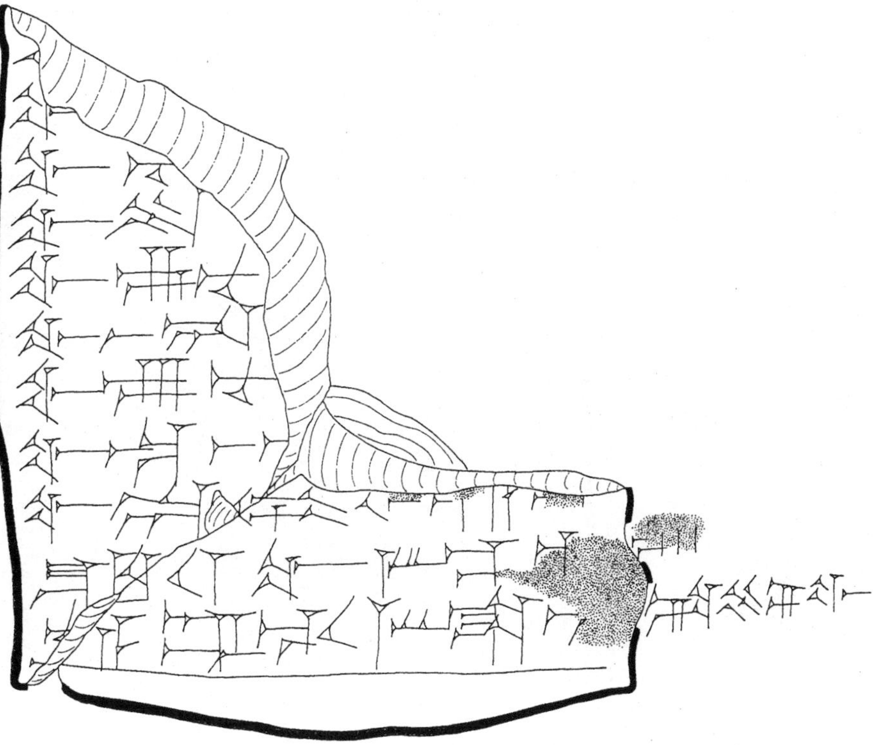

LEFT EDGE

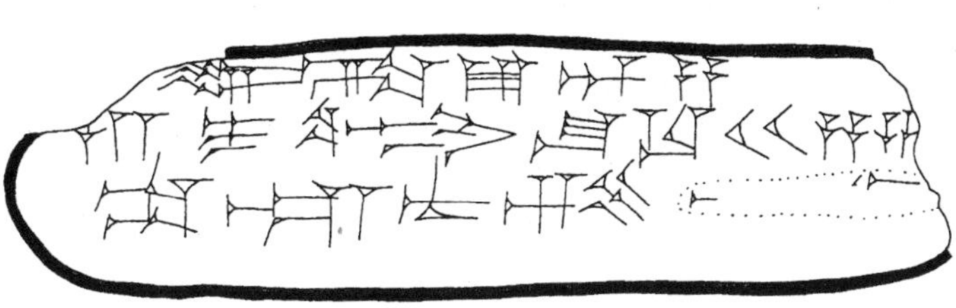

ERASURE

29

OBVERSE

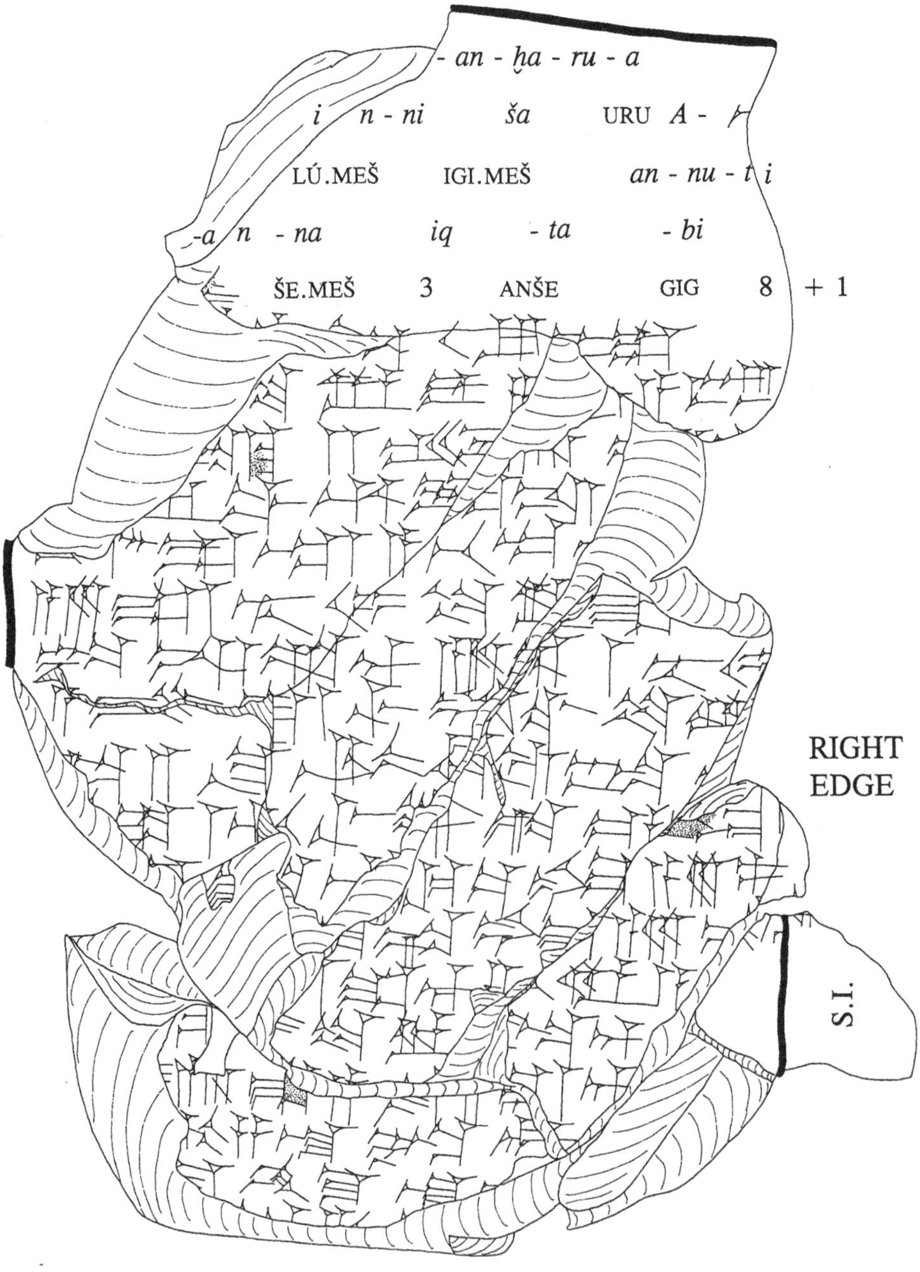
- an - ḫa - ru - a
i n - ni ša URU A -
LÚ.MEŠ IGI.MEŠ an - nu - t i
-a n - na iq - ta - bi
ŠE.MEŠ 3 ANŠE GIG 8 + 1
RIGHT EDGE
S.I.

29

REVERSE

25’

30’

35’

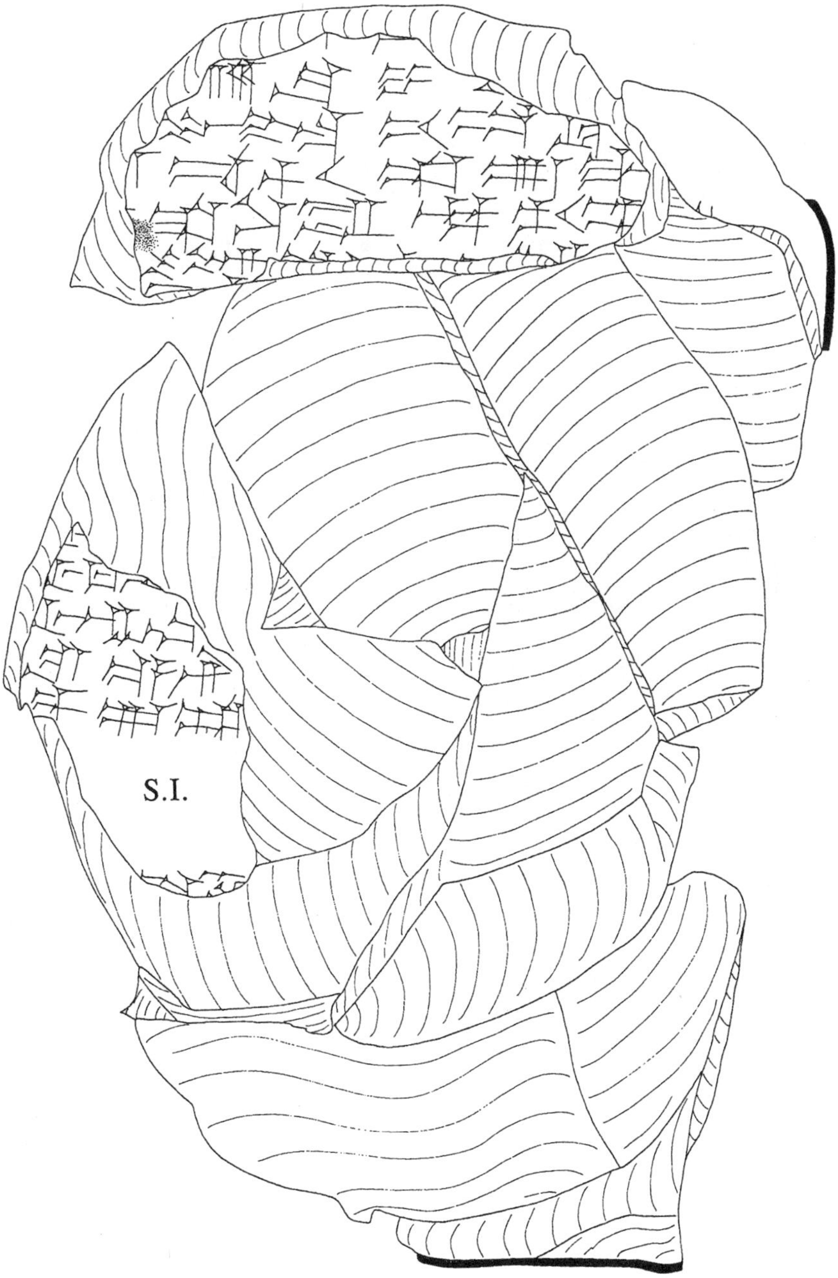

29

LEFT EDGE

30

OBVERSE

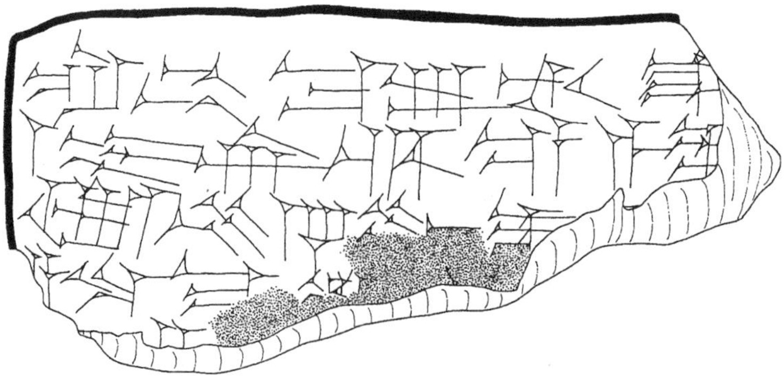

5

END OF OBVERSE DESTROYED

31

OBVERSE

BEGINNING OF OBVERSE DESTROYED

1'

5'

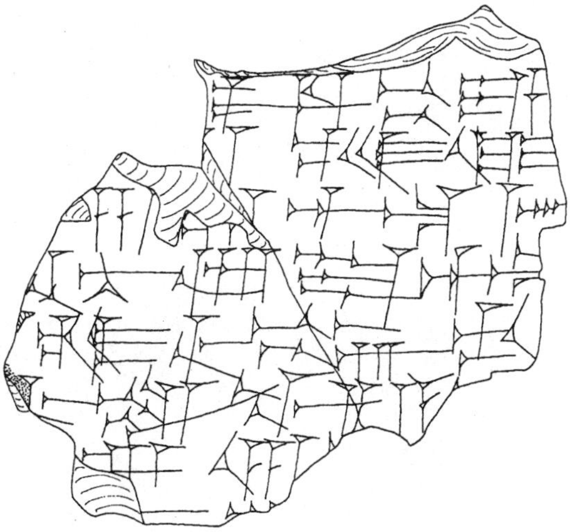

END OF OBVERSE DESTROYED

32

OBVERSE

1

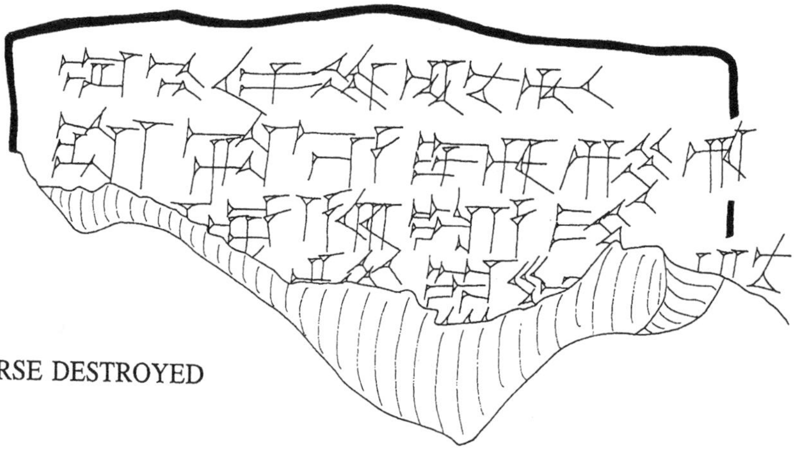

5

END OF OBVERSE DESTROYED

REVERSE

BEGINNING OF REVERSE DESTROYED

6'

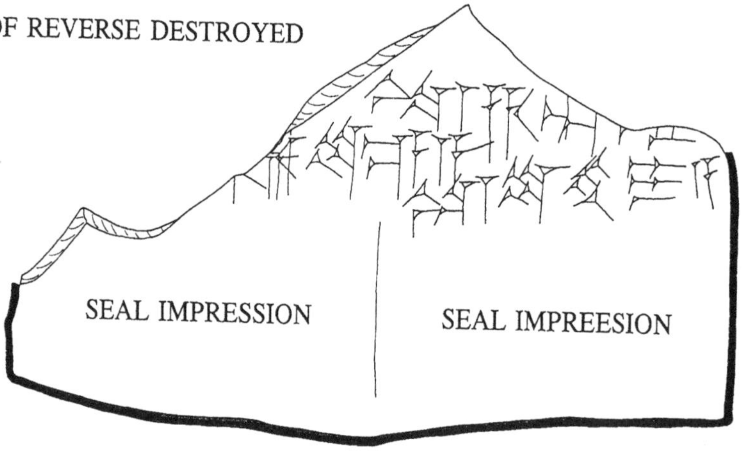

UPPER EDGE

9'

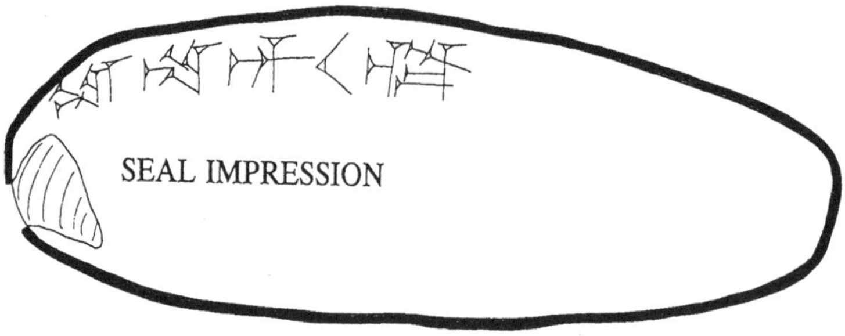

LEFT EDGE

10'

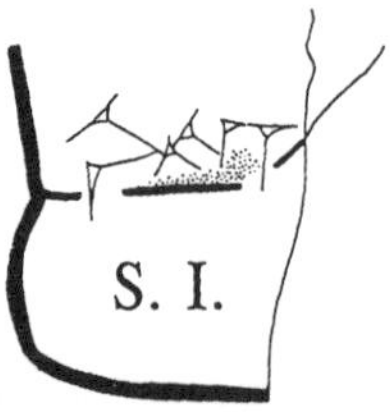

33

OBVERSE

1

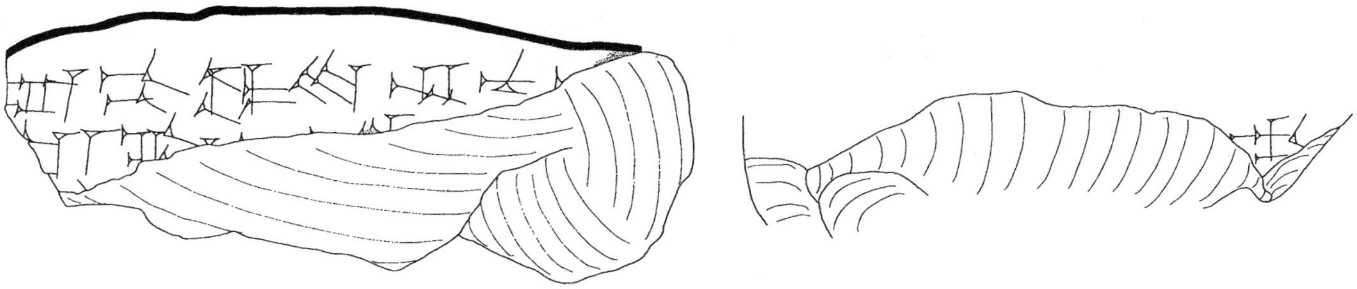

END OF OBVERSE DESTROYED

33

REVERSE

BEGINNING OF REVERSE DESTROYED

4’

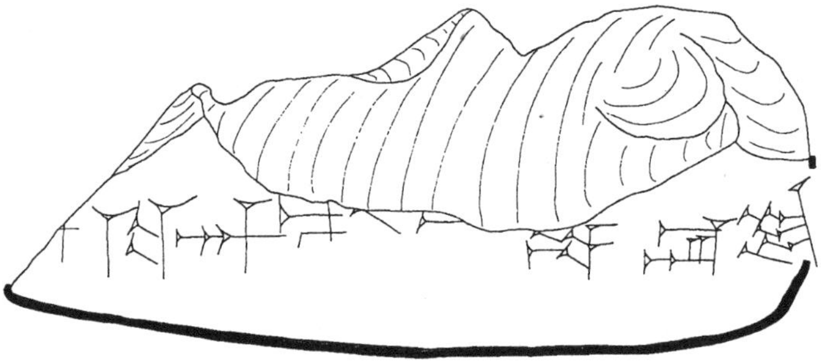

UPPER EDGE

6’

34

OBVERSE

1

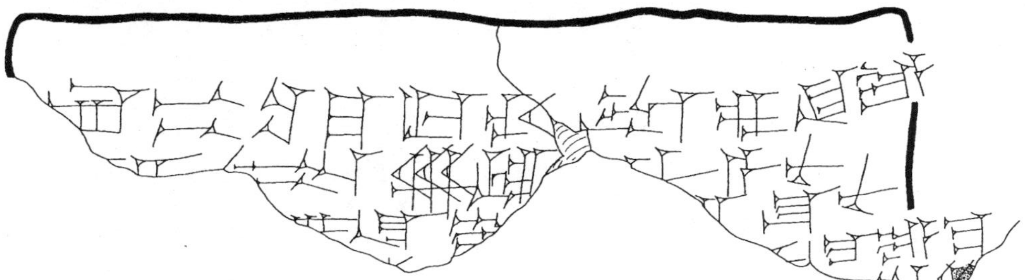

5

END OF OBVERSE DESTROYED

REVERSE

BEGINNING OF REVERSE DESTROYED

6’

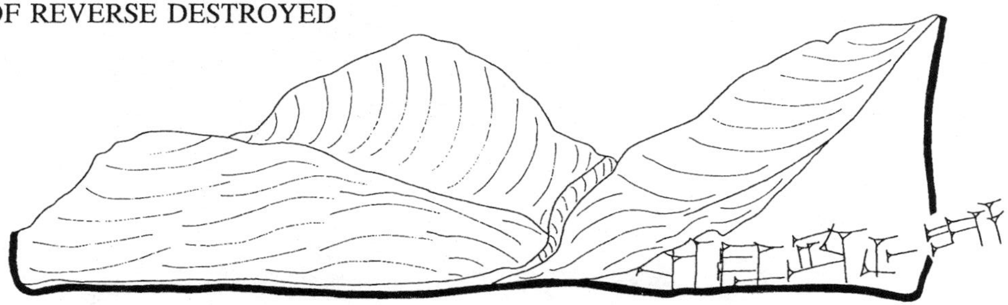

34

UPPER EDGE

7'

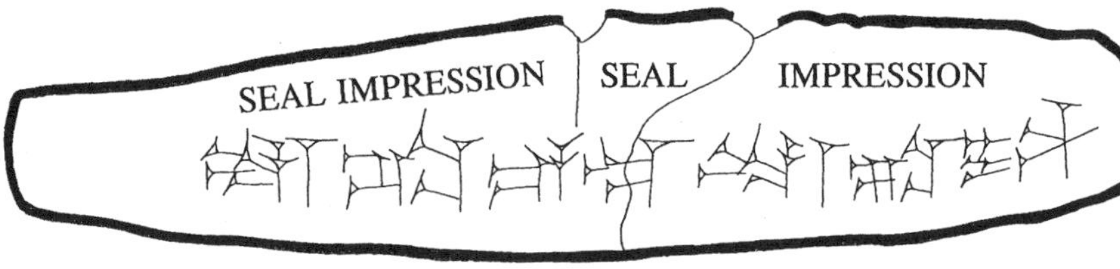

35

OBVERSE

5

10

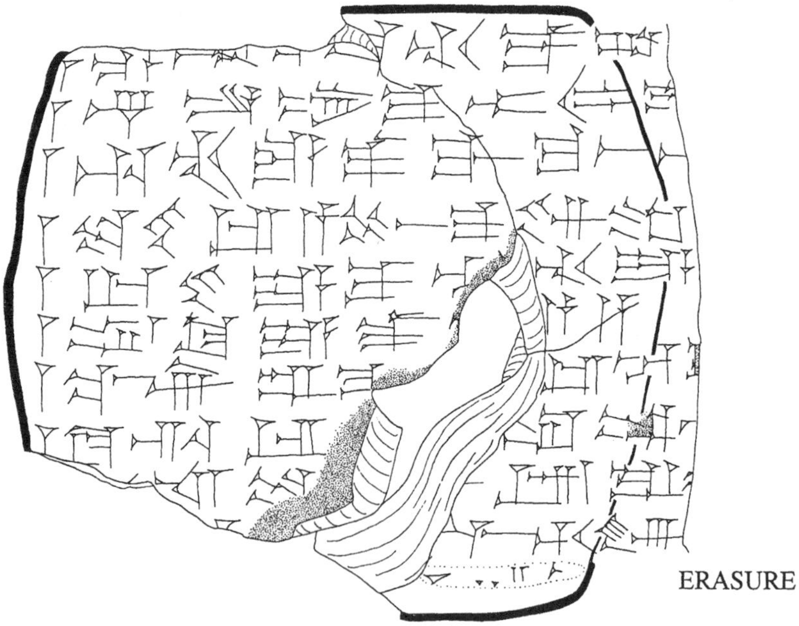

LOWER EDGE

11

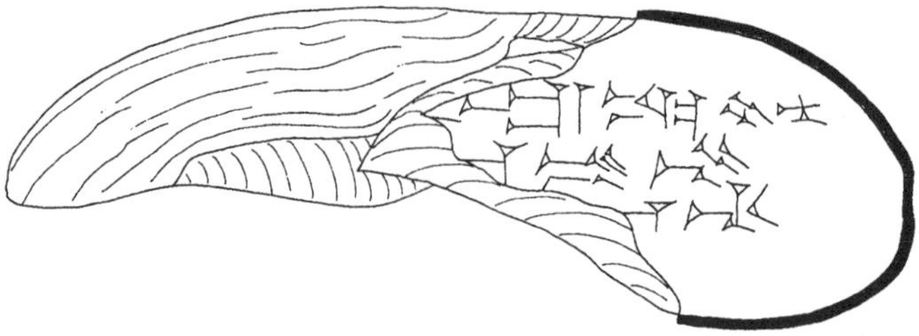

36

OBVERSE

1

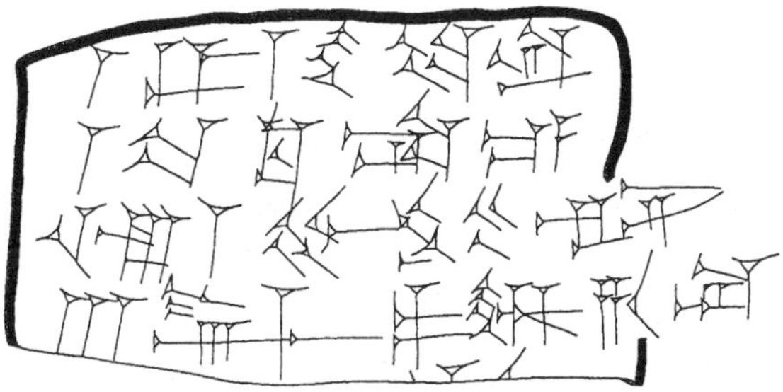

5

END OF OBVERSE DESTROYED

REVERSE

BEGINNING OF REVERSE DESTROYED

6'

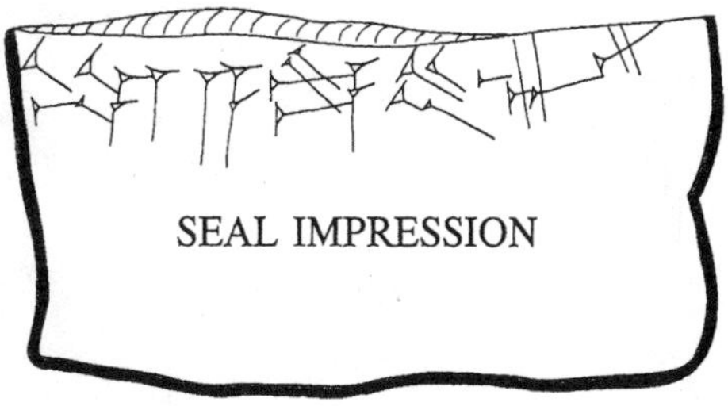

37

UPPER EDGE

OBVERSE

2

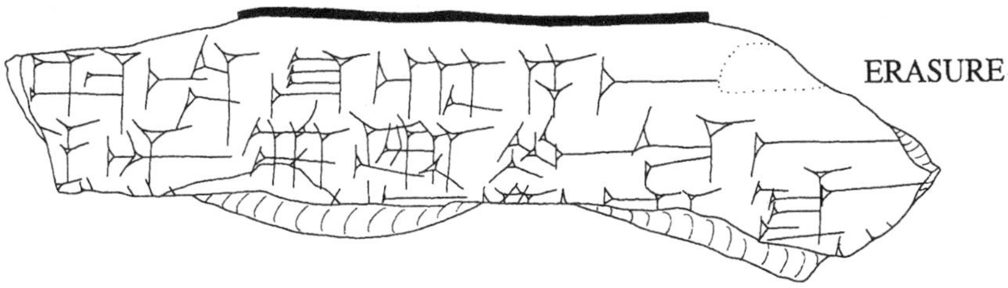

END OF OBVERSE DESTROYED

38

REVERSE

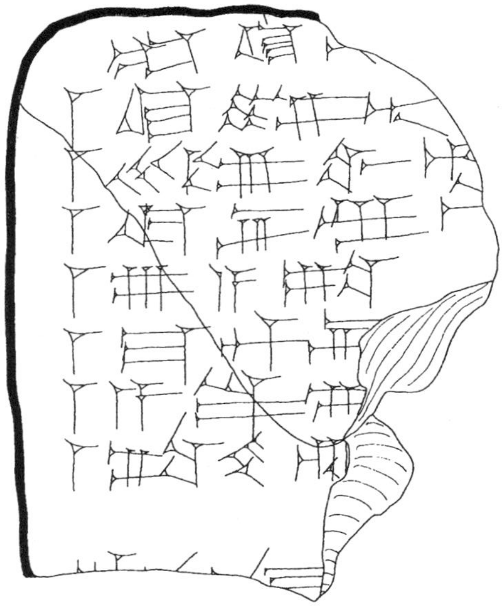

END OF REVERSE DESTROYED

39

REVERSE

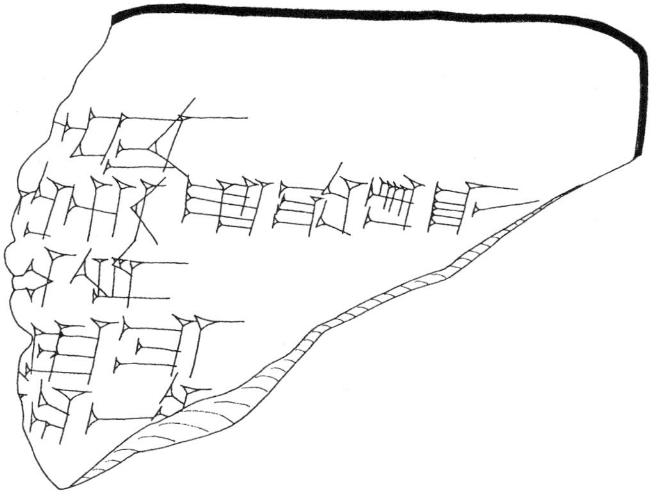

END OF REVERSE DESTROYED

40

OBVERSE

BEGINNING OF OBVERSE DESTROYED

1’

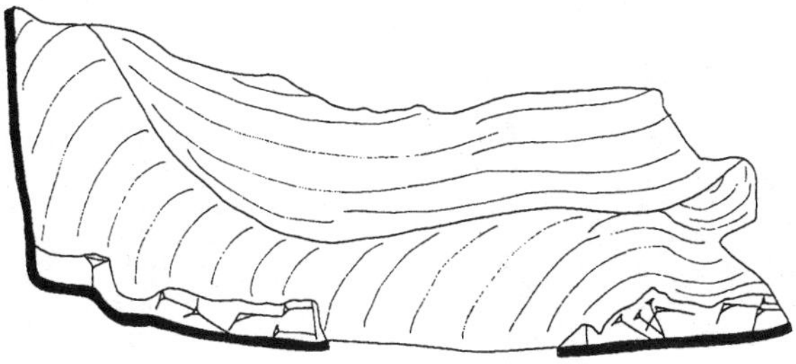

LOWER EDGE

2’

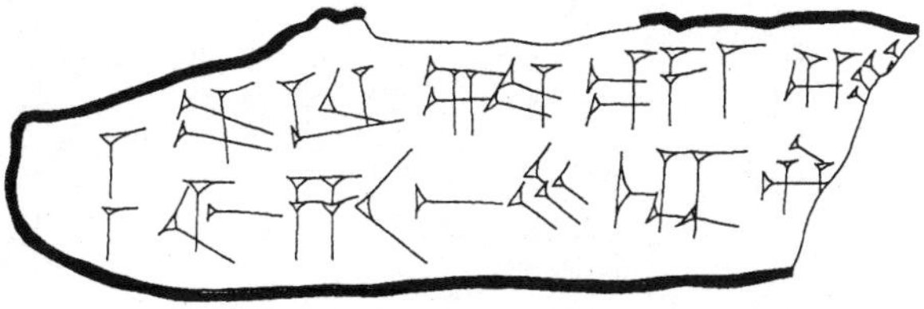

REVERSE

4’

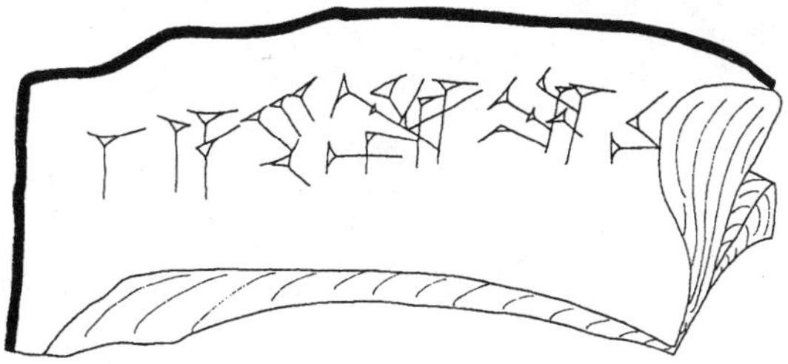

END OF REVERSE DESTROYED

41

OBVERSE

1

5

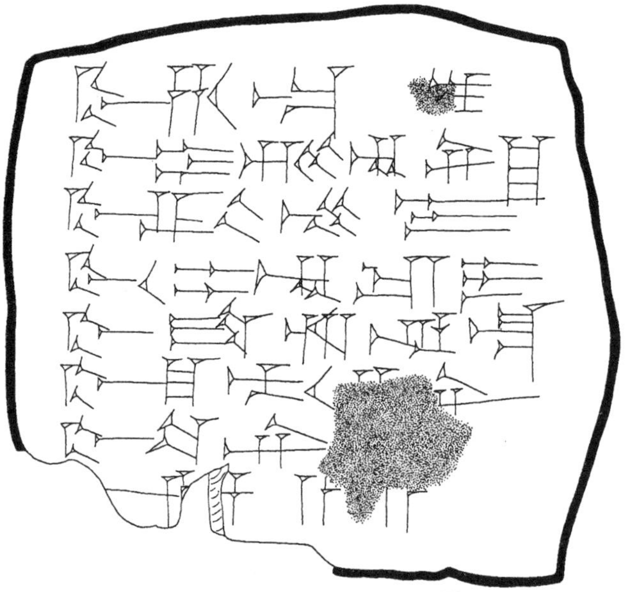

LOWER EDGE

9

REVERSE

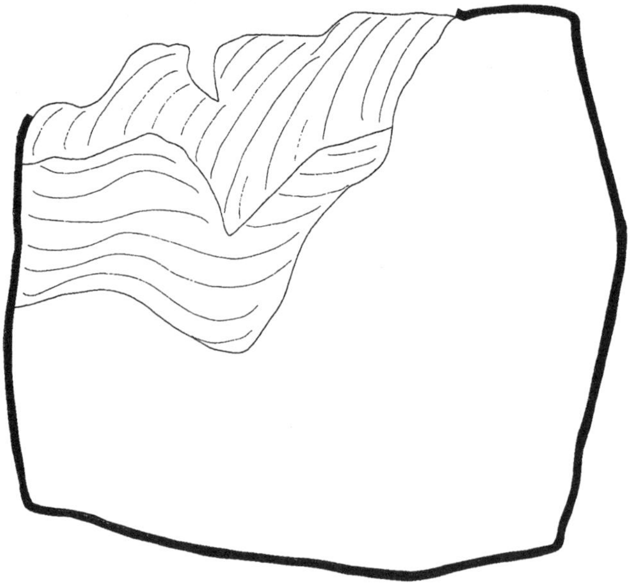

42

REVERSE

1'

5'

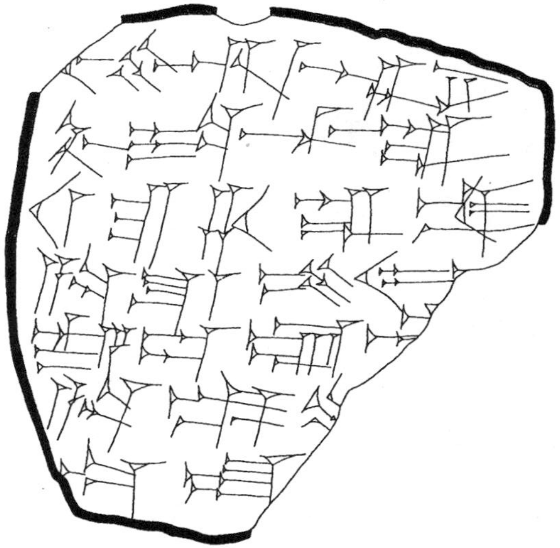

43

OBVERSE

BEGINNING OF OBVERSE DESTROYED

1'

5'

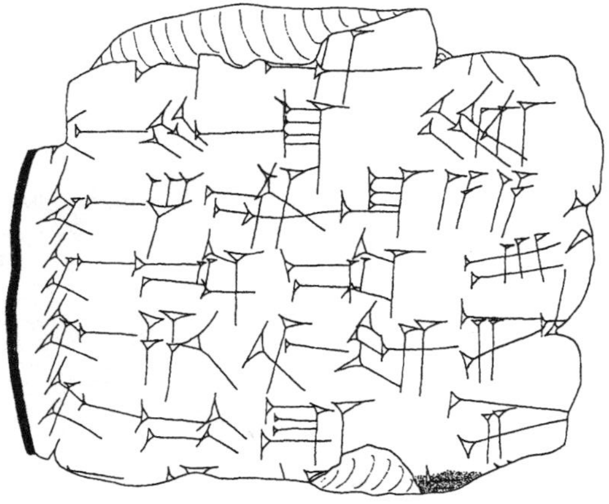

44

OBVERSE

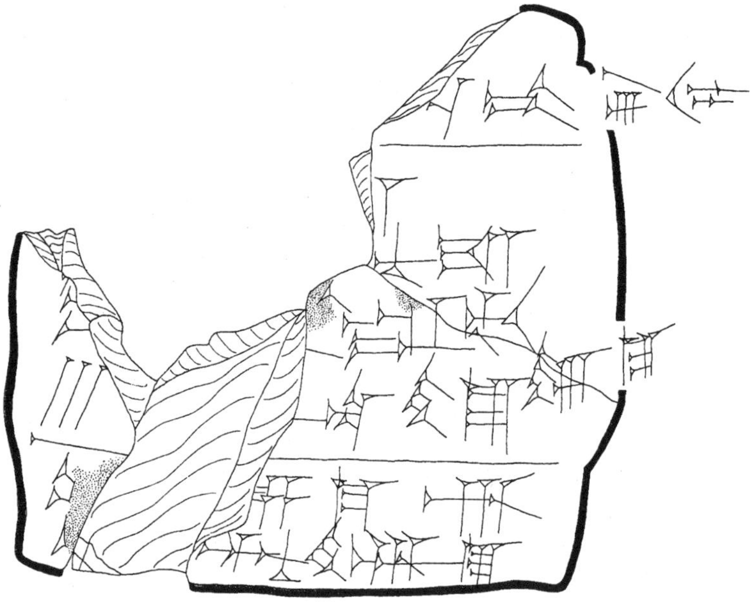

LOWER EDGE

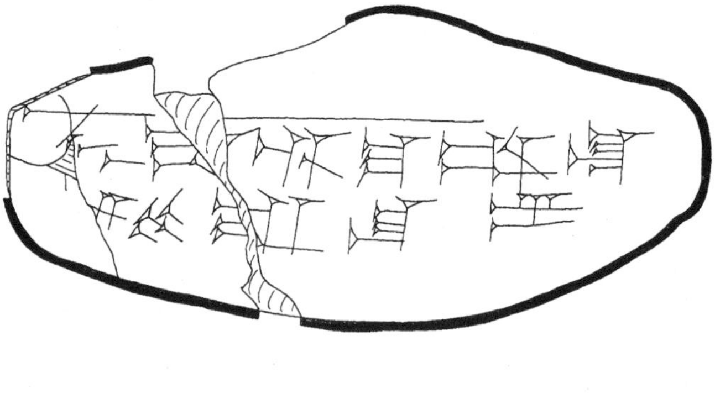

44

REVERSE

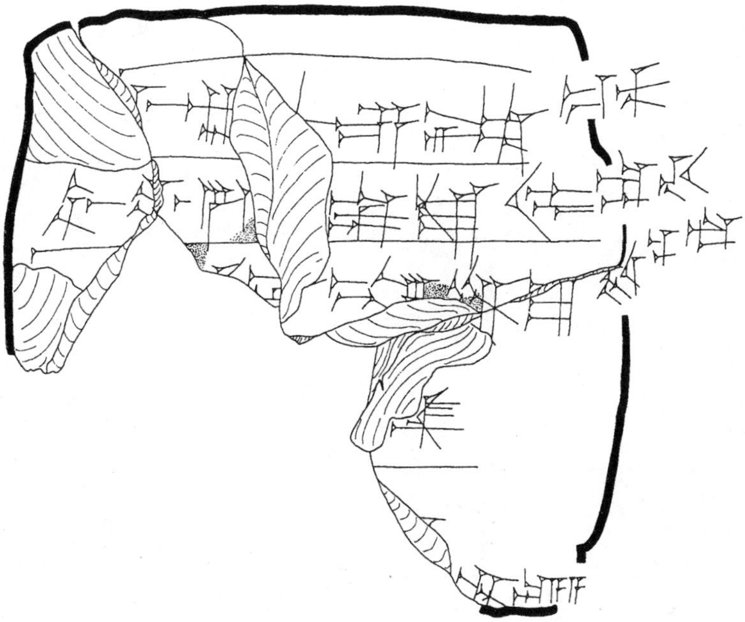

45

REVERSE

BEGINNING OF REVERSE DESTROYED

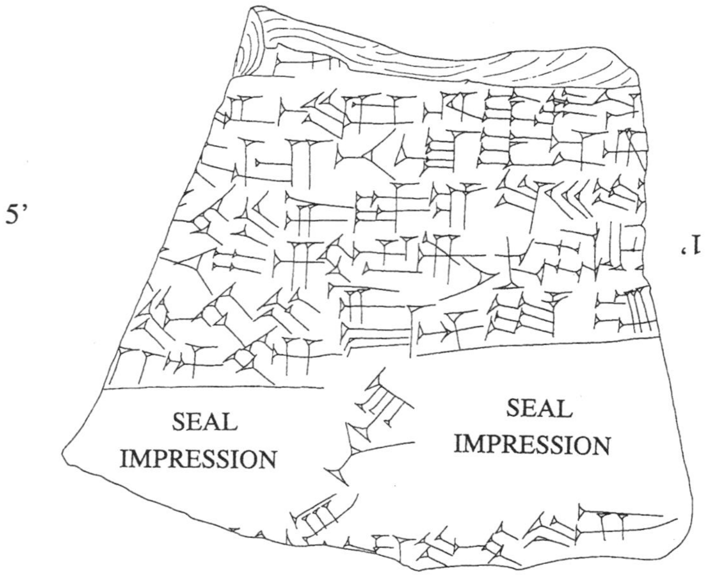

END OF REVERSE DESTROYED

46

REVERSE

BEGINNING OF REVERSE DESTROYED

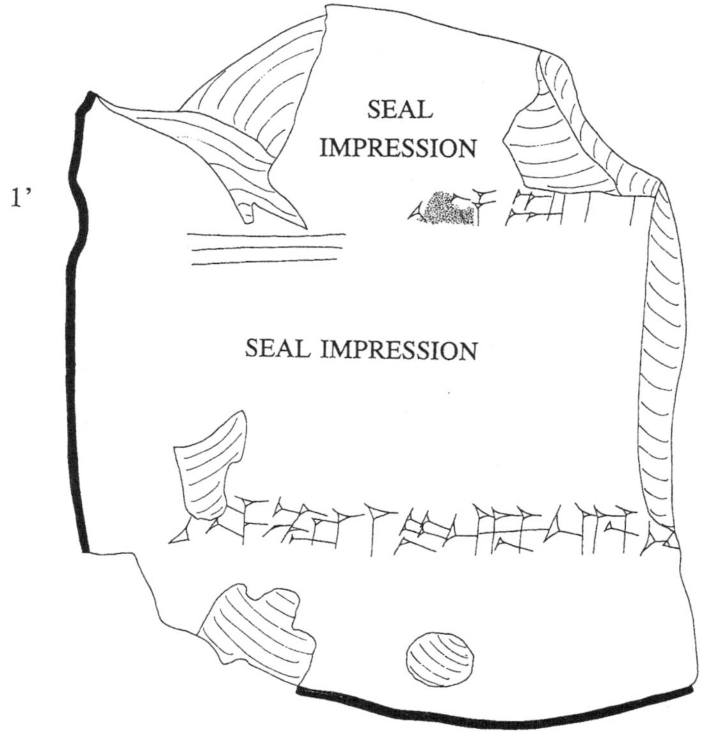

47

OBVERSE

1

5

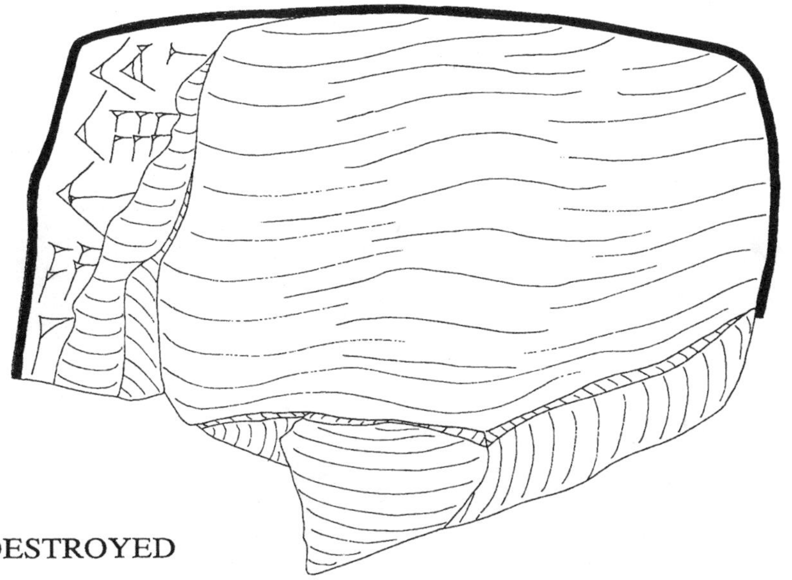

END OF OBVERSE DESTROYED

REVERSE

BEGINNING OF REVERSE DESTROYED

6’

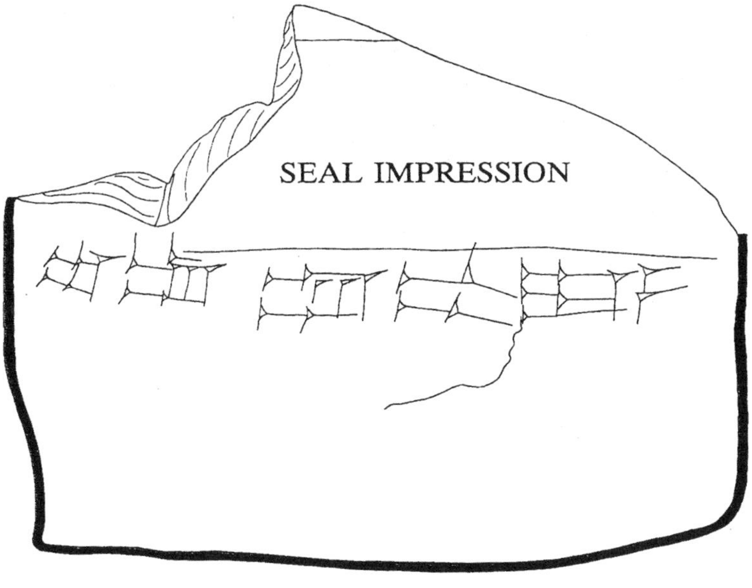

48

OBVERSE

FOR BEGINNING OF OBVERSE SEE HSS 16, 425

5

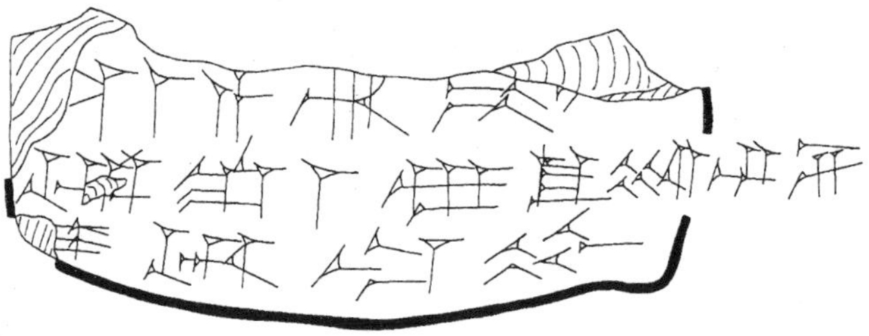

LOWER EDGE

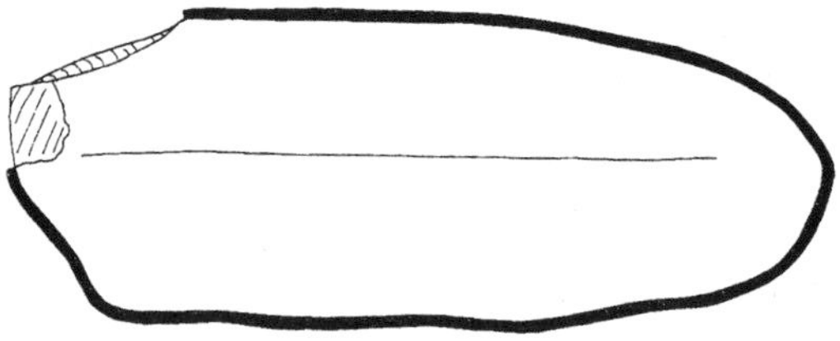

REVERSE

8

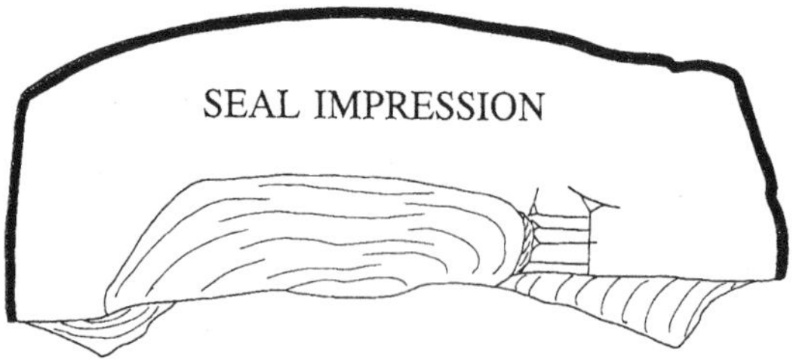

FOR END OF REVERSE SEE HSS 16, 425

49

REVERSE

1

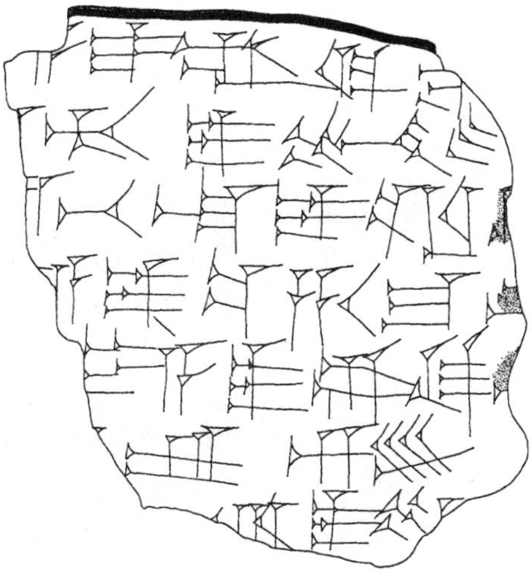

5

END OF REVERSE DESTROYED

50

OBVERSE

1

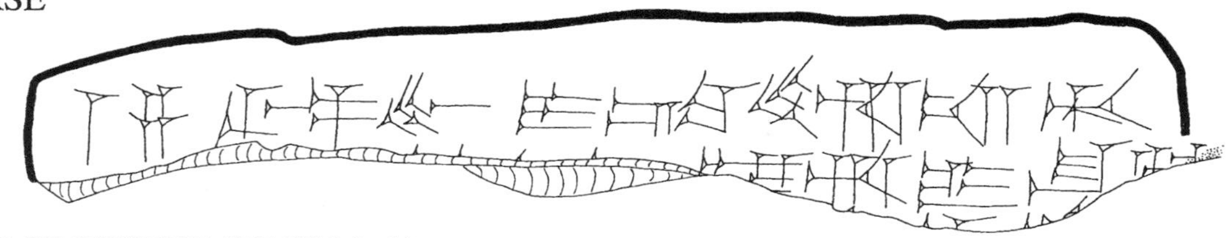

FOR END OF OBVERSE SEE HSS 9, 11

REVERSE

FOR BEGINNING OF REVERSE SEE HSS 9, 11

41

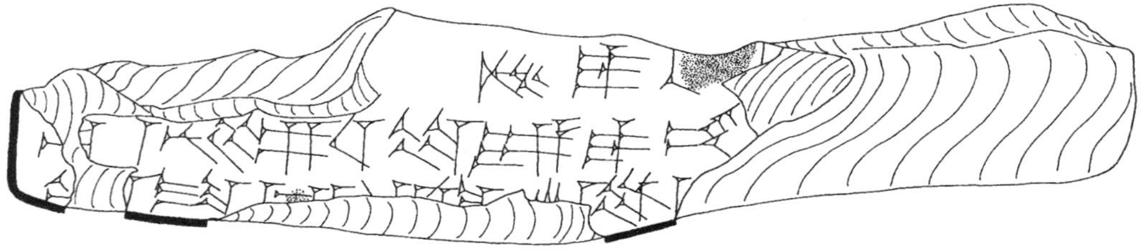

UPPER EDGE

45

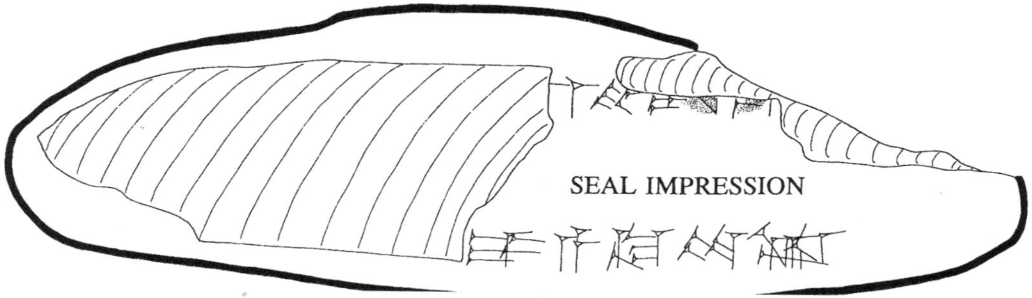

51

REVERSE

BEGINNING OF REVERSE DESTROYED

2’

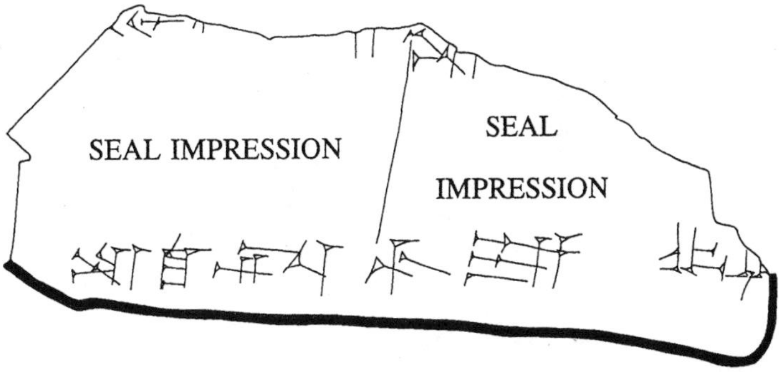

3’

UPPER EDGE

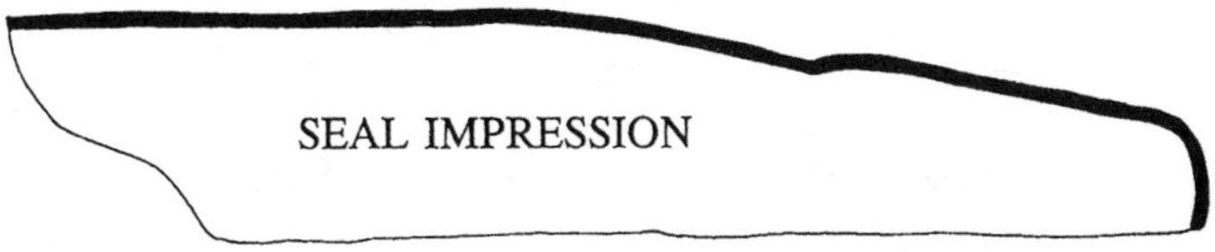

52

OBVERSE

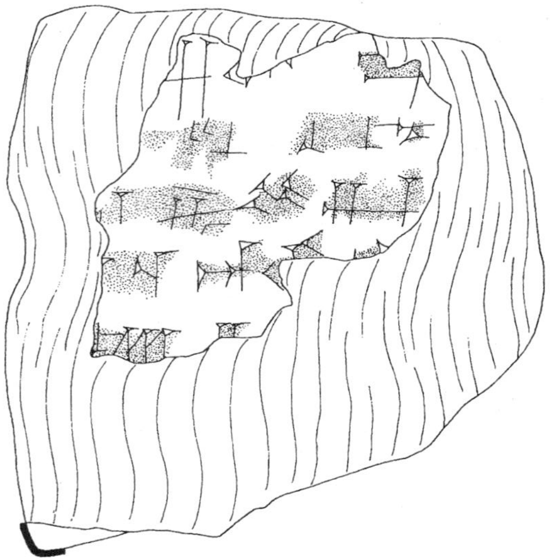

1

5

REVERSE

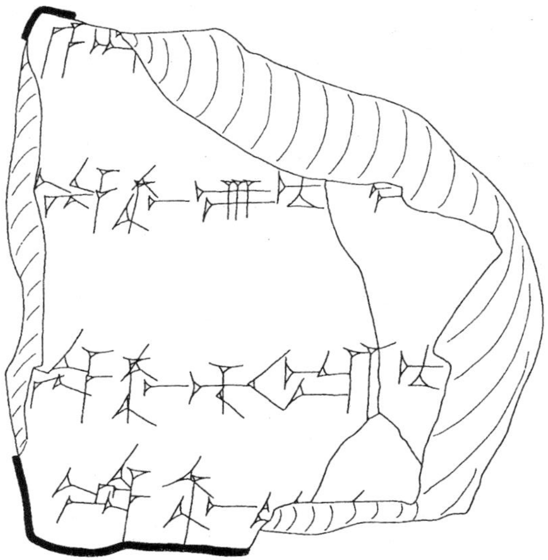

6'

53

OBVERSE

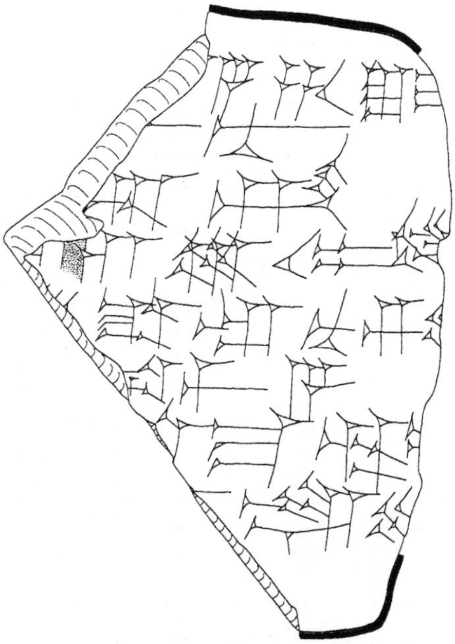

LOWER EDGE

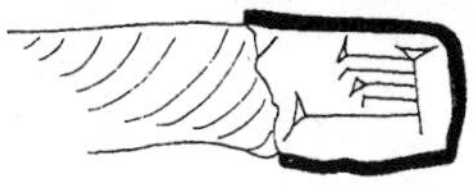

54

OBVERSE

1

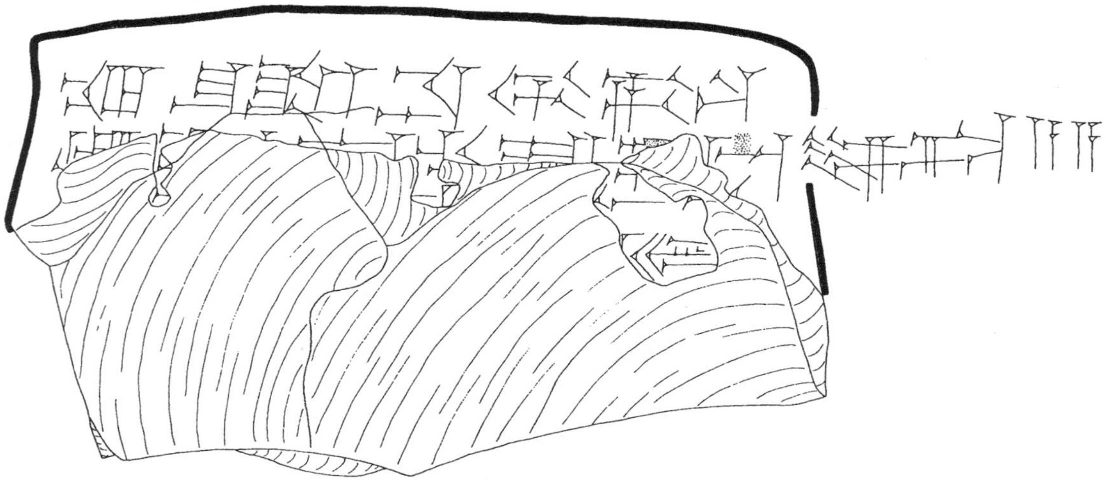

END OF OBVERSE DESTROYED

54

REVERSE

BEGINNING OF REVERSE DESTROYED

5'

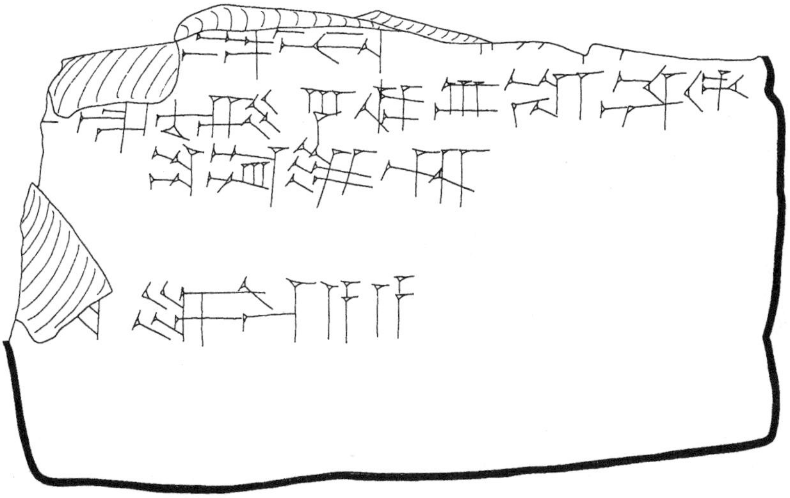

UPPER EDGE

9'

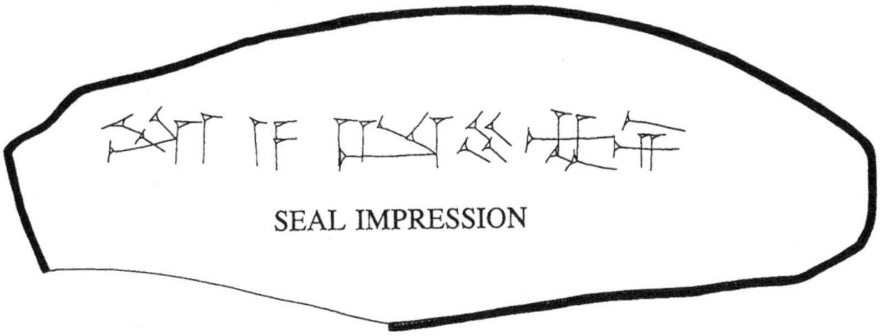

LEFT EDGE

10'

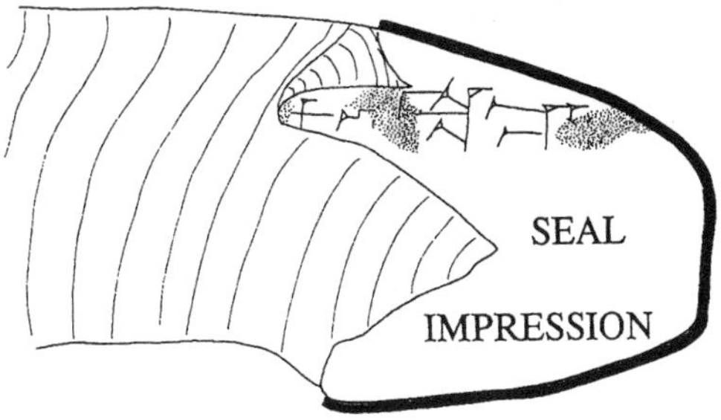

55

OBVERSE

1

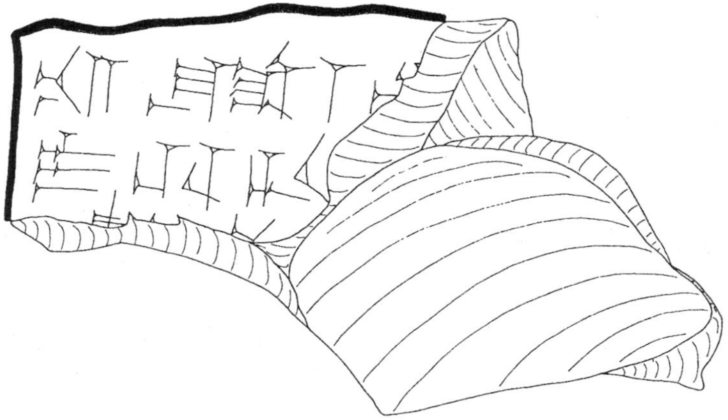

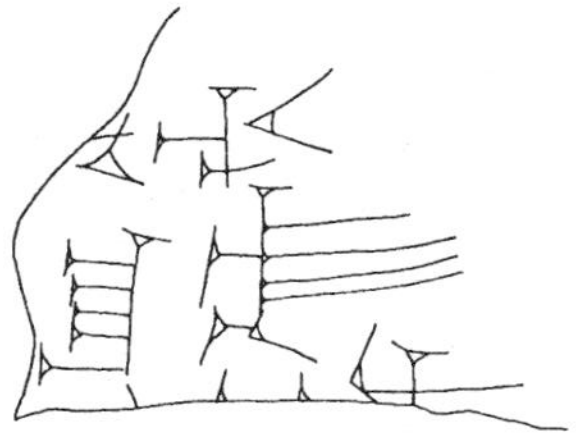

5

END OF OBVERSE DESTROYED

REVERSE

BEGINNING OF REVERSE DESTROYED

6'

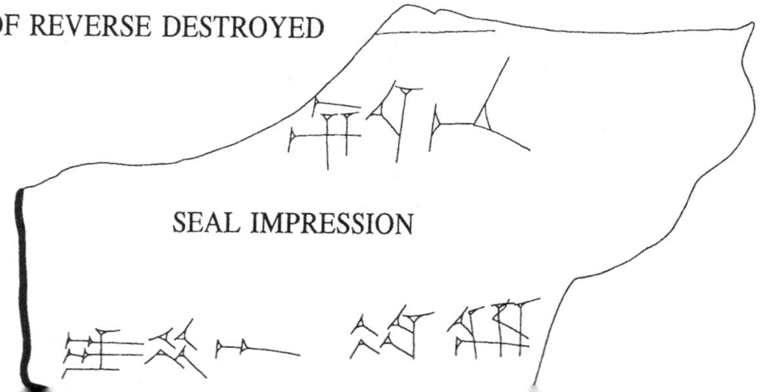

55

UPPER EDGE

8'

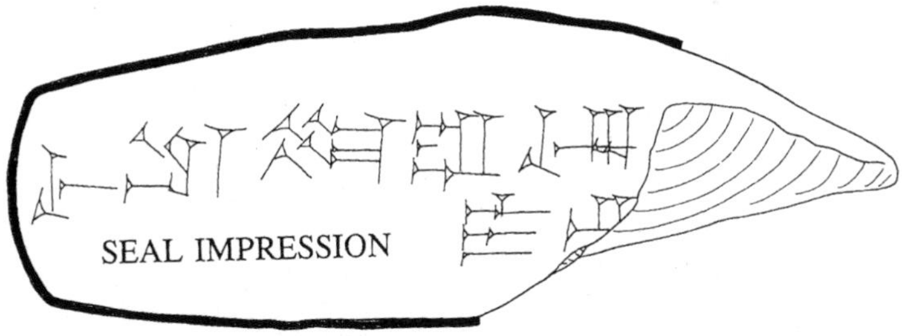

LEFT EDGE

10'

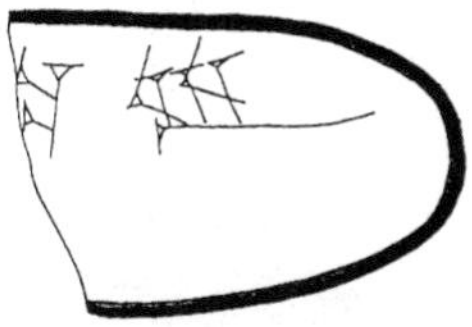

56

OBVERSE

BEGINNING OF OBVERSE DESTROYED

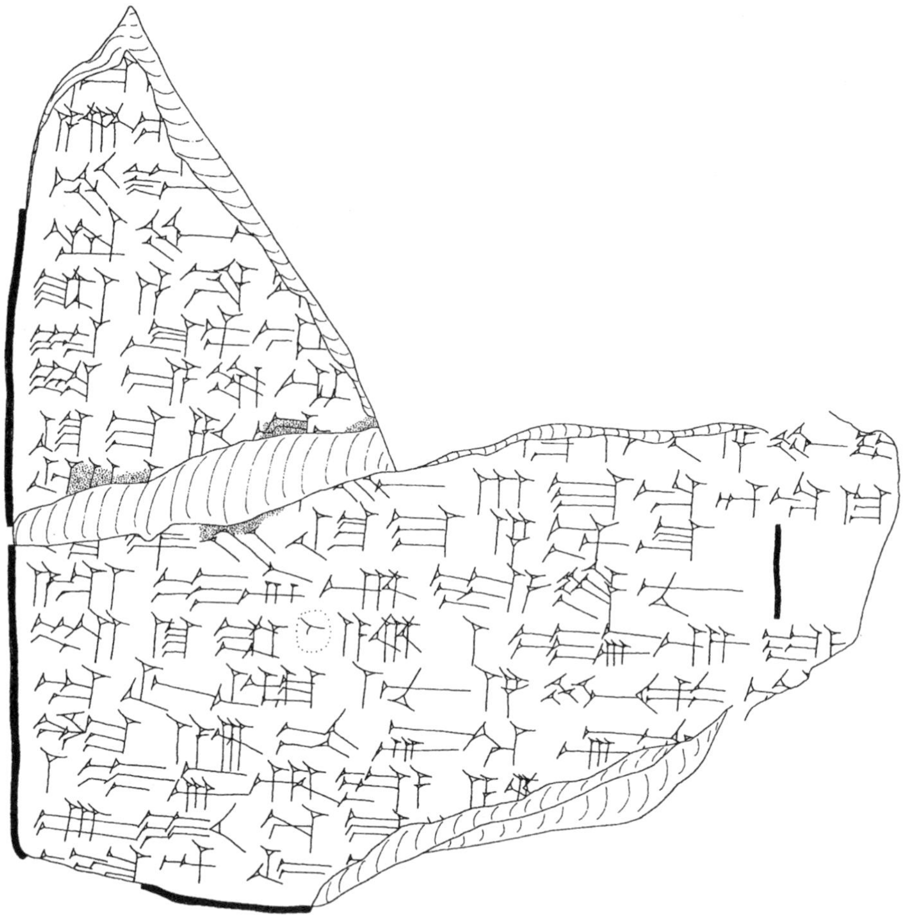

LOWER EDGE

56

REVERSE

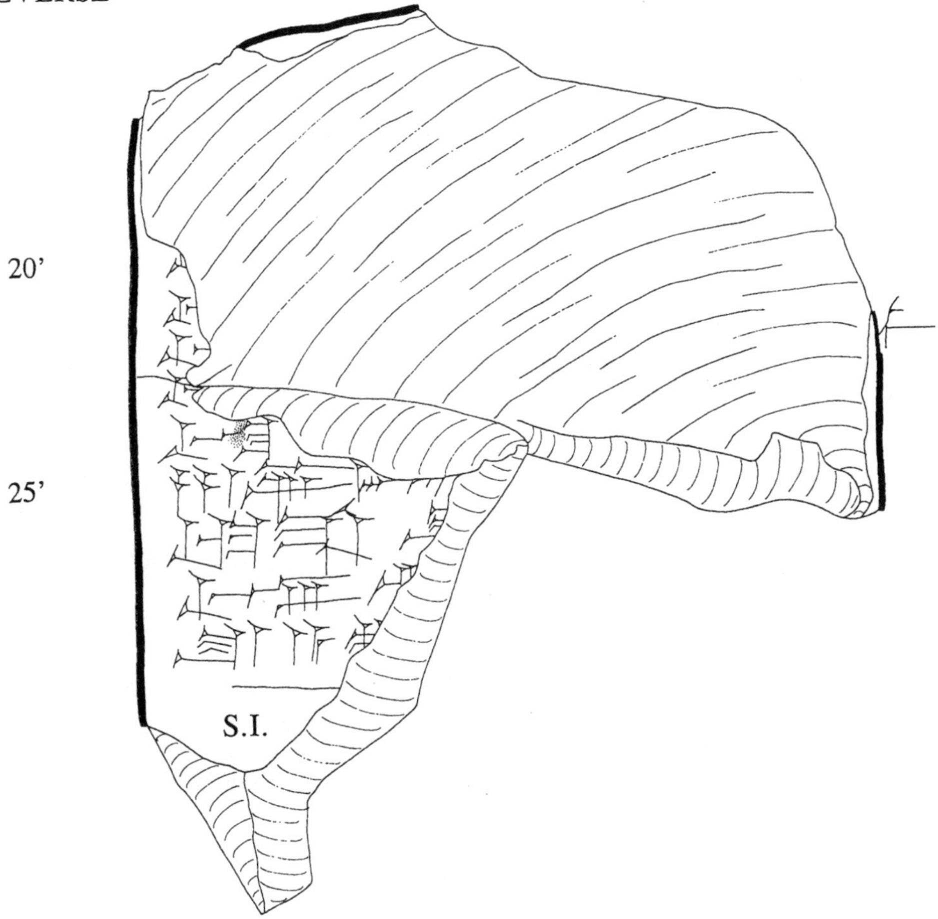

END OF REVERSE DESTROYED

LEFT EDGE

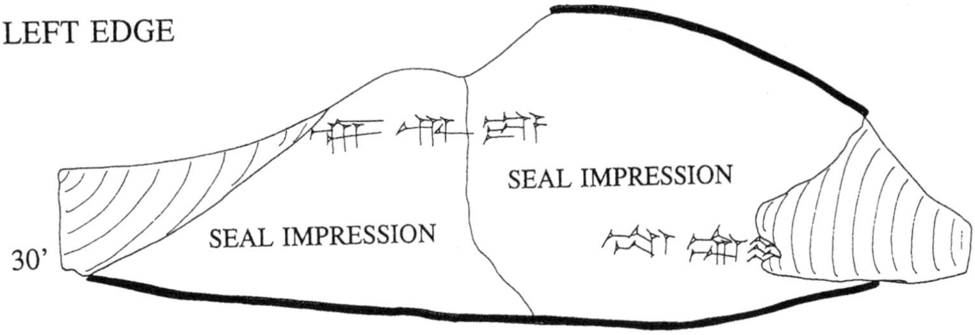

57

OBVERSE

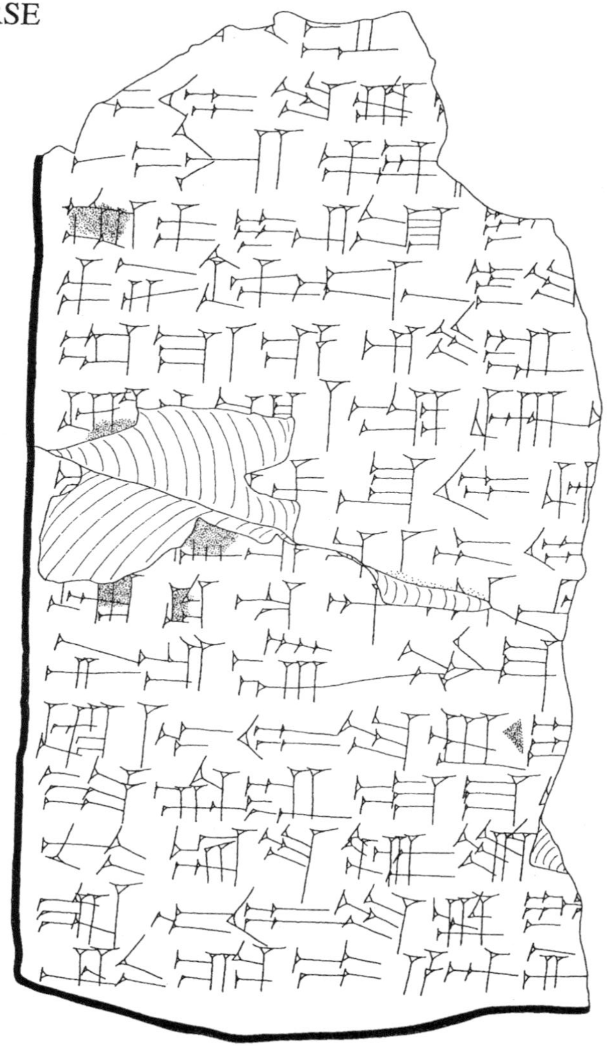

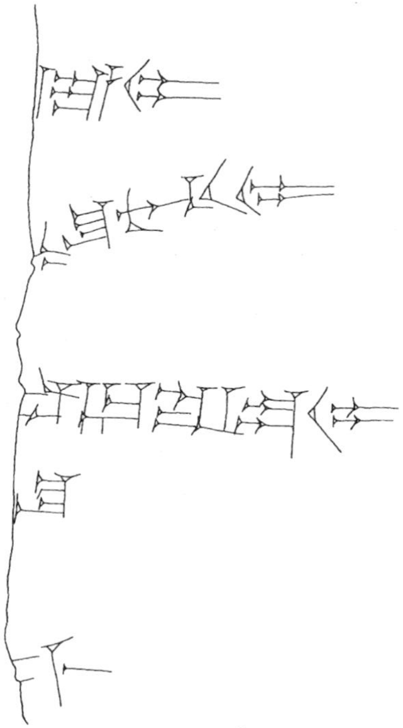

57

LOWER EDGE

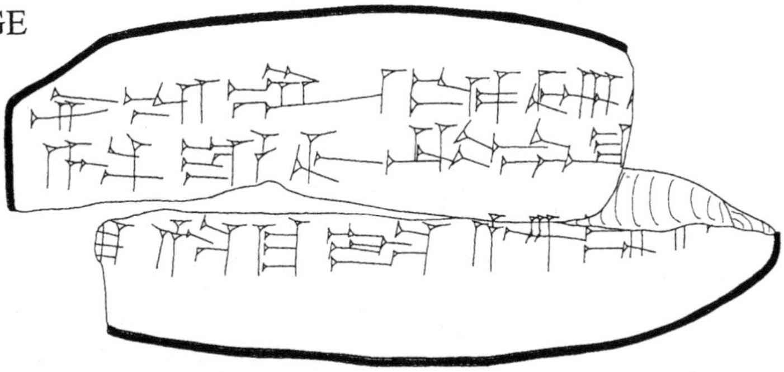

REVERSE

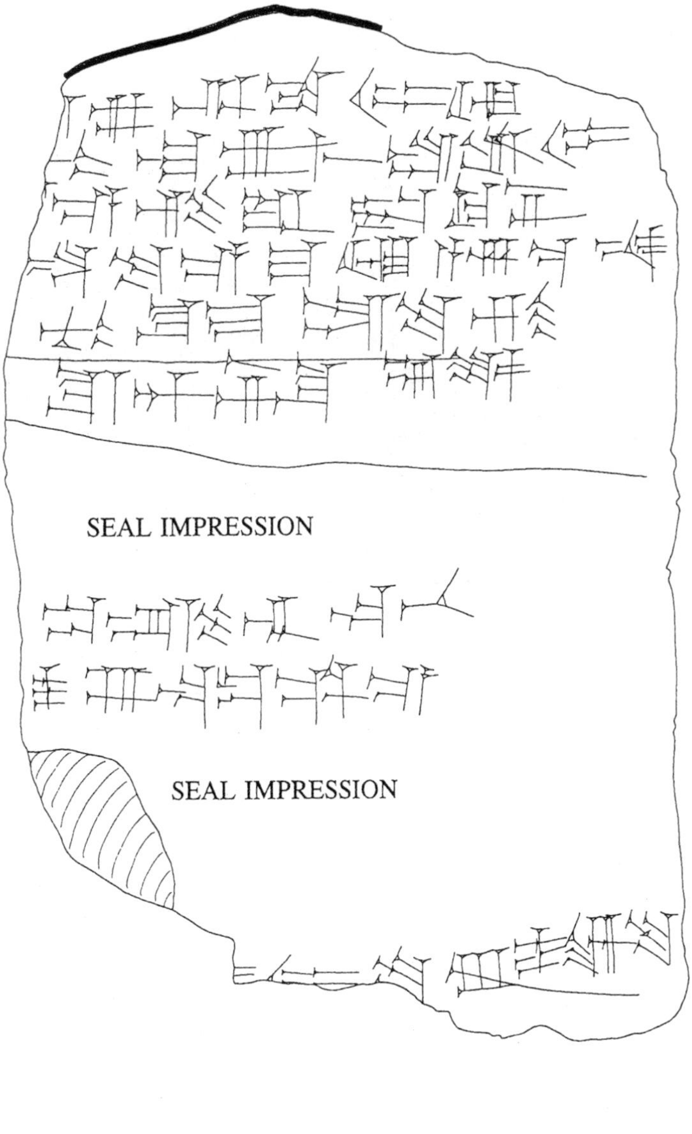

57

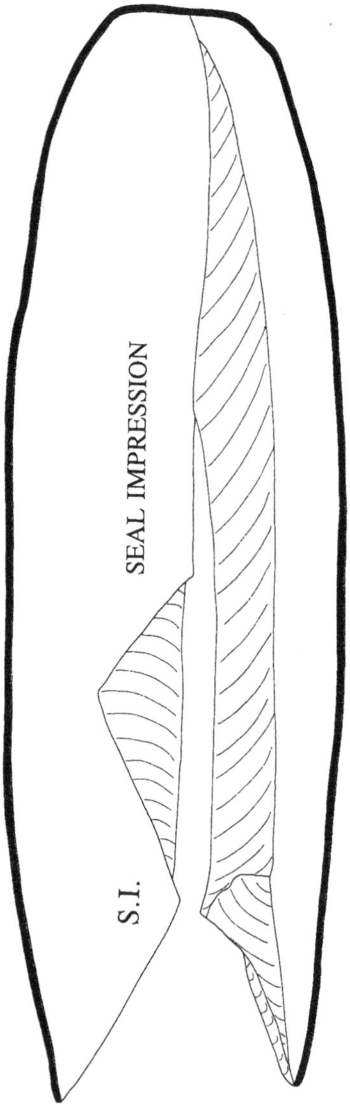

LEFT EDGE

58

OBVERSE

BEGINNING OF OBVERSE DESTROYED

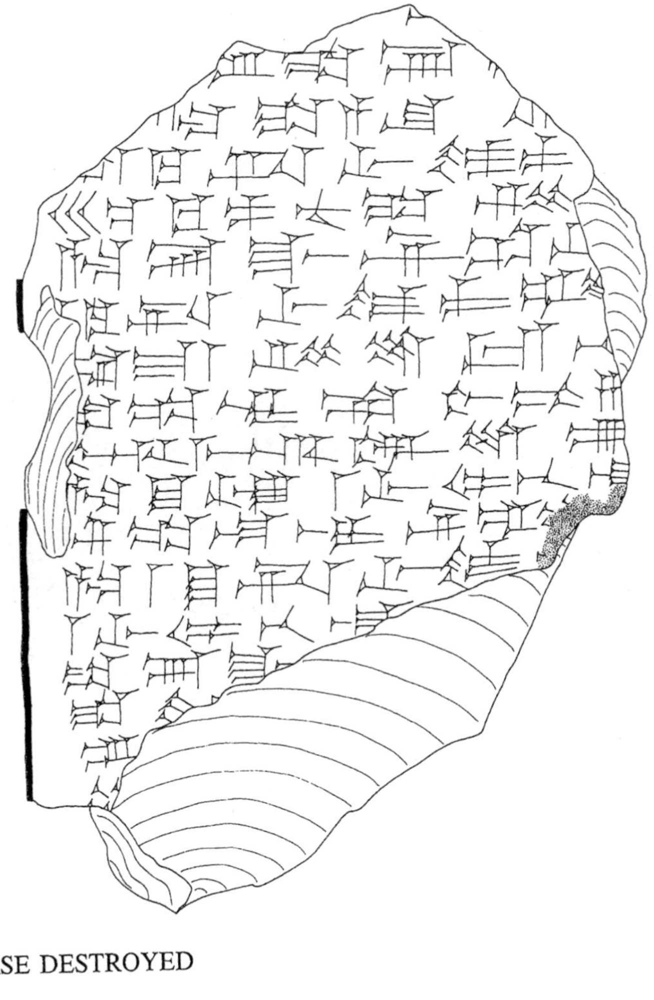

END OF OBVERSE DESTROYED

59

OBVERSE

BEGINNING OF OBVERSE DESTROYED

RIGHT EDGE

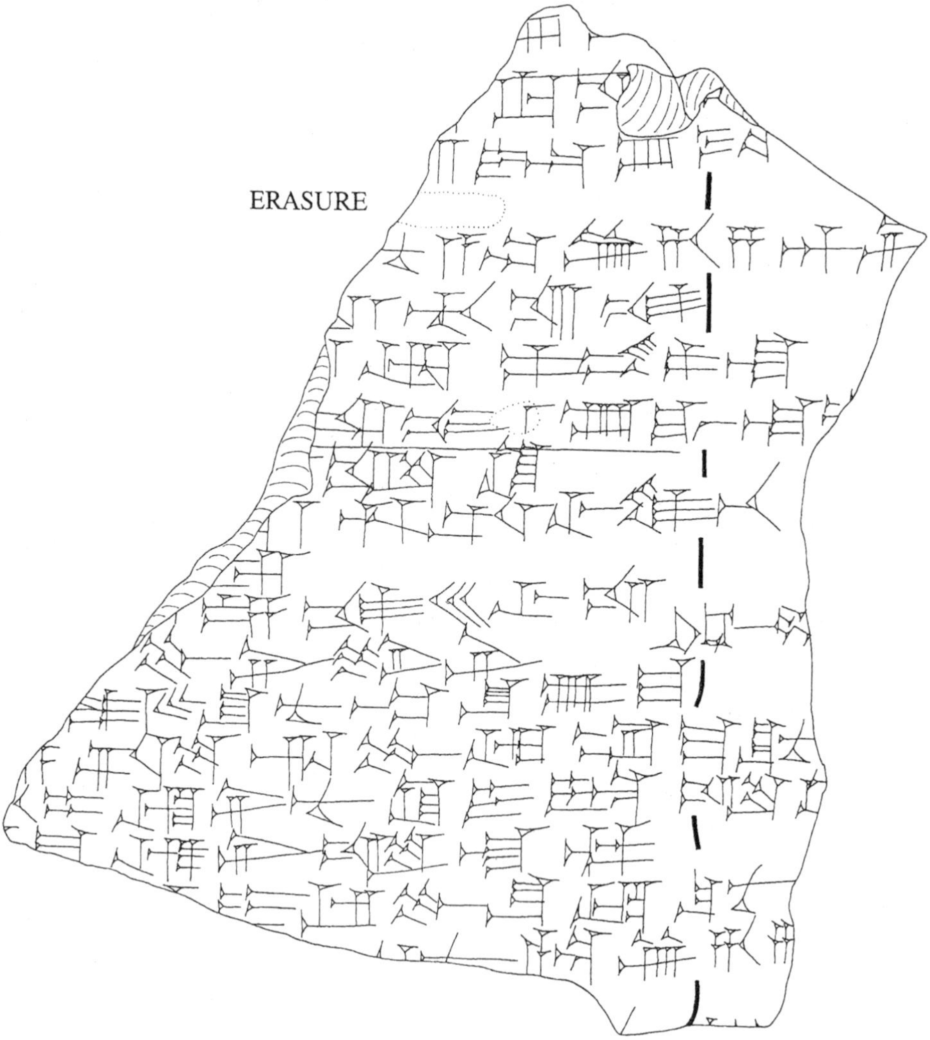

END OF OBVERSE DESTROYED

60

OBVERSE

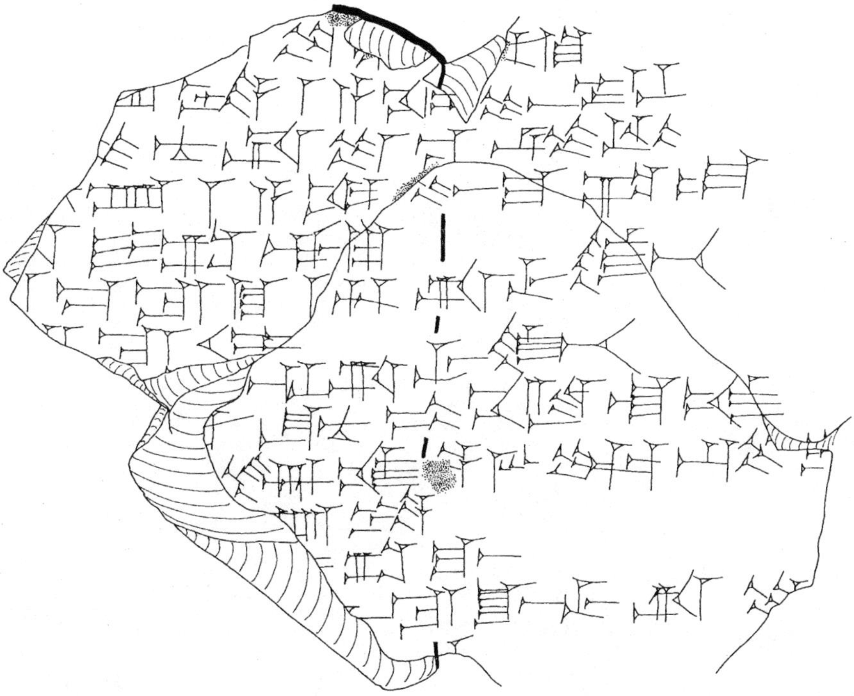

END OF OBVERSE DESTROYED

60

REVERSE

BEGINNING OF REVERSE DESTROYED

15’

20’

25’

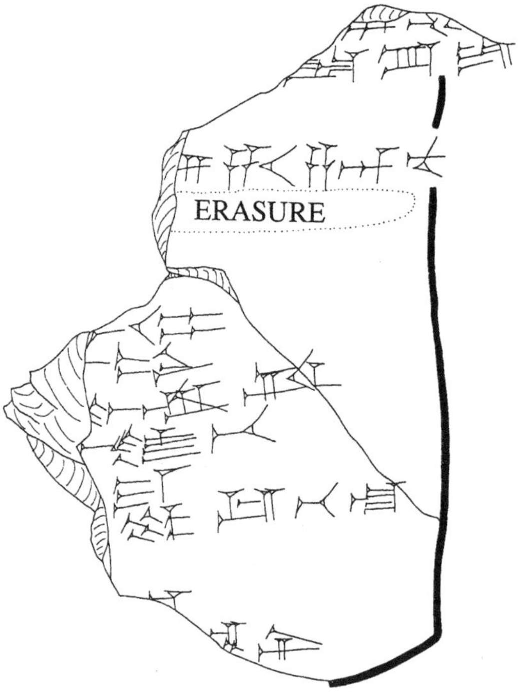

UPPER EDGE

30’

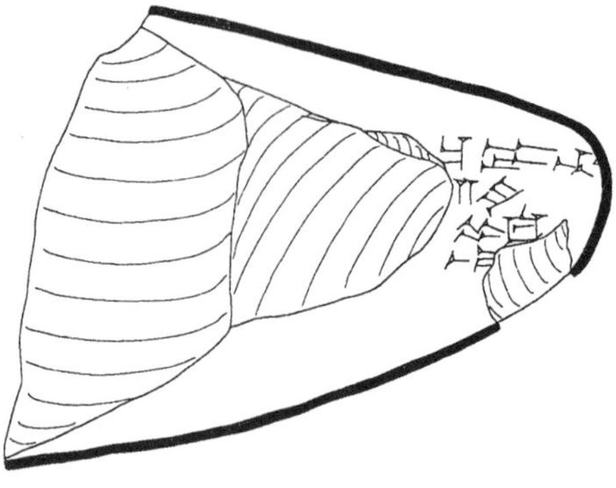

61

OBVERSE

BEGINNING OF OBVERSE DESTROYED

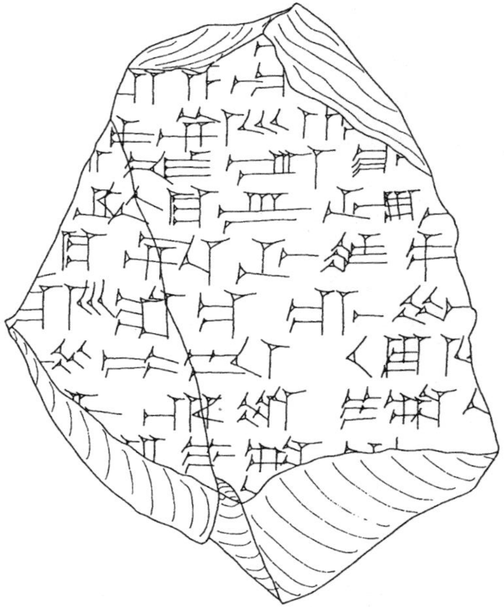

END OF OBVERSE DESTROYED

62

REVERSE

BEGINNING OF REVERSE DESTROYED

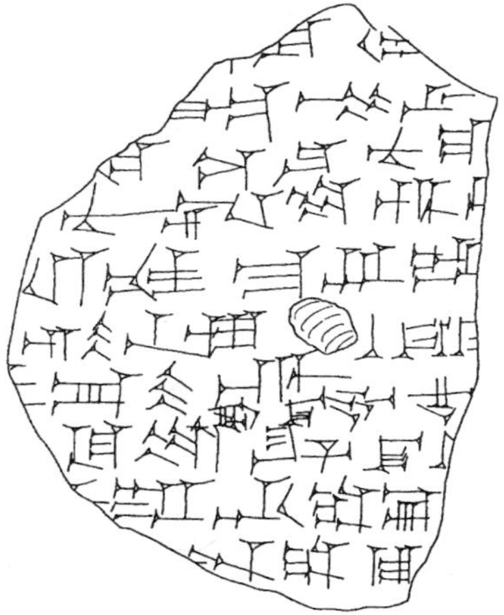

END OF REVERSE DESTROYED

63

OBVERSE

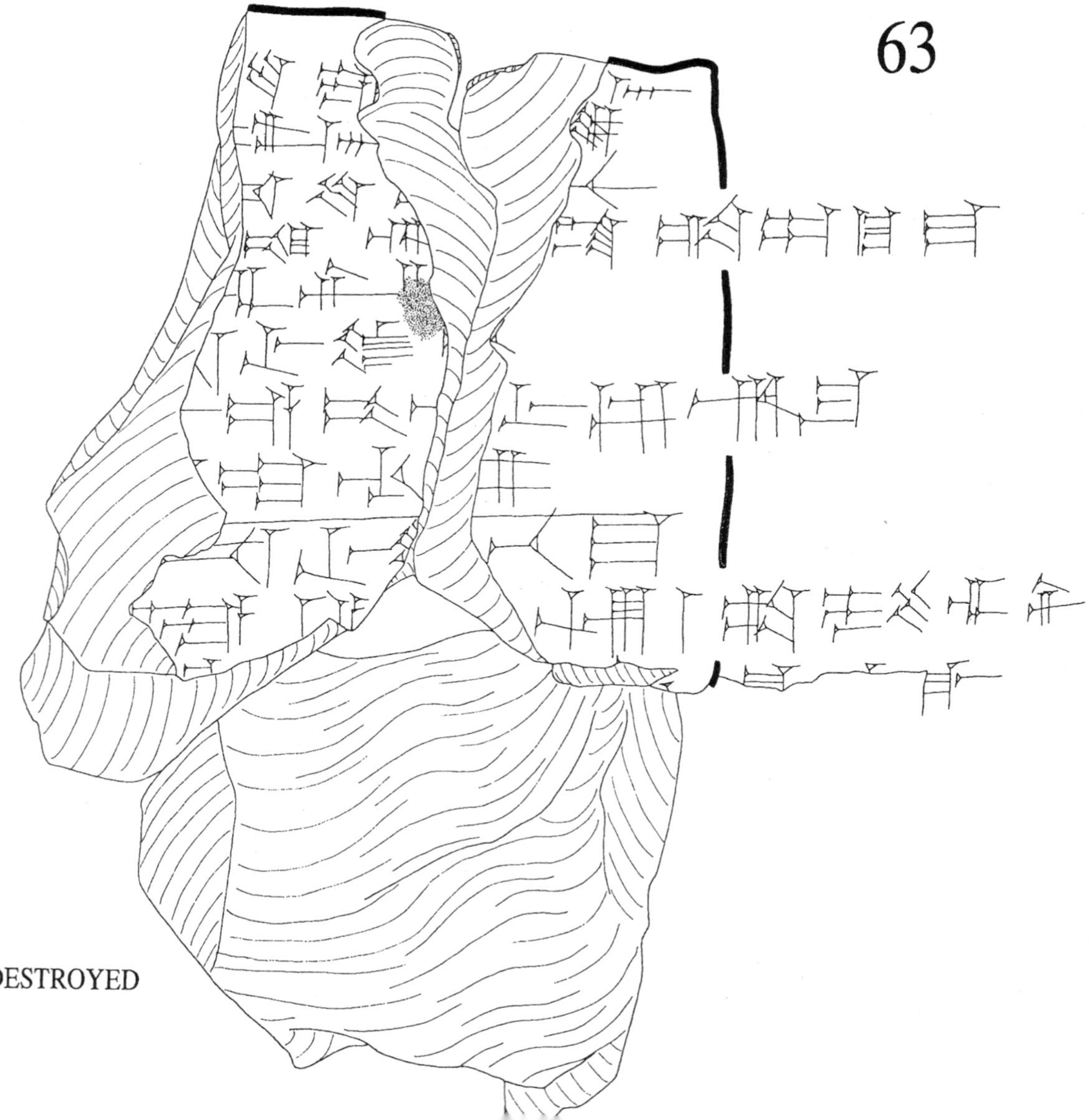

END OF OBVERSE DESTROYED

63

REVERSE

BEGINNING OF REVERSE DESTROYED

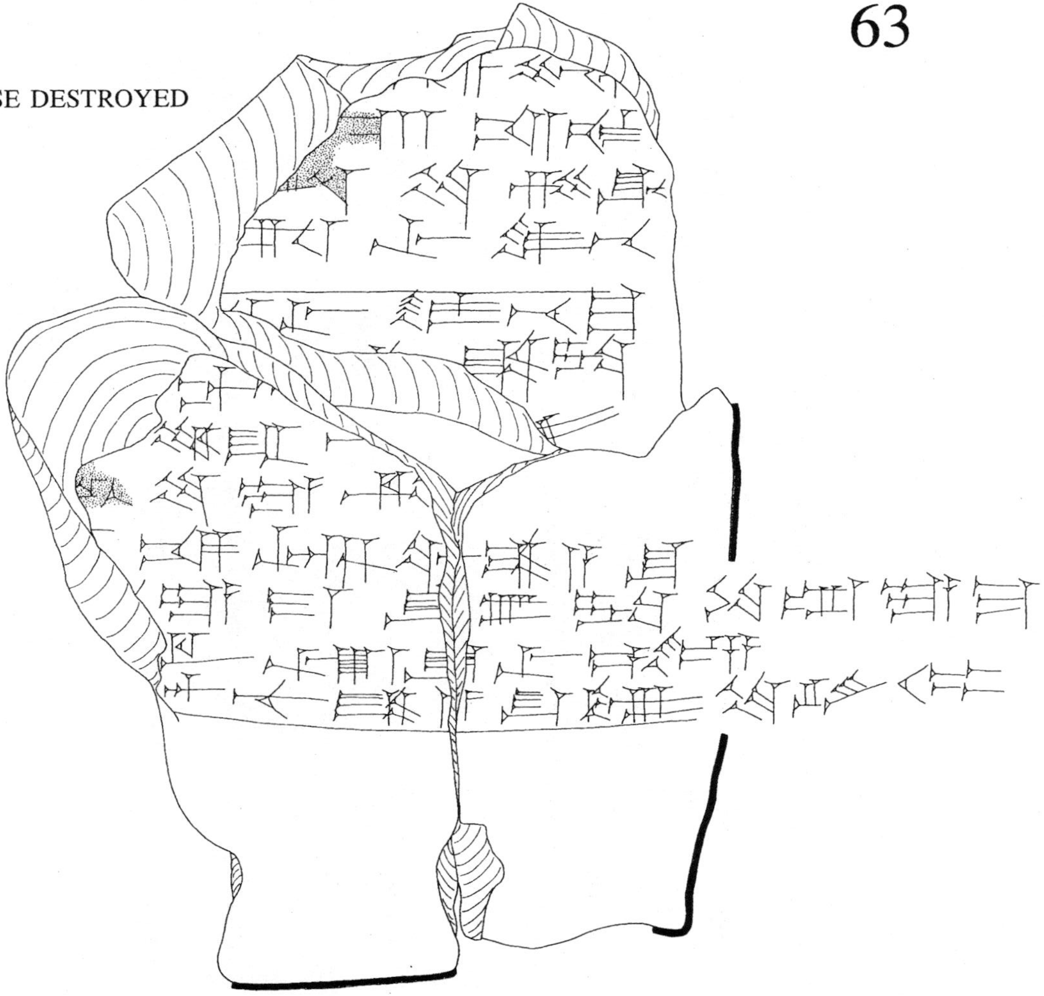

64

OBVERSE

1

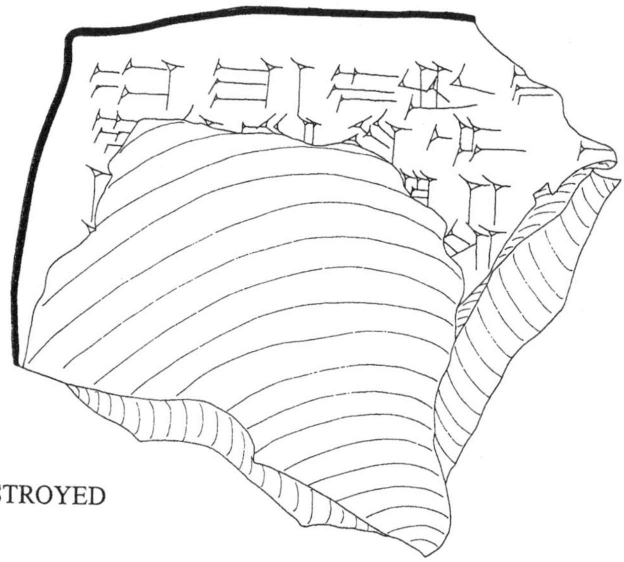

END OF OBVERSE DESTROYED

REVERSE

BEGINNING OF REVERSE DESTROYED

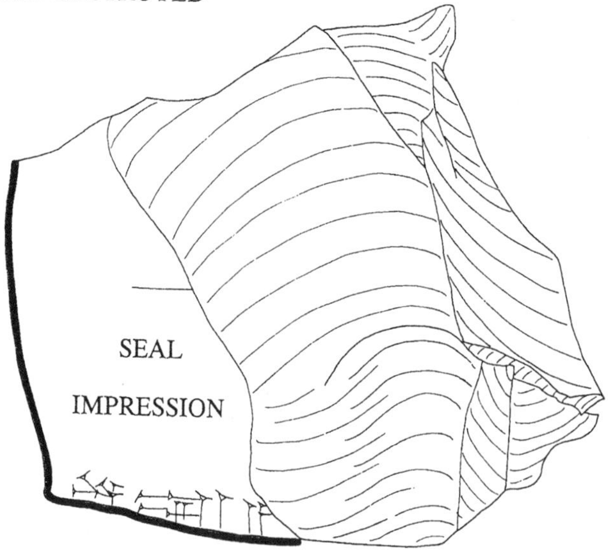

5’

64

UPPER EDGE

6’

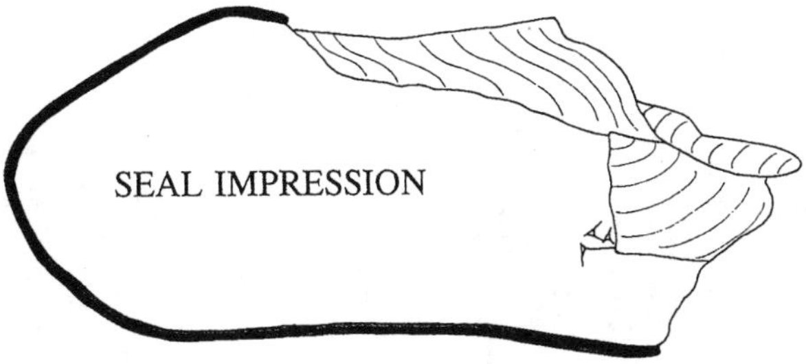

65

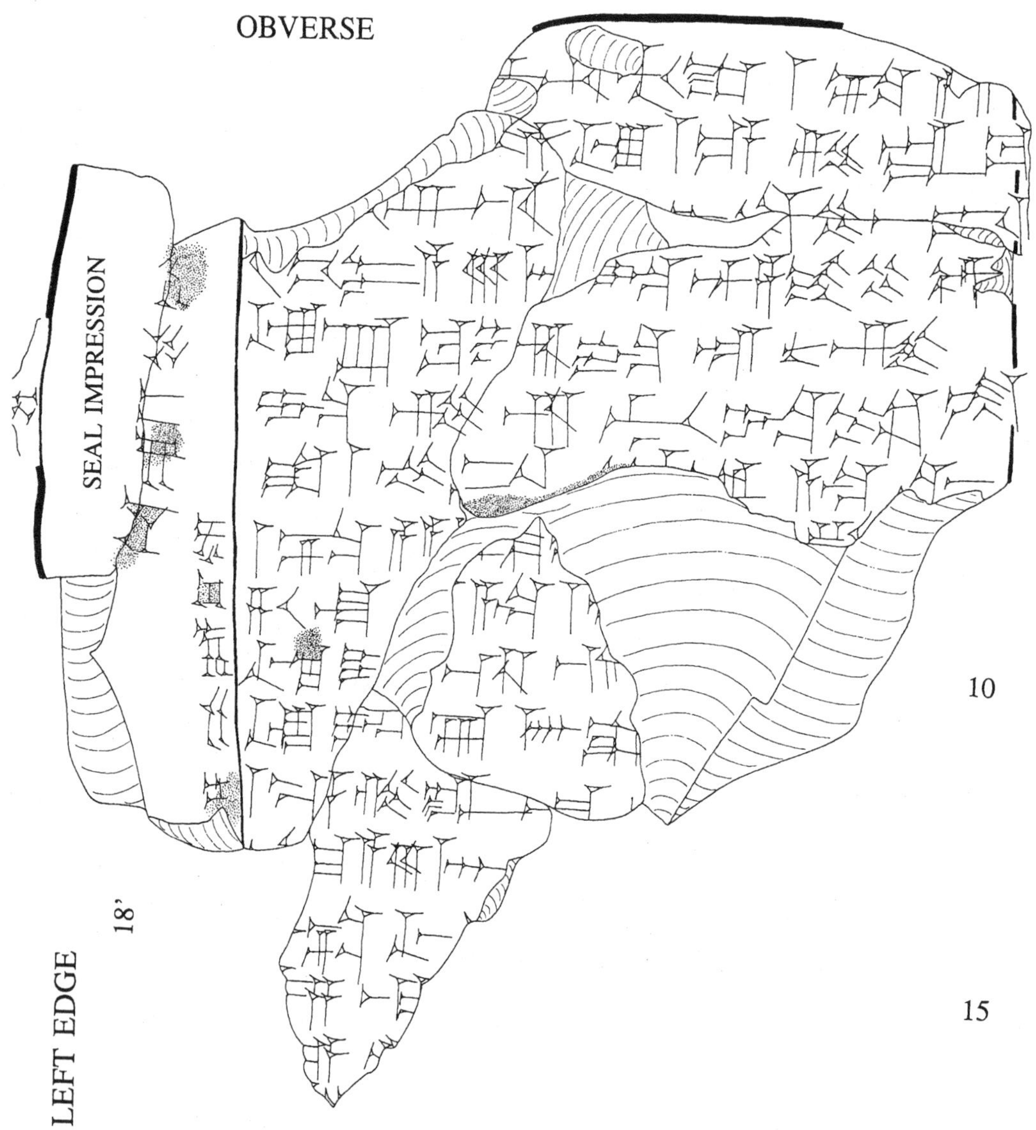
OBVERSE
SEAL IMPRESSION
10
15
18'
LEFT EDGE
END OF OBVERSE DESTROYED

Part V

Lexical Index

J. FINCKE – G. WILHELM

AKKADIAN

AMORITE

EBLAITIC

HITTITE

HURRIAN

Kassite

Luwian

Sanskrit

Sumerograms

Studies on the
Civilization and Culture of
NUZI AND THE HURRIANS

***

Volume 1. *In Honor of Ernest R. Lacheman on His Seventy-fifth Birthday, April 29, 1981*. Edited by M.A. Morrison and D.I. Owen. Winona Lake: Eisenbrauns, 1982. Pp. xxi + 496. ISBN 0-931464-08-0.

Volume 2. *General Studies and Excavations at Nuzi 9/1*. Edited by D.I. Owen and M.A. Morrison. Winona Lake: Eisenbrauns, 1987. Pp. ix + 723 + 1 foldout. ISBN 0-931464-37-4.

Volume 3. *Joint Expedition with the Iraq Museum at Nuzi VII: Miscellaneous Texts*. By E.R. Lacheman and M.P. Maidman Edited by D.I. Owen and M.A. Morrison. Winona Lake: Eisenbrauns, 1989. Pp. xii + 307. ISBN 0-931464-45-5.

Volume 4. *The Eastern Archives of Nuzi and Excavations at Nuzi 9/2*. Edited by D.I. Owen and M.A. Morrison. Winona Lake: Eisenbrauns, 1993. Pp. xii + 420. ISBN 0-931464-64-1.

Volume 5. *General Studies and Excavations at Nuzi 9/3*. Edited by D.I. Owen. Winona Lake: Eisenbrauns, 1995 . Pp. ix + 357. ISBN 0-931464-67-6.

Volume 6. *Two Hundred Nuzi Texts from the Oriental Institute of the University of Chicago*, Part 1. By M.P. Maidman. Edited by D.I. Owen. Bethesda: CDL Press, 1994. Pp. xvi + 440. ISBN 1-883053-05-6.

Volume 7. *Edith Porada Memorial Volume*. Edited by D.I. Owen and G. Wilhelm. Bethesda: CDL Press, 1995. Pp. x + 159. ISBN 1-883053-07-2.

Volume 8. *Richard F.S. Starr Memorial Volume*. Edited by D.I. Owen and G. Wilhelm. Bethesda: CDL Press, 1996. Pp. 484. ISBN 1-883053-10-2.

Volume 9. *General Studies and Excavations at Nuzi 10/2*. Edited by D.I. Owen and G. Wilhelm. Bethesda: CDL Press, 1997. ISBN 1-883053-26-9; in preparation.